Dear John

Heres wishing you a
very happy 50th

Love Bridget Jim
& family xx

THE WORLD ATLAS OF
WINE

We dedicate the sixth edition of this Atlas to Len Evans
who enlarged the world of wine for us all

HUGH JOHNSON   JANCIS ROBINSON

THE WORLD ATLAS OF WINE

SIXTH EDITION

Mitchell Beazley

HUGH JOHNSON JANCIS ROBINSON

THE WORLD ATLAS OF WINE
Hugh Johnson, Jancis Robinson

First published in Great Britain in 1971 by Mitchell Beazley, an imprint of Octopus Publishing Group Ltd, an Hachette Livre UK Company, 2–4 Heron Quays, London E14 4JP

Managing Editor Gill Pitts

Assistant Editor Julia Harding MW

Research/Editorial Assistant Philippa Bell

Commissioning Editor Susanna Forbes

Additional Research Sarah Ahmed

Art Director Tim Foster

Executive Art Editor Yasia Williams-Leedham

Designer Colin Goody

Production Manager Peter Hunt

Cartographic Editor Zoë Goodwin

Gazetteer Andrew Johnson

Index John Noble

Picture Research Jenny Faithfull

Revisions and new cartography for the sixth edition: Cosmographics

Original cartography: Clyde Surveys Ltd

Printed and bound in China

How the maps work

The maps in this Atlas vary considerably in scale, the level of detail depending on the complexity of the area mapped. There is a scale bar with each map. Contour intervals vary from map to map and are shown in each map key. Serif type (eg MEURSAULT) on the maps indicates names and places connected with wine; sans serif type (eg Meursault) mainly shows other information.

Each map page has a grid with letters down the side and numbers across the bottom. To locate a château, winery, etc, look up the name in the Gazetteer (pages 385–399), which gives the page number followed by the grid reference.

Every effort has been made to make the maps in this Atlas as complete and up to date as possible. In order that future editions may be kept up to this standard, the publishers will be grateful for information about changes of boundaries or names that should be recorded.

Previous page *Cabernet Franc, Touraine, France*

Right *Peter Lehmann winery, Barossa, Australia*

Contents

Foreword

Wine consciousness is not yet a universal phenomenon. Will I be able to write that again when the seventh edition of this Atlas comes around? It has spread so far, so fast, that parts of Asia, considered a long-shot export market when we last went to press, are now making and exporting wines themselves. Traditional ways of approaching the subject must be, you would think, more and more precarious, perhaps even irrelevant, with such seismic movement going on.

And certainly since wine began to be of interest beyond a smallish circle, mainly in Europe, the terms of discussion have shifted this way and that. If the emphasis began on the geography of vineyards, soil, and climate, at the time of my first edition in 1971, by the 1980s grape varieties had moved to centre stage.

The secrets of quality were decreed at one time to be in chemical analysis and control. Before long physical factors were deemed more important. Biochemistry came next, with mystery making an unexpected comeback in the enigmatic form of biodynamics. From grape varieties the emphasis had moved, meanwhile, to their growers: the human element was given a prominence it had never had before, and wine joined the activities ruled by the cult of celebrity. New ways of marketing to new consumers make swings of fashion hard to ignore. If a single movie can make farmers pull up one grape variety to plant another you have to ask if there is anything fundamental to plot about wine at all.

Not much, you have to conclude, for the millions of hectolitres that fill the branded bottles on supermarket shelves around the world. Commodity wine is a reality, whether it wears a varietal label or a geographical one. The important thing is that it is, with ever fewer exceptions, competently made.

Yet it is hard for wine truly to become commonplace. For most consumers round the world even everyday wines convey good times, conversations, and cheerfulness. There is a sad segment who never want to pay more than the minimum for their drink, or indeed their food. Battery chickens were invented for them – and indeed battery wines. For those who travel, though, those who eat out, cook, and share pleasures with friends, it is choices that matter: the choices between flavours and cultures. Simple and sophisticated are both in fashion. So are Italian and Asian, French and fusion. The idea of a one-style-fits-all food culture seems remote today; almost absurd. As with food, so with wine. If there is a fashion today it is diversity.

HOCUS POCUS?

So where does diversity begin? Where it always has, in the fields, the regions, and countries where wine is made, with the people who make it and their intentions. Among the fleeting fashions of the past quarter century was an attempt to dismiss terroir, the sense of place in wine, as mere hocus pocus. New regions sometimes described it as the snobbery of the long-established, jealous for their reputations. Strange, or not so strange, that as they in turn find their feet, watch their maturing vines, and taste the maturing wine of their own vintages these very regions are plotting out their own distinctive terroirs, finding their own sense of place. From bold assertions that soil and climate are perfect in whole wide valleys a more experienced generation is making its own distinctions. Lighter soils or steeper slopes, more morning mist or evening breeze are not the first thing you may notice on a young farm, but when after 10 or 20 years you retaste the wines, you will know where the grapes ripen first and where the frost strikes; where to plant Cabernet and where Merlot. If there is a universal trend in wine labelling it is naming more individual plots whose wines have the distinctive quality or character to justify a premium. They are the real meat for the reader of this Atlas.

The element you will find missing from this book, for lack of space, is an attempt to describe the beauty of its prime subject. In covering the facts of geography, the aspects of soil and climate, culture, and ambition that shape the almost incredible variety on offer the experience itself has had to be left aside. You will find elsewhere in our respective work the appreciations of individual wines that justify the geographical detail. It is glass by glass that wines attract us, sometimes disappoint us or wonderfully often ravish our senses. What we calmly describe here as a peppery Syrah, a honeyed Riesling, or a ripe and structured Côte de Nuits has held our attention, stimulated our taste-buds, and excited our wonder for whole happy evenings.

The discussion of fine wines, groping in our vocabularies for descriptions and explanations, is not an affectation, nor is it provoked by commonplace tastes and sensations. Certain wines have within them a natural vigour, an inbuilt eloquence, that expresses as nothing else does the forces that made them. You cannot trace a strawberry to a field, or a fish to a stream, or a gem to a mine, in the act of enjoying it. It is possible with wine, and not only to the place where it was made, and to the fruit that gave it flavour, but to the year the fruit ripened and even to the vintner who conducted operations. Does anything else so fully justify an atlas of its origins?

MIDNIGHT OIL

Jancis has taken the main burden of travel, research, and writing what was originally my compilation on her shoulders and those of her able and amply qualified assistant Julia. To say I am grateful is an understatement. As she writes I read what are often revelations to me with fascination. Sometimes I comment, occasionally adjust, but the work I began has now become hers, and only she, I firmly believe, is capable of doing it. To the others involved in everything from map-making to picture research and proof-reading we are both deeply in debt. I have to single out Gill Pitts as the most capable and dedicated, as well as cheerful and tireless editor. Good books are not made without such midnight oil burners. I have worked with a lot of people during the 36 years this work has been underway. We have never been a happier or more united crew.

Introduction

For the second time it has been a particularly instructive honour to revise this classic wine reference, producing a book that, with 400 pages, is bigger and (to judge from the intensity of our team effort over the last two years) better than it has ever been. This ever more demanding task has forced me to confront just how rapidly the world of wine has changed since the last edition was published in 2001, two days after the New York horizon, and much else besides, was changed for ever.

It may be just six years since the 5th edition appeared (previous editions were published in 1971, 1977, 1985, and 1994), but if there is one overall characteristic affecting the world today, and the wine world no less, it is acceleration, and in particular acceleration of the pace of change. We have to run, or at least rewrite and redraw, to keep this book at the forefront of wine book publishing, where it has been for the last 36 years.

We have only to look at the extraordinary flowering of interest in both consuming and producing wine throughout the world in the early years of this century to see some of the impetus for this acceleration. When I began writing about wine in the mid-1970s, it was with some trepidation. In many quarters wine (and food) were seen as shockingly frivolous subjects. A life devoted to either could easily be viewed as a waste of a good education.

Today things are very different. It sometimes seems as though there is scarcely a man of letters, sporting hero, or captain of industry – and yes, an increasing proportion of female connoisseurs too – who does not profess their love of wine, increasingly often to the extent of setting up their own label or estate, or at the very least investing in a sizeable personal wine collection.

Overtaking beer and liquor, wine has become the strong drink of choice in the world's dominant economy, and the USA also looks set fair to become the world's most important importer of wine, as well as having become by far the biggest single producer of it outside Europe. The charms, and posited health benefits, of wine have finally conquered the world, including making substantial inroads into many parts of Asia, a continent once thought immune to the wine virus.

But as the army of wine lovers swells, and as communications within that army have become so extraordinarily rapid and efficient, on a truly global scale, trends in wine that might have taken a generation to take effect can now be observed spreading round the world between one vintage and the next.

THE PENDULUM OF FASHION

To take just one example of how rapidly the pendulums of fashion now swing, Chardonnay mania seemed a particular threat when the last edition was written. An obsession with red wine seems to have replaced it in the intervening years, and we can now choose from a dazzling array of so-called heritage grapes, varieties rescued from near extinction in their homeland. Another example of rapid change: when the last edition was assembled, organic viticulture was regarded as almost a fringe activity, its biodynamic counterpart beyond the pale. Today, as we become increasingly aware of the perils we face on a planetary scale, there are few vine-growers unaware of the need to address issues of sustainability in the vineyard, and followers of the arcane runes of biodynamics now include a significant number of highly regarded wine producers.

Perhaps inevitably the most notable overall development between this edition and the last has been the observable changes in climate virtually everywhere and their effects on what sort of wines are produced where. There have been obvious beneficiaries of global warming such as vine-growers on the northern (and occasionally southern) fringes of the world's wine map. Canada, England, and especially Germany are now able to ripen grapes much more reliably than they could even one edition ago. Technology in general, refrigeration and irrigation in particular, has so far been able to sustain viticulture in its traditional strongholds closer to the equator, and it has allowed the development of some new wine regions even closer than ever before. But it is clear that in many parts of the world, notably the less glamorous parts of Australia and California, but also in some areas of Spain,

access to good-quality, affordable water will be a critical concern over coming years.

As more and more vine-growers harness such technological advances as satellite-based navigation to zoom in on micro-variations between small blocks within the same vineyard, for instance, we have seen the macro extent of the world's wine map evolve, even if between the fifth and sixth editions of this Atlas, expansion has been driven as much by social factors as by climatological ones. Asia may have been hardly a force in wine at all until the late 1990s, but it is likely to play an increasingly important part in shaping where wine is made and consumed. Acknowledging that China is already the world's sixth most important grower of grapevines, we have increased coverage of this vast continent in this edition, and doubtless will again in the next.

In recognition of the intense sophistication of California's legion of extremely adept wine producers, we have provided much more detailed coverage of the Napa Valley this time, with detailed maps of Rutherford, Oakville, and Stags Leap District. Also in North America, but much further north, we have included for the first time a map of British Columbia's Okanagan Valley in western Canada, a relatively new source of interesting.

The wine map of Australia continues to extend itself into cooler corners, so that our coverage of this important force in the world of wine has developed considerably too, including a new map of the Limestone Coast in South Australia for this edition as well as further detail of Barossa Valley, Eden Valley, McLaren Vale, and Adelaide Hills. Coverage of New Zealand, with the world's most southerly vineyards, has been extended to maps of both Martinborough and Central Otago, a sign of this country's newfound prowess with Pinot Noir, while the historic but still rewarding South African Constantia region also benefits from a map of its own.

But wine has been evolving in Europe too, as witness our brand new maps of several German regions, Kremstal and Kamptal in Austria, the Peleponnese in Greece, and Toro in Spain. Keeping track of Spain's constantly evolving wine map has been a particular challenge over recent years, although the last edition already saw a complete overhaul of Spanish coverage in this Atlas. France has always been mapped in particular detail, not least because her wine history is so long, so intricate, and so minutely codified. Nevertheless we are particularly pleased with an entirely new and extremely useful map of the precise soil types to be found in one of France's most varied wine appellations, and one in the most obvious state of flux today, St-Emilion.

Of all the things we buy, wine is more geographically traceable than almost anything else. It is one of the very few things we can pluck off a shelf or wine list and tell from one glance who made it, when, and exactly where it comes from. All the more reason then for any keen wine lover to have to hand something that can be consulted anywhere – in a car, a field, a wine shop, or by a fireside – and can show in as much detail as possible the precise spot on the globe that was responsible for each bottle.

We are proud that the maps in this Atlas continue to set the standard as the wine lover's reference even in the era of Google Earth and the manifold resources of the internet. Of course these uniquely wine-friendly maps, of differing levels of complexity according to subject matter, are the great strength of this book, but they are just part of what the book has to offer. In providing comment on what is to be found in and around the vineyard, winery, and glass, we are keenly aware of our role as interpreters in an increasingly complex wine world.

Hugh's original texts are such a delight to read that in the fifth edition I updated them with a particularly light touch, but, such has been the speed of change this century that I have had, regretfully in many cases, to make a much higher proportion of revisions to keep this reference as useful and topical as possible. The maps have also been revised more energetically than ever, as Andrew Johnson, who slaved over them to provide the Gazetteer, observed.

The aim, as always, is to provide not a textbook but an enthusiastic, well-informed introduction to each region. Hugh and I try to take the reader by the hand and explain what makes each place special, and how it imprints its particular characteristics on the wines made there. But constant changes in climate, technique, fashion, and regulations mean that these descriptions need frequent revision. Despite superficial appearances, and this magical drink's satisfyingly visceral, sustained appeal, there is little that is timeless about wine.

Towards the end of the 20th century there was a trend, especially in wine regions outside Europe, for producers to source grapes from an array of different growers and blend, so that location of winery has become no sure guide to provenance of grapes. However, as more and more alert winemakers become obsessed by the individual characteristics of each plot of vines, we are seeing an increasing proportion of single-vineyard wines – which is why in this edition we have been keen to add more notable individual vineyards to many of our maps, even those outside Europe.

I am thrilled to see, however, after decades during which winemakers and grape varieties, not to mention scores, threatened to take precedence over what really creates wine, that the world of wine is increasingly preoccupied by its most important aspect, geography.

HOW THIS ATLAS WORKS
The maps have been put together with the consumer, not the wine bureaucrat, in mind. If an appellation – AC, DOC, DO, AVA, GI, or South African ward, for example – exists but is of no practical interest to the wine drinker, our policy is to omit it. If the name of a region, area, or district is in common wine parlance, even if it has not yet been granted an official designation, we have tended to include it.

We have marked those wineries we think are of particular interest to the world's wine lovers, whether on the basis of the quality of their wine or their local importance. It is becoming increasingly difficult in some parts of the world, however, to pinpoint exactly where a winemaking enterprise is based. Many operations, particularly but by no means exclusively in California and Australia, have a "cellar door", sales outlet, or tasting room in a quite different location from where they actually produce the wine (which in some cases may even be in a contract winery or custom crush facility). In such cases we have marked the former location as being where they choose to present themselves to wine lovers. Wine producers are not marked on the exceptionally detailed Côte d'Or maps, however, since these concentrate on vineyards rather than cellars – which tend to be huddled together in the same village backstreets anyway.

The famous skills and work ethic of the Chinese are now being trained on vine-growing and winemaking, as shown here with Merlot grapes grown for the Austrian-owned Bodega Langes in Hebei province. Bordeaux red wine grapes dominate China's newer plantings.

Note that in order to make it easier to distinguish between wine-related names and place names, all wine names, whether appellations or wineries, are in type with serifs (for example, the appellation of MEURSAULT) whereas geographical names are in sans serif type (for example, the village of Meursault).

In deciding the order of different regions within countries, we have tried very roughly to go from west to east and from north to south, although like all rules this has its exceptions. Within France (a notable exception to the above rule), the Vins de Pays wines have their own section but their labels tend to appear on the geographically relevant page.

The policy in choosing which labels to feature on these pages (a wine publishing innovation when it was introduced in the first edition) is stricter than before. I have tried as far as possible to make the labels shown reflect my personal choice of the best wines made in that particular country, region or district. The vintage shown on the label has no particular relevance, although at the time of publication they are generally current and eminently respectable. These choices should have a track record over many vintages, or at least several in the most embryonic wine regions. The number of labels shown on each page is often determined far more by page design than qualitative considerations. Nor should anything qualitative be read into the order in which the labels are shown on the page. Aesthetics, geography, grape varieties, and ease of caption writing have all variously played their part in this.

PERSONAL THANKS
First of all I am as eager as ever to thank Hugh Johnson, who could not have been a more generous, supportive, good-humoured, not to mention talented, collaborator. He seems to have been even more closely involved with this sixth edition than the fifth, scrutinizing every image and map, reading every word, and often rewriting some of mine, sprinkling Johnson gold dust throughout the extensively revised texts that illuminate the maps.

As so often over the past two years, I have relied extremely heavily on the knowledge, diligence, and memory of my assistant and fellow Master of Wine Julia Harding, who has herself developed a network of extremely generous informants in vineyards, wineries, and laboratories around the world. (I suppose we should also acknowledge a huge debt at this point to the magic of email, without which this revision would have taken nearly twice as long to complete)

And Hugh, Julia, and I, not to mention publisher and originator Mitchell Beazley, have been quite exceptionally lucky in our managing editor Gill Pitts who, as with the fifth edition, truly has achieved what on paper looks to be impossible in such a relatively short time – much of it at the expense of her weekends but not, miraculously, her sense of humour. So efficient have she and Julia been that I have hardly seen cartographic editor Zoë Goodwin at all

ABBREVIATIONS

The following most common abbreviations are used in the key facts boxes and throughout the text:

ft	feet	**AC**	Appellation Contrôlée
g	grams	**AVA**	American Viticultural Area
ha	hectares	**DO**	Denominación de Origen
hl	hectolitres	**EU**	European Union
in	inches	**GI**	Geographic Indication
kg	kilograms	**INAO**	Institut National de l'Origine et de la Qualité
km	kilometres		
l	litres	**OIV**	Organisation International de la Vigne et du Vin
m	metres		
mm	millimetres		

while she wove her particular, essential brand of magic. All I have done is benefit hugely from her efficiency, expertise, and daunting level of consistency.

The same is largely true of the rest of this admirable team, although I have been delightedly and directly aware of Sarah Ahmed's research skills, and the hard work and tenacity that has been displayed by Philippa Bell over the past months, whose unenviable job it has been to track down often the most obscure labels from all over the world. I have also had the pleasure of direct discussions with art director Tim Foster and art editor Yasia Williams, which were always stimulating, well-informed, and rewarding. Hugh and I are enormously grateful to all those specified on p.4, who have managed to get this book from our furrowed brows to crisp, beautiful, physical reality.

Other hard-working éminences grises in the cartographic field were Alan Grimwade and his team at Cosmographics.

Enormous thanks are also due to everyone cited in, and particularly those inadvertently missed off, the list of Acknowledgments on p.400. We have prevailed upon the goodwill of a vast array of informants all over the world and can only bless them and the way improved technology has allowed us to communicate with such satisfying, almost dangerous (in terms of meeting deadlines), speed. Any faults in this book are much more likely to be mine than theirs, and they certainly cannot be held responsible for the many opinions expressed in this book, and certainly not for such tendentious issues as choices of labels.

As ever, however, I owe most to Nick and our children, Julia, Will, and Rose, all of whom are now old enough to see that perhaps someone would buy my books after all.

KEY FACTS

Many of the maps are augmented by compact tables of each region's vital statistics, location, grape varieties grown, viticultural challenges, and, most importantly, meteorological data.

These key facts, based on weather data kindly supplied in 2000 by Australians Dr Richard Smart and John Gwalter, necessarily rely on the location of weather stations with records over many years. In many cases, weather stations, denoted by an inverted red triangle on the maps, are located on the edge of towns rather than in vineyards themselves, which means that because of urban development and different elevations, they may experience slightly different, often warmer, temperatures than the vineyards themselves. On the other hand, most wine regions have experienced slightly higher temperatures in the years since the data were assembled, thanks to climate change. We have not altered the data since 2000 and are confident that they are still reasonably accurate and provide a useful basis for comparison between regions (which is one of their main purposes).

Compare these very different sets of statistics for the hot, dry climate of Mendoza and the much cooler, wetter one of Bordeaux. On the accompanying graphs, curves are shown for the mean, or average, maximum and minimum temperatures plotted for each month. The average rainfall for each month is also represented. The Mendoza data runs from July through to June, that for Bordeaux from January to December.

Latitude / Altitude (ft/m)
In general, the lower the latitude, or nearer the equator, the warmer the climate. But this can be offset by altitude, an important factor also determining likely diurnal temperature variability: the higher the vineyard, the greater the difference between day (maximum) and night (minimum) temperatures.

Mean July/January temperature (°F/C)
Average temperature in what is usually the warmest month, a reliable guide to the likely temperature throughout the growing season. Studies in Australia by Richard Smart and Peter Dry have shown that the temperature experienced throughout the vines' growing period can be simply but accurately described by comparing the mean temperature for what is normally the warmest month: July in the northern hemisphere and January in the southern.

Annual rainfall (in/mm)
Average total precipitation indicating the likely availability of water.

Harvest month rainfall (in/mm)
Average rainfall during the month when most of the grapes are most likely to be picked (although this can vary according to variety and individual year); the higher the rainfall, the greater the risk of rot.

Chief viticultural hazards
These are generalizations and may include

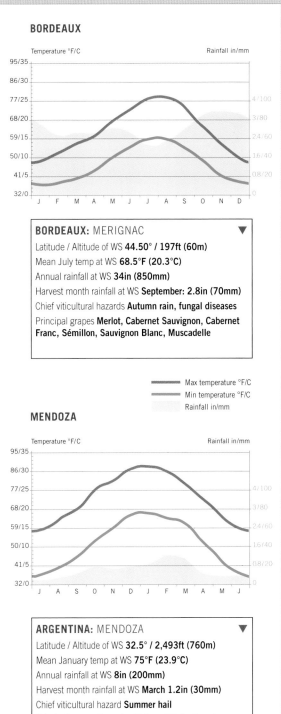

BORDEAUX

BORDEAUX: MERIGNAC ▼
Latitude / Altitude of WS **44.50° / 197ft (60m)**
Mean July temp at WS **68.5°F (20.3°C)**
Annual rainfall at WS **34in (850mm)**
Harvest month rainfall at WS **September: 2.8in (70mm)**
Chief viticultural hazards **Autumn rain, fungal diseases**
Principal grapes **Merlot, Cabernet Sauvignon, Cabernet Franc, Sémillon, Sauvignon Blanc, Muscadelle**

— Max temperature °F/C
— Min temperature °F/C
Rainfall in/mm

MENDOZA

ARGENTINA: MENDOZA ▼
Latitude / Altitude of WS **32.5° / 2,493ft (760m)**
Mean January temp at WS **75°F (23.9°C)**
Annual rainfall at WS **8in (200mm)**
Harvest month rainfall at WS **March 1.2in (30mm)**
Chief viticultural hazard **Summer hail**
Principal grapes **Bonarda, Malbec, Criolla Grande, Cereza, Cabernet Sauvignon, Barbera, Sangiovese**

climate-related challenges such as spring frost or autumn rain as well as endemic pests or vine diseases. See glossary for explanations.

Principal grapes
By no means exhaustive list of the varieties most commonly grown for wine in the region.

The World of Wine

The world's wine map is no longer composed of two neat bands through the temperate zones of each hemisphere. Global warming and the increasingly sophisticated art of tropical viticulture is changing the shape of the map as you read this.

Europe may still dominate the list of the world's most important vine-growers, based on the most recent set of statistics available from the OIV, but Asia in general, and China in particular, is moving up the ranks at extraordinary speed. As throughout Asia, wine is far from the only product of these new vineyards – see all those countries marked † in the lists for those which produce a significant proportion of fresh and dried grapes, and whose average yields are therefore distorted. (The world's 25th, 26th, and 32nd most important vine-growers, Iraq, Afghanistan, and Yemen, respectively, have been omitted from the list because they do not officially produce wine.) The Americas and Australia have also become far more important vine-growers than they were in the mid-1990s, with significant new plantings in Australia, Chile, and the USA, although the rate of planting in each of these countries had slowed by the mid-2000s.

Thanks to the parlous state of vineyards in some Eastern European countries, the world's total vineyard area barely increased between 1998 and 2004, but the world's total production of wine increased by almost 14% over the same period, due largely to more efficient viticulture and more reliable summers. But even though global wine consumption rose by 8% in the same period, we are still left with the dominant problem of European viticulture: over-production of the sort of wine no-one wants to drink any more. Europe's creaking machinery for propping up prices by distilling surplus wine into industrial alcohol, and paying farmers to pull out vines in less satisfactory areas, continues to be the subject of apparently endless debate. Countries such as Argentina and South Africa do their best to dispose of their surpluses via grape concentrate and brandy-based drinks.

DISTRIBUTION OF THE WORLD'S VINEYARDS

(in 1,000s hectares)

Rank	Country	2004	1998	%Change
1	Spain	1,200	1,180	1.7
2	France	889	914	-2.7
3	Italy	849	899	-5.6
4	Former Soviet Reps*	587	788	-25
5	Turkey †	570	602	-5.3
6	China †	471	194	143
7	USA	398	364	9.3
8	Iran †	296	270	9.6
9	Portugal	247	260	-5
10	Romania	222	253	-12
11	Argentina	213	210	1.4
12	Chile †	189	144	31
13	Australia	164	98	67
14	South Africa	133	111	20
15	Greece	130	129	0.8
16	Germany	102	106	-3.8
17	Bulgaria	97	109	-11
18	Algeria †	95	56	70
19	Hungary	83	131	-37
20	Brazil †	74	60	23
21	Serbia & Montenegro*	72	106	-32
22	Egypt †	71	56	27
23	India †	65	43	51
24	Morocco †	50	50	0
27	Austria	49	49	0
28	Syria †	46	86	-46
29	Mexico †	42	41	2.4
30	Slovakia & Czech Rep	31	33	-6
31	South Korea	25	30	-17
33	Tunisia †	23	27	-15
34	Japan	20	22	-9.1
35	Slovenia	17	-	-
36	Cyprus †	17	20	-15
37	Lebanon †	15	26	-42
38	Switzerland	15	15	0
39	Peru †	11	11	0
40	Uruguay	9	11	-18
41	Jordan †	4	15	-73
	World total	**7,591**	**7,519**	**0.9**

	acre	ha

The hectare (100 ares) is the equivalent of 2.47 acres.

HECTOLITRES The hectolitre (100 litres) is the commonest measure for wine production. It equals 22 imperial gallons (26.4 US gallons).

---- International boundary

▬ Vineyards

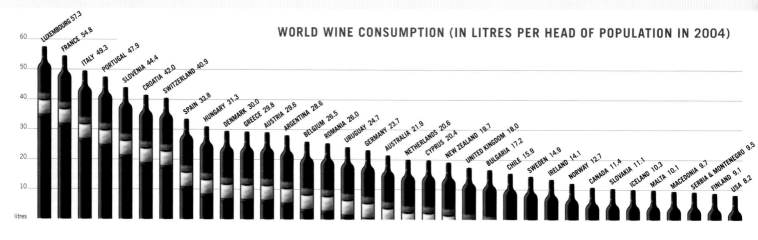

WORLD WINE CONSUMPTION (IN LITRES PER HEAD OF POPULATION IN 2004)

LUXEMBOURG 57.3, FRANCE 54.8, ITALY 49.3, PORTUGAL 47.9, SLOVENIA 44.4, CROATIA 42.0, SWITZERLAND 40.9, SPAIN 33.8, HUNGARY 31.3, DENMARK 30.0, GREECE 29.8, AUSTRIA 29.6, ARGENTINA 28.6, BELGIUM 26.5, ROMANIA 26.0, URUGUAY 24.7, GERMANY 23.7, AUSTRALIA 21.9, NETHERLANDS 20.6, CYPRUS 20.4, NEW ZEALAND 19.7, UNITED KINGDOM 18.0, BULGARIA 17.2, CHILE 15.9, SWEDEN 14.9, IRELAND 14.1, NORWAY 12.7, CANADA 11.4, SLOVAKIA 11.1, ICELAND 10.3, MALTA 10.1, MACEDONIA 9.7, SERBIA & MONTENEGRO 9.5, FINLAND 9.1, USA 8.2

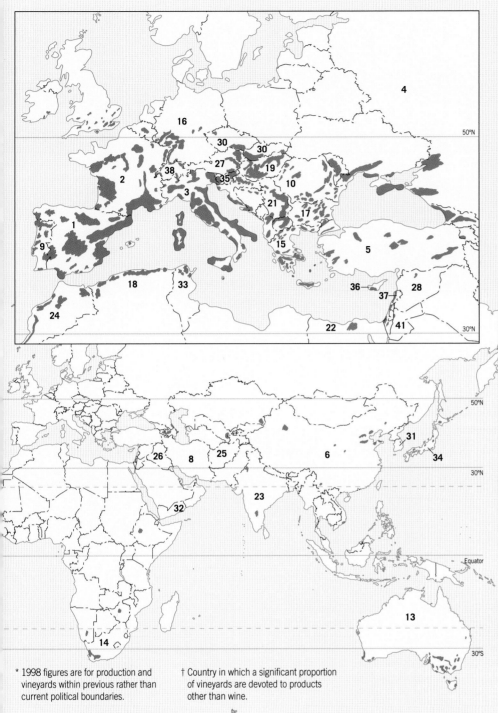

WINE PRODUCTION (in 1,000s hectolitres)			
Country	2004	1998	Yield 2004 hl/ha
North America			
USA	20,169	20,450	50
Canada	522	343	–
Latin America			
Argentina	15,464	12,673	73
Chile †	6,301	5,475	33
Brazil†	3,925	2,782	53
Uruguay	1,126	1,132	125
Mexico†	1,100	1,112	26
Peru †	130	120	12
Bolivia †	20	20	–
Europe			
France	57,386	52,671	65
Italy	53,000	54,188	62
Spain	42,988	30,320	36
Former Soviet Reps*	12,386	15,093	21
Germany	10,047	10,834	99
Portugal	7,481	3,621	30
Romania	6,166	5,002	28
Hungary	4,340	4,180	52
Greece	4,295	3,826	33
Austria	2,735	2,703	59
Bulgaria	1,949	3,308	20
Serbia & Montenegro*	1,740	4,025	24
Switzerland	1,159	1,172	77
Slovakia & Czech Rep	949	940	31
Slovenia	506	–	30
Luxembourg	156	160	–
Albania	100	105	–
Malta	70	32	–
United Kingdom	17	12	–
Belgium	2	1	–
Africa			
South Africa	9,279	8,156	70
Algeria †	770	360	8
Tunisia †	375	352	16
Morocco †	350	298	7
Europe/Middle East			
Cyprus †	404	710	23
Turkey †	250	278	0.4
Lebanon †	150	186	10
Israel †	60	90	–
Far East			
China †	11,700	3,550	24
Japan	862	1,301	43
Australasia			
Australia	13,811	7,415	84
New Zealand	642	606	–
World total	**294,882**	**259,602**	**39**

* 1998 figures are for production and vineyards within previous rather than current political boundaries.

† Country in which a significant proportion of vineyards are devoted to products other than wine.

The world's total consumption of wine continues to rise gradually overall, even though it has declined markedly since 1998 in all 10 countries with the highest average per capita wine consumption, with the exception of Portugal and Switzerland, where it has remained steady. The global increase is chiefly thanks to more enthusiastic consumption in so many countries outside the top 10, notably the vast American market as well as the other big wine importers, Germany and the UK.

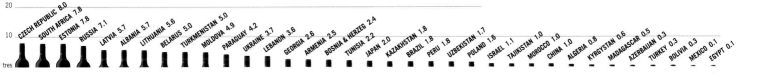

The Ancient World

Wine is far older than recorded history. It emerges with civilization itself from the East. The evidence from tablets and papyri and Egyptian tombs fills volumes. Mankind, as we recognize ourselves, working, quarrelling, loving, and worrying, comes on the scene with the support of a jug of wine. Pharaonic wine, however vividly painted for us to see, is too remote to have any meaning. Our age of wine, with still-traceable roots, begins with the Phoenicians and Greeks who colonized the Mediterranean, starting about 1100BC in the case of the Phoenicians, about 350 years later in the case of the Greeks. It was then that wine began to arrive where it was to make its real home: Italy, France, and Spain.

The Greeks called Italy the Land of Staked Vines (see p.153), just as the Vikings called America Vínland for the profusion of native vines they found circa AD1000. North Africa, Spain, Provence, Sicily, the Italian mainland, and the Black Sea had their first vineyards in the time of the Greek and Phoenician Empires.

ANCIENT GREECE

The wines of Greece herself, no great matter for much of modern times, were lavishly praised and documented by her poets. There was even a fashionable after-dinner game in Athens that consisted of throwing the last few mouthfuls of wine in your cup into the air, to hit a delicately balanced dish on a pole. Smart young things took coaching in the finer points of *kottabos*. But such treatment of the wine, and the knowledge that it was almost invariably drunk as what we would call "a wine cup", flavoured with herbs, spices, and honey and diluted with water (sometimes even seawater) seems to question its innate quality. That the wines of different islands of the Aegean were highly prized for their distinct characters is indisputable. Chios in particular was a supplier in constant demand. Whether the wines would appeal to us today we have no way of knowing.

Greeks industrialized winegrowing in southern Italy, Etruscans in Tuscany and further north, and Romans followed. So much was written about wine and winemaking in ancient

Rome that it is possible to make a rough map (far right) of the wines of the early Roman Empire. The greatest writers, even Virgil, wrote instructions to winegrowers. One sentence of his – "Vines love an open hill" – is perhaps the best single piece of advice that can be given to a European wine-grower. Others were much more calculating, discussing how much work a slave could do for how little food and sleep without losing condition. Roman wine-growing was on a very large scale, and business calculation was at the heart of it. It spread right across the Empire, so that Rome was eventually importing countless ship-loads of amphoras from her colonies in Spain, North Africa – the entire Mediterranean. Since Pompeii was a tourist resort and considerable *entrepôt* for the wine trade, its remarkable survival gives us a great deal of detailed evidence.

How good was Roman wine? Some of it apparently had extraordinary powers of keeping, which in itself suggests that it was well made. The must was frequently concentrated by heating, and wine was stored over

EARLY WINE VESSELS

3000BC
Babylonian

There are earlier wine vessels, in Georgia in particular, but this elaborate creation indicates the importance of wine in ancient Mesopotamia. According to Herodotus, the Mesopotamians imported their wine down the Euphrates. The drinking spout on this vessel seems to link it with Spain's *porrón*.

c.1900BC
Ancient Egyptian

We know more about the viticulture, oenology, and table manners of the Pharoahs than those of almost any other era. They kept vintage-dated single-vineyard wines and drank them in cups of precious metal. This silver beaker was found at the Montu temple near Luxor.

560–530BC
Ancient Greek

The Greeks developed the ceremonial use of wine at symposiums, drinking sessions when the wine was mixed with water and spices in beautifully decorated jars. This clay amphora (a jar with two handles) is painted with a conventional scene from the cult of the god of wine, Dionysus.

Ancient Egyptian grape harvest, from the tomb of Kha'emwese at Thebes, circa 1450BC. The whole process of Egyptian wine-growing and winemaking is vividly illustrated in surviving paintings.

hearths to be exposed to smoke to achieve what must have been a madeira-like effect.

ROME'S GREAT VINTAGES

Rome's great vintages were discussed and even drunk for longer than seems possible; the famous Opimian – from the year of the consulship of Opimius, 121BC – was being drunk when it was 125 years old.

The Romans had all that is necessary for ageing wine, although they did not use the materials as we do. Glass, for example, was not used for wine storage. Wooden barrels were used only in Gaul (which included Germany). Like the Greeks, the Romans used earthenware amphoras. They hold about 35 litres.

Most Italians of 2,000 years ago probably drank wine very like some of their less sophisticated descendants today; young, rather roughly made, sharp or strong according to the vintage. Even the Roman method of cultivation of the vine on trees, the festoons which became the friezes on classical buildings, was still practised until recently in parts of the south of Italy and (especially) northern Portugal.

The Greeks took wine north to southern Gaul. The Romans domesticated it there. By the time they withdrew from what is now France in the 5th century AD, the Romans had laid the foundations for almost all of the most famous vineyards of modern Europe.

Starting in Provence, which had had Greek-planted vineyards already for centuries, they moved up the Rhône Valley and into the Languedoc, the Provincia Narbonensis. At the beginning of the 21st century we still have no clear evidence of exactly when viticulture started in Bordeaux. The earliest mention is in the works of the poet Ausonius in the 4th century AD (Ausonius lived in St-Emilion, perhaps even at Château Ausone), but it probably began long before this.

All the early developments were in the river valleys, the natural lines of communication, which the Romans cleared of forest and cultivated, at first as a precaution against ambushes.

*Starting in Caucasia or Mesopotamia **1** in perhaps 6000BC, the vine was cultivated in Egypt and Phoenicia **2** in about 3000BC. By 2000BC it was in Greece **3** and by 1000BC it was in Italy, Sicily, and North Africa **4**. In the next 500 years it reached at least Spain, Portugal, and the south of France **5**, and probably southern Russia as well. Finally (see map below) it spread with the Romans into northern Europe **6**, getting as far as Britain.*

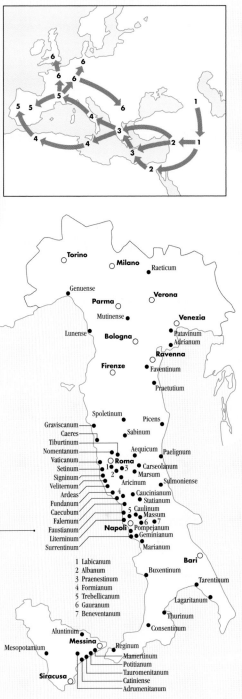

Besides, boats were the best way of moving anything so heavy as wine. Bordeaux, Burgundy, Trier on the Mosel (where the museum preserves a fully laden and manned Roman wine-boat in stone) probably all started as merchant-centres for imported Italian or Greek wine, and then planted their own vines.

By the first century there were vines on the Loire and the Rhine; by the second in Burgundy, and by the fourth in Paris (not such a good idea), in Champagne, and on the Mosel. Burgundy's Côte d'Or remains the least easy vineyard to account for, having no convenient navigable river. It lay where the main road north (to Trier on the Mosel, the northern Rome) skirted the rich province of Autun. Presumably the Autunois saw the commercial opportunity, then found they had chosen a golden slope. The foundations had been dug for the French wine industry we still know.

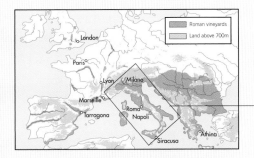

Roman vineyards and wines in AD100 The map above shows the approximate distribution of the grapevine *Vitis vinifera* throughout the Roman Empire in AD100. It displays a remarkably close correspondence with the vineyards of the 21st century, although there is much less in Spain and Portugal, and less in France but vastly more in Eastern Europe (and apparently also in Britain). The map on the right is a reconstruction of wine-growing in Italy in the same year. Names of modern cities are shown in bold; wine names in non-bold type.

---

c.500BC

Thracian

The land north of Greece was famous for its artistry in precious metals. This solid gold rhyton, a deer's head decorated with nymphs, was found at Panagyurishte in Bulgaria in the 20th century. It implies the utmost respect for the wine it contained.

400BC

Etruscan

The Etruscans, who inhabited the country between Tuscany and Rome, were the first in Italy to appreciate wine, before the colonizing Greeks brought it to the south. Perhaps this bronze jug is a portrait of some young man. Much about Etruscan life remains a mystery.

AD100

Roman

The Romans used all the materials we know, including glass, for their wine-drinking. The most recherché material, though, was fluorspar, a mineral found in Persia that gave a unique flavour to the wine drunk from it. Tycoons apparently chewed their fabulously valuable goblets.

The Middle Ages

Out of the Dark Ages that followed the fall of the Roman Empire we gradually emerge into the illumination of the medieval period, to see in its lovely painted pages an entirely familiar scene: people enjoying drinking wine. Winemaking methods were not to change in their essentials until the 20th century. The Church was the repository of the skills of civilization in the Dark Ages – indeed the continuation of Rome's Imperial administration under a new guise. The Emperor Charlemagne recreated an Imperial system – and took great and famous pains to legislate in favour of better wine.

As expansionist monasteries cleared hillsides and built walls around fields of cuttings, and as dying wine-growers and departing crusaders bequeathed it their land, the Church came to be identified with wine – not only as the Blood of Christ, but as luxury and comfort in this world. Cathedrals and churches, but above all the multiplying monasteries, owned or created most of the greatest vineyards of Europe.

The Benedictines, from their great mother-houses of Monte Cassino in Italy and Cluny in Burgundy, went out and cultivated the finest vineyards, until their way of life became notorious: "Rising from the table with their veins swollen with wine and their heads on fire." Their great monasteries included Fulda near Frankfurt, Lorsch near Mainz, and major establishments in Alsace, Switzerland, Bavaria, and Austria.

Reaction came in 1098, when Saint Robert of Molesme split from the Benedictines and founded the ascetic order of the Cistercians, named for their new abbey of Cîteaux, within walking distance of the Côte d'Or. The Cistercian order was explosively successful, founding not only the great walled vineyards of the Clos de Vougeot in Burgundy and the Steinberg in the Rheingau, beside their abbey of Kloster Eberbach, but magnificent monasteries all over Europe – and eventually, of course, becoming as notorious for their gluttony as the Benedictines. Alcobaça in Portugal seems to have been their Michelin 3-star establishment.

The one important exception to domination by the Church was the thriving vineyard of Bordeaux, where development was simply commercial, with a single market in view. From 1152 to 1453 the great Duchy of Aquitaine, most of western France, was united by marriage to the crown of England and bent its efforts to filling great annual wine fleets with hogsheads of light claret, the *vin nouveau* the English loved.

But it was within the stable framework of the Church and the monasteries, in which tools and terms and techniques seemed to stand still, that the styles of wine and even some of the grape varieties now familiar to us slowly came into being. Few things in the medieval world were so strictly regulated. Wine and wool were the two great luxuries of northern Europe in the Middle Ages. Trade in cloth and wine made fortunes – most notably in Flanders and the great annual fairs that took place in Champagne, attracting merchants even over the Alps. No region became more obsessed with wine than Germany, where vast barrels known as "tuns" were built for great vintages. The Heidelberg tun held the equivalent of 19,000 dozen bottles. Connoisseurship may have been rudimentary, but in 1224 the King of France held an international tasting. "The Battle of Wines" included 70 entries, from Spain, Germany, and Cyprus as well as all over France. The judge was an English priest. Cyprus won.

The technology of winemaking scarcely changed during the medieval period – or for centuries after. Grape varieties were selected and developed and refinements made, but the harvest scene here is different only in style and costume from one you could have seen in most of Europe early in the 20th century. Donkey transport was benign, efficient, and of course sustainable. This early 16th century tapestry is one of five depicting the vintage, woven at Tournai in the southern Netherlands and now at the great museum of the arts of wine at Château Mouton Rothschild in the Médoc.

The Evolution of Modern Wine

Up to the start of the 17th century wine was in the unique position of being the one and only wholesome and – up to a point – storable beverage. It had no challengers. Water was normally unsafe to drink, at least in cities. Ale without hops very quickly went bad. There were no spirits, nor any of the caffeine-containing drinks that appear essential to life today.

Europe drank wine on a scale it is difficult to conceive of; our ancestors must have been in a perpetual fuddle. It is hard to have confidence in the descriptions of wine that survive from before about 1700. With the exception of Shakespeare's graphic tasting notes, "a marvellous searching wine, and it perfumes the blood ere one can say 'What's this?'," they tend to refer to royal recommendations or miraculous cures rather than to taste and style.

In the 17th century all this changed, starting with chocolate from Central America, then coffee from Arabia and finally tea from China. At the same time the Dutch developed the art and commerce of distilling, turning huge tracts of western France into suppliers of cheap white wine for their stills; hops turned ale into more stable beer and great cities began to pipe the clean water they had lacked since Roman times. The wine industry was threatened with catastrophe unless it developed new ideas.

It is no coincidence that we date the creation of most of the wines we consider classics today from the second half of the 17th century. But these developments would never have succeeded without the timely invention of the glass wine bottle. Since Roman times wine had spent all its life in a barrel. Bottles, or rather jugs, usually of pottery or leather, were used simply for bringing it to table. The early 17th century saw changes in glassmaking technology that made bottles stronger and cheaper to blow. At about the same time some unknown thinker brought together the bottle, the cork, and the corkscrew.

Bit by bit it became clear that wine kept in a tightly corked bottle lasted far longer than wine in a barrel, which was likely to go off rapidly after

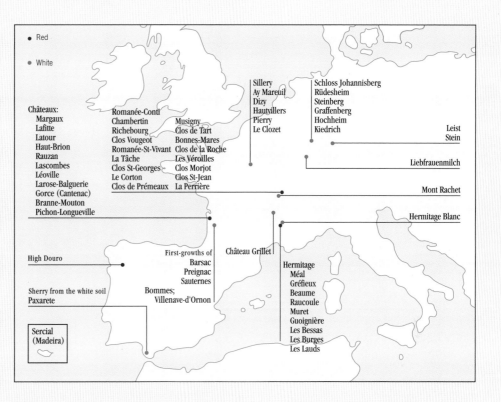

the barrel was broached. It also aged differently, acquiring a "bouquet". The *vin de garde* was created and with it the chance to double and treble the price of wines capable of ageing.

It was the owner of Château Haut-Brion who first hit on the idea of what we might call "reserve" wines: selected, later-picked, stronger, carefully made, and matured. In the 1660s he opened London's first restaurant, under his own name, Pontac's Head, to publicize his produce.

In the early 18th century, burgundy changed its nature too. The most delicate wines, Volnay and Savigny, were once the most fashionable. Now these *vins de primeur* began to give way to the demand for long-fermented, dark-coloured *vins de garde*, especially from the Côte de Nuits. In Burgundy at least, though, the master-grape, Pinot Noir, had been identified and made mandatory. Champagne, too, adopted Pinot

It is fascinating to compare A Jullien's 1866 classification of the world's great wines with our modern ideas. In his Topographie de Tous les Vignobles Connus he listed the vineyards shown on this map (in their original spelling).

Noir in emulation. Germany's best vineyards were being replanted to Riesling. But most other regions were still experimenting.

The wine that benefited most from the development of the bottle was the fiery port the English had started to drink in the late 17th century – not out of choice, but because the duty on their preferred French wine was raised to prohibitive levels by an almost uninterrupted state of war. They had doubts about it at first, but as the century, and their bottles, grew older, their opinion of it rose sharply. The trend is graphically illustrated by the way the port bottle changed shape within a century (see below).

THE EVOLUTION OF THE PORT BOTTLE

In 1708 the port bottle was still a carafe; by 1793 it had approached its modern proportions. With the discovery that bottled wine improved with keeping, bottles were designed to be "laid down", enabling the emergence of vintage wine.

first wine-rush. This was the world phylloxera struck (see pp.18–19). At the time, when it caused the pulling up of almost every vine, it seemed like the end of the world of wine.

In retrospect the rationalization of planting, the introduction of grafting, and the enforced selection of the most desirable grape varieties together made a chance for a great new beginning. But it was a slow and tortuous start, with every sort of setback in glut, fraud, Prohibition, Depression, World War – and bad weather. In 40 years (to take Bordeaux as the sample) only 11 vintages could be described as generally good. It was against this depressing background that the French government made the first moves towards regulation in the fledgling regime of Appellations Contrôlées (see p.52). The notion of terroir was codified for the first time.

SCIENCE AND INDUSTRY

The 20th century saw two revolutions in the world of wine: the first scientific, the second industrial. As it began, the practical significance of Pasteur's science was just sinking in; fermentation was no longer a mystery but a process that could be controlled. Bordeaux had opened the first university department dedicated to oenology, at the same time as Montpellier, Geisenheim, Davis in California, and Roseworthy in Australia opened departments for the study of viticulture. The established wine world had enough problems to solve; the emerging one had every decision to take, starting with which varieties to plant.

But it was not until the 1950s, as America struggled out of the chaotic legacy of Prohibition, and Europe began to recover from World War II, that anything like prosperity returned to châteaux, wineries, and domaines.

For the warm countries of the New World the true revolution came with refrigeration and the ability to cool the fermenting must. Almost the only aromatic, balanced, and profitably ageable table wines therefore came from northern Europe. Once that nut was cracked, California took to varietal wines like a religion.

In 1866, André Jullien published the figures for the alcoholic strengths of recent vintages. By today's standards the burgundies are formidable: Corton 1858, 15.6%; Montrachet 1858, 14.3%; Volnay 1859, 14.9%; Richebourg 1859, 14.3%. In contrast, Bordeaux wines of the same two years ranged from 11.3% (St-Emilion Supérieur) to a mere 8.9% (Château Lafite).

The low natural strength of the Bordeaux wines explains what seems today a curious habit of the old wine trade. Up to the mid-19th century the wines for England – which was most of the best of Bordeaux – were subjected to what was known as *le travail à l'anglaise*. One recipe called for the addition of 30 litres of Spanish wine (Alicante or Benicarlo), two litres of unfermented white must, and a bottle of brandy to each barrel of claret. The summer after the vintage the wine was set to ferment again with these additives, then treated as other wines and kept for several years in wood before shipping. The result was strong wine with a good flavour, but "heady and not suitable for all stomachs". It fetched more than natural wine.

Today's preoccupation with authenticity, even at the expense of quality, makes these practices seem abusive. But it is as if someone revealed as a shocking practice the addition of brandy to port. We like Douro wine with brandy in it; our ancestors liked Lafite laced with Alicante. (And tastes change; today we like Douro wine without brandy as well.)

In the 19th century, champagne was sweeter and fuller in colour and flavour – although otherwise very like it is today. Port and sherry had both been perfected. There was more stronger sweet wine: Málaga and Marsala were in their heydays. Madeira, Constantia, and Tokay (as it was then called) were as highly regarded as Germany's Trockenbeerenauslesen.

The wine trade was booming. In the wine-growing countries an unhealthy amount of the economy rested on wine: in Italy in 1880 it was calculated that no less than 80% of the population more or less relied on wine for a living. Both Italy (in Tuscany and Piemonte) and Spain (in Rioja) were creating their first modern export wines. California was in the midst of its

EVOLUTION OF WINE PRODUCTION IN BORDEAUX

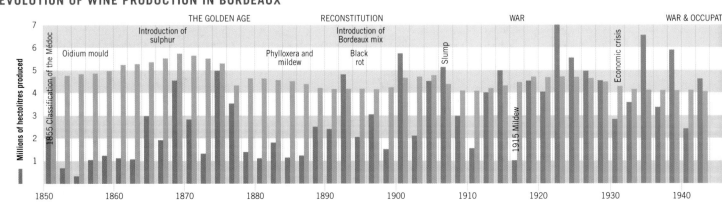

Not many varieties: Zinfandel was California's own grape, but Chardonnay was "the sole source of the great French white burgundies", Cabernet "the premier red grape of the Bordeaux area of France". Their names became incantations, their wines categories that no winery could be without. Australia, whose founding wine-growers planted Shiraz, Semillon, and Riesling, had to hurry to introduce the grapes the whole world started to want.

The modern world of wine started in the 1960s, with the almost simultaneous appearance of new wineries with high ambitions in California and Australia, and perhaps more significantly the launch by E & J Gallo of cheap palatable table wines (even if they were labelled "Chablis" and "Hearty Burgundy") to cater to a completely new public.

OAK AS MAKE-UP

Armed with the science to improve quality, and with technology that accelerated with demand, ambitious winemakers felt there were no heights they could not scale. The great discovery of the 1960s was that French oak barrels, used judiciously, could give wines from very different terroirs more than a passing resemblance to the "classics" of France. No single factor did more to close the gap between French wine and its imitators.

Sadly it was a trick that soon got out of control as novices confused the taste of oak with the taste of good wine. Over-use of oak as flavouring, making wines that refresh no-one, is still a widespread problem, not only in the New World, but among French, Italian, and Spanish producers who have lost confidence in their own taste and bend to the wind of fashion.

The 21st century started with the greatest supplies (indeed a potentially embarrassing glut) of good wine from more sources than the world has ever known. Added to all the scientific and technological advances, the great leap at the end of the 20th century was in communication, hence in worldwide competition.

There are few, if any, secrets today in a world which used to play its cards close to the chest. The "flying winemaker" was an invention of the 1980s: a high-tech professional, usually Australian, originally commissioned to make wine in Europe in Australia's winter, now often making many wines at the same time all over the world. Winemakers, flying or earthbound, sometimes seem to be in constant confessional, spewing out every detail of their doings on back-labels. The ever-present danger of a global village, of course, is that marketing takes over from the people with wine-stained hands. Marketeers play safe. Their advice will flood the market with what sold last year rather than what a vineyard is best capable of.

The danger of sameness, of every producer aiming at the global market with a "me-too" wine, has been well aired. To most consumers, it must be said, it is not a danger at all. Base-level wine drinkers make up the majority, and what they want is continuity. Variety equals confusion and loss of confidence. To Anglo-Saxons the reassurance of labels in English has been another big factor in the success of New World wines.

On the other hand, the world's wine drinkers are slowly but measurably trading-up and taking more interest in what they are drinking. Quality wine is gaining at the expense of table wine – a trend that a future surplus at all levels will only accelerate.

The days are passing when, for example, branded Chardonnays can slug it out in the marketplace on the basis of low price and lots of advertising. As consumers learn more about wine, and about their own tastes, they are prepared to spend more. It became clear in the last decades of the 20th century that the days of the nondescript are numbered. The vineyards of the Midi that once produced *vin ordinaire* are now the home of Vins de Pays. Few grudge the premium, and success spurs the producers.

There are many reasons to believe in the survival of variety. Indeed in its revival, as ambitious New World growers replace Cabernet and Merlot with Sangiovese, Nebbiolo, Tempranillo, Touriga Nacional, and vast tracts of Syrah or, more likely thanks to Australia's increasing influence, Shiraz. But there are heartening signs that wine producers all over the world are taking new interest and delight in what they and they alone have to offer today's increasingly discerning consumer, whether it be very special local conditions or an almost extinct indigenous grape variety. This does not make learning about wine any easier, but wine is naturally complex, and all the better for it.

The term "flying winemaker" was originally applied to Nigel Sneyd, when Tony Laithwaite of the UK company Bordeaux Direct brought him over from Australia in 1987 to supervise the vintage at the St-Vivien co-op in the Dordogne.

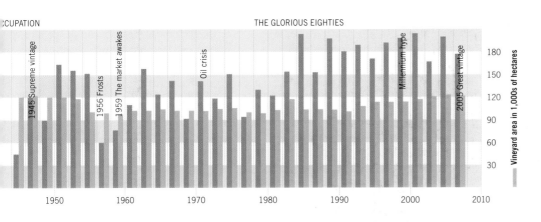

OCCUPATION

THE GLORIOUS EIGHTIES

1945 Supreme vintage
1956 Frosts
1959 The market awakes
Oil crisis
Millennium hype
2005 Great vintage

180
150
120
90
60
30

Vineyard area in 1,000s of hectares

1950   1960   1970   1980   1990   2000   2010

Left Bordeaux's vineyard area and wine production in relation to wars, pests, diseases, slumps, booms, and the weather, plotted up until 1988 by Philippe Roudié of Bordeaux University. Two great chemical aids, sulphur (against oidium mould) and Bordeaux mixture (copper sulphate and lime), against mildew had immediate effect. The 1990s were dominated by arguments over prices. Will the new century see warmer and warmer vintages? They have been as irregular as ever up to now.

The Vine

It is an extraordinary fact that this wonderfully varied and evocative drink we call wine is the fermented juice of a single fruit, the grape. Every drop of wine we drink is made from rain (and in hotter regions irrigation water) recovered from the ground by the mechanism of the plant that bears grapes, the vine, and in the presence of sunlight converted by photosynthesis into fermentable sugar, with a little help of nutrients from the soil.

For the first two or three years of its life a young vine is too busy creating a root system and building a strong woody stalk to bear more than a few grapes. Thereafter, left to nature, it would rampage away, bearing some fruit but spending much more of its energy on making new shoots and putting out long, wandering branches of leafy wood, ideally seeking out a tree to climb, until it covered as much as an acre (nearly half a hectare) of ground, with new root systems forming wherever the branches touched the soil.

This natural form of reproduction, known in French as *provignage*, was used to make a vineyard in ancient times. To prevent the grapes rotting or the mice getting them, since they lay on the ground, little props were pushed under the stems to support each bunch. If the vine grew near trees, it used its tendrils to climb them to dizzy heights. The Romans planted elms especially for the purpose. Freelance labour was hired for the vintage; it was too dangerous to risk your own slaves.

Modern vines, of course, are not allowed to waste their precious energy on being "vigorous" – making long, leafy branches – however much they may try (see p.31). Better-quality grapes grow in moderately fertile soil on a vine that is pruned in winter and regularly cut back to a very limited number of buds.

Like most other plants, vines will reproduce from seed, but the seeds rarely turn out like their parents. Instead viticulturists propagate vines asexually by taking cuttings so that they can be sure that the offspring are the same as the mother vine. Pips are used only for experimenting with new crosses between different varieties.

For planting a new vineyard cuttings are either planted to take root on their own or grafted onto a rootstock, a rooted cutting of another species specially selected for the soil type or resistance to drought or nematodes (tiny worms) for instance.

Nurserymen should try to take cuttings only from plants that are healthy and free of virus. The little grafted "slips" are planted out for a season until they form roots. If there is any danger of virus infection, tissue-cultured vines, grown from only the virus-free growing-tip, have to be nurtured in a laboratory to become a rooted plant.

As a vine grows older its principal roots penetrate deeper into the ground in search of water and nutrients. In very general terms, the younger the vine, the lighter and less subtle the wine – although vines can produce delicious fruit in their first year or two, when yields are naturally low and the available flavour is concentrated into relatively few grapes. Somewhere between three and six years after being planted, the vine stabilizes, filling the space allotted to it above ground. It produces increasingly flavourful grapes and therefore more and more concentrated wine, presumably thanks to an increasingly complex root system which regulates the supply of water and nutrients.

Yields typically start to decline after 25 or 30 years (or the vine succumbs to disease or is of an unfashionable grape variety), when vines tend to be pulled out as uneconomic. Wine from vines older than this generally command a premium and may be labelled the produce of old vines, *vieilles vignes* in French.

The best soils (see pp.26-27) drain quickly and often deeply, sometimes drawing the roots down to great depths to find a stable but not too generous water supply. At the same time the vine constantly grows new feeder roots near the surface.

PESTS AND DISEASES

The European vine family, called vinifera, or "wine-bearing", has countless enemies, the worst of them diseases and pests introduced far too recently (mostly from America) for it to have developed any natural resistance. In the 19th century, first powdery mildew (oidium) and then downy mildew attacked Europe's vines – and vinifera vines planted in the New World. Laborious remedies were discovered for these two fungal diseases, though both still need treatment by regular spraying. Another common reason for the persistent drone of tractors spraying vineyards in the growing season is rot, specifically the malign form of botrytis fungus (as opposed to the benevolent form, which can produce such exceptional sweet white wines as those described on p.102). This botrytis bunch rot, also called grey rot, can impart a fatally mouldy taste to grapes, and is increasingly resistant to anti-rot chemicals (see pp.30-31 for alternative strategies). Fungal diseases are a particular problem in damp climates or where the vine's leaves are particularly dense.

Towards the end of the 19th century, soon after a cure for the two mildews had been developed, a far more dangerous scourge was observed and, eventually, identified. The phylloxera louse feasts on the roots of the vine and eventually kills it. It almost destroyed the entire European vineyard, until it was discovered that native American vines (phylloxera came from America) are immune. Virtually every vine in Europe had to be replaced with a vinifera cutting grafted onto a rooted cutting from an American vine, a phylloxera-resistant rootstock.

Some of the world's newer wine regions (Chile and parts of Australia being the most obvious examples) have yet to experience this predatory aphid, and so happily plant their vinifera vines

THE VINE THROUGH THE YEAR

BUDS DEVELOP

As early as March in northern Europe and September in the southern hemisphere, the buds left after winter pruning start to swell and the first signs of green can be seen emerging from the gnarled wood. This happens when temperatures reach about 50°F (10°C).

LEAVES SEPARATE

Within 10 days of budbreak, leaves start to separate from the bud and embryonic tendrils begin to be visible, and are all too vulnerable to frost, which can strike as late as mid-May or mid-November in cooler districts of the northern and southern hemispheres respectively. Late pruning of the vine can delay budbreak.

FLOWERING BEGINS

Between 6 and 13 weeks after budbreak the crucial flowering of the vine begins with the emergence of tiny caps of fused petals. These look very like miniature versions of the grapes that will be formed here once the caps fall, exposing the stamens so that they can be fertilized by pollen to create the berries.

directly as ungrafted cuttings. In Oregon and New Zealand, however, this has proved a short-term stratagem, and in the 1980s vine-growers in northern California learnt to their cost that rootstocks have to be very carefully chosen if they are to offer reliable resistance to phylloxera. Hundreds of thousands of acres there had to be replanted with more suitable, truly phylloxera-resistant rootstocks, and strict quarantine rules are in force in many wine regions.

The parts of the vine that grow above ground are on the menu for a whole menagerie, too. Red spiders, the grubs of the cochylis and eudemis moths, various sorts of beetles, bugs, and mites find it nutritious. The latest enemy to viticulture is the Asian lady beetle, which releases a body fluid that even in tiny amounts taints the wine. Most of these pests can be controlled by the various chemical sprays to which so many vines are subjected throughout the summer. Meanwhile, the growing band of organic and biodynamic vine-growers are experimenting with more natural methods such as predators, pheromones, and biopesticides.

THE SPREAD OF PHYLLOXERA

1863 Phylloxera louse discovered in southern England.

1866 Found in southern Rhône Valley and the Languedoc, France.

1869 Phylloxera reaches Bordeaux.

1871 Discovered in Portugal and Turkey.

1872 Phylloxera found in Austria.

1874 The louse spreads to Switzerland.

1875 Phylloxera found in Italy and also as far afield as Victoria, Australia, in late 1875 or early 1876.

1878 Phylloxera reaches Spain. Grafting of vines onto resistant American rootstocks begins in France.

1881 Presence of phylloxera confirmed in German vineyards.

1885 The louse is discovered in Algeria.

1897 Phylloxera found in Dalmatia (Croatia).

1898 Spreads to Greece.

1980s Phylloxera-affected vines found in northern California.

1990s Diseased vines discovered in Oregon and in New Zealand (pictured left).

2006 Isolated outbreak in Victoria's Yarra Valley, Australia.

PESTS, DISEASES, AND THEIR EFFECTS ON THE VINE

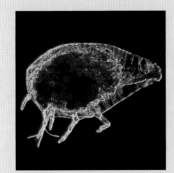

The phylloxera louse is shown in all its sinister detail by this light micrograph. Native to North America, it reached Europe on steamships able to cross the Atlantic fast enough for it to survive on the botanical specimens collected by Victorians. American vines are resistant to it, and grafting European vines onto American roots is the only effective defence.

Fungal diseases such as downy and powdery mildew as well as various sorts of rot are the vine's chief enemies except in the most arid climates. The most effective weapon in the vigneron's armoury against them is spraying vines with fungicides based on copper, traditionally copper sulphate or Bordeaux mixture. The copper leaves the vines this alarming bright blue colour.

Leafroll virus is a complex of different viruses which turns vine leaves a deep red and causes them to curl downwards. While the vines are often gloriously photogenic, the wines are seriously lean because the disease slows the whole ripening process, and it tends to reduce yields by up to 50%. Leafroll virus is present all over the world but has been a particular problem in South Africa.

Pierce's Disease is spread by this leaf hopper, the glassy-winged sharpshooter, whose ability to fly long distances has put a wide range of northern California vineyards at risk. Vines die within five years of first succumbing to this bacterial disease, showing first as dead spots on the leaves, which eventually fall off. No grape varieties are resistant and there is no known cure.

FLOWERING EFFECTS

The size of the eventual crop depends on the success of pollination. Poor weather during the 10- to 14-day flowering can result in coulure, whereby the stalks of an excessive number of very small berries shrivel, causing them to drop off, and also millerandage: different-sized berries on the same bunch.

VERAISON

The place of such buds as escape frost and rain is taken by hard, green baby grapes in June/December. These grapes swell during the summer and in August/February undergo veraison, whereby they soften and turn reddish or yellow. The ripening process begins and sugars start to build rapidly inside the grape.

FULL RIPENESS

Measuring ripeness and in particular deciding what constitutes perfect ripeness has been the focus of much recent research. Dark-skinned varieties should certainly have uniformly deep-coloured skins, but stems and stalks should start to lignify (turn woody) and grape seeds should show no sign of greenness.

International Grapes

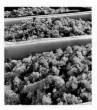

If geography determines the nuances of how a wine tastes, the raw material is the grape variety or varieties that go into the wine. Since the mid-20th century, varieties have played an increasingly important role in the language of wine. Today far fewer wine drinkers know the name Chablis, for instance, than know the name of the grape from which wines in this northern French appellation are made: Chardonnay. It is much easier to get to grips with a handful of well-known grape names than to know all the possible place names that could be found on wine labels, which is why "varietal labelling" has become so popular. That said, blends of two or more varieties are becoming increasingly common at the expense of monovarietal wines.

A passing acquaintance with the particularly well-travelled varieties described on these pages would provide a good start to anyone's wine education. At least some of the most obvious characteristics outlined in italics below each grape name should be more or less guaranteed in any varietally labelled bottle – which includes the great majority of wine produced outside Europe and an increasing proportion of European, even French, wine.

But to progress in terms of wine knowledge, to start to understand most of the good and great wines of Europe and to understand the subtleties of wines made elsewhere, you need to satisfy some geographical curiosity. A book like this can help to explain more than any other why Hermitage tastes different from another wine made from the same grape, Syrah, grown 30 miles (48km) upstream on the differently angled slopes of Côte-Rôtie.

CROSS-SECTION OF A PINOT NOIR GRAPE TOWARDS THE END OF THE RIPENING PROCESS.

Brush What remains attached to the stem when grapes are destemmed at the winery, or knocked off the bunch during mechanical harvesting.

Stem (or stalk) As grapes reach full physiological ripeness, stems turn from green and fleshy to brown and woody. Stems can make a wine taste tart and astringent.

Pulp (or flesh) This is wine's main ingredient by volume, containing grape sugars, acids, and, mainly, water. The flesh of almost all wine grapes is this grey colour.

Pip (or seed) The number, size, and shape of pips is different for different grape varieties. All pips release bitter tannins if crushed.

Skin The most important ingredient in red wines, containing a high concentration of tannins, colouring matter, and compounds which determine the eventual wine's flavour.

PINOT NOIR

Cherry, raspberry, violets, game, mid-ruby hue

This most elusive grape is relatively early ripening and extremely sensitive to terroir. Planted somewhere hot, it will ripen too fast and fail to develop any of the many fascinating flavour compounds its relatively thin skins can harbour. Pinot Noir's perfect place on earth is Burgundy's Côte d'Or, where, if the clones, vine-growing, and winemaking techniques are right, it can convey intricate differences of terroir. So haunting are great red burgundy's charms that growers everywhere try to emulate them, but so far only New Zealand, Oregon, and the coolest corners of California and Australia have had much luck. It is rarely blended for still wine, but with Chardonnay and its cousin Pinot Meunier it is part of the standard recipe for champagne.

RIESLING

Aromatic, delicate, racy, expressive, rarely oaked

Riesling is to white wine what Cabernet Sauvignon is to red: it can make entirely different wines in different places and can age magnificently. Mispronounced (it is "Reessling"), underrated, and underpriced for most of the late 20th century, Riesling is slowly becoming more fashionable. The wine tends to be powerfully scented, reflecting minerals, flowers, lime, and honey depending on its provenance, sweetness, and age. Riesling makes great botrytized wines in its homeland, Germany, but thanks to global warming it also makes fine, firm dry wines there too. Riesling is still the noblest grape of Germany and Alsace and is widely admired in Australia and Austria.

SYRAH/SHIRAZ

Black pepper, dark chocolate, notable colour, and tannin

In its northern Rhône Valley home Syrah most famously makes great, dark, long-lived Hermitage and Côte-Rôtie (where it is traditionally perfumed with a little Viognier). It is now planted all over southern France, where it is commonly used in blends. Syrah tastes quite different in Australia, where, called Shiraz, it is the country's most planted red grape, making dense, rich, potent wines in places as warm as Barossa, though it can still have a hint of black pepper in the cooler reaches of Victoria. Today growers all over the world are experimenting with this easy-to-love grape, whose wines, however ripe, always have a savoury kick at the end.

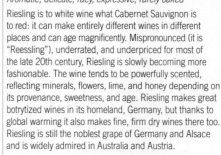

CABERNET SAUVIGNON

Blackcurrant, cedar, high tannin

Synonymous with serious red wine capable of ageing into subtle splendour. For this reason Cabernet Sauvignon is also the best-travelled red wine variety, but since it is a relatively late ripener it is viable only in warmish climates. Some years it may not ripen fully even in its homeland, the Médoc/Graves. But when it does, the colour, flavour, and tannins packed into the thick skins of its tiny, dark blue berries can be remarkable. With careful winemaking and barrel ageing, it can produce some of the longest-living and most intriguing reds of all. In Bordeaux and increasingly elsewhere it is blended with Merlot and Cabernet Franc, although it can make delicious unblended wine if grown somewhere as warm as Chile or northern California, its second home.

CHARDONNAY

Broad, inoffensive – unless over-oaked

The white burgundy grape, but so much more versatile than Pinot Noir. Chardonnay can be grown and ripened without difficulty almost everywhere except at the extremes of the wine world (its early budding can put it at risk of spring frost damage). It has become the world's best-known white wine grape, perhaps because (unlike Riesling, for example) it does not have a particularly strong flavour of its own, which is one reason why it responds so well to barrel fermentation and/or oak ageing. It routinely takes on whatever character the winemaker desires: vivacious and sparkling, refreshingly unoaked, rich and buttery, or even sweet.

MERLOT

Plump, soft, and plummy

Cabernet Sauvignon's traditional, slightly paler, fleshier blending partner, especially in Bordeaux, where its earlier ripening makes Merlot so much easier to grow that it is the most planted grape there. Easier to ripen than Cabernet Sauvignon in cooler vintages, it is more alcoholic in warmer ones. Its bigger berries and thinner skins mean generally less tannic, more opulent, wines that can be enjoyed sooner. Merlot also has an independent existence as a varietal, particularly in the USA, where it is regarded as easier to drink (if more difficult to admire) than Cabernet, and in northeast Italy, where it is easier to ripen. It reaches its apogee in Pomerol, where it can result in voluptuous, velvety essences. Especially common in Chile.

SAUVIGNON BLANC

Grass, green fruits, razor-sharp, rarely oaked

Piercingly aromatic, extremely refreshing, and, unlike most of the grapes on these pages, best drunk relatively young. Sauvignon Blanc's original home in France is the Loire, particularly in and around Sancerre and Pouilly-sur-Loire for Pouilly-Fumé, where it can vary considerably according to vintage. Grown in too warm a climate it can lose its characteristic aroma and acidity and can be too heavy in much of California and Australia. Provided the vine's tendency to excessive vigour is tamed by canopy management, Sauvignon Blanc does particularly well in New Zealand, notably Marlborough, as well as in cooler parts of South Africa. In Bordeaux it is traditionally blended with Sémillon for both dry and luscious sweet wines.

GEWURZTRAMINER

Lychees, roses, heady, high alcohol, deep-coloured

Gewurztraminer is a devil to spell – and often loses its Umlaut – but a dream to recognize. Its distinctive aroma, so strong that it earned the grape the prefix *gewürz*, or "spice", in German, can easily be tiring, especially if combined with high residual sugar in the wine. But the best examples of Gewurztraminer from Alsace, where it is most revered, have an undertow of body and nerve, as well as a savoury finish, which stops them from cloying. Sufficient acidity is the key. Some fine examples have also emerged from New Zealand's East Coast, Chile, British Columbia, Oregon, and Alto Adige. Gewurztraminer grapes are characteristically deep pink and the wine is almost always a particularly deep golden, sometimes pinkish, colour as a result.

SEMILLON

Figs, citrus, lanolin, full-bodied, rich

Sémillon is included here on the strength of the exceptional quality of the sweet wine produced from it, particularly in Sauternes and Barsac, where it is traditionally blended 4:1 with Sauvignon Blanc, together with a little Muscadelle. Its relatively thin skins make Sémillon (Semillon outside France) highly susceptible to the botrytis mould that can in the right conditions concentrate the grapes miraculously with noble rot. It is the most planted white grape in Bordeaux, where it is also responsible for some fine, oaked dry wines, especially in Graves. Australia's Hunter Valley also has a special affinity with it, making long-lived, complex, mineral-scented dry wines from early-picked grapes, and South Africa has some venerable Semillon vines.

Regional Grapes

The grape varieties featured here and on the previous page are some of the best-known varieties of the European *vinifera* species of the *Vitis* genus, which also includes American and Asian vine species, and Virginia creeper.

In parts of the USA, wine is made from American vines, which are usefully resistant to many of the fungal diseases that commonly attack vines (outlined on p.18), but species such as *labrusca* have a particularly strong "foxy" flavour (characteristic of Concord grape jelly) which non-locals find off-putting. American and Asian vines can, however, be extremely useful for breeding new varieties for particular conditions. Hundreds of hybrids have been bred by crossing them with European vinifera varieties, notably so that they will ripen in regions with short growing seasons. Some Mongolian vine species, for example, can be useful for breeding to incorporate cold resistance into the resulting vines.

Because many (though by no means all) hybrids produce inferior wine they have at times been scorned, and in Europe are officially outlawed. Many European vine breeders have concentrated on crossing various vinifera varieties to respond to a particular need or environment. Müller-Thurgau, for example, was an early crossing developed specifically to ripen in sites where Riesling would not.

Growers need to decide more than which variety and rootstock to plant. The life of a vine is usually about 30 years (although in fashion-conscious regions the variety is sometimes changed by simply lopping off the plant above ground and grafting on a new, more desirable variety). Just as important can be the choice of clone(s) of the favoured variety. Nurserymen have long observed, selected, and propagated particular plants with special characteristics: high or consistent yield; good resistance to various pests, diseases, and environmental extremes; early ripening, and so on. Today a grower can choose either a single clone or, usually better, several different clones.

Not all vines come with labels attached, of course. The science of vine identification by observation of precise variations in grape and leaf shape, colour, and so on, is known as ampelography. It has revealed various fascinating relationships between varieties, but none quite so radical as the recent discoveries enabled by DNA analysis of different varieties. This exact science has shown that Cabernet Franc and Sauvignon Blanc, for example, are the parents of Cabernet Sauvignon, and that Chardonnay, Aligoté, the Beaujolais grape Gamay, the Muscadet grape Melon de Bourgogne, Auxerrois, and a dozen others are all the progeny of Pinot Noir and the obscure but historic grape Gouais Blanc. Further revelations are expected.

GRENACHE NOIR

Pale, sweet, ripe, useful for rosé

Grenache is widely planted round the Mediterranean and is the most planted grape of the southern Rhône, where it is often blended with Mourvèdre, Syrah, and Cinsault. It is also widely grown in Roussillon, where, with Grenache Blanc and Grenache Gris, its high alcohol levels are useful for the region's famous Vins Doux Naturels (see p.144). As Garnacha it is the most planted red grape in Spain. As Cannonau in Corsica, and as Grenache in California or Australia, it is revered only if the vines are very old or if blended with Syrah and Mourvèdre.

SANGIOVESE

Savoury, lively, variable: from prunes to farmyard

Italy's most planted grape, in its many forms, and particularly common in Central Italy, most gloriously in Chianti Classico, Montalcino (as Brunello), and Montepulciano (as Vino Nobile). The least noble clones, overproduced, make light, tart red wine – oceans of it in Emilia-Romagna. The traditional Chianti recipe diminished it with the white grape Trebbiano as well as the local Canaiolo and a bit of deep Colorino. Today Tuscany's many ambitious producers coax maximum colour and flavour from it. Sangiovese is increasingly planted elsewhere.

CABERNET FRANC

Leafily aromatic, refreshing, rarely heavy

The less intense, softer progenitor of Cabernet Sauvignon. Because it ripens earlier, Cabernet Franc is widely planted in the Loire and on the cooler, damper soils of St-Emilion, where it is often blended with Merlot. In the Médoc/Graves it is planted as an insurance against Cabernet Sauvignon's failure to ripen. Much more resistant to cold winters than Merlot, it can make appetizing wines in New Zealand, Long Island, and Washington. In northeast Italy it can taste positively grassy, and reaches its silky apogee in Chinon, Bourgueil, Saumur-Champigny, and Anjou-Villages.

TEMPRANILLO

Tobacco leaves, spice, leather

Spain's most famous grape. As Tinto Fino or Tinto del País it provides the backbone of Ribera del Duero's lively, deep-flavoured reds. In Rioja it is blended with Garnacha. In Catalunya it is known as Ull de Llebre, in Valdepeñas Cencibel. In Navarra it is often blended with Bordeaux grapes. As Tinta Roriz it has long been used for port and is increasingly respected as a table wine grape in Portugal, where in the Alentejo it is known as Aragonês. Its early budding makes it vulnerable to spring frosts, its thin skins to rot, but it is increasingly valued internationally for fine wine.

MOURVEDRE

Animal, blackberries, alcoholic, tannic

This is a grape that needs considerable sunshine to ripen and is by far the most important grape in Bandol, Provence's most noble wine, although it has to be aged with care. Throughout southern France, and South Australia, it adds flesh to Grenache and Syrah blends in particular. In Spain, as Monastrell, it is the country's second most planted red grape and is associated more with heft than quality. It was known, and somewhat overlooked, as Mataro in both California and Australia until being renamed Mourvèdre and enjoying a new lease of life with glamorously Gallic associations.

NEBBIOLO

Tar, roses, violets, orange with black tints

Piemonte's answer to Pinot Noir. In Barolo and Barbaresco it responds to every nuance of aspect and elevation. It will ripen only on the most favoured of sites. When fully ripe it is exceptionally high in tannins and acids, if not pigments, but long cask and bottle ageing can result in hauntingly seductive wines. Nebbiolo makes a wide range of other, usually lesser, wines in northwest Italy (in Valtellina and Gattinara for example), but like Pinot Noir it has shown a reluctance to travel. Some Americans and Australians keep trying to prove otherwise.

ZINFANDEL

Warm berry flavours, alcohol, sweetness

Zinfandel was regarded as California's own grape for a century, until it was established that, as Primitivo, it was known on the heel of Italy at least as early as the 18th century. DNA analysis has now established its origins as Croatian. The vine ripens unevenly but some berries build almost unparalleled sugars so that "Zin" can be as strong as 17% alcohol. It is more commonly grown to produce enormous crops of much less intense wine in California's Central Valley, much of it stripped of colour, flavoured with aromatic Muscat or Riesling, and sold as (pale pink) White Zinfandel.

MALBEC

Spicy and rich in Argentina, gamey in Cahors

Malbec is a conundrum. It has long been a blending grape all over southwest France, including Bordeaux, but is the dominant grape only in Cahors, where, known as Côt or Auxerrois, it has typically made rustic, sometimes rather animal wines suitable for only medium-term ageing. Emigrés took it to Argentina, where in Mendoza it was so clearly at home that it has become the country's most popular red grape and makes gloriously velvety, concentrated, lively wines, high in alcohol and extract. It thrives particularly in Mendoza's Luján de Cuyo district.

TOURIGA NACIONAL

Tannic, fireworks, occasionally porty

Portugal's most famous port grape, although just one of a wide range of distinctive grapes grown in the Douro Valley, such as the unrelated Touriga Franca, Tinta Barroca, Tinto Cão, and Tinto Roriz (Tempranillo). It is increasingly bottled as a varietal wine throughout Portugal, and is an increasingly important ingredient in Dão. It is also likely to be planted much more widely throughout the wine world for it is by no means short of class and personality. Touriga Nacional is always extremely high in tannin, alcohol, and colour, not least because it is naturally unproductive.

CARMENERE

Firm, Bordeaux-like, can be slightly green

Historic, very late-ripening Bordeaux variety which is hardly found in Bordeaux today but it is common in Chile, where pre-phylloxera cuttings were introduced in the 1850s. For long Carmenère was confused with Merlot but it has now been distinguished in the vineyard. The grapes have to be fully ripe if the resulting wines, which are always very deep in colour, are to avoid a certain green tomato-leaf character and many growers think Carmenère is best blended with other Bordeaux varieties. It is also found in northeastern Italy.

PINOT GRIS

Full, golden, smoky, pungent

This fashionable grape has its power base in Alsace, where, with Riesling, Gewurztraminer, and Muscat, it is regarded as a noble grape variety, responsible for some of the region's most powerful, if quite soft, wines. This pink-skinned mutation of Pinot Noir is a cousin of Chardonnay. In Italy it is known as Pinot Grigio and can produce both characterful and decidedly dull dry whites. Growers elsewhere dither between calling it Gris or Grigio without necessarily any significance for style. It is a speciality in Oregon and, increasingly, New Zealand.

CHENIN BLANC

Extremely versatile; honey, and damp straw

Chenin Blanc is the grape of the middle Loire, sandwiched between the Melon de Bourgogne of Muscadet and the Sauvignon Blanc of the Upper Loire. Much misunderstood, it makes sometimes ordinary dry wine in both California and South Africa, where it is widely planted, but in the Loire it can make nervy, age-worthy, distinctive wines of all stages of sweetness. Botrytized Loire Chenins such as Vouvray can be great, long-lived, sweet whites. In the Loire Chenin Blanc also makes lightly honeyed, dry, still wines, and some characterful sparkling Saumur and Vouvray.

MUSCAT BLANC

Grapey, relatively simple, often sweet

This is the finest sort of Muscat and has small berries (*petits grains* in French) which are round rather than oval like those of the less noble Muscat of Alexandria (Gordo Blanco or Lexia in Australia, where this lesser variety is grown for the table). As Moscato Bianco in Italy, the finer Muscat is responsible for Asti and many fine, light fizzes. It also makes great sweet wines in southern France and Greece. Australia's strong, sweet, sticky Muscats are made from a dark-skinned version, Brown Muscat. Spain's Moscatel is usually Muscat of Alexandria. Muscat Ottonel is different and lighter.

VIOGNIER

Heady, full-bodied, hawthorn blossom, apricots

Fashionable, distinctive variety that has now travelled from its home in Condrieu, northern Rhône, to virtually all corners of the wine world. Unless fully ripe, its distinctively seductive aroma does not develop, which means that most memorable examples are relatively alcoholic; the trick is to keep the acidity too. California and Australia have managed it. Best drunk young, it is increasingly blended with the other Rhône white grapes: nervy but aromatic Roussanne and big, almondy Marsanne – especially in southern France. Sometimes fermented with Syrah/Shiraz to stabilize it.

PINOT BLANC

Lively, light, Chardonnay-like

Lighter-skinned mutation of Pinot Noir which has often been confused with its cousin Chardonnay in the vineyard, especially in Italy, where it is called Pinot Bianco. It is the everyday, inoffensive grape of Alsace, related to Auxerrois and sometimes called Clevner. It can make substantial wines, including wonderfully rich Trockenbeerenauslesen, in Austria as Weissburgunder. It is also popular in southern Germany and Alto Adige for its full-bodied dry whites. The grape is relatively low in acidity and flavour compounds so Pinot Blanc is generally drunk young.

MARSANNE

Almond, marzipan aromas, very full-bodied

Along with Roussanne, this is the characteristic grape variety of white Hermitage in the northern Rhône. It is now planted throughout the southern Rhône as well as in Australia, especially in the state of Victoria. In southern France and in California, especially the Central Coast, Marsanne is often blended with varieties such as Roussanne, Rolle/Vermentino, Grenache Blanc, and Viognier. Its wines tend to be deep golden, heady, and alcoholic. Marsanne is also grown to a limited extent in Switzerland and northeast Spain.

Wine and Weather

After the vine comes the weather, the second most important ingredient in wine and the great variable. Climate, the expected, long-term, averaged weather in any given region puts the overall limits on what can be grown and how well, but it is the vagaries of a single year's weather that make or break a vintage. A single phenomenon such as hail or frost can also affect quantity rather than quality, sometimes decimating the size of a crop. Hail is as disastrous as spring frost, although fortunately it tends to be localized.

Many factors influence climate, of which temperature and rainfall are undoubtedly the most important. Sunlight is, of course, vital for photosynthesis, but temperature is more critical, especially in cool climates. The climate of a wine region crucially affects not only the choice of grape variety but also the sort of wine it can produce. Cool-climate wines tend to be lower in alcohol and higher in acidity than those made in hot climates, whose flavours may be less refined but more emphatic. Without sufficient rainfall or warmth, grapes will not ripen properly. An excess of either may well prejudice the quality of wine made from those grapes.

Mean temperatures (the average of daily maximum and minimum temperatures) in the final month of ripening need normally to fall between 60 and 70°F (15 and 21°C) to produce fine table wines (hotter climates can make good table wines, and extremely good fortified wines). Winters need to be sufficiently cool to allow the vine its revitalizing winter sleep. But if temperatures regularly fall below about 5°F (-15°C) in winter (see the Former Soviet Republics, p.278, for example), then the risk of even dormant vines fatally freezing may be uneconomically high and some winter protection may be needed.

The difference between winter and summer temperatures is important. In continental climates such as those of the Finger Lakes, Ontario, and eastern Germany, where this difference is great and where the climate is affected principally by a large landmass, temperatures fall so rapidly in autumn that there is a risk that grapes will simply not ripen fully. In maritime climates, moderated by nearby sea or ocean, there is a much less marked difference between summer and winter temperatures. In warmer maritime climates such as Margaret River in Western Australia, winters may not always be cold enough for the vines to fall dormant, and organic viticulture may be difficult because pests and diseases are not always killed off in the winter. In cooler maritime climates such as Bordeaux in France and Long Island in New York, the weather during flowering, the crucial, quantity-determining vine event in early summer, can often be unsettled or cool, which can prejudice both how much fruit is set and how even is the setting.

Temperatures also vary throughout the day. Air temperature is usually highest in early afternoon and lowest at dawn. Some regions have a much more marked contrast between day and night temperatures than others and are said to have a large diurnal temperature variation. (The significance of topography is discussed in the section on terroir.)

The vine needs water as well as warmth. An average annual rainfall of at least 20in (500mm) is generally required (and 30in/750mm or more in hotter climates where evaporation from the soil and transpiration from the leaves are much greater) to promote sufficient photosynthesis to ripen grapes. Many wine regions have much less rainfall than this, but growers with access to irrigation water – generally from rivers, aquifers, dams, and wells – make up for the shortage. Some varieties such as La Mancha's Airén grown as bushvines are particularly tolerant of near-drought conditions.

If a vine runs short of water, it is said to suffer water stress and tends to produce smaller grapes with thicker skins. Although this tends to reduce total yields, it can up to a certain point result in wines with real concentration of flavour and colour. Severe drought, however, stops the ripening process completely as the vine goes into survival rather than reproductive mode and results in unbalanced wines (see p.26).

Availability of irrigation water rather than any climatic aspect is what limits the spread of the vine in many regions with hot summers, notably in the southern hemisphere and California. In theory there is no upper limit on annual rainfall. Even flooded vineyards can recover quickly, especially in winter, and parts of Galicia in northern Spain and the Minho in northern Portugal, for example, can receive an average of more than 60in (1,500mm) of rain a year. It is the timing of rain that is critical. If there is very heavy rainfall just before harvest, especially after a period of relatively dry weather, grapes can swell quickly and sugar, acids, and such flavours as have been built up may rapidly become diluted (see p.32 for details of how winemakers can try to compensate). Prolonged wet weather during the second half of the growing season also tends to encourage the fungal diseases to which vines are prone, and rotten grapes can be the distasteful result (although modern vine farmers wage war with an array of sprays and vine training techniques, and are much less likely than their predecessors to be forced into picking grapes before they are fully ripe).

Wind can play an important part too. Winds can be beneficial by cooling hot vineyards and drying out damp ones, in Corsica or southern Uruguay, for example, but constant wind stress, as in the Salinas Valley of Monterey in California, can stop photosynthesis and delay the ripening process. Vine-growers in more exposed parts of the southern Rhône Valley have to install windbreaks to minimize the effects of the notorious mistral, and the hot, dry zonda of Argentina is feared rather than welcomed by wine producers.

Frost in late spring when the season's buds are vulnerable is a grower's nightmare. Portable heaters such as these at Stag's Leap Wine Cellars in Napa Valley are designed to keep temperatures above vine freezing point.

Terroir

There is no precise translation for the French word terroir. Terrain comes nearest, but has a less specific, less emotive connotation. Perhaps this is why many Anglo-Saxons long mistrusted it as a Gallic fancy: a conveniently mystical way of asserting the superiority of French soil and landscape and the unknowable peculiarities that give French wines special qualities.

Yet there is no mystery about terroir. Everyone – or at least every place – has one. Your garden and mine have terroirs; probably several. The front and back of a house almost certainly offer different growing conditions for plants. Total natural growing environment is all that terroir means, and the existence of the Aboriginal near-equivalent *pangkarra* suggests the concept is deeply rooted as part of mankind's relationship to the Earth.

At its most restrictive, the word means soil. By extension, and in common use, it means much more. It embraces the soil itself, the subsoil and rocks beneath it, its physical and chemical properties and how they interact with the local climate, the macroclimate of the region, to determine both the mesoclimate of a particular vineyard and the microclimate of a particular vine. This includes for example how quickly a patch of land drains, whether it reflects sunlight or absorbs the heat, its elevation, its degree of slope, its orientation to the sun, and whether it is close to a cooling or sheltering forest or a warming lake, river, or the sea.

Thus, if the foot of a slope is frost-prone, it will have a different terroir from that of the hillside down which the cold air drains, even if the soil is the same (which is why, for instance, vines are not planted in the Willamette Valley in Oregon at altitudes below 200ft/60m). In general, the higher the altitude, the cooler the average temperature, especially at night (which explains why viticulture is possible at all as close to the equator as, say, Salta in Argentina), although some hillside vineyards in northern California can be warmer than the valley floor because they lie above the fog line.

Similarly, an east-facing slope that catches the morning sun may have identical soil to a west-facing slope that warms up later and holds the evening rays, but its terroir is different and the wine it produces will be subtly different too. In the case of the meandering Mosel in Germany at the northern limit of vine cultivation, even the precise orientation of a slope can determine whether great wine or no wine can be produced from it.

The single most important aspect of terroir, however, given that vines have been planted somewhere with summers that are warm and dry enough for them to stand a chance of ripening, is the extent to which water and nutrients are available. If a vine is planted on fertile soils with a high water table, such as those of some of the least favoured sites on the floor of the Napa Valley in California, or the Wairau Valley in Marlborough, New Zealand, vines will have almost constant access to water and may indeed be waterlogged for part of the growing season. The vine's natural instinct will be to become "vigorous", growing shoots and leaves at such a rate that there is danger they will shade any fruit. Over-vigorous vines produce unripe grapes and wines that actually taste leafy and green because they have put all their energy into vegetative growth rather than ripening grapes.

However, if a vine is planted in very infertile soil with access to barely any water, so that supplies are severely restricted, such as in many of the traditional vineyards of southern Spain, southern Italy, and northern Africa, photosynthesis virtually stops for a significant part of the summer. The vine suffers such water stress it "shuts down" and, in order to survive, the vine has to use up, or respire, some of the energy that should have gone into ripening. The only reason sugars build up in the grapes under these circumstances is from the gradual evaporation of water from the berries. Few interesting flavour compounds are formed, tannins do not ripen and the result can be extremely unbalanced wines that are high in alcohol but have harsh, unripe tannins, less intense flavours, and dangerously unstable colours.

There are all sorts of viticultural tricks that can compensate for these natural disadvantages (canopy management and controlled irrigation are respectively the most obvious for the extreme environments described above) and the result can be some extremely good wine. Some growers and winemakers choose to manage their vineyards in such a way as to override or minimize the effect of terroir characteristics, by blending from diverse or distant regions or by manipulating the wine in the winery; others wish to express environmental effects in their wines as eloquently as possible. Some producers might suggest that the traditional

PRECISION VITICULTURE: UNDERSTANDING VINEYARD VARIABILITY

The tools of precision viticulture allow a grower to understand, and so better manage, vineyard variability. In this example, yield mapping has been used in conjunction with a high resolution electromagnetic soil survey and elevation mapping to identify zones of characteristic performance within the block. Yields can vary 10-fold (between 2 and 20 tonnes/ha, for example) within vineyards managed in exactly the same way throughout.

In this example, an 18 acre (7.3ha) vineyard in Coonawarra, Australia, the variation in topography drives variation in soil depth. This in turn drives variation in soil water availability, which controls variation in yield. However, the block is essentially flat with a mere 4ft (1.2m) difference in elevation from the lowest to the highest point – yet clearly, the variation in the land underlying the vineyard exerts enormous influence on its productivity.

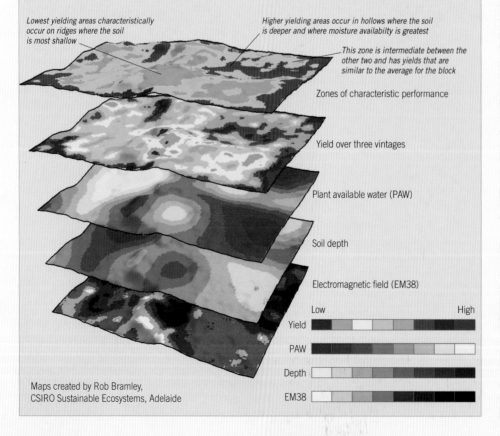

Lowest yielding areas characteristically occur on ridges where the soil is most shallow

Higher yielding areas occur in hollows where the soil is deeper and where moisture availabilty is greatest

This zone is intermediate between the other two and has yields that are similar to the average for the block

Zones of characteristic performance

Yield over three vintages

Plant available water (PAW)

Soil depth

Electromagnetic field (EM38)

Low — High

Yield

PAW

Depth

EM38

Maps created by Rob Bramley,
CSIRO Sustainable Ecosystems, Adelaide

winemaking practices of their own region have themselves become part of the terroir.

So what sort of terroir naturally produces great wine? Research into the crucial interaction between soil and water and vine nutrition has developed considerably over the last 50 years, and in the last 10 years, sophisticated technology has allowed a far greater understanding of very localized terroir effects. See the panel below left for an example of this in practice.

In Burgundy, the vineyards that have over time proved – without the use of such hi-tech analysis – to produce the finest wines tend to be those in the middle of the famous Côte d'Or where the combination of marl, silt, and limestone that has ended up there (see p.57) seems most propitious for adequate but restricted water supply and therefore wine quality. The panel on the right illustrates a recent example of vineyard development on a well-established property in Bordeaux, where soil analysis has shown that even with a long history of vine-growing, it is easy to overlook some of the best plots.

It should be said, however, that superior terroirs have a way of perpetuating themselves that is not entirely natural. The owner of Grand Cru land can afford to maintain it to perfection with drainage ditches, the precise amount and quality of fertilizer, and ideal cultivation techniques, while such cosseting is uneconomic for a less glorified plot. Terroirs depend on man and his money for their expression, as witness the dip in Château Margaux's performance between 1966 and 1978 when the owner could no longer afford to maintain his first-growth in the style it merited.

Some organic and biodynamic wine-growers suggest that the term terroir should also apply to all the flora and fauna of the land, visible or microscopic, and that terroir is inevitably changed by chemical fertilizers and other soil additions that have been imported from outside the ecosystem of the local vineyard. And you could also argue that centuries of monoculture and such wholesome practices as ploughing and planting cover crops have almost certainly altered the land that was originally classified. But the interesting thing is just how much different, even adjacent, plots of land can vary in their effect on the resultant wine even when they have been nurtured in exactly the same way.

VINEYARD ZONING

Soil mapping has become an exact and exacting science. Growers with access to the technology can now acquire soil maps at very high resolution to decide which plot of land to buy, how to modify various parts of it, and exactly which variety to plant where. In existing vineyards, especially larger ones where yield and ripening may vary greatly from one part of the vineyard to another, vine vigour can be measured using similarly sophisticated methods such as remote sensing via aerial imagery and yield monitoring and mapping. This process, now generally referred to as precision viticulture, allows growers the luxury of, for example, picking each

UNEARTHING TERROIR

In Bordeaux in the 1960s and 1970s, Gérard Seguin's studies of the Médoc showed that the very best soils were not particularly fertile ("medium potential", soil scientists call them) and drained quickly and deeply, drawing the roots down to great depths, up to 23ft (7m) in Margaux, to find a stable water supply. Subsequent research by Bordeaux's Cornelis van Leeuwen and others has shown that it is not so much soil depth as water availability that matters for wine quality. So much so that the water-holding capacity of richer soils can be too great if roots go deep. On heavy clay in Pomerol (for example Château Pétrus), rooting depth tends to be only about 4.3ft (1.3m) and on the limestone soils of St-Emilion (for example Château Ausone), rooting ranges from 6.6ft (2m) on the slopes to 1.3ft (0.4m) on the plateau (see map on p.111). However, in clay soils there must be enough organic matter to allow water to move freely.

Despite unsubstantiated suggestions that wines taste of the minerals in the soil, it seems, based on current knowledge, that drainage and water availability, rather than precise chemical composition, are the key to the perfect soil for great wine.

This photo illustrates an example of "medium potential" land, recently unearthed at Château Olivier in Bordeaux. The estate comprises 470 acres (190ha) of land within the Pessac-Léognan appellation, but only about a quarter of that area is planted with vines. In 2002 research was undertaken to see if any of the unplanted plots of land might offer even better or more interesting terroir than some of the existing vineyards. Working with consultants Denis Dubourdieu and Xavier Choné, they dug 6.6–10ft (2–3m) pits in more than 200 locations to study the soil profile.

In the plot called Bel Air on the western side of the property they discovered a small area of land on an outcrop of gravel on a glacial terrace that was even older than the main part of the Château Olivier vineyard. The soil is compacted gravel, that is small stones within a matrix of sandy clay. This drains well and restrains the vigour of the vine, while the small proportion of clay provides a regular, consistent but limited supply of water.

This soil is particularly suited to the later-ripening Cabernet Sauvignon, which tends to be more prone to unripeness due to vintage variation than Merlot, a more precocious variety. Selecting the right variety is a critical adjunct to terroir identification.

topsoil, 8–16in (20–40cm) thick, rich in organic matter

depth of compacted gravel ranges from 6.6 to 16.4ft (2–5m); 50–60% gravel within a matrix of sandy clay with iron (orange when the iron is oxidized, grey when reduced)

plot within a vineyard at just the right moment– but it is only an option where the potential quality and price of the wine are high enough to justify the costs. The kind of vineyard "zoning" illustrated in the panel on the left, where terroir is understood at a very small scale, helps the grower make even better wine, and potentially make more money.

More and more wines made in the New World are now labelled not just with their region of origin but with the name of a vineyard – partly from increased awareness of the different potentials of each vineyard, and also perhaps from increased competition. It is now obvious that AN Other Chardonnay, however beautifully dressed and carefully described on its back label, has to draw credibility – and, more important, character – from more than just varietal flavour and nicely judged oak maturation.

The Wine-grower's Year

For someone who grows grapes and makes wine, every act in vineyard and cellar is centred on the most important time of the year, the harvest and the winemaking weeks immediately after it. There is much variation between regions and producers, but the following is a rough outline of each month's key operations. The northern hemisphere month is specified first in the headings; vineyard task above cellar task.

JANUARY / JULY

Pruning This chilly operation is usually done by hand in the middle of winter. The dry shoots, or *sarments* as the French call them, are increasingly popular for barbecues. Early budding vine varieties may be pruned deliberately late so as to delay budbreak and minimize frost risk.

Malolactic fermentation should be well under way in the cellar, either in tanks or barrels. Constant supervision and analysis is needed to check the progress of the lactic bacteria (the agents of this change) and the acid levels.

FEBRUARY / AUGUST

Pruning continues in the vineyard. The now fully exposed wires, posts, and stakes are mended if necessary.

Topping up Wine contracts in cold weather so topping up reduces the risk of harmful oxidation by making sure that the "ullage" space between the barrel and the wine's surface is minimal. Bungs, usually plastic, must also be airtight. If the bung is kept at the top of the barrel rather than at an angle, where it is kept fully moist, topping up has to be more frequent – perhaps once or twice a week.

MARCH / SEPTEMBER

Ploughing is a spring operation and is one of the main ways to control weeds in the vineyard. Mechanical ploughing, using sensors to avoid damaging the trunks, is very common. But some growers are returning to horse-drawn ploughs, especially on steep slopes or to avoid compacting the soil.

Bottling of wines that are designed to be drunk young. In smaller wineries this means booking a mobile bottler and ensuring all wines to be bottled are finished and stable.

JULY / JANUARY

Spraying against pests and disease gets into full swing. Rain and humid weather promote the fungal diseases that plague so many vines. Spraying techniques vary from one man with a tank on his back, to tractor-mounted spray contraptions, to aerial spraying by helicopter.

Bottling of fine wines in their second year before summer kicks in. The precise timing of bottling can vary according to the state of the wine, the efficiency of the bottle factory, and the cellar staff's sporting preoccupations.

AUGUST / FEBRUARY

Veraison Red wine grapes soften and turn from green to red. Increasingly growers also perform a summer or green harvest, whereby less ripe or excess bunches are removed. The aim is to channel the remaining sunshine and nutrients into fewer berries, making more concentrated wine. This can backfire if severe drought follows, giving dry berries and unbalanced wine.

In warm regions the winery must be prepared for vintage, which may even have already started in the hottest regions.

SEPTEMBER / MARCH

Harvesting is the most common and vital operation this month, although possibly even more important is deciding exactly when to pick (see p.32). Pickers must be hired, organized, and in some cases fed and housed. Alternatively, picking machines and drivers must be ready.

In the winery this is the most exhausting period of the year when the truly dedicated may work around the clock. All the necessary winemaking equipment and additions such as yeast, sugar, acid, and so on, must be in place.

APRIL / OCTOBER

Desuckering Cutting off vine suckers neatens up the vine and concentrates energy into the young shoots that have emerged.

Racking, moving wine from one container to another with the aim of leaving behind potentially harmful sediment such as the lees of fermentation. This is usually done immediately after the alcoholic fermentation – a bit of aeration does no harm to most very young wines. A wine may be racked up to three or four times during its first year in barrel.

MAY / NOVEMBER

Frost damage protection Not *Star Wars* but a gas flame-thrower, towed by tractor, and one of several ways of protecting vines against catastrophe if the temperature falls below freezing point. Other methods include spraying with water to coat the buds in ice, the traditional little "smudge pot" portable heaters, heated wires, and wind machines or even helicopters to break up the cold air.

Start to prepare and assemble wine orders so that they can be despatched before the heat of summer.

JUNE / DECEMBER

Shoot positioning is particularly important in damp climates, where vines tend to be vigorous. Young shoots are tied onto wires so that the vine is in a good position to turn sunlight into a decent crop of good-quality grapes. A stable period of fine weather is needed while the vines flower (see p.18) to produce a large crop; unsettled weather may eliminate the need for a green harvest in August/February.

Fine wines may well be racked again over the next few weeks, certainly before the real heat of summer.

OCTOBER / APRIL

Even after the grapes have been picked, sunny weather can continue to build up carbohydrate reserves in the vine, helping it withstand winter and produce shoots in spring.

Punching down the cap of skins that have floated to the surface of the fermentation vat is essential to keep it moist, aerate the wine, and encourage the extraction of colour and flavour from the skins. This has to be done every day and requires considerable force. Various mechanical alternatives have been devised.

NOVEMBER / MAY

Vine leaves turn yellow, gold, and then, especially if the leaves are infected with a virus, a beautiful red. After the first frost they drop off. Any cover crops may be sown now.

Fining, or clarification, for serious red wines in their second year with whisked egg whites; these attract tiny particles of solids remaining in the wine before falling to the bottom of the barrel. Other fining agents include special forms of clay and gelatin. First-year wines may be transferred from fermentation vat to barrel about now.

DECEMBER / JUNE

In the vineyard cuttings may be taken for propagating young vines. The vines are now dormant and will withstand winter cold so long as the temperature does not fall below about -4°F (-20°C). Pruning may start.

Early tastings of the new wines begin. Some decisions may be taken about how different lots of wine will be used. Malolactic fermentation should be under way by now, whether in barrel or tank, encouraged by the introduction of special lactic bacteria and the warming of the cellar.

Making Wine in the Vineyard

We now know something about which grape variety to plant and the likely effect of weather, climate, and local environment on the vine. But how about choosing exactly where and how to plant vines? Vineyard site selection, while virtually unknown in the traditional wine regions of Europe, where inheritance, appellation laws, and planting rights tend to dictate vineyard location, is becoming an increasingly important and exact science.

A prospective vineyard investor needs to know that a commercially viable quantity of healthy grapes is likely to be ripened on that site every year. Acting on a hunch is one possible tactic but close analysis of topography, climate, and soil data is safer (see p.26).

Crude statistics on temperature, rainfall, and sunshine hours can help, but need careful interpretation. High average summer temperatures may look good on paper for instance, but photosynthesis effectively stops above a certain temperature (between about 85 and 95°F, or 30 and 35°C) depending on the location, so ripening could be adversely affected if there are too many very hot days. Wind, excluded from many sets of meteorological statistics, can also stop photosynthesis by closing the stomata, the tiny openings on leaves and berries that regulate the process.

In cooler areas, the critical aspect of temperature evaluation is whether grapes will ripen reliably. If average summer and autumn temperatures are relatively low for viticulture (such as those for England or Luxembourg), or if autumn usually arrives early with either predictable rains (as in Oregon) or a substantial drop in temperature (as in British Columbia), then relatively early ripening varieties may have to be planted. Chardonnay and Pinot Noir are fine for the Pacific Northwest but even they ripen too late for vineyards furthest from the equator. Riesling will ripen on the most favoured sites in the Mosel in northern Germany, but would be marginal for much of England and Luxembourg (even if global warming is changing this). Seriously early ripening varieties such as, respectively, Seyval Blanc and Müller-Thurgau, have been regarded as safer choices.

The average summer rainfall and its likely timing would give a useful indication of the likelihood of fungal diseases such as those described on p.18. Monthly rainfall totals, with measurements of likely evaporation, should give any would-be vigneron an idea of whether any irrigation is needed. If the site is in an area where supplementing natural rainfall is allowed, then comes the big question of whether there is a suitable source and quantity of water nearby. Precise control of timing and rates of irrigation is an increasingly important way of shaping the quality as well as quantity of the wine produced. Lack of water is likely to be the most significant brake on vineyard expansion in California,

ANALYSING GRAPE JUICE

A portable spectrometer (right) analyses the sugar content of a drop of grape juice in the vineyard. During the ripening process the levels of acidity (mainly tartaric and malic acids) fall while the fermentable sugars (mainly fructose and glucose) rise. As harvest approaches vine-growers constantly monitor the build-up of grape sugars, as well as the weather forecasts, in order to decide when to pick.

With dark-skinned grapes in particular many winemakers nowadays prefer to wait for a state known as "physiological ripeness". At this point the skins start to shrivel slightly, the stalks turn from green to brown and the grape is ripe enough to be pulled easily off the stalk, even if spectrometer analysis suggested a sufficient sugar level was reached some days before.

Measurements of sugar content

Specific gravity	1.060	1.065	1.070	1.075	1.080	1.085	1.090	1.095	1.100	1.105	1.110	1.115	1.120	1.125
°Oechsle	60	65	70	75	80	85	90	95	100	105	110	115	120	125
Baumé	8.2	8.8	9.4	10.1	10.7	11.3	11.9	12.5	13.1	13.7	14.3	14.9	15.5	16.0
Brix	14.7	15.8	17.0	18.1	19.3	20.4	21.5	22.5	23.7	24.8	25.8	26.9	28.0	29.0
% Potential alcohol V/V	7.5	8.1	8.8	9.4	10.0	10.6	11.3	11.9	12.5	13.1	13.8	14.4	15.0	15.6

Argentina, and, especially, Australia, in many parts of which water is either unavailable or too saline thanks to excessive deforestation.

Water may be needed for other purposes, too. At the coolest limits of viticulture, the length of the frost-free season and likelihood of spring frosts are crucial factors. In Ontario and the northeastern states of the USA, for example, the total number of frost-free days governs the length of the growing season and therefore which grape varieties are likely to ripen. In Chablis and the cool Casablanca Valley of Chile, water is needed for sprinkler systems to protect young vines from frost by covering them with a layer of ice, but in Casablanca there is a distinct shortage of available water – frost having proved an unforeseen hazard.

The soil, or more likely soils, of any prospective vineyard site needs careful analysis, generally by taking a series of soil samples at regular intervals, together with measurements of elevation and water availability. The diagrams on p.26 map the results of soil and water information gathered using more sophisticated techniques and equipment.

The fertility of the soil is a key ingredient in the likely quality of wine produced there. The soil should be neither too acid nor too alkaline and have a suitable degree of organic matter (the remains of other plants, animals, and insects) and minerals such as phosphorus, potassium, and nitrogen. Phosphorus is vital for photosynthesis and is rarely lacking in the soil. Too much potassium can result in wines dangerously high in pH and low in acidity. Too much nitrogen (a common ingredient in fertilizers and manure) can result in excessively vigorous vines that put all their energy into growing leaves rather than ripening grapes so

that the bunches are dangerously shaded by an increasingly dark, heavy canopy of leaves and shoots. The phenomenon is particularly common on very fertile soils, typically relatively young soils such as those in New Zealand and the floor of the Napa Valley. Vigour also varies with the variety of vine and rootstock. Vigorous vines need special treatment, as outlined in the panel below right.

DESIGNING A VINEYARD

Once a vine-grower has selected a site or cleared a vineyard for replanting he or she must design the vineyard. The orientation of the rows, the ideal distance between the vines, how best to train them, the height of the posts (and, later, wires), and the number of buds to keep when pruning must all be taken into consideration. Should the vine rows run north–south so as to allow the leaves the maximum chance to absorb sunshine? Will it be necessary to create terraces on a hillside site – more expensive to design and maintain – so that rows of vines follow contour lines, allowing tractors and people to move easily along them?

Then comes one of the most important decisions of all: how close to plant the vines, both between and within rows, based on the sort of yields the vine-grower is aiming for (see p.84 for more on yields). In Mediterranean climates, where it is frequently too hot and dry, a restricted water supply in low-latitude vineyards can dictate widely spaced traditional bushes with a vine density of less than 1,000 vines per hectare and naturally low yields.

New World vineyards were once typically planted in warm or hot regions, often on fertile virgin soil, which threatened to oversupply the vine with nutrients. Growers left spaces as wide as 12ft (3.7m) for vineyard machinery between

the rows, and often left 8ft (2.4m) between vines, resulting again in a vine density of just over 1,000 vines per hectare, though for very different reasons. This economized on plants, posts, and wires – and the labour involved in installing them – and made cultivation and mechanical harvesting easy. But all too often the price paid was excessive vigour, sprawling canopies burying their own fruit and most of the leaves needed for photosynthesis in deep shade. Not only do such grapes not ripen properly, resulting in wines that belie the climate with unattractively high acidity and unripe tannins, but the wood destined to carry the next year's crop does not ripen either. The embryo buds on the cane need exposure to the sun to make them fruitful. Too many layers of leaves thus start a vicious spiral of smaller crops and more foliage year by year. Liberal irrigation could result in economically viable yields per hectare, but each vine would be required somehow to ripen too heavy a charge of grapes.

This stereotype, now much modified, contrasts markedly with the traditional vineyards of Bordeaux and Burgundy, where yields per hectare are generally much lower, and yields per vine lower still. Here vines are planted as densely as 10,000 vines per hectare at intervals of 3ft (1m) along rows just 3ft (1m) apart (worked by *tracteurs-enjambeurs* that straddle the vines). Each vine is kept deliberately small, typically trained according to the single or double Guyot system (see below left). Planting and labour costs are much higher, but the grapes are given the maximum chance to ripen with beneficial effects on the quality of the wine. Over the last few decades there has been considerable progress in what is known as canopy management, based on a wider range of vine-training systems, designed to spread out and control the canopy of even the most vigorous vines (see the lyre system, for example, below right).

Other important decisions throughout the year include whether to cultivate between the rows or leave grass or other cover crops to grow, whether to ignore the sprawling shoots of summer or to trim them off, and whether to "green harvest" to reduce the number of bunches before or during ripening (see p.28). Patterns of solutions to all these puzzles (see the Bordeaux vineyard below left, for example) have evolved, over centuries of sometimes unconscious experimentation in Europe, into models appropriate to local conditions and some of the world's most precious vineyards and most universally admired wines.

These choices may well be influenced, or reduced, by the grower's overall philosophy of farming. More and more growers are adopting organic or biodynamic viticulture. Both approaches prohibit the use of all agrochemicals and synthetic fertilizers which may leave residues, although limited amounts of sulphur-based sprays are used to control mildew. Biodynamic

The insectary on the biodynamically farmed Benziger Estate in Sonoma Mountain, a paradise for beneficial mites, bugs, butterflies, and birds, is a gloriously colourful part of their strategy to practise natural pest control.

growers rely on homeopathic doses of strange-sounding preparations (see photo on p.349) and, even more controversially, plan their work in the vineyard and cellar according to the lunar calendar. Results can be impressive, even if the science behind it remains a mystery – even to those who practise it.

Vine-growing is, after all, like all farming, utterly dependent on nature and local practicalities. Of all aspects of wine production it is rightly recognized as the single most important, and demanding, factor determining exactly how wine tastes.

VIGOUR AND CANOPY MANAGEMENT

LOW-VIGOUR VINES

Bordeaux vineyards such as this one in the Sauternes region tend to be densely planted, up to 10,000 vines per ha, and trained low on a simple vertical trellis such as the single or double **Guyot** since the soils are not particularly fertile and the climate is generally temperate. With careful pruning and shoot and leaf removal, the grower can obtain the ratio of fruit to leaves that is needed to fully ripen the berries before the temperatures drop.

HIGH-VIGOUR VINES

In more fertile soils, vines can produce a slightly larger crop without loss of quality as long as the training system provides sufficient foliage to ripen the crop without shading the fruit. The **lyre** system, shown here at Kumeu River in New Zealand, splits the canopy in two to maximize photosynthesis but it must be carefully managed to avoid excessive shading. Vine density is relatively low, which suits higher vigour soils. Expensive netting may also be needed to keep birds off.

Making Wine in the Cellar

If in the vineyard nature is ultimately in charge, man takes over in the winery, chai, cantina, bodega or Keller. Winemaking basically consists of a series of decisions dictated by the grapes and their condition and by the style of wine the winemaker has set his or her heart on or has been asked to produce. Occasionally these conflict. The diagrams on pages 36 and 37 show the steps involved in making two very different sorts of wine: a relatively inexpensive unoaked white and a high-quality, traditionally made, barrel-aged red wine.

CONSTITUENTS OF GRAPE JUICE

Water	70–80%
Carbohydrates	15–25%
Organic acids	0.3–1%
Tannins	0.01–0.1%
Nitrogenous compounds	0.03–0.17%
Minerals	0.3–6%

The carbohydrates in grape juice are mainly the sugars fructose and glucose, and the organic acids are mainly malic and tartaric. "Nitrogenous compounds" include proteins, primary amino acids, and ammonia, all of which are important nutrients for the yeast which enable it to convert the sugars into alcohol. The most significant mineral is potassium but it constitutes a maximum of 0.25% of the juice. The sodium content is minimal (0–0.02%); this high ratio of potassium to sodium is often recommended in the diets of cardiac patients.

HARVESTING THE GRAPES

The winemaker's first and possibly most important decision is when to pick. He or she should have been monitoring the sugar and acid levels in the grapes and their general health in the weeks leading up to the usual harvest date.

Decisions on harvest date need to be taken in conjunction with the weather forecast. If, for example, the grapes are not quite ripe enough but rain is predicted, the decision is whether to leave the grapes on the vine and hope that there will be sufficient warm, dry weather afterwards for them to ripen fully. Some varieties are much more sensitive than others to the exact date of harvest. Merlot, for example, can easily lose quality – a certain liveliness in the wine – if kept too long on the vine, whereas Cabernet Sauvignon is much more tolerant of a few extra days. If the grapes are already suffering from fungal disease (see p.19), the rain will exacerbate this so the best decision may be to pick the grapes just slightly less ripe than ideal. White wine is much more forgiving of a few rotten grapes than red in which the colour is rapidly lost and the wine tainted by a mouldy taste.

The winemaker, in conjunction with whomever is in charge of labour, also has to decide at what time of day to pick. In hot climates grapes are generally picked either at night (easier by machine, with big spotlights) or very early in the morning in order to deliver the grapes to the winery as cool as possible. In the old days grapes would be thrown into the back of trucks and sit in the sun, often squashed and increasingly oxidized, so that they arrived at the winery having lost a substantial proportion of their primary fruit flavour. Nowadays any winemaker with pretensions to quality will insist that grapes arrive as cool and undamaged as possible in small stable units, typically little plastic, stackable boxes, which keep the bunches whole (although whole bunches are an impossibility if the grapes are picked by machine since they operate by literally shaking the grapes off the vine).

Machines are used increasingly in the vineyard, not just for picking but for pruning and lifting training wires during the growing season. But the greatest wines in the world are still picked by hand, no matter how expensive and elusive the pickers, because they can both snip whole bunches off the vine and also make intelligent decisions about which fruit to pick.

PREPARING GRAPES FOR FERMENTATION

Once the grapes arrive at the winery they may be deliberately chilled – some hot-climate wineries even have cold rooms where grapes may be kept for hours or days until a fermentation vat is available. Even more likely at a top-quality winery in any climate is that the grapes are subject to further selection. One of the most obvious winery innovations in the 1990s was the installation of sorting tables, typically a slow-moving belt onto which grapes are tipped to be minutely examined before arriving at the crusher or crusher-destemmer. (Mechanical crushing releases the all-important juice and replaces the human foot – still used for some high-quality port.)

Most white grapes are destemmed before going to be pressed because stems can be astringent and would spoil a light, aromatic wine. For some full-bodied white wines, however, and most top-quality sparkling and sweet white wine, the winemaker may choose to put whole bunches into the press. This is because the stems can act as useful conduits of the juice to help drainage – and in any case only the first portion of it, the so-called "free-run" juice, may be used.

For white wines winemakers must decide whether they are going to make the wine protected as much as possible from oxygen, preserving every ounce of fresh fruit flavour (preventing oxidation and stunning ambient yeasts right at the start with added sulphur dioxide; complete destemming; low temperatures throughout; and so on), or to adopt deliberately oxidative techniques, exposing the grapes to oxygen and aiming for secondary, more complex flavours rather than the pure, unadorned hit of primary aromas. Riesling,

Chardonnay grapes are pumped into the press at the modest Meursault winery of Pierre Morey, who is also the winemaker at the much more luxurious Domaine Leflaive in Puligny-Montrachet. Note the sorting table in the background. Rubber boots are a winemaking prerequisite.

Sauvignon Blanc, and other aromatic grape varieties tend to be vinified protectively, while most top-quality Chardonnay, including white burgundy, is made oxidatively. Oxidative handling may include a period of deliberate "skin contact", not as exciting as it sounds, but a few hours either in the press before it is turned on or in a special holding tank, during which further flavour will be leeched into the must from the skins. If the skins are allowed contact with juice for white wine for too long, however, they impart far too much astringency – which is why grapes for white wine, unlike red wine grapes whose skins are needed for colour and tannin, are pressed before fermentation.

The harsher the pressing process, the tougher the resultant white wine. Over the years, presses have been designed with increasing ingenuity to squeeze out the juice as gently as possible, without breaking the pips or extracting astringency from the grape skins. Pneumatic presses, which operate by using an inflatable rubber bag to press the grapes against the inside walls of a horizontal cylinder, are now most common. Some of them are completely insulated from oxygen for protective juice handling. Winemakers are increasingly careful to separate different portions of what flows from the press, the earliest juice being the finest and least astringent.

At this stage, particularly protectively made white wines may be clarified, cleared of all the little grapey fragments still in suspension. Centrifuges were once used for this, but they can easily spin out too many solids and flavour. More usual today is to let solids settle to the bottom of a holding tank and then run off the clear juice into the fermentation tank. It is important at this stage that fermentation still hasn't started, which is why low temperatures and sulphur additions are important.

Red wine grapes meanwhile are usually crushed and destemmed, although a few handfuls of stems may be deliberately thrown into the fermentation vat to increase the tannin level, and some particularly traditional winemakers, especially in Burgundy, like to ferment whole bunches. This works only in climates with growing seasons long enough to ripen the stems fully as well as the fruit, otherwise the stems would make the wine taste horribly tough. (Most Australian red grapes, for example, would have unacceptably low acid levels if not picked until the stems were ripe.)

A very particular exception to the destemming rule for reds is a fermentation technique called carbonic maceration, characteristic of Beaujolais, some Côtes du Rhône, and especially good for naturally tannic varieties such as Carignan in the Languedoc-Roussillon, where the aim is to produce fruity wines without much tannin. Whole bunches are put into a sealed fermentation vat, the bottom layer of grapes is crushed by the weight of grapes above and starts fermenting naturally, giving off carbon dioxide. The whole vat becomes saturated in carbon dioxide, under whose influence the whole grapes in the upper part of the vat

undergo a special sort of internal fermentation, whose products have a characteristic soft, bubble-gum or banana-like smell.

THE FERMENTATION PROCESS

Following crushing and pressing of white grapes and crushing of red ones, the winemaker has to make decisions about conventional fermentation, the miraculous transformation of sweet grape juice into much drier, more complex-flavoured wine. If yeast (naturally present or added) is put into contact with grape sugars, it converts them into alcohol, heat, and carbon dioxide. The riper the grapes, that is the higher the sugar level, the stronger the wine they are capable of making. Fermentation vats naturally warm up as the process gets under way, so in warmer climates they may well need cooling jackets or internal cooling to keep the "must", as the pulpy mixture between grape juice and wine is known, below the temperature at which precious flavour compounds may be boiled off. The gas that is generated can make a winery a heady – and dangerous – place at harvest time, where the smell is an intoxicating mixture of carbon dioxide, grapes, and alcohol, especially if the fermentation vats are open-topped, as for many traditional red wines.

Although white wines are made in sealed vats so as to protect the must from damaging oxidation and avoid any browning, a vat full of red must has its own protection, the thick "cap" of skins that float on the surface.

Many aspects of winemaking have been subjected to detailed scrutiny and improvement over the last few decades, but yeast still presents some mystery and controversy. The winemaker's initial choice is whether or not to use specially selected and prepared yeast, so-called cultured yeast, as opposed to relying on the strains of yeast that are naturally in the atmosphere, called wild or ambient yeast.

In new wine regions there may be no choice; wine yeasts need time to build up a population and in the early years the only ambient strains available are more likely to be harmful than benevolent. With a small but increasing number of exceptions, most New World wines are therefore made by adding specially cultured yeast to the must, which may, if it has been chilled, need warming before fermentation can be persuaded to start. (Once one vat has started, the addition of fermenting must from it will kick-start a second, but some winemakers believe in deliberately macerating red grapes for a few days before fermentation.)

Cultured yeast, typically selections from yeast naturally present in other, more established wine regions, behaves predictably. Particularly powerful yeast can be chosen for high-alcohol wines, those which encourage coagulation of sediment may be useful for sparkling wines. The choice of cultured yeast can also have a significant influence on the flavour of the wine, for example enhancing particular aromas or highlighting the fresh fruit character. Traditionalists, however, prefer to leave everything to the ambient yeast in the belief

Punching down the cap of grapeskins (pigeage in French) that naturally floats on top of fermenting red wine at Spice Route in Swartland, South Africa. It is important to encourage as much contact as possible between cap and liquid because all the colour, flavour and tannins are in the skins.

that, while their behaviour may not be quite as predictable, they add more interest to the wine's flavour. It is not going too far to regard them as an aspect of terroir.

The winemaker's nightmare is a "stuck fermentation", when fermentation stops before all the sugar has been converted into alcohol and the winemaker is left with a dangerously vulnerable mixture, which can all too easily fall prey to oxidation and nasty bacteria. The level of alcohol in a finished wine is an effective weapon against many bacteria.

The exact pace – time and temperature – of a red wine fermentation is critical to the sort of wine that results. The warmer the fermentation (up to the dangerous flavour-evaporation limit), the more flavour and colour will be extracted. Long, cool fermentations tend to result in light, fruity wines, but if a fermentation is too short and hot, the wine will also be low in body and flavour. The temperature rises as fermentation gets under way, but is generally between about 72 and 86°F (22 and 30°C) for full-bodied red wines, and cooler, sometimes as low as 54°F (12°C), for aromatic white wines.

To extract tannins, flavour, and colour from the grape skins during red wine fermentation, the cap and the must need to be encouraged to commune with each other. This is generally done by either pumping the must over the cap or by physically punching it down into the liquid, although there is an increasing array of mechanical and computerized ways of submerging the cap. The science of this process, and any post-fermentation maceration designed to extract and soften tannins, has become extremely exact, and a key factor in how much more palatable many young red wines are today.

Gentle handling of the grapes, must, and wine is generally, though not universally, considered to be a factor in ultimate wine quality. Where money is no object, or if a winery is conveniently built into a hillside, winery design and equipment harness the force of gravity to avoid the use of pumps (as shown on pp.38–39).

IMPROVING ON NATURE

It is at the fermentation stage, red or white, that the winemaker decides whether or not to add acid or sugar. French winemakers, apart from those in the far south, have been adding sugar to fermentation vats to increase the alcohol content (not sweetness) of the final wine for 200 years, ever since this process, now called chaptalization, was proposed by the agriculture minister Jean-Antoine Chaptal. The AC laws incorporate detailed limits to the amount of sugar (or, nowadays, concentrated grape must) that may be added, generally the equivalent of no more than an additional 2% of alcohol. In practice, thanks to warmer summers, better canopy management (see p.31) and anti-rot strategies, growers are now able to pick grapes riper and riper so that less and less additional sugar is needed.

In less ripe vintages in cooler climates, winemakers may also decide to exclude a portion of juice from the red wine fermentation vat so as to improve the all-important ratio of flavour- and colour-filled skins to juice (a practice called *saignée* in France). This traditional practice is sometimes replaced by more mechanical

Chromatography spotting provides a visual guide as to how a wine is progressing through its malolactic fermentation. The first spot is tartaric acid (present in all the wines), the second spot is malic acid, and the highest is lactic acid. Tests will be repeated until the malic acid spot disappears.

manipulation: concentration based on evaporation under vacuum or reverse osmosis.

Winemakers in warm climates on the other hand routinely add ("adjust" is the word they prefer) acidity to musts from grapes that have ripened to sugar levels that are only dreamt of in northern France, but whose natural acidity has dropped to an unappetizingly low level on the way. Tartaric acid, grapes' natural acid, is the acid of choice. There is another, arguably more natural, way in which winemakers can accentuate the acidity of a wine. Alcoholic fermentation of any wine may be followed by a second sort of fermentation, the "malolactic", in which the grapes' harsher malic (appley) acids are converted into softer, lactic (milky) acids. Understanding and mastery of this second fermentation, by warming the wine and sometimes adding special lactic bacteria, was the key factor in the mid-20th century in making red wines drinkable younger by lowering the overall acidity and adding some extra flavours as well.

But those extra flavours may not be necessary or desirable in an aromatic, probably protectively made white wine, and if the malolactic fermentation is deliberately suppressed (by filtering or fining the necessary yeasts and proteins out of the wine), the effect is to make the wine taste crisper. In practice malolactic fermentation is encouraged in most good-quality Chardonnay to add texture and flavour, and in warmer climates it is compensated for by added acidity.

Malolactic fermentation is invariably good for red wine and in recent years a fashion has emerged for conducting it not in large tanks as was the rule, but in individual barrels. This needs much more labour and supervision so is warranted only for high-quality wines, but the short-term result at least is a perceptibly smoother, more seductive texture, a characteristic that some wine tasters have come to associate with quality. Increasingly, therefore, winemakers who wish their wines to show well in youth are running red wine out of the fermentation vat just before the end of fermentation into barrels, where the wine will finish its alcoholic and then its malolactic fermentation.

An increasingly controversial issue, particularly in warmer climates such as California and parts of Australia, is high alcohol levels in wine, generally the result of picking grapes later to get more flavour and the inevitable consequence of higher sugar levels. As with must concentration, various mechanical methods, again based on evaporation or reverse osmosis, may be used to reduce the alcohol level of the finished wine. However, some producers prefer to find alternative strategies in the vineyard so that the raw material is in better balance to begin with.

While some top-end red wines finish their alcoholic fermentation in barrel, full alcoholic fermentation in barrel has become de rigueur for

any full-bodied white wine with aspirations to a high price. By the end of the 20th century, oak had become The Other Ingredient in wine, such a high proportion of good to great wine both red and white being matured if not fermented in small oak barrels. Indeed, practically all serious red wine undergoes the smoothing process of maturation in oak, and all but the most aromatic and lively whites are both fermented and matured in small (225 litre) oak barrels.

However a wine is matured after fermentation it will have to be bottled. Before a wine is subjected to this often rather brutal process, the winemaker has to be sure it is stable: that it does not contain any potentially dangerous bacteria and will not do anything inconvenient if subjected to extreme temperatures. It must be clarified, for the wine is still likely to be cloudier than the consumer has come to expect. Inexpensive white wines are often therefore put into a tank and fiercely chilled so that any tartaric acid that remains in solution is precipitated before bottling and won't reappear as (completely harmless but worrying-looking) crystals in the bottle later on. The great majority of wine of either colour is filtered in some way so as to remove any danger of refermentation, and fined (see p.29) so that any remaining particles drop out of the wine. Filtration is a heavily political subject among wine folk, however. Overdone, it can remove flavour and the potential for ageing; underdone, it can leave the wine prey to harmful bacteria and refermentation, particularly if the bottle gets too warm. But as wine ages, it can be hard to tell the difference between filtered and unfiltered wine, except of course by the amount of sediment in the bottle.

Oak and Alternatives

Oak has been used for storing wine for centuries because it is both watertight and easy to work. Its more recently appreciated attributes, however, are that oak flavours have a natural affinity for those of wine, adding more complex compounds, and, perhaps more importantly, its physical properties are unparalleled for gently clarifying and stabilizing, while deepening the colour of a red and softening the texture of any well-made wine.

Fermenting a white wine in barrel, provided it has not been stripped of all of its solids and left defenceless against the assault of all the tannins and pigments in the oak, makes the wine much smoother in texture yet deeper in flavour. Another white winemaking ploy to give the wine a more creamy texture, whether the wine was fermented in barrel or tank, is regularly to stir the lees of the fermentation. This may also impart some of their often rather milky flavour to the wine.

White wines may be barrel-aged for as few as three months to take up just a little oak flavour (the older the barrel, the less flavour and oak tannins). Serious red wines are usually matured for longer, up to 18 months, or possibly more in older or larger oak casks. To separate the new wine from the larger particles of the lees, the so-called gross lees, the wine is generally racked (see p.29) into a clean barrel quite soon after fermentation and several times thereafter, generally more often in Europe than in the New World. Racking aerates the wine, softening its tannins and minimizing the risk of nasty odours building up in the barrel. Some wine is always lost by evaporation, however, and the barrels need regular topping up, another process that beneficially exposes the wine to a little air and softens its rough edges. The winemaker's job during barrel maturation is regularly to taste the contents of each barrel, and to judge not just when the wine should be racked but also when it is ready for bottling.

An alternative, occasionally a supplement, to barrel ageing, is to add tiny, measured doses of oxygen to a wine in tank or barrel. This technique of micro-oxygenation has become increasingly popular but its application is still more of an art than a science.

While micro-oxygenation is a way of imitating the way barrels aerate wine, oak chips, staves and fragments of various shapes and sizes can be used to replicate the flavour effect of oak barrels without their considerable cost. They may also improve texture and make the colour more stable. The use of such alternatives is not free of controversy but it does have a history: French agronomist Olivier de Serres refers to "vin de coipeau" (*copeaux,* that is "wood chips", in modern French) in his book *Théâtre d'Agriculture* published in 1600. He explains how they should be prepared and suggests that they will help clarify the wine, making it drinkable younger, and add an attractive aroma.

The use of fire during barrel-making enables the oak staves to be bent into place and toasts the insides. Micro-oxygenation of wine in stainless steel tanks (above) may not be as dramatic, but it can have a very similar effect on texture.

WHERE OAK COMES FROM

The important factors in barrel maturation are the size and age of the cask (the older or larger the barrel, the less oak flavour it will impart), length of time in cask, how heavily the barrel was toasted (a heavily toasted barrel will impart fewer wood tannins but more spicy or roasted flavours), how well the oak was seasoned (stacked outside to lose its harshness) before being made into a barrel, and the provenance of the oak (although this has usually to be taken on trust from the cooper).

American oak can be attractively sweet with a vanilla note. Baltic oak was admired at the end of the 19th century. Eastern European oaks are enjoying a revival, but French oak is still generally revered above all other – not least because the forests in the regions mapped here have been so well managed.

Limousin is wide-grained, tannic, and generally more suitable for brandy than wine. The oaks of Tronçais, a single, large government-owned forest in the Allier département, grow so slowly that the wood is tight-grained and considered excellent for wine. Vosges oak is similar, light in colour and preferred by some winemakers. Others simply ask for oak from "le Centre". Winemakers tend to have a range of favourite coopers rather than sticking to just one.

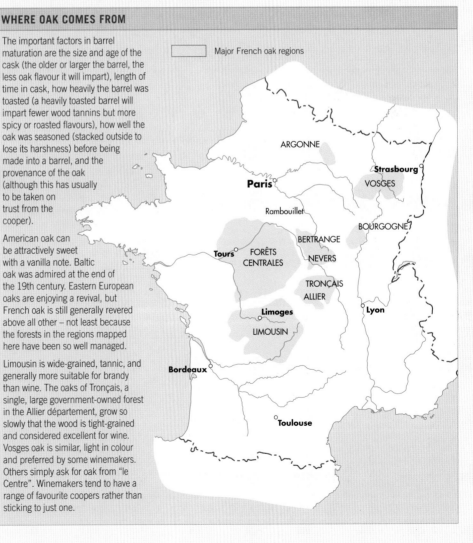

Major French oak regions

ARGONNE
Strasbourg
VOSGES
Paris
Rambouillet
BOURGOGNE
BERTRANGE
Tours
FORÊTS
CENTRALES
NEVERS
TRONÇAIS
ALLIER
Lyon
Limoges
LIMOUSIN
Bordeaux
Toulouse

How Wine is Made

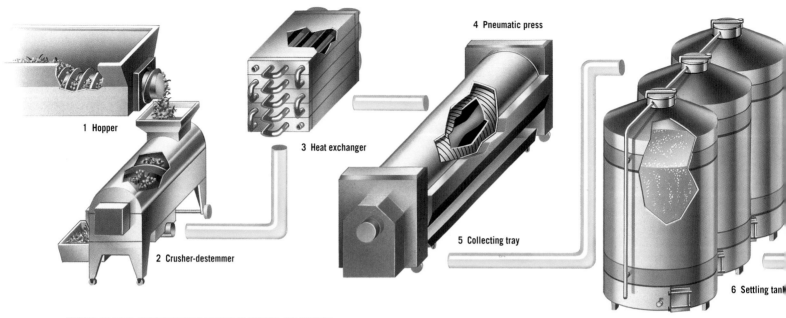

1 Hopper

2 Crusher-destemmer

3 Heat exchanger

4 Pneumatic press

5 Collecting tray

6 Settling tank

HOW MASS-PRODUCED WHITE WINE IS MADE

In this example of an inexpensive white wine made protectively in a well-equipped winery in a warm region, the grapes will have been picked by machine. A truck backs up to the winery and fills the hopper **1** with bunches of grapes, and usually some "MOG" (material other than grapes, such as leaves) as well. The screw feeds the grapes into the crusher-destemmer **2**. Grapes are crushed by rollers in the hopper. A rotating cylinder perforated with holes big enough to allow grapes, but not large, potentially astringent stem fragments or leaves, then destems the grapes. The resulting mixture of grapes and pulp may well then be pumped through a heat exchanger **3** to cool it down. This slows down the oxidation process, helping to prevent the loss of flavour and too early a start to the fermentation. Sulphur dioxide is often added for the same reason. The pulp is pumped into the pneumatic press **4** and the rubber membrane is slowly inflated, pressing the grape pulp against the perforated stainless steel cylinder but keeping the pips whole so as not to release their bitter oils. The juice is collected in the lower tray **5** from which it is pumped to the stainless steel settling tanks enclosed in cooling jackets **6**. Here the juice may be covered with a blanket of inert gas such as carbon dioxide to prevent oxidation. Special enzymes may be added to encourage some of the

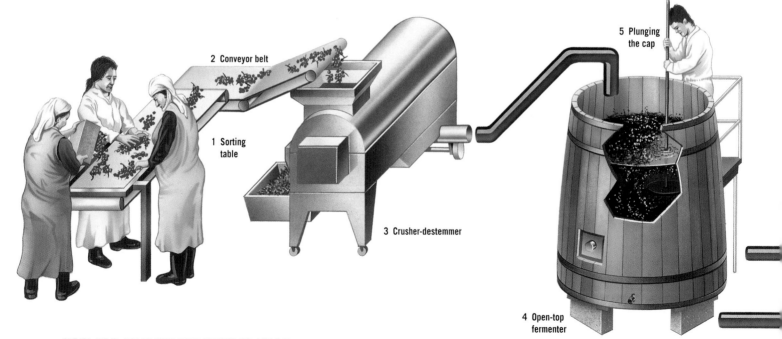

2 Conveyor belt

1 Sorting table

3 Crusher-destemmer

5 Plunging the cap

4 Open-top fermenter

HOW TOP-QUALITY RED WINE IS MADE

This diagram shows how a typical fine red wine is made in the most traditional way possible. Hand-cut bunches of grapes are gently transferred from small containers, designed to prevent the grapes being crushed in transit from vine to winery, onto a sorting table **1**. Any unripe, damaged or mouldy grapes are cut out and any other matter removed by hand. The conveyor belt **2** carries the bunches to the crusher-destemmer **3** (see **2** above), where the stalks are removed and most of the grapes are crushed. The settings can be adjusted according to how many stems and whole grapes are required. For less tannic grapes such as Pinot Noir, some or all of the stems may be retained at this stage to give the wine structure. The grape must, including the all-important skins for colour, flavour, and tannin, is then pumped into an open-top fermenter **4**, which these days is often made of stainless steel, but traditionally was made of oak, concrete, or even slate. Here yeasts naturally present in the atmosphere will slowly set in motion the alcoholic fermentation. Some winemakers cool the must before fermentation to give some extra skin contact time, others heat the must immediately to encourage the alcoholic fermentation. Sugar levels start to fall as the level of alcohol rises and the carbon dioxide given off pushes up the grape skins and pulp to form a cap, which protects the

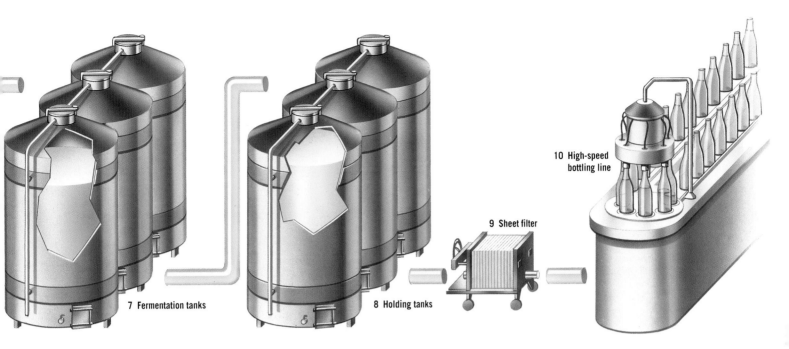

7 Fermentation tanks

8 Holding tanks

9 Sheet filter

10 High-speed bottling line

suspended solids to settle out of the liquid after about 24 hours in the settling tanks. The now much cleaner grape juice is pumped into temperature-controlled stainless steel fermentation tanks **7**. The juice is inoculated with a strain of specially selected cultured yeast. The temperature is kept low for inexpensive white wines, usually between 54 and 63°F (12 and 17°C) to preserve fresh, fruity aromas. However, the higher the temperature, the faster the

fermentation and the sooner the fermentation tank can be used for another batch of grapes. The length of the fermentation can vary from a few days to a month, the carbon dioxide escaping through a valve not shown here. The wine is racked off the lees, becoming even cleaner, and put into holding tanks **8** protected from oxygen. The wine is then stored at a low temperature until required to fill an order so as to keep it as fresh as possible. It may

have to be blended and is then cold-stabilized – chilled to almost 32°F (0°C) to precipitate tartrate crystals – and probably fined. All commercial wines are then filtered to remove any potentially harmful bacteria. It may be pumped through a sheet filter **9**, or a membrane filter, to remove any particles held in suspension. The star-bright wine is then bottled by means of a high-speed bottling line **10** just before being shipped, keeping storage costs low.

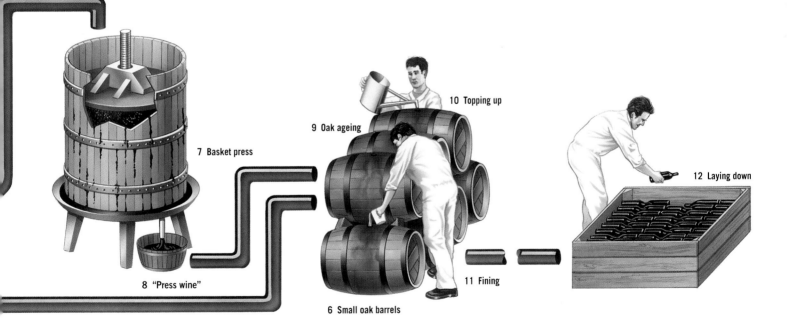

7 Basket press

8 "Press wine"

9 Oak ageing

10 Topping up

6 Small oak barrels

11 Fining

12 Laying down

must against oxidation. The cap is regularly plunged down **5** or broken up by pumping the must over it to prevent its drying out. After the alcoholic fermentation is over, some winemakers allow an extended period of maceration to extract even more phenolics from the skins, while others transfer the wine into small oak barrels **6** before all the sugar has been fermented into alcohol. In either case, the second, malolactic fermentation takes place. The solids left

at the bottom of the fermentation vat are then transferred to a press, in this case a traditional basket press **7**, where the "press wine" is squeezed out and collected below **8**. This press wine is much more tannic and in cooler regions usually kept separate, in warmer ones blended immediately to add valuable structure. The wine is then aged in oak barrels **9** for up to 18 months. Evaporation means that these barrels will have to be topped up **10**, and the wine will

occasionally be "racked" off its sediment into a new barrel to aerate it and prevent the build-up of harmful compounds. The wine will also probably be fined **11**, clarified by adding a fining agent that attracts any suspended solids, and lightly filtered to ensure that it is microbiologically stable. Before bottling, a final blend may be made. After careful bottling the wine is laid down in bins **12** and stored for bottle ageing; it is labelled and capsuled just before despatch.

Anatomy of a Winery

In 1993, when French entrepreneur François Pinault and his family acquired the Pauillac first-growth Château Latour after 30 years of British ownership, they knew that the winery needed substantial reconstruction and redesign. Architect and stage designer Bruno Moinard eventually won the commission and the first vintage to be vinified in the brand new *cuviers*, the tank halls where fermentation takes place, was 2001.

Château Latour's president, Frédéric Engerer, was determined that neither grapes nor must should be subjected to the potentially harmful effects of pumping, which can break open grapes and possibly risk oxidation. Grapes are accordingly picked into shallow plastic crates – not beautiful but extremely practical, easily washable and with minimal risks of grapes at the bottom being crushed by those

above. As in many luxurious modern wineries, the design had to allow grapes and must to move by gravity alone, which dictated that the grape reception area be as high as possible.

One crucial aspect of the new design is the provision of stainless steel fermentation tanks of very different sizes, so that lots of grapes from different parcels of vineyard, with their different characteristics, can be kept separate right through the winemaking process until the vital blending decisions are made. These *assemblages* are made on the basis of extensive tastings during the first winter, which determine which lots of wine go into the *grand vin* Château Latour itself, which into the second wine, Les Forts de Latour, and which into the third wine, Pauillac de

Château Latour. In the larger *cuvier*, tanks vary in size between 106 and 166hl, but in the smaller one at right angles to it they may be as small as 12hl or even 1hl, enough to fill only about 120 bottles, for trial microvinifications.

After *assemblage* the blends are put into barrel and aged in the first-year and then the second-year barrel cellars, or *chais*, and in different proportions of new oak, for many months. Generally before the heat of the summer of the second year after harvest, the wine is bottled, the majority of it labelled immediately, although it is not shipped before November so as to minimize the risk of any heat damage en route. Château Latour's wines are made in a very similar way to that shown on the bottom half of pp.36–37.

Smaller tanks These are used to vinify grapes from smaller plots and for winemaking experiments. It is a great advantage for maximizing individual terroir and varietal characteristics to have many different-sized tanks. Individual tanks may be designed for specific blocks

Administrative offices

Blending tank This enormous tank holds 2,000hl, the equivalent of more than 266,000 bottles. The wine spends very little time here but its purpose is to ensure the final wine, determined by an intricate series of tastings, is a completely homogeneous blend

Second-year barrel cellar Before the heat of the summer the casks are brought down to the basement, for a further ageing period of 11–13 months

First-year barrel cellar At the beginning of December after the harvest, the wine is put into French oak barrels to begin the maturation process. New barrels are used every year for the *grand vin*, Château Latour, and a proportion of new oak for Les Forts de Latour, the second wine

Grape waiting room At the height of the harvest, when the sorters cannot keep up with the volume of grapes arriving at the winery, the grapes wait here. They are kept as briefly as possible in batches according to which vineyards they come from

Sorting tables The grapes are hand-sorted in two stages with two lines of parallel tables to increase capacity. The first sorting removes leaves, stalks, and imperfect berries. The healthy berries are raised by conveyor belt to the destemmer, and then the destemmed berries are sorted to remove any stem fragments before the grapes go by conveyor into the crusher. A skilled team of 20 people can sort around 3 tonnes an hour

Grape reception Hand-picked grapes are delivered from the surrounding vineyards in small plastic crates. The crates are fork-lifted on pallets to the upper floor

Laboratory Any good winery of any size will have some equipment for wine analysis, and others should use external specialist labs. Quality control involves a full chemical analysis of wine throughout its various stages, particularly malolactic fermentation

The exterior of the almost fortress-like working parts of Château Latour, dramatically lit at night, as seen from the road to the quite separate château itself, with its bedrooms, reception rooms, and, for some, memories of great mature vintages.

Video room for visitors

Tasting room for visitors

Wine library Samples of earlier vintages are stored in this vaulted cellar. They serve as a collection for research purposes and some may be used for special tastings and entertaining

Bottling line Hygiene and accuracy of fill are the chief requirements for fine wine. For minimal effects of oxygen there should be a gap of less than 0.4in (10mm) between the bottom of the cork and the surface of the wine in the bottleneck when it is young, although this will increase during ageing as the cork absorbs wine

Fermenting room There are 68 stainless steel water-cooled tanks, ranging from 12hl to 166hl, so that the grapes from each vineyard plot can be vinified separately. Fermentation takes about one week and maceration one or two weeks, then the wine is run off into clean tanks for the malolactic fermentation. These tanks can also be used after the wine has been aged in barrels for storage and technical analysis

Pneumatic press What is left after the new wine has been run off goes to the press so that any remaining wine can be separated from the solids left at the bottom of the tank. This is known as the press wine and some of it may be included in the blend for the final wine

Concentrator This piece of technology, based on the principles of vacuum evaporation, is rarely used or needed, but it can be used to remove excess water from the juice in a very wet vintage, especially if it rains at harvest. It was last used in 1997

Stoppering Wine

Wine can be stored only if there is an effective and appropriate stopper. The three corks of varying quality and age pictured below are all susceptible to cork taint – even the cheap agglomerate versions made of cork chips glued together. (The old champagne cork shows the effect of years of compression; the long cork has been in a bottle of Bordeaux for several decades.) A cork that has come into contact with both chlorine and mould will develop the thoroughly off-putting mustiness associated with trichloroanisole, or TCA, which, when transmitted to the liquid, results in unpleasantly "corked" or "corky" wine. Cork producers are trying to upgrade their production techniques, but many wine producers have become so exasperated by the incidence of cork taint that they have adopted alternative stoppers.

Synthetic corks, usually made of plastic, are the most popular, particularly with New World producers. They come in a wide range of styles and quality levels, allowing wine drinkers to continue the cork-pulling ritual beloved by many without any risk of cork taint, although they are not always easy to get back in the bottle, and are not generally suited to wines made for ageing in bottle.

Some producers have adopted screw caps instead, particularly for aromatic wines such as Riesling, or simple fruity reds for early drinking, for which no oxygen ingress is thought necessary for ageing. There are concerns that in the long term wine will age differently, and very possibly less gracefully, under stoppers other than natural cork, or that the potentially airtight seal of a screw cap or Vino-Lok will cause other unwanted flavours.

Cork bark, stacked here for seasoning, is not thick enough to be removed from the tree until it is 25 years old, and in Portugal it may be removed only every nine years. Corks are basically cylinders punched lengthwise out of bark like this and, while they may have their faults, they are the ultimate in recyclable stoppers.

STOPPERS

Champagne cork
Ordinary cork
Agglomerate cork
Synthetic cork
Screw cap
Vino-Lok

Storing Wine

If good wine is worth paying extra for (which in the majority of cases it is) it is worth keeping and serving (see overleaf) in good condition.

There is nothing mysterious or difficult about handling wine. But doing it well can add vastly to the pleasure of drinking it – and doing it badly can turn nectar into sludge. Wine asks only to be kept lying quietly in a dark, cool, ideally slightly damp place. Strong light can harm wine, particularly sparkling wine, over an extended period. Warmth speeds up reactions so the warmer any wine is kept, the faster and less subtly it will mature. And if a bottle of wine is kept in a very dry place, air may start to penetrate the cork.

Wine storage is a problem for almost everyone. Few houses today come with underground cellars like the one opposite, the perfect place for keeping a collection. One option is to pay someone else to store your wine for you in ideal conditions. This has the obvious disadvantages of continuous expense and loss of spontaneity, but it does shift the responsibility onto a professional's shoulders. Many fine wine merchants offer this service. The best truly monitor your wine collection and advise you when to drink what. The worst have been known to abscond with their clients' wine. Most are delighted to act as brokers in a fine wine market owned by their clients. Any professional wine warehouse should be able to guarantee ideal temperature and humidity, and a sound tracking and retrieval system.

Wine collectors without their own cellars who are determined to keep their bottles about them have to improvise. Some go so far as to build their own extensive cellars from scratch, either excavating or heavily insulating. The USA in particular has several specialists in cellar design and construction. In Europe, a more common installation is not a many-roomed wine mansion with en suite tasting and viewing facilities but a utilitarian concrete cylinder, basically a spiral staircase encircled by horizontal wine storage spaces which can be sunk into the ground. This is hardly practical in, for example, an often-torrid apartment block. For these circumstances, and for very hot climates, specially controlled wine storage cabinets are available, but they are hardly economical in terms of either investment, space, or energy use.

In cooler climates it may be easier to find a corner of a house or flat that can be converted into a small private wine "cellar" (and remember that every cellar begins with a single bottle). Many older townhouses in Britain were built with coal holes, often under the pavement. With good insulation from excessive damp, which may cover labels with so much mould they are illegible, these can provide excellent wine storage.

Spaces under stairs are also favourites for wine storage. They tend to be naturally dark but can also easily be converted into a cupboard. Wine can also be stored in disused fireplaces, or in any room that is used so little that it is relatively cool.

Wine is not over-fussy about temperature: anything from 45 to 64°F (7–18°C) will do, although 50°F (10°C) would be ideal. What matters more is that it varies as little as possible (next to an uninsulated boiler or water heater will not do). No wine will stand alternate boiling and freezing. In high temperatures it will not only age faster, but there is also the danger of the cork's expanding and contracting so rapidly that it stops being a perfect seal and lets oxygen in. If there is any sign of seepage, drink the wine as soon as possible. But if coolness is impracticable, steady moderate warmth will do. Just beware very high temperatures, above 95°F (35°C), which could rob the wine of its subtlety. This is why fine wine today is generally shipped either in temperature-controlled containers or only at cool times of year.

No special equipment is needed in a cellar, coal hole, or cupboard. Traditionally, bottles have always been kept lying horizontally so as to prevent the cork from drying, shrinking, and letting in air, whether they are stored in a case or individually. (Stacking bottles upside down achieves the same end, but labels and capsules are more difficult to read.) Bottles can be stacked in a pile if they are all the same, but as they are more likely to vary it is better to keep them in a rack for easy identification and retrieval of each one.

There are several good arguments for buying certain wines young, at their opening price, and

This wine cellar has grown organically. Unopened wooden cases of young wines are stored elsewhere. Ready-to-open bottles are arranged for ease of access in horizontal wine racks inserted into traditional bins in which bottles of the same type would have been stacked on top of each other.

"laying them down" in cellar or cupboard until they reach perfect maturity. Many fine wines simply never come on the market again after they are first offered – or if they do, as in the case of the rarest red bordeaux or California cult Cabernets, for example, it will be at several times the release price. Do not think that all fine wine will appreciate in value, however; it all depends on the vagaries of the market, and even currency movements. With more modest wines the only object of cellaring the wine is to be able to drink them in good condition when they have matured to suit your taste.

One of the under-sung pleasures associated with owning even a modest wine collection is that of handling, sorting, cataloguing (if you are that way inclined), rearranging, and choosing from such a varied selection of packages of potential delight.

For some wine collectors, keeping records is a substantial part of the fun. Specially designed cellar books are available and are the most traditional method of recording what was bought, from whom, and at what price, as well as when individual bottles were opened and how they tasted. Some people also record who shared these bottles and what food was served. Modern cellar records are more likely to be electronic.

Wine and Time

There is a myth about wine that refuses to wither, let alone die, which is that all wine improves with age. One of wine's most magical properties is that some of it is capable of evolving and improving for decades, and very occasionally centuries. The great majority of wine made today, however, is ready to drink within a year or less of being bottled, and some wines are best drunk straight off the bottling line.

Almost any inexpensive wine, especially whites and rosés, as well as such light-bodied, low-tannin reds as those made from Gamay (Beaujolais, for example), Grignolino, Dornfelder, Jaen, Lambrusco, Portugieser, the Australian crossing Tarrango, and some of the simpler Pinot Noirs, are at their best young. The pleasure in them is a matter of freshness and youthful fruitiness before it starts to fade. As a general rule, the more expensive a wine, even when quite young, the more it is designed to be aged. One of the very few white grapes that makes high-quality, often highly priced wine which can be at its most appealing in youth is Viognier, whose seductive perfume, usually accompanied by relatively low acidity, tends to fade after two or three years in bottle. Champagne and other top-quality sparkling wines are the only other highly priced unfortified wines that are generally ready to drink straight off the shelf.

Most of the great white wines and practically all the best reds, however, are sold long before they are ready to drink. Such wines are grown to be aged. When young they contain an unresolved complex of acids and sugars, minerals and pigments, tannins and all sorts of flavour compounds. Good wines have more of these things than ordinary wines, and great wines more than good wines. Which is why, in the end, they have more flavour and character. But it takes time for these elements, the primary grape-derived aromas and the secondary ones of fermentation and in many cases oak, to interact, to resolve themselves into a harmonious whole and for the distinct scent of maturity, called (by analogy with flowers) the bouquet, to form. Time, and oxygen.

It was not until Louis Pasteur was asked by Napoleon III in 1863 to find out why so much wine went bad on its way to the consumer, to the great detriment of the French wine trade, that the role of oxygen was discovered. Pasteur established that too much contact with air allows the growth of harmful bacteria that turn the wine into vinegar. On the other hand, he found that it was very slight amounts of oxygen acting gradually that make wine mature. There is enough oxygen in the headspace between the liquid and the cork and dissolved in a bottle of wine to account for an ageing process lasting for years. Pasteur showed, by sealing wine in test tubes, alternately full and half-full, that the oxygen in a half-full tube caused the same

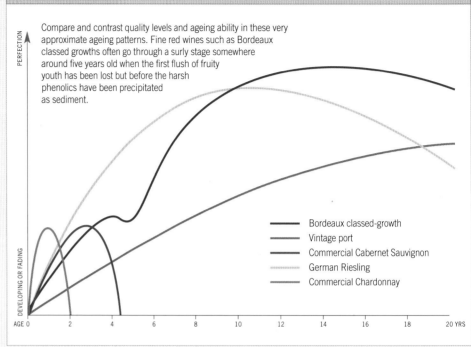

HOW WINE AGES

Compare and contrast quality levels and ageing ability in these very approximate ageing patterns. Fine red wines such as Bordeaux classed growths often go through a surly stage somewhere around five years old when the first flush of fruity youth has been lost but before the harsh phenolics have been precipitated as sediment.

PERFECTION

DEVELOPING OR FADING

AGE 0   2   4   6   8   10   12   14   16   18   20 YRS

— Bordeaux classed-growth
— Vintage port
— Commercial Cabernet Sauvignon
····· German Riesling
— Commercial Chardonnay

deposit in a few weeks as is found in very old bottles, and that it affected colour in exactly the same way as extreme old age.

In fact he immensely speeded up the process that happens in a bottle: the oxygen in the wine acts on its constituents to mature them, but beyond the period of maturity it continues to act and from then on the wine deteriorates.

Pasteur found that barrel-aged wine has several opportunities to absorb oxygen: first of all through the staves; then when it is being racked from one barrel to another and being topped up.

The ageing that takes place in bottle is a totally different process – almost the opposite in fact. Rather than absorbing oxygen the wine gradually loses it. The life of all its constituents is dependent on the very small amount in solution, and the headspace, or "ullage", between the wine and the cork. As the oxygen supply diminishes, the possibilities for further change are being reduced – so the process of ageing wine in bottle is "reductive" as opposed to oxidative.

A youthful fine red wine goes into bottle from barrel containing a mix of tannins, pigments, flavour compounds (these three known collectively as phenolics), and the more complex compounds formed by them. In the bottle, tannins continue to interact with pigments and acids to form new compounds and larger molecules which are eventually precipitated. This means that as it ages, it loses colour and astringency, but gains complexity, and sediment. In fact, holding a bottle of fine wine up to the light to examine how much sediment there is gives a good clue as to how mature it is – although the more heavily a wine has been filtered before bottling, the less sediment will form.

The equivalent process in white wines, which have a much lower charge of phenolics, is less well understood, but gradual oxidation turns the phenolics gold and eventually brown as primary and secondary fruity and "winey" aromas and crisp acids mellow into honeyed, nutty or savoury complexities. If the main preservative of red wine is tannin, of white it is acidity. White wines with sufficient acidity (and sufficient substance to balance it) will mature as long as reds – or in the case of some botrytized sweet whites, German Rieslings, Tokajis, and Loire Chenin Blancs (all particularly high in acidity), even longer.

REACHING A PEAK

The most frequently asked question about any specific wine is "When will it be at its best?" The inconvenient truth is that even a wine's maker can only guess, and often the answer is clear only after a wine has started to decline, to lose fruit and flavour at such a rate that the acidity, or sometimes tannins, starts to dominate. All that is predictable about fine wine is its unpredictability.

Those who buy wine by the case of a dozen bottles and monitor the wine's progress bottle by bottle frequently find that a wine seems wonderfully opulent in youth, then goes through a sullen, dumb stage (when many of the complex compounds are formed) before emerging as an even more magnificent wine afterwards.

Bottle variation, even of different bottles from the same case, is a common phenomenon. The case may have been filled with bottles from different lots (many bottles nowadays have lot numbers marked on the glass) but often there is no rational explanation, just further proof that wine is a living, capricious entity.

It is certainly true that different vintages of the same wine vary enormously in their ageing ability. Red grapes with thick skins, typically the product of a dry year, are likely to age longer than those from wet years, whose skin to pulp ratio is much lower. Similarly, white wines made from grapes grown in a cool year are likely to need longer before their acidity mellows to an acceptable level.

Another factor – quite apart from storage conditions, which are discussed on p.41 – is the size of bottle in which a wine is stored. The amount of headspace is usually constant no matter what the size of the bottle, which means that there is twice as much oxygen per volume of wine in a half-bottle as in a bottle, and only half as much in a magnum (two bottles in one). The ageing effect of that oxygen is therefore much faster in a half-bottle and much slower in larger bottles. This is why halves seem to deteriorate so rapidly and why collectors will pay a premium for the large bottle sizes. Stately ageing is deemed the best.

But, in very general terms, it is possible to say which sorts of wine are most worthy of ageing, or "laying down" as English parlance has it. In approximately descending order of potential life in bottle for red wines, to take some obvious candidates for the cellar, are well-made examples of vintage port, Hermitage, classed-growth claret, Bairrada, Aglianico, Madiran, Barolo, Barbaresco, Brunello di Montalcino, Côte-Rôtie, fine red burgundy, Châteauneuf-du-Pape, Chianti Classico Riserva, Georgian Saperavi, Ribera del Duero, Dão, Australian Cabernet and Shiraz, California Cabernet, Rioja, Argentine Malbec, Zinfandel, New World Merlot, and New World Pinot Noir.

By far the most important body of wines that positively demand to be kept are the Crus Classés of Bordeaux. A generation ago such wines were made to endure, on the assumption that they would be kept a minimum of seven or eight years, and more likely 15 or more. Today's wine drinker is less patient. Modern taste looks for softer tannins (the all-important flattering "mouthfeel") and riper flavours that mean the wine can be drunk after a mere five years or so. California can manage this style virtually every year, but Bordeaux still depends on nature: the 1986 Bordeaux vintage, for example, is determinedly old-fashioned; some are still obdurate.

Red burgundy poses fewer problems because its tannins are rarely obtrusive enough to make patience essential, although some Grands Crus are so obviously stuffed with substance in youth that it would be a shame, and a great waste of money, to drink them at less than 10 years old. All but the very finest white burgundies mature even faster, and Chardonnay is not usually a particularly long-lived grape variety.

The majority of all fine wine kept in professional storage in the UK is stored by Octavian in this warehouse, 90ft (27m) below the Wiltshire countryside in what is basically a disused limestone quarry.

OLD AND NEW

The red on the left is a four-year-old South Australian Shiraz, still very deep in hue with some suggestion of purple and its deep tint right out to the rim. On the right is another New World wine from a deeply coloured grape, an eight-year-old California Cabernet. See how the colour is less intense, much less blue, and more orange with a much paler rim – the effects of bottle age.

The white on the left is a two-year-old California Chardonnay but it could be almost any young white wine. A Riesling would be greener, a Muscadet almost water-white. The wine on the right is a 15-year-old Grand Cru white burgundy. Notice how white wines also acquire a brown tinge with age but gain rather than lose colour.

In general terms the white wines that most obviously benefit from bottle age, in declining order of longevity, are fine examples of Tokaji, Sauternes, Loire Chenin Blanc, German Riesling, Chablis, Hunter Valley Semillon, sweet Jurançon, white burgundy from the Côte d'Or, and dry white Bordeaux. Most sherry, madeira, and sparkling wine is ready to drink as soon as it is bottled, although vintage and de luxe champagne should have enough guts to withstand and benefit from further ageing in bottle.

When to drink a wine is of course partly a matter of personal, even national, taste. The British have notoriously had a penchant for old wine, while the French and Americans frequently drink their fine wines a decade before the British. What is sure is that almost all wine is now being made so that early drinking is at least possible, if not always desirable.

Enjoying Wine

Wine is not a solitary drink. It is essentially sociable, and one of the greatest pleasures it has to offer is the sharing of it. The more thought that goes into the process of sharing, the more pleasure it can give. One option is to dash to the nearest wine store at the last minute and pull the cork just before serving a chilly, cloudy red or lukewarm white, but wine is as sensitive as most wine drinkers and rewards those prepared to undertake a little basic planning. This means some realistic advance calculation of the likely number of bottles and types of wines you will need.

Some of the attentions paid to wine are frivolous, some of the rituals absurd. Others such as the **order of serving** can make all the difference between mere satisfaction and real delight. It is no affectation, but simply making the most of a good thing, to serve more than one wine at anything other than the most casual meal. A young wine served first tends to show off the qualities of an older one; a white wine is usually good at ushering in a red one; a light wine a massive one; a dry wine a sweet one. But many of these combinations played the other way round can be disastrous for the second wine. In the same way that a really good wine puts in the shade a lesser wine served after it, so a dry white wine served after a red may lose much of its appeal.

The question of **how much to serve** is more difficult. In a normal 75cl bottle, there are six to eight glasses of wine (which means generous glasses filled one-third full, not small ones filled to the brim). At a light lunch one glass per person might be enough, whereas at a long dinner, five or six might not be too much. A total of half a bottle per person (perhaps one glass of white wine and two of red) is a reasonable average for most people and occasions – but the circumstances and mood of the meal, and above all how long it goes on, are the deciding factors. There is a golden rule for hosts: be generous but never pressing, and be sure to pour copious quantities of water too.

If the number of wine drinkers at the table calls for more than one bottle with each course, consider serving two slightly different wines together – perhaps different vintages of the same wine/producer or the same grape but of different provenance. (To avoid confusion, try to serve different wines in glasses of different shapes and/or sizes.)

Once likely quantities have been decided, bottles containing sediment can be stood up in time for it to fall to the bottom of the bottle – which can take anything from a few minutes to a few days, depending on the structure and quantity of the sediment. Even more importantly, this preparation allows time for all bottles to be brought to their ideal temperature.

Nothing makes more difference to enjoying wine than its **temperature**. It is possible to both flatter and deceive by manipulating the serving temperature, and all too easy to make a fine wine taste coarse by getting it wrong. Stone-cold claret and lukewarm Rieslings are abominations – not because they offend any

Cut the foil, possibly taking it off completely if you want to see all of the bottleneck. Take the cork out gently, keeping the bottle (and sediment) as still as possible.

Having wiped the lip of the bottle (with particular care if the foil was so old it may have contained lead), hold the bottle in one hand and the decanter in the other. Pour steadily, ideally with the bottleneck against a strong source of light such as a naked lightbulb or a candle. Bottles are usually stored in wine racks with their labels uppermost.

Continue to pour until you see the sediment (if any) moving into the lower neck of the bottle. Then stop when the dregs start to move dangerously close to the rim. If there is much more sediment than this, stand the wine for longer, stopper the decanter, and try again later, although some wines throw a "bottle deposit" which sticks irrevocably to the sides.

rule of etiquette, but simply because the wines taste so far from their best. And there are several good reasons why this should be so.

Our sense of smell (and hence the greater part of our sense of taste) is susceptible only to vapours. Red wine generally has a higher molecular weight – and is thus less volatile, or smelly, than white. The object of serving red wine *chambré*, at what is known as room temperature, is to warm it to the point where its aromatic elements begin to vaporize – which is at a progressively higher temperature for more solid and substantial wines. An aromatic light red such as Beaujolais or cool-climate Pinot Noir can be treated as a white wine; even cold, its volatility is almost overwhelming. On the other hand, a full-scale red wine such as a Brunello or a Shiraz may need the warmth of the room, of the cupped hand around the glass, and possibly of the mouth itself to volatilize its complex constituents.

Tannins are much more obvious at low temperatures. Thus, the warmer a tannic young red wine is served, the softer, more generous, and more evolved it will taste. The illusion of maturity can be created for a young Cabernet or red Bordeaux, for example, by judiciously serving it on the warm side, which will increase the apparent flavour and decrease its astringency. Pinot Noir or red burgundy, however, tends to be lower in tannin and more naturally aromatic. This explains the long tradition of serving red burgundy cooler than red Bordeaux, almost straight out of the cellar.

Cold is also necessary to counterbalance the richness of very sweet wines, even if doing so may mask some of their flavours. On the chart on the right, most of the sweetest white wines are entered at the coldest point. It is a good idea to pour them very cold and let them warm up slightly while you sip them: the process seems to release all their aroma and bouquet. This balancing act is explained by the fact that, like tannin, acidity tastes more pronounced at lower temperatures, so whites whose acidity needs to be emphasized, whether because they are high in sugar, over-aged, or from particularly hot climates, can be given apparent zip by serving them particularly cool.

The chart sets out in some detail the wide range of temperatures that bring out the best in different wines. It is based on personal experience, often modified in discussions (not to mention arguments) with other wine-lovers. But it is worth remembering that when the term *chambré* was invented, the prevailing temperature in French dining rooms was unlikely to have been above 60°F (15 or 16°C). A wine served too hot lacks refreshment value and is practically very difficult to cool down, whereas a wine served too cool will naturally approach room temperature and can easily be warmed by cupping the glass in a hand.

It is easier to serve white wine at the right temperature than red as it can be put in a refrigerator. But the fastest way to cool a bottle is to put it in a bucket of ice and water (not ice alone, which will not touch much of the

bottle), or a special cooling jacket. In a very warm room (and especially a hot garden) it is a good idea to keep the bottle in the bucket between pourings – or, if it is already chilled, in a vacuum bottle cooler which does not entail water and drips. This may mean pouring the wine initially a bit too cold but it will warm up all too quickly in the glass. A useful tip for large quantities (several bottles in a big bucket) is to make a monster block of ice by putting a polythene bag of water in the deep-freeze: the bigger the block the slower it thaws. Tall Germanic bottles should be put in the water upside-down for a few minutes first to cool the wine in the neck.

Persuading a red wine to reach the right temperature is harder. If it starts at cellar temperature, it can take several hours in a normal room to raise it 10 or 12 degrees. The kitchen is the logical place – but many kitchens are well over 68°F (20°C), especially while dinner is cooking. At this sort of temperature red wines may be thrown out of balance; the alcohol starts to vaporize and produces a heady smell, which masks the wine's character. Some of its flavour may even be lost for ever.

One practical way of warming red wine in a hurry is first to decant it, then to stand the decanter in water at about 70°F (21°C). It does

no harm to heat the decanter (within reason) first. Microwave ovens also come into their own for heating wine bottles in a hurry. The danger, however, is being too impatient and heating the wine beyond the point of no return. A little experimentation with a bottle of water would be prudent. And remember to remove anything metallic.

It may be difficult to get a red wine to the optimum temperature, but there are also times when it is necessary to make an effort to keep it there. Vacuum bottle coolers, or even ice buckets, may be needed when serving red wine in hot climates or high temperatures. In a restaurant, do not hesitate to ask for an ice bucket if your red wine has been served too warm. You will be continuing a long and noble tradition of connoisseurship.

Serving wine out of doors presents its own demands, quite apart from getting the temperature right. A subtle bouquet, particularly of a red wine, is much more likely to be stolen by a passing breeze than if the same wine were served indoors. Bold, assertive wines generally show better outside than cellar treasures, which are best reserved for the dining room.

The next, rather obvious, step is **opening the bottle(s)**. In most cases this means removing the foil, or capsule, and pulling the cork. Foils

WINE AND TEMPERATURE

This chart suggests the ideal temperature for serving a wide range of wines. "Room temperature" is low by modern standards: all the better for fine wine. White and pink wines are in yellow; reds and fortifieds in purple. The top (°C) and bottom (°F) lines give the more general guidance on ideal serving temperatures.

	DOMESTIC FRIDGE TEMPERATURE					IDEAL CELLAR TEMPERATURE					ROOM TEMPERATURE			
SWEET WINES				DRY WHITES			LIGHT REDS				FULL-SCALE REDS			
°C4	5	6	7	8	9	10	11	12	13	14	15	16	17	18
		MUSCADET		CHABLIS		GRAND CRU CHABLIS								
				MACON		CHINON			BEST WHITE		RED BURGUNDY			
		GEWURZTRAMINER					BURGUNDIES & GRAVES							
		& PINOT GRIS		BEAUJOLAIS NOUVEAU		BEAUJOLAIS CRUS								
		SANCERRE/POUILLY			SAUTERNES			COTES DU RHONE			TOP RED RHONE			
		ALSACE RIESLING					WHITE RHONE	(RED)					VINTAGE PORT	
			JURANÇON					LANGUEDOC-						
			FINO &					ROUSSILLON REDS	ORDINARY RED					
ALIGOTE			MANZANILLA		TAWNY PORT				BORDEAUX					
TOKAJI		NON-VINTAGE CHAMPAGNE				AMONTILLADO		MADEIRA				FINE RED BORDEAUX		
						MONTILLA				MADIRAN				
SPARKLING WINE										BANDOL				
(eg SEKT, CAVA)			BEST CHAMPAGNE											
EISWEIN			GOOD GERMAN &		BEST DRY		BEST SWEET							
			AUSTRIAN WINE		GERMAN WINE		GERMAN WINE							
SWEET LOIRE/CHENIN BLANC										CHIANTI CLASSICO		BEST PORTUGUESE		
				VALPOLICELLA		CHIANTI			RISERVAS		REDS			
ASTI							SICILIAN REDS			SUPER TUSCANS				
			SOAVE				BARBERA/DOLCETTO			BAROLO				
VINHO VERDE &			VERDICCHIO					PUGLIAN REDS		RIBERA DEL DUERO				
RIAS BAIXAS										NAVARRA & PENEDES		& PRIORAT		
						TOKAJI ASZU				RIOJA				
MOSCATO &			FENDANT							CHILEAN REDS				
MOSCATEL			LAMBRUSCO					LIGHT ZINFANDELS			ARGENTINE REDS			
										PINOTAGE				
		CHENIN BLANC								CALIFORNIA/AUSTRALIAN/				
		MOST CHARDONNAYS			TOP CALIFORNIA/AUSTRALIAN				OREGON PINOT NOIR				
MOST MUSCATS						CHARDONNAYS		NZ PINOT NOIR			BEST CALIFORNIA			
		NZ SAUVIGNON		CALIFORNIA							CABERNETS &			
		NEW WORLD RIESLING		SAUVIGNON BLANC			OLD HUNTER				ZINFANDELS			
			LIQUEUR MUSCAT		VALLEY SEMILLON					TOP AUSTRALIAN			
PINK WINES									URUGUAYAN TANNAT		CABERNET/SHIRAZ			
°F 39	41	43	45	46	48	50	52	54	55	57	59	61	63	64

are usually cut neatly just below the rim of the bottle so as to keep the look of the bottle intact but this is just convention. Special foil cutters are a strictly optional boon.

Corkscrews are surprisingly varied; corkscrew collectors can be even more obsessive than wine collectors. Below are some of the better designs. The only essentials in a corkscrew that does actually incorporate a screw is that it is a hollow helix rather than a solid shaft, which could pierce the cork straight through and give no leverage, and that it ends in a good, sharp point.

Opening bottles of sparkling wine requires a special technique. Well-chilled bottles that have not recently been agitated make the least fuss when opened (warm, shaken fizz can spume alarmingly, and wastefully). It is worth remembering that the pressure inside a champagne bottle is not dissimilar to that inside the tyre of a truck, so an unguarded cork pushed out of a bottle can do a great deal of damage. After taking off the foil and untwisting the wire muzzle, hold the cork down into the bottleneck while gently twisting the bottle off it, ideally at an angle. The cork should pop out discreetly with minimum loss of liquid. Seriously recalcitrant champagne corks can be persuaded to turn by a "champagne star" that fits into the four grooves in the top of the cork to give more torque.

Very old corks can pose problems. They can easily disintegrate under the pressure of a corkscrew, particularly one of the more powerful modern designs. The two-pronged sort, the so-called butler's friend (because it theoretically enabled him to replace the contents of a bottle with inferior wine without having pierced the cork), can be useful for such bottles. Vintage port is one of the longest-living wines and gave rise to the traditional port tongs, tongs of metal specially designed to make a clean incision through a bottleneck under a very old cork after being heated in an open flame.

Vintage port is also necessarily associated with one of wine's most controversial rituals: **decanting**, or pouring wine from its original bottle into another container, usually a glass carafe, before serving it. The most obvious reason for doing this is to leave behind any crunchy and often bitter sediment that has formed in the bottle (and there will be a great deal in a bottle of mature vintage port). The other, more contentious, reason is to aerate the wine, exposing it to the oxygen which Pasteur found so powerful a tool in ageing a wine (see p.42).

Decanting is much discussed but little understood, largely because its effect on a given wine is unpredictable. There is a mistaken idea that it is something you only do to ancient bottles with lots of sediment – a mere precautionary measure to get a clean glass of wine. But experience shows that it is usually young wines that benefit most. The oxygen they contain has had little chance to take effect. But the air in the decanter works rapidly and effectively. In a matter of a few hours it can often induce the opening of what was a closed bud. This means you are more likely to get every single molecule of the scent and flavour you paid for. Some strong young wines – Barolo springs to mind – can benefit from even as much as 24 hours in a decanter. An hour makes all the difference to others. A good rule of

CORKSCREWS

The most common foil cutter **1** can rapidly become addictive. **2** is a classic old corkscrew suitable for use on even the most ancient cork, while **3** is the design most commonly used by wine waiters because it incorporates a knife for cutting the foil. **4** is the notorious butler's friend model, while **5** is the relatively expensive Leverpull, which extracts corks with just two easy movements, twisting the cork off the screw with a further two. **6** is the champagne star for twisting the most obdurate champagne corks.

DECANTERS

Virtually any neutral-tasting container can be used as a decanter but glass is perfect in that it shows off the wine's colour – and the ideal decanter has a stopper so that delicate wines are not exposed to more oxygen than necessary. **7** is a typically shaped bottle-sized decanter, although magnum sizes are useful for maximum aeration of particularly tight, closed wines. **8** is an English design of 1800 with three glass rings for a good grip.

GLASSES

All of these glasses (**9–12**) conform to the basic requirements of a good wine glass, having a stem and a bowl that allows swirling without any loss of wine. Glass **10** is the standard shape and size of tasting glass agreed by an international panel for official standards organizations many years ago, but some tasters, particularly non-professionals, may find it a little constricting.

thumb is that young, tannic, alcoholic wines need, and can withstand, much earlier decanting than old, lighter-bodied wines. But full white wines such as white burgundies can benefit from decanting too – and will look even more beguiling in a decanter than reds.

Those who feel most passionately opposed to decanting argue that there is a danger of losing some fruit and flavour while the wine is poured into and evolves in the decanter. Better, they feel, to pour straight from the bottle, taste and evaluate the wine's state of maturity, and aerate in the glass if necessary by swirling the wine around. It is certainly true that some very old wines can lose such charm as remains extremely rapidly after decanting, yet these are the wines most likely to have a heavy deposit. Trial and individual taste are the surest guides.

The technique of decanting is illustrated on p.44. The only essential equipment is a carafe and a corkscrew. If the wine is very young and unevolved, it will do no harm at all to swirl it about a bit in the decanter, exposing it to even more oxygen, and if the surface area of the wine in the decanter is extensive, it may even help to leave the decanter unstoppered.

It was once widely believed that pulling the cork from a bottle of wine and leaving it unstoppered to "breathe" would have a marked effect on the wine. In reality the area of wine in a bottle-neck is too small to make much difference.

The amount of oxygen in a half-empty bottle of wine on the other hand can have an enormous, usually harmful, effect on the wine. This is especially marked on **leftovers** in an unfinished bottle. For this reason, leftover wine is generally best kept in a smaller bottle of about the same capacity as the leftovers so that it is exposed to very little oxygen. And the process of deterioration can be slowed by keeping the leftovers in a refrigerator, low temperatures having the effect of slowing chemical reactions.

The wine drinker requires one more vital piece of equipment: **glasses**. Wonderfully complicated experiments and blind tastings have shown that a slight modification to the basic shape can accentuate what certain types of wine have to offer. But there is no absolute need to have different glasses for different wines. White wines have traditionally been served in smaller glasses than red – perhaps because some are more naturally aromatic and need less headspace – but this is mere convention.

Strong and sweet wines are usually served in smaller quantities than dry table wines, so there is logic to using a small glass for them, and sparkling wines appreciate a nice long trajectory for each bubble, which means a tall, narrow glass.

It may seem too obvious to mention, but wine glasses should be clean, that is polished and untainted with smells of detergents or cupboards. Although some can withstand modern dishwashers, most are best rinsed with hot water and polished by hand with a linen cloth, ideally when still hot. Cupboard or cardboard smells usually come from keeping glasses upside down, on a shelf or in a box. This may be necessary on open shelves, but it is better to keep them right way up in a clean, dry, airy cupboard. Sniff them before putting them on the table. It is good practice for the nose.

SPECIAL GLASSES

Generally speaking the basic wine shape will suit almost any wine, but champagne and sparkling wines tend to taste best, and keep their fizz longest, if served in particularly tall glasses such as **14**, some of which go in towards the rim too. Glass **15** is quite big enough for port, while the traditional sherry copita **16** is almost a pastiche of the standard wine glass. Some people like their red burgundy served in goldfish bowls such as **13**.

WINE COOLERS

The traditional way of cooling a bottle of wine is to leave it in an ice bucket such as **17** filled with a fast-cooling mixture of water and ice cubes. A sleeve or cooling jacket **18** filled with coolant and kept in the freezer can be just as effective (and is a lot more portable), while a vacuum bottle cooler **19** will efficiently keep bottles cool, or warm, no matter what the ambient temperature.

13

14

15

16

17

18

19

Tasting and Talking about Wine

A great deal of wine, even good or great wine, flows over tongues and down throats of people who drink it but don't actually taste it. They are not attuned to it; not receptive to what it has to offer. They are pre-occupied or deep in conversation; they have just drunk whisky or gin which numb the senses; they have a cold; or they have simply never been told about how to get the most out of every mouthful.

Nothing the winemaker can do dispenses with the need for a sensitive and interested drinker. If the sense of taste were located in the mouth (where our impulses tell us it is), anyone swallowing a mouthful of wine would get all the sensations it has to offer. But in fact the nerves that receive anything more distinctive than the basic sensations of sweet, sour, salt, and bitter, such as the complex flavours of wine, are located higher in the head and deeper in the brain, at the top of our noses.

The most sensitive bit of what we call our sense of taste is actually our sense of smell. The real organ of discrimination is in the upper nasal cavity, where in normal breathing the air never goes. And the only sensations that can reach it are the vapours of volatile substances. To reach the brain the vapours of wine need to be inhaled (either through the nose or, less effectively, the back of the mouth) into the upper part of the nasal cavity, where they are sensed by a thousand different receptors, each sensitive to a particular group of related aromas. Amazingly, we humans are apparently able to distinguish up to 10,000 different smells.

It is often remarked how these smells stir memories far more rapidly and vividly than other sensations. From the position of the olfactory bulb, nearest neighbour to the temporal lobe where memories are stored, it seems that smell, the most primitive of our senses, may have a privileged position of instant access to the memory bank.

Experienced tasters often rely on the immediate reaction of their memory to the first sniff of a wine. If they cannot relate it straight away to wines they have tasted in the past they must fall back on their powers of analysis, located in the parietal lobe. In the frontal lobe their judgement of the wine is formed (to be stored in turn in the temporal lobe for future reference). The range of reference available is the great difference between an experienced taster and a beginner. There is little meaning in an isolated sensation, though it may be very pleasant. Where the real pleasures of wine tasting lie are in the cross-references, the stirring of memories, the comparisons between similar and yet subtly different products of the same or neighbouring ground. Wines differ from one another in terms of colour, texture, strength, structure, body, and length, as well as their complex of flavours. A taster takes all these into account.

Tastings come in many different forms, from the simple act of enjoyment round a friendly

HOW TO TASTE AND APPRECIATE WINE

Eyes

Pour a tasting sample into the glass so that it is no more than a quarter full. First check the wine is clear (cloudiness or fizziness indicate a fault) and look straight down on to it to see how intense the colour is (the deeper a red, the younger the wine and/or thicker-skinned the grapes, a valuable clue if tasting a mystery wine "blind"). Red wines become paler with age, white wines deeper. Tilt the glass away from you against a white background and observe the colour in the middle of the liquid and at the rim. All wines turn slowly brown with age and the rim is the first place where any brick colour is noticeable in a red. Young reds are more purplish-blue than brick. Old reds lose colour completely at the rim. The glossier the colour and the more subtly shaded its different colour gradations, the better the wine.

Nose

Take one sniff with all your concentration, then swirl the wine around and sniff once more. The stronger the impression, the more intense the aroma or bouquet. A subtle, maturing wine may need the swirl before it gives off much smell. If you are tasting blind, this is the moment when you are hoping for a massive intuitive clue, some relationship to something from your tasting memory bank. If you are tasting to assess the wine, note whether it smells clean (most wines do nowadays), intense, and what the smell reminds you of. It is much easier to remember a smell if you can attach words to it. As you taste or drink the wine (and these two activities can feel very different) notice how the smell changes. Good wines tend to become more interesting, inexpensive commercial wines often less so, with time. A very small percentage of the population is anosmic, unable for some physical reason to use the sense of smell to the full.

Mouth

This stage involves taking a good mouthful of wine and exposing all of the taste buds distributed over the tongue and insides of the cheeks to it. If the nose is best at sensing the subtle flavours in a wine, the mouth is best at measuring its constituents: tip of the tongue usually for sweetness, upper edges for the all-important acidity, back of the tongue for bitterness, insides of the cheeks for drying tannins, and the entrance to the throat for any burning excess of alcohol. Once a mouthful has been swallowed or, by professionals, spat out, a judgement can be made as to whether all these elements are in balance (young reds are often deliberately high in tannins) and how persistent the wine is on the palate – a good indicator of quality. At this stage the wine can be judged, possibly even identified, in its entirety.

table to the professional blind tasting tests involved in qualifying as a Master of Wine. One which puzzles many wine neophytes is the tasting ritual acted out in so many restaurants whereby the wine waiter pours a small sample of the chosen wine for you to taste. The purpose of this is for you to check that the wine is firstly at the right temperature and secondly that it is not obviously faulty, most usually tainted by some degree of TCA (see p.40). You cannot send it back just because you don't like it.

What is much harder than appreciating wine is communicating its sensations. There is no notation of taste, as there is of sound or colour; apart from the words used for its basic dimensions such as strong, tart, tough, sweet, salt, and bitter, every word in the language of taste is borrowed from the other senses. And yet words, by giving an identity to sensations, help to clarify them. Assembling a vocabulary is a crucial element in becoming a wine connoisseur.

From talking about wine to writing about it is but a step – which few wine drinkers ever take. Yet there is a strong case for keeping notes on what you drink or taste in a more or less organized way. In the first place, having to commit something to paper makes you concentrate; the prime requirement for being able to taste wine properly at all. In the second it makes you analyse and pin labels on the sensations passing across your palate. In the third it is an aide-mémoire: when somebody asks you what a wine is like you can look it up and say something definite. In the fourth it allows you to extend comparison between wines over time – either the same wine a year later, or different but related wines on different occasions.

In short, keeping tasting notes is like keeping a diary: obviously a good idea, but hard to get off the ground. A little guidance may help. Professional tasting sheets are often divided into three, to remind tasters to make a note of the appearance of the wine, how it smells, and the impact of the wine on the palate. There may even be a fourth space for overall impressions. Different tasters evolve their own tasting language and shorthand and there is no point in being too prescriptive. The single most important note to be made is the full name of every wine tasted. A date can be useful on tasting notes too in case you ever have the chance to monitor the same wine later in its life and make comparisons. And a note of the place and/or fellow tasters may help to jog your memory when you come to read these (usually increasingly illegible) notes again.

Are scores appropriate for judging wine? Under some professional circumstances, such as competitions or judging panels, they are unavoidable – either as symbols, or the numbers that have become such a powerful weapon in wine retailing today. The habit of applying points out of 100 to wines has been seized on with delight by a new generation of wine buyers around the world, for it offers an international scoreboard (reflected often by a similarly calibrated international marketplace), and can be understood no matter what your native language. But,

despite the apparent accuracy and precision of a score out of 100, let no-one forget that wine tasting is an essentially subjective process. A score that is the average of a panel can be deeply suspect, an average which tends to exclude any wine with real individuality (which is bound to displease someone). And even the pronouncements of a single palate can be misleading. We all have our own likes and dislikes among wine flavours and styles. We all begin with one set of preferences and then our taste evolves and continues to change throughout our wine-drinking lives. The best judge of the right styles of wine for your palate is you. There are no absolutes of right and wrong in wine appreciation.

The most charismatic taster of and talker about wine of them all, the late Len Evans OBE AO, who virtually single-handedly turned Australia into a wine-drinking and wine-producing nation. He is seen here in 2003 at one of his famous tutorials for a hand-picked, crack corps of tasters.

Every wine competition tends to have its own way of presenting wines' attributes and tasters' impressions of them. Below, from left to right, are the approved scoresheets for top wine shows in France, Australia, and Argentina. Note the complete anonymity of the wines being judged.

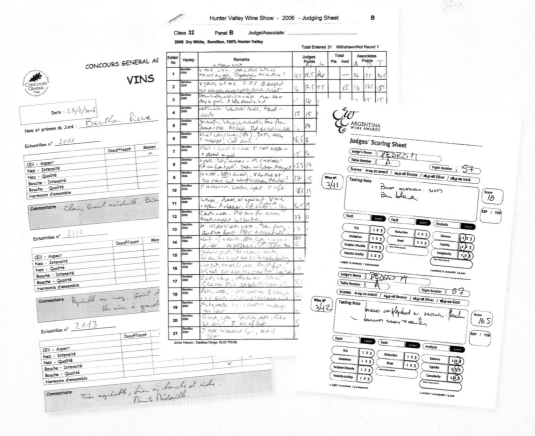

Klein Constantia estate in South Africa's Constantia ward, a new map in this edition.

The World of Wine

France

It would be as impossible to think of France without wine as it is to think of wine without France. The map shows France's administrative départements and, more important to national pride and international pleasure, her many and varied wine regions. Names such as Burgundy and Champagne have long been so redolent of greatness in wine that, much to the disgust of the French, they have in their time been liberally borrowed without apology. The pale mauve areas on the map that shadow the famous regions show how much more widely the vine was grown in France as recently as the mid-20th century. Today vines in these lesser areas have been largely replaced by other crops (see each département's total vineyard area on the blue grape bunches) although vines are still widely grown in the Charentes (for cognac) and in the flatlands of the Languedoc-Roussillon, also known as the Midi, despite concerted attempts to persuade farmers there to rip out the vines that are most obviously surplus to requirements.

Glut is always a problem in such archaic vineyards as those of the Midi. It is aggravated today by France's falling wine consumption. The export market is only interested in quality – which, despite all, France still supplies to a higher level, and in greater variety, than any other country.

The French national character, and its preoccupation with matters of the heart, palate, and liver, partly explains this. But geography is the key. France, washed by the Atlantic and lapped by the Mediterranean, is uniquely well-situated. In *l'hexagone*, between ocean, sea, and the influence of the continent to the east, almost all possibilities are covered. Soils are just as varied, with more of the precious *calcaire* (limestone), so propitious to wine quality, than any other country. Climate change, so far, has been largely beneficial.

But France not only has good vineyards; she defines, classifies, and controls them in more detail than any other country. It started with the Appellation d'Origine Contrôlée, born in the 1920s, which broke new ground by restricting the use of a geographical name to wines made in a precisely specified area. The law also stipulates which grape varieties may be grown, the maximum crop per hectare (yield), minimum grape ripeness, how the vines are grown, and to a certain extent how the wine is made. AOCs (or ACs for short) are administered by the Institut National des Appellations de l'Origine et de la Qualité (INAO). Today there is much discussion about whether the much-imitated AC regulations are a national treasure or an unnecessarily restrictive straitjacket, stifling experimentation and handicapping France in its rivalry with the products of the much more liberal New World.

Just below the AC category, which now constitutes about half of all French wine, are VDQS wines (Vins Délimités de Qualité Supérieure), sort of ACs-in-waiting, which represent only about 1% of each harvest. The second biggest category of French wine is Vins de Pays, the "country wines" described on pp.152–53. At the bottom of the ladder of quality is the shrivelling underbelly of Vin de Table.

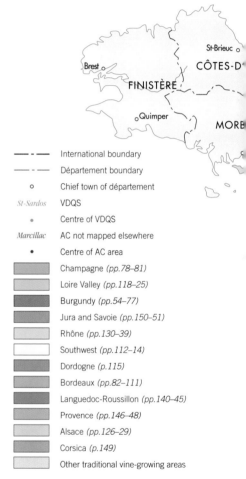

— · —	International boundary
— – —	Département boundary
○	Chief town of département
St-Sardos	VDQS
•	Centre of VDQS
Marcillac	AC not mapped elsewhere
•	Centre of AC area
▧	Champagne *(pp.78–81)*
▧	Loire Valley *(pp.118–25)*
▧	Burgundy *(pp.54–77)*
▧	Jura and Savoie *(pp.150–51)*
▧	Rhône *(pp.130–39)*
▢	Southwest *(pp.112–14)*
▧	Dordogne *(p.115)*
▧	Bordeaux *(pp.82–111)*
▧	Languedoc-Roussillon *(pp.140–45)*
▧	Provence *(pp.146–48)*
▧	Alsace *(pp.126–29)*
▧	Corsica *(p.149)*
▧	Other traditional vine-growing areas

Proportional symbols

 40   Area of vineyard per département in thousands of hectares (no figure given if area <1000 hectares)

THE LANGUAGE OF THE LABEL

The appellation is often printed much larger than the name of the producer, even though the latter can be a surer guide to quality.

QUALITY DESIGNATIONS

Appellation (d'Origine) Contrôlée (AC) wines whose geographical origins, varietal make-up, and production methods are precisely regulated – generally the best and certainly the most traditional

VDQS AC-in-waiting

Vin de Pays "country wine", often from areas larger than AC zones, in which non-traditional varieties and higher yields are allowed (see p.152)

Vin de Table basic wine for which no geographical origin, grape variety or vintage may be stated on the label

OTHER COMMON EXPRESSIONS

Blanc white

Cave (*coopérative*) co-operative winery

Château wine estate or even farm, typically in Bordeaux

Coteaux de, Côtes de typically hillsides

Cru literally a "growth", a specified superior plot of land

Cru classé *cru* that has been distinguished by an important classification such as the 1855 in Bordeaux (discussed on p.82)

Domaine vineyard holding, Burgundy's generally smaller-scale answer to château

Grand Cru literally "great growth": in Burgundy, the finest vineyards; in St-Emilion, nothing special

Méthode classique, méthode traditionnelle sparkling wine made using the same method as for champagne

Mis (en bouteille) au château/domaine/á la propriété estate-bottled wine made by the same enterprise as grew the grapes

Négociant merchant bottler, an enterprise that buys in wine or grapes (cf domaine)

Premier Cru literally "first growth": in Burgundy, a notch down from Grand Cru; in the Médoc, one of the top four châteaux

Propriétaire-récoltant owner-vine-grower

Récoltant vine-grower (and, outside France, winemaker)

Récolte vintage

Rosé pink

Rouge red

Supérieur usually just slightly higher in alcohol

Vieilles vignes old vines and therefore in theory denser wine, though the "old" is unregulated

Vigneron vine-grower

Villages suffix denoting selected communes, or parishes, within an appellation

Vin wine

Viticulteur vine-grower

BELGIQUE

LUXEMBOURG

DEUTSCHLAND

SCHWEIZ

ITALIA

ESPAÑA

Calais

Lille

PAS-DE-CALAIS

NORD

Arras

SOMME

Amiens

Somme

AISNE

Charleville-
Mézières

Meuse

ARDENNES

Laon

MEUSE

Metz

MOSELLE

MEURTHE-
ET-
MOSELLE

Nancy

Toul

Côtes de Toul

Bar-le-Duc

VOSGES

Épinal

BAS-
RHIN

Strasbourg

6

Colmar

9

HAUT-
RHIN

Rhin

Moselle

SEINE-MARITIME

le Havre

Rouen

Seine

OISE

Beauvais

Oise

Aisne

Reims

MARNE

Châlons-en-
Champagne

21

Marne

VAL-D'OISE
Pontoise

SEINE
ST-
DENIS

PARIS

HAUTE-
DE-SEINE
Versailles

SEINE-
ET-MARNE

VAL DE
MARNE

Evry

Melun

Aube

Seine

Troyes

HAUTE-
MARNE

Chaumont

HAUTE-
SAÔNE

Vesoul

Belfort

BELFORT

DOUBS

Besançon

Doubs

ÉVRE
-INE

urg

CALVADOS

St-Lô

Caen

ORNE

Alençon

EURE

Evreux

YVELINES

ESSONNE

EURE-
ET-LOIR

Chartres

MAYENNE

Laval

SARTHE

le Mans

LOIR-ET-
CHER

Blois

Orléans

LOIRET

YONNE

Auxerre

6

Chablis

CÔTE-D'OR

Dijon

Beaune

10

Loire

MAINE-ET-LOIRE

Angers

Coteaux d'Ancenis

20

Montoire-sur-le-Loir

INDRE-
ET-
LOIRE

Tours

10

8

4

NIÈVRE

1

CHER

Bourges

Loire

Nevers

le Creusot

SAÔNE-ET-LOIRE

10

JURA

2

Lons-le-
Saunier

L. Léman

HAUTE-
SAVOIE

Annecy

Anches

17

2

Thouars

Vins du Thouarsais

VENDÉE

le Roche-sur-Yon

fs Vendéens

DEUX-
SÈVRES

Haut-Poitou

Poitiers

2

VIENNE

Niort

2

Châteauroux

INDRE

1

Châteaumeillant
Châteaumeillant

Guéret

CREUSE

ALLIER

Moulins

St-Pourçain-
sur-Sioule

St-Pourçain

13

Mâcon

Bourg-en-Bresse

AIN

Belley

Bugey

Chambéry

2

SAVOIE

HAUTE-
VIENNE

Limoges

PUY-DE-DÔME

Clermont-
Ferrand

Côtes d'Auvergne

LOIRE

Roanne

Côte Roannaise

Boën-sur-Lignon

Côtes du
Forez

RHÔNE

22

Lyon

ISÈRE

St-Étienne

Grenoble

Isère

la Rochelle

CHARENTE-
MARITIME

40

CHARENTE

Angoulême

39

DORDOGNE

Périgueux

Tulle

CORRÈZE

CANTAL

Aurillac

HAUTE-LOIRE

le Puy

Mende

LOZÈRE

12

Tournon

19

Valence

Die

Clairette de Die

DRÔME

Rhône

HAUTES-ALPES

Gap

ALPES-DE-

125

Bordeaux

GIRONDE

Libourne

15

Garonne

LOT

Cahors

Lot

6

Estaing

Marcillac-
Vallon
Marcillac

Rodez

AVEYRON

Entraygues

Vins d'Entraygues et du Fel

Vins d'Estaing

Côtes de Millau

GARD

64

Nîmes

97

Avignon

VAUCLUSE

53

Coteaux de Pierrevert

Pierrevert

Digne

HAUTE-PROVENCE

ALPES-
MARITIMES

Nice

LANDES

Mont-de-Marsan

Buzet

Côtes du Brulhois

LOT-ET-
GARONNE

Agen

la Villedieu-du-Temple

TARN-ET-
GARONNE

Lavilledieu

Montauban

Gaillac

Albi

3

Côtes
du Quercy

Tarn

8

TARN

HÉRAULT

Montpellier

11

BOUCHES-
DU-
RHÔNE

Draguignan

VAR

31

Toulon

Marseille

18

GERS

Côtes de St-Mont

Auch

2

St-Sardos

2

HAUTE-
GARONNE

Toulouse

Narbonne

80

AUDE

Carcassonne

Côtes de la
Malepère

Tursan

Geaune

St-Mont

Adour

PYRÉNÉES-
ATLANTIQUES

Pau

2

Tarbes

HAUTES-
PYRÉNÉES

Foix

ARIÈGE

Perpignan

33

PYRÉNÉES-
ORIENTALES

1:3,625,000

Km 0   50   100   150 Km

Miles 0   50   100 Miles

N

Burgundy

The very name of Burgundy has a sonorous ring. Is it the chapel- or the dinner-bell? Let Paris be France's head, Champagne her soul; Burgundy is her stomach. It is a land of long meals, well-supplied with the best materials (Charolais beef to the west, Bresse chickens to the east, and such super-creamy cheeses as Chaource and Epoisses). It was the richest of the ancient duchies of France. But even before France became Christian it was famous for its wine.

Burgundy is not one big vineyard, but the name of a province that contains several distinct and eminent wine regions. By far the richest and most important is the **Côte d'Or**, Burgundy's heart, composed of the **Côte de Beaune** to the south and the **Côte de Nuits** to the north, the ancestral home of Chardonnay and Pinot Noir. In any other context the Chardonnays of **Chablis**, the reds and whites of the **Côte Chalonnaise**, and the whites of the **Mâconnais** (all equally part of Burgundy) would in themselves be the stars. Immediately south of the Mâconnais is **Beaujolais**, quite different from Burgundy in scale, style, soil, and grape (see pp.72–74).

For all its ancient fame and riches, Burgundy still feels simple and rustic. There is hardly a grand house from one end of the Côte d'Or to the other – none of the elegant country estates that stamp the Médoc as a creation of leisure and wealth in the 18th and 19th centuries. Most of the few big holdings of land, those of the Church, were broken up by Napoleon. Burgundy is still one of the most fragmented of France's important wine-growing districts. The average holding may be bigger than it used to be, but is still a mere 15 acres (6ha).

The fragmentation of Burgundy is the cause of the single great drawback of its wine: its unpredictability. From the geographer's point of view the human factor is unmappable, and in Burgundy, more than in most places, it needs to be given the limelight. For even having pinned down a wine to one particular *climat* (plot of vines) in one particular commune in one particular year, it could still, in many cases, have been made by any one of six or seven people owning small parcels of the land, and reared in any one of six or seven cellars. *Monopoles*, or whole vineyards in the hands of one grower, are rare exceptions. Even the smallest grower has parcels in two or three vineyards. Bigger ones may own a total of 50–100 acres (20–40ha) spread in small lots in a score of vineyards throughout the Côte. Clos de Vougeot's 125 acres (50ha) are divided among more than 90 growers.

For this very reason about 65% of burgundy is still bought in barrel from the grower when it is new by négociants (or shippers), who blend it with other wines from the same appellation to achieve marketable quantities of a standard wine. This is offered to the world not as the product of a specific grower, whose production

of that particular wine may be only a cask or two, but as the wine of a given district (be it as specific as a vineyard or as vague as a village) *élevé* – literally, reared – by the shipper.

Reputations of the larger négociants vary enormously but Bouchard Père et Fils, Joseph Drouhin, Faiveley, Louis Jadot, and Louis Latour (for its best whites) are reliable, Boisset has improved enormously and all are significant vineyard owners themselves. The end of the 20th century saw the emergence of a number of ambitious young négociants making some of Burgundy's best wines with Dominique Laurent and Verget leading the field in red and white wine-rearing respectively. Today an increasing number of respected growers also have their own négociant business.

There are nearly 100 Appellations Contrôlées in Burgundy. Most refer to geographical areas and appear in detail on the following pages.

Built into these geographical appellations is a quality classification which is practically a work of art in itself (explained in detail on p.58). However, the following appellations can be applied to wine made from grapes grown in any part of Burgundy, including vineyards within famous communes whose soil and situation are below par: Bourgogne (for Pinot Noir or Chardonnay), the rarely seen red or white wine Bourgogne Grand Ordinaire (for a mixture of local Burgundian grapes), and, Burgundy's house red and white respectively, Bourgogne Passetoutgrains (for a mixture of Gamay with at least a third Pinot Noir), and Bourgogne Aligoté (for the relatively tart white wine that is made from Burgundy's other white grape). There are also such recondite mini-appellations as **Bourgogne Vézelay**, an obeisance to a single village blessed by gastronomy as well as by the Church.

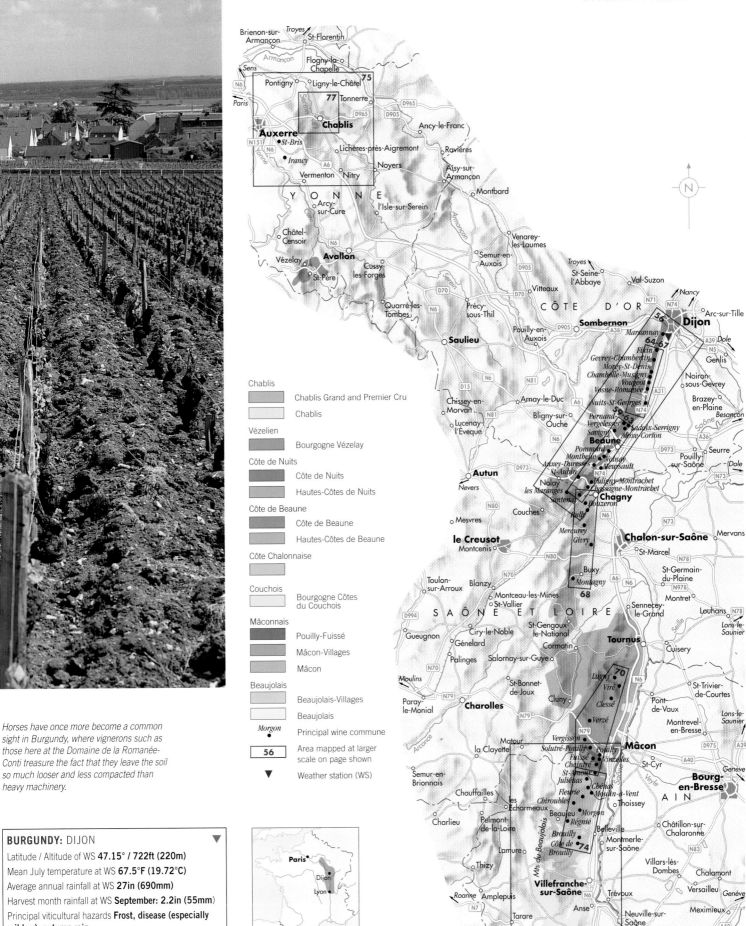

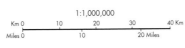

Chablis

Chablis Grand and Premier Cru

Chablis

Vézelien

Bourgogne Vézelay

Côte de Nuits

Côte de Nuits

Hautes-Côtes de Nuits

Côte de Beaune

Côte de Beaune

Hautes-Côtes de Beaune

Côte Chalonnaise

Couchois

Bourgogne Côtes du Couchois

Mâconnais

Pouilly-Fuissé

Mâcon-Villages

Mâcon

Beaujolais

Beaujolais-Villages

Beaujolais

Morgon • Principal wine commune

56 Area mapped at larger scale on page shown

▼ Weather station (WS)

Horses have once more become a common sight in Burgundy, where vignerons such as those here at the Domaine de la Romanée-Conti treasure the fact that they leave the soil so much looser and less compacted than heavy machinery.

BURGUNDY: DIJON ▼

Latitude / Altitude of WS **47.15° / 722ft (220m)**

Mean July temperature at WS **67.5°F (19.72°C)**

Average annual rainfall at WS **27in (690mm)**

Harvest month rainfall at WS **September: 2.2in (55mm)**

Principal viticultural hazards **Frost, disease (especially mildew), autumn rain**

Principal grape varieties **Pinot Noir, Chardonnay, Gamay, Aligoté**

1:1,000,000

Km 0   10   20   30   40 Km

Miles 0   10   20 Miles

Côte d'Or: The Quality Factor

A Burgundian understandably feels a certain reverence towards the rather commonplace-looking ridge of the Côte d'Or – like the Athenians towards an unknown god. One is bound to wonder at the fact that a few small parcels of land on this hill give superlative wines, each with its own positive personality, and that others do not. Surely one can discover the factors that distinguish one parcel from another – giving to some grapes more sugar, thicker skins, or generally more character and distinction.

One can. And one cannot. Soil and subsoil have been analyzed time and again. Temperature and humidity and wind direction have been recorded; wines have been minutely analyzed… yet the central mystery remains. One can only put down certain physical facts, and place beside them the reputations of the great wines. No one has yet proved conclusively how the two are connected (even if wine-loving geologists are attracted to the Côte d'Or like moths to a flame).

The Côte lies along an important geological fault line where the seabed deposits of several different geological epochs, each rich in calcium from defunct shellfish, are exposed like a sliced layer cake. Exposure has weathered their rocks into soils of different ages and textures; the varying degrees of slope have mixed them in different proportions. Minor local fault lines which lie at right angles to the Côte add variations to the mix.

The altitude of the mid-slope is roughly constant at about 820ft (250m). Higher, on the thinly soiled hard rock cap of the hill, the climate is harsher; grapes ripen later. Lower down, where the soil is more alluvial, valley mists and unseasonal frosts are more common and full ripeness more difficult to achieve.

The Côte faces east with a bias to the south, locally skewed (especially in the Côte de Beaune) to full south and even west exposure. Along its lower part, generally about a third of the way up, runs a narrow outcrop of marlstone, making calcareous clay soil. Marl by itself would be too rich a soil for the highest quality wine, but in combination with the stones and scree washed down from the hard limestone higher up it is perfect. Erosion continues the

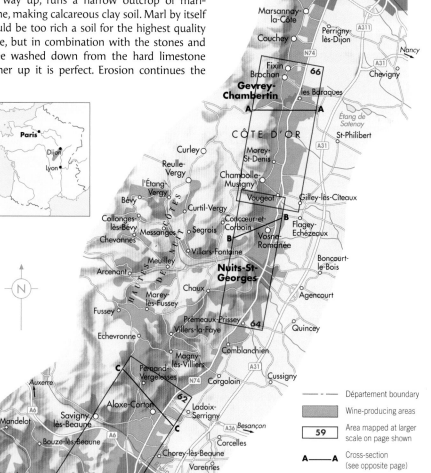

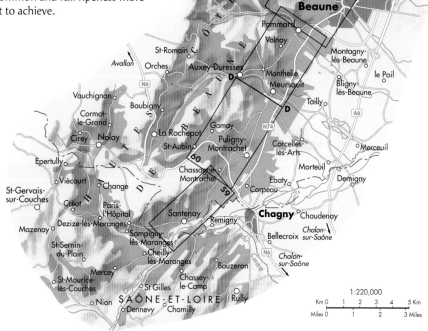

blending below the actual outcrop, the distance depending on the angle of incline.

In the Côte de Beaune the marly outcrop, or Argovien, is wider and higher on the hill; instead of a narrow strip of vineyard under a beetling brow of limestone there is a broad and gentle slope vineyards can climb. The vines almost reach the scrubby peak in places.

On the dramatic isolated hill of Corton the soil formed from the marlstone is the best part of the vineyard, having only a little tree-covered cap of hard limestone above it. In Meursault the limestone reappearing below the marl on the slope forms a second and lower shoulder to the hill, limy and very stony; excellent for white wine.

Such illustrations are only random examples of the varied structure of the Côte. And with each change of soil comes a change in drainage and aspect, in the temperature of the soil – in any one of a hundred factors that affect the vine and therefore the wine.

Burgundy has been the northernmost area in Europe to produce great red wine. It is vital that the Pinot Noir vines ripen before the cold and damp of autumn sets in. The climate peculiar to each vineyard, the so-called mesoclimate (see p.26), in combination with the physical structure of the land, has the most decisive effect. The best vineyards of the Côte face due east; it is the morning sun they need, to warm the ground gradually and retain the heat all day. They are sheltered from the southwest, from the most rain-bearing wind – but not so sheltered as to be frost pockets on still nights.

The other, unmappable, quality factor is the grower's choice of vines and the way they are pruned and trained. There are more or less vigorous clones of the classic varieties, and a grower who chooses the most productive, prunes inadequately, or over-fertilizes the soil, inevitably compromises quality. Today the pursuit of quality has the upper hand over greed and growers are increasingly aware of the need to revitalize the soil after years of over-enthusiatic use of agrochemicals. Organic and biodynamic viticulture are increasingly popular here, particularly with the younger generation.

The Côte d'Or is mapped in more detail here than any other wine region partly because of its singular pattern of varying mesoclimates and soils but also because of its unique history. Of all regions this is the one where wine quality has been studied the longest – certainly since the 12th century when Cistercian and Benedictine monks were already eager to distinguish one *cru* from another and explore their potential.

The Dukes of Burgundy of the house of Valois in the 14th and 15th centuries did everything possible to encourage and profit by the region's wines. Every generation since has added to the sum of local knowledge that is expressed in the *climats* and *crus* of the hills that stretch from Dijon to Chagny.

The map opposite gives the essential overview. At the top of the not-very-impressive hills is a broken plateau with abrupt scarps (steep hills) where geological fault-lines protrude. This is the **Hautes-Côtes**, divided into those of Beaune and those of Nuits, rising to over 1,300ft (400m) and subject to lower temperatures and exposure that puts their crop a good week behind the Côtes below.

This is not to say that in their more sheltered east- and south-facing combes the Pinot Noir and Chardonnay vines cannot produce generally lightish but sometimes fine wines of true Côte d'Or character, and in exceptionally hot years such as 2003 and 2005 the Hautes-Côtes, like the cooler corners of the Côte d'Or itself, come into their own. The best communes in the Hautes-Côtes de Beaune include Nantoux, Echevronne, La Rochepot, and Meloisey; in the Hautes-Côtes de Nuits, where red wines dominate, Marey-lès-Fussey, Magny-lès-Villers, Villars-Fontaine, and Bévy.

At the southern tip of the Côte de Beaune is **Maranges**, responsible for delicate reds from the three communes just west of Santenay bearing the suffix -lès-Maranges.

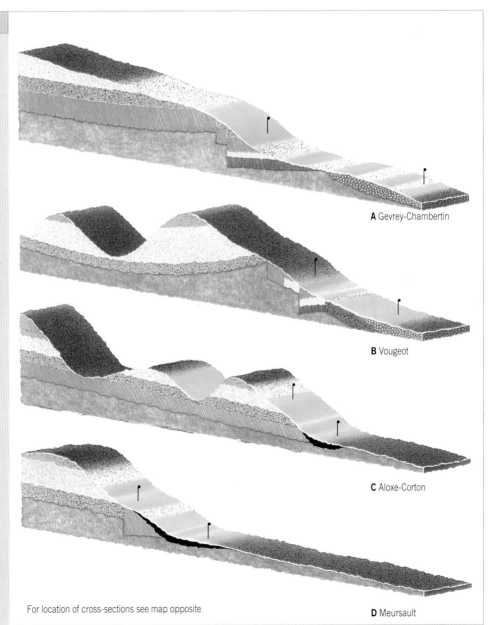

VARIATIONS IN SURFACE SOIL

A cross-section of the Côte d'Or through four great vineyards as shown on the map opposite. The surface (soil) derives from the rock both under it and higher up the hill. In Gevrey-Chambertin immature soil or rendzinas (see key) persists low down until the layer of marlstone. On and below the marlstone is good calcareous brown earth on limestone in a well-sheltered position (Chambertin). A mixture of soils continues into the valley, giving good vineyard land. At Vougeot the marlstone outcrops twice. Below the top outcrop is Grands Echézeaux; on and below the second Clos de Vougeot. The hill of Corton has a broad band of marlstone almost to the top; the best vineyards are on it. But on this steep gradient growers constantly have to collect soil from the bottom and carry it back up the slope. Where limestone debris falls from above, white wine is grown (Corton-Charlemagne). At Meursault the marlstone is again high and broad but its benefit is felt lower where it forms stony soil on a limestone outcrop. The best vineyards are on this convex ramp.

Soil

Skeletal calcareous brown earth
Normal calcareous brown earth
Skeletal gley calcareous brown earth
Normal gley calcareous brown earth
Brown earth
Rendzinas (immature soils)
Limits of vineyard area

Rock

Argovien (marlstone)
Bajocien Supérieur (marlstone)
Callovien and Bathonien Supérieur (soft limestone, clay or shale)
Bathonien Moyen and Inférieur (hard limestone)
Bajocien Inférieur (sandy limestone)
Oligocène Supérieur (various: limestones, sandstones and clay)
Quaternary pebbles
Rauracien (hard limestone)
Loess

A Gevrey-Chambertin

B Vougeot

C Aloxe-Corton

For location of cross-sections see map opposite

D Meursault

Côte d'Or

The Côte d'Or – the Côte de Beaune and the Côte de Nuits, separated only by a few miles where vines give way to marble quarries – is an irregular escarpment some 30 miles (50km) long. Its top is a wooded plateau; its bottom the beginning of the plain-like valley of the River Saône. The width of the slope varies from a mile and a half to a few hundred yards – but all the good vineyards lie in this narrow compass.

The classification of the qualities of the land in this strip is the most elaborate on earth, further complicated by slight differences in nomenclature and spelling between different producers. Based on classifications going back nearly 200 years, it divides the vineyards into four classes and stipulates the precise labelling of each wine accordingly.

Grands Crus are the first class, of which 30 are effectively in operation today, mainly in the

The Hospices de Beaune was founded in the mid-15th century by the Duke of Burgundy's Chancellor Nicolas Rollin and his third wife Guigone de Salin. The hospital, or Hôtel-Dieu, is endowed with vineyards from around Beaune and is therefore able to provide its services for free.

Côte de Nuits. Each has its own appellation. The single, simple vineyard name – Musigny, Corton, Montrachet, or Chambertin (sometimes prefixed by "Le") – is the patent of Burgundy's highest nobility.

Premiers Crus, the next rank, use the name of their commune, followed by the name of the vineyard (or, if the wine comes from more than one Premier Cru vineyard, the commune name plus the words Premier Cru). Examples would be, respectively, "Chambolle-Musigny, (Les) Charmes" or, if the wine were a blend between Charmes and another Premier Cru vineyard or two, then the name would be "Chambolle-Musigny Premier Cru".

Some Premiers Crus are better than others, which is hardly surprising since there are 622 in all. Perrières in Meursault and Rugiens in Pommard, as well as Les Amoureuses in Chambolle-Musigny and Clos St-Jacques in Gevrey-Chambertin, can command prices in excess of lesser Grands Crus such as Clos de Vougeot and Corton.

Appellation Communale is the third rank; that is, with the right to use a commune name

such as Meursault. These wines are often referred to as "village" wines. The name of a specific vineyard, or *lieu-dit*, is permitted – and increasingly used – on the label of these wines but it must be printed in smaller type than the commune name. A few such vineyards, while not officially Premiers Crus, can be considered to be in the same class.

Fourth, there are less propitiously sited vineyards even within some famous communes (typically on lower-lying land east of the main road, the N74), which have only the right to call their wine Bourgogne. Their produce may be clearly inferior, but not by any means always. There are growers here who offer some of the Côte d'Or's rare bargains.

The consumer must remember to distinguish the name of a vineyard from that of a commune. Many villages (Vosne, Chassagne, Gevrey, etc.) have affixed their name to that of their best vineyard. The difference between Chevalier-Montrachet (from one famous vineyard) and a Chassagne-Montrachet (from anywhere in a big commune) is not obvious, but it is vital.

THE LARGER WINE MERCHANTS OF BEAUNE

1 Chanson Père & Fils
2 Bouchard Aîné & Fils
3 Patriarche Père & Fils
4 Caves de la Reine Pédauque
5 Joseph Drouhin
6 Louis Latour
7 Remoissenet Père & Fils
8 Bouchard Père & Fils
9 Louis Jadot
10 Champy
11 Albert Bichot
12 Jaffelin
13 Camille Giroud

The world famous Hospices de Beaune charity wine auction (below) is held every November on the third Sunday of the month.

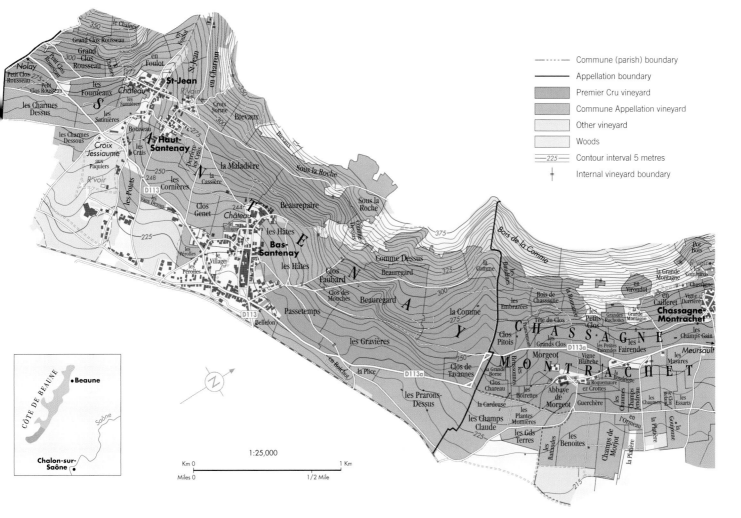

Côte de Beaune: Santenay

The maps on this and the following eight pages trace the vineyards of the Côte d'Or from south to north. Unusually for this Atlas the orientation of the maps has been turned through between 45 and 90 degrees so that in each section the intricacies of the Côte lie across the page.

The Côte de Beaune starts without a great explosion of famous names. It leads in gradually, from the relatively obscure villages of Sampigny, Dézize, and Cheilly, which share the one well-known *cru* of Maranges (all beyond the limits of this map; see p.56), into the commune of **Santenay**. After the hamlet of Haut-Santenay and the little town of Bas-Santenay (a spa frequented by local gamblers and bons viveurs) the Côte half-turns to take up its characteristic slope to the east.

This southern end of the Côte de Beaune is the most confused geologically and in many ways is atypical of the Côte as a whole. Complex faults in the structure of the hills

make radical changes of soil and subsoil in Santenay. Part of the commune is analogous to parts of the Côte de Nuits, giving deep, if not exquisitely fine, red wine with a long life. Other parts give light wine more typical of the Côte de Beaune. Some of the highest vineyards have proved too stony to pay their way. Les Gravières (the name draws attention to the stony ground, as the name Graves does in Bordeaux) and La Comme are the best *climats* of Santenay.

As we move into **Chassagne-Montrachet** the quality of these excellent red wine vineyards is confirmed. The name of Montrachet is so firmly associated with white wine that few people expect to find red here at all. But most vineyards from the village of Chassagne south grow at least some red wine: Morgeot, La Boudriotte, and (overleaf) Clos St-Jean are the most famous. These red wines are naturally tough, tasting more like a rustic Gevrey-Chambertin than, say, a Volnay, although the

tendency nowadays is to vinify them in a way that maximizes their rather fragile fruit.

Visiting at around the time of the French Revolution, Thomas Jefferson reported that white wine-growers here had to eat hard rye bread while red wine men could afford it soft and white. But Le Montrachet (mapped overleaf) had been famous for white wine since the 16th century, and at least part of the village's soil is much better suited to Chardonnay than to Pinot Noir. White wine-growing really took over in the second half of the 20th century as the world fell in love with Chardonnay. Nowadays Chassagne-Montrachet is known to the world chiefly for its dry but succulent, golden white wine scented with flowers or sometimes hazelnuts.

▼ It is not surprising that there are two Moreys here. Families run deep and wide in the Côte d'Or. Colin-Deléger is also related to a host of Colins (see overleaf) and there is even a Colin-Morey. Burgundy is not easy.

Côte de Beaune: Meursault

This is the heartland of white burgundy – but not only white: a surprising amount of red is made here too. A side valley in the hills just north of Chassagne leading up to the hamlet of **St-Aubin**, home of well-priced, slightly earthy wines, divides the vineyards in two. South of it there is excellent white wine but the emphasis is on red. North, on the border of Puligny, there is the best white wine in Burgundy, if not the whole world.

The Grand Cru Montrachet earns its fame by an incredible concentration of the qualities of white burgundy. At its incomparable best it has (given 10 years) more scent, a brighter gold, a longer flavour, more succulence and yet more density; everything about it is intensified – the mark of truly great wine. Perfect exposure to the east, yet an angle which means the sun is still flooding down the rows at nine on a summer evening, and a sudden streak of limestone soil are factors giving it an edge over its neighbours. So much greater is demand for than supply of this illustrious wine, however, that expensive disappointments are by no means unknown.

The other Grands Crus grouped about it are marginally less famous, not quite so perfectly situated, but their wines can sometimes be more carefully made. Chevalier-Montrachet tends to have less depth (its soil is stonier; the best has been used for renewing Le Montrachet). Bâtard-Montrachet lies on heavier ground and often fails to achieve quite the same finesse (though it can take as long to age). Les Criots (in Chassagne) and Bienvenues belong in the same class – as at their best do the Puligny Premiers Crus Les Pucelles, Les Combettes, Les Folatières, and Le Cailleret (and the best of Meursault's Les Perrières).

There is a real distinction between **Puligny-Montrachet** and **Meursault** even though the vineyards of the one flow without a break into the other. In fact the hamlet of Blagny – which makes excellent wine high up on stony soil – is in both, and boasts a typically complicated appellation: Premier Cru in Meursault, Blagny Premier Cru in Puligny-Montrachet, and AC Blagny when (which is rare) the wine is red.

Pulignys tend to be rather more delicate and refined than Meursault, not least because the water table here is higher and it is more difficult to dig cellars deep enough for the wines to be

◀ Only the top four of these great white burgundies are officially classified Grand Cru but many would put the Premier Cru Coche-Dury Perrières on a par with them. Lafon and Leflaive were pioneers of biodynamic viticulture. Lafarge and d'Angerville make great Volnay.

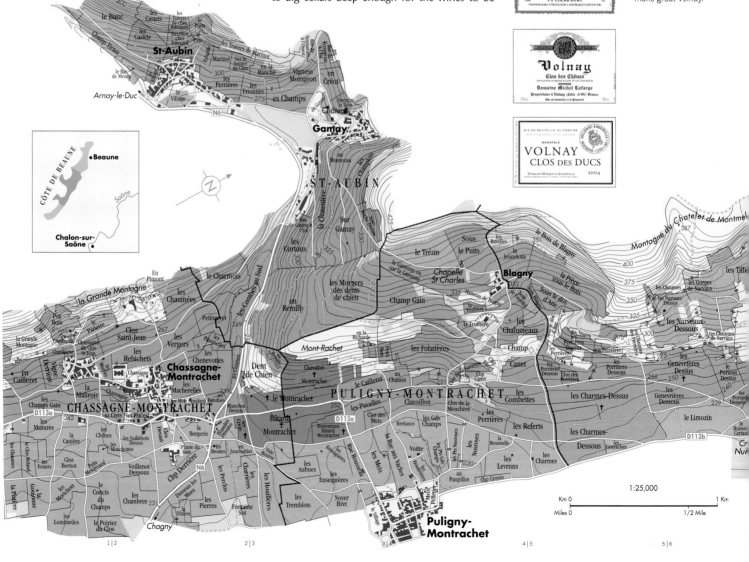

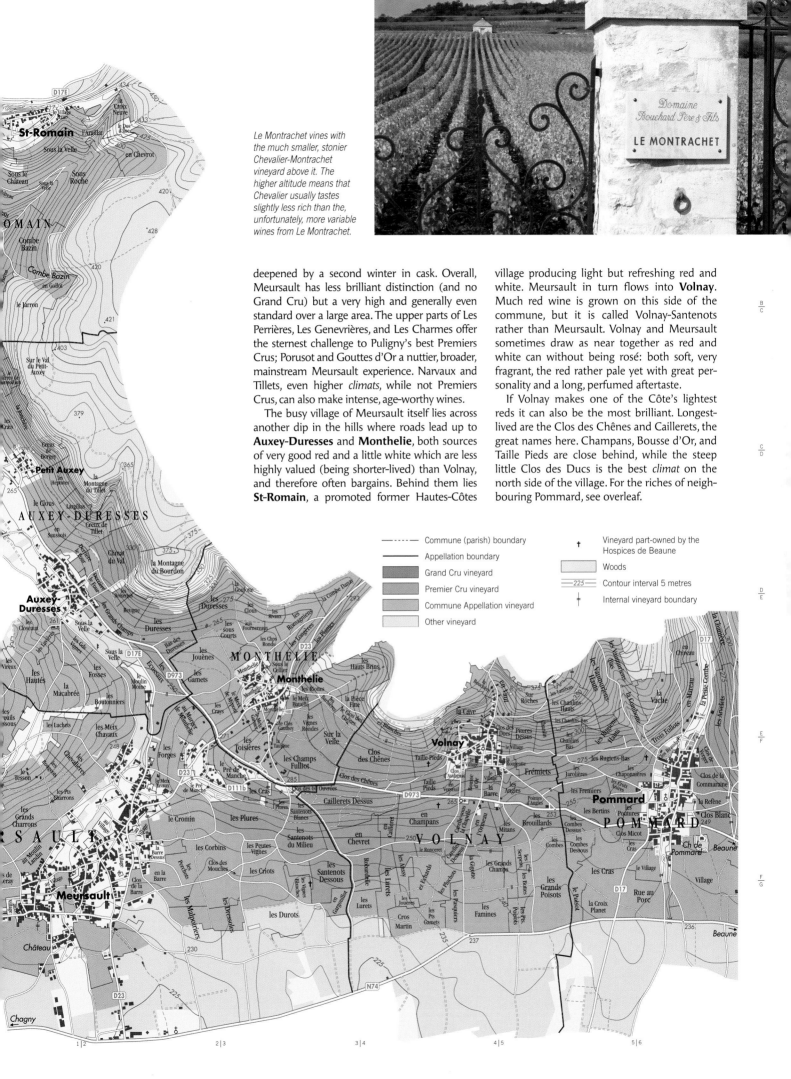

Le Montrachet vines with the much smaller, stonier Chevalier-Montrachet vineyard above it. The higher altitude means that Chevalier usually tastes slightly less rich than the, unfortunately, more variable wines from Le Montrachet.

deepened by a second winter in cask. Overall, Meursault has less brilliant distinction (and no Grand Cru) but a very high and generally even standard over a large area. The upper parts of Les Perrières, Les Genevrières, and Les Charmes offer the sternest challenge to Puligny's best Premiers Crus; Porusot and Gouttes d'Or a nuttier, broader, mainstream Meursault experience. Narvaux and Tillets, even higher *climats*, while not Premiers Crus, can also make intense, age-worthy wines.

The busy village of Meursault itself lies across another dip in the hills where roads lead up to **Auxey-Duresses** and **Monthelie**, both sources of very good red and a little white which are less highly valued (being shorter-lived) than Volnay, and therefore often bargains. Behind them lies **St-Romain**, a promoted former Hautes-Côtes

village producing light but refreshing red and white. Meursault in turn flows into **Volnay**. Much red wine is grown on this side of the commune, but it is called Volnay-Santenots rather than Meursault. Volnay and Meursault sometimes draw as near together as red and white can without being rosé: both soft, very fragrant, the red rather pale yet with great personality and a long, perfumed aftertaste.

If Volnay makes one of the Côte's lightest reds it can also be the most brilliant. Longest-lived are the Clos des Chênes and Caillerets, the great names here. Champans, Bousse d'Or, and Taille Pieds are close behind, while the steep little Clos des Ducs is the best *climat* on the north side of the village. For the riches of neighbouring Pommard, see overleaf.

-------	Commune (parish) boundary
———	Appellation boundary
▉	Grand Cru vineyard
▉	Premier Cru vineyard
▉	Commune Appellation vineyard
▉	Other vineyard

†	Vineyard part-owned by the Hospices de Beaune
▉	Woods
—225—	Contour interval 5 metres
✝	Internal vineyard boundary

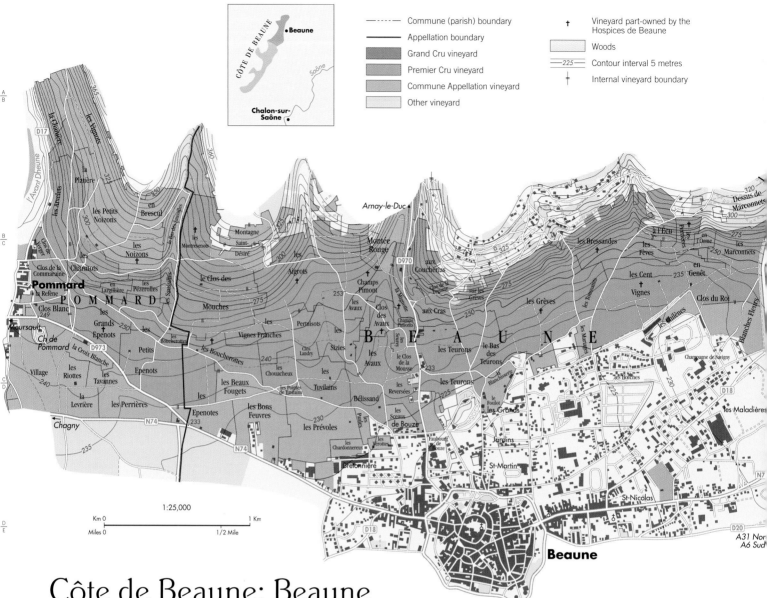

Côte de Beaune: Beaune

You might expect the **Pommard** vineyards bordering Volnay (mapped on the previous page) to give the most Volnay-like, fragrant, and ethereal wines. But Burgundy as ever foxes expectations. The commune boundary marks a soil change that makes Les Rugiens (ruddy, as its name suggests, with iron-rich earth) Pommard's standard-bearer for a different style entirely: dark, heady, and tannic. Many vineyards entitled to the simple Pommard village appellation, which make up about a third of the commune, produce wines in this style which can lack grace and distinction. But there are two or three exceptional Premiers Crus – above all Rugiens and Epenots – and four or five fine growers. It is worth remembering that in Burgundy the grower counts as much as the vineyard, and the saying goes, "There are no great wines; only great bottles of wine."

Pommard's most prestigious vineyard is the lower part of Les Rugiens (Les Rugiens-Bas on the map on p.61), just above the western side of the village. One of the best *cuvées* of the

Hospices de Beaune annual charity auction, Dames de la Charité, is made from Rugiens and Epenots combined. The Clos de la Commaraine and the wines of the growers Courcel, Comte Armand, and de Montille are some of Pommard's finest; sturdy wines that need 10 years to develop the lovely savoury character of the best burgundy.

In the string of famous vineyards that occupy what the Burgundians call "the kidney of the slope", at about the 800ft (250m) line above **Beaune**, a large proportion belongs to the city's négociants: Drouhin, Jadot, Bouchard Père et Fils, Chanson, and Patriarche among them. Drouhin's part of the Clos des Mouches is celebrated for both red and its exquisite white while a part of Les Grèves belonging to Bouchard Père et Fils is known as the Vigne de l'Enfant Jésus and makes another marvellous wine. No Beaune is a Grand Cru; the best is usually gentle wine, lasting well but not demanding to be kept the 10 years or more that a Romanée or Chambertin would.

Travelling north from Beaune the road crosses a plain, and the hills and vineyards retreat. Ahead looms the prow of Corton, the one isolated hill of the whole Côte d'Or, with a dark cap of woods. Corton breaks the spell that prevents the Côte de Beaune from having a red Grand Cru. Its massive smooth slide of hill, vineyard to the top, presents faces to the east, south, and west; all excellent. Indeed, it has not one but two Grand Cru appellations: for white wine and red, covering most of the hill. The white, Corton-Charlemagne, is grown on the upper slopes to the south and west, where debris from the limestone top is washed down, whitening the brown marly soil. What is truly strange is that only in the last 100 years or so has Charlemagne been planted with Chardonnay. This massive, often superlative white wine, at best a rival to Montrachet, is a relatively recent conversion.

The big tannic red is grown in a broad band all round – too broad on the east-facing slopes, where some of the lower Grand Cru land is

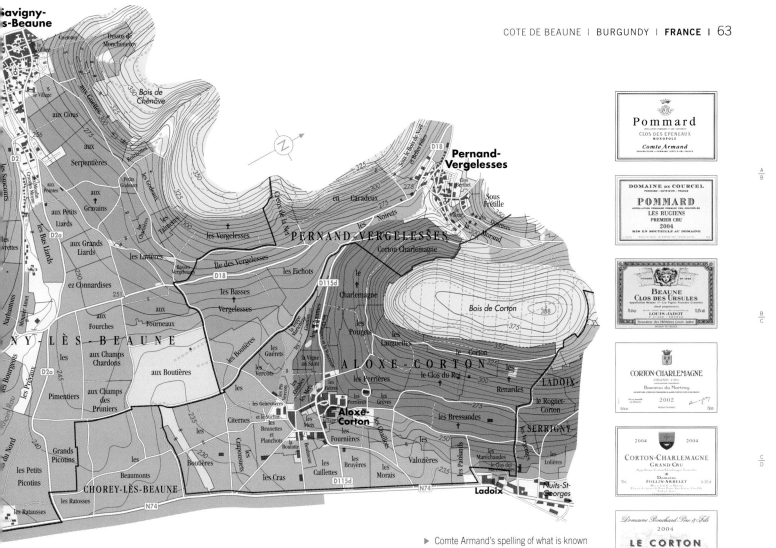

▶ Comte Armand's spelling of what is known elsewhere as Epenots is typical of the refusal by Burgundy's legion of proud, independent producers to adopt uniform rules.

frankly inferior. Top red Cortons come only from Le Corton itself, Les Bressandes, Le Clos du Roi, and Les Renardes. Confusingly, the part marked Corton-Charlemagne on the map grows both white wine (above) and red Corton (below). There is an Alice in Wonderland air about the legalities, but none whatsoever about the wine.

Aloxe-Corton is the appellation of the lesser wines (red and white) grown below the hill to the south, while **Pernand-Vergelesses** round the back has some notably cooler east-facing Premier Cru vineyards as well as some of the hill of Corton's west-facing Grand Cru slopes.

If **Savigny** and Pernand are slightly in the background it is only because the foreground is so imposing. The best growers of both make wines up to the highest Beaune standard, now fully reflected in their price. Up a side valley, Savigny, producing wines that are "*Nourrissants, Théologiques, et Morbifuges*" according to local publicity, can be a marvel of finesse. **Chorey** is even lower down the flanks of this magnificent hill.

The hill of Corton with its topknot of trees. Pinot Noir is planted mainly on the south-facing slopes in the centre, while the Chardonnay vines producing Corton-Charlemagne receive less direct sunlight on western slopes on the left.

Côte de Nuits: Nuits-St-Georges

More "stuffing", longer life, and deeper colour are the signs of a Côte de Nuits wine compared with a Volnay or a Beaune. This is red wine country: white is a rarity.

The line of Premiers Crus, wriggling its way along the hills of the Côte de Nuits, is threaded with clutches of Grands Crus. These are the wines that express with most intensity the inimitable sappy richness of Pinot Noir. The line follows the outcrop of marlstone below the hard limestone hilltop, but it is where the soil has a mixture of silt and scree over the marl that the quality really peaks. Happily, this corresponds time and again with areas that enjoy the best shelter and most sun.

The wines of Prémeaux go to market under the name of **Nuits-St-Georges**. The quality is very high and consistent: big strong wines which at their best almost approach the style of Chambertin. Like Clos de l'Arlot, Clos de la Maréchale is a *monopole*, returned from its long-term tenant, the family firm of Faiveley, to its owner JF Mugnier in time for the 2004 vintage. Les St-Georges and Vaucrains vineyards just over the commune boundary produce wines with tense, positive flavours that demand long bottle age – something that cannot be said of most Côte de Nuits-Villages, a junior appellation for the extreme northern and southern ends of the Côte de Nuits.

Unlike bustling Beaune, Nuits is a not a town for tourists, but it is the home of a number of négociants. The Premiers Crus leading north into **Vosne-Romanée** are a worthy introduction to that extraordinary parish.

Vosne-Romanée is a modest little village with only its uncommon concentration of famous names on the backstreet nameplates to suggest that the world's most expensive wine lies beneath your feet. The village stands below a long incline of reddish earth, with the Romanée-St-Vivant vineyard nearest the village. The soil is deep, rich in clay and lime. Mid-slope is La Romanée-Conti with poorer, shallower soil. Higher up, La Romanée tilts more steeply; it seems drier and less clayey. On the right the big vineyard of Le Richebourg curves around to face east-northeast. Up the left flank runs the narrow strip of La Grande Rue, and beside it the long slope of La Tâche. These are among the most highly prized of all burgundies.

Romanée-Conti and La Tâche are both *monopoles* of the Domaine de la Romanée-Conti, which also has substantial holdings in both Richebourg and Romanée-St-Vivant (and Echézeaux and Grands Echézeaux for good measure). For the finesse, the velvety warmth combined with a suggestion of spice, and the almost oriental opulence of their wines, the market will seemingly stand any price. Romanée-Conti is the most perfect of all, but the entire group has a family likeness: the result of vineyard site, small crops, old vines, late picking, and inordinate care.

Clearly one can look among their neighbours for wines of similar character at less stupendous prices (though frighteningly similar prices in the case of Domaine Leroy). All the other named vineyards of Vosne-Romanée are splendid. Indeed, one of the old textbooks on Burgundy remarks drily: "There are no common wines in Vosne." The Premier Cru Malconsorts just south of La Tâche deserves special mention.

The big, some would say too big, 75-acre (30-ha) Echézeaux Grand Cru – which includes most of the violet *climats* around that marked Echézeaux du Dessus on the map – and the smaller Grands Echézeaux are really in the commune of Flagey, a village too far east to feature on our map which has been absorbed (at least oenologically) into Vosne. Grands Echézeaux has more regularity, more of the lingering intensity that marks the very great burgundies, and certainly higher prices.

One high stone wall surrounds the 125 acres (50ha) of the Clos de Vougeot; the sure sign of a monastic vineyard. Today it is so subdivided that it is anything but a reliable label on a bottle. But it is the *climat* as a whole that is a Grand Cru. The Cistercians used to blend wine of the top, middle, and sometimes bottom slopes to make what we must believe was one of the best burgundies of all... and one of the most consistent, since in dry years the wine from lower down would have an advantage, in wet years the top slopes. It is generally accepted, however, that the middle and especially top of the slope tend to produce the best wine today. There are wines from near the top in particular (just outside the Clos) that can be almost as great as their northern neighbour Musigny. The name of the grower, as ever, must be your guide.

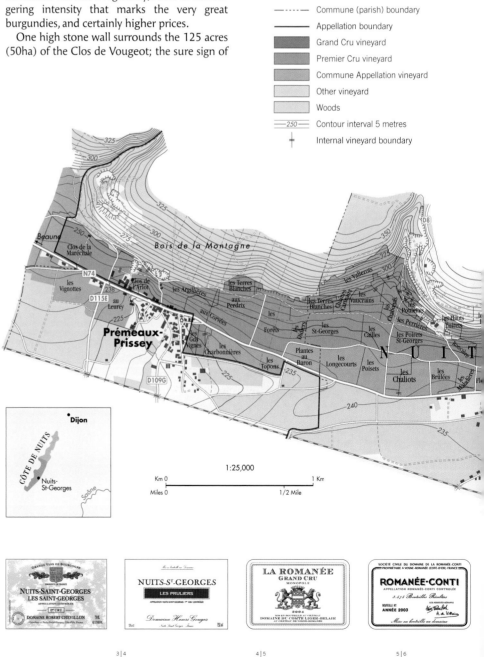

Prémeaux-Prissey church below the Argillières vineyard. Wine from this vineyard is sold under the much more famous name of the town to the north, Nuits-St-Georges, despite its proximity to this village at the southern end of the Côte de Nuits.

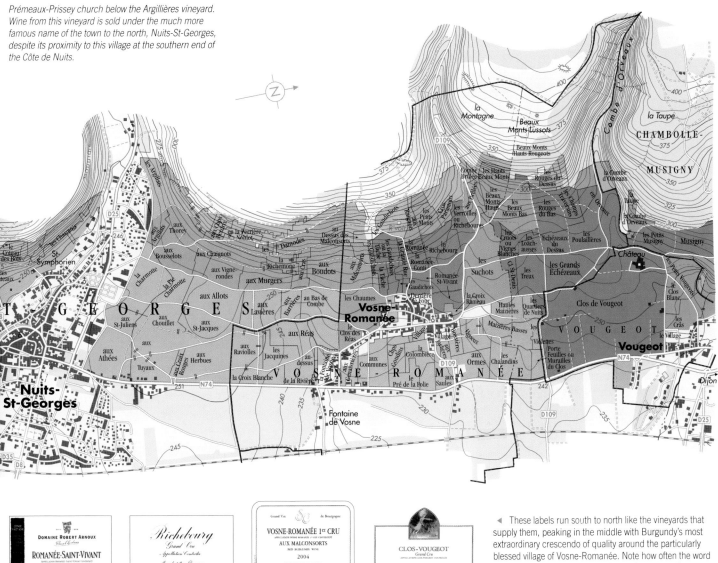

◄ These labels run south to north like the vineyards that supply them, peaking in the middle with Burgundy's most extraordinary crescendo of quality around the particularly blessed village of Vosne-Romanée. Note how often the word Romanée recurs. La Romanée vineyard was recently restored to its former owner.

Côte de Nuits: Gevrey-Chambertin

The finest, longest-living, eventually most velvety red burgundies are made at this northern end of the Côte d'Or. Nature adds rich soil to the perfect combination of shelter and exposure provided by the hills. The narrow marlstone outcrop, overlaid with silt and scree, follows the lower slopes. From it Chambertin and the Grands Crus of Morey and Chambolle draw their power: wines of weight and muscle, unyielding when young, but the best will offer unmatched complexity and depth of flavour when mature.

The Grand Cru Musigny stands apart, squeezed in under the barren limestone crest, obviously related to the top of the Clos de Vougeot. The slope is steep enough to oblige the vignerons to carry the brown limy clay, heavy with pebbles, back up the hill after prolonged rainy weather. This and the permeable limestone subsoil allow excellent drainage. Conditions are just right for a wine with plenty of body.

The glory of Musigny is that it covers its undoubted power with a lovely, haunting delicacy of perfume; a uniquely sensuous savour. A great Musigny makes what is so well described as a "peacock's tail" in your mouth, opening to reveal ever more ravishing patterns of flavour. It is not as strong as Chambertin, not as spicy as Romanée-Conti – but it fully warrants ten to 15 years' ageing. Bonnes-Mares is the other Grand Cru of Chambolle. It starts as a tougher wine than Musigny, and ages perhaps a little slower, never quite achieving the tender grace of its neighbour. Les Amoureuses and Les Charmes – their names perfectly expressive of their wine – are among the best Premiers Crus of Burgundy. But any **Chambolle-Musigny** is likely to be very good.

The commune of **Morey-St-Denis** is overshadowed in renown by its five Grands Crus. Clos de la Roche, with little Clos St-Denis (which gave its name to the village), like Chambertin, are wines of great staying power, strength and depth, fed by soil rich in limestone. The Clos des Lambrays is a *monopole* promoted to Grand Cru rank in 1981, now making seductive wines. Clos de Tart, the *monopole* of the house of Mommessin, is consistently fine, intense, and exotic. Morey has more than 20 tiny Premiers Crus, few of whose names are well-known but whose general standard is very high. The vineyards climb the hill, finding soil higher up than anywhere else in the area. The lofty, stony Monts-Luisants even produces some white wine.

Gevrey-Chambertin has a vast amount of good land. Suitable vineyard soil stretches further from the hill here than elsewhere; some

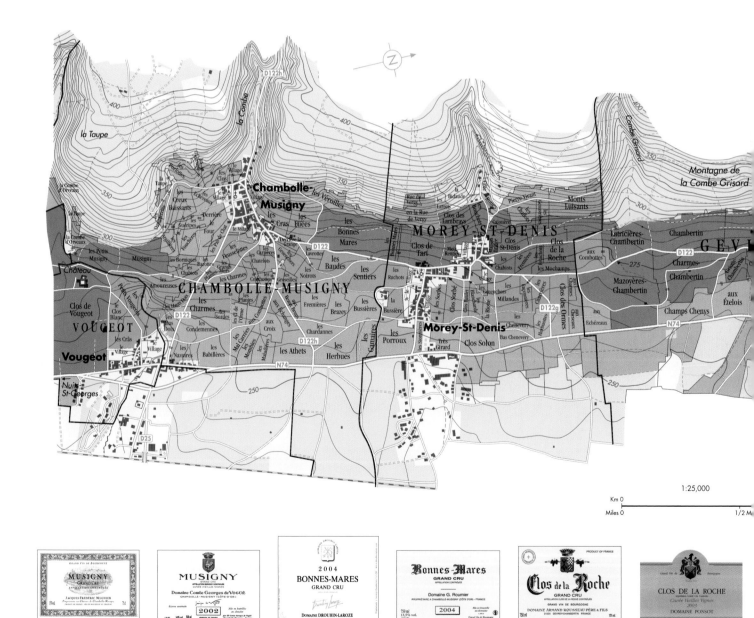

1:25,000

This backstreet of Chambolle-Musigny could hardly express the appeal of Burgundy's villages better with its sun-worn, gentle stone, its proudly maintained tidiness, and shutters suggesting benevolently warm summers. Burgundy is a favoured destination for gastronomic tourists, many walking or cycling through famous vineyards.

east of the main road is still appellation Gevrey-Chambertin rather than plain Bourgogne. Its two greatest vineyards, Chambertin and Clos de Bèze, face east on a gentle slope just under the woods. They were acknowledged Grands Crus at a time when the citizens of Gevrey were quarrelling with the worthies of Beaune who were handing out the honours. Otherwise their constellation of vineyards – Mazis, Latricières, and the rest – would probably have been Grands Crus in their own right, too. They have the right to add Chambertin after their names, but not (like Clos de Bèze) before. Burgundian wine law can be more subtle than theology.

The commune also has a slope 160ft (50m) higher with a superb southeast exposure. Its Premiers Crus – Cazetiers, Lavaut St-Jacques, Varoilles, and especially Clos St-Jacques – are arguably peers of the Grands Crus. There are more famous individual vineyards in this village than in any other in Burgundy. The slopes to the north, once called the Côte de Dijon, were until the 18th century considered to be among the best. But growers were tempted to grow bulk wine for the city and planted the "disloyal" Gamay. Brochon became known as a "well of wine". Today its southern edge is included in Gevrey-Chambertin; the rest of its vineyards have only the right to the appellation Côte de Nuits-Villages.

Fixin, however, has some tradition of quality with the Premiers Crus La Perrière, Les Hervelets, and Clos du Chapître potentially up to the standards of Gevrey-Chambertin. **Marsannay**, which is situated just off the map to the right, specializes in delicious Pinot Noir rosé, some flirtatious red, and a little ordinary white.

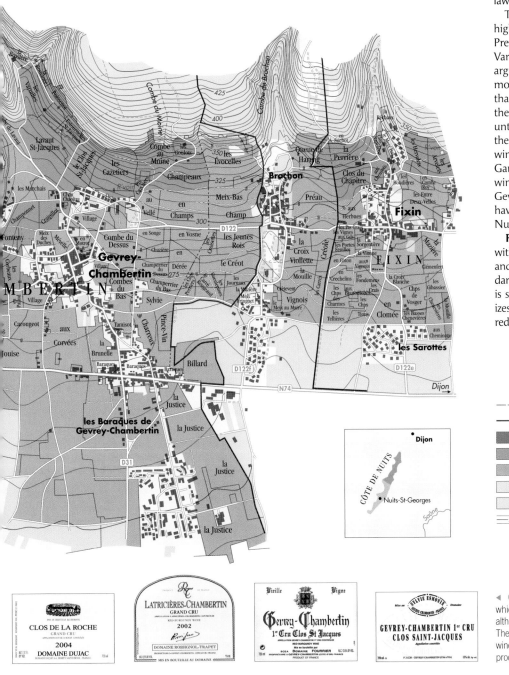

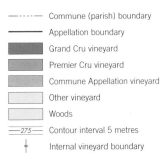

--------- Commune (parish) boundary

————— Appellation boundary

Grand Cru vineyard

Premier Cru vineyard

Commune Appellation vineyard

Other vineyard

Woods

══275══ Contour interval 5 metres

┼ Internal vineyard boundary

◀ Chambolle, Morey, and Gevrey boast a host of vineyards which can claim to express the apogee of red burgundy – although labelling is recondite even by Burgundian standards. The Bonnes-Mares and Clos de la Roche labels are in fact for wines made in Chambolle or Morey. Other great Gevrey producers include Rousseau and the Dugats.

Côte Chalonnaise

So close is the north of the Côte Chalonnaise to the southern tip of the Côte d'Or that it is surprising that most of its wines taste so perceptibly different, like slightly undernourished country cousins. The rolling, pastoral hills south of Chagny are in many ways a continuation of the Côte de Beaune, although the regular ridge is replaced here by a jumble of limestone slopes on which vineyards appear among orchards and pasture. These vineyards rise to a markedly higher altitude than those of the Côte de Beaune, resulting in a slightly later harvest and a more precarious ripening process. The Côte Chalonnaise, once called the "Région de Mercurey", was named for its proximity to Chalon-sur-Saône to the east.

The map shows only the most celebrated, central strip of the Côte, specifically the five major communes that give their names to the appellations Rully, Mercurey, Givry, Montagny, and Bouzeron, and some of their better-known vineyards situated on mainly east- and south-facing slopes.

In the north **Rully** makes more white than red. The white is brisk, high in acid, in poor vintages ideal material for sparkling Crémant de Bourgogne and in good vintages lively, apple-fresh, lean white burgundy that can be exceptional value. Rully reds also tend to leanness – but are not without class.

Mercurey is much the best-known appellation, accounting for two in every three bottles of Côte Chalonnaise red. Pinot Noir here is on a par with a minor Côte de Beaune: firm, solid, almost rough when young, but ageing well. The négociants Antonin Rodet and Faiveley are among the important producers.

There has been rampant Premier Cru inflation here, the total number in Mercurey alone rising from five in the 1980s to over 30 on more than 250 acres (100ha) of vineyard today. This significantly higher proportion of Premiers Crus than in the Côte d'Or to the north is characteristic of the Côte Chalonnaise; the resulting modest premium is worth paying.

Mercurey's neighbour **Givry** is the smallest of the four major appellations and is almost as dedicated to red wine. It is often lighter, easier, and more enjoyable young than Mercurey, although the Clos Jus, recovered from scrubland in the late 1980s, is producing solidly powerful wine that is well worth ageing.

Montagny to the south is the one all-white appellation and includes neighbouring Buxy, whose co-operative is probably the most successful in southern Burgundy. The whites here are fuller and the best are more like minor Côte de Beaune wines than the leaner Rullys. The firm of Louis Latour long ago discovered what good value they can be and is responsible for a significant proportion of total production.

Bouzeron, the village just north of Rully, has its own appellation exclusively for the wines of one grape. Indeed it is the only appellation for a single-village Aligoté white in Burgundy; a reward for perfectionist winemaking by, among others, Aubert de Villaine, the co-owner of the Domaine de la Romanée-Conti.

The whole area, Bouzeron included, is a good source of generic red and white burgundy sold under the Bourgogne appellation.

This Mercurey village scene well conveys the sense of the Côte Chalonnaise's being slightly off the beaten track, although vignerons here are rapidly catching up with the level of ambition now evident in the Côte d'Or.

▼ These producers of superior Chalonnaise wines are part of the new wave, which includes such domaines as Stéphane Aladame, Vincent Dureuil-Janthial, François Lumpp, Saint-Jacques, and Tupinier-Bautista.

Map legend:

Canton boundary
Commune (parish) boundary
Appellation boundary
■ RENÉ BOURGEON Notable producer
Premier Cru vineyard
Other vineyard
Woods
—200— Contour interval 20 metres

Mâconnais

The town of Mâcon on the Saône, 35 miles (55km) south of Chalon, gives its name to a wide, hilly, and profoundly rural area which is increasingly recognized as producing extremely interesting whites on its own account. With its characteristic limestone subsoil, overlaid either with clay or alluvial topsoil, this is definitively white wine country. The slightly warmer climate than that of the Côte d'Or suits the Chardonnay grape, which seems gloriously at home in the Mâconnais and now accounts for almost 90% of all Mâconnais wine.

The Beaujolais vine Gamay is still the mainstay of Mâcon Rouge. When grown on limestone as opposed to the granite of Beaujolais to the south, Gamay can take on a hard, rustic edge so Mâcon Rouge is rarely thrilling. An increasing proportion of land however is devoted to Pinot Noir, which is sold as the rather more valuable Bourgogne Rouge.

The locator map overleaf shows which section of the greater Mâconnais region is mapped in detail. The mauve area to the north and west of this section is responsible for the most basic Mâcon Blanc, Rouge, and a little Rosé. Mâcon-Villages should in theory guarantee superior quality from the region's best villages, but in practice applies to virtually all white Mâcon. A surer guide to white wine quality is to seek out wines sold under the name of one of the 26 villages allowed on wine labels, some of which are marked on the map. Of these, some also have the right to the red Beaujolais-Villages appellation that extends into the southern end of the Mâconnais at the bottom of the map.

In this buffer zone, the villages of Chasselas, Leynes, St-Vérand, and Chânes also qualify for the strange appellation of convenience **St-Véran**. It applies to Chardonnay grown on the southern and northern fringes of the Pouilly-Fuissé appellation mapped in detail on p.71. Soils in southern St-Véran tend to be red, acidic, and sandy, producing very different and generally much simpler, leaner wines than the luscious ones made on the limestone of Prissé and Davayé to the north of Pouilly-Fuissé.

Pouilly-Vinzelles and **Pouilly-Loché**, lying just to the east of the central Pouilly-Fuissé zone, are theoretical alternatives to the real thing, but are in very short supply.

Vines alternate with pasture in the commune of St-Vérand, which, sort of, lends its name to the particularly disparate appellation of St-Véran. It was created for what might be called the Pouilly-Fuissé fringes in the year this Atlas was first published, 1971.

◄ There could be no greater compliment to this southern Burgundian outpost than the arrival of Lafon and Leflaive, the most admired producers of Meursault and Puligny-Montrachet respectively, from the Côte d'Or. Thévenet is an old hand while newcomers Bret Brothers have already established a dazzling reputation.

Mâcon-Prissé, also grown on limestone, can be good value and Lugny, Uchizy, Chardonnay (the lucky village with the name of the grape), and Loché all have their fans as providers of keenly priced, plump burgundian Chardonnay. Two of the best villages however are Viré and Clessé, both on the strip of limestone which threads its way north through the region vaguely parallel to the main north–south A6 autoroute from the Pouilly-Fuissé cluster of excellence and then up to form the backbone of the Côte d'Or. A special AC, **Viré-Clessé**, was created in 1999 for the wines of these villages and several more (see map).

You will not find the brilliance of Montrachet or Corton-Charlemagne in the Mâconnais but there is no shortage of strong, stylish, well-made answers to the Chardonnays of the New World, wines with a perceptibly French accent whose ranks swell with every vintage.

EASTERN MACONNAIS

— - — - — Département boundary

———— Canton boundary

———— Viré-Clessé

• Azé Village which may append its name to Mâcon and/or is entitled to AC Mâcon-Villages

Leynes • Commune entitled to AC St-Véran

DOM MICHEL ■ Notable producer

Pouilly-Fuissé

Pouilly-Vinzelles

Pouilly-Loché

St-Véran

Mâcon-Villages

Woods

71 Area mapped at larger scale on page shown

Co-operatives are particularly important in the Mâconnais, with that of Lugny in the north responsible for one of Louis Latour's best-selling wines, Les Genièvres. The Sologny co-op is close to both the Lafon and Leflaive operations in the west of the area mapped here.

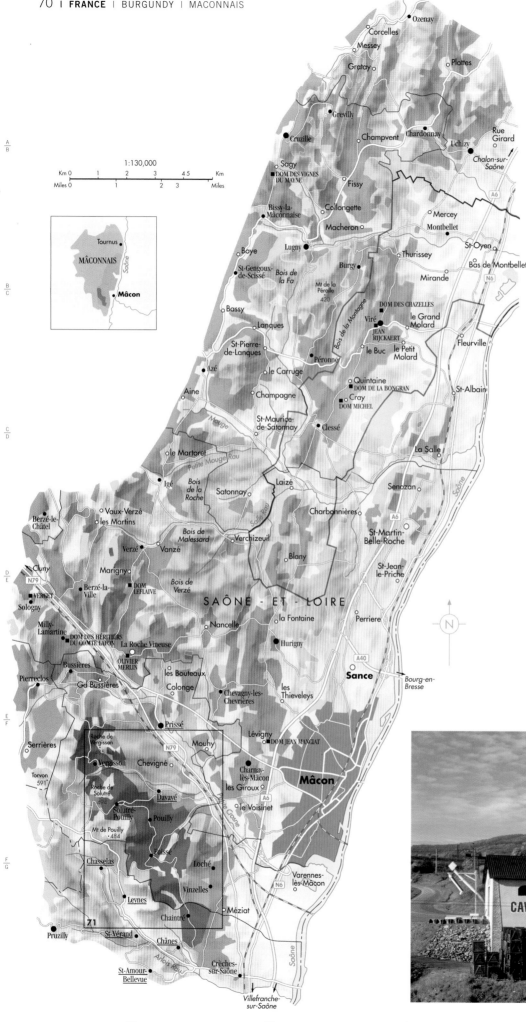

1:130,000

Km 0   1   2   3   4 5   Km
Miles 0   1   2   3   Miles

MÂCONNAIS

Tournus

Saône

Mâcon

Ozenay
Corcelles
Messey
Gratay
Plottes
Grevilly
Champvent
Chardonnay
Rue Girard
Cruzille
Uchizy
Chalon-sur-Saône
Sagy
DOM DES VIGNES DU MAYNE
Fissy
Bissy-la-Mâconnaise
Collongette
Macheron
Mercey
Montbellet
Boye
Lugny
Thurissey
St-Oyen
St-Gengoux-de-Scissé
Burgy
Mirande
Bas de Montbellet
Bois de la Fa
Mt de la Péralle 420
DOM DES CHAZELLES
le Grand Molard
Bassy
Viré
JEAN RIJCKAERT
le Petit Molard
Lanques
Bois de la Montagne
le Buc
Fleurville
St-Pierre-de-Lanques
Péronne
Quintaine
DOM DE LA BONGRAN
Azé
le Carruge
Cray
DOM MICHEL
St-Albain
Aine
Champagne
St-Maurice-de-Satonnay
Clessé
le Martoret
La Salle
Igé
Bois de la Roche
Satonnay
Laizé
Senozan
Vaux-Verzé
les Martins
Bois de Malessard
Verchizeuil
Charbonnières
Berzé-le-Châtel
Verzé
Vanzé
Blany
St-Martin-Belle-Roche
Marigny
Bois de Verzé
SAÔNE - ET - LOIRE
St-Jean-le-Priche
Cluny
Berzé-la-Ville
DOM LEFLAIVE
la Fontaine
Perriere
VERGET
Sologny
Nancelle
Milly-Lamartine
DOM DES HÉRITIERS DU COMTE LAFON
La Roche Vineuse
Hurigny
Bussières
OLIVIER MERLIN
les Bouteaux
Pierreclos
Gd Bussières
Colonge
Chevagny-les-Chevrières
les Thieveleys
Sance
Bourg-en-Bresse
Prissé
Lévigny
DOM JEAN MANCIAT
Serrières
Roche de Vergisson
Mouhy
Torvon 591
Vergisson
Chevigné
Charnay-lès-Mâcon
les Giroux
Mâcon
Roche de Solutré
Davayé
le Voisinet
Solutré-Pouilly
Pouilly
Mt de Pouilly 484
Faisse
Chasselas
Loché
Varennes-lès-Mâcon
Leynes
Vinzelles
Méziat
St-Vérand
Chaintré
Pruzilly
Chânes
Crèches-sur-Saône
St-Amour-Bellevue
Villefranche-sur-Saône

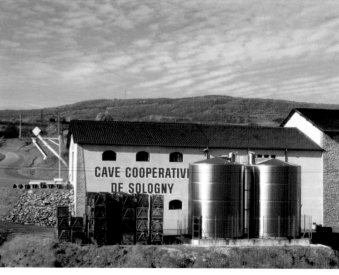

CAVE COOPERATIVE DE SOLOGNY

Pouilly-Fuissé

Mâconnais wines were traditionally associated with simplicity and value rather than excellence, but close to the Beaujolais border is a pocket of white wine-growing with distinction of a different order. The Pouilly-Fuissé district is a sudden tempest of wave-shaped limestone hills, rich in the alkaline clay the Chardonnay vine loves.

The map shows how the five very different Pouilly-Fuissé villages shelter on the lower slopes; the contour lines alone are enough to suggest just how irregular the topography is, and how varied the vineyards. Vines on the south-facing, open slopes of Chaintré may ripen a full two weeks before those on the north-facing slopes of Vergisson, whose wines can be some of the most full-bodied in a long, late vintage. The village of Solutré-Pouilly shelters under the pale pink rock of Solutré, while the twin villages of Pouilly and Fuissé are relatively low-lying and peaceful, but for the constant prowl of wine-loving tourists.

The best Pouilly-Fuissé is full to the point of richness and capable of sumptuous succulence with time. Perhaps a dozen small growers make wines that frequently reach these heights, applying wildly varying policies on oak, lees-stirring, and the occasional addition of second-crop berries to add acidity to what can be a too-fat wine. Others may be bland in comparison, virtually indistinguishable from Mâcon-Villages, their producers leaning heavily on Pouilly-Fuissé's international fame.

After a period of stagnation in the 1980s, the appellation is now in flux, and flowing quite noticeably in the right direction. The most obvious catalyst was the miniature Domaine Guffens-Heynen of Vergisson, run by the wine-making firebrand Jean-Marie Guffens and his talented vine-grower wife. The previous leader of Pouilly-Fuissé, Château de Fuissé, has had to raise its game, but now this area can boast a host of over-achievers such as the Bret Brothers, J-A Ferret, Robert-Denogent, Daniel Barraud, and Olivier Merlin (based just to the north of this zone on excellent land on the west-facing slopes of La Roche Vineuse).

The recent cycle of popularity, lassitude, and recovery here provides a universal lesson. In the 1980s few wines were more fashionable, especially in the USA, than the virtually unpronounceable "Pwee-Fwee-say". As a result producers grew complacent and sold all manner of heavily sulphured, tart, thin whites under this name, at robust prices. By the early 1990s they found themselves with cellars full of unwanted wine. Hence today's welcome quality revolution.

----- Commune (parish) boundary

■ DANIEL BARRAUD Notable producer

En Servy Noted vineyard

▢ Vineyards

▢ Woods

──200── Contour interval 10 metres

1:35,714

Km 0 ———————— 1 Km

Miles 0 ———————————————— 1 Mile

▼ Some of the stars of this zone, so easy to confuse with Pouilly-Fumé in the Loire, where Sauvignon Blanc rather than Chardonnay is the dominant grape variety. Jean Rijckaert was once Jean-Marie Guffens' business partner but has branched out on his own.

It is difficult to miss the Roche de Solutré. It marks the southern end of the limestone plateau on which all great burgundy is grown. Some of the richest Pouilly-Fuissé is grown here.

Beaujolais

In one of the marriages of grape and ground the French regard as mystical, in Beaujolais' sandy clay over granite the Gamay grape, undistinguished virtually everywhere else, can produce uniquely fresh, vivid, fruity, light but infinitely swallowable wine. *Gouleyant* is the French word for the way fine Beaujolais slips ineffably down the throat.

Lightness is not a fashionable virtue, and even committed wine drinkers may overlook Beaujolais, not least because the popularity of Beaujolais Nouveau every late November in the late 1970s and 1980s and the associated rapid cashflow conferred a dangerous complacency on the region. Today there are serious efforts to make more serious wine.

The Beaujolais region stretches 34 miles (55km) from the granite-based hills immediately south of Mâcon, the southern end of Burgundy, to the much flatter land northwest of Lyon. Beaujolais in total produces almost as much wine as the rest of the Burgundy wine regions put together and, as one would expect, the region is far from homogeneous. Its soil divides it sharply, just north of Villefranche, the region's capital. South of here in "Bas" Beaujolais the soil is clay, the wine plain Beaujolais. Its villages remain obscure: the highest their wine can aspire to is the extra degree of alcohol that enables them to qualify as Beaujolais Supérieur. From this deep well nearly 70 million litres of wine a year are drawn – and rapidly drunk.

Very fresh and new (and natural), it can be the ultimate bistro wine, served by the *pot* in Lyon's famously authentic *bouchons* (small brasseries). Too often however its alcohol has been exaggerated by adding sugar to the juice, sacrificing its racy, almost stinging fragrance and easy-flowing lightness to become merely raw and heavy. Plain "Bas" Beaujolais rarely keeps well. Even in a good vintage its clay soil is too cold to ripen full flavours in the Gamay grapes – although there are notable exceptions.

The northern part of the region, "Haut" Beaujolais, is granite-based, with a variously sandy topsoil that drains, warms, and ripens the Gamay, often to perfection. Thirty-eight of its communes, marked in the areas coloured blue and mauve on the map, have the right to the appellation **Beaujolais-Villages**. Their vineyards climb the wooded mountains to the west to heights above 1,480ft (450m).

It is almost always worth paying more for a -Villages wine for its extra concentration. Only individual growers who bottle (very much the minority) tend to use the names of the Beaujolais-Villages communes. Most Beaujolais is sold by merchants, who blend a generalized "-Villages" to their clients' tastes.

The 10 places marked in magenta within the mauve area on the map have the right to use their own names on labels and are expected to show distinct characteristics of their own.

These are the Beaujolais Crus, mapped in detail overleaf and lying just south of the Mâconnais, close to Pouilly-Fuissé. In this northern region a small amount of Beaujolais Blanc is also made – indeed some villages can sell their red wine as Beaujolais-Villages and their white as Mâcon-Villages.

The Gamay grape is in its element here. Each Gamay vine in Beaujolais was traditionally staked individually (although trellising is now allowed in the better vineyards). Its plants are almost like people, leading independent lives: after ten years they are no longer trained, but merely tied up in summer, standing free. A Gamay vine can live longer than a human.

The great majority of Beaujolais today is made by semi-carbonic maceration, in which whole bunches of grapes go into a subsequently sealed vat uncrushed and the grapes, at least at the top of the vat, begin fermenting internally – a high-speed fermentation that emphasizes the characteristic smell and flavour of the fruit and minimizes tannins and malic acid. But there are significant signs of a return to the old, more burgundian methods

Gamay vines in Régnié, the most recent addition to the ranks of Crus Beaujolais, are grown as tradition dictates in the heartland of Beaujolais – without wires but trained up a single stake en gobelet. This gives the vine roughly the same shape as a goblet.

of vinification, some producers even willingly reintroducing oak casks to make much more age-worthy wines.

Well off the map to the west, over a mountain ridge and in the Upper Loire basin in fact, are three much smaller regions similarly devoted to the Gamay grape (see the map of France on p.53). The **Côte Roannaise**, on south- and southeast-facing slopes of the Loire near Roanne, also enjoys a granite base and several individual domaines here can produce wines that have the same refreshing integrity as Beaujolais in its purest form. Further south, growing Gamay on similar soils, the **Côtes du Forez** is dominated by a single, superior co-op. **Côtes d'Auvergne** is even more extensive, almost plumb in the centre of France near Clermont-Ferrand, and makes light reds and rosés from Gamay, and a little light white.

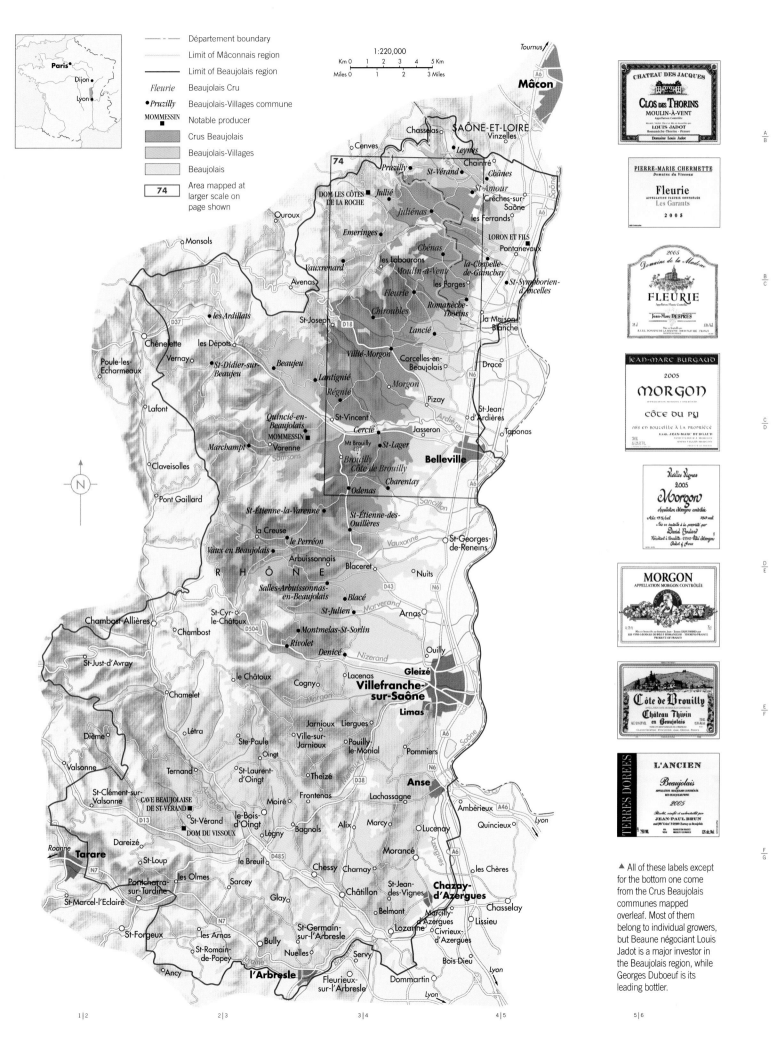

Paris
Dijon
Lyon

Département boundary
Limit of Mâconnais region
Limit of Beaujolais region
Fleurie Beaujolais Cru
• *Pruzilly* Beaujolais-Villages commune
■ MOMMESSIN Notable producer

Crus Beaujolais
Beaujolais-Villages
Beaujolais

74 Area mapped at larger scale on page shown

1:220,000
Km 0   1   2   3   4   5 Km
Miles 0   1   2   3 Miles

Tournus

Mâcon

Chasselas
SAÔNE-ET-LOIRE
Vinzelles
Cenves
Leynes
Chaintré
Pruzilly
St-Vérand
Chânes
St-Amour
Crêches-sur-Saône
les Ferrands
Ouroux
DOM LES CÔTES DE LA ROCHE
Jullié
Juliénas
Emeringes
Chénas
Monsols
LORON ET FILS
Pontanevaux
Vauxrenard
les Labourons
Moulin-à-Vent
la-Chapelle-de-Guinchay
Avenas
les Pacres
St-Symphorien-d'Ancelles
les Ardillats
Fleurie
Romanèche-Thorins
St-Joseph
Chiroubles
Lancié
la Maison Blanche
Chénelette
Vernay
les Dépots
St-Didier-sur-Beaujeu
Beaujeu
Villié-Morgon
Corcelles-en-Beaujolais
Drace
Lafont
Lantignié
Morgon
Régnié
Pizay
St-Jean-d'Ardières
Quincié-en-Beaujolais
St-Vincent
Cercié
Jasseron
Taponas
Marchampt
MOMMESSIN
Varenne
Samsons
Mt Brouilly
St-Lager
Belleville
Claveisolles
Brouilly Côte de Brouilly
Pont Gaillard
Charentay
Odenas
Sancillon
St-Étienne-la-Varenne
St-Étienne-des-Ouillères
St-Georges-de-Reneins
la Creuse
le Perréon
Vauxonne
Vaux en Beaujolais
Arbuissonnais
Blaceret
Nuits
RHÔNE
Salles-Arbuissonnas-en-Beaujolais
Blacé
St-Cyr-le-Châtoux
Marverand
St-Julien
Arnas
Chambost-Allières
St-Romain-Montmelas-St-Sorlin
Chambost
Rivolet
Denicé
Nizerand
St-Just-d'Avray
le Châtoux
Ouilly
Chamelet
Cogny
Lacenas
Gleizé
Villefranche-sur-Saône
Limas
Dième
Jarnioux
Liergues
Létra
Ste-Paule
Ville-sur-Jarnioux
Pouilly-le-Monial
Pommiers
Valsonne
Oingt
Théizé
Anse
Ternand
St-Laurent-d'Oingt
St-Clément-sur-Valsonne
Frontenas
Lachassagne
Ambérieux
CAVE BEAUJOLAISE DE ST-VÉRAND
Moiré
Alix
Marcy
Lucenay
Quincieux
Lyon
St-Vérand
le-Bois-d'Oingt
Dareizé
DOM DU VISSOUX
Légny
Bagnols
Morancé
les Chères
Roanne
Tarare
St-Loup
le Breuil
Chessy
Charnay
St-Jean-des-Vignes
Chazay-d'Azergues
Chasselay
Pontcharra-sur-Turdine
les Olmes
Sarcey
Glay
Belmont
Marcilly-d'Azergues
Lissieu
St-Marcel-l'Eclairé
St-Germain-sur-l'Arbresle
Lozanne
Civrieux-d'Azergues
les Arnas
Bully
Nuelles
Servy
Bois Dieu
Ancy
St-Romain-de-Popey
Turdine
l'Arbresle
Fleurieux-sur-l'Arbresle
Dommartin
Lyon

CHÂTEAU DES JACQUES
CLOS DES THORINS
MOULIN-À-VENT
Appellation Contrôlée
LOUIS JADOT
Romanèche-Thorins - France
Domaine Louis Jadot

PIERRE-MARIE CHERMETTE
Domaine du Vissoux
Fleurie
APPELLATION FLEURIE CONTRÔLÉE
Les Garants
2005

2005
Domaine de la Madone
FLEURIE
Appellation Fleurie Contrôlée
Jean-Marc DESPRÉS

JEAN-MARC BURGAUD
2005
MORGON
CÔTE DU PY
mis en bouteille à la propriété

Vieilles Vignes
2005
Morgon
appellation Morgon contrôlée
Daniel Bouland

MORGON
APPELLATION MORGON CONTRÔLÉE

Côte de Brouilly
Château Thivin
en Beaujolais

TERRES DORÉES
L'ANCIEN
Beaujolais
APPELLATION BEAUJOLAIS CONTRÔLÉE
2005
JEAN-PAUL BRUN

▲ All of these labels except for the bottom one come from the Crus Beaujolais communes mapped overleaf. Most of them belong to individual growers, but Beaune négociant Louis Jadot is a major investor in the Beaujolais region, while Georges Duboeuf is its leading bottler.

The Crus of Beaujolais

The hazy blue hills mapped here, often wooded on their heights but densely planted with vines below, are home to the 10 individual Crus of Beaujolais. Its whole extent is 15 miles (24km) by less than half as much. And yet the wines at their best display to perfection the effects of terroir on a single grape, Gamay. Each Cru has a personality which good growers explore and express with as much vigour as the vintage allows. They range from crisply fragrant wines to drink young to rich brooding bottles that need several years for their heady pungency to evolve.

All the Cru vineyards are sited sufficiently high for frost damage to be relatively rare; the best on east and south slopes, sheltered from the lively westerlies. Soils range from decomposing basalt (in Morgon) to limestone (in parts of St-Amour). Underlying it all is the granite of ancient volcanoes – obviously so in the stump of Mont Brouilly, with its acid, sandy soils.

Brouilly, not a specific village, is the largest of the Beaujolais Crus, its 3,000 acres (1,200ha) of vines filling most of the southern quarter of the map. With a production at times approaching 700,000 cases, it can best be described as variable. **Côte de Brouilly** on the slopes of Mont Brouilly can reach appropriately greater heights; especially wines from the southeastern slopes.

Morgon, the second largest of the Crus, is one of the most distinctive in terms of soil and savour. It centres on the Mont du Py, whose Côte du Py slope of schist rich in manganese gives more rigour than any other Cru, and almost as much breadth and substance as Moulin-à-Vent.

Régnié to the west has only had Cru status since 1988. Its soils are relatively sandy and so the wines tend to be soft and forward. To the north, **Chiroubles** is Beaujolais at its prettiest, both as wine and village.

Fleurie is central in every way. Good young Fleurie epitomizes the spirit of the region: the scent is strong, the wine fruity and silky, limpid; a joy to swallow. The transition to the severity of **Moulin-à-Vent**, like the Brouillys an area rather than a commune, is a tale of terroir writ large. Here the soil is rich in iron and manganese, probably but unprovably implicated in the concentration, dumbness even, of its young wines and their ability to age for 10 years into something Burgundian in character.

Chénas, the smallest Cru, has lost most of its best land to Moulin-à-Vent. **Juliénas** is Fleurie-like in youth but at best fatter, fleshier and spicier with the backbone to keep it going for five years. Juliénas is steep, ideally sheltered and drained. No Cru has a higher overall standard. **St-Amour** provides a final stage from Beaujolais to St-Véran and the Mâconnais.

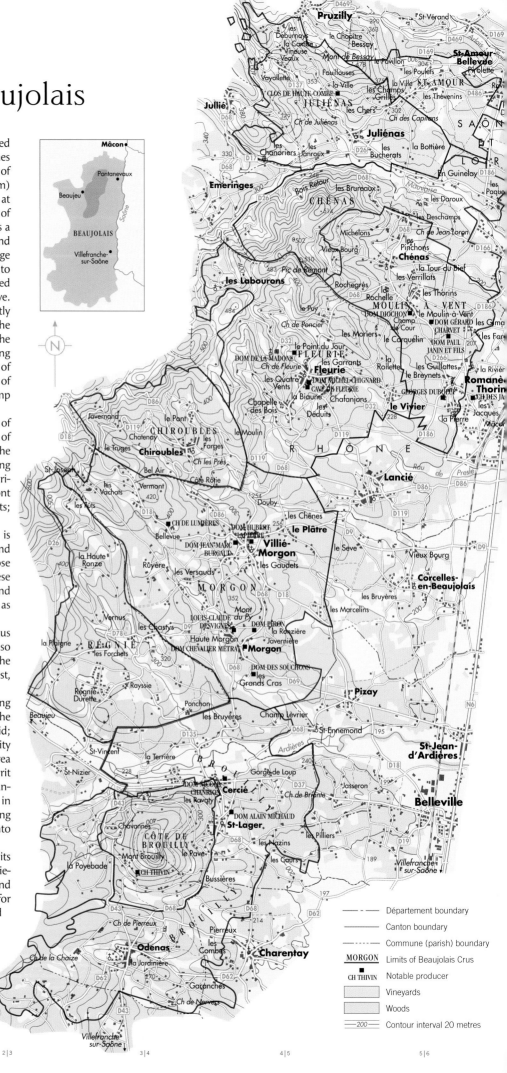

1:75,000

	Département boundary
	Canton boundary
	Commune (parish) boundary
MORGON	Limits of Beaujolais Crus
CH THIVIN	Notable producer
	Vineyards
	Woods
200	Contour interval 20 metres

Chablis

Chablis, for all its fame one of the wine world's most under-estimated treasures, is almost the sole survivor of what was once a vast wine-growing region; the main supplier to Paris, only 110 miles (180km) away to the northwest. In the late 19th century its département, the Yonne, had 100,000 acres (40,000ha) of vines – many of them red – and fulfilled what was to become the role of the Midi. Chablis' waterways flowing into the River Seine were thronged with wine-barges, except in spring when they were cleared for the massive *flottage* of firewood to the capital from every upstream forest.

First phylloxera crushed, then the railways bypassed the wine-growers of the Yonne, leaving it one of France's poorest agricultural regions. The second half of the 20th century saw a great renaissance and a fresh justification for its renown. For Chablis is one of the great inimitable originals. Chardonnay responds to its cold terroir of limestone clay with flavours no-one can reproduce in easier (or any other)

wine-growing conditions – quite different even from those of the rest of Burgundy to the south. Chablis is hard but not harsh, reminiscent of stones and minerals, but at the same time of green hay; when it is young it actually looks green, which many wines are supposed to. Grand Cru Chablis, and even some of the best Premier Cru Chablis, tastes important, strong, almost immortal. And indeed it does last a remarkably long time; a strange and delicious sort of sour taste enters into it when it reaches about ten years of age, and its golden-green eye flashes meaningfully. (Chablis fanatics know it can go through a less exciting wet wool phase that can put others off. So much the worse for them.)

Cool-climate vineyards need exceptional conditions to succeed. Chablis lies 100 miles (160km) north of Beaune – and is therefore nearer to Champagne than to the rest of Burgundy. Geology is its secret: the outcrop of the rim of a wide submerged basin of limestone

and clay. The far rim, across the English Channel in Dorset, gives its name, Kimmeridge, to this unique pudding of prehistoric oyster-shells. Oysters and Chablis, it seems, have been related since creation. The hardy Chardonnay variety (known here as the Beaunois – the vine from Beaune) is Chablis' only vine. Where the slopes face the sun it ripens excellently.

Chablis and **Petit Chablis**, the much-expanded outlying area, are not the only appellations of the Yonne. **Irancy** has long grown Pinot Noir to make light red burgundy. The Sauvignon Blanc grown around St-Bris-le-Vineux, unusual for this part of France, has its own appellation **St-Bris** (it was awarded AC status in 2001), while the Chardonnay and Pinot Noir grown there is sold as **Bourgogne Côte d'Auxerre**, except for that around Chitry which is labelled **Bourgogne Chitry**. **Bourgogne Epineuil** comes from around that village west of Tonnerre. Are such distinctions worthwhile? They do no harm.

The slope of these vineyards for Bourgogne Chitry, one of a rash of relatively recent, relatively minor regional appellations on the outlying fringes of Chablis country, helps to minimize the risk of frost damage to young vines.

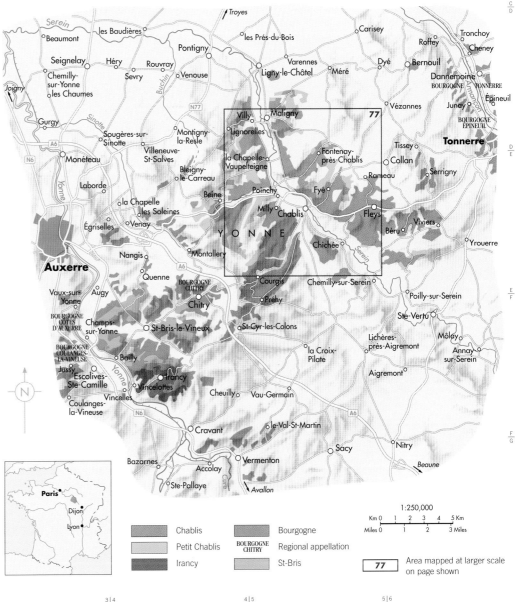

1:250,000

	Chablis		Bourgogne
Petit Chablis		**BOURGOGNE CHITRY** Regional appellation
Irancy		St-Bris

77 Area mapped at larger scale on page shown

The Heart of Chablis

The classification of Chablis into four grades is one of the clearest demonstrations anywhere in the northern hemisphere of the importance of southern slopes: Grand Cru wines always taste richer than Premiers Crus, Premiers Crus than plain Chablis, and Chablis than Petit Chablis.

All the Grands Crus lie in a single block looking south and west over the village and the river, their total 247 acres (100ha) representing only 2% of the total Chablis vineyard area. In theory each of the seven has its own style. Many regard Les Clos and Vaudésir as best of all. Certainly they tend to be the biggest in flavour. But more important is what all have in common: intense, highly charged flavour on the scale of the best whites of the Côte de Beaune but with more of a nervy edge – which, with age, leads to noble complexity. Grand Cru Chablis must be aged, ideally for 10 years, and many examples are still majestic at 20, 30, or even 40.

Les Clos is the biggest, with 64 acres (26ha), and best-known; many would also say the first in flavour, strength, and lasting-power. Fine vintages of Les Clos can develop an almost Sauternes-like perfume in time. Les Preuses should be very ripe, round, and perhaps the least stony in character, while Blanchot and Grenouilles are usually highly aromatic. Valmur is some critics' ideal: rich and fragrant; others prefer the definition and finesse of Vaudésir. La Moutonne, a small plot straddling Vaudésir and Les Preuses, is not officially classified as a Grand Cru but should be, and the name can be found on labels. Bougros comes last in most

accounts – but the hallmark of the producer is often more distinctive than that of the precise plot on this relatively homogeneous slope.

There are 79 named Premiers Crus, but the lesser-known ones have long since been permitted to go to market under the names of the dozen or so best-known. The map opposite shows both the old names and the new ones that are now in common use. The Premiers Crus vary considerably in exposure and gradient; certainly those on the north bank of the River Serein, flanking the Grands Crus to the northwest (La Fourchaume, for example) and east (Montée de Tonnerre and Mont de Milieu), have the advantage. A Premier Cru Chablis will generally have at least half a degree of alcohol less than a Grand Cru, and be correspondingly less impressive and intense in scent and flavour. Nonetheless, it should still be a highly stylish wine and can last at least as long as a Premier Cru white from the Côte d'Or. Its principal fault, these days, is likely to be dilution as a result of over-production.

The 1970s and 1980s saw a very substantial increase in the authorized vineyard area – the cause of continuing controversy among growers. The issue dividing them is the soil. Conservatives credit the Kimmeridgian marl with unique properties; their opponents claim the same for the closely related Portlandian that crops up much more widely in the area. The INAO has favoured the latter, thus allowing expansion to a total of more than11,400 acres (4,600ha) by 2006. In 1960 there was more land dedicated

There are almost as many smudge pots as vines in the Grand Cru Bougros vineyard with Les Preuses in the background. They are lit to raise the temperature above freezing point when spring frost threatens the first shoots of the growing season. A more modern alternative is spraying the vines with water, which becomes a protective layer of ice.

to Premier Cru Chablis than straight Chablis. Today, although Premier Cru land has expanded considerably, nearly four times as much vineyard is allowed to produce unqualified Chablis.

Some say that quality has suffered as a result of this expansion. It remains, as it always will this far from the equator, very uneven from year to year as well as variable (particularly in style) from grower to grower. Most growers today favour tank-fermented, unoaked, fresh wines. Some producers have shown that oak can have special properties to offer some of their better wines.

The quantity made each year can vary enormously for Chablis vineyards are still perilously subject to frost damage.

Grand Cru Chablis, largely ignored by the world's fine wine traders, remains even now half the price of Corton-Charlemagne. Parity would be closer to justice.

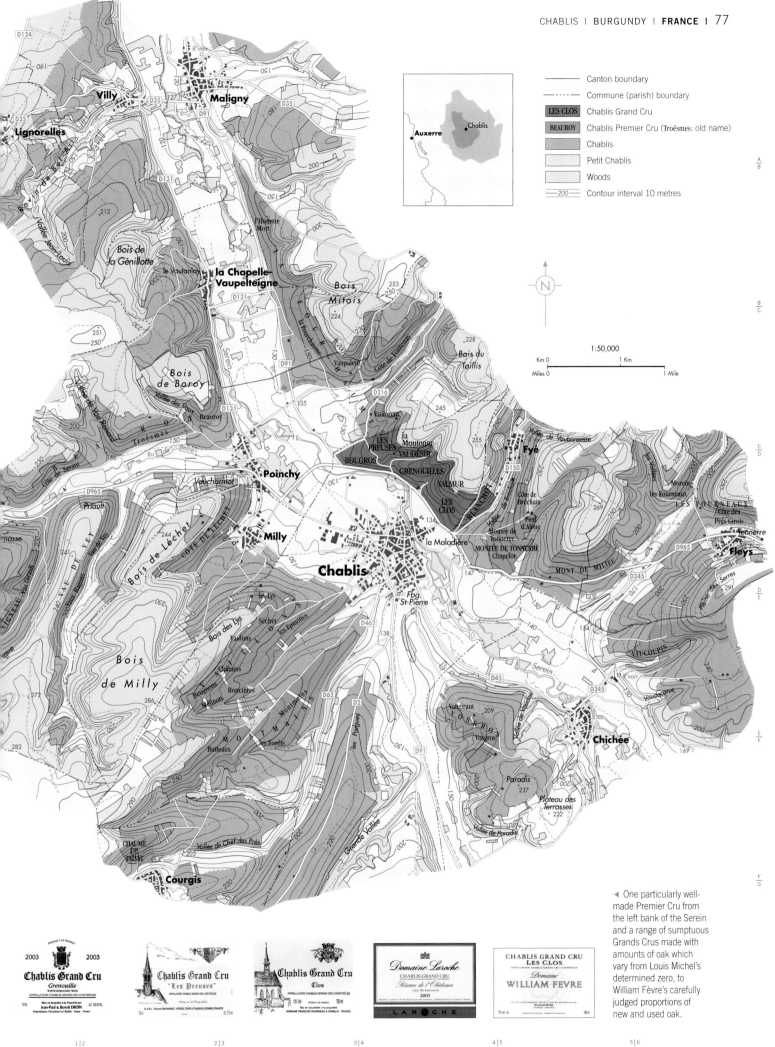

Canton boundary
Commune (parish) boundary
LES CLOS Chablis Grand Cru
BEAUROY Chablis Premier Cru (Troêsmes: old name)
Chablis
Petit Chablis
Woods
——200—— Contour interval 10 metres

Auxerre • • Chablis

Yonne

N

1:50,000
Km 0 1 Km
Miles 0 1 Mile

D124
Villy
Maligny
Lignorelles
D35
D91
D35
127
150
061
D131
212
l'Homme
Mort
Bois de
la Génillotte
le Vautanlay
la Chapelle-
Vaupelteigne
Bois
Mitais
253
250
D131a
224
251
250
Serein
Bois
de Baroy
Vaupulent
Côte de Fontenay
228
Bois du
Taillis
D91
130
150
Vallée des Vaux
135
de Fontenay
D216
Beauroy
D131
150
Ru de Beine
Vallée de Vau Renard
156
Troêsmes
Vaudorent
245
255
Vallée de Vaubarousse
Côte de Savant
LES
PREUSES
la
Moutonne
Fye
D965
Veucharmot
Poinchy
BOUGROS VAUDÉSIR
GRENOUILLES
VALMUR
D150
250
Côte de
Bréchain
269
Priault
Côte de Léchet
Bois de Léchet
CÔTE DE LÉCHET
Milly
BLANCHOT
LES
CLOS
134
Vallée de Bréchain
Pied
d'Aloue
Chablis
la Maladière
MONTÉE DE TONNERRE
Chapelot
Montée de
Tonnerre
Morein
les Fourneaux
LES FOURNEAUX
Côte des
Prés Girots
Tonnerre
D965
Fleys
244
241
les Lys
Séchet
les Epinottes
Fbg
St-Pierre
147
MONT DE MILIEU
D345
241
D462
138
D345
VAUCOPIN
Bois des Lys
Vaillons
250
VAILLONS
Châtains
Ropcières
Sécher
272
Bois
de Milly
286
Beugnons
Mélinots
MONTMAINS
Montmains
les Forêts
D62
D2
les Pargues
Serein
D45
Vaugiraut
209
VOSGROS
(Vosgros)
Chichée
282
Butteaux
250
Les Forêts
D91
150
169
Paradis
237
Plateau des
Terrasses
222
Vallée de Paradis
CHAUME
DE
TALVAT
Vallée de Chef des Prés
205
Courgis
220
Grande Vallée
200
150

◄ One particularly well-
made Premier Cru from
the left bank of the Serein
and a range of sumptuous
Grands Crus made with
amounts of oak which
vary from Louis Michel's
determined zero, to
William Fèvre's carefully
judged proportions of
new and used oak.

A/B
B/C
C/D
D/E
E/F
F/G

Champagne

To be champagne, a wine must do more than sparkle. It must come from the Champagne region in northeast France. This is a basic tenet of wine law in France, throughout Europe and now, thanks to tenacious negotiation, in much of the rest of the world. It would be claiming too much to say that all champagne is better than any other sparkling wine. But the best champagne has a combination of freshness, richness, delicacy, and raciness, and a gently stimulating strength that no sparkling wine from anywhere else has yet achieved.

Part of Champagne's secret lies in its combination of latitude and precise position. The latitude in the key facts panel opposite is higher than for any other wine region in this Atlas

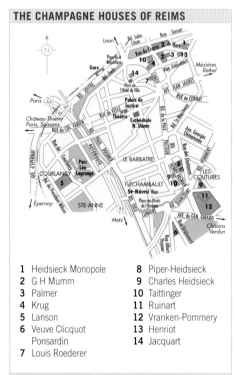

THE CHAMPAGNE HOUSES OF REIMS

1 Heidsieck Monopole	8 Piper-Heidsieck
2 G H Mumm	9 Charles Heidsieck
3 Palmer	10 Taittinger
4 Krug	11 Ruinart
5 Lanson	12 Vranken-Pommery
6 Veuve Clicquot	13 Henriot
Ponsardin	14 Jacquart
7 Louis Roederer	

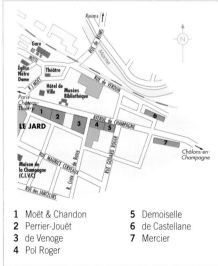

THE CHAMPAGNE HOUSES OF EPERNAY

1 Moët & Chandon	5 Demoiselle
2 Perrier-Jouët	6 de Castellane
3 de Venoge	7 Mercier
4 Pol Roger	

(except for England – whose best sparkling wines are fair copies of champagne). Even before global warming brought an increase in average ripeness, Champagne's proximity to the sea helped to ripen grapes this far from the equator and temperatures in the ripening month of July are higher than in Germany's Franken, California's Santa Maria, and New Zealand's Marlborough. This means that the relatively early ripening varieties grown in Champagne reliably reach just the right levels of sugar and acidity before autumn sets in. Higher temperatures have brought embarrassingly generous crops, however, as the vines adjust to warmer growing seasons.

Champagne, whose soil and climate have so much to offer, is only 90 miles (145km) northeast of Paris, centred on a small range of hills rising from a plain of chalk and carved in two by the River Marne. The map overleaf shows Champagne's heart, but the whole region is much more extensive. The Marne département still produces more than two-thirds of all champagne, but there are vineyards in the Aube to the south that specialize in vigorous, fruity Pinot Noir (about 22% of the region's total), and the mainly Pinot Meunier vineyards on the banks of the River Marne extend westwards well into the Aisne département (about 9%).

Demand for champagne is higher than ever and by 2004 all of the official champagne-producing area of 81,191 acres (32,871ha) (delimited in 1927) had been planted, with the Champenois still arguing about how it might be extended. Only 10% of this precious vineyard belongs to the large exporting houses responsible for the worldwide reputation of champagne who tend to blend ingredients from all over the region to produce their wines. The rest is owned by more than 19,000 growers, many of whom are part-time.

More and more of these growers, well over 2,000 at the last count, are making and selling their own wine rather than selling grapes to the *maisons*, although they sometimes do that as well. The growers' champagnes, which are increasingly highly regarded, now account for almost a quarter of all sales. Just over a tenth of all champagne is put on the market by one of the co-ops established in Champagne's dog days in the early 20th century. But the champagne market is still dominated by the famous names, the big houses of Reims and Epernay shown left – together with a few, such as Bollinger of Ay, based outside the two Champagne towns.

Because it is obviously so successful here, the champagne recipe has been much copied. Take Pinot Noir, Pinot Meunier, and Chardonnay grapes and apply a kid-glove process now called the "traditional method" (the Champenois having objected even to the world's admiring use of the old term "champagne method").

The grapes are pressed, in four-ton lots, so gently that the juice is very pale, even from the

Louis Roederer's super de luxe champagne Cristal can be spotted across a crowded restaurant because of its clear glass and golden label, but it is also distinguished by its traditional lack of a punt, the hollow in the base of a bottle that helps the pourer, and makes stacks of the bottles so much more secure.

LANGUAGE OF THE LABEL

Most NV names include Brut, Cuvée, or Reserve. Bollinger uses the English spelling of Special.

Blanc de blancs all-Chardonnay champagne

Blanc de noirs champagne made exclusively from dark-skinned grapes

Cuvée a blend, which all champagne is

Non-vintage (NV) champagne containing wines from more than one year

Réserve much used but meaningless term

Vintage wine from a single year

SWEETNESS LEVELS

Extra brut bone dry

Brut dry

Sec dryish

Demi-sec medium sweet (despite the name)

Doux relatively sweet

BOTTLER CODES

NM *négociant-manipulant*, champagne-maker who buys in grapes

RM *récoltant-manipulant*, grower who makes his or her own wine

CM *coopérative de manipulation*, a co-op

RC *récoltant-coopérateur*, grower selling wine made by a co-op

MA *marque d'acheteur*, buyer's own brand

dark-skinned Pinots Noir and Meunier, and only a precisely prescribed amount of juice from each lot may be used for champagne. (Most of the increasingly popular rosé champagne is made by deliberately adding some red wine to the white.)

The juice ferments lustily at first. In the past it slowed down, the doors would be thrown open to let in the autumnal chill and fermentation stopped. The wine spent a chilly winter, still with the potential of more fermentation latent in it.

So it used to be shipped. England in the 17th century was an eager customer for barrels of this delicate, rather sharp wine. The English bottled it on arrival, in bottles that were stronger than any known in France. It re-fermented in spring: the corks went pop and the beau monde found that they had created a sparkling wine. Whether or not it was the English who did it first (and the inhabitants of Limoux claim to have made the first brut sparkling wine, in the 16th century), premature bottling was vital to the process that changed Paris's favourite local wine into a prima donna.

For the wine continued to ferment in the bottle and the gas given off by the fermentation dissolved in the wine. If the natural effect was encouraged by adding a little sugar and a little more yeast, what had been a pretty but very light wine was found to improve immeasurably, gaining strength and character over a period of two years or more. Above all, the inexhaustible bubbles gave it a miraculous liveliness. Today sugar and yeast are added to the fully fermented dry wine so that a second fermentation takes place in the bottle.

The chief difference between champagne brands lies in the making of the *cuvée*, as the blend of dry base wines is called. Everything depends on experience in assembling the young wines – which are sometimes deepened by a dose of older, reserve wine – and on how much the house is prepared to spend on raw materials. As described overleaf, the quality and character of vineyards even in the heart of Champagne vary considerably.

Another crucial ingredient in champagne quality is the length of time the producer leaves the wine on the lees of the second fermentation in bottle. The longer the better, and certainly longer than the mandatory minimum of 15 months for non-vintage and three years for vintage champagne, for it is contact with this sediment as much as anything that gives champagne its subtle flavour.

The reputation of an established house is based on its non-vintage wines, blended so that no difference is noticeable from year to year. Styles vary from the challenging concentration of a Krug or a Bollinger to the seductive delicacy

of a Taittinger, with Pol Roger and Louis Roederer as models of classical balance.

The industrialization of champagne began with the widow Clicquot in the early 19th century. Her achievement was a way of cleaning the wine of its sediment (unavoidable when it re-ferments in bottle) without losing the bubbles, which involved *remuage*, literally shaking by hand the sediment on to the cork in gradually upended bottles. Today this is largely done mechanically in large computer-controlled pallets. The neck of the bottle is then frozen, a plug of murky ice shoots out when the bottle is opened, leaving perfectly clear wine behind to be topped up by wine with varying *dosages* of sweetness.

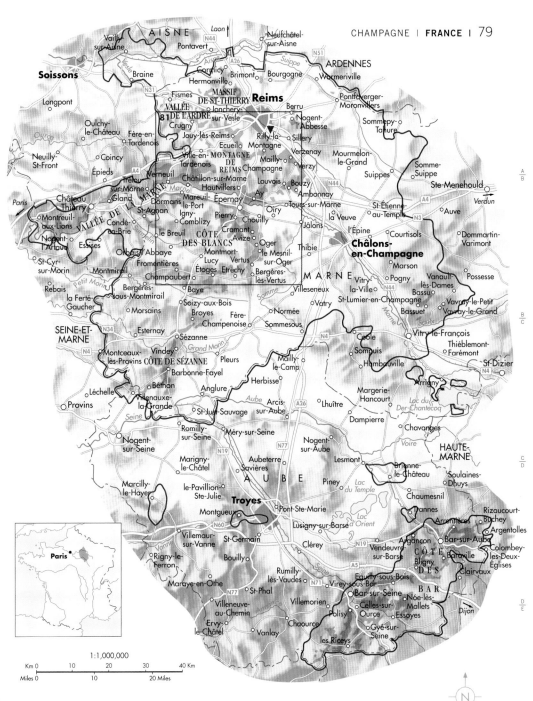

1:1,000,000

Km 0   10   20   30   40 Km
Miles 0   10   20 Miles

– – – – Département boundary

———— Limit of Champagne AC

▨ Wine-producing areas

81 Area mapped at larger scale on page shown

CHAMPAGNE: REIMS ▼
Latitude / Altitude of WS **49.19° / 295ft (90m)**
Mean July temp at WS **66°F (18.9°C)**
Annual rainfall at WS **25in (630mm)**
Harvest month rainfall at WS **September: 1.8in (45mm)**
Chief viticultural hazards **Spring frost, fungal disease**
Principal grapes **Pinot Noir, Pinot Meunier, Chardonnay**

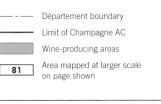

◀ A truly luxurious line-up, although most other houses have their answers to these de luxe *cuvées*. Other obvious candidates include Bollinger's RD, Laurent-Perrier's Grand Siècle, Veuve Clicquot's Grande Dame, Perrier Jouët's Belle Epoque, and Pol Roger's Sir Winston Churchill.

The Heart of Champagne

What lies beneath the vines is Champagne's trump card. Not only can cool, damp cellars be easily hewn from chalk, but it retains moisture and acts as a perfectly regulated vine humidifier which actually warms the soil and produces grapes rich in nitrogen – particularly useful for making yeast work effectively.

Today three grapes dominate. Meaty Pinot Noir is most planted (38% of the vineyards) having overtaken Pinot Meunier, a sort of country cousin that is easier to grow and ripen, obviously fruity but not so fine. Plantings of refreshing, potentially creamy Chardonnay have also increased, to 28% of the total.

Although today an increasing number of champagnes are emerging from single vineyards, the traditional and still usual plan is to combine the qualities of the best grapes from the distinct parts of the region. In this marginal climate full ripeness is the exception, and slight variations of slope and aspect are crucial.

The Montagne de Reims, the wooded "mountain" of the city where France's kings were crowned (it rises to less than 1,000ft/300m), is planted with Pinot Noir and to a lesser extent Pinot Meunier. Pinot planted on such north-facing slopes as those of Verzenay and Verzy produce base wines notably more acid and less powerful than those grown on the much more propitious southern flanks of the Montagne de Reims at Ay but can bring a particularly refined, laser-etched delicacy to a blend. Montagne wines contribute to the bouquet, the headiness and, with their firm acidity, to what the French call the "carpentry" – the backbone of the blend.

The village of Bouzy, whose lower slopes can be too productive for top quality champagne, is famous with English-speakers for obvious reasons, but also because it makes a small quantity of still red wine. The comparatively tart still wines of the Champagne region – both white and occasionally light red – are sold under the Coteaux Champenois appellation.

The Vallée de la Marne in the west has a succession of south-facing slopes which trap the sun and make these the fullest, roundest, and ripest wines, with plenty of aroma. These too are predominantly black-grape vineyards, famous for Pinot Noir in the best-exposed sites but with Pinot Meunier and, increasingly, Chardonnay planted elsewhere.

The east-facing slope south of Epernay (topographically not unlike the Côte de Beaune) is the Côte des Blancs, planted with Chardonnay that gives freshness and finesse to a blend. Champagne made with 100% Chardonnay is sold as Blanc de Blancs. Cramant, Avize, and Le Mesnil are three villages with long-respected names for their (unblended) wine. (The Côte de Sézanne is effectively a slightly less distinguished extension of the Côte des Blancs.)

These (and all Champagne-appellation) vineyards have what you might call a concealed classification – concealed because it is never mentioned on the labels. The *échelle* (ladder) *des crus* gives the grapes of every commune a percentage rating. Until this century an indicative grape price was agreed for the harvest as a whole. A grower in one of the Grand Cru communes would be paid 100% of the price. Premiers Crus would receive between 99% and 90%, according to their place on the ladder, and so on down to 80% for some of the outlying areas. Now the grape price is agreed on an individual basis between the grower and the producer, although the vineyard ratings may still apply – and some would like to see the ratings revised to distinguish more precisely between different vineyards' potential.

Such super-luxury "prestige" brands as Dom Pérignon, Krug, Pol Roger's Sir Winston Churchill, Roederer Cristal, Perrier-Jouët's Belle Epoque, Veuve Clicquot's La Grande Dame, and Taittinger's Comtes de Champagne naturally have the highest average *échelle* rating in their constituent wines. Krug and Bollinger have long been exponents of fermenting their base wines in oak. An increasing number of other producers, including many of the more ambitious growers, are following suit. The resulting wines – it should never be forgotten that champagne is a wine – can suffer if served too young or too cool. The cheapest champagnes have little to offer at any stage.

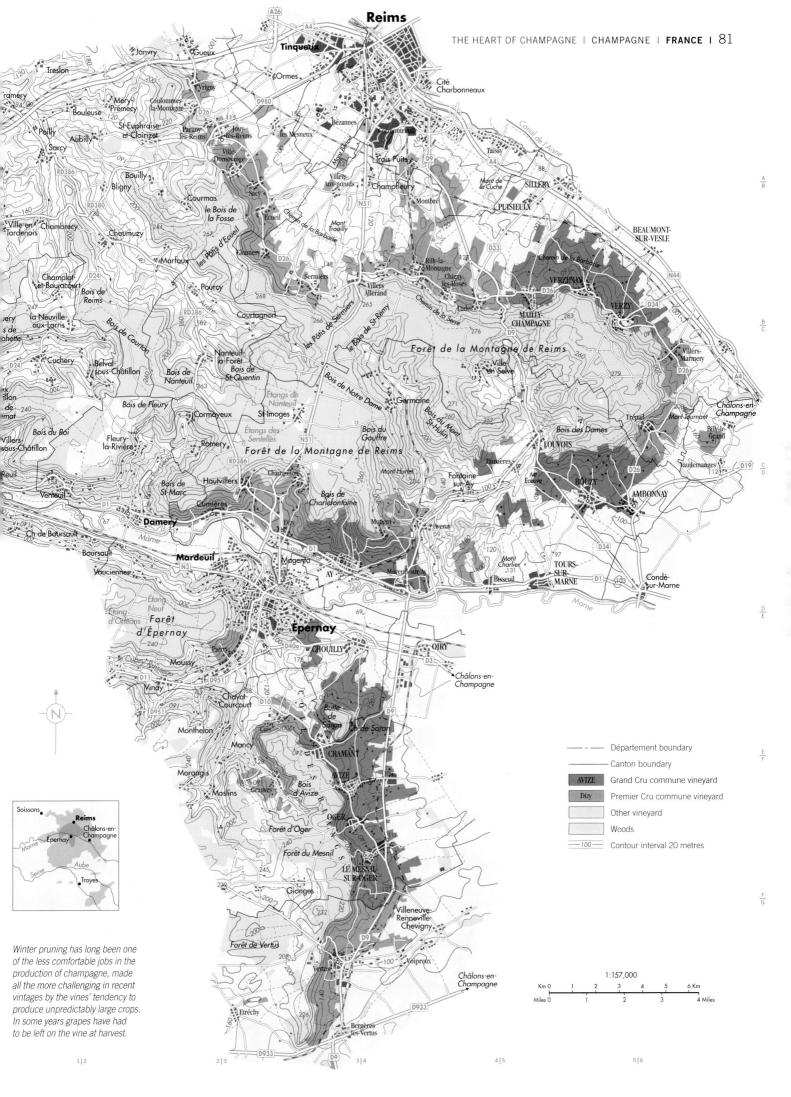

Legend:

AVIZE — Grand Cru commune vineyard
Dizy — Premier Cru commune vineyard
Other vineyard
Woods
— Département boundary
— Canton boundary
—100— Contour interval 20 metres

1:157,000

Km 0 1 2 3 4 5 6 Km
Miles 0 1 2 3 4 Miles

Winter pruning has long been one of the less comfortable jobs in the production of champagne, made all the more challenging in recent vintages by the vines' tendency to produce unpredictably large crops. In some years grapes have had to be left on the vine at harvest.

Bordeaux

As Burgundy's appeal is unashamedly sensual, Bordeaux's is more cerebral. On the one hand is the nature of the wine itself: at its best indescribably subtle in nuance and complexity. On the other is the sheer intellectual challenge of so many estates, or châteaux as they are called here, in so many regions and subregions.

Bordeaux is the largest fine wine district on earth. The whole département of the Gironde, named after its most important estuary, is dedicated to wine-growing. All of its wine is Bordeaux. Its production, 6 million hectolitres in 2005, dwarfs that of all French wine regions except for the vast Languedoc-Roussillon. Red wines outnumber white by eight to one.

The great red wine areas are the Médoc, north of the city of Bordeaux, and to the south the best of the Graves, Pessac-Léognan, on the west bank of the Garonne. These are the so-called "left bank" wines. The "right bank" consists of St-Emilion and Pomerol along the north bank of the Dordogne. The country between the two rivers is called Entre-Deux-Mers, a name found only on bottles of its dry white wines, although this region also makes three-quarters of all the red wine sold as AC Bordeaux and Bordeaux Supérieur. In the far south of the map opposite lies Bordeaux's centre of sweet white wine production.

Some of the fringe appellations mapped here are rarely seen on bottles outside the region, although fine wines carrying the northern right bank appellations Côtes de Bourg (some good white wines) and Côtes de Blaye are becoming more and more common, with the simple appellation Blaye usually signifying particularly ambitious reds. An umbrella AC, Côtes de Bordeaux, is proposed for some of these lesser known names (see p.99).

Bordeaux's great glories are its finest red wines (the world's archetypes for blends of Cabernet and Merlot), the tiny production of very sweet, golden Sauternes which can live even longer, and some unique dry whites made in the Graves. But not all Bordeaux is glorious; the region is too big, and expanded towards the end of the 20th century. The most favoured areas, for the reasons outlined overleaf, may be capable of producing some of the world's greatest wines and can command some of the world's highest prices. In less glamorous areas, however, are far too many vine-growers without the incentive, will or, in some cases, the physical ability to produce interesting wine.

The marginality of Bordeaux's climate means that in some years basic red Bordeaux looks a very puny thing alongside the Cabernets so reliably ripened in much of the New World. The straight Bordeaux appellation, which is applied to more red wine than the total South African or German vintage each year, too rarely upholds the glory of this world-famous region. After much debate on how to solve this problem, including the uprooting of less favoured

vineyards, a Vin de Pays de l'Atlantique was created in 2006 for wine in all three colours.

Compared with Burgundy the system of appellations in Bordeaux is simple. The map opposite shows them all. Within them it is the wine châteaux (sometimes grand estates, sometimes no more than a smallholding with cellar attached) that look after their own identification problem. On the other hand there is a form of vineyard classification by quality built into the system in Burgundy that is missing in Bordeaux. Here, in its place, is a variety of local château classifications, unfortunately without a common standard.

By far the most famous is the classification of the wines of the châteaux of the Médoc – and Château Haut-Brion of the Graves – which was finalized in 1855, based on their value as assessed by Bordeaux brokers at the time. Its first-, second-, third-, fourth-, and fifth- "growths", or crus, represent the most ambitious grading of agricultural produce ever attempted.

It succeeded in identifying the soils with the highest potential, as the following pages detail. Where present standards depart from it there is usually an explanation (an industrious proprietor in 1855 and a lazy one now, or, more likely nowadays, vice versa). Even more to the point, in many cases land has been added, or exchanged; the vineyard is not precisely the same. The vineyards of a château rarely surround it in a neat plot. More often by now they are scattered and intermingled with those of their neighbours. They can produce annually anything from 10 to 1,000 barrels of wine, each holding the rough equivalent of 300 bottles, or 25 cases. The best vineyards make a maximum of 5,000 litres from each hectare of vines, the less good ones considerably more (see panel overleaf).

The super-luxury first-growths, which can easily make as many as 200,000 bottles of their principal wine, or *grand vin*, as opposed to a second wine blended from the less successful vats, traditionally fetch about twice the price of the second-growths, but thereafter a fifth-growth may fetch more, for example, than a second if it is better run. The system adopted on the maps that appear on the following pages is simply to distinguish between classed-growths (in areas where they exist) and the vineyards that surround them.

One notable development at the end of the 20th century was the emergence, particularly on the right bank, of *microcuvées* – wines made by *garagistes,* so-called because their production of a few hundred cases a year is small enough to be vinified in a garage. With the exception of the prototypes Le Pin of Pomerol and Château Valandraud of St Emilion, few of these *microcuvées* have established a durable market and reputation – a fact that does not seem to have discouraged anyone from trying.

Of greater long-term significance for the region is the vast improvement in viticultural practices that has been effected since the mid-1990s. Far more producers nowadays are able to harvest fully ripe grapes, not just because of climate change but thanks to stricter pruning throughout the year, higher trellising, more careful canopy management, and more cautious use of agrochemicals.

Bordeaux's Quai des Chartrons was once famous as the centre of its wine trade, then suffered from an air of neglect, but now plays an important part in the city's revamp. There are still no fewer than 400 wine merchants in and, especially, around Bordeaux.

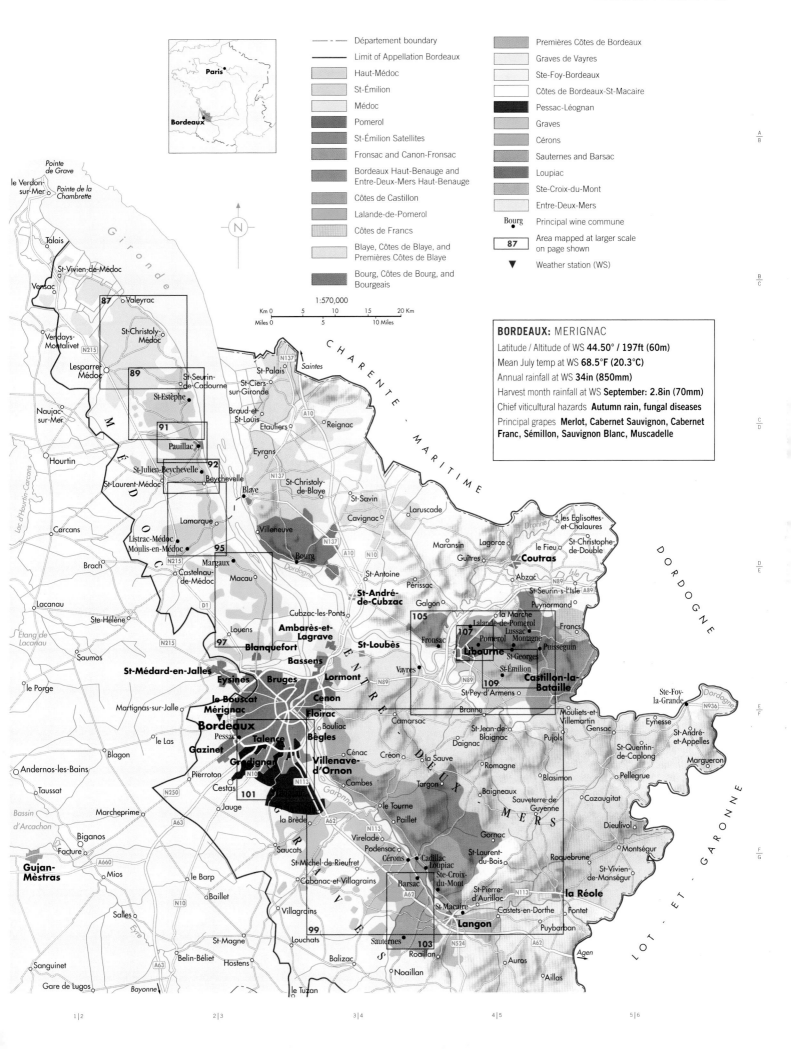

Département boundary
Limit of Appellation Bordeaux
Haut-Médoc
St-Émilion
Médoc
Pomerol
St-Émilion Satellites
Fronsac and Canon-Fronsac
Bordeaux Haut-Benauge and Entre-Deux-Mers Haut-Benauge
Côtes de Castillon
Lalande-de-Pomerol
Côtes de Francs
Blaye, Côtes de Blaye, and Premières Côtes de Blaye
Bourg, Côtes de Bourg, and Bourgeais

Premières Côtes de Bordeaux
Graves de Vayres
Ste-Foy-Bordeaux
Côtes de Bordeaux-St-Macaire
Pessac-Léognan
Graves
Cérons
Sauternes and Barsac
Loupiac
Ste-Croix-du-Mont
Entre-Deux-Mers

Bourg Principal wine commune
87 Area mapped at larger scale on page shown
▼ Weather station (WS)

1:570,000
Km 0   5   10   15   20 Km
Miles 0   5   10 Miles

BORDEAUX: MERIGNAC
Latitude / Altitude of WS **44.50° / 197ft (60m)**
Mean July temp at WS **68.5°F (20.3°C)**
Annual rainfall at WS **34in (850mm)**
Harvest month rainfall at WS **September: 2.8in (70mm)**
Chief viticultural hazards **Autumn rain, fungal diseases**
Principal grapes **Merlot, Cabernet Sauvignon, Cabernet Franc, Sémillon, Sauvignon Blanc, Muscadelle**

Bordeaux: The Quality Factor

The quality and quantity of wine the Bordeaux region produces each year may vary quite markedly, but as the world's biggest resource of fine wine, it clearly has some advantages. Its position near the sea and being threaded with rivers gives it a moderate and stable climate with relatively few frosts severe enough to kill vines in winter or harm buds in spring. Europe's biggest forest, on the ocean side and in the Landes département to the south, protects it from strong salt winds and moderates rainfall. The weather during flowering in June is variable, which is why the crop size varies too, but summers and, particularly, autumns are usually reliably warm and sunny. Both average temperature and rainfall are slightly higher than in Burgundy – compare the statistics on p.83 and p.55 – which means that Bordeaux can successfully grow later-ripening grape varieties.

Merlot, Cabernet Sauvignon, Cabernet Franc, and Petit Verdot are the main grapes grown for red wines, in that order of declining importance, with some Malbec still grown north of the Gironde. Sémillon and an increasing proportion of Sauvignon Blanc are the main white wine grapes (supplemented by Muscadelle in sweet wine districts and some Ugni Blanc towards Cognac country). Because these grapes all flower at slightly different times, growing a mix of them can provide the château owner with some insurance against a few days of bad weather at the critical time in June, and against a particularly cool autumn which may fail to coax Cabernet Sauvignon to its full ripeness.

Practically all Bordeaux wine estates therefore are planted with a mixture of grape varieties, the proportions varying according to local conditions, tradition, and, increasingly, fashion. The fleshiness of Merlot long made it a natural filler for Bordeaux Cabernet's more angular frame but in the late 20th century it was particularly popular with both growers and drinkers, perhaps because both vines and wines ripen conveniently early. Cabernet Franc, which flowers and ripens after Merlot but sooner than Cabernet Sauvignon, offers additional insurance cover and, often, an attractive aroma. Petit Verdot ripens latest of all but when it does ripen fully, which it does increasingly thanks to global warming, it can add sumptuously spicy top notes to a Médoc blend.

It is a right bank tradition to favour the early ripening Merlot over Cabernet Sauvignon, which predominates in the Médoc and Graves. The fleshy Merlot is more usually supplemented by Cabernet Franc rather than Cabernet Sauvignon in Pomerol and, especially, St-Emilion.

WHAT MAKES THE WINE

Some of the factors affecting the varying qualities and character of Bordeaux wine are shown in this diagram of the basin of the Gironde.

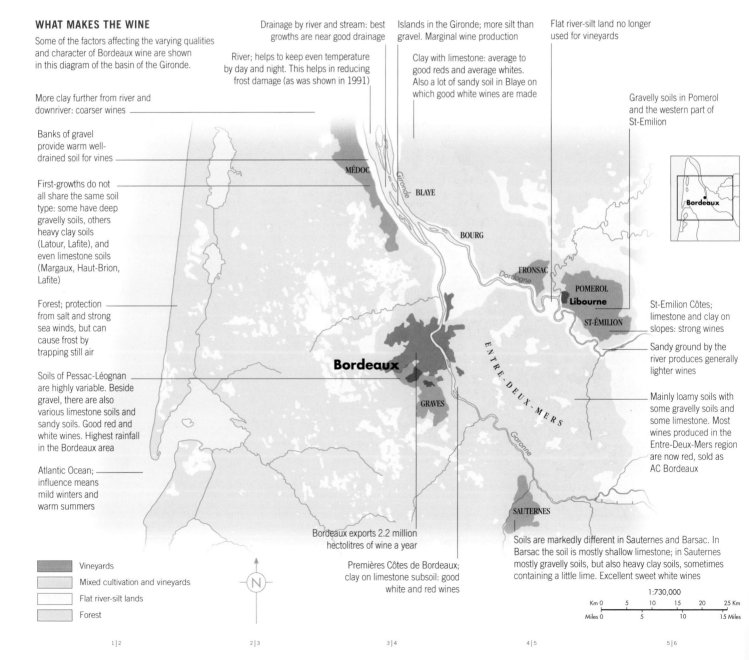

More clay further from river and downriver: coarser wines

Banks of gravel provide warm well-drained soil for vines

First-growths do not all share the same soil type: some have deep gravelly soils, others heavy clay soils (Latour, Lafite), and even limestone soils (Margaux, Haut-Brion, Lafite)

Forest; protection from salt and strong sea winds, but can cause frost by trapping still air

Soils of Pessac-Léognan are highly variable. Beside gravel, there are also various limestone soils and sandy soils. Good red and white wines. Highest rainfall in the Bordeaux area

Atlantic Ocean; influence means mild winters and warm summers

Drainage by river and stream: best growths are near good drainage

River; helps to keep even temperature by day and night. This helps in reducing frost damage (as was shown in 1991)

Islands in the Gironde; more silt than gravel. Marginal wine production

Clay with limestone: average to good reds and average whites. Also a lot of sandy soil in Blaye on which good white wines are made

Flat river-silt land no longer used for vineyards

Gravelly soils in Pomerol and the western part of St-Emilion

St-Emilion Côtes; limestone and clay on slopes: strong wines

Sandy ground by the river produces generally lighter wines

Mainly loamy soils with some gravelly soils and some limestone. Most wines produced in the Entre-Deux-Mers region are now red, sold as AC Bordeaux

MÉDOC

BLAYE

BOURG

Gironde

FRONSAC

Dordogne

POMEROL

Libourne

ST-ÉMILION

Bordeaux

ENTRE-DEUX-MERS

GRAVES

Garonne

SAUTERNES

Bordeaux exports 2.2 million hectolitres of wine a year

Premières Côtes de Bordeaux; clay on limestone subsoil: good white and red wines

Soils are markedly different in Sauternes and Barsac. In Barsac the soil is mostly shallow limestone; in Sauternes mostly gravelly soils, but also heavy clay soils, sometimes containing a little lime. Excellent sweet white wines

Vineyards

Mixed cultivation and vineyards

Flat river-silt lands

Forest

N

1:730,000

Km 0   5   10   15   20   25 Km

Miles 0   5   10   15 Miles

In fact, as Château Figeac proves, Cabernet Sauvignon can indeed be persuaded to ripen on the gravelly western plateau of St-Emilion but if grown on those parts of the plateau where limestone is the dominant soil type it tends to produce very hard, tannic wine and so is not commonly planted on the right bank. This is one of the reasons that the two banks tend to produce such very different styles of wine.

This difference in varietal mix, unknown in Burgundy for example, is just one (important) factor in explaining the huge differences that can be found between the wines of one property and another. The status of the vineyard is another factor. Success breeds success, meaning more money to spend on costly care of the land (see panel) – or on buying more. Differences that were originally marginal can thus increase over the years, and this certainly helps to explain the vast difference in quality between, say, a classified growth and its unclassified neighbour.

But there are clearly marked differences in soil structure and soil type all over the Bordeaux region – however difficult it can be to identify a precise soil type with, say, first-growth quality (see the notes on the left of the map opposite). Even within one part of Bordeaux, the Médoc being perhaps the most intriguing example, the soil is said to "change at every step". And a look at the map on p.83 shows how one portion of it, between St-Julien and Margaux, is an exception to the streak of superlative wine quality that otherwise exists going north from Margaux. It also suggests that there is something very special about the plateau of Pomerol and St-Emilion.

In very general terms Bordeaux soils have developed on either Tertiary or Quaternary deposits, the former generally giving way to clay or limestone soils, the latter made up of alluvial sandy gravels left in gentle mounds hundreds of thousands of years ago by melted glaciers from the Massif Central and the Pyrenees.

These gravels, still fully exposed unlike the other gravels deposited in most of the rest of southwest France, are most marked in the Graves (hence the name), Sauternes, which is effectively a continuation of it, and the Médoc.

Dr Gérard Séguin of the University of Bordeaux undertook some of the first key studies of how Bordeaux soils relate to wine quality. He studied the gravely soils of the Médoc where deep-rooted vines produce great wine because the gravels so carefully regulate the water supply. His most notable discovery was that a supply of moisture to the vine that was no more than moderate was much more important than the exact composition of the soil.

His successor Cornelis van Leeuwen has probed further and discovered that there is no absolute correlation between how deep the roots go and how good the wine is. Old vines plus deep gravels happen to be the perfect recipe in some parts of the Médoc, in Margaux for instance, but in Pomerol vines seem perfectly capable of making great wine from vines that penetrate less than 5ft (1.5m) into Château Pétrus's heavy clays. The key factor for quality is the regulation of water supply – just slightly less than the vine wants – rather than the depth of the roots, which can vary from 23ft (7m) in Margaux, to 6.5ft (2m) on the Côtes, the steep limestone hillside on top of which the town of St-Emilion perches, such as at Château Ausone, and just 1.3ft (0.4m) on the plateau west of St-Emilion.

One general observation about the relationship between soil and wine quality, especially marked in Bordeaux, is that the best sites stand out most clearly in lesser vintages and are able to maintain consistently quality. Other sites, superficially similar and often very close, produce wine that is more marked by the deficiencies of the vintage, although increasingly sophisticated viticulture mitigates this. Perhaps the explanation lies in the unalterable (and perhaps invisible) properties of the soil?

The Domaine de l'Ile de Margaux produces wine that is eligible only for the Bordeaux Supérieur appellation since the vines are grown on flat alluvial silt – although its island status has kept it free of phylloxera all this time.

PRODUCTION COSTS

The table below gives the most recent (2004) estimates of production costs in euros for a typical AC Bordeaux (A), a typical well-run Médoc château (B), and a classed-growth (C). Much more new oak, for example, is used for C than B, and none for A. First-growths may cost even more to run but the rewards are even greater than for a so-called "super second". Some of the *microcuvées*, largely a right bank phenomenon, have more care lavished on them than even the first-growths in the hope of attracting prices based on their rarity.

Most Bordeaux properties are run on bank borrowings, however, typically a value of around €1.8 million per ha for a top classed-growth, which would be amortized over 15 years, with a fixed interest rate of about 4.5%. (It is sometimes said that the Crédit Agricole bank owns France's entire *vignoble*). This would add at least €100,000 per ha each year to costs, and therefore almost €20 per bottle to the figure at the bottom of column C. And, of course, the costs in the table leave the wine unbottled, unmarketed, and untransported. Production costs look incredibly low compared with the selling price of the *grand vin*, but this represents only a proportion of the wine sold by the château.

	A	B	C
Number of vines per ha	3,330	6,500	7,800
Harvest costs per ha	314	1,572	2,700
Total viticultural costs per ha	5,030	17,780	20,000
Average yield (hl per ha)	58	58	40
Total viticultural costs per hl	87	306	500
Barrel ageing	–	182	550
Total costs per hl	87	488	1,050
Total costs per bottle	0.65	3.66	7.88

Source: Conseil Interprofessionnel du Vin de Bordeaux (CIVB) and AXA Millésimes

Northern Médoc

Geographically, the Médoc is a great tongue of flat or barely undulating land isolated from the body of Aquitaine by the broad brown estuary of the Gironde. In common usage its name is given to more fine wine than any other name in the world: Margaux, St-Julien, Pauillac, St-Estèphe, and their surrounding villages are all "Médoc" in location and in style. But the appellation Médoc is both more limited and less prestigious. It is more clearly understood under its former name of Bas- (meaning lower) Médoc. The term Bas was dropped for reasons of – shall we say? – delicacy. But the fact remains. The lower Médoc, the tip of the tongue, the farthest reaches of the region, has none of the high points, either physically or gastronomically, of the Haut-Médoc to its south.

The well-drained dunes of gravel give way to lower, heavier, cooler, and more clay-dominated land north of St-Estèphe, with St-Seurin, the last commune of the Haut-Médoc, riding a characteristic hump between areas of channelled marsh. North and west of here is fertile, long-settled land, with the bustling market town of Lesparre as its capital since the days of English rule six centuries ago.

Until recently, vineyards took their place here with pasture, orchard, and woodland but after an orgy of planting they have spread to cover almost all the higher ground where gravel lightens the clay, centring on the villages of St-Yzans, St-Christoly, Couquèques, By, and Valeyrac along the banks of the Gironde Estuary, and covering much of the interior in St-Germain-d'Esteuil, Ordonnac, Blaignan (Caussac), and (the biggest) Bégadan. In and around these villages are some of the Bordeaux producers who have been hardest-pressed, encouraged to invest in both vineyard and cellar by what seemed to be a buoyant market in the late 1990s, only to find that the market was really only interested in the more famous châteaux to the south. There are no classed-growths here, but there is the greatest concentration of the best of the rest, worthy Crus Bourgeois and even one of only nine properties deemed Crus Bourgeois Exceptionnels (by a controversial classification in 2003, subsequently annulled) together with a further 13 Crus Bourgeois Supérieurs.

The Cru Bourgeois Château Potensac, classified Exceptionnel in 2003, has the same perfectionist owners as Château Léoville-Las-Cases in St-Julien and is situated on the same slight plateau as La Cardonne and the well-run Tour Haut-Caussan. Other properties temporarily officially classified Crus Bourgeois Supérieurs are Châteaux Castéra at St-Germain; Loudenne overlooking the Gironde near St-Yzans-de-Médoc; the well-distributed Greysac, reliable if light Patache d'Aux, improving Rolland de By, beguiling La Tour de By, and enterprising Vieux Robin of Bégadan; Bouranc and d'Escurac of Civrac-en-Médoc; Les Ormes Sorbet of Couquèques; and Les Grands Chênes of St-Christoly-Médoc.

But there are many other notable wines such as Châteaux Preuillac, Haut-Condissas, Laulan Ducos, and the defiantly modern Goulée developed by the team at Château Cos d'Estournel in St-Estèphe which can all offer some of Bordeaux's best red wine value.

The clearest way to see the difference between Médocs Haut and Bas is to compare the career of a Cru Bourgeois mapped here with a Cru Bourgeois from one of the pages that follow. When young, there may be little to distinguish them: both are vigorous (like the vines on the rich soils of the Bas-Médoc), tannic, dry, and "très Bordeaux". At five years, though, the Haut-Médoc wine is finding that fine-etched personality, that clean transparency of flavour, that will go on developing. The Bas-Médoc has begun to soften, but remains a sturdy, rather rustic wine, often deep-coloured, satisfying, and savoury rather than enlightening and inspiring. At 10 years of age there has been more softening, but usually at the expense of "structure"; not the refining of character that we find further south.

This windmill belongs to Château Tour Haut-Caussan, where proprietor Philippe Courrian lavishes classed-growth care on this Cru Bourgeois Supérieur, even though it can be difficult to persuade the market to pay classed-growth prices for it.

▶ Six more sources of great red Bordeaux value made with enormous care – classic Médoc except for Goulée, which is a deliberate attempt to fit Northern Médoc fruit into a modern shape.

St-Estèphe

The gravel banks which give the Haut-Médoc and its wines their character and quality, stretching along the shore of the Gironde, sheltered from the ocean to the west by forest, begin to peter out at St-Estèphe. It is the northernmost of the four famous communes that are the heart of the Médoc. A *jalle* – the Médoc word for a stream – divides it from Pauillac, draining on the one hand the vineyards of Château Lafite, on the other three of the five classed-growths of St-Estèphe: Châteaux Cos d'Estournel, Cos Labory, and Lafon-Rochet.

There is a distinction between the soils of St-Estèphe and Pauillac to the south: as the gravel washed down the Gironde diminishes there is a stronger mixture of clay found in it. Higher up in Margaux, there is very little. In St-Estèphe it is heavier soil, which drains more slowly. This is why vines grown in St-Estèphe seem to withstand particularly hot, dry summers, such as those of 1990 and 2003, better than those in the well-drained gravels to the south. Even in less extreme weather the wines tend to have more acidity, are fuller and more solid, and often have less perfume – but they fill your mouth with flavour. They have traditionally been sturdy clarets which can become venerable without losing vigour. In recent years, however, the general tendency to make red Bordeaux to the same bigger, bolder model has had the effect of blurring some of the differences between St-Estèphe and wines from other communes.

Cos d'Estournel is the most spectacular of the classed-growths. It has an eccentric Chinese-pagoda'd edifice, impressively crowning the steep slope up from the Pauillac boundary, overlooking the meadows of Château Lafite. Together with Château Montrose, overlooking the river, it makes the biggest and best of the St-Estèphes; strong wines with a dark colour and a long life. "Cos", as it is nearly always called (with the S pronounced), has particular power and succulence, partly perhaps because of a high proportion of Merlot in the vineyard but also because of marked determination at its helm. The situation of Montrose on its gravel mound overlooking the Gironde anticipates that of Latour in Pauillac just to the south. Some find a similar echo in its intense, tannic, deeply flavoured wine. Classic Montrose vintages take 20 years to mature although recently the wines have been easier to read in youth.

Of the other two classed-growths near Cos d'Estournel, Château Cos Labory often seems content to be full of fruity flavour at a fairly young age. Lafon-Rochet, revamped in the 1960s by Guy Tesseron, a cognac merchant, was the first Médoc château to be rebuilt in the 20th century and now makes particularly reliable wines. Calon-Ségur, north of the village of St-Estèphe and the northernmost classed-growth of the Médoc, is as solid as any St-Estèphe and usually rather more robust and stolid than either Cos d'Estournel or Montrose when young. Some 250 years ago the Marquis de Ségur, owner of both Lafite and Latour, reputedly said his heart was at Calon. It still is, on the label (see below).

Above all, St-Estèphe is known for its Crus Bourgeois, which were temporarily reclassified as Exceptionnels, Supérieurs, and straight Crus Bourgeois in 2003. No fewer than four of the nine Exceptionnels are on the plateau south and west of the village. Châteaux Phélan Ségur and de Pez are both outstanding producers of very fine wine. Pez has an extraordinary historical record: as the property of the Pontacs of Haut-Brion its wine was sold as Pontac in London in the 17th century – possibly before any other growth of the Médoc. Today it belongs to the champagne house of Louis Roederer. Château Les Ormes de Pez nearby benefits from the same strong management as at Château Lynch-Bages in Pauillac while Château Haut-Marbuzet to the south between Montrose and Cos d'Estournel is usually made sweet and oaky.

Among the dozen worthy Crus Bourgeois Supérieurs (more than any other commune), Château Meyney is unusual in the Médoc for having monastic origins. Its situation by the river, neighbour to Montrose, might make one

Monsieur d'Estournel insisted on as much attention to detail in the construction of what is today Château Cos d'Estournel as the current owner does in viticulture and winemaking at this prominent second-growth.

look for finer wine with more potential for development. In practice it is sturdy and often good value, just like Châteaux Beau-Site, Le Boscq, Chambert-Marbuzet (under the same ownership as Haut-Marbuzet), Clauzet, Le Crock, La Haye, the relative newcomer Lilian Ladouys, Petit Bocq, Tour de Marbuzet, Tour de Pez and Tronquoy-Lalande – all Crus Bourgeois Supérieurs which demonstrate the commune's solid virtues but are usually ready to drink much sooner than the classed-growths.

Among a bevy of no fewer than 20 straight Crus Bourgeois, Château Marbuzet is notable for being under the same ownership as Cos d'Estournel.

To the north of St-Estèphe the gravel bank diminishes to a promontory sticking out of the *palus* – the flat river-silted land beside the estuary on which no wine of quality grows. On top of the promontory in the little village of St-Seurin-de-Cadourne a cluster of notable wines are made, such as the gentle Château Coufran, the more tannic Château Verdignan, the sometimes admirable Château Bel Orme Tronquoy de Lalande, and, most notable of all, on a classic mound near the river, Château Sociando-Mallet whose flamboyantly ambitious wines have been known to trounce

▼ *The grandees of the commune, with the grandest wines of all on the right. The Montrose and Sociando-Mallet labels have both been redesigned to move all but what the proprietors see as the most important information to the back label.*

first-growths in blind tastings. The owner operates outside the Cru Bourgeois system.

North of St-Seurin is the end of the Haut-Médoc: any wine grown beyond that point qualifies for the appellation Médoc, plain and simple. The beautiful Château Loudenne, over-looking the Gironde and which flew the British flag for over a century (until 1999), occupies its first gravel knoll.

West of St-Estèphe, further from the river, Cissac and Vertheuil lie on stronger and less gravelly soil at the forest's edge. Château Cissac is the outstanding growth: for long vigorous enough to be a Pauillac, although, like so many red Bordeaux, especially here, it has been soft-ened since the early 1990s.

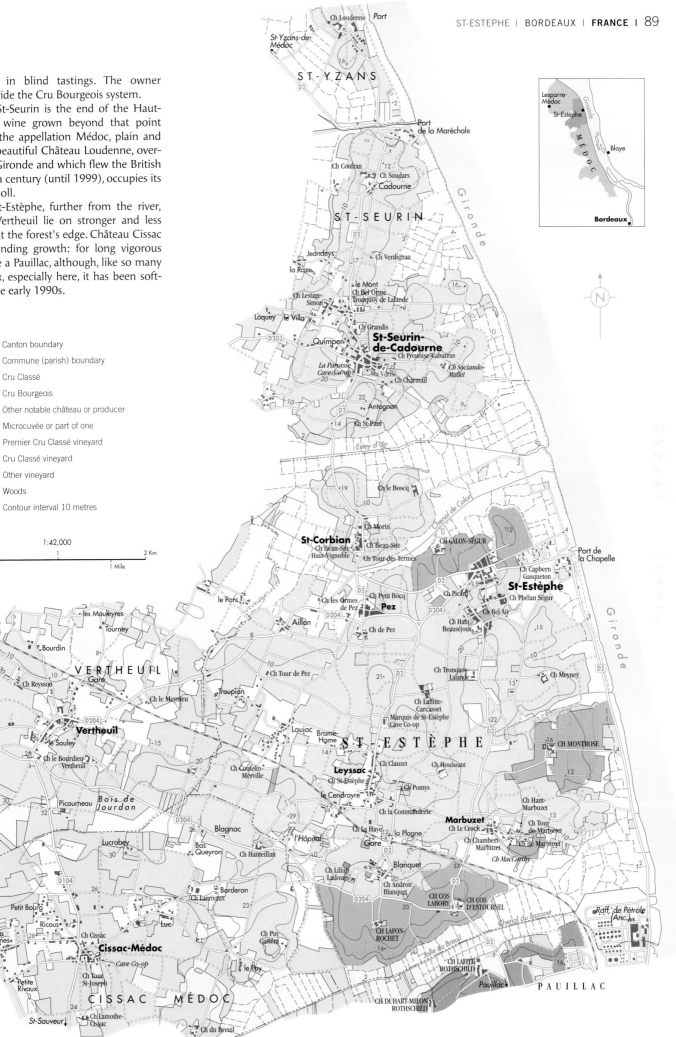

	Canton boundary
	Commune (parish) boundary
CH COS LABORY	Cru Classé
Ch de Pez	Cru Bourgeois
Ch Sociando-Mallet	Other notable château or producer
	Microcuvée or part of one
	Premier Cru Classé vineyard
	Cru Classé vineyard
	Other vineyard
	Woods
20	Contour interval 10 metres

1:42,000

Pauillac

If one had to single out one Bordeaux commune to head the list, there would be no argument. It would be Pauillac. Châteaux Lafite, Latour, and Mouton Rothschild, three out of the first five of the famous 1855 classification of the Médoc and Graves, are its obvious claim. But many red Bordeaux enthusiasts would tell you that the wines of Pauillac have the quintessential flavour they look for – a combination of fresh soft-fruit, oak, dryness, subtlety combined with substance, a touch of cigar-box, a suggestion of sweetness, and, above all, vigour. Even the lesser growths approach the enthusiasts' ideal.

At Pauillac the gravel mounds, or *croupes*, of the Médoc get as near as they ever do to being hills. The highest part, with Châteaux Mouton Rothschild and Pontet-Canet on its summit, reaches 100ft (30m) – quite an achievement in this coastal area, where a mere swelling of the ground provides a lookout point.

The town of Pauillac is the biggest of the Médoc. Happily, its long-established oil refinery has ceased operation and become a mere (though colossal) depot. Its old quay has become a marina; a few restaurants have opened. The Cazes family of Château Lynch-Bages have endowed the sleepy hamlet of Bages with a Michelin-starred restaurant, Château Cordeillan-Bages, and an all-day brasserie and smart bakery. So far, that's it. Pauillac could scarcely be called animated.

The vineyards of the châteaux of Pauillac are on the whole less subdivided than in most of the Médoc. Whereas in Margaux (for example) the châteaux are bunched together in the town, and their holdings in the surrounding countryside are inextricably mixed up – a row here, a couple of rows there – in Pauillac whole slopes, mounds, and plateaux belong to a single proprietor. One would therefore expect greater variations in style derived from terroir. One is not disappointed.

The three great wines of Pauillac are all dramatically different. Châteaux Lafite Rothschild and Latour stand at opposite ends of the parish; the first almost in St-Estèphe, the second almost in St-Julien. Oddly enough, though, their characters tend in quite the opposite direction: Lafite more towards the smoothness and finesse of a St-Julien, Latour more towards the emphatic firmness of a St-Estèphe.

In a typical year Lafite, which with 250 acres (100ha) is one of the biggest vineyards in the Médoc, makes about 700 barrels of its top wine, or *grand vin*; a perfumed, polished, and quintessentially elegant production in a unique circular subterranean *chai*. Even more of its second label Carruades is made.

The firmer and more solid Latour (whose inner workings are illustrated on pp.38–39), seems to spurn elegance, expressing its supremely privileged situation on the hill nearest the river in robust depths that can take decades to reveal their complexity. Latour has the great merit of evenness over uneven vintages. Even the château's second wine, Les Forts de Latour, from separate parcels of land shaded as for a Cru Classé to the west and northwest of the château, is considered and priced as a second-growth. A junior selection, still often richly savoury, is sold simply as Pauillac.

Mouton Rothschild is a third kind of Pauillac: strong, dark, full of the savour of ripe blackcurrants and at its best exotic. No visitor to Pauillac should miss the little museum of works of art connected with wine – old glass, paintings, tapestries – as well as the very fine *chais*, which make Château Mouton Rothschild the showplace of the whole Médoc.

Smelling the richness and feeling the force of Cabernet Sauvignon in these wines, it is strange to think that it is a mere 150 years since it was recognized as the best vine for the Médoc. Up to that time even the first-growths had established the superiority of their terroirs with a mixture of less distinguished grape varieties – above all Malbec. But the best Cabernet Sauvignon is famously slow to mature. Given the 10 or often even 20 years they need (depending on the quality of the vintage), these wines reach into realms of perfection where they are rarely followed. But millionaires tend to be impatient: too much is drunk far too young.

The southern approach to Pauillac, the D2, is flanked by the two rival second-growth halves of the historic Pichon estate. For years Pichon-Lalande (as Château Pichon Longueville Comtesse de Lalande is known) had the better name, but it is now given a run for its money by Château Pichon-Longueville, as the property once known as Pichon-Baron now styles itself. The key ingredient here has been investment on a massive scale by the insurance group AXA, which has restored the distinctively turreted château itself, erecting a dramatic visitors' centre and perhaps the first building in the Médoc which would naturally be called a winery. (In Bordeaux *cuviers* are generally full of fermentation tanks and *chais* are stacked with barrels.)

Yes, tourism is alive and well in the Médoc. This is not Paris but Bages, the hamlet just south of Pauillac and the fiefdom of the Cazes family of Lynch-Bages. Note, visitors may catch up with their emails over their croissants.

Château Lynch-Bages, though "only" a fifth-growth, has long been loved, particularly in Britain, for its richly spicy wine – a sort of Mouton for not-quite-millionaires – together with its second wine Château Haut-Bages Averous. The mystery château meanwhile has been Pontet-Canet, the biggest Cru Classé of all. Superbly sited as a neighbour to Mouton, it is however utterly different: tannic and reserved where Mouton is open and opulent. Recent vintages have been impressive.

Château Duhart-Milon belongs to the Rothschilds of Lafite, and Châteaux d'Armailhac and Clerc Milon to Mouton. All three clearly benefit from the wealth and technical knowledge of their proprietors and managers. Châteaux Batailley and the usually finer Haut-Batailley lie back from the river in the fringe of the woods. Like Haut-Batailley, the

▼ A sweep upwards in status, and price, from left to right here, although after a period during which the first-growths released their wines at the same opening price, Latour is increasingly out in front of the other two first-growths that flank it below.

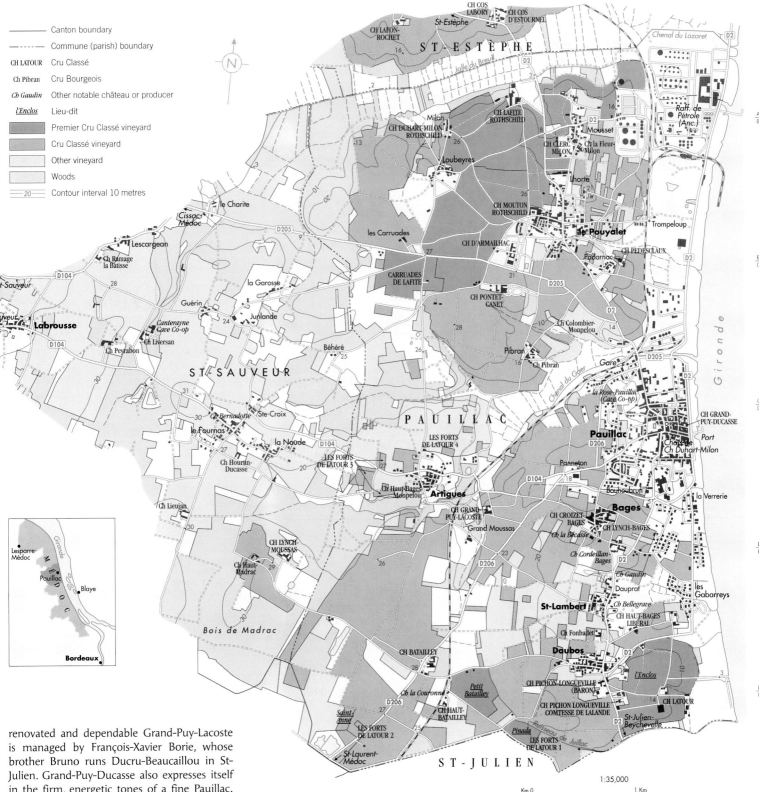

Canton boundary

- - - - - Commune (parish) boundary

CH LATOUR Cru Classé

Ch Pibran Cru Bourgeois

Ch Gaudin Other notable château or producer

l'Enclos Lieu-dit

Premier Cru Classé vineyard

Cru Classé vineyard

Other vineyard

Woods

—20— Contour interval 10 metres

renovated and dependable Grand-Puy-Lacoste is managed by François-Xavier Borie, whose brother Bruno runs Ducru-Beaucaillou in St-Julien. Grand-Puy-Ducasse also expresses itself in the firm, energetic tones of a fine Pauillac. Lacoste is one continuous vineyard on high ground, surrounding its château, while the Ducasse property is scattered in three separate parcels to the north and west of Pauillac and its old château is situated right on the quay in the town itself.

Château Haut-Bages Libéral, its vineyards superbly sited in St-Lambert, has acquired new premises and a new lease of life. Château Lynch-Moussas, run in conjunction with Château Batailley, sells consistently good wine at modest prices. Châteaux Croizet-Bages and Pedesclaux are fifth-growths that have serious

rivals in Pauillac's four 2003 Crus Bourgeois Supérieurs: Colombier-Monpelou, propitiously sited next to the much improved Château Pontet-Canet; Fonbadet in St-Lambert, with old vines and serious wine; Haut-Bages Monpelou (under the same ownership as Batailley); and the AXA-owned and cosseted Pibran. The local co-operative, under the name of La Rose-Pauillac, is also making creditable wine, though in diminishing quantities.

The map includes part of the next parish to the west, St-Sauveur. There are no wines of outstanding quality here; the Crus Bourgeois marked, however, are respectable and useful. Château Liversan belongs to the owner of Châteaux Patache d'Aux and Le Boscq to the north; Château Peyrabon is a big, well-run vineyard; Château Bernadotte was acquired by Pichon-Lalande's owner in 1993; and the wine of Ramage la Batisse is fragrant and serviceable.

St-Julien

No other commune in Bordeaux has so high a proportion of classed-growths as St-Julien. It is a small commune, with the smallest production of the famous four of the Médoc. Yet almost all of St-Julien is superlative wine-growing land: typical mounds of gravel, not as deep as in Pauillac, but all are either close to the river or sloping south to the considerable valley (considerable by Médoc standards, that is) drained by the Jalle du Nord and the Chenal du Milieu.

Thus the great châteaux divide into two groups: the riverside estates epitomized by the Léovilles around the village of St-Julien itself, and the southern group centred on the village of Beychevelle, led by Château Beychevelle, Branaire-Ducru, and Ducru-Beaucaillou, and reaching back inland with Châteaux Gruaud Larose and Lagrange. Around Beychevelle is a cluster of superior but unclassified chateaux, including the solid Gloria.

If Pauillac makes the most striking and brilliant wine of the Médoc, and Margaux the most refined and exquisite, St-Julien forms the transition between the two. With comparatively few exceptions its châteaux make rather round and gentle wine – gentle, that is, when it is mature: it starts as tough and tannic in a good year as any.

The principal glory of the commune is the vast estate of Léoville on the boundary with Pauillac, once the biggest in the Médoc, now divided into three. Château Léoville-Las-Cases has the most extensive vineyards of the three, with 240 acres (almost 100ha). Its dense, almost austere, long-lived wine is so obviously "classic", and the Delon family who run it so astute, that Léoville-Las-Cases is sometimes priced almost at first-growth levels. Léoville Barton runs it close, and belongs to the old Irish family of Barton, who moved to Bordeaux as merchants early in the 18th century. Anthony Barton lives in the beautiful 18th-century

Château Langoa Barton next door, and makes his two wines side by side in the same *chai*. Langoa is usually reckoned the slightly lesser wine of the two, but both are among the finest of clarets in a traditional manner and are never less than good value, even in tricky years. Léoville Poyferré has had a more chequered past, but has justified its great name with excellent forceful wines since the 1980s.

To the south of the Léovilles, Bruno Borie's Château Ducru-Beaucaillou with its Italianate mansion has established a style of its own, distinct in emphasizing finesse at a very high level, while its neighbour Branaire-Ducru is somehow a little less polished. On the other hand, Château Beychevelle and its neighbour St-Pierre convey finesse and elegance with an easy plumpness that is intensely seductive.

Château Gruaud Larose begins the "inland" section of St-Julien with wines whose richness and drive puts them in the very top rank. There

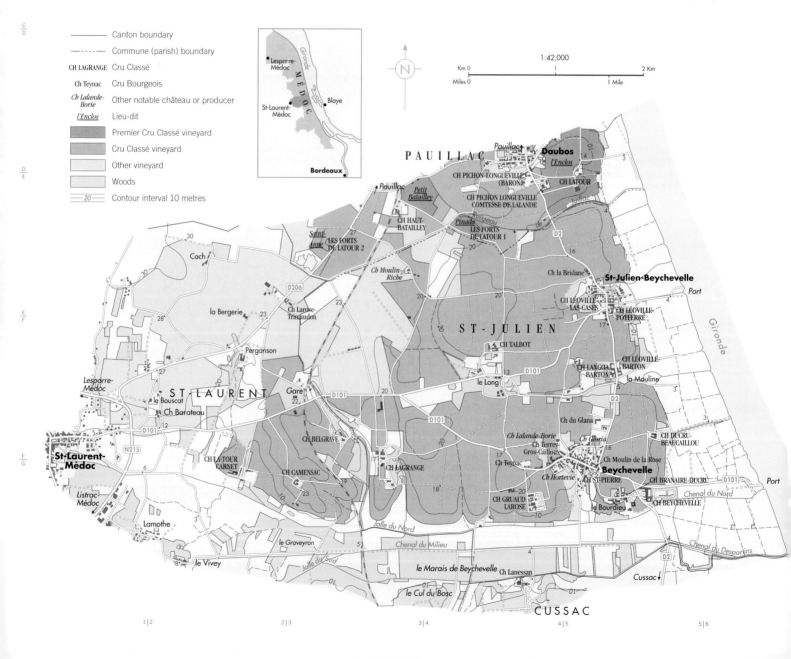

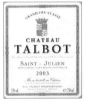

▲ The top three labels are all supplied by what was originally one estate. Every one of them offers the drinker claret of the most archetypal sort – an appetizing dry red designed for the table, after a prolonged period in the cellar.

is scarcely a more reliable château in Bordeaux than this traditionally fashioned jewel in the Merlaut family's crown. Château Talbot, which occupies the central high ground of the commune, may be a shade less fine, but is consistently dense, smooth, and savoury, perhaps owing almost as much to winemaking skill as to its site.

The last of the classed-growths, Château Lagrange, used to be very highly regarded for its rich, substantial wine. Suntory of Japan have brought it back into focus since they acquired it in 1984. It lies far back in the country in the sleepy hinterland on the border of St-Laurent (whose appellation is Haut-Médoc) and in a group with three other classed-growths, all in different stages of resurrection. La Tour Carnet is most advanced and nowadays makes alluring wine. Camensac, now owned by the Merlaut family of Gruaud Larose, was replanted a few years later by the owner of the huge and popular Cru Bourgeois Larose-Trintaudon. Its wine is gaining substance and recognition.

The second-year chai at Château Langoa Barton, where Château Léoville Barton is also made, shows just how much wine is available each year – but owner Anthony Barton, one of the Médoc's few resident classed-growth owners, has never been accused of greed in his pricing.

Château Belgrave has also, like so much in the Médoc since the early 1980s, been restored, in this case by négociants Dourthe – but this hinterland never manages to produce quite the class of the vineyards closer to the Gironde.

St-Julien is not prime bourgeois country but Châteaux du Glana, Moulin de la Rose, and Terrey-Gros-Cailloux were all ranked Crus Bourgeois Supérieurs in 2003.

Central Médoc

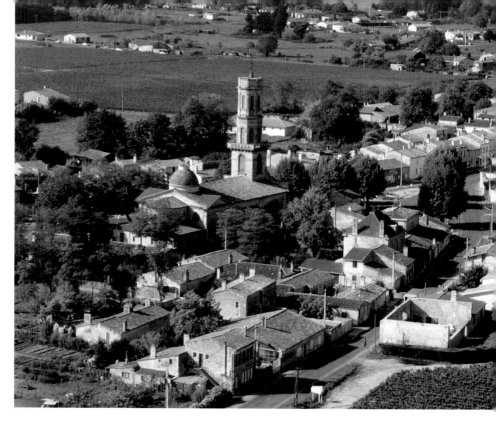

This is the bridge passage of the Médoc, the mezzo forte between the andante of St-Julien and the allegro of Margaux. Four villages pass without a single classed-growth; their appellation simply Haut-Médoc. Here the gravel mounds rise less proudly above the river and the water table is much higher, leaving vines watered more readily and the wines they produce generally less complex. The commune of Cussac maintains some of the momentum of St-Julien – indeed there are moves to have some of its land reclassified as such. But this is the stretch of the drive up the Haut-Médoc during which the dedicated wine tourist (if a passenger) can enjoy a little snooze.

This, even more than St-Estèphe, is Cru Bourgeois country, with a significant proportion of the 2003 Crus Bourgeois Supérieurs, and no fewer than two of the nine Crus Bourgeois Exceptionnels in Moulis: Châteaux Chasse-Spleen and Poujeaux. Both lie on the outskirts of the little hamlet with the grand name of Grand Poujeaux well west of Arcins where the gravel ridges rise and fan out inland, culminating at Grand Poujeaux and at Listrac. These two communes are dignified with appellations of their own instead of the portmanteau "Haut-Médoc". In recent years Listrac and Moulis have risen steadily in estimation.

Quality rises with the gravel and its water-metering effects. Chasse-Spleen can be viewed almost as an honorary St-Julien for its smoothness, its accessibility, and yet its firm, oak-aged structure. Château Poujeaux can be just as impressive if usually rather more robust and less subtle. Between these two properties, the village of Grand Poujeaux is surrounded by a knot of properties with "Grand Poujeaux" in their names: Gressier, Dutruch, La Closerie, and Branas (the latter two not Crus Bourgeois), all reliable for stout-hearted, long-lived reds with the flavour that makes the Médoc unique. Just north of here, Château Maucaillou on the other side of the railway track that leads up the Médoc can sometimes offer exceptional value.

Listrac even further inland has a higher plateau, limestone beneath its gravel, and a name for tough, tannic wines that need time. The name here is Fourcas: of the three châteaux that bear it, Hosten and Dupré are those to watch. Much replanting and infilling has recently enlarged the vineyard considerably here.

Today's thoroughly modernized Château Clarke, with 130 acres (53ha) of vines and lying just within Listrac, was the creation of the late Baron Edmond de Rothschild. The twin châteaux Fonréaud and Lestage south of the village of Listrac have 182 acres (74ha) between them. These redeveloped estates temper the Listrac austerity and make rounder wines, which can only help to make the appellation better known.

In the north of the area mapped, the Cru Bourgeois Supérieur Château Lanessan faces St-Julien across the canal that separates the parishes. Lanessan and its neighbour Caronne Ste-Gemme (largely in St-Laurent) are well-run estates whose owners can afford high standards. Otherwise Cussac has little of the all-important gravel. The forest here comes close to the river. Château Beaumont occupies its best outcrop. Its wine is easy, fragrant, quick to mature – and correspondingly popular. Oddly Château Tour du Haut-Moulin in Vieux Cussac is just the opposite: dark, old-fashioned, needing years – but worth the wait.

The riverside here is worth a visit to see the handsome 17th-century battlements of the Fort-Médoc – an anti-English precaution now turned to peaceful uses. At Lamarque an earlier fortress, the splendid Château de Lamarque, has established a name for carefully made, satisfyingly full-bodied wine with the true stamp of the Médoc on it. Lamarque is the Médoc's link with Blaye on the other side of the Gironde: a regular car-ferry service runs from the pier.

A good deal of replanting has given the area a more purposeful look in recent years.

The busy little town of Lamarque. Its chief significance for the wines of the Médoc is arguably as home to the region's most respected specialist consultant oenologist Jacques Boissenot and his son and successor Eric.

Château Malescasse was one of the first to be restored. And in the next commune south, Arcins, the big old properties of Château Barreyres and Château d'Arcins have been hugely replanted by the Castels, whose empire stretches from Morocco to Britain's Oddbins stores. They and their well-managed neighbour Château Arnauld are steadily making Arcins better known. The village's chief claim to fame, however, is still the little Lion d'Or, the Médoc's wine trade canteen.

Beyond the Estey de Tayac, in the southeast corner of the area, we enter the sphere of Margaux. The extensive Château Citran is now owned by the Merlaut family. It and the smaller Villegeorge (off this map to the south, but a Cru Bourgeois Supérieur to watch) lie in the commune of Avensan. Both are well known, and approach Margaux in style.

Soussans is among the communes whose AC is not merely Haut-Médoc but Margaux, a name some proprietors just north of here would like to appropriate. Châteaux La Tour de Mons and Paveil de Luze both qualify as Crus Bourgeois Supérieur, the latter being for a century the stylish country resort of one of the great merchant families of Bordeaux, making the kind of easy, elegant wines the family liked.

◄ Labels for those who are not label hunters but who appreciate value. Over the last few years winemaking expertise down in these lower ranks has improved just as much as at the top, although prices have not risen nearly as much.

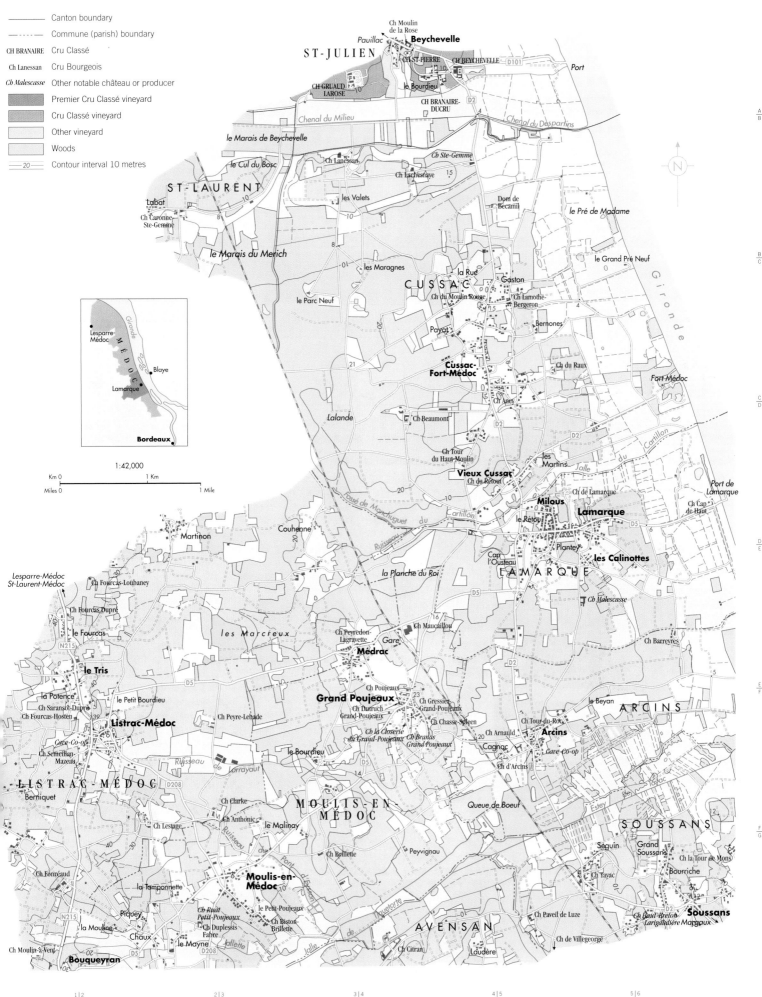

Canton boundary
Commune (parish) boundary
CH BRANAIRE Cru Classé
Ch Lanessan Cru Bourgeois
Ch Malescasse Other notable château or producer
Premier Cru Classé vineyard
Cru Classé vineyard
Other vineyard
Woods
20 Contour interval 10 metres

1:42,000

Km 0   1 Km
Miles 0   1 Mile

Ch Moulin
de la Rose
Pauillac
Beychevelle
ST-JULIEN
CH ST-PIERRE CH BEYCHEVELLE
D101
Port
CH GRUAUD
LAROSE
le Bourdieu
CH BRANAIRE-
DUCRU
D2
Chenal du Milieu
Chenal du Despartins

le Marais de Beychevelle
Ch Ste-Gemme
ST-LAURENT
le Cul du Bosc
Ch Lanessan
Ch Lachesnaye
15
les Valets
Dom de
Becamil
le Pré de Madame
Labat
Ch Caronne-
Ste-Gemme
le Marais du Merich
les Maragnes
le Grand Pré Neuf
la Rue
CUSSAC
Gaston
le Parc Neuf
Ch du Moulin Rouge
Ch Lamothe-
Bergeron
21
Payat
Bernones
Ch du Raux
Cussac-
Fort-Médoc
Fort Médoc
Lalande
Ch Beaumont
D2
D2
Ch Tour
du Haut-Moulin
les Martins
Jalle
Vieux Cussac
Ch du Retout
Ch de Lamarque
Port de
Lamarque
Milous
Lamarque
Ch Cap
de Haut
le Retout
Couhenne
Martinon
Cap
l'Ousteau
Plantey
les Calinottes
la Planche du Roi
LAMARQUE
Lesparre-Médoc
St-Laurent-Médoc
Ch Fourcas-Loubaney
Ch Malescasse
Ch Fourcas-Dupré
le Fourcas
les Marcreux
Ch Peyredon-
Lagravette
Ch Maucaillou
Ch Barreyres
N215
Gare
16
le Tris
Médrac
la Potence
le Petit Bourdieu
Ch Saransot-Dupré
Ch Poujeaux
23
le Beyan
ARCINS
Ch Fourcas-Hosten
Grand Poujeaux
Ch Gressier-
Grand-Poujeaux
Listrac-Médoc
Ch Dutruch
Grand-Poujeaux
Ch Chasse-Spleen
Ch Tour-du-Roc
Cave-Co-op
Ch la Closerie
du Grand-Poujeaux
Ch Brillas
Grand Poujeaux
Ch Arnauld
Arcins
Ch Semeillan-
Mazeau
le Bourdieu
Cagnac
Cave-Co-op
LISTRAC-MÉDOC
D208
Ch d'Arcins
Berniquet
Ch Clarke
MOULIS-EN-
MÉDOC
Queue de Boeuf
SOUSSANS
Ch Anthonic
Ch Lestage
le Malinay
Séguin
Grand
Soussans
Ch Fonréaud
Ch Brillette
Peyvignau
Bourriche
Ch la Tour de Mons
la Tamponnette
Ch Tayac
Piquey
Ch Ruat
Petit-Poujeaux
le Petit-Poujeaux
Moulis-en-
Médoc
Ch Paveil de Luze
Soussans
la Mouline
Ch Duplessis
Fabre
Ch Biston-
Brillette
AVENSAN
Ch Haut-Breton
Larigaudière Margaux
Chaux
le Mayne
D208
Ch Moulin-à-Vent
Bouqueyran
Ch Citran
Laudère
Ch de Villegeorge

Gironde

MÉDOC
Lesparre-
Médoc
Blaye
Lamarque
Bordeaux

1|2   2|3   3|4   4|5   5|6

Margaux and the Southern Médoc

Margaux and Cantenac, the village just south of it, are considered to make the Médoc's most polished and fragrant wine. Their historical record says so; and contemporary reality is slowly catching up. There are more second- and third-growths here than anywhere, and a new broom has been sweeping through the southern Médoc.

The map shows a rather different picture from Pauillac or St-Julien. Instead of the châteaux being spread out evenly over the land, they are huddled together in the villages. An examination of the almost unliftable volumes of commune maps in the *mairie* shows a degree of intermingling of one estate with another that is far greater than in, say, Pauillac. One would therefore look to differences in grape varieties, technique, and tradition more than changes of soil to try to explain the differences between the châteaux.

In fact the soil of Margaux is the thinnest and gravelliest in the Médoc, so that vines may root

The 17th-century manor house of Château d'Issan enjoys one of Bordeaux's most romantic situations, entirely surrounded by the moat of an old fortified castle. And the wine? When it's good, it's very, very good.

up to 23ft (7m) deep for their steady but meagre supply of water. The result is wines that start life comparatively supple, although in poor years they can turn out thin. In good and great years, however, all the stories about the virtues of gravel are justified: there is a delicacy about archetypal Margaux, and a sweet haunting perfume, that can make it the most exquisite claret of all.

The wines of Châteaux Margaux and Palmer are the ones that most often reach such heights. Château Margaux is not only a first-growth of the Médoc, it is the one that most looks the part: a pediment at the end of an avenue; the air of a palace with *chais* to match. After under-investment from the late 1950s, the Mentzelopoulos family acquired it in 1978 and has been making superlative wine ever since. Their seminal oaked white Pavillon Blanc de Château Margaux, grown on the western limit of the map opposite, being white, qualifies only as a humble AC Bordeaux. The third-growth Château Palmer, however, can present a formidable challenge and, unlike so many red Bordeaux today, acutely expresses its origins.

Château Lascombes (owned successively by American wine writer Alexis Lichine, English brewers Bass, and an American investment syndicate) is a case where buying more land diluted second-growth quality in the 1970s and '80s. Things have been slowly improving, however – with no shortage of outside help. Next door the recently revived third-growth Château Ferrière is producing convincing Margaux with characteristic finesse.

Of the famous pair which used to be the big Rauzan estate, as famous in the 18th century as Léoville was in St-Julien, Rauzan-Ségla (once Rausan-Ségla) is today much the better, having been reformed in the 1980s and taken firmly in hand from 1994 by the family behind the fashion house Chanel. The smaller Rauzan-Gassies still lags far behind second-growth standards and shows little inclination to narrow the gap.

There are several distinguished pairs of châteaux in Margaux. The two second-growths Brane-Cantenac and Durfort-Vivens are owned by different members of the ubiquitous Lurton family, yet make distinctly different wine: the Brane fragrant and almost melting, the Durfort

much less generous. A tiny vestige of the third-growth Desmirail has been resurrected to join them as a third bowstring.

Fourth-growth Pouget is the often forceful brother of third-growth Boyd-Cantenac. Malescot St-Exupéry (which can be miraculously scented and one of the best of Margaux) and the small third-growth Château Marquis d'Alesme-Becker belong to the Zuger brothers Roger and Jean-Claude respectively and some competitive instinct is now in evidence.

Still in Margaux proper, fourth-growth Château Marquis de Terme, although rarely seen abroad, now makes rather good wine, and third-growth Château d'Issan (see photo) has one of the best situations in Margaux, with its vineyard sloping gently towards the river.

In Cantenac itself, the château of Prieuré-Lichine was deservedly famous for making some of Margaux's most consistent claret when it was owned by Alexis Lichine – and also for being the first to admit passers-by in a way which has, remarkably, only just become accepted practice. Château Kirwan was once in eclipse but has been restored and began to shine again in the 1990s. Yet another tale of restoration and renewed quality has been the lonely Château du Tertre, isolated on high ground well inland in Arsac, under the same dynamic Dutch ownership as Château Giscours. Château Cantenac-Brown, which competes for the prize of ugliest Médoc château (it looks like a Victorian English school), flanks Brane-Cantenac and makes some of Margaux's most solid wine.

There are three more important classed-growths before the Haut-Médoc vineyards give way to the northern suburbs of Bordeaux: Giscours, whose half-timbered farm buildings face a most impressive sweep of vines and harbour a particularly flattering style of wine; Cantemerle, a perfect Sleeping Beauty château, deep in a wood of huge trees and quiet pools, whose wine is more known for elegance; and the top-flight Château La Lagune, a neat 18th-century building under the same ownership as Paul Jaboulet Aîné of the Rhône Valley.

Dauzac, the fourth classed-growth of this southern area and managed by the Lurton family, has raised its sights. Its neighbour Siran is one of Margaux's pair of Crus Bourgeois Exceptionnels, the other being Labégorce-Zédé, under the same ownership as nearby Labégorce since 2005. Both Siran and Château d'Angludet, owned and inhabited by the Sichel family, can make wine of classed-growth quality.

1:42,000
Km 0 | 2 Km
Miles 0 | 1 Mile

SOUSSANS
Ch Devrem-Valentin
Marsac
Pauillac
Ch Marsac Séguineau
Soussans
Ch Haut-Breton-Larigaudière
le Cadéos
Ch Labégorce-Zédé
Relais de Margaux
Cru Monplaisir 1
Dom de l'Île Margaux
Île de Macau
Bessan
Ch Labégorce
Richet
MARGAUX
le Pez
la Halle
D2
CH MARQUIS D'ALESME-BECKER
Ch la Gurgue
Port d'Issan
Gironde
Ch Bel-Air Marquis-d'Aligre
CH LASCOMBES
CH MARGAUX
D105
Vire Fougasse
CH FERRIÈRE
CH MALESCOT-ST-EXUPÉRY
Cru Monplaisir 2
Île des Vaches
Pavillon Blanc
Margaux
Ch Pontac-Lynch
D105
CH DURFORT-VIVENS
CH MARQUIS DE TERME
Issan
CH D'ISSAN
Lagunegrand
Mathéou
Ch Martinens
CH RAUZAN-GASSIES
CH PALMER
les Eycards
CH RAUZAN-SÉGLA
D2
Grange Neuve
D105
CH PRIEURÉ-LICHINE
Cantenac
CH CANTENAC-BROWN
CANTENAC
CH KIRWAN
la Mail
Péséou
CH BRANE-CANTENAC
CH DESMIRAIL
Jean Faure
CH BOYD-CANTENAC
Ch Siran
la Bastide
Benqueyre
CH POUGET
Port de Labarde
Gassion
CH DAUZAC
D209
Blanchard
Ch d'Angludet
Marois de Labarde
la Métairie
Larrieu Terrefort
Labarde
LABARDE
Ligondras
Ferme Suzanne
Macau
D105
CH GISCOURS
Pied de Port
CH DU TERTRE
Bern
Clos de May
ARSAC
Ch Maropallia
les Trois Moulins
Maucamps
Ch Monbrison
MACAU
Ch Maucamps
la Mouline
Ch Cambon la Pelouse
Ch Mille Roses
D211
D210
Arsac
Cambon-la-Pelouse
D2
CH CANTEMERLE
Fellonneau
Labric
Lafont
Fronton
Gasteau
les Carrayes
Ch de Gironville
Ch de Girouville
Ch d'Arche
Ludon-Médoc
Lesparre-Médoc
MÉDOC
Gironde
Paloumey
CH LA LAGUNE
Feydieu
Bouscarrut
les Lauriers
Blaye
le Petit Feydieu
D211
D210
Peyquem
LE PIAN-MÉDOC
LUDON-MÉDOC
Margaux
le Pian-Médoc
la Taste
Bordeaux
Ch de Malleret
Haras
Bordeaux
Ch d'Agassac

Legend

— Canton boundary
--- Commune (parish) boundary
CH MARGAUX Cru Classé
Ch Martinens Cru Bourgeois
Ch Bel-Air Marquis-d'Aligre Other notable château or producer
Ch Marojallia Microcuvée or part of one
Premier Cru Classé vineyard
Cru Classé vineyard
Other vineyard
Woods
—25— Contour interval 5 metres

A|B
B|C
C|D
D|E
E|F
F|G

◄ Change is the keynote of Bordeaux. A new proprietor or just a new determination can change the wine style and fortune of a château. Of these 11 properties, only the grandest of all, first-growth Château Margaux, has had the same hand on the tiller, and the tiller set in exactly the same direction, for the last 30 years.

CHÂTEAU MARGAUX
GRAND VIN
2000
PREMIER GRAND CRU CLASSÉ
MARGAUX

Château
RAUZAN-SEGLA
MARGAUX
2005

GRAND CRU CLASSÉ EN 1855
CHÂTEAU
BRANE-CANTENAC
MARGAUX
2000
APPELLATION MARGAUX CONTRÔLÉE
MIS EN BOUTEILLE AU CHÂTEAU

1|2   2|3   3|4   4|5   5|6

Graves and Entre-Deux-Mers

There is much more to the **Graves** region than its most famous communes of Pessac and Léognan, conjoined in a single appellation, (mapped overleaf). The southern end of this zone of scattered vines has been coming to life, too. Nondescript whites have given place to fresh, lively, dry wines – and to a new wave of reds with deep, sappy fruit and ripe tannins. Langon is now a regular resort of buyers looking for flavour and value. In central and southern Graves a number of the old properties, notably in the once-famous parishes of Portets, Landiras, and St-Pierre-de-Mons, have new owners and new philosophies.

The ability of Graves soil to make red and white wine equally well is seen at Châteaux de Chantegrive in Podensac and Rahoul in Portets, and in properties dotted around Arbanats and Castres-Gironde. Clos Floridène at Pujols-sur-Ciron and Château du Seuil, like so many successful properties situated close to the Garonne, excel at understated, oak-aged dry whites from the Sauvignon Blanc and Sémillon grapes that seem so at home in this quiet southern corner of the Gironde, even if the proportion of white wine produced in the Graves AC is hardly more than a quarter and continues to fall.

The extent of this map northwards and eastwards is testament to the efforts being made in some of Bordeaux's even less glamorous wine areas. Most of the wine sold as lowly AC Bordeaux is made in the **Entre-Deux-Mers**, the wedge of pretty farmland between the Garonne and Dordogne rivers, even if the name Entre-Deux-Mers itself is reserved on wine labels for the harmless dry white produced there, in much smaller quantity.

But an increasing number of producers of red wines that qualify for no grander an AC than Bordeaux or the slightly stronger Bordeaux

Supérieur are seriously trying to make wines of note, notably by tending their vineyards much more carefully and reducing yields. Many of them are marked on this map, which includes the most interesting part of Entre-Deux-Mers.

A number of substantial châteaux, and the odd exceptional co-op, have changed the aspect of the region, especially of the parishes in the north of this map towards the Dordogne and St-Emilion, from one of mixed farm and orchard to vinous monoculture. Some of the most successful flag-bearers were the Lurton family's excellent Château Bonnet south of Grézillac, the Despagne family's versatile Château Tour de Mirambeau south of Branne, the Courcelle family's Château Thieuley near Créon, and Château Toutigeac in the little-used sub-appellation **Haut-Benauge**. Many of these make even more successful dry whites (from Sémillon and Sauvignon grapes) than reds. Château de Sours of St-Quentin-de-Baron has even managed to sell its deep pink Bordeaux rosé *en primeur*.

But there are signs of even more exciting winecraft in Entre-Deux-Mers, as well there might be in the far north where limestone soils can be uncannily similar to parts of the St-Emilion appellation. The Despagnes have created Girolate, a hand-made Merlot garage wine, out of one of the most densely planted vineyards in all Bordeaux. Northwest of this map, Château de Reignac near St-Loubès (see p.83), has achieved similarly dizzy prices, thanks to the singlemindedness of owner Yves Vatelot. While Pierre Lurton, winemaker at Châteaux Cheval Blanc and d'Yquem no less, brings a certain glamour to the region via his own property Château Marjosse, near Grézillac.

Since the **Premières Côtes de Bordeaux** encircle the sweet white appellations of Cadillac, Loupiac, and Ste-Croix-du-Mont, it is

hardly surprising that good sweet wines are produced here too. Those made in the south of the zone are sold as **Cadillac** while the dry whites are sold as straightforward Bordeaux. One of Bordeaux's leading oenologists, Denis Dubourdieu, at Château Reynon at Béguey near the town of Cadillac has succeeded with fresh Sauvignon white and a particularly toothsome red. Château Fayau at Cadillac is keeping up the local tradition of sweet, fruity white.

Legend:

■ VILLA BEL AIR	Notable producer
	Barsac
	Cadillac and Premières Côtes de Bordeaux
	Cérons
	Côtes de Bordeaux-St-Macaire
	Entre-Deux-Mers
	Bordeaux Haut-Benauge and Entre-Deux-Mers Haut-Benauge
	Graves
	Loupiac
	Pessac-Léognan
	Premières Côtes de Bordeaux
	Ste-Croix-du-Mont
	Sauternes
101	Area mapped at larger scale on page shown

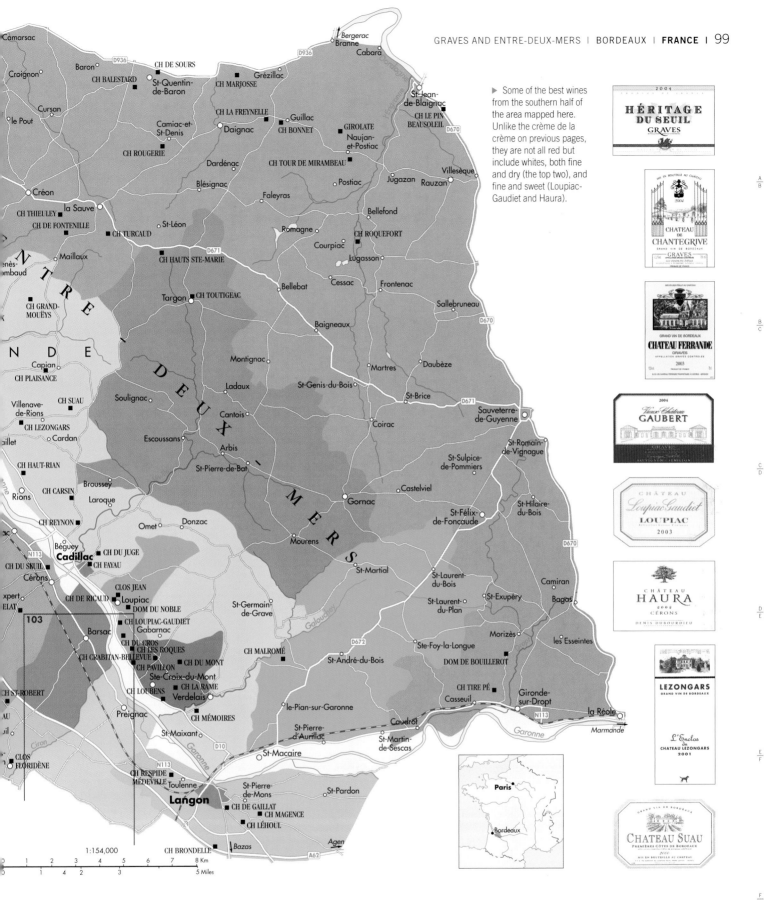

▶ Some of the best wines from the southern half of the area mapped here. Unlike the crème de la crème on previous pages, they are not all red but include whites, both fine and dry (the top two), and fine and sweet (Loupiac-Gaudiet and Haura).

There are plans to introduce an alternative umbrella AC **Côtes de Bordeaux** for the two appellations here, and three more on the right bank (see p.82), that include the word Côtes in their name: Premières Côtes de Bordeaux (possibly with Côtes de Bordeaux-St-Macaire), Côtes de Bourg, Premières Côtes de Blaye, Côtes de Castillon, and Côtes de Francs. The idea is to increase recognition, not to blend between these different Côtes appellations.

It is too much to claim that the liquorous **Ste-Croix-du-Mont** has become a money-making proposition, as it once used to be, but three châteaux – Loubens, du Mont, and La Rame – make great efforts, and in neighbouring **Loupiac** both Châteaux Loupiac-Gaudiet and de Ricaud are ready to run the risks inherent in making truly sweet, rather than just semi-sweet, wine (see p.102). **Côtes de Bordeaux-St-Macaire** is a little-seen white AC from this zone.

Just across the River Garonne, to the north of Barsac in the Graves lies **Cérons**, a separate appellation long forgotten (it includes Illats and Podensac), which has found new prosperity (at Château d'Archambeau, for example) by making mainstream white and red under the Graves appellation, largely abandoning its tradition of a style midway between Graves Supérieures (the sweetish white of Graves) and Barsac that was softly rather than stickily sweet.

Pessac-Léognan

It was here, in the southern outskirts of the city of Bordeaux, that the whole concept of fine red Bordeaux was launched, in the 1660s, by the owner of Château Haut-Brion. Its arid sand and gravel had already supplied the region and its export market with its best red wine since at least 1300, when the archbishop who became Pope Clement V (of Avignon) planted what is now Château Pape Clément.

Pessac-Léognan is the modern name for the heartland of the Graves, mapped in its entirety on the previous two pages. Pine trees have always been the main crop of this sandy soil. The vineyards are clearings, often isolated from one another in heavily forested country crossed by shallow river valleys. The map opposite shows how the city and its oldest vineyards reach out into the forest, which continues (as the Landes) south and west from here to the Basque foothills of the Pyrenees.

Now the city has swallowed all the vineyards in its path except the superlative group on the deep gravel soils of Pessac: Haut-Brion and its neighbour and stablemate La Mission Haut-Brion, Les Carmes Haut-Brion, and Picque Caillou (north and west of Haut-Brion respectively and off this map) and, further out of town, the archi-episcopal Pape Clément.

Châteaux Haut-Brion and La Mission are found with difficulty, deep in the suburbs, on opposite sides of the old Arcachon road which runs through Pessac. Haut-Brion is every inch a first-growth, a suave equilibrium of force and finesse with the singularity of great Graves: hints of earth and fern, tobacco and caramel; a flavour not so high-toned but frequently more intriguing than even a Lafite or a Margaux. La Mission tastes denser, riper, more savage – and often just as splendid. In 1983 the American owners of Haut-Brion bought its old rival, including Château La Tour Haut-Brion also made within the old La Mission estate – not to unite the vineyards but to continue the match. The game is played out each year, not just between the two famous reds, but between their incomparably rich white sisters too, Châteaux Haut-Brion Blanc and Laville Haut-Brion. There are few more vivid examples of what terroir, the uniqueness of each piece of ground, means on this Bordeaux soil.

Although the majority of wine produced in the vineyards mapped here is red, with much the same grape recipe as in the Médoc, most Pessac-Léognan properties also produce some white of sometimes superlative quality within

Who would have thought that wine would be seen as an essential part of a fashionable beauty treatment, as here at the spa, hotel, and restaurant adjacent to Château Smith Haut Lafitte? There's a range of grape-based creams and potions too.

the same appellation. The commune of Léognan, well into the forest, is the hub of this map. Domaine de Chevalier is its outstanding property, despite its modest appearance. The domaine has never had a château. Although its *chai* and *cuvier* have been impeccably rebuilt and its vineyard considerably expanded in the late 1980s and early 1990s, it retains the air of a farm in a clearing in the pines, but the wines once again have substance as well as finesse. Only about 1,000 cases of a magnificently long-lived barrel-fermented white made from Sauvignon and Sémillon are made each year so it is never a bargain.

Château Haut-Bailly is the other leading classed-growth of Léognan; unusual in these parts for making only red wine, but deeply and persuasively. Château de Fieuzal's red has provided a serious challenge for some time, however – and its white is also very fine, if in decidedly limited quantities, as is the way with the top Graves properties. Malartic-Lagravière is similar, and has been thoroughly modernized since being acquired by the Belgian Bonnie family in 1997.

Château Carbonnieux is different. This old Benedictine establishment was for long much more famous for its reliable white than for its light red, although the red has gained weight recently. Château Olivier, surely Bordeaux's

oldest and most haunting château building, produces both colours and is also the subject of long-term renewal. (See Terroir, pp.26–27.)

No Graves property has had a more obvious face-lift recently than Château Smith Haut Lafitte in the commune of Martillac, which marks the southern limit of Pessac-Léognan. Not only does it make a very successful red and white, the property now boasts in Les Sources de Caudalie a hotel, restaurants, and a grape-based spa (see above). Improvements at Château Latour-Martillac to the south have been on a more modest scale.

The prophet and prime mover here is André Lurton: founder of the local growers' organization; owner of Châteaux La Louvière, de Rochemorin, the classified Couhins-Lurton (virtually all the properties mentioned here were classified in 1959), and de Cruzeau (south of Latour-Martillac and mapped on p.99); and the driving force behind much of the recent renewal. Château Bouscaut, also classified, if by no means the best, is owned by his niece Sophie Lurton.

▼ All four of the truly great wines represented on the right below belong to the same family, descendants of the American Clarence Dillon who bought first-growth Château Haut-Brion in 1935, when St-Emilion first-growth Château Cheval Blanc was also for sale – so unprofitable was Bordeaux wine production.

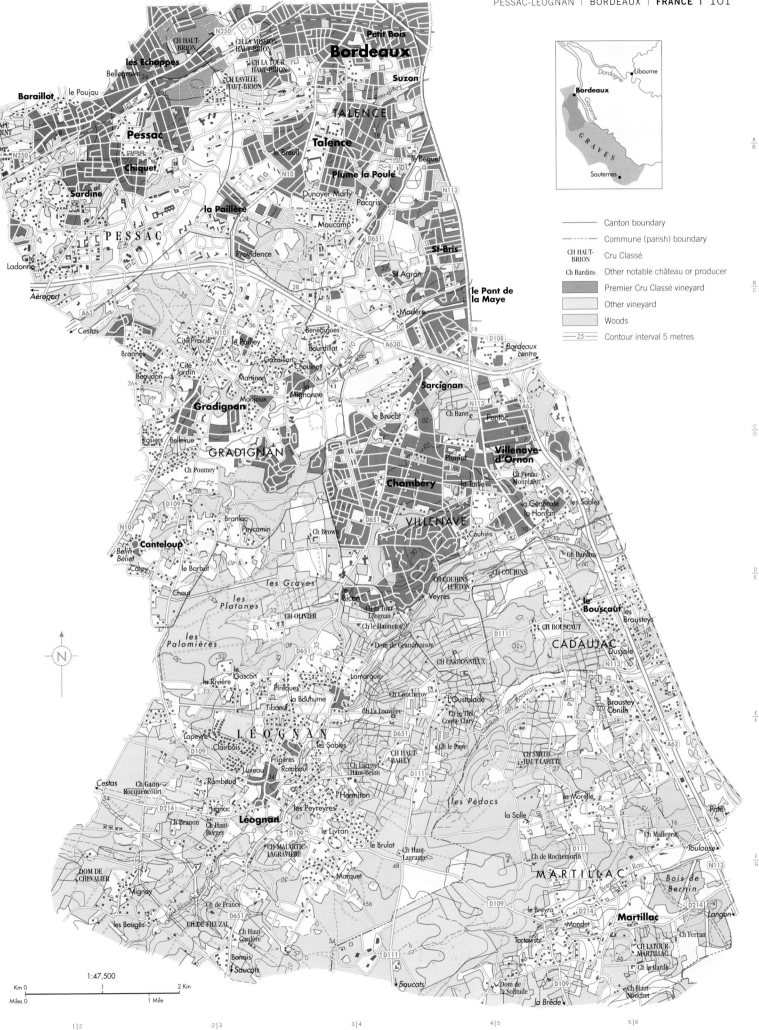

Canton boundary
Commune (parish) boundary
CH HAUT-
BRION
Cru Classé
Ch Bardins
Other notable château or producer
Premier Cru Classé vineyard
Other vineyard
Woods
25
Contour interval 5 metres

1:47,500

Km 0   1   2 Km
Miles 0   1 Mile

Sauternes and Barsac

All the other districts of Bordeaux mapped in this Atlas make wines that can be compared with, and preferred to, one another. **Sauternes** is different: arguably under-appreciated but incomparable, it is a speciality which finds few real rivals. Potentially one of the world's longest-living wines, it depends on local conditions and on a very unusual fungus and winemaking technique. In great vintages the results can be sublime: a very sweet, rich-textured, flower-scented, glittering golden liquid. In some years it can frankly fail to be Sauternes (properly so-called) at all.

Above all it is only the best-situated and best-run châteaux of Sauternes – and in this we include Barsac – that make such nectar. Ordinary Sauternes is just sweet white wine.

The local conditions in this warm and fertile corner of Aquitaine include the mists that form along the little River Ciron on autumn evenings, lasting till after dawn. The special technique which only the well-financed châteaux can afford to employ is to pick over the vineyard as many as eight or nine times, typically beginning in September and sometimes going on until November. This is to take full advantage of the peculiar form of mould (known as *Botrytis cinerea* to the scientist, or pourriture noble – "noble rot" – to the poet) which forms, capriciously, on the Sémillon, Sauvignon Blanc, and Muscadelle grapes during the mild, misty nights, then multiplies in the heat of the day to reduce the grape skins to brown pulp. Instead of affecting the blighted grapes with a flavour of rot, this botrytis engineers the escape of the greater part of the water in them, leaving the sugar, acids, and the flavouring elements in the juice more concentrated than ever. The result of painstaking fermentation of extremely rich grape juice and ageing in small barrels is wine with an intensity of flavour, a smooth, unctuous texture, and exceptional ageing potential which can be made no other way.

But it does mean picking the grapes as they shrivel, sometimes berry by berry – and the proprietors of little-known châteaux can afford only to pick the entire crop at once, and hope for botrytis to be as concentrated on that date as possible.

Production is absurdly low, since evaporation is actually encouraged. From each one of its 250-odd acres (roughly 100ha) Château d'Yquem, the greatest of the Sauternes producers and now owned by the deep-pocketed but commercially astute LVMH, makes fewer than a thousand bottles of wine. A first-class Médoc vineyard makes five or six times as much.

The risk element is appalling, since humid weather in October can turn the mould into the noxious fungus known as grey rot and rob the grower of all chance of making sweet wine, and sometimes of making any wine at all. Costs are correspondingly high and the price of even

the finest Sauternes (with the exception of Yquem), makes it one of the least profitable wines to the grower. Prices have been rising gradually but few wine drinkers realize just how underpriced great sweet white Bordeaux is compared with its red counterpart.

Sauternes was the only area outside the Médoc to be classed in 1855. Château d'Yquem was made a First Great Growth – a rank created for it alone in all Bordeaux. Strangely, for its dominant hilltop position, it has a "perched", therefore unusually high, water-table that keeps its vines growing well even in drought. Eleven other châteaux were made first-growths and 12 more were classed seconds.

Five communes, including Sauternes itself, are entitled to use the name. **Barsac**, the biggest of them, has the alternative of calling its wine either Sauternes or Barsac.

Styles of Sauternes vary almost as much as standards, even if most of the finest properties cluster around Yquem. Château Lafaurie-Peyraguey can taste as floral as it sounds; AXA's Château Suduiraut in Preignac is typically lush and sumptuous; Château Rieussec (owned by the Rothschilds of Lafite) is often deep-coloured and rich. Other current top performers include Clos Haut-Peyraguey and Châteaux de Fargues (run by the Lur-Saluces family which used to own Yquem), Raymond-Lafon, and La Tour Blanche,

Grapes like these, concentrated by the revered Botrytis cinerea fungus, are guided into the basket of a thoroughly traditional basket press at Yquem. Once it is full it is wheeled across the presshouse to be subjected to the overhead press. The aim is to press very, very gently but very, very firmly.

which doubles as a winemaking school. A quite different but long-living style of unoaked wine is made at Château Gilette. In Barsac Châteaux Climens, Coutet, and Doisy-Daëne lead the field with wines slightly fresher in feeling than Sauternes. The increasing proportion of diligently made nectar from this part of the wine world deserves a far more appreciative following.

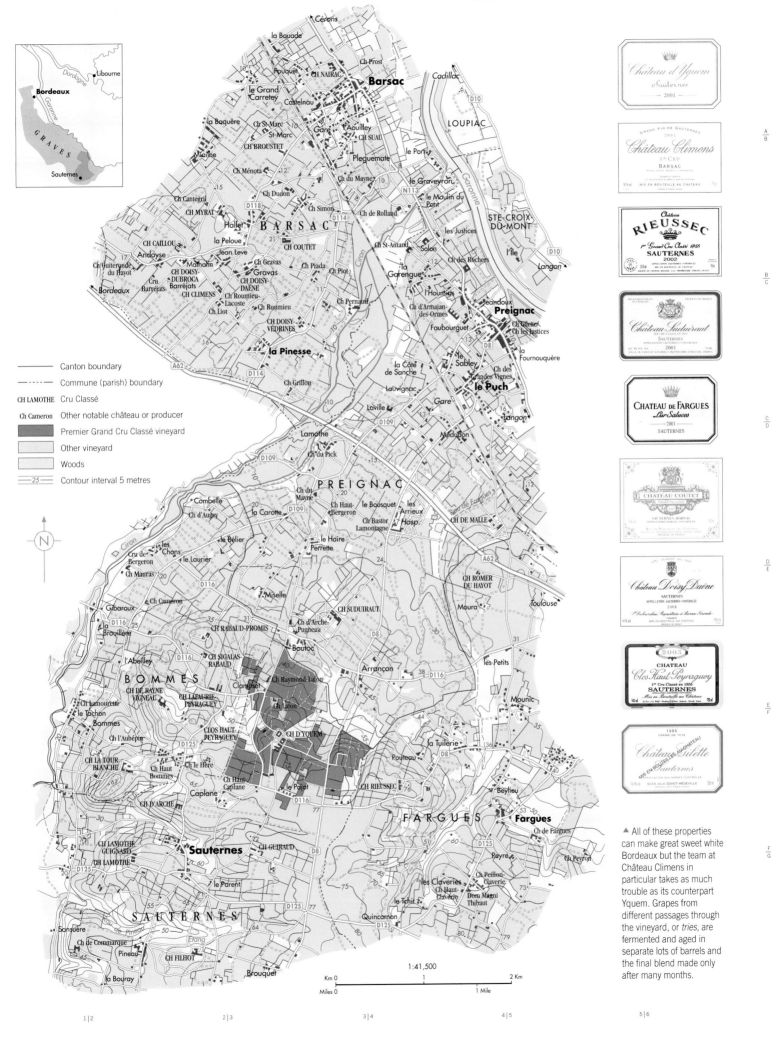

All of these properties can make great sweet white Bordeaux but the team at Château Climens in particular takes as much trouble as its counterpart Yquem. Grapes from different passages through the vineyard, or *tries*, are fermented and aged in separate lots of barrels and the final blend made only after many months.

The Right Bank

This map provides an overview of Bordeaux's most dynamic region, named "right bank" by Anglo-Saxons in contrast to the Médoc and Graves on the "left bank" of the Gironde. The French call it the Libournais after its ancient capital, Libourne, Bordeaux's second centre of wine commerce. Historically Libourne supplied northern Europe with simple and satisfying wines from its neighbouring vineyards, Fronsac, St-Emilion, and Pomerol. Belgium was Libourne's chief market.

Today two of these names are as famous as any and more expensive than most. Pomerol and St-Emilion are described in detail on succeeding pages, but what we can see here are the wine areas that surround them and, to judge from the many notable producers mapped, just how lively they are in the 21st century.

A good example, and the most distinctive, are the twin appellations of **Fronsac** and **Canon-Fronsac**, west of Libourne. When the leading Libourne négociant J-P Moueix, which had until then been the most significant proprietor, apparently washed its hands of them in 2000, selling several notable properties to the Halley family of French supermarket Carrefour fame, many saw this as the beginning of the end. But in fact it has signalled a surge for this gentle wooded district of sudden hills, with several well-heeled outsiders supplying the will and means to give Fronsac in particular a vigour it has lacked for centuries.

There was a time when Fronsac was widely admired as a historic region in its own right and it is certainly true that its best wines are distinguished by being not just splendidly fruity in typical right bank manner, but also more characterfully rigorous, more tannic when young. They are rustic in style compared with the high gloss of, say, the finest Pomerol, but they are improving year by year with investment in modernization. The limestone slopes along the river are known as Canon-Fronsac, although even locals can sometimes be at a loss to describe what differentiates the two appellations.

The outlying vineyards of Pomerol are clustered around the villages of Néac and **Lalande-de-Pomerol** and qualify for the appellation named after the latter. They are generally less vivid than wines from the plateau of Pomerol itself but the key to quality as in much of the area mapped on these two pages is often investment by the owner of a grander property. Thus, for example, La Fleur de Boüard in Lalande-de-Pomerol benefits from the equipment and expertise of the family that owns Château Angélus in St-Emilion.

A similar phenomenon is evident in the easternmost appellations of the right bank, **Côtes de Castillon** and (off the map to the east) **Côtes de Francs**. Both Château Les Charmes Godard and Château Puygueraud are part of the many holdings of the Belgian Thienpont family (others include Vieux Château Certan and Le Pin). In Côtes de Castillon, only the western sector of which is mapped here, Château d'Aiguilhe shares an owner with Château Canon-la-Gaffelière in St-Emilion, Château Joanin Bécot is part of a major conglomeration of smarter right bank properties, and Clos Puy Arnaud is a sister property to St-Emilion's Troplong Mondot.

St-Emilion's so-called "satellites" are four villages north of the town, **Montagne**, **Lussac**, **Puisseguin**, and **St-Georges**, which are all

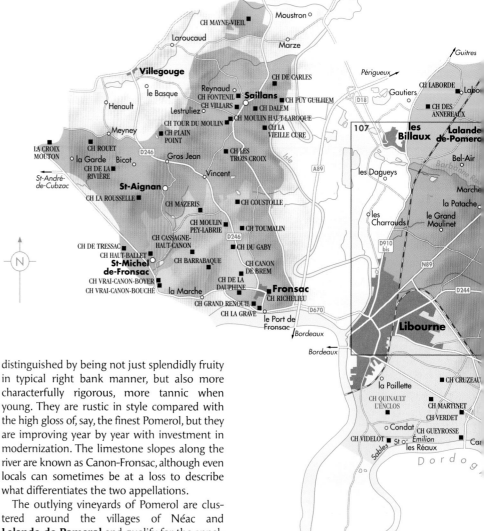

Vineyards near Cassoret, in the Côtes de Francs, one of the many outlying appellations on the right bank whose fortunes were revived in the late 20th century. Vines are often trained higher than in the grander St-Emilion appellation to the west to allow (cheaper) picking by machine rather than by hand.

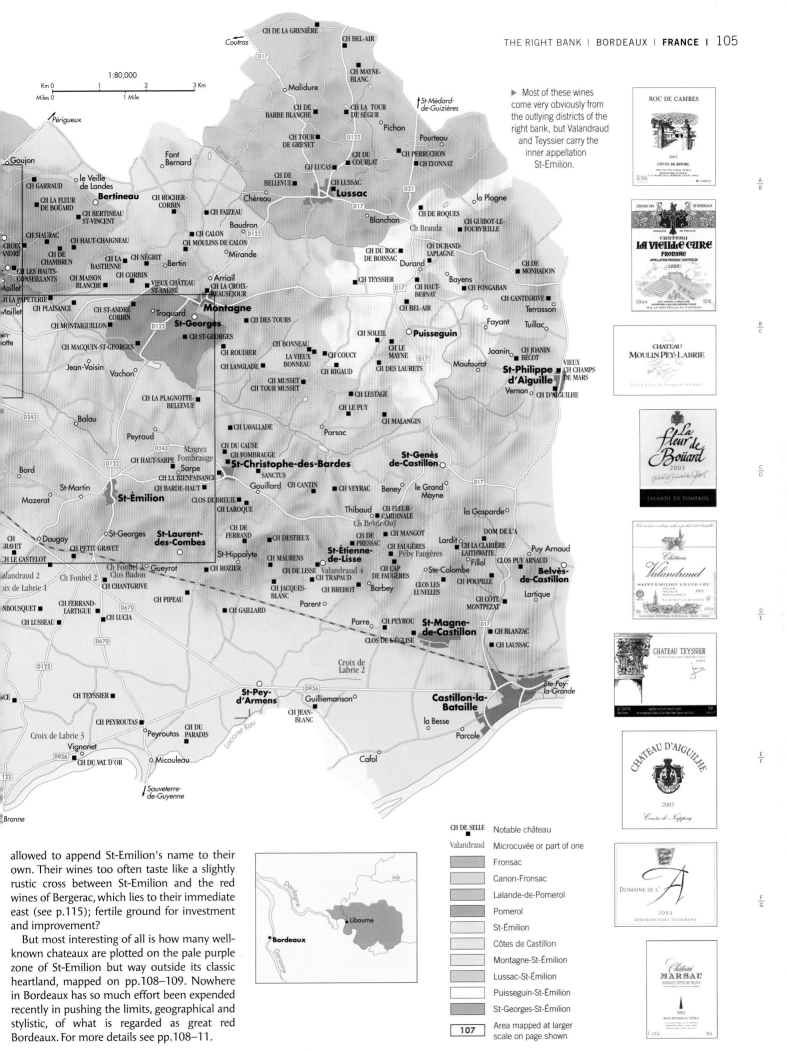

▶ Most of these wines come very obviously from the outlying districts of the right bank, but Valandraud and Teyssier carry the inner appellation St-Emilion.

Map labels:

CH DE LA GRENIÈRE · CH BEL-AIR · Coutras · CH MAYNE-BLANC · Malidure · St-Médard-de-Guizières · CH DE BARBE BLANCHE · CH LA TOUR DE SÉGUR · Pichon · CH TOUR DE GRENET · CH DU COURLAT · Pourteau · CH PERRUCHON · CH LYONNAT · CH LUCAS · CH DE BELLEVUE · CH LUSSAC · **Lussac** · la Plagne · CH GARRAUD · le Veille de Landes · CH ROCHER-CORBIN · Chéreau · CH DE ROQUES · Font Bernard · Goujon · CH LA FLEUR DE BOÜARD · CH BERTINEAU ST-VINCENT · CH FAIZEAU · Baudron · Ch Branda · CH GUIBOT-LE-FOURVIEILLE · **Bertineau** · CH SIAURAC · CH HAUT-CHAIGNEAU · CH CALON · CH MOULINS DE CALON · Mirande · CH DU ROC DE BOISSAC · Durand · CH DURAND-LAPLAGNE · CH DE MONBADON · CROIX ANDRÉ · CH DE CHAMBRUN · CH LA BASTIENNE · CH NÉGRIT · Bertin · CH TEYSSIER · Bayens · CH FONGABAN · CH LES HAUTS-CONSEILLANTS · CH MAISON BLANCHE · CH CORBIN · VIEUX CHÂTEAU ST-ANDRÉ · Arriail · CH HAUT-BERNAT · CH CANTEGRIVE · Terrasson · Maillet · CH LA CROIX-BEAUSÉJOUR · CH BEL-AIR · H LA PAPETERIE · CH PLAISANCE · CH ST-ANDRÉ CORBIN · **Montagne** · Fayant · Tuillac · CH MONTAIGUILLON · Troquard · CH DES TOURS · CH SOLEIL · **Puisseguin** · Joanin · CH JOANIN BÉCOT · **St-Georges** · CH ST-GEORGES · CH BONNEAU · CH LE MAYNE · VIEUX CH CHAMPS DE MARS · CH MACQUIN-ST-GEORGES · CH ROUDIER · LA VIEUX BONNEAU · CH COUCY · **St-Philippe d'Aiguille** · Jean-Voisin · Vachon · CH LANGLADE · CH RIGAUD · CH DES LAURETS · Vernon · CH D'AIGUILHE · CH MUSSET · CH TOUR MUSSET · CH LESTAGE · Balau · CH LA PLAGNOTTE-BELLEVUE · CH LE PUY · Peyraud · CH LAVALLADE · Parsac · CH MALANGIN · Bord · Magrez Fombrauge · CH DU CAUSE · St-Martin · CH HAUT-SARPE · CH POMBRAUGE · **St-Christophe-des-Bardes** · **St-Genès de-Castillon** · Mazerat · Sarpe · SANCTUS · CH LA BIENFAISANCE · Gouillard · CH CANTIN · CH VEYRAC · Beney · le Grand Mayne · St-Martin · CH BARDE-HAUT · CH FLEUR-CARDINALE · la Gasparde · **St-Émilion** · CLOS DUBREUIL · Thibaud · Ch Belair-Ouÿ · CH LAROQUE · CH DE FERRAND · St-Hippolyte · CH DE PRESSAC · DOM DE L'A · St-Georges · CH DESTIEU · CH MANGOT · Lardit · CH LA CLARIÈRE LAITHWAITE · Puy Arnaud · **St-Laurent-des-Combes** · CH FAUGÈRES · Péby Faugères · Fillol · CLOS PUY ARNAUD · GRAVET · CH PETIT GRAVET · Gueyrot · CH MAURENS · **St-Étienne-de-Lisse** · CH CAP DE FAUGÈRES · **Belvès-de-Castillon** · CH LE CASTELOT · Ch Fonbel 3 · CH ROZIER · CH DE LISSE · Valandraud 4 · Ste-Colombe · CH POUPILLE · Clos Badon · CH TRAPAUD · CLOS LES LUNELLES · Lartique · Valandraud 2 · CH FONBEL · Clos Badon · CH CHANTGRIVE · CH JACQUES-BLANC · CH BREHOT · Barbey · CH CÔTE MONTPEZAT · oix de Labrie 1 · Ch Fonbel 2 · CH FERRAND-LARTIGUE · CH PIPEAU · Parent · CH GAILLARD · Parre · CH PEYROU · **St-Magne-de-Castillon** · CH BLANZAC · CH LUSSEAU · CH LUCIA · CLOS DE L'ÉGLISE · CH LAUSSAC · Croix de Labrie 2 · Ste-Foy-la-Grande · CH TEYSSIER · **St-Pey-d'Armens** · Guilliemanson · **Castillon-la-Bataille** · CH PEYROUTAS · CH JEAN-BLANC · la Besse · Croix de Labrie 3 · Peyroutas · CH DU PARADIS · Parcole · Vignonet · Micouleau · Cafol · CH DU VAL D'OR · Sauveterre-de-Guyenne · Branne

Rivers/roads: Lavie Rau · Lacoret Rau · D17 · D21 · D122 · D243 · D670 · D936 · Périgueux

---

allowed to append St-Emilion's name to their own. Their wines too often taste like a slightly rustic cross between St-Emilion and the red wines of Bergerac, which lies to their immediate east (see p.115); fertile ground for investment and improvement?

But most interesting of all is how many well-known chateaux are plotted on the pale purple zone of St-Emilion but way outside its classic heartland, mapped on pp.108–109. Nowhere in Bordeaux has so much effort been expended recently in pushing the limits, geographical and stylistic, of what is regarded as great red Bordeaux. For more details see pp.108–11.

Inset map: Dordogne · Isle · Libourne · **Bordeaux** · Garonne

Legend:

CH DE SELLE ■ Notable château
Valandraud — Microcuvée or part of one
Fronsac
Canon-Fronsac
Lalande-de-Pomerol
Pomerol
St-Émilion
Côtes de Castillon
Montagne-St-Émilion
Lussac-St-Émilion
Puisseguin-St-Émilion
St-Georges-St-Émilion
107 — Area mapped at larger scale on page shown

Wine labels (right margin): ROC DE CAMBES 2001 CÔTES DE BOURG · CHÂTEAU LA VIEILLE CURE FRONSAC 2000 · CHATEAU MOULIN PEY-LABRIE · La fleur de Boüard 2003 LALANDE DE POMEROL · Château VALANDRAUD SAINT-EMILION GRAND CRU 2003 · CHATEAU TEYSSIER 2004 · CHATEAU D'AIGUILHE 2003 · DOMAINE DE L'A 2003 · Château MARSAU BORDEAUX CÔTES DE FRANCS 2004

Pomerol

Although Pomerol is, relatively speaking, a new star in the firmament of Bordeaux, its most sought-after wines can fetch a higher price than the much larger first-growths of the Médoc, and an astonishing number of small properties, for an area no bigger than St-Julien, are generally agreed to be among the best in the whole of Bordeaux.

Pomerol is such a curious corner of the world that it is hard to get your bearings. There is no real village centre. Almost identical small roads criss-cross the plateau apparently at random. Every family seems to make wine, and every house stands apart among its vines. The landscape is evenly dotted with modest houses – each rejoicing in the name of château. The church stands oddly isolated too, like yet another little wine estate. And that is Pomerol; there is nothing more to see.

Geologically it is another big gravel bank, slightly rising and falling but remarkably flat overall. Towards Libourne the soil tends to be sandy while to the east and north, where it meets St-Emilion, it is often enriched with clay.

What grows here is the gentlest, richest, most velvety, and instantly appealing form of red Bordeaux. Good Pomerols have deep colour without the marked acidity and tannin that often go with it, a ripe-plummy, even creamy smell, and sometimes a great concentration of all their qualities: the striking essence of a great wine.

Pomerol is a democracy. It has no classification, and indeed it would be very hard to devise one. There is no long tradition of steady selling to build on. Châteaux are small family affairs and subject to change as individuals come and go. Nor is the complexity of the soil, as it switches from gravel to gravelly clay to clay with gravel, or from sandy gravel to gravelly sand, exactly reflected in vineyard boundaries.

There is a good deal of agreement, however, about which are Pomerol's outstanding vineyards. Château Pétrus was for years allowed by all to come first, with perhaps Trotanoy as runner-up – though Vieux Château Certan ("VCC") would contest this. Then along came Le Pin, microscopic even by Pomerol standards (hardly five acres/3ha), the creation of Jacques Thienpont, a member of the Belgian family that also owns VCC.

Wine made in such tiny quantity can be hand-reared with what was originally the exceptionally demanding technique of conducting the second softening malolactic fermentation in individual barrels. The result is an ultra-wine, with an excess of everything, including charm (and of course scarcity), and this has been reflected in prices sometimes higher than those of Pétrus.

The map opposite distinguishes in capitals the growths whose wines currently fetch the highest prices. Clos l'Eglise and Châteaux Clinet, L'Eglise-Clinet (how confusing these names are), and La Fleur de Gay are relatively

recent jewels in the Pomerol crown. Châteaux La Fleur-Pétrus, La Conseillante, L'Evangile, Lafleur, and Latour à Pomerol all have long track records of excellence.

The tight grouping of these châteaux on the clay soil is an indication of their character as well as their quality. These properties generally make the densest, fleshiest, and most opulent wines. Rather than being overwhelmed by the complications of Pomerol it is worth knowing that the average standard here is very high. The village has a name for reliability. Bargains, on the other hand, are not often found.

The most potent influence in the district is the *négoces* (merchant-houses) of Libourne, led with authority and style by the family firm of Jean-Pierre Moueix, which either owns or manages a high proportion of the finest properties. They renamed and rebuilt Hosanna (once Château Certan Guiraud) next to Pétrus, and nearby Providence (formerly Château la Providence) was relaunched by the Moueixes with the 2005 vintage.

One advantage that has certainly helped the popularity of this little region is the fact that its wines are ready relatively soon for Bordeaux. The chief grape here is not the tough-skinned

A familiar sight for those attempting to navigate the monocultural plateau of Pomerol. Can all these famous châteaux really be so close together? Yes, because they are all so small – which does nothing to keep prices down.

Cabernet Sauvignon, whose wine has to live through a tannic youth; in Pomerol it is Merlot, secondary in the Médoc, that is the leading vine. Great growths have about 70–80% Merlot, with perhaps 20% Cabernet Franc, known here as Bouchet. The greatest Pomerol, Pétrus, is almost exclusively Merlot, growing in almost pure clay – with astonishing results.

Even the best Pomerol has produced all its perfume and achieved its dazzling finesse within a dozen years or so, and many are already attractive at five years old.

◄ The average annual total production at each of these top Pomerol properties varies from 600 to 3,000 cases of wine – and prices tend to vary inversely. The trick should be to find a property whose size is as great as its ambition – but this is far from easy in a very small appellation which has already been subdivided many a time.

St-Emilion

The ancient and beautiful town of St-Emilion, epicentre of what is currently Bordeaux's most seismic wine region, is propped in the corner of an escarpment above the Dordogne. Behind it on the sand and gravel plateau vines flow steadily on into Pomerol. Beside it along the ridge they swoop down steep limestone slopes (the Côtes) into the plain.

It is the little but much-visited rural gem of the Bordeaux region – inland and upland in spirit, Roman in origin, hollow with cellars, and heady with wine. Even the church at St-Emilion is a cellar: cut, like them all, out of solid rock. The hotel restaurant in the town square is actually on the church roof, and you sit beside the belfry to eat your lampreys stewed in red wine *à la bordelaise*.

St-Emilion makes rich red wine. Before many people can really come to terms with the dryness and slight asperity of Médoc wines, they love the solid tastiness of St-Emilion. The best made in ripe and sunny seasons grow almost sweet as they mature.

The grapes of St-Emilion are the plump Merlot and the Cabernet Franc. Cabernet Sauvignon can have problems ripening in this climate, less tempered by the ocean, especially in its damper, cooler soils. On the whole the wines here take less time to reach perfection than Médoc wines, if a little longer than Pomerols: say four years for the wine of a poor vintage; eight and upwards for a good one. Yet the best can live as long.

The classification of St-Emilion is much more rigorously topical than that of the Médoc. Every

10 years or so (most recently in 2006) it revises its candidates for Premiers Grands Crus Classés and Grands Crus Classés. Other St-Emilions may be described as Grand Cru without the Classé (careful label inspection is needed). There are currently 13 of the first, plus Cheval Blanc and Ausone in a separate – seemingly permanent – super-category of two, and 46 of the second. The plain Grands Crus run into hundreds. The most recent promotions to Premier Grand Cru Classé were Châteaux Pavie Macquin and Troplong Mondot, and even quite famous properties may be demoted.

But there is an increasing number of wines, some of them highly sought-after, which operate outside the classification system. In the early

◀ St-Emilion's admirable classification system, updated every 10 years, promoted both Troplong Mondot and Pavie Macquin to Grand Cru Classé status in 2006. La Mondotte, a special plot cossetted by the owners of Château Canon-la-Gaffelière, is coincidentally geographically very close to Château Tertre Roteboeuf, which also operates outside the official classification. Ausone and Cheval Blanc are top of the tree.

MONTAGNE-ST-ÉMILION

ST-GEORGES-ST-ÉMILION

Ch Franc Maillet
Ch Vieux Maillet
Guadeleyrat
Ch le Bon Pasteur
Ch Haut-Maillet
la Croix Chante-Caille
Ch l'Evangile
Montagne
Ch Croqué Michotte
le Jura
Ch Grand-Corbin-Despagne
Ch Haut Corbin
Ch la Grave Figeac
Ch Corbin Michotte
Ch Corbin
Vieux Château St-André
Maison Neuve
Montagne
CH CHEVAL BLANC
Ch la Dominique
Ch Grand Corbin
Chasteau
Ch Jean Voisin
Vachon
Ch Ripeau
Clos Grand Faurie
Ch Trimoulet
Sarrensot
CH FIGEAC
Ch Chauvin
le Fougueyrat
la Rose
Ch la Fleur
Merissac
Petit Montlabert
Bézineau
Ch Dassault
la Croix Figeac
Clos de l'Oratoire
Peyraud
Barrail Figeac (Hotel)
Ch la Marzelle
Ch Rol Valentin
Ch Moulin du Cadet
Ch Cap-de-Mourlin
Ch Haut-Segottes
Balau
Ch Larmande
Ch Faurie de Souchard
Côte de Baleau
Ch Laniote
Ch Fonroque
le Cadet
Ch Yon-Figeac
Ch la Gomerie
Ch Petit Faurie de Soutard
St-Christophe-des-Bardes
Ch Laroze
Ch Soutard
Ch Clos des Jacobins
Ch Cadet-Piola
Magnan
Ch Cadet-Bon
St-Christophe-des-Bardes
Jacquemeau
Ch Franc Mayne
Ch Gaudet-St-Julien
Ch Balestard la Tonnelle
Sarpe
Clos de Sarpe
Ch Grand Mayne
Ch Grand-Pontet
le Rivalon
Bord
le Dôme
Ch Bellevue
Ch Grandes Murailles
Clos St-Julien
Ch la Coupaude
Ch Sansonnet
CH TROTTEVIEILLE
Gaubert
CH BEAU-SÉJOUR BÉCOT
CLOS FOURTET
Ch Villemaurine
Couvent des-Jacobins
Ch la Serre
St-Christophe
le Barrail
CH ANGÉLUS
Clos St-Martin
CH BEAUSÉJOUR HÉRITIERS DUFFAU-LAGARROSSE
Ch Bergat
Ch le Prieuré
CH CANON
Ch Bardel Haut
Fonrazade
Ch Gracia
Mazerat
St-Émilion
Ch la Clotte
CH PAVIE MACQUIN
Ch Roylland
Ch Matras
Ch de Valandraud
CH TROPLONG MONDOT
Ch Berliquet
Ch de Valandraud
CH MAGDELAINE
Clos La Madeleine
CH AUSONE
Ch Moulin St-Georges
ST-LAURENT
Pin de Fleur
CH BÉLAIR
les Carrières
Libourne
Ch Carteau Côtes Daugay
Ch Fonplégade
CH LA GAFFELIÈRE
St-Georges
Ch Pavie Décesse
la Mondotte
Ch Tertre-Daugay
St-Georges Côte Pavie
Ch Bellevue Mondotte
Ch l'Arrosée
Godeau
Ch lé Tertre Roteboeuf
Castillon-la-Bataille
Cave Co-op
CH PAVIE
Ch Rochebelle
St-Laurent des-Combes
Ch Canon-la-Gaffelière
Valandraud 3
Ch Larcis Ducasse
vers D670
l'Arsis
Ch Bellefont-Belcier
Ch Lassègue
Gueyrot

Libourne
Bordeaux
Isle
Dordogne
Garonne

Canton boundary
Commune (parish) boundary
CH AUSONE   Premier Grand Cru Classé (2006)
Ch Laroze   Grand Cru Classé
Ch la Fleur   Other notable château
Ch Rol Valentin   Microcuvée or part of one
Premier Grand Cru Classé (A) vineyard
Other vineyard
Woods
—25—   Contour interval 5 metres

1:26,400

Km 0   1 Km
Miles 0   1/2 Mile

1980s Château Tertre Roteboeuf was one of the first properties to be taken under new, fanatical management and pushed to the limits of quality and desirability without seeking official rank. Since then, dozens if not hundreds of the 800-odd châteaux to be found within this appellation have been modernized, and their wines made generally smoother, less rustic, and more concentrated.

Another new, arguably less benevolent, wave began in the early 1990s with the emergence of Château Valandraud, a fiercely unfiltered, concentrated wine conjured up by local négociant Jean-Luc Thunevin from a few tiny parcels of vines. This was the first of St-Emilion's "microcuvées" or "garage wines" (so-called because they tend to be made in such small quantities they can be made in a garage) and it spawned an army of them, appearing as if from nowhere. Those which seem to have established at least some reputation are marked in magenta on the map but many came and went without reaping the expected financial rewards. The formula is to produce extremely obvious wines in quantities minute enough (generally less than 1,000 cases) to create demand. It often works.

Meanwhile, the extensive St-Emilion appellation has also attracted more than its fair share of newcomer investors who have typically bought vineyard, invested heavily in winemaking equipment, and hired one of several high-profile oenologists who specialize in this area. Michel Rolland, Stéphane Derenoncourt, and Pascal Chatonnet are the best-known. In this respect, and even in the style of some of its more deliberately modernist wines, St-Emilion has a certain unexpected similarity with California's Napa Valley. The hand of man and mammon can seem particularly powerful here.

There are two distinct districts of St-Emilion, not counting the lesser vineyards of the river plain and the parishes to the east and northeast that are allowed to use the name (described and mapped on pp.104–105). See opposite for more detail on the particularly varied soil types throughout the St-Emilion appellation.

One group of the finest châteaux lies on the border of Pomerol, on the western edge of St-Emilion's sandy and gravelly plateau. The most famous of this group is Cheval Blanc, a trim, cream-painted house in a grove of trees which is far from suggesting the splendid red wine, one of the world's most beautifully balanced, that its predominantly Cabernet Franc vines produce. Of Cheval Blanc's neighbours, it is the big Château Figeac which comes nearest to its level, but in a more restrained, reticent though eventually very fragrant style, from even more gravelly soil and with, unusually, a significant proportion of Cabernet Sauvignon.

The other, larger, group, the Côtes St-Emilion, occupies the escarpment around and to the east of the town towards St-Laurent-des-Combes. A particularly propitious, south-facing slope flanks the southern tip of the town from Tertre Daugay via the Pavies to Tertre Roteboeuf. The plateau ends so abruptly that it is easy to see just how

Château Bélair is the next door neighbour of first-growth Château Ausone and, similarly, can boast extraordinary cellars created from limestone, quarried to build the town of St-Emilion which lies above.

thin a layer of soil covers the soft but solid limestone in which the cellars are hewn (see above). At the revitalized Château Ausone, the jewel of the Côtes, in one of the finest situations in all Bordeaux overlooking the Dordogne Valley, you can walk into a cellar with vines, as it were, on the ground floor above you.

The Côtes wines may not be quite so fruity as the "Graves" wines from the plateau (the name Graves is confusingly applied to them because of their gravel soil), but at their best they are some of the most perfumed and "generous" wines of Bordeaux. They are typically more alcoholic than wine from the Médoc. The Côtes provide shelter from the north and west, an incline towards the sun, and relative immunity to frost. On the plateau around Château Cheval Blanc, on the other hand, a slight dip in the ground acts as a sump in which freezing air can collect on cloudless winter nights.

In a remarkably short time St-Emilion has been transformed from a sleepy backwater into a hotbed of ambition and heavily touted new labels, but the comfort of St-Emilion to the ordinary wine-lover is the number of other châteaux of moderate fame and consistently high standards which can provide utterly enjoyable and relatively affordable wine.

THE TERROIRS OF ST-EMILION

The soil map of the St-Emilion appellation below, based on extensive research undertaken by Cornelis Van Leeuwen at the University of Bordeaux for the Syndicat Viticole de St-Emilion, shows just how dramatic are the variations in terroir within this complex appellation.

Much of the land south of the main road to Bergerac looks distinctly unpromising, with its recent alluvial deposits from the Dordogne, which are gravelly closer to the river's flood plain, sandy further away. Moving uphill towards St-Emilion itself we encounter sandy soils which we would expect to produce relatively light wine, but this soon gives way to the limestone base that is so obvious to visitors to the town. Soft *molasses du Fronsadais* (the same soil type as is found in Fronsac) forms the lower slopes and the much harder *calcaire à Asteries* the plateau, with clay-rich topsoil. It is hardly surprising that such good wine can be made from grapes grown on the so-called Côtes. These slopes around the town are the result of the work of the Dordogne, Isle, and then Barbanne rivers on Tertiary deposits in the Quaternary period. Note, too, the islands that are richer in loam than clay, particularly the one north of St-Hippolyte.

But northwest of the town is an extensive swathe of quite different shallow sandy soils that is relieved most dramatically by the mound of gravel on the Pomerol border where Châteaux Figeac and Cheval Blanc are to be found.

This map explains very clearly why Figeac and Cheval Blanc can taste so similar, and why the two Premiers Grands Crus Classés A, Cheval Blanc and Ausone, are so very different in style.

In theory terroirs don't change but Alain Vauthier's new regime at Château Ausone has entailed landscaping the Côtes. The wines have certainly changed enormously – they have been much more concentrated since 1995.

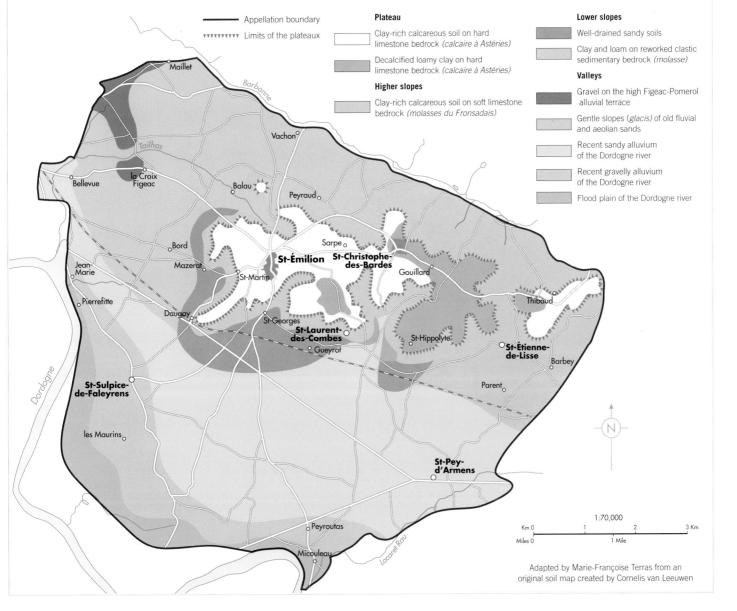

Appellation boundary

Limits of the plateaux

Plateau

Clay-rich calcareous soil on hard limestone bedrock (*calcaire à Astéries*)

Decalcified loamy clay on hard limestone bedrock (*calcaire à Astéries*)

Higher slopes

Clay-rich calcareous soil on soft limestone bedrock (*molasses du Fronsadais*)

Lower slopes

Well-drained sandy soils

Clay and loam on reworked clastic sedimentary bedrock (*molasse*)

Valleys

Gravel on the high Figeac-Pomerol alluvial terrace

Gentle slopes (*glacis*) of old fluvial and aeolian sands

Recent sandy alluvium of the Dordogne river

Recent gravelly alluvium of the Dordogne river

Flood plain of the Dordogne river

1:70,000

Km 0   1   2   3 Km
Miles 0   1 Mile

Adapted by Marie-Françoise Terras from an original soil map created by Cornelis van Leeuwen

Wines of the Southwest

South of the great vineyard of Bordeaux, west of the Midi, and sheltered from the Atlantic by the forests of the Landes, the vine flourishes in scattered areas which still have strong local gastronomic traditions, each by a river – the vine's old link to distant markets. This was the "High Country" that the jealous merchants of Bordeaux excluded from the port until their own wine (sometimes, to compound the injury, beefed up with sturdier stuff made upstream) was sold. The Bordeaux grape varieties may dominate the areas on the fringes of the Gironde département where Bordeaux wine is made (including wines of the Dordogne discussed overleaf), but elsewhere in this southwestern corner is France's most varied collection of indigenous wine grapes, many peculiar to their own small appellation.

Cahors, famous for the depth and longevity of its wines since the Middle Ages, is typical. Although it is often softened by some Merlot, it eschews both Cabernets Sauvignon and Franc and depends for its soul and flavour on a grape known here as Côt, in Argentina and Bordeaux as Malbec. Thanks to this grape, and to summers that are generally warmer than Bordeaux's, Cahors tends to be fuller and more vigorous, if a little more rustic, than typical red Bordeaux. But phylloxera literally decimated the region's vineyards, railways from the Languedoc severely reduced demand for their produce, and the fierce winter of 1956 ravaged such vineyards as remained.

Nowadays the busy town of Cahors finds itself upstream of most vineyards. Today, as shown on p.114, maize and sunflowers are also to be found on the three alluvial terraces above the River Lot planted with vines, of which the upper two are most highly regarded for their wine. Vineyards, reminiscent of English gardens with their neat grass and vine hedges, have also been planted higher up on the rocky *causses*. Cahors has attracted more than what seems its fair share of inward investment from well-heeled outsiders, whether from Paris or New York, and wine styles have evolved accordingly with some of the more expensive bottlings almost rivalling Mendoza's in build and obvious oak influence. A few dozen wines are chosen by a panel as representing Cahors Excellence each vintage.

As far again upstream from Cahors as Cahors is from the Gironde département boundary (and therefore marked on the map of France on p.53 rather than here) are the vineyards of the Aveyron département. Up in wild country are the last vestiges of the Massif Central's once-flourishing vignoble. **Marcillac** is the most important wine, a peppery red made from Fer Servadou, potentially hard as iron. Its multi-hued neighbours, **Vins d'Entraygues et du Fel** and **Vins d'Estaing**, are rare and becoming rarer, in contrast to the **Côtes de Millau** to the south whose mountain reds are made from a thorough southwestern cocktail of grapes.

The hill country around the River Tarn west of Albi, and downstream of the magnificent gorge cut by the river into the Cévennes, seems tame by comparison. Its rolling green pastureland is gentle in both aspect and climate, studded with beautiful towns and villages of which 73 are contained within the appellation

Gaillac. Wine was probably made here long before vines were cultivated downstream in Bordeaux but, as in Cahors, the phylloxera louse crippled the wine trade. It has been revived with real enthusiasm only in the last decade or so. Much of this is because of increased sophistication in matching the varied terroirs of Gaillac to its decidedly various vine varieties. The most characteristic red wine ingredients are the peppery local Braucol (Fer Servadou) and much lighter Duras. Syrah is a welcome intruder, Gamay less so for early-

Like most southwestern wine regions, the sporadic hillside vineyards of Irouléguy in the western Pyrenees are planted with indigenous vine varieties such as Petit Courbu, the Mansengs, and Tannat, a sign of just how long wine has been made here.

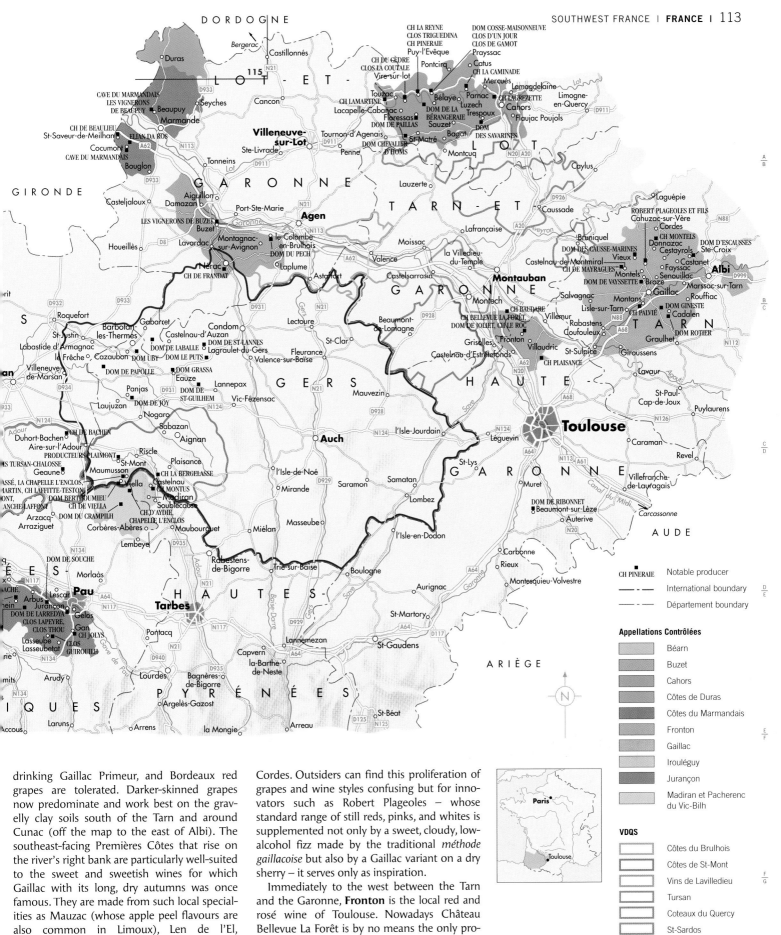

DORDOGNE

LOT-ET-

GIRONDE

GARONNE

TARN-ET

GERS

HAUTE-

GARONNE

TARN

AUDE

ARIÈGE

PYRÉNÉES

Appellations Contrôlées

Béarn

Buzet

Cahors

Côtes de Duras

Côtes du Marmandais

Fronton

Gaillac

Irouléguy

Jurançon

Madiran et Pacherenc du Vic-Bilh

VDQS

Côtes du Brulhois

Côtes de St-Mont

Vins de Lavilledieu

Tursan

Coteaux du Quercy

St-Sardos

Vin de Pays

Côtes de Gascogne

CH PINERAIE ■ Notable producer

— · — · — International boundary

— · — · — Département boundary

115 Area mapped at larger scale on page shown

drinking Gaillac Primeur, and Bordeaux red grapes are tolerated. Darker-skinned grapes now predominate and work best on the gravelly clay soils south of the Tarn and around Cunac (off the map to the east of Albi). The southeast-facing Premières Côtes that rise on the river's right bank are particularly well-suited to the sweet and sweetish wines for which Gaillac with its long, dry autumns was once famous. They are made from such local specialities as Mauzac (whose apple peel flavours are also common in Limoux), Len de l'El, Muscadelle, Sauvignon Blanc, and the relatively rare Ondenc. Modern white wines are typically off-dry and made with varying degrees of sparkle, including the gently fizzing Perlé, and are a speciality of the limestone vineyards to the north, notably around the hill town of

Cordes. Outsiders can find this proliferation of grapes and wine styles confusing but for innovators such as Robert Plageoles – whose standard range of still reds, pinks, and whites is supplemented not only by a sweet, cloudy, low-alcohol fizz made by the traditional *méthode gaillacoise* but also by a Gaillac variant on a dry sherry – it serves only as inspiration.

Immediately to the west between the Tarn and the Garonne, **Fronton** is the local red and rosé wine of Toulouse. Nowadays Château Bellevue La Forêt is by no means the only producer to make limpid, fruity red of the florally scented native Négrette grapes, mixed with sundry others of the southwest (and sometimes Syrah or Gamay). **Vins de Lavilledieu** and **Côtes du Brulhois** are similar wines made downstream, the latter stiffened by Tannat.

North of the vast sweep of vineyards devoted to Armagnac (and increasingly diverted into inexpensive crisp white Vin de Pays des Côtes de Gascogne), on the left bank of the Garonne, lies the appellation **Buzet**, whose production, from vineyards scattered over 27 communes of orchard and farm, is largely in the hands of one well-organized co-op. Its top wine, Château de Gueyze, stands comparison with a good Médoc.

The **Côtes du Marmandais**, even further north, has an excellent co-operative. Abouriou grapes spice up the Bordeaux blend that characterizes these parts.

The remaining wine regions on this map historically depended on the port of Bayonne rather than Bordeaux. The general **Béarn** appellation and its **Béarn-Bellocq** enclave, encompass the red, white, and rosé wines made outside the celebrated wine zones of Madiran and Jurançon, the two true jewels of the southwest.

Madiran is Gascony's great red wine, grown on clay and limestone hills along the left bank of the River Adour. The local red grape, Tannat, is well-named for its dark and tannic, tough and vigorous wines, often blended with some Cabernet and Pinenc (Fer Servadou). The region's dynamic winemakers differ on whether and how to tame these monsters, using varying degrees of new oak and even deliberate (micro-)oxygenation. Some of these wines can be drunk earlier but after seven or eight years fine Madiran is truly admirable: aromatic, full of flavour, fluid, and lively, well able to withstand both comparison with classed-growth Bordeaux and an accompanying *confit de canard*.

The winemaking talent of this region has been turning its attention to the local white too, not least the Plaimont co-operative union, which dominates production of the **Côtes de St-Mont** and has done much to rescue local vine varieties from extinction. Sweet and dry white **Pacherenc du Vic-Bilh** is made within the Madiran zone from Arrufiac, Petit Courbu, Gros and Petit Manseng grapes, and is more exciting every year, but tends to be overshadowed by its counterpart south of Pau, Jurançon.

Jurançon is one of France's most distinctive white wines, a tangy, green-tinged essence made in a wide range of sweetness levels on the steep Pyrenean foothills of Béarn. Gros Manseng grapes are responsible for the dry, earlier-picked Jurançon Sec while the smaller, thicker-skinned Petit Manseng berries are much more suitable for leaving on the vine into November, and sometimes even December, to shrivel and concentrate both sugars and acidity

The lazy River Lot is still flanked by some Cahors vines but the most admired vineyards are up to 650ft (200m) above the river on the stony limestone causses, where the yields are much lower and the wines have more structure.

(noble rot is not a feature of Jurançon). These sweet *moelleux* wines are lively enough to drink, as the French do, at the beginning of a meal, with the local foie gras for instance, and are perhaps closer to Vouvray in style than to the weight of a good Sauternes. Wines labelled Vendange Tardive are richer, made from even more shrivelled grapes picked during at least two passages through the vineyard.

Tursan, downstream of Madiran, is being revitalized, although red wines outnumber the interesting whites made from Baroque grapes.

The tiny appellation of **Irouléguy** makes France's only Basque wine: firm, refreshing rosé, red, and white wines of the local grapes, including Tannat, Petit Courbu, and the Mansengs, grown on south-facing terraces as high as 1,300ft (400m) above the Atlantic, their labels heavily adorned with Xs.

◀ Very varied labels for very varied wines. The Rotier Gaillac is a sweet wine of extraordinary intensity, Le Faite the top bottling of the innovative Plaimont group of co-ops, yet both are almost local secrets. Other obvious candidates would be the Marmandais wines of Elian da Ros and Château de Beaulieu.

Dordogne

The Bordeaux right bank's beautiful hinterland, the *bastide* country of the Dordogne leading back into the maze of green valleys cut into the stony upland of Périgueux, has long been a favourite with tourists. For them, the new dedication in the region's vineyards and cellars is a bonus.

Even the small **Côtes de Duras** appellation, effectively a bridge between Entre-Deux-Mers and Bergerac, produces a number of thoroughly respectable wines from Bordeaux grapes. Some reds, some sweet whites, but in particular zesty, dry Sauvignon Blanc.

Traditionally the wines of **Bergerac** were seen as country bumpkins beside the sophisticates of Bordeaux. The most ordinary red and dry white wines of the Dordogne département's catch-all appellation still resemble the most basic AC Bordeaux, with the same shortcomings, but there is now a critical mass of producers determined to prove that Bergerac can produce far more serious wines – of all three hues and, in whites, all sweetness levels. Luc de Conti of Château Tour des Gendres, a biodynamic convert, deserves considerable, although not exclusive, credit. Thanks to a combination of lower yields and mastery of cellar hygiene and oak ageing, the new wave of ambitious wine producers (not all of them French) is producing deep-flavoured, well-structured wines to rival some of Bordeaux's smartest appellations.

The grapes are the same as Bordeaux's. The climate is a little more extreme than that of the Atlantic-influenced Gironde, and there is limestone on higher ground. The range of whites is wide, if confusing, and worth exploring. Bergerac Sec can be a forceful dry white made from any combination of Sémillon and Sauvignon Blanc (although some serious sweet white is also produced, mainly for local consumption). Côtes de Bergerac distinguishes superior reds made within the Bergerac zone according to stricter rules.

Within the greater Bergerac region are many individual appellations – so many that some are virtually ignored. **Rosette**, for example, occupies a rather magnificent amphitheatre of vines north of the town of Bergerac, but only a handful of growers choose to sell their delicate, slightly sweet whites under this name. In the same area the appellation **Pécharmant** is celebrated almost exclusively locally for its full-bodied, sometimes-oaked reds.

Just over the departmental boundary from the Côtes de Castillon (see p.104) is the

complex **Montravel** white wine zone in which **Côtes de Montravel** and **Haut-Montravel** are sweeter wines coming from respectively the north and east of the area. Straight Montravel made all over the zone is a dry wine, made with increasing confidence, often using both Sauvignon Blanc and oak, while Sémillon is king of the sweet wines, which are remarkably like the best sweet whites made over the border in Côtes de Francs. Muscadelle is allowed here too. Merlot-dominated Montravel red now has its own appellation but the wine may be declassified to Bergerac if it does not pass muster with the local tasting committee.

The most distinctive, most glamorous wines of this part of France are sumptuously sweet, white, and made in dispiritingly small quantities in two zones southwest of the town of Bergerac. Indeed, the total production of **Saussignac**,

Monbazillac's western neighbour and home to some extraordinarily determined producers, is only a few thousand cases.

The total output of Bergerac's most famous wine, **Monbazillac**, is 30 times greater and average quality has improved considerably since 1993 when machine picking was abandoned in favour of several selective harvests by hand. Much lighter doses of sulphur dioxide have become the norm. Like the Sauternes region, Monbazillac lies just east of where a tributary flows into the left bank of a major river (in this case the Gardonette and the Dordogne). The permitted grapes are also the same, but the wines are not, one reason perhaps being Muscadelle's particular aptitude in Monbazillac. Botrytis may sweep through the vineyards of Monbazillac when there is none in Sauternes. The best young Monbazillacs, such as those of Château Tirecul La Gravière, are more exuberant, more sprightly than the best young Sauternes, whereas mature Monbazillac takes on an amber nuttiness that is decidedly uncharacteristic of Bordeaux's most famous sweet white wine.

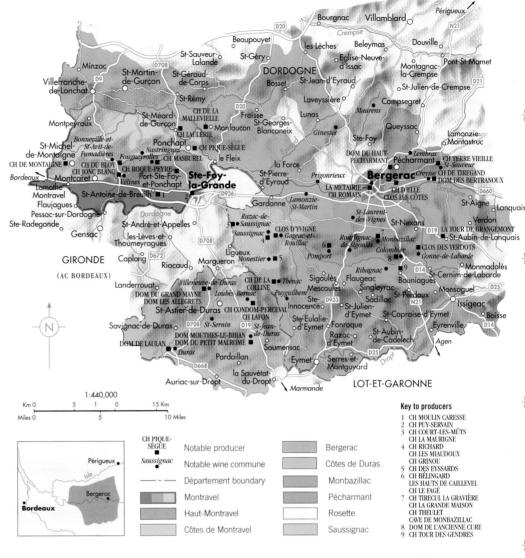

Km 0 ... 15 Km
Miles 0 ... 10 Miles

1:440,000

CH PIQUE-
SÈGUE ● Notable producer
Saussignac ● Notable wine commune
— — — Département boundary
Montravel
Haut-Montravel
Côtes de Montravel

Bergerac
Côtes de Duras
Monbazillac
Pécharmant
Rosette
Saussignac

Key to producers
1 CH MOULIN CARESSE
2 CH PUY-SERVAIN
3 CH COURT-LES-MÛTS
 CH LA MAURIGNE
4 CH RICHARD
 CH LES MIAUDOUX
 CH GRINOU
5 CH DES EYSSARDS
6 CH BÉLINGARD
 LES HAUTS DE CAILLEVEL
 CH LE FAGÉ
7 CH TIRECUL LA GRAVIÈRE
 CH LA GRANDE MAISON
 CH THEULET
 CAVE DE MONBAZILLAC
8 DOM DE L'ANCIENNE CURE
9 CH TOUR DES GENDRES

◄ Three great white wines with Miadoux's most voluptous red and the flagship dry white of Luc de Conti, who has acted as unofficial team leader for today's new generation of Bergerac vignerons. Gloire de Mon Père is the luscious red counterpart.

la Grande Vignolle

DOMAINE

Vineyards between the Loire and Domaine Filliatreau in Saumur-Champigny, which is built into the calcareous tuffeau that characterizes this popular appellation. Here the tuffeau is typically yellower, softer, and sandier than further upstream around Bourgueil and Chinon, where it is generally white.

LIATREAU

Loire Valley and Muscadet

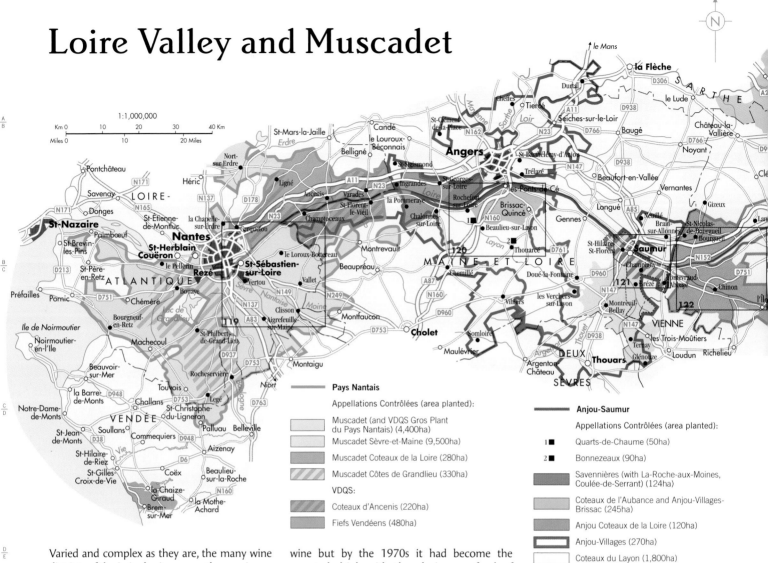

Pays Nantais

Appellations Contrôlées (area planted):

- Muscadet (and VDQS Gros Plant du Pays Nantais) (4,400ha)
- Muscadet Sèvre-et-Maine (9,500ha)
- Muscadet Coteaux de la Loire (280ha)
- Muscadet Côtes de Grandlieu (330ha)

VDQS:

- Coteaux d'Ancenis (220ha)
- Fiefs Vendéens (480ha)

Anjou-Saumur

Appellations Contrôlées (area planted):

1 ■ Quarts-de-Chaume (50ha)
2 ■ Bonnezeaux (90ha)
- Savennières (with La-Roche-aux-Moines, Coulée-de-Serrant) (124ha)
- Coteaux de l'Aubance and Anjou-Villages-Brissac (245ha)
- Anjou Coteaux de la Loire (120ha)
- Anjou-Villages (270ha)
- Coteaux du Layon (1,800ha)
- Saumur (1,450ha)
- Saumur-Champigny (1,500ha)
- Coteaux de Saumur (12ha)

Varied and complex as they are, the many wine districts of the Loire basin are worth mapping as a whole, for although they are so far-flung (see the map of France on p.53 for the outlying ones), with wide variations of climate, soil, and tradition, and four or five important grape varieties, the wines do have a family likeness. They are light and invigorating, with palpable acidity. The classic word for them is charming; the classic mystery that they are not more widely appreciated outside northern France. These wines are unwarranted casualties of the modern wine drinker's obsession with weight and strength.

It does not help that well over half of all Loire wines are white. They divide clearly between the dry wines to the east (Sancerre and Pouilly) and west (Muscadet), with the often-sweeter wines of Touraine and Anjou in the middle, made from the Loire's own grape, the much-traduced Chenin Blanc. The best reds of Touraine and Anjou, however, have all of the fragrance and charm of Cabernet Franc. New(ish) oak is used more than ever for both reds and whites; sulphur noticeably less. The best-known wines of the Loire are described and mapped on these and the next six pages.

Brittany's wine country – one might almost say Neptune's vineyard – is the Pays Nantais, the home of **Muscadet**. Muscadet was the first modern success story for the Loire. In the mid-20th century it was a little-known country

wine but by the 1970s it had become the accepted drink with the glorious seafood of northern France and the vineyard area accordingly doubled in size. Today it is being reined back to the most suitable sites. Muscadet is not expensive, and yet is perfect in context – very dry, slightly salty, but firm rather than acid: in fact in hot years it can lack acidity. Beside a plate of shrimps, oysters, or mussels it becomes one of gastronomy's most convincing clichés.

Muscadet is the name of the wine, not of a place or a grape (which in Muscadet's case is a cousin of Chardonnay, Melon de Bourgogne). The **Sèvre-et-Maine** region, which is mapped opposite in detail, has 85% of Muscadet's vineyards, densely planted on low hills of varied origin including most notably gneiss and granite. The heart of the district lies around Vertou, Vallet, St-Fiacre, and La Chapelle-Heulin – the area where the wines are ripest, liveliest, and most scented.

Muscadet Coteaux de la Loire made well inland on steep slopes of schist or granite tends to be a little leaner, while **Muscadet Côtes de Grandlieu**, made on sandy, stony soils, is suppler and riper than most.

Muscadet has traditionally been bottled *sur lie* – straight from the fermentation vat, unracked – the lees deepening both flavour and texture (as, in a different way, they do in champagne). The best producers are, happily,

determined to throw off Muscadet's reputation as a simple wine, carefully coaxing from their vines much healthier, riper grapes, experimenting with extended lees ageing, distinguishing between different soil types, and treating some of the most concentrated fruit to oak ageing in almost Burgundian idiom.

Outside the areas mapped in detail, **Jasnières** produces some fine, challengingly dry, Chenin Blanc and necessarily light reds and rosés from local Pineau d'Aunis grapes within the confusingly named **Coteaux du Loir** zone.

Cheverny meanwhile flourishes in myriad forms, of which some quite piercing Sauvignon Blanc is probably best; sharp, dry whites made from Romorantin are labelled **Cour-Cheverny**.

Irregular quality dogs growers this far north. Although global warming is having a marked effect, ripeness in many Loire vineyards can vary so widely from one year to another that they seem hardly to produce the same wine. A fine autumn ripens grapes almost to raisins, but a wet one can deliver a very acid product. Hence the importance of the sparkling wine industry here.

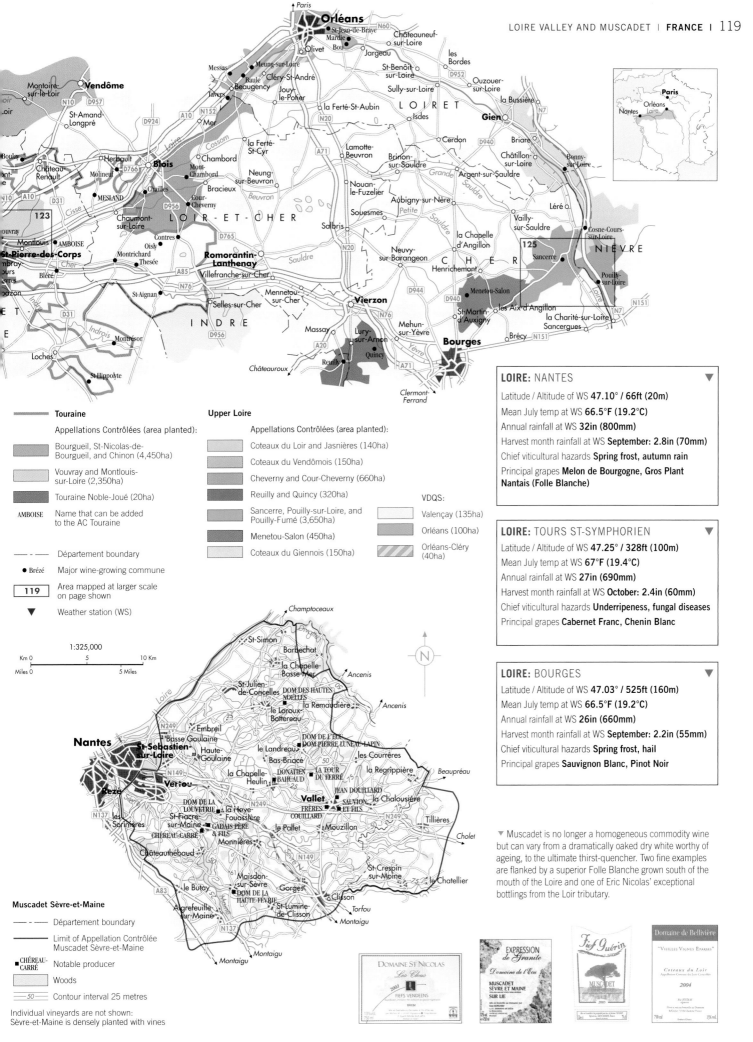

Touraine

Appellations Contrôlées (area planted):

Bourgueil, St-Nicolas-de-Bourgueil, and Chinon (4,450ha)

Vouvray and Montlouis-sur-Loire (2,350ha)

Touraine Noble-Joué (20ha)

AMBOISE Name that can be added to the AC Touraine

— - — Département boundary

● Brézé Major wine-growing commune

119 Area mapped at larger scale on page shown

▼ Weather station (WS)

Upper Loire

Appellations Contrôlées (area planted):

Coteaux du Loir and Jasnières (140ha)

Coteaux du Vendômois (150ha)

Cheverny and Cour-Cheverny (660ha)

Reuilly and Quincy (320ha)

Sancerre, Pouilly-sur-Loire, and Pouilly-Fumé (3,650ha)

Menetou-Salon (450ha)

Coteaux du Giennois (150ha)

VDQS:

Valençay (135ha)

Orléans (100ha)

Orléans-Cléry (40ha)

1:325,000

Km 0   5   10 Km
Miles 0   5 Miles

Muscadet Sèvre-et-Maine

— - — Département boundary

——— Limit of Appellation Contrôlée Muscadet Sèvre-et-Maine

■ CHÉREAU-CARRÉ Notable producer

Woods

—50— Contour interval 25 metres

Individual vineyards are not shown: Sèvre-et-Maine is densely planted with vines

LOIRE: NANTES ▼

Latitude / Altitude of WS **47.10° / 66ft (20m)**

Mean July temp at WS **66.5°F (19.2°C)**

Annual rainfall at WS **32in (800mm)**

Harvest month rainfall at WS **September: 2.8in (70mm)**

Chief viticultural hazards **Spring frost, autumn rain**

Principal grapes **Melon de Bourgogne, Gros Plant Nantais (Folle Blanche)**

LOIRE: TOURS ST-SYMPHORIEN ▼

Latitude / Altitude of WS **47.25° / 328ft (100m)**

Mean July temp at WS **67°F (19.4°C)**

Annual rainfall at WS **27in (690mm)**

Harvest month rainfall at WS **October: 2.4in (60mm)**

Chief viticultural hazards **Underripeness, fungal diseases**

Principal grapes **Cabernet Franc, Chenin Blanc**

LOIRE: BOURGES ▼

Latitude / Altitude of WS **47.03° / 525ft (160m)**

Mean July temp at WS **66.5°F (19.2°C)**

Annual rainfall at WS **26in (660mm)**

Harvest month rainfall at WS **September: 2.2in (55mm)**

Chief viticultural hazards **Spring frost, hail**

Principal grapes **Sauvignon Blanc, Pinot Noir**

▼ Muscadet is no longer a homogeneous commodity wine but can vary from a dramatically oaked dry white worthy of ageing, to the ultimate thirst-quencher. Two fine examples are flanked by a superior Folle Blanche grown south of the mouth of the Loire and one of Eric Nicolas' exceptional bottlings from the Loir tributary.

Anjou

The ideal and goal of Anjou has traditionally been sweet white wine, the product of autumn sunshine and noble rot. In the past, years without their benison produced little of value. But the last decade has seen a far more ambitious approach to dry white wine here too, amounting almost to a revolution. Seriously fine dry (Sec) white is now produced every year, thanks to picking by hand rather than the ubiquitous machine harvester, the strictest selection at harvest, and the sensitive use of oak.

The grape that gives us all this is the Chenin Blanc, called locally Pineau de la Loire. It can reach thrilling ripeness, sweetness with near perfect acid balance, in the southeast of the area mapped here, in the **Coteaux du Layon**. Here the Parisian Basin bumps up against the Massif Amoricain, creating buttes fully exposed south-southwest to the sun and to drying

winds straight off the Atlantic, which help to concentrate the grape sugars. The particularly well-protected **Quarts de Chaume** with only 120 acres (under 50ha) and **Bonnezeaux** (about double that) are outstanding enough to have appellations of their own, like Grands Crus in Burgundy.

The elusive River Aubance, parallel with the Layon to the south, also sees great sweet white wines, when Nature co-operates. **Coteaux de l'Aubance** has been invaded by what can seem like an army of talented wine producers.

Savennières lies north of the Loire, on one of its rare steep south-facing banks. Again it is Chenin Blanc, but here the wine is dry, as dense and rich in substance as it is rigid in structure. This combination of concentration and acidity deserves years in bottle. Within Savennières two

Grands Crus have their own sub-appellations: **La Roche aux Moines** with less than 70 acres (just under 30ha) and **La Coulée de Serrant** with a mere 12 fiercely biodynamic acres (5ha).

These are historically the most distinguished wines of Anjou, but the region's basic Anjou appellation has also been in a state of benevolent transformation. **Anjou Blanc** can nowadays be firm and characterful. Even the sickly **Rosé d'Anjou** is being overtaken by the delicately scented, off-dry rosé **Cabernet d'Anjou**.

Although soils here seem generally better suited to whites, Cabernet Franc has its place here too. Anjou's growers are mastering their vines and new oak barrels to become accomplished producers of aromatic reds. The best of these, occasionally stiffened by Cabernet Sauvignon, earn the appellation **Anjou-Villages**. In the best vintages they can provide the subtle thrill of a great Touraine red at half the price.

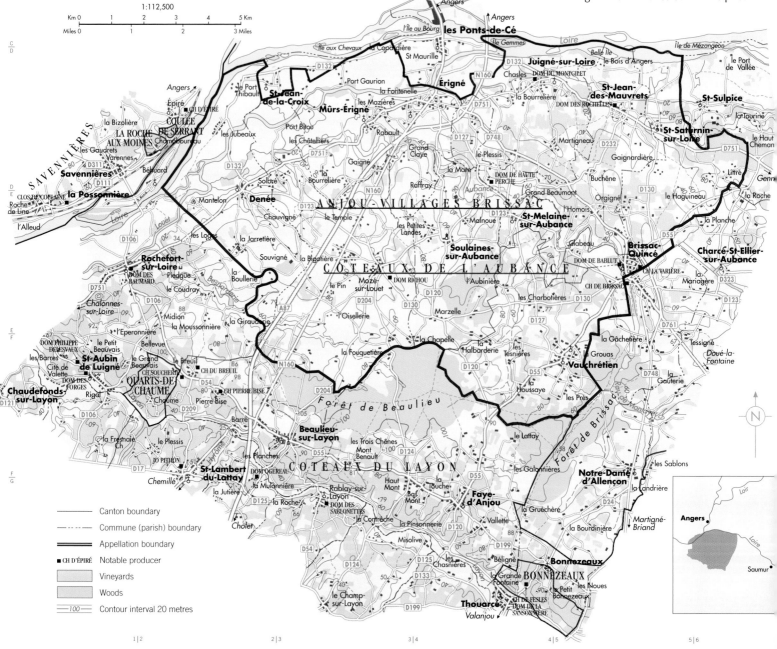

1:112,500

| Canton boundary |
| Commune (parish) boundary |
| Appellation boundary |
| CH D'ÉPIRÉ Notable producer |
| Vineyards |
| Woods |
| 100 Contour interval 20 metres |

Saumur

Carbon dioxide has long been vital to the wine economics of the Saumur region. As in Champagne it makes a virtue of acidity. Sparkling Saumur (appellation Mousseux) mops up the Chenin Blanc (and up to 10% Chardonnay) grown all over Saumur, and even parts of Anjou's Coteaux du Layon and Coteaux de l'Aubance, too tart to enjoy as a still wine.

The town of Saumur, lying 30 miles (48km) upstream of Angers, is the Loire's Reims and Epernay rolled into one, with kilometres of cellars carved in the soft local tuffeau. It is in the nature of Chenin Blanc to make more flirtatious fizz than the grapes used for champagne, but the best sparkling Saumurs – Brut and made by the traditional method – are not without ambition. They may have a component that was fermented in oak and another that has benefited from considerable age. In contrast, Crémant de Loire may contain grapes grown virtually anywhere in this long eastward stretch of the Loire but rules governing its production are stricter and the wines, generally, finer than Saumur Mousseux.

▼ A selection of some of the finest and most representative wines of both Anjou and Saumur today: three great sweet Anjou Chenins, one dry from Saumur, and a delicious red (Saumur-Champigny) whose maker Philippe Vatan is no fan of oak for his reds.

Still Saumur, without bubbles, comes in all three hues. It is much riper overall than it was a decade or two ago, but today much the most important wine made in the greater Saumur region is the fashionable red **Saumur-Champigny** from a small enclave of vineyards on the left bank of the River Loire. Vines are densely planted along the white cliffs by the river while inland, around the important wine centre of St-Cyr-en-Bourg with its reliable co-op, the local tuffeau becomes yellower and sandier and tends to produce slightly lighter wines.

A high proportion of cellars, such as these at Domaine des Vernes in this central stretch of the Loire, are hewn out of the tuffeau which provides the sort of temperature and humidity control that would cost a fortune to replicate elsewhere.

This is one of Cabernet Franc's most refreshing expressions, from tuffeau-dominated land that is effectively an extension of the best red wine country of Touraine just over the département boundary. As elsewhere in the Loire, reds are deeper and stronger thanks to the much-improved vine-growing, and climate change.

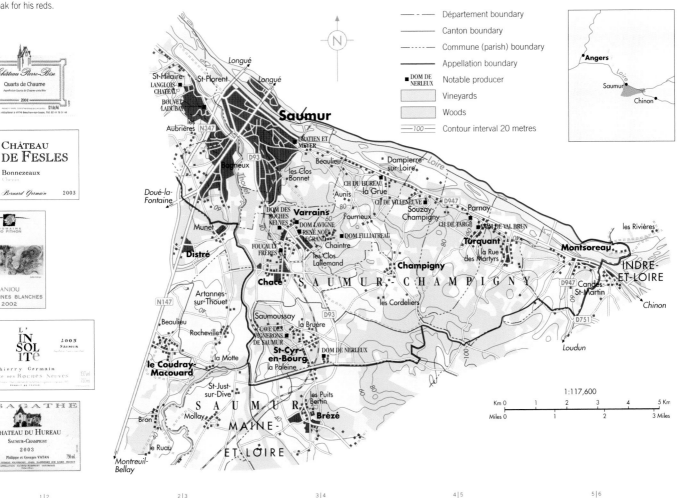

Chinon and Bourgueil

St-Nicolas-de-Bourgueil, Bourgueil, and Chinon make Touraine's and the Loire's best red wines. Saumur-Champigny (see previous page) is the only one that comes close. At this Atlantic-influenced western end of the Touraine, Cabernet Franc – known here as Breton – makes vigorous wine with raspberry fruitiness and the rasping savour of a freshly sharpened pencil. In an average year the purple new wine is excellent, drunk cool, within a few months of the vintage. In outstandingly ripe years such as 1997, 2003, and 2005, the wine has the substance and structure, like a good red bordeaux, to mature for a decade. For its quality it is absurdly undervalued.

Chinon makes the silkiest, most tender wine of the district from a patchwork of varied soils – whose produce is increasingly vinified separately. Vineyards on riverside sand and gravel make lighter, earlier-drinking styles of Chinon. Tuffeau, particularly the south-facing slopes of Cravant-les-Coteaux east of Chinon and the plateau above Beaumont to the west, tends to produce wines with the structure of a good **Bourgueil**, where steeper slopes and more limestone in the soil make wine which can improve for up to 10 years in bottle. **St-Nicolas-de-Bourgueil** has very similar soils to Bourgeuil.

A hundred years ago Chinon's wine was rated the equal of Margaux. In charm, if not in force or structure, it can come surprisingly close today and production is expanding accordingly. Very little white wine is made in Chinon.

The greater Touraine region produces a host of other, usually less serious, reds, rosés, and whites, all called **Touraine** but sometimes with the geographical suffixes Amboise, Azay-le-Rideau, or Mesland. **Touraine Noble Joué** is an unusually dry, characterful rosé, or vin gris, made on the southern outskirts of Tours between Esvres and Joué-lès-Tours from Pinots Meunier, Noir, and Gris. A dizzying range of grapes is allowed but light Gamay is characteristic for reds, and Sauvignon, sometimes extremely good value, for zesty whites.

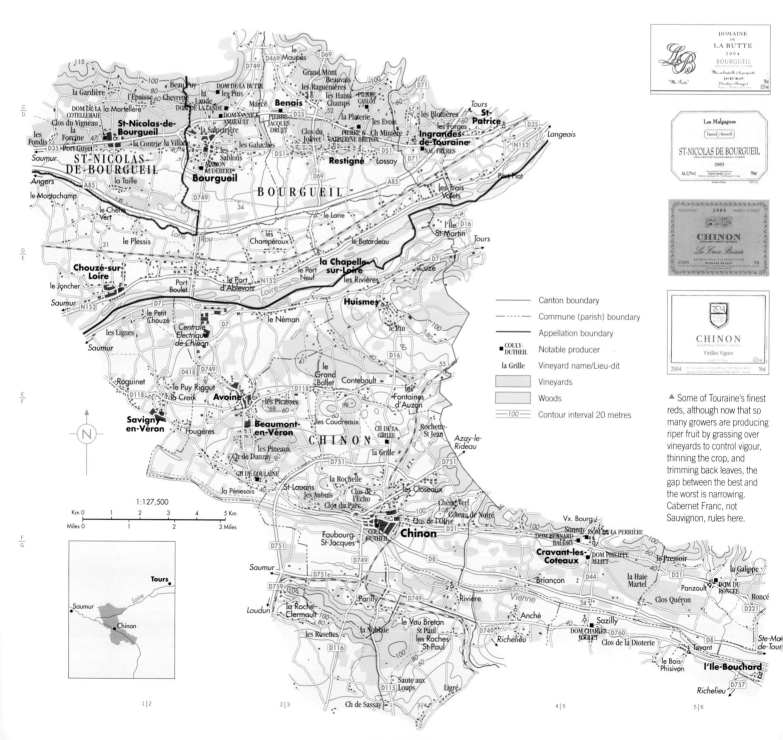

Some of Touraine's finest reds, although now that so many growers are producing riper fruit by grassing over vineyards to control vigour, thinning the crop, and trimming back leaves, the gap between the best and the worst is narrowing. Cabernet Franc, not Sauvignon, rules here.

———	Canton boundary
– – –	Commune (parish) boundary
········	Appellation boundary
■ COULY-DUTHEIL	Notable producer
la Grille	Vineyard name/Lieu-dit
▒	Vineyards
░	Woods
—100—	Contour interval 20 metres

1:127,500

Km 0 1 2 3 4 5 Km
Miles 0 1 2 3 Miles

Vouvray and Montlouis-sur-Loire

Everything royal and romantic about France is summed up in this land of renaissance châteaux, ancient towns, and beguiling white wines that lies along a short stretch of the immense but gentle Loire.

Low hills of soft tuffeau flank the river along the reach from Noizay to Rochecorbon. For centuries they have provided both cellars and cave-dwellings to the wine-growers of the district. The Chenin Blanc here, although often tarter than in Anjou, at its best is sweet with the distinct taste of honey. What distinguishes it more than anything, however, is its long life. For a comparatively light wine its longevity is astonishing. You may expect port to live for half a century, but in a pale, firm, rather delicate wine the ability to improve and go on improving for so long in bottle is matched only occasionally in Germany. Acidity is the key.

The first distinction in **Vouvray** is whether any given bottle is dry (*sec*), off-dry (*sec-tendre*, an unofficial but increasingly popular style), medium dry (*demi-sec*), sweet (*moelleux*), or for that matter sparkling. The influence of the Atlantic meets that of the continent here; the weather varies enormously from year to year, as does the ripeness and health of the grapes. Vouvray therefore alters character radically from vintage to vintage: some years dry and austere, requiring many years' softening in the bottle (although less now that sulphur is added more sparingly); every now and then a gloriously rich expression of noble rot, requiring several different harvests through each vineyard. Less successful vintages may be converted into very good sparkling wines, which have a honeyed character and an ageing potential that sets them apart from sparkling Saumur.

Normally only the richer vintages carry the name of one of the handful of famous vineyards on the best slopes, where clay and gravel overlie the riverside tuffeau. The best-known producer, Huet (since 2005 co-owned with an estate in Tokaj; a sign of the times?), owns three: Le Haut Lieu above the cellars, Le Mont, whose wines are the most concentrated, and the Clos du Bourg, favourite of winemaker Noël Pinguet and the first of his conversions to biodynamic viticulture in the late 1980s.

Montlouis-sur-Loire has very similar conditions to Vouvray (even locals can find the wines difficult to differentiate), without the perfect sheltered, south-facing situation of the first rank of Vouvray's vineyards along the Loire. Soils tend to be slightly sandier and so Montlouis is stereotypically a little lighter and less intense, and more Montlouis is destined to be made sparkling.

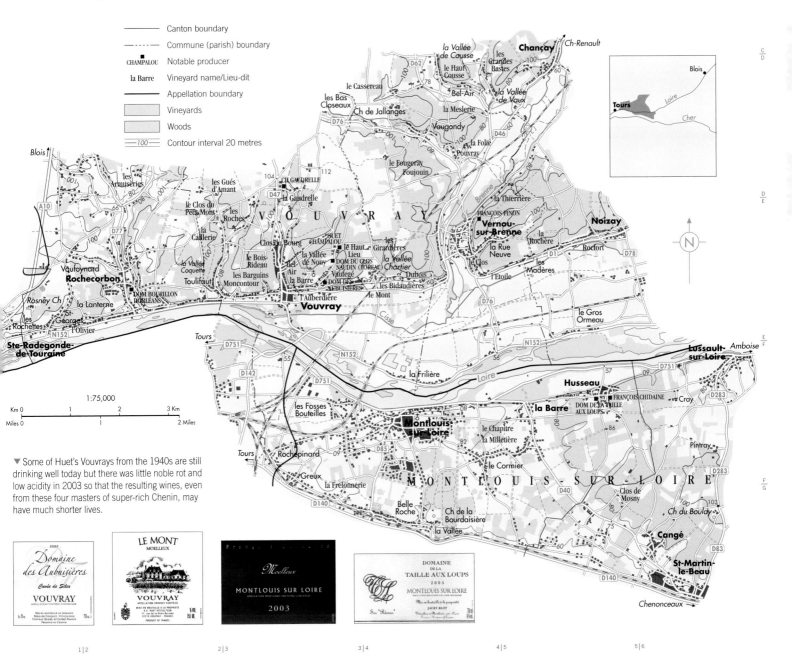

▼ Some of Huet's Vouvrays from the 1940s are still drinking well today but there was little noble rot and low acidity in 2003 so that the resulting wines, even from these four masters of super-rich Chenin, may have much shorter lives.

Pouilly and Sancerre

The crisp white wines of Pouilly and Sancerre are perhaps the easiest to recognize in France. On these limestone and clay hills bisected by the upper reaches of the River Loire, in a near-continental climate, Sauvignon Blanc can make better, certainly finer and more complex, wine than anywhere else in the world. But it does so all too rarely. The popularity of **Sancerre**, and **Pouilly-Fumé** made across the river, has allowed some less-than-thrilling examples on to our shelves and wine lists.

Pouilly-sur-Loire is the town; its wine is only called Pouilly-Fumé when it is made from the Sauvignon Blanc grape, often known here as Blanc Fumé. Its other grape, Chasselas, makes wine so mild that its survival here is a mystery. (Neither has anything to do with Pouilly-Fuissé, the white wine of Mâcon described on p.71.)

It would be a brave taster who maintained he or she could always tell a Pouilly-Fumé from a Sancerre. The best of each are on the same level; the Sancerre perhaps slightly fuller and more obvious, the Pouilly-Fumé more perfumed. Many Pouilly vineyards are lower than those of Sancerre, which lie at altitudes of 650–1,150ft (200–350m) flanking the hilltop town, but most of the best are to the north of Pouilly itself. The soils here have a high proportion of clay-flint (silex) which confers the potential for ageworthy, almost acrid wines described as having a gunflint (*pierre à fusil*) character. Silex is also common in the Sancerre vineyards on the slopes across the river from Pouilly and east of the town, while those in the west of the Sancerre appellation tend to be *terres blanches*, white limestone soils with a high proportion of clay resulting in rather sturdier wines. In between these two zones, the limestone is often mixed with pebbles and the wines more linear and refined.

A total of 14 villages, and three hamlets, have the right to produce Sancerre. The two best Sancerre vineyards are generally acknowledged to be the pebbly, calcareous Chêne Marchand in the village of Bué, which makes particularly mineral, finely etched Sancerre, and the Monts Damnés in Chavignol, where kimmeridgean marl (clay-limestone) produces broader wines. The silex of Ménétréol gives steelier wine – provided the winemaker is committed to quality.

The total area of Sancerre vineyard more than trebled in the last quarter of the 20th century and by 2005 had reached 6,700 acres (2,700ha), almost two and a half times the extent of the Pouilly-Fumé *vignoble*.

In the more homogeneous Pouilly, de Ladoucette's Disneyland-original Château du Nozet may be the biggest and best-known estate, but Didier Dagueneau has pioneered seriously low yields and experimentation with oak (echoed by Vincent Pinard, Henri Bourgeois, Alphonse Mellot, and other leading produers in Sancerre).

Such ambitious producers are understandably interested in proving that their wines are worth ageing, but – in stark contrast to the great white wines of Vouvray, for example – the great majority of Sancerre and Pouilly-Fumé reaches its appetizing, flirtatious peak within a year or two of bottling. However, a current project to favour cuttings descended from pre-1950 plants rather than modern clones may eventually result in longer-lasting wine

Sancerre's other passion is its Pinot Noir, popular in the region though rarely seen outside it. Its rare rosé form can be a beauty, but some red versions can be disconcertingly light to those expecting a lesser red burgundy. It may represent only about a seventh of total production (and none at all within the Pouilly-Fumé appellation), but some of the more ambitious producers are determined to prove that in good years it can provide just as much pleasure as many a wine at a similar price from the Côte de Beaune.

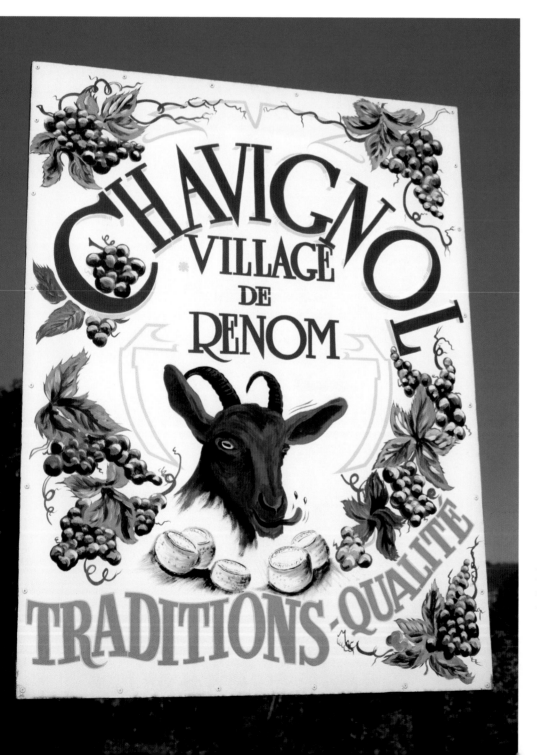

There is little doubt about the gastronomic traditions of the village of Chavignol just northwest of Sancerre, the base for such masters as the Cotats, who believe that once Chavignol's wines were more important than Sancerre's.

1:172,500

Km 0   5   10 Km
Miles 0   5 Miles

----- Département boundary

——— Canton boundary

----- Commune (parish) boundary

■ COTAT   Notable producer

le Paradis   Vineyard name/Lieu-dit

——— Appellation boundary

    Vineyards

    Woods

—200— Contour interval 20 metres

▲ Some innovative labelling here, from Pouilly's enfant terrible Didier Dagueneau for his particularly flinty Silex *cuvée*, which must be one of the region's longest-lived wines, and for Henri Bourgeois' similarly dense Sancerre from silex soils.

Well inside the great bend of the river are the other so-called Vignobles du Centre (see the map of the Loire Valley on p.119). The historic vineyards of Quincy and Reuilly, and a rapidly expanding fragment at Menetou-Salon, also make fruity Sauvignon Blancs and pale Pinot Noir to compete with Sancerre, at keener prices.

Quincy on largely sandy soils is the most rustic of these three appellations and applies only to white wine. **Reuilly** makes an increasing amount of all three colours on well-exposed steep limestone marl (clay-limestone) and gravel and sand terraces. **Menetou-Salon**, thanks to a high proportion of limestone, has its own charm. The best can certainly rival the laziest exponents of its neighbour to the east Sancerre.

Crottins, the little cylinders of local goat's cheese high in acidity and salt, have long been a proven match for those living around Sancerre. For others this is often the first combination to demonstrate just how well white wine partners cheeses of all sorts.

Alsace

The wine of Alsace reflects the ambivalent situation of a border province. There are two possible physical boundaries between France and Germany: the Rhine and the crest of the Vosges, which run parallel 15 miles (25km) west of the river. The Rhine has been the political frontier through most of history, but the mountains have always been the line that makes the great climatic, stylistic, even linguistic difference. Alsace has never been German, except in periods of military occupation. Its language and its market may be, but its soul is entirely French. Alsace makes Germanic wine in the French way. The tone is set by the climate, the soil, and the choice of grape varieties: all comparable with German wine regions, the nearest of which is Baden just across the Rhine.

Traditionally, Alsace winemakers sought bone dry, firm, strong wines, fermenting every ounce of the sugar produced by the long dry summers of Alsace and, often, adding even more (chaptalizing) to make the wine even stronger. This contrasted with the traditional German model of feather-light wines with natural grape sugar lingering delicately therein. But of late these two stereotypes have been moving towards each other. The average residual sugar level of Alsace wine has been increasing while German wines are becoming drier and stronger. The best producers on both sides of the Rhine are proud that all of this is a result of lowering yields and concentrating on what each grape has to offer. But consumers complain that Alsace wine is becoming more difficult to match with food, and that labels give them too few clues as to how sweet the wine is likely to taste.

The major clues on Alsace labels, most unusually for France, are varietal. The grapes that give their names and special qualities to the wines of Alsace are the Riesling of the Rhine – responsible here and in Germany for the best wine of all – Sylvaner, Muscat, Pinots Blanc, Gris, and Noir, and the uniquely perfumed Gewurztraminer. Gewurztraminer is the perfect introduction to the province. You would not think that so fruity a scent could come from a wine that can be so clean and dry. *Würze* means spice in German – although a more accurate description would make mention of rose petals, grapefruit, and, sometimes, lychees.

Gewurztraminer has its place with some of the richest of the very rich Alsatian dishes: goose or pork. But many Alsatians consider Riesling their true *grand vin*. It offers something

Zind Humbrecht's Clos St-Urbain on the particularly steep, south-facing slope of the Grand Cru Rangen well south of the Alsace heartland. The volcanic base is especially well suited to ripening Gewurztraminer and Pinot Gris to the limit.

much more elusive: a balance of hard and gentle, flowery and strong, which leads you on and never surfeits. Those that don't tend to favour Pinot Gris (once called Tokay d'Alsace), which makes the fullest-bodied but least perfumed wine of the region; it has an obvious place at table as an alternative to a white burgundy.

Alsace Muscat is usually a blend of Muscat Ottonel and Muscat Blanc grapes. At its best it keeps all of Muscat's characteristic grapey scent, but makes a dry wine as clean as a whistle: a playful apéritif.

Klevener de Heiligenstein is a grape speciality of the area round the village of Heiligenstein just north of Barr, in a limestone-dominated area which extends as far north as Ottrott. The lightly spicy, sometimes slightly buttery wine is relatively light in alcohol, and in good vintages it can age well.

Much more important is Pinot Blanc – a name used both for Pinot Blanc itself, the everyday grape of Alsace which usually manages to transmit some of the characteristic smokiness of the

region's whites, and for the softer Auxerrois (the two are frequently blended). To keep matters complicated the Auxerrois is sometimes labelled Klevner, or even Clevner. It is also the most common base wine for sparkling Crémant d'Alsace made by the traditional method, which at its best can rival the Crémants of Burgundy and the Loire.

In a class above the commonest wines of the region comes Sylvaner. Alsace Sylvaner is light and sometimes attractively tart. Without the tartness it can be a little dull and coarse in flavour. It is often the first wine to be served at an Alsatian dinner, to build up to the main wine, the Riesling.

The lesser grapes, Chasselas and Knipperlé (which can shine on poor, granitic soils), are not usually identified on the label. Very young,

◀ René Muré has one of the most exciting plantings of the often-underestimated Sylvaner grape, just as old-vine Chasselas in such hands as Schoffit of Nonnenberg near Colmar (see overleaf) can be transformed into something admirably out of the ordinary.

particularly in the summer after a good vintage, they are so good that visitors should not miss them by insisting on a smarter one with a name. The term Edelzwicker (noble mixture) is usually applied to a mixture of grape varieties but rarely noble ones.

Of these grapes, only Riesling, Pinot Gris, Gewurztraminer, and Muscat – the Alsace grape nobility – are generally allowed the controversial Alsace Grand Cru appellation discussed overleaf, although the quality of old Sylvaner vines in Zotzenberg north of Mittelbergheim has earned Grand Cru status. Those sites so far approved as Grands Crus that are not within the areas mapped in more detail overleaf are numbered on the map opposite, many of them clustered on a patch of particularly well-favoured clay-limestone due west of Strasbourg on some of the lowest-lying vineyard land of the Bas-Rhin département. Steinklotz is particularly well-known for Pinot Gris and Pinot Noir, Altenberg de Bergbieten for Riesling. In the bottom left-hand corner of the map, 12 miles (20km) south of the main concentration of Haut-Rhin Grands Crus, is the historic Rangen vineyard, which rises steeply above the village of Thann. Schoffit and Zind-Humbrecht make superbly rich wines, especially Riesling and Pinot Gris, from these warm volcanic soils. In general the vineyards of the Bas-Rhin are less sheltered by the Vosges and produce rather lighter wines.

One of the attractions of Alsace for winemakers and more intellectual connoisseurs is the mosaic of soil types within the region and the challenge of matching grapes to them. But what distinguishes Alsace from other French wine regions is its low rainfall (see statistics overleaf). A quick comparison with other pages shows that only Perpignan is drier than Colmar, and even Toulon in Provence is wetter than Strasbourg. Drought may sometimes plague vineyards here but ripeness is usually guaranteed.

Like its counterparts from the Loire and from Germany, Alsace wine is essentially about fruit rather than oak. If oak is used at all it is generally in the form of old oval casks incapable of imparting oak flavour. André Ostertag of Epfig is exceptional in using barriques. Similarly, most Alsace winemakers have deliberately suppressed the second malolactic fermentation for their whites, but it is generally necessary to soften the 6% or so of Alsace wine that is red and made from Pinot Noir grapes. Colours and styles vary enormously from the traditional tart, dark rosé to some deep crimson, oaky wines made from barrel-aged, low-yield fruit. As in Germany, the holy grail of perfect red Pinot is hard for winemakers to ignore, but harder still to achieve.

Another challenge for the region's winemakers is to make the most of its finest autumns when seriously ripe grapes can be picked to make either Vendange Tardive wines or, even sweeter, rarer, and generally botrytized, Sélection de Grains Nobles made from several different pickings. A late-picked Gewurztraminer has perhaps the most exotic smell of any wine in the world, and can at the same time keep a remarkable cleanness and finesse of flavour.

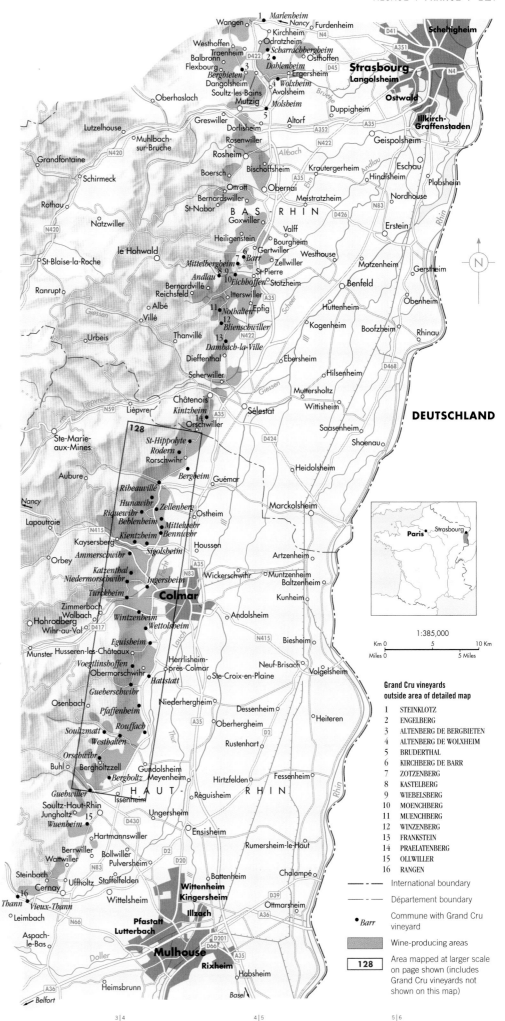

1:385,000

Km 0 — 5 — 10 Km
Miles 0 — 5 Miles

Grand Cru vineyards outside area of detailed map

1   STEINKLOTZ
2   ENGELBERG
3   ALTENBERG DE BERGBIETEN
4   ALTENBERG DE WOLXHEIM
5   BRUDERTHAL
6   KIRCHBERG DE BARR
7   ZOTZENBERG
8   KASTELBERG
9   WIEBELSBERG
10 MOENCHBERG
11 MUENCHBERG
12 WINZENBERG
13 FRANKSTEIN
14 PRAELATENBERG
15 OLLWILLER
16 RANGEN

— — — International boundary
— · — · Département boundary

• *Barr* Commune with Grand Cru vineyard

▨ Wine-producing areas

[128] Area mapped at larger scale on page shown (includes Grand Cru vineyards not shown on this map)

The Heart of Alsace

The map on these pages lays the heart of the Alsace vineyard on its side, making it directly comparable with the maps of the Côte d'Or. The north lies to the right. As in Burgundy, a range of east-facing hills provides an ideal environment for the vine. Spurs and re-entrants offer extra shelter and a privileged sunwards tilt in places where the vines face east, southeast, or south. A dense pine forest nearby can lower the average temperature of a vineyard by a full degree centigrade compared with one next to a planting of young oaks. Every nuance of the unfolding landscape is echoed in the alignment of the vine rows to catch each minute of sunlight.

And Alsace is sunny. The high Vosges to the west are the secret of these vineyards, which lie along the mountain flank at an altitude of 600–1,200ft (180–360m), in a green ribbon that is rarely more than a mile wide. The lorry drivers grinding their way up through Kaysersberg towards St-Dié invariably encounter a thick bank of clouds as they reach the crest of the Vosges, with clouds banking up to the west. The

higher the mountains are, the drier the land they shelter from moist west winds. The map shows the central stretch of the Haut-Rhin vineyards, clustered under the wooded slopes to the north and south of the city of Colmar – where the mountains can keep the sky clear of clouds for weeks on end. In this protected climate, classic firm Riesling thrives.

Ironically, the wine-growing conditions are so ideal that Alsace has been seen during long periods of its troubled history as a source of *vin ordinaire* or reliable blending material – rather as France once regarded Algeria. Hence the lack of a long-hatched hierarchy of the better and the best vineyards in the manner of the Côte d'Or.

Instead the modern wine industry developed through the enterprise of farmers (many of them working land that has been in the family since the 17th century) turning merchant and branding their own and their neighbours' wines, distinguishing them only by their grapes. Such famous names as Hugel, Dopff, Trimbach, Humbrecht, Becker, Kuehn, or Muré are the result. Alsace also had France's first co-operative cellar, in 1895, and such co-operatives as Eguisheim, Kientzheim, Beblenheim, and Westhalten rank high among some of the better producers today.

The Grand Cru appellation (see p.127), an attempt to designate the best vineyards which was launched in 1983, is a change in emphasis which is not without its problems. The Grands Crus, marked on the map in violet, are slowly changing the way Alsace wines are perceived. Their restricted yields and increased levels of ripeness offer at least theoretically a higher quality level. They should promote the wines from being a mere varietal (an expression of a grape) to enjoying appellation status in the fullest sense: the specific linkage of terroir and grape variety based on soil, situation and – up to a point – tradition.

But the Alsace wine trade has until recently been organized to sell individual combinations of brands and varieties rather than shared vineyards, whose exact boundaries are the subject of much dispute anyway. The most famous names outside the region such as Hugel and Trimbach are merchants first and growers

ALSACE: COLMAR ▼

Latitude / Altitude of WS **47.55° / 689ft (210m)**

Mean July temp at WS **66.4°F (19.1°C)**

Annual rainfall at WS **23in (590mm)**

Harvest month rainfall at WS **September: 2.4in (60mm)**

Chief viticultural hazards **Soil erosion, occasional drought**

Principal grapes **Pinot Blanc, Riesling, Gewurztraminer, Pinot Gris, Sylvaner, Pinot Noir**

Département boundary

Commune (parish) boundary

SPOREN Grand Cru vineyard

Other vineyard

Altenburg Other leading vineyard

Woods

200 Contour interval 20 metres

▼ Weather station (WS)

second. This emphasis on individual vineyards has the effect of transferring power from the merchants to the growers and has not, therefore, been universally welcomed.

The Grand Cru decrees stipulate which grapes may be grown in each Grand Cru, and blends such as that allowed for Altenberg de Bergheim may be sanctioned by each Grand Cru's management committee. Many site/variety associations are already well in place, usually on the basis of growing and tasting experience, which often turns out to have some geological link. At Guebwiller at the southern end of this stretch of vineyards, for example, the sandstone of Kitterlé is famous for its luscious wines from a range of grape varieties, particularly those grown by Schlumberger. Just north of here at Westhalten the more limestone slope of Zinnkoepflé faces due south and concentrates Gewurztraminer and Riesling to new heights, whereas the marls and sandstone of the southeast-facing Vorbourg at Rouffach have a particular affinity for Muscat.

Hatschbourg at Voegtlingshofen is a splendid vineyard of marl and limestone ripening dense-textured Pinot Gris and Gewurztraminer, like Goldert next door. Eichberg at Eguisheim grows fine Gewurztraminer and Riesling on marl and sandstone while Hengst at Wintzenheim is famous for the same varieties.

The granite underpinnings of the Vosges produce Rieslings with extra richness when they influence vineyards such as Turckheim's Brand and Kientzheim's Schlossberg. At Riquewihr the clay marls of Schoenenbourg also produce glorious Riesling, although the clays of the Sporen south of the village are more suitable for Gewurztraminer.

Nonetheless some producers, especially those with a certain reputation, eschew the Grand Cru system. The finest Riesling in Alsace, some would say the world, is grown in Trimbach's Clos Ste-Hune within the Rosacker Grand Cru above Hunawihr. The word Rosacker is never mentioned on the label because the Trimbachs do not believe that the rest of this mainly limestone vineyard matches Clos Ste-Hune in quality.

Indeed, the word Clos, signifying a self-contained vineyard often within another, can be shorthand for quality, as in Domaine Weinbach's Clos des Capucins at the foot of the Schlossberg slopes in Kientzheim; Muré's Clos St-Landelin within the Vorbourg vineyard; and Zind-Humbrecht's Clos Hauserer near the Hengst Grand Cru, Clos Jebsal near Turckheim, Clos St-Urbain in Thann's Grand Cru Rangen (on the map on p.127), and Clos Windsbuhl near Hunawihr.

Best to concentrate on the view above head level in the narrow streets of Riquewihr in high season. And the Vosges Mountains, which we have to thank for every bottle of delicious Alsace wine, are never far from view.

But while the concepts of the Grand Cru and Clos appeal to many winemakers, others may produce equally fine selections simply as *cuvées* of their best grapes. Alsace, it seems, will always be in dispute.

Not that the casual tourist will feel anything but pampered. A signposted Route des Vins takes a meandering course the whole length of the Alsace wine country, calling at some of the prettiest wine towns in the world. Riquewihr and Kaysersberg are the most beautiful, and the city of Colmar, the capital of Alsace, has a magnificent collection of timber-framed houses which date from the 15th century.

Between the settlements the high-trained vines block out the view along the narrow lanes, until you reach a ridge and suddenly see the gleaming green sea rolling against the mountains disappearing in a haze in the distance.

◀ Grand Cru wines from growers, plus three wines that are effectively brands belonging to the merchants Léon Beyer (a Gewurztraminer specialist), Hugel, and Trimbach. The modest Clos Ste-Hune label belies it reputation, and price. But it can be worth ageing for a decade or two

Northern Rhône

The valley of the Loire and the valley of the Rhône are two sides of the same coin. Most Loire wine is white, most Rhône red. In each case there is a wide variety of wine styles but they all have something in common; in the case of the Rhône, substance.

Rhône red wines vary from the intensely concentrated and tannic, ruby-black or purple-black in youth, to relatively simple but solid alcoholic fruit juice. The best have depth, length, and mature to a lingering harmony comparable to the greatest wines of Bordeaux. White wines are in the minority and tend to headiness, but thanks to much-improved wine-making can now be as notable as all but the best of the red.

The vineyards around the Rhône Valley fall naturally into two groups: the north (*septentrionale*, as the French call it), with less than a tenth of total production, almost all fine wine, and the much more diverse south (*méridionale*), where the landscape is quite different. In the course of the Rhône as it flows from Switzerland through France, the country changes from oak forest, where the vine shares the fields with peach trees and nut trees, to the herbal scrub and olive groves of Provence. A quick comparison of the rainfall (see key facts panels on pages 131 and 137) in the two regions is enough to explain why the northern Rhône is so much greener and less Mediterranean than the south. The break comes at about Montélimar, where for a short stretch the vine is absent from the broad valley.

In the north the vine perches on terraced cliffs of crumbling granite wherever the best exposure to the sun can be found. The grape of the northern Rhône is Syrah, alias Shiraz. But the northern Rhône can also boast three highly distinctive and fashionable white wine grapes – Marsanne, Roussanne, and Viognier – even if they make relatively little wine in total.

On the following pages the best areas of the northern and southern Rhône are mapped in detail. Côte-Rôtie, Condrieu, and Hermitage, the most majestic Rhône wines, all belong in the northern sector. Around them lie several others of strong local character, long traditions, and evolving reputations.

Cornas, for example, is the stubborn country cousin to the noble Hermitage, made of the same Syrah grapes grown on granite and with just as much authority and power, if less finesse. The appellation today shows encouraging signs of rejuvenation via the likes of Stéphane Robert of Domaine du Tunnel, Vincent Paris, and Eric and Joël Durand. Over recent years total plantings on Cornas's east-facing amphitheatre of terraces, so sheltered from the river's influence that they ripen particularly early, have grown to 257 acres (104ha). Jean-Luc Colombo and his experiments with heavy oaking and the venerable Auguste Clape are perhaps the most famous Cornas producers, but are no longer the only ones with an international reputation.

The temptation to stretch a good name to breaking point has overtaken **St-Joseph**, the west-bank appellation to the north of Cornas, which now stretches almost 40 miles (60km) from Guilherand in the St-Péray appellation to well north of the village of Chavanay in Condrieu. It was once a group of six communes, of which Mauves, which has similar granitic soils to the hill of Hermitage across the river, was arguably the best. But since 1969 St-Joseph has been allowed to expand into a total of 26 communes, and to grow from 240 to 2,445 acres (almost 1,000 ha). A St-Joseph should be the sappiest, fastest-maturing

Those designing new, fully mechanized vineyards in, for example, Australia must be completely bemused by these Côte-Rôtie vineyards with their slopes of up to 60%. It is easy to see how wines produced at the top and bottom of the slope would differ.

northern Rhône red without losing its Syrah nerve. Fortunately since the 1990s an increasing proportion has been grown on the steep granite river banks rather than at the bottom of these slopes or on the much cooler plateau. Wines from the latter are difficult to distinguish from a northern **Côtes du Rhône**, the catch-all appellation of the Rhône Valley which applies to 50 communes north of Montélimar (and 113 in the south). The names of the original six St-Joseph communes, Glun, Mauves, Tournon, St-Jean-de-Muzols, Lemps, and Vion, together with Chavanay in Condrieu country to the north, remain pointers to the best wines. Fine, sometimes vineyard-designated, wines are made here by the likes of Jean-Louis Chave, Stéphane Montez, Chapoutier, and Jean Gonon. St-Joseph also produces one of the Rhône's least-known but most persuasive and food-friendly whites, often better than its red, from the Hermitage grapes Marsanne and Roussanne.

Traditional-method wines seem somehow out of place in this rustic, southern environment. But **St-Péray**, south of Cornas, has an old name for its heavyweight, golden sparkling (and sometimes still) wine made from Roussanne and Marsanne. On the River Drôme, off the map to the east, totally different grapes (Clairette and Muscat) respectively make two different styles of sparkling wine: substantial **Crémant de Die** made mainly from Clairette grapes and featherlight, grapey **Clairette de Die Tradition** (so called even though Clairette may not account for more than a quarter of the mainly Muscat blend). Light, still wines in all three colours are sold locally as **Châtillon-en-Diois**.

The narrowness of the northern Rhône Valley has limited any expansion of the most venerable appellations here, but some growers are experimenting with areas not blessed with AC status. Some of the more energetic producers of Côte-Rôtie and Condrieu (see overleaf) have sought out specially favoured granite slopes on the opposite, left bank of the river such as at Seyssuel between Vienne and Lyon for recent plantings of Syrah and Viognier. The produce of these vineyards outside the approved areas must be sold as Vins de Pays, in this case often des Collines Rhodaniennes (see the map on p.153). Similarly, well-financed producers from further north such as Louis Latour of Beaune and Georges Duboeuf of Beaujolais are capitalizing, with keenly priced Vins de Pays, on the potential and low land prices of the Coteaux de l'Ardèche.

RHÔNE: VALENCE ▼

Latitude / Altitude of WS 44.55° / **525ft (160m)**

Mean July temp at WS **72.5°F (22.5°C)**

Annual rainfall at WS **33in (840mm)**

Harvest month rainfall at WS **September: 5in (130mm)**

Chief viticultural hazards **Poor weather at flowering, fungal diseases**

Principal grapes **Syrah, Viognier**

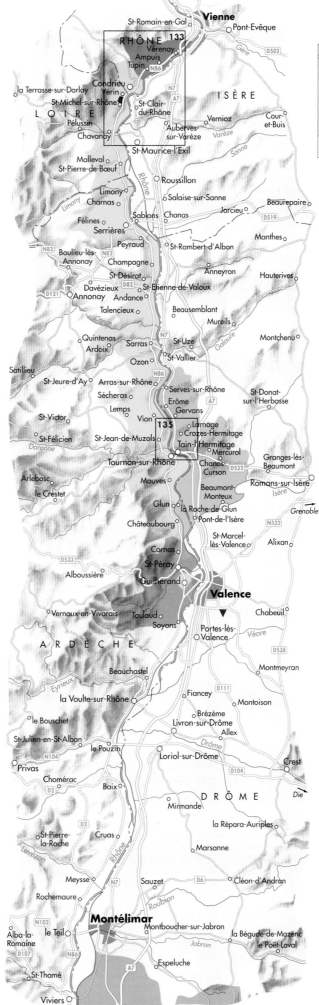

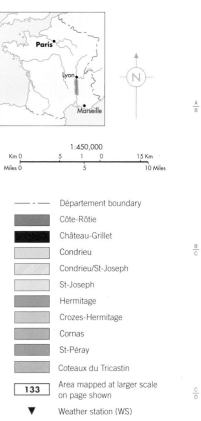

Département boundary

Côte-Rôtie
Château-Grillet
Condrieu
Condrieu/St-Joseph
St-Joseph
Hermitage
Crozes-Hermitage
Cornas
St-Péray
Coteaux du Tricastin

133 Area mapped at larger scale on page shown

▼ Weather station (WS)

▲ The northern Rhône is not chock full of bargains, but savoury Syrahs are some of the best-value wines produced there.

Côte-Rôtie and Condrieu

Côte-Rôtie's ribbon of vineyards, hugging the granite western walls of the valley at Ampuis in perilous terraces, have only recently known worldwide fame. Until the spotlight of fashion picked out the single-minded Marcel Guigal and his exceptional wines in the 1980s, Côte-Rôtie was an insider's wine, astonishing all who discovered it with its magical soft-fruity finesse, southern in warmth but closer to a great red burgundy in the way firm tannin supported delicate flavours – in marked contrast to the sheer mass of Hermitage, the northern Rhône's most famous emissary.

Like Hermitage, Côte-Rôtie is certainly Roman or earlier in origin. Up to the 19th century its wine was sold by the vase of 76 litres (20 gallons), the measure of a double amphora. It long maintained its almost secret niche as one of France's greatest wines. When this Atlas was first published, in 1971, the total area of vineyards was only 173 acres (70ha) and dwindling. Its price barely justified the hard work involved in cultivating the back-breakingly steep terraces. The world has since "discovered" Côte-Rotie, prices have risen steeply, and in 35 years the vineyard area has more than tripled to 555 acres (225 ha), definitively overtaking Hermitage in terms of the amount of wine produced.

As the name implies, this southeast-facing slope (so steep that gradients can reach 60% in places and pulleys, even monorails, have to be used to transport anything as heavy as a box of grapes) is indeed roasted (*rôtie*) in summer. Many parts of this strip of vineyards, sometimes barely 1,640ft (500m) wide, are exposed to the sun all day. The hard rock (schist in the north) from which these riverside plots are hewn retains every degree of heat, which is why newer plantings on the plateau above rarely ripen anything like as fully and have arguably diluted Côte-Rôtie's reputation.

It may seem obvious where the boundaries should be: the northwestern one at the top of the famously roasted slope and the southeastern boundary now formed by the N86, the road that winds down the right bank of the Rhône south of Lyons, but just how far northeast and southwest true Côte-Rôtie terroir extends has been disputed for centuries. All are agreed, however, that the original vineyards are centred on the two most obvious slopes above the little town of Ampuis, the Côte Blonde on a

south-facing spur just south of town and the southwest-facing bank that is the Côte Brune to the north. The Côte Blonde, being part of the greater Massif Central, has much more granite, sometimes visible at the surface, with notably soft topsoils, comprising many different plots of sandy/slaty soil with a pale limestone element. These produce softer, more charming, earlier-developing wines than those produced on the almost equally extensive and even more varied Côte Brune, whose schist and heavier clay are darkened by iron and whose wines are traditionally tougher. The limestone content of the soils here is particularly variable, but it is not sought out by growers of Syrah as it would be by those growing the grapes of Burgundy.

The local map of individual vineyards lists even more than those mapped here, which include those most likely to be found on labels. Being equal in quality but not in style, the wines of the Côtes Blonde and Brune were in the past blended by merchants to produce a unified Côte-Rôtie. But today there is also a fashion for vineyard-designated bottlings, a trend accelerated by the dominant figure in the appellation, the perfectionist Marcel Guigal. By bottling separately wines labelled La Mouline (Côte Blonde), La Landonne, and La Turque (Côte Brune), after ageing them in new oak for a daring and dramatic 42 months, he has come as close as any grower to creating a new

It is easy to see why elaborate systems of pulleys are needed to tend these century-old Syrah vines in Côte-Rôtie. Only parts of the Mosel Valley in northern Germany rival it for difficulty.

Romanée-Conti. These are wines for millionaires, impressed by power and pungency, but not always for lovers of the classic gentle Côte-Rôtie, matured in barrels that are themselves mature. Traditionalists might be more satisfied by wines from such as Gangloff and Jasmin, and Rostaing's Côte Blonde bottling.

The picture is further complicated by the divergence between the names on Guigal labels, the most famous names of Côte-Rôtie, and those on local maps. The toughest, longest-lived of all Guigal's wines comes from La Landonne vineyard, which is also bottled by Jean-Michel Gérin and René Rostaing. But this is the only one of Guigal's internationally traded so-called "La La" wines that is an officially recognized plot. La Mouline, a Guigal brand name, is a sumptuous velvety monster produced from holdings in the Côte Blonde as marked on the map. La Turque, another Guigal brand, is made from vines also marked on the map high above the centre of Ampuis, while the more traditional Côte-Rôtie bottling under Guigal's more recently acquired Château d'Ampuis label is a blend from seven quite different vineyards from both Côtes Brune and

◄ Guigal's La Mouline is the most approachable of the so-called "La La" Côte-Rôties, and is made from the oldest vines. The Condrieu producers here are all relative newcomers who have firmly established their reputations.

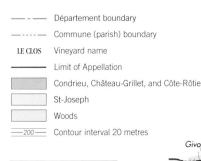

Département boundary
Commune (parish) boundary
LE CLOS Vineyard name
Limit of Appellation
Condrieu, Château-Grillet, and Côte-Rôtie
St-Joseph
Woods
200 Contour interval 20 metres

1:61,540

But Côte-Rôtie is far from a one-man appellation. Gilles Barge, the Bonnefonds, Bernard Burgaud, Clusel-Roch, Jamet, Ogier, and Jean-Michel Stéphan and many other producers based in Condrieu or St-Joseph can all make wines of great interest. Merchants with particularly significant Côte-Rôties include Chapoutier, Delas, Duclaux, Jaboulet, Vidal-Fleury (owned by Guigal), and, of course, Guigal itself.

It is not just geography that distinguishes Côte-Rôtie from Hermitage. In theory Côte-Rôtie growers have long been allowed to add up to 20% of Viognier to perfume and stabilize the Syrah on which the wine depends. Guigal's La Mouline is often enlivened by more than 10% Viognier, but 2–5% is the most common proportion. (This technique was widely taken up elsewhere, particularly in Australia, in the early 21st century.)

The extraordinarily heady, recognizably perfumed Viognier grape with its aromas of apricots and may blossom is the speciality of the even smaller appellation of **Condrieu** into which the Côte-Rôtie vineyards merge to the south, where schist and mica give way to granite. Many of the local growers make both of these sought-after white and red wines, much as the bigger merchants would like to acquire their wines or, preferably, their vineyards. At one time Condrieu was more commonly encountered as a sweet but relatively obscure wine. The difficulty of growing such an unreliable, disease-prone, low-yielding vine as Viognier on the often relatively inaccessible slopes above the village of Condrieu compared unfavourably with other much easier, more

lucrative crops for which the area was well known. By the 1960s the total planted area of the Condrieu appellation, created in 1940, had shrunk to barely 30 acres (12ha). Fortunately, the charms of Viognier in general and Condrieu in particular were so obvious that an increasingly international fan club developed. The variety is now much more widely planted in the Languedoc, California, and Australia than in Condrieu. But the enthusiasm has been sufficient to identify new clones of Viognier (not all of them predicated on wine quality) and encourage a new blast of creative energy in Condrieu itself.

Among the top producers of classical, fragrant, almost exclusively dry Condrieu are Georges Vernay with his Coteau du Vernon, Pierre Dumazet, André Perret, and Guigal, who now produces a de luxe bottling, La Doriane, blended from grapes grown on the Côte Châtillon and Colombier vineyards. Younger, equally ambitious producers who have also been experimenting with late-picked, botrytized, and oaked versions include Yves Cuilleron, Yves Gangloff, Pierre Gaillard, and François Villard.

All this creativity demands vineyards and Condrieu has been growing, to more than 320 acres (130ha) by 2005. The Condrieu appellation ambles north from the village of Chavanay, where growers may also produce St-Joseph, and the higher granite content in the soil is said to imbue some minerality in the wines, as far north as the hills north of Condrieu itself, which can yield particularly rich Viognier.

New sites are not always in the awkward inaccessible spots where the finicky Viognier vine flourishes – not least because, in order to produce an economic crop level, it should be sheltered from the cool, north wind at flowering time. The most favoured vineyards in Condrieu tend to have a powdery, mica-rich topsoil called locally *arzelle*. They include Chéry, Chanson, Côte Bonnette, and Les Eyguets. Condrieu combines alcoholic power with a haunting but surprisingly fragile aroma. It is one of the very few luxury-priced whites that should be drunk young.

The most unusual Viognier of all is **Château-Grillet**: 9.4 acres (3.8ha) in a privileged amphitheatre of vines which has carved out its own appellation, an enclave within Condrieu's territory. The wine's price has recently reflected more its rarity than its obvious quality. It can be so muted as to be positively surly in youth, although it can emerge as a beauty after several years in bottle.

Blonde. Guigal's grip on the town of Ampuis continues to tighten. It seemed inevitable that he would acquire and glamorously renovate the down-at-heel Château d'Ampuis right on the river's edge and he has since installed his own cooperage in its extensive and now carefully manicured grounds.

Hermitage

The imposing hill of Hermitage may be world-famous but it really is as limited as the map opposite suggests. With just over 320 acres (130ha) of vines, the entire Hermitage appellation is not that much more extensive than, say, Château Lafite in Pauillac. And, unlike appellations to the north such as St-Joseph, expansion is limited by long-standing decree. But Hermitage has long been celebrated as one of France's most glorious wines. So much so that the records of Bordeaux producers shipping in Hermitage to beef up their own wines are extensive and date from the mid-18th century at least. Wine merchant André Jullien's celebrated survey of the world's finest vineyards, *Topographie de Tout les Vignobles* published in 1866 (see p.15), lists the individual *climats*, or small plots, of Hermitage alongside Château Lafite and Romanée-Conti as among the best red wines of the world. The town of Tain l'Hermitage squeezed on to the narrow river bank at the foot of the hill of Hermitage was known as Tegna in Roman times and its wines were celebrated by both Pliny and Martial.

France's main north–south artery the Rhône, and its accompanying roads and railway, snakes under its narrow terraces, making the vineyard's magnificent stance looking south down the river above Tain familiar to millions.

The slopes of Hermitage, uniquely in the northern Rhône, are on the river's left bank and face due south, and they are well protected from cold winds from the north. This granitic outcrop was once an extension of the Massif Central until the river burrowed a course round its western rather than eastern flank. It amounts to just 331 acres (134ha), much of it, especially on the western side closest to the Massif Central, terraced, heat-retaining granite which rises to almost 1,150ft (350m). The slopes may not be quite as steep as those of Côte-Rôtie but they are still steep enough to outlaw mechanization, and make repairing the ravages of erosion a back-breaking annual task. The topsoil that slides down the hill after heavy storms is made up largely of decomposed flint and limestone with glacial deposits that are alpine in origin at the eastern end.

Although for the red wines of Hermitage nothing but Syrah is planted, each *climat* is subtly different in terms of soil type, exposition, and altitude with some benefiting from the shelter provided by a natural amphitheatre. As long ago as the late 19th century Jullien felt confident in listing Hermitage's *climats* in order of merit: Méal, Gréfieux, Beaume, Raucoule, Muret, Guoignière, Bessas, Burges, and Lauds. Spellings have changed but the *climats* remain and, although Hermitage is typically, and possibly ideally, a blend from several different *climats*, their names have been seen on an increasing proportion of wine labels as the urge to get to grips with individual vineyard characteristics has taken hold of both producers and consumers.

In general the lightest, most aromatic red wines come from the higher *climats*: Beaume and L'Hermite, beside the chapel on top of the hill (see above) after which Jaboulet's famous Hermitage La Chapelle is named. Relatively fleshy wines come from Péléat. Les Gréffieux, in which Chapoutier has the largest holding, makes elegant, aromatic wines while Le Méal can produce extremely powerful wines. The particularly granitic Bessards, turned south-southwest at its western end, tends to produce the most tannic and longest-lived wines, such as Chapoutier's exceptionally concentrated

The chapel high up in that part of the constricted Hermitage appellation known as L'Hermite. Much higher than this, Syrah vines may struggle to ripen some years. The key to Hermitage's strength is its granitic soil, which acts as a storage heater, and its southern aspect.

Pavillon Ermitage (using the old spelling, which seems to be making a comeback).

The adjective "manly" has stuck to Hermitage ever since it was first applied to it (even if in recent years the supposedly feminine Côte-Rôtie seems to have taken a dose of testosterone). Hermitage, once used extensively

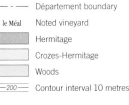

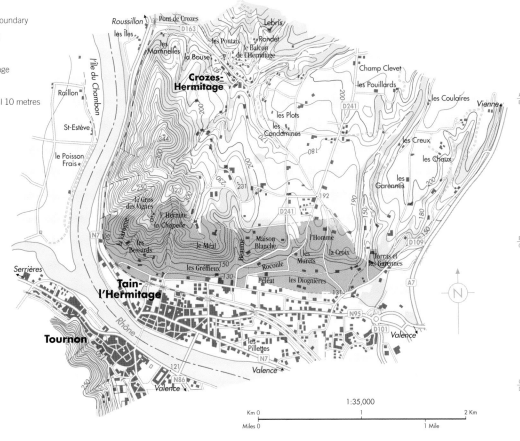

1:35,000

to strengthen fine red Bordeaux, has almost the qualities of port without the added brandy. Like vintage port, Hermitage throws a heavy sediment in, often onto, the bottle (it needs decanting) and improves for many years until its scent and flavour are almost overwhelming.

Young Hermitage of a good vintage is as closed and tannic as any young great red, but nothing can restrain its abounding perfume and the fistfuls of fruit that seem to have been crammed into the glass. As it ages the immediacy of its impact does not diminish, but its youthful assault gives way to the sheer splendour of its mature presence. You could not drink it and fail to be impressed.

Unlike the appellations of Condrieu and Côte-Rôtie lying to the north, Hermitage has long been fashionable. Virtually all of the available land has therefore been planted and there has been little opportunity to extend the vineyard area.

The appellation is dominated by just four producers: Domaine Jean-Louis Chave, based across the river in Mauves just south of Tain's twin town Tournon, and the large merchant houses of Chapoutier, Jaboulet, and the smaller Delas, whose names, aimed at all that traffic motoring along below, adorn the walls that prop up their terraces.

But there has been another opportunity for enthusiastic newcomers to this wine area, joined by an increasing number of local producers keen to bottle the fruit of their own labours rather than sell it to the excellent co-operative, the Cave de Tain l'Hermitage. Like most great wines, Hermitage has its shadow. **Crozes-Hermitage** is to the Grand Cru what a village Gevrey-Chambertin is to Le Chambertin. Crozes, the village round the back of the hill, gives its name to an appellation that extends almost 10 miles (16km) both north and south of Tain and Hermitage itself, including about 250 acres (100ha) of vineyard, only a fraction of them mapped here (see also the map on p.131).

Until the 1990s only one Crozes wine, Paul Jaboulet's Domaine de Thalabert made in one of Crozes' most successful areas just north of

Beaumont-Monteux, was regularly comparable with a Hermitage and much of the rest was pallid stuff. Today, however, we can choose from two basic styles – one full of youthful blackcurrant fruit for early drinking and the other, more serious bottlings that mimic the sheer weight of Hermitage and can be kept for up to 10 years. The better merchants and growers such as Alain Graillot, Belle, Domaine Pochon, Domaine Marc Sorrel, and Domaine du Colombier led the way but new merchants such as Tardieu Laurent and the Tain co-op are also responsible for some admirable bottlings. The likes of Domaines Yann Chave, Combier, des Entrefaux, des Remizières, and Gilles Robin are also producing Crozes-Hermitage, and some of them Hermitage itself, that is increasingly to be reckoned with.

Crozes-Hermitage can also be white, and the Hermitage hill was historically almost as famous for its white wine, from Roussanne and, mainly, Marsanne grapes, which even today accounts for about a quarter of the Hermitage vines. Jullien named Raucoule as the best vineyard for white Hermitage and it is still known for the aroma of its whites. Today Chante-Alouette is the best-known name.

Besides being a vineyard (though not one that is named on the traditional maps of Hermitage), it is a trademark of Chapoutier and a thoroughly remarkable, often misunderstood, wine. Golden, dry, and full with a remarkably delicate, eventually nutty flavour, it should ideally mature, like red Hermitage, for a decade at least, although the current incumbent, Michel Chapoutier, is making this full-bodied white much more approachable in youth too.

Another white wine that was for long an Hermitage speciality and was resurrected by Gérard Chave in the 1970s is the extraordinarily long-lived sweet *vin de paille* of Hermitage, made in tiny quantities in very ripe years from grapes that are traditionally shrivelled on straw (*paille*) mats. Bottles from the 19th century still exist as the appellation's oldest souvenirs and are said to be still hauntingly rich.

▼ Le Chevalier de Sterimberg is the only white wine here, based unusually on Roussanne grapes. It belongs to the once-dominant merchant house of Paul Jaboulet Aîné, which, after a period of stagnation, was taken over by the owner of Bordeaux's Château La Lagune in late 2005.

Southern Rhône

The funnel end of the Rhône Valley, where it releases its traffic to the Mediterranean, has a place in every traveller's affections. History and natural history combine to make it one of the richest regions of France for interests of every kind. Who cannot picture the vast engineering of the Romans, lizards alert on its slumbering stones, plots of early vegetables screened from the mistral, the pines and almonds yielding to olive groves in the far south – and always, on hillside or plain, sand or clay, the cross-stitch of vines?

These vines lie baking on broad terraces of smooth, round stones warmed by the sun, almost invariably a rich mix of varieties. In the south the dominant grape for red wines is the versatile Grenache, increasingly supplemented by Syrah and Mourvèdre. The heart of the region, the vineyard that sums up all its qualities, is Châteauneuf-du-Pape (see overleaf). Around it is a cluster of villages with their own

sweet, spicy story to tell, related by a swelling band of ambitious producers. There is a clear path for promotion for wine villages in the southern Rhône. Once their wines have established a reputation, they can apply to have the name of their village officially recognized on the label.

The most common appellation is **Côtes du Rhône**, a general one for the red, white, or rosé of the Rhône Valley, encompassing more than 100,000 acres (40,300ha). Its annual crop can be three times as much as that of Beaujolais, and not very much less than all of Bordeaux.

Within this there is, of course, wide variation of quality and style, lighter soils and cooler climes making lighter wines. Some Côtes du Rhône is extremely ordinary, but even this portmanteau appellation has its treasures, often but not always the lesser wines of producers in grander appellations. The archetype was Château de Fonsalette from the same stable as the famous Château Rayas of Châteauneuf-du-

Pape. Coudoulet de Beaucastel is Château de Beaucastel's riposte. But there are achievers in outlying areas too, such as those whose labels are shown at the bottom of the next page.

Grenache must now account for at least 40% of all red Côtes du Rhône; its most usual but by no means only blending partners being Syrah and Mourvèdre. White and rosé wines account for just 2% and 4% of production respectively.

The **Côtes du Rhône-Villages** appellation is a very distinct step up, and one that can offer some of France's best value. Of the 95 communes eligible for the -Villages suffix, all of them in the south, the 20 best have the right to append their names to the already cumbersome moniker Côtes du Rhône-Villages. These favoured villages are marked in italics on this map and some of the best-known are mapped in detail overleaf. Others that have established some degree of fame outside their own region include Valréas, Visan, and, on the right bank of the Rhône, Chusclan, which, with nearby Laudun, has a reputation for fine rosés as well as reds. The two northernmost of the Côtes du Rhône-Villages, Rousset-les-Vignes and St-Pantaléon-les-Vignes, used to sell their wines as Haut-Comtat, a name little seen today.

Between these northern villages and the Rhône lies **Coteaux du Tricastin** in a parched mistral-swept landscape better known in the past for its truffles than its wine. Mourvèdre will not ripen so far from the Mediterranean so it is Cinsault that bolsters fruity Grenache and stiffening Syrah here. Wines from the likes of Domaine Gramenon made here can be aged for longer than the usual two or three years.

Also reflecting higher altitudes and cooler conditions than most Côtes du Rhône is **Côtes du Ventoux**. The tradition here was for reds and rosés that were light in every way and lively when very young, but producers such as Fondrèche and Pesquié are now making increasingly serious wine.

Lying on the right bank of the Rhône, the **Côtes du Vivarais** is almost invariably like featherweight Côtes du Rhône thanks to conditions that are exceptionally cool for this torrid part of France.

Much hotter and more Mediterranean-influenced are the vineyards of the **Costières de Nîmes** north of the Camargue, now rightly considered a westward extension of the vineyards mapped overleaf rather than part of the Languedoc.

Can you not hear the cicadas croaking on this sleepy afternoon in Gigondas under the much-painted Dentelles de Montmirail? Gigondas was one of the first southern Rhône villages to earn its own appellation.

Nîm

CH DE LA TU

oM

Montpellier

oUchaud

DOM DE
PIERRES

Vauvert

CH DE BECK

CH ROUBAU

Étang
Charn

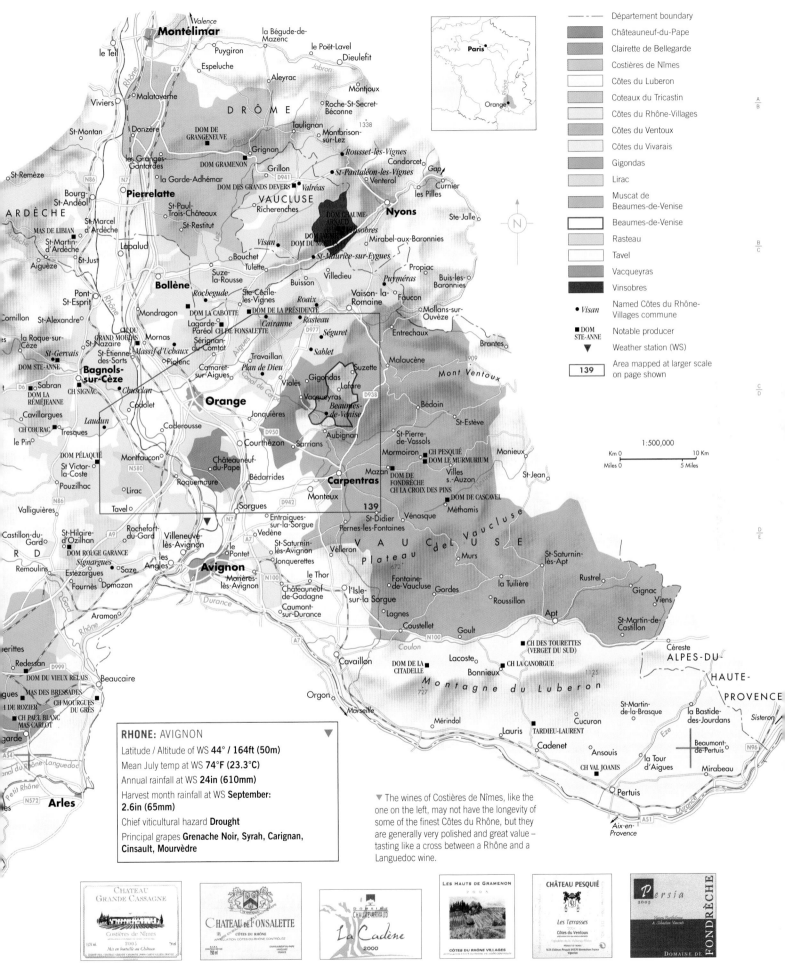

Legend:

- — · — Département boundary
- Châteauneuf-du-Pape
- Clairette de Bellegarde
- Costières de Nîmes
- Côtes du Luberon
- Coteaux du Tricastin
- Côtes du Rhône-Villages
- Côtes du Ventoux
- Côtes du Vivarais
- Gigondas
- Lirac
- Muscat de Beaumes-de-Venise
- Beaumes-de-Venise
- Rasteau
- Tavel
- Vacqueyras
- Vinsobres
- • *Visan* — Named Côtes du Rhône-Villages commune
- ■ DOM STE-ANNE — Notable producer
- ▼ — Weather station (WS)
- 139 — Area mapped at larger scale on page shown

1:500,000
Km 0 ——— 10 Km
Miles 0 ——— 5 Miles

RHONE: AVIGNON ▼

Latitude / Altitude of WS **44°** / **164ft (50m)**

Mean July temp at WS **74°F (23.3°C)**

Annual rainfall at WS **24in (610mm)**

Harvest month rainfall at WS **September: 2.6in (65mm)**

Chief viticultural hazard **Drought**

Principal grapes **Grenache Noir, Syrah, Carignan, Cinsault, Mourvèdre**

▼ The wines of Costières de Nîmes, like the one on the left, may not have the longevity of some of the finest Côtes du Rhône, but they are generally very polished and great value – tasting like a cross between a Rhône and a Languedoc wine.

Châteauneuf-du-Pape and Environs

Châteauneuf-du-Pape is the renowned centrepiece of the southern Rhône, just north of Avignon on hills dominated by a ruined papal summer palace. It is mapped here with its most famous neighbouring villages either across the Rhône or east of a wedge of land too flat and fertile for serious wine production. The meaty, spicy red wine of Châteauneuf has the distinction not only of having the highest minimum strength of any French wine (12.5% alcohol, though in practice usually over 14%) but also of being the first to be so regulated. In 1923 its most famous grower, the late Baron Le Roy of Château Fortia, delimited the land arid enough to support both lavender and thyme, thereby laying the foundation stones for France's famous Appellation Contrôlée (AC) system.

Some 100,000hl of wine a year are made here, 95% of it red but hugely variable in quality. Most is good to average; lightened in colour (not alcohol) by increasing the proportion of Grenache grapes so that it can be drunk after a mere year or two. Many Châteauneuf estates, however, like Bordeaux châteaux, produce classic dark and deep wines, each using its own cocktail of the 13 permitted grape varieties to make more or less spicy, more or less tannic or smooth, shorter- or longer-lived wine. Grenache is the backbone of the AC, often blended with Mourvèdre and Syrah together with some Cinsault, Counoise (a local speciality), and small amounts of Vaccarèse, Picpoul Noir, Terret Noir, and the light-skinned Grenache Blanc, Clairette, Bourboulenc, Roussanne (which is much easier to grow in the southern than the northern Rhône), and the neutral Picardan. Château de Beaucastel and Clos des Papes, unusually, persist with all 13.

Modern winemaking methods and a global taste for Mediterranean wines have seen established performers such as the Châteaux de Beaucastel, Rayas, and La Nerthe, Domaine du Vieux Télégraphe, and Clos des Papes joined by a host of sometimes idiosyncratic individuals such as Henri Bonneau, André Brunel at Les Cailloux, and the Férauds at Domaine du Pegaü, whose limited edition bottlings appeal so much to the fine wine collector. Their reds, always rich and spicy but often tough in youth, can age to sumptuous, sometimes gamey, depths of flavour and their rare whites, succulent from an early age, develop exotic scents, occasionally reminiscent of orange peel, after seven or eight years. Many producers use heavy burgundy-shaped bottles embossed according to which of several rival factions they belong to.

The Châteauneuf-du-Pape cliché is the *galet*, the rounded, heat-absorbing stone found almost exclusively in some of its vineyards, but in reality soils within this relatively small area are much more varied. The famous vineyards of Rayas, for instance, have hardly any *galets* but quite a high proportion of both clay and sand. Wine produced on the predominantly north-facing vineyards between Mont-Redon and Orange tends to be lighter and more elegant with much softer tannins than those of hotter sites. The use of new wood, size of cask, and the proportion of Mourvèdre in the blend are also responsible for the extraordinary variation in style among Châteauneufs made today.

Châteauneuf-du-Pape is surrounded by more than 100 communities that produce Côtes du Rhône; the named Côtes du Rhône-Villages communes are marked in magenta, mainly in the north of the map. Some, however, have won their own appellation. **Gigondas**, producing a tight-knit powerhouse of a red needing five or six years' ageing from a hot bowl of vineyards beneath the Dentelles de Montmirail, rivals Châteauneuf-du-Pape itself. Ambitious producers such as Domaine Santa Duc and Château de St-Cosme have successfully experimented with new oak while traditionalists such as Domaine de Cayron still make sumptuously heady wines.

Vacqueyras earned its own appellation in 1990 and, although generally more restrained than Gigondas, it can also offer the spice and herbs of the southern Rhône at a fair price. **Vinsobres** (see map, p.137) and **Beaumes-de-Venise** gained AC status for their chunky reds from 2004. **Cairanne** and **Rasteau** have also proved themselves worthy of AC status, even if by mid-2006 all they could officially muster was an appellation for Rasteau's rather rustic strong and sweet Vins Doux Naturels (see p.144). Beaumes-de-Venise has long been celebrated for its own strong, sweet, golden Muscat VDN.

The named Côtes du Rhône-Villages wines are all characters worthy of closer study. Sablet,

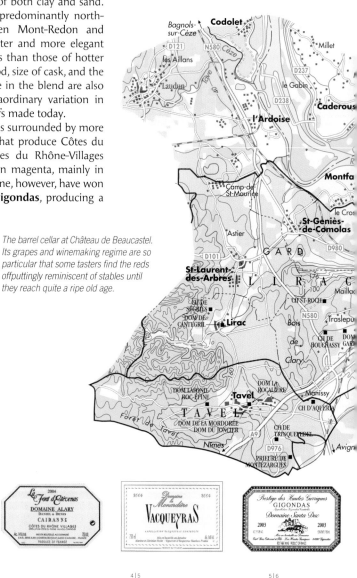

The barrel cellar at Château de Beaucastel. Its grapes and winemaking regime are so particular that some tasters find the reds offputtingly reminiscent of stables until they reach quite a ripe old age.

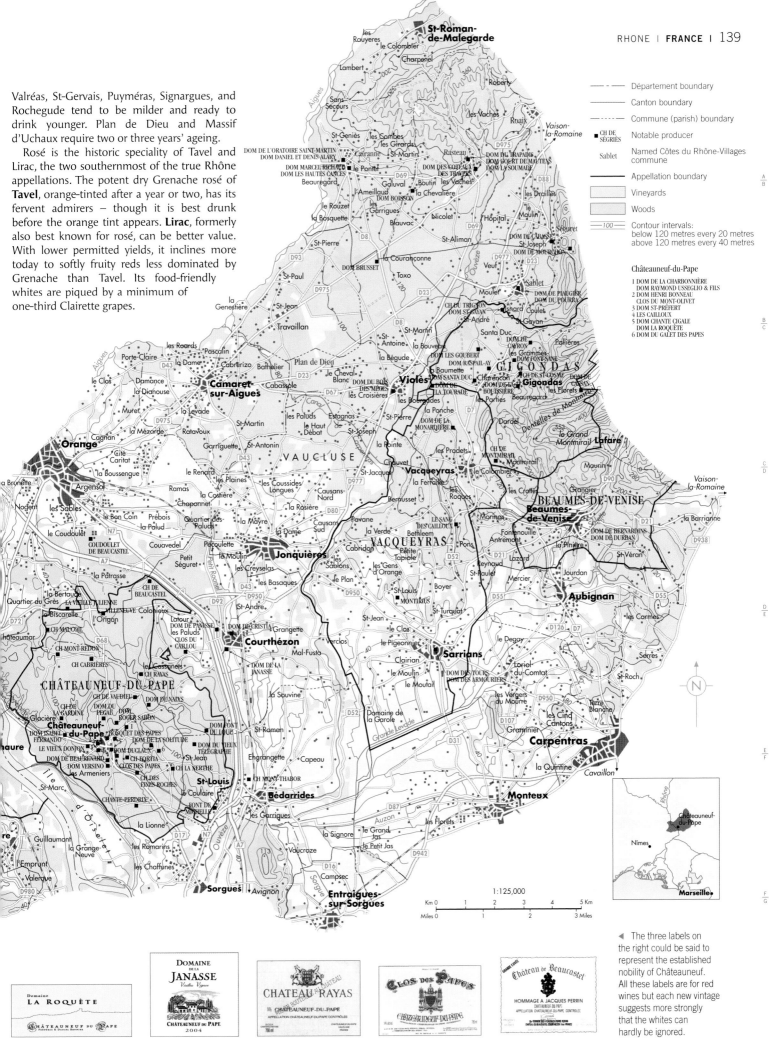

Valréas, St-Gervais, Puyméras, Signargues, and Rochegude tend to be milder and ready to drink younger. Plan de Dieu and Massif d'Uchaux require two or three years' ageing.

Rosé is the historic speciality of Tavel and Lirac, the two southernmost of the true Rhône appellations. The potent dry Grenache rosé of **Tavel**, orange-tinted after a year or two, has its fervent admirers – though it is best drunk before the orange tint appears. **Lirac**, formerly also best known for rosé, can be better value. With lower permitted yields, it inclines more today to softly fruity reds less dominated by Grenache than Tavel. Its food-friendly whites are piqued by a minimum of one-third Clairette grapes.

Département boundary
Canton boundary
Commune (parish) boundary
Notable producer
Named Côtes du Rhône-Villages commune

Appellation boundary
Vineyards
Woods

Contour intervals:
below 120 metres every 20 metres
above 120 metres every 40 metres

Châteauneuf-du-Pape
1 DOM DE LA CHARBONNIÈRE
  DOM RAYMOND USSEGLIO & FILS
2 DOM HENRI BONNEAU
  CLOS DU MONT-OLIVET
3 DOM ST-PRÉFERT
4 LES CAILLOUX
5 DOM CHANTE CIGALE
  DOM LA ROQUÈTE
6 DOM DU GALET DES PAPES

1:125,000

The three labels on the right could be said to represent the established nobility of Châteauneuf. All these labels are for red wines but each new vintage suggests more strongly that the whites can hardly be ignored.

Western Languedoc

The Languedoc, described in more detail overleaf, is France's open back door, its melting pot, its link with more southerly climes. While most of the region is firmly Mediterranean, its far west is influenced by the Atlantic. All of its highest, wildest wine regions are mapped on these pages. The character of their wines shades from Rhône-like (or at least Rhône-influenced) in the east to something more like Bordeaux in structure, if not in flavour, in higher and more western vineyards.

Of the two most important appellations of the western Languedoc, **Minervois** is slightly more civilized, more polished. The terrain is not quite so rugged as that of Corbières, although at its northern limit where vineyards push up into the foothills of the dominating Montagne Noire, their hold on the rocky, *garrigue*-covered foothills of the Cévennes looks every bit as precarious as that of the gnarled Corbières vines on what are effectively the foothills of the Pyrenees. Clinging above the village of Minerve are some of the appellation's highest, latest-ripening vineyards, overlooking a south-facing amphitheatre. Just downhill in a wide sweep west, the Petit Causse is a belt of clay-limestone in the best circle seats. The vineyards around La Livinière produce so many wines which seem to combine the rugged scents of the high vineyards with the suave suppleness of lower altitude wines that they have earned their own appellation.

To the southwest is Clamoux, where Atlantic influence begins, in the form of higher acid levels and a slightly lighter style. The subregions of Argent Double, hotter, drier land sloping down towards the River Aude, and Serres, closest to the Mediterranean, provide much of the dreary blended Minervois found at come-hither prices in every French supermarket. The producers' names on the map are those of more ambitious individuals and co-operatives making particularly supple wine.

Although more than 94% of all Minervois is red, and 4% is now rosé, the ancient Bourboulenc grape underpins some increasingly fine white blends of Maccabéo, Grenache Blanc, Marsanne, Roussanne, and Rolle, with oak nowadays often a well-integrated component.

Bourboulenc, commonly called Malvoisie, comes into its own on a strange western outpost of the Languedoc appellation (described in detail overleaf) called La Clape, an eccentric detached limestone massif that in Roman times was an island south of the port of Narbo (today's Narbonne). These whites really are marine-, not to say iodine-, scented. An increasing array of sweet wines are also made in Minervois, not least aromatic **Muscat de St-Jean de Minervois**.

The **Corbières** landscape is even more dramatic: a geological chaos of mountain and valley reaching from the sea 40 miles (60km) back into the Aude département. Limestone alternates with schist, clays, marls, and sandstone; the influence of the Mediterranean with intermittent influence from the Atlantic blowing down the Aude Valley and over its western hills.

Red Corbières, other than at its most mundane, tastes less tamed and more concentrated, often rather tougher, than Minervois, whose vineyards enjoy less extreme summers. Drought and summer fires are constant threats in many parts of the varied Corbières appellation, which has always been a hotbed of local politics. A major reshuffle in 1990 divided Corbières into no fewer than 11 climatic zones, but those of St-Victor, Quéribus, and Termenès in the far southwest have since been amalgamated into Hautes-Corbières, and the low, barren hills around Boutenac have earned their own appellation **Corbières-Boutenac**.

Fitou, granted the Languedoc's first appellation in 1948 and a longstanding producer of Rivesaltes VDN (see p.144), consists of two distinct enclaves within Corbières: a clay-limestone band around the saltwater lagoons on the coast and a patch of mountainous schist 15 or so miles (24km) inland, separated by a great wedge of Corbières. For much of the 1980s and 1990s, Fitou lagged behind its northern neighbours but today producers such as Domaine Maria Fita and Bertrand-Bergé are giving the two prominent co-operatives, Mont Tauch and Cascastel, a run for their money. The proportion of Grenache is increasing at the expense of Carignan in Fitou Montagneux, while Syrah and Mourvèdre are gaining ground in Fitou Maritime.

The extent of the cooling Atlantic influence here is most graphically seen in the western hills south of Carcassonne where **Limoux** long ago established at least a national reputation for its fine traditional method fizz, whether Blanquette, based on the original Mauzac grape, or the more delicate Crémant de Limoux made from Chardonnay and Chenin Blanc. Still white Limoux is oak-fermented, obviously raised in a much cooler environment than expected

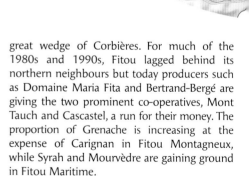

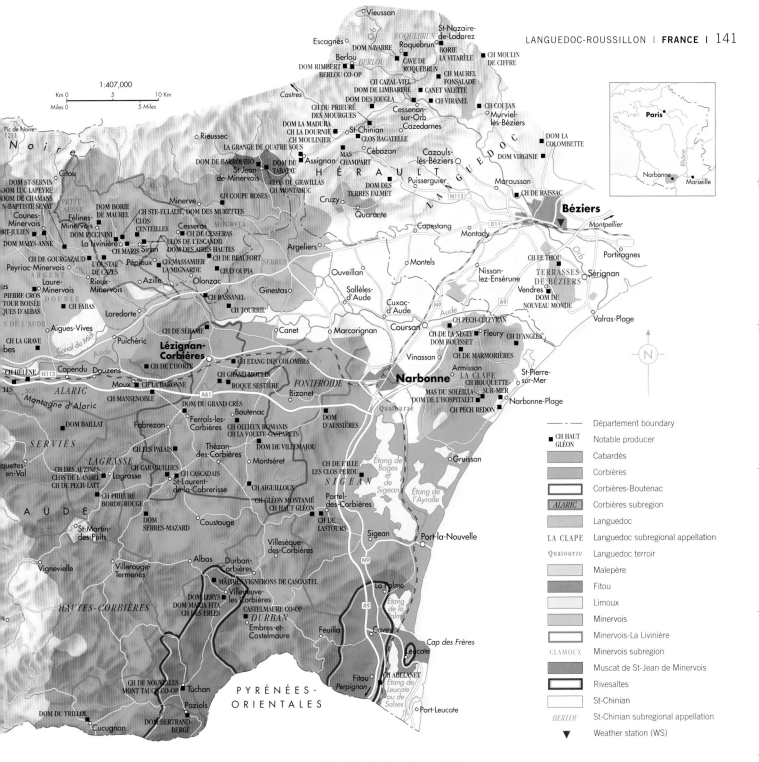

Légende / Legend:

------	Département boundary
■ CH HAUT GLÉON	Notable producer
	Cabardès
	Corbières
	Corbières-Boutenac
ALARIC	Corbières subregion
	Languedoc
LA CLAPE	Languedoc subregional appellation
Quatourze	Languedoc terroir
	Malepère
	Fitou
	Limoux
	Minervois
	Minervois-La Livinière
CLAMOUX	Minervois subregion
	Muscat de St-Jean de Minervois
	Rivesaltes
	St-Chinian
BERLOU	St-Chinian subregional appellation
▼	Weather station (WS)

this far south, and based on Chardonnay. The relatively recent red Limoux appellation is for oaked blends of which Merlot must constitute half and the rest may be drawn from the other Bordeaux grapes and Grenache and Syrah.

All of these wines have much finer acidity than those made in the warmer eastern Languedoc, as do those of the **Côtes de la Malepère** to the immediate north. Malepère wines, never blockbusters, are dominated by Merlot and Malbec (or Côt). Just north of

Carcassonne, **Cabardès** is the only appellation in which Mediterranean and Atlantic (Bordeaux) grapes are mandatorily combined. The increasingly well made wines reflect this.

St-Chinian is mapped on this page but is described overleaf with its neighbour Faugères.

▼ A selection of the many appellations mapped here, with Fitou the only one pre-dating 1985, plus Chloé, an impressive blend of Bordeaux varieties grown in the relatively cool, high vineyards near Roquetaillade. Mansenoble is a suave Corbières.

LANGUEDOC: BEZIERS ▼

Latitude / Altitude of WS **43° / 262ft (80m)**

Mean July temp at WS **73.4°F (23°C)**

Annual rainfall at WS **28in (710mm)**

Harvest month rainfall at WS **September: 2.5in (65mm)**

Chief viticultural hazards **Drought**

Principal grapes **Carignan, Grenache Noir, Cinsault, Syrah, Merlot, Cabernet Sauvignon**

Eastern Languedoc

The sweep of vines around France's central Mediterranean coastline has only relatively recently joined the French wine mainstream. For years it was merely the provider of pale red *vin ordinaire*, the produce of overcropped vines, often as much from the appellation areas shaded on the map opposite as from the flatlands of the coastal hinterland. But today there is no shortage of evidence of the quality of wine that can be coaxed from these more propitious zones, generally on higher ground and poorer soils; wines with real local character, a strong French accent, and remarkably attractive prices. While most of the maps in this book show the extent of all the vineyards in a particular region, the vine has been planted so extensively in the area mapped here that only those areas producing Appellation Contrôleé wines are highlighted.

The big challenge not just for France but for the European Union in the early 21st century is what to do about those Languedoc vineyards that do not qualify for AC status, particularly those planted with varieties capable of producing only the most basic Vin de Table. The Languedoc-Roussillon is still the biggest wine region in the world with over 721,500 acres (292,000ha) of vines in 2005 (Bordeaux had 375,000 acres/151,600ha). A total of 30,000 individuals and their families depended on their own vines for income in the late 1990s. Thanks to an expensive programme of subsidies and careful managing of planting rights, that total had been reduced to just over 24,000 by 2005, but it still represents a powerful social force, and one that has a long tradition of militant protest.

Relatively few of these vine-growers also make wine. A good two-thirds of them, a higher proportion than in any other French wine region, take their grapes straight to the local co-op, of which there are still more than 200 in the Languedoc-Roussillon, almost half of them in the Hérault département mapped opposite. These co-ops are increasingly amalgamating in an attempt to pool resources and gain stature in the competitive modern wine market, but they vary enormously in their abilities to make and sell exportable wine. A considerable proportion of Europe's wine surplus, which was forecast to be an embarrassing 27 million hl, or almost half of total French wine production, by 2010, is still produced in the area mapped here.

▼ The enigmatic neck label below belongs to the top bottling of Château Puech Haut. The Servières is based on brilliant cherry-like Cinsault. No other wine region can offer such a wide range of grape varieties as are represented here.

But wine enthusiasts should concentrate on the wines that emerge from the coloured zones of the eastern Languedoc appellations. The most exciting wines tend to be made by passionate individuals, often first-generation wine producers who would, in another age, have signed up for more conventional professions. They typically operate where the Romans grew vines (some of the first in Gaul) on hillsides with such poor, shallow soils that nothing else would flourish.

The Coteaux du Languedoc appellation, which in 2006 was recast simply as the over-arching regional appellation **Languedoc**, is by far the most important, and most varied. Its subregional appellations and terroirs (see the names in magenta) encompass most, but not all, of the likely spots for top quality viticulture in the eastern Languedoc – as the distribution of notable producers clearly shows.

One of the most obviously distinctive terroirs within the Languedoc is Pic-St-Loup in the far north of the area mapped here on the foothills of the dramatic Cévennes. The wines produced on the flanks of the rocky finger that is the Pic-St-Loup itself, north of Montpellier, by such estates as Clos Marie, Mas Bruguière, Domaine de l'Hortus, and Châteaux de Cazeneuve, de Lancyre, and Lascaux are obviously the products of southern sunshine. They reflect the herbs of the region but also the definition conferred by altitude and relatively cool nights. The subregional appellation Terrasses du Larzac, encompassing the terroirs of Montpeyroux and St-Saturnin, north of Clermont-l'Hérault, is even higher and and makes even more intense wines, with some of the wild character to be found in the hills of Corbières to the southwest. The pioneer, in the 1970s, was the Mas de Daumas Gassac. Producers such as Domaines l'Aiguelière, d'Aupilhac (with Cinsault and old-vine Carignan), Font Caude, and La Sauvageonne have confirmed the high potential of these windy hills.

The zone of Grés de Montpellier incorporates a wide swathe of vineyards with varied soils southwest and north of this ancient university city but which all benefit from the moderating influence of sea breezes throughout the heat of high summer. The medieval town of Pézenas lends its name to a subregional wine appellation extending north of the town as far as Cabrières, rich in the schist that characterizes both Faugères to the immediate west and its neighbour St-Chinian mapped on the previous page.

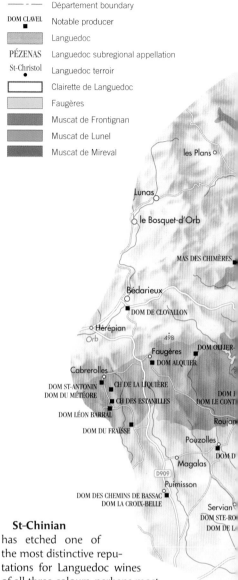

	Département boundary
DOM CLAVEL ■	Notable producer
	Languedoc
PÉZENAS	Languedoc subregional appellation
St-Christol ●	Languedoc terroir
	Clairette de Languedoc
	Faugères
	Muscat de Frontignan
	Muscat de Lunel
	Muscat de Mireval

St-Chinian
has etched one of the most distinctive reputations for Languedoc wines of all three colours, perhaps most characterfully from the rugged schists of the north and west of the zone at altitudes often well above 1,970ft (600m) in spectacularly mountainous country. There are fine whites, Carignan-marked reds from St-Chinian-Berlou, and St-Chinian-Roquebrune reds more heavily influenced by Rhône varieties, particularly sharply etched Syrah grown on schist. Vines grown at lower altitudes on the bizarre purple clay and limestone soils around the village of St-Chinian itself tend to be softer and more supple. **Faugères** is made up almost entirely of schist and demands hard work on meagre soils and vineyards up to 2,300ft (700m) overlooking Béziers, the plain, and the much less promising vineyards that stretch towards the coast.

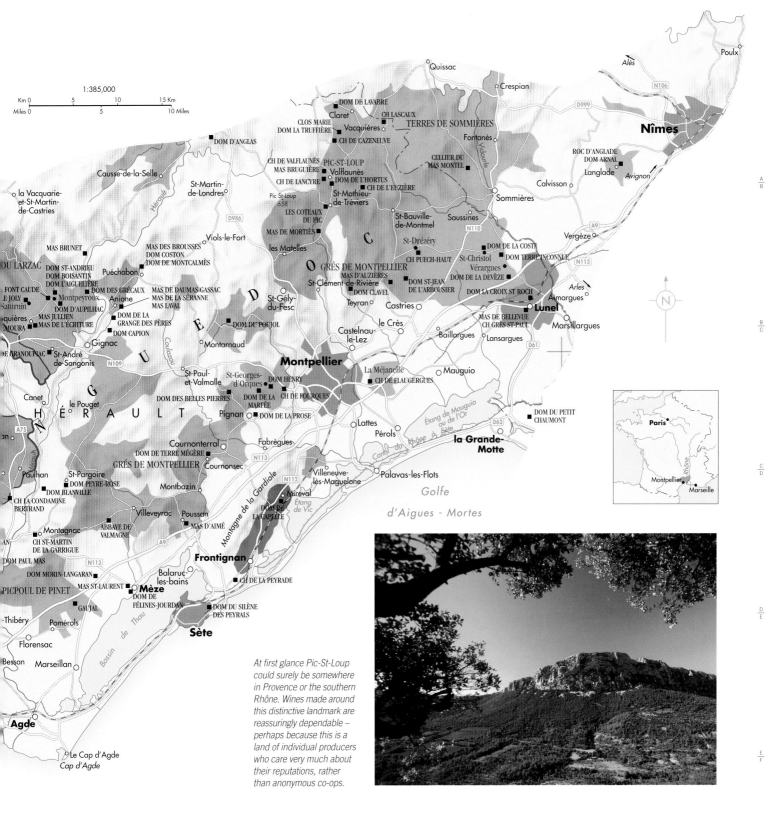

At first glance Pic-St-Loup could surely be somewhere in Provence or the southern Rhône. Wines made around this distinctive landmark are reassuringly dependable – perhaps because this is a land of individual producers who care very much about their reputations, rather than anonymous co-ops.

Of the vast production of the Languedoc, more than 80% is red, and mainly blends of Mediterranean varieties such as Carignan (still France's most planted grape, traditionally vinified by carbonic maceration in an effort to soften it) with increasing proportions of Grenache, Syrah, Mourvèdre, or Cinsault. White winemaking has become increasingly sophisticated, however, and there are now many intriguing blends of such grapes as Grenache Blanc, Clairette, Bourboulenc, Picpoul, Roussanne, Marsanne, and Viognier.

Clairette du Languedoc and **Picpoul de Pinet** are white wines embraced by the AC system. The first is now made, just north of Pézenas, in an increasingly fresh style to flatter what can be a very refreshing grape variety while the second, most unusually for France, is a varietal appellation, in this case dependent on the quirky, lemon-scented Picpoul grape grown between Pézenas and the sea. These represent the tradition of the Languedoc as much as the sweet golden Vins Doux Naturels based on Muscat, of which Muscat de Frontignan was once world famous. Muscats de Mireval and de Lunel south of Nîmes rarely show the zest of a Frontignan wine.

Those are the principal appellations of the eastern Languedoc but most producers, whether in an AC zone or in the flatlands in between, make a range of Vins de Pays (considered in detail on pp.152–53). And many, particularly but not exclusively those outside the official appellation zones, make nothing but Vins de Pays – whether carrying the name of some small local Vin de Pays zone or the more internationally recognizable Vin de Pays d'Oc with a grape name. The reliably hot summers can ripen a usefully wide range of grape varieties and here at least French prejudice against *vins de cépage* – those that Anglo-Saxons call varietal wines – is much less marked.

The Languedoc has proved that it can play a decent game on that horribly level playing field which is home to the most basic producers of the New World. Fortunately for us all, it has also proved that it can produce serious, terroir-driven essences of southern France too.

The traditional product of the upper Agly Valley is Vin Doux Naturel, seen here ageing not inside in cask but, following one local tradition, in the hot sun in glass bonbonnes – 3,024 of them at Mas Amiel in the Maury appellation.

Roussillon

Roussillon, whose wines are currently in an exciting state of flux, is so much more than a suffix, being very different both physically and culturally from the Languedoc. Its inhabitants consider themselves Catalans who happen to find themselves in France, but only since 1659. Their yellow and red striped banners are everywhere, their local dialect with its double Ls more closely resembles Spanish than French.

The landscape here may be more dramatic – at the eastern end of the Pyrenees the peaks of the Canigou, snow-covered most of the year, swoop more than 7,500ft (2,500m) down to the Mediterranean – but the region is softer, less wild than the rocky lower contours of the Corbières hills to the north. Sunshine (an average of 325 days a year) helps, and explains the fields and groves (and vineyards) of fruit and vegetables to which the Perpignan plain and Agly, Têt, and Tech valley floors are devoted. The effects of that sunshine are concentrated by the east-facing amphitheatre created by the Corbières, Canigou, and Albères mountains which separate modern France from Spain.

This means that France's first fruits of the season regularly come from here, and the vineyards on the plain are some of the driest and hottest in France, their low bushes yielding only modest quantities of fully ripe Grenache grapes of all hues as early as mid-August. They have traditionally been used for the most basic of Roussillon's famous Vins Doux Naturels (VDN). These once-popular apéritifs are not in fact naturally sweet wines, as the name implies, but part-fermented grape juice stopped from becoming wine by adding alcohol, the timing of this being dictated by the sweetness and strength sought.

Roussillon makes 90% of all of France's Vins Doux Naturels, and **Rivesaltes**, made in a vast area of Roussillon mainly from Grenache Noir, Blanc, and Gris, is France's most popular VDN by far. It is styled either Ambré, Grenat, or Tuilé, according to whether it was respectively made from pale-skinned grapes, dark-skinned grapes, or made mainly from Grenache Noir and deliberately exposed to air.

Muscat de Rivesaltes comes from the same generous zone, incorporating all but the highest vineyard land of the Pyrénées-Orientales département, together with the two enclaves of Fitou in the Aude mapped on p.141. Permitted yields are lower for the Muscat, and the wine, made from Muscat of Alexandria with some Muscat Blanc grapes, is generally finer, although most are best drunk young.

But it is the curious inland region of the upper Agly Valley, with its distinctive black schist around Maury in the far northern uplands of Roussillon, that has become the focus of the most exciting recent wine activity in Roussillon. The sheer quality of its deep-flavoured reds and firm, long-living, mineral-scented dry whites has drawn a host of winemakers from all over the world to join pioneer Gérard Gauby, a convert to biodynamic viticulture. At the time of writing this dramatic landscape does not even have its own appellation but **Maury** has one for its VDN, mostly rosé or red, which can be as noble and certainly as long-lived as a good Banyuls.

Banyuls is France's finest VDN, grown at yields that sometimes average less than 20hl/ha on France's southernmost vineyards, steep windswept terraces of brown schist sloping to the sea just north of a rather sleepy Spanish frontier post. Grapes vary considerably but come predominantly from ancient Grenache Noir bushes ripened to almost record levels, often shrivelling to raisins on the vine. For Grand Cru Banyuls, made only in particularly good years, 30 months of barrel-ageing and 75% of Grenache Noir is mandatory. Ageing techniques and therefore hues and wine styles vary just as widely as for port (see p.221), and sometimes for similar reasons. Pale wines heady with rancio flavour may result from long ageing in old wooden barrels in relatively warm conditions, while Rimage wines are aged, like vintage port, at a much more stately pace in bottle.

Dry wines made from the vineyards devoted to Banyuls are called after the pretty fishing port of **Collioure**, famously home to artists and anchovy packers. Deep crimson essences, almost more Spanish than French, also testify to the robust alcohol levels achieved by the vines, mainly Grenache but increasingly supplemented by Syrah and Mourvèdre. Powerful white Collioure is also made from Grenache Blanc and Gris.

The dry wines of Roussillon are certainly easier for outsiders to understand than its VDN, even if they are evolving in style and composition every year. **Côtes du Roussillon** is the base level, still made largely from old-vine Carignan with Grenache, Cinsault, and, particularly, Syrah and Mourvèdre playing an increasingly important role. Many reds and whites, including Agly's best, are sold as Vin de Pays des Côtes Catalanes. Roussillon can boast an exotic palette of pale-skinned grape varieties which can be transformed into heady, perfumed dry table wines (see key facts panel).

Côtes du Roussillon-Villages are bolder, more positive wines (reds only) thanks to even lower yields and higher strength. This appellation is

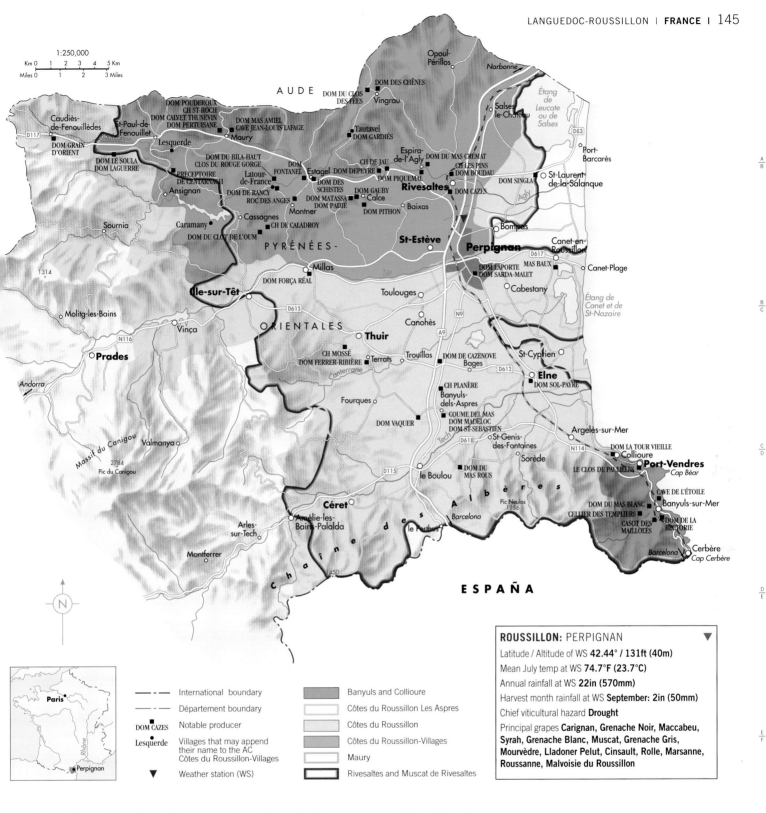

1:250,000

| Km 0 | 1 | 2 | 3 | 4 | 5 Km |
| Miles 0 | | 1 | | 2 | 3 Miles |

AUDE

Opoul-
Périllos

Narbonne

DOM DU CLOS
DES FÉES
DOM DES CHÊNES
Vingrau

Caudiès-
de-Fenouillèdes
St-Paul-de-
Fenouillet
DOM POUDEROUX
CH ST-ROCH
DOM CALVET THUNEVIN
DOM PERTUISANE
DOM MAS AMIEL
CAVE JEAN-LOUIS LAFAGE

Tautavel
DOM GARDIÉS

Salses-
le-Château

Étang
de
Leucate
ou de
Salses

D117
DOM GRAIN
D'ORIENT
Lesquerde
Maury
Espira-
de-l'Agly
DOM DU MAS CRÉMAT
CH DE JAU
CH LES PINS
DOM BOUDAU

Port-
Barcarès

DOM LE SOULA
DOM LAGUERRE
DOM DU BILA-HAUT
CLOS DU ROUGE GORGE
PRÉCEPTOIRE
DE CENTARNACH
Latour-
de-France
DOM
FONTANEL
Estagel
DOM DEPEYRE
DOM PIQUEMAL
DOM SINGLA
St-Laurent-
de-la-Salanque

A
B

Ansignan
DOM DE RANCY
ROC DES ANGES
DOM DES
SCHISTES
DOM GAUBY
DOM MATASSA
DOM PADIÉ
Calce
Rivesaltes
DOM CAZES

Caramany
Cassagnes
Montner
DOM PITHON
Baixas
Bompas

Sournia
CH DE CALADROY
PYRÉNÉES-

DOM DU CLOT DE L'OUM
St-Estève
Perpignan
Canet-en-
Roussillon

1314
Millas
Têt
D617
MAS BAUX
DOM LAPORTE
DOM SARDA-MALET
Canet-Plage

Molitg-les-Bains
DOM FORÇA RÉAL
Toulouges
Cabestany

B
C

Ile-sur-Têt
D615
ORIENTALES
Canohès
A9

Étang de
Canet et de
St-Nazaire

Vinça
N9

Andorra
N116
Prades
Thuir
Trouillas
St-Cyprien

CH MOSSÉ
DOM FERRER-RIBIÈRE
Terrats
DOM DE CAZENOVE
Bages
D612
Elne
DOM SOL-PAYRE

Massif du Canigou
Canterrane
CH PLANÈRE
Banyuls-
dels-Aspres

C
D

Valmanya
Fourques
DOM VAQUER
COUME DEL MAS
DOM MADELOC
DOM-ST-SEBASTIEN
St-Genis-
des-Fontaines
Sorède
Argelès-sur-Mer

2784
Pic du Canigou
D115
Tech
D618
DOM DU
MAS ROUS
LE CLOS DE PAULILLES
DOM LA TOUR VIEILLE
Collioure
Port-Vendres
Cap Béar

Céret
le Boulou
Pic Neulos
1256
CAVE DE L'ÉTOILE
Banyuls-sur-Mer

Arles-
sur-Tech
Amélie-les-
Bains-Palalda
Albères
Barcelona
DOM DU MAS BLANC
CELLIER DES TEMPLIERS
CASOT DES
MAILLOLÉS
DOM DE LA
RECTORIE

Montferrer
Chaîne des
le Perthus
1450
Barcelona
Cerbère
Cap Cerbère

D
E

ESPAÑA

N

Paris
Rhône
Perpignan

– – – International boundary

— — Département boundary

DOM CAZES Notable producer

Lesquerde Villages that may append
their name to the AC
Côtes du Roussillon-Villages

▼ Weather station (WS)

Banyuls and Collioure

Côtes du Roussillon Les Aspres

Côtes du Roussillon

Côtes du Roussillon-Villages

Maury

Rivesaltes and Muscat de Rivesaltes

ROUSSILLON: PERPIGNAN ▼

Latitude / Altitude of WS **42.44° / 131ft (40m)**

Mean July temp at WS **74.7°F (23.7°C)**

Annual rainfall at WS **22in (570mm)**

Harvest month rainfall at WS **September: 2in (50mm)**

Chief viticultural hazard **Drought**

Principal grapes **Carignan, Grenache Noir, Maccabeu,
Syrah, Grenache Blanc, Muscat, Grenache Gris,
Mourvèdre, Lladoner Pelut, Cinsault, Rolle, Marsanne,
Roussanne, Malvoisie du Roussillon**

restricted to the northern third of the area and allows the villages of Latour-de-France, Lesquerde, Tautavel, and Caramany their own sub-appellations. Many of these wines offer good value for firm, solid, age-worthy wines whose aromas come from the soil rather than from following international fashion.

The early 21st century appellation **Côtes du Roussillon Les Aspres** was devised expressly for superior wines from those villages not included in Côtes du Roussillon-Villages. There has been no shortage of work for wine bureaucrats in this, the southernmost wine region of France.

▼ An array of some of the newest stars in all of France – truly exciting and distinctive dry whites and reds, together with two of the better products of the vineyards around Collioure, one strong, the other very strong and sweet.

Provence

Provence! The name alone has such resonance, let alone the place, that visiting wine drinkers were long prepared to forgive a region whose most distinctive offering used to be an excess of over-strong and under-flavoured rosé.

Happily this quintessentially Mediterranean region has been invaded by the same sort of individuals hellbent on upgrading quality as have been making their mark elsewhere. An increasing proportion of rosé, Provence's most important and increasingly fashionable wine, is gently made, intriguingly perfumed, and dry enough to be the perfect foil for the garlic and olive oil that characterize the region's cuisine. Seriously interesting reds are also being made all over Provence.

A glance at the map explains why these reds may vary considerably in character. The classic appellation **Côtes de Provence** alone, France's most extensive, encompasses the northern outskirts of Marseille, the southern flanks of the Montagne Ste-Victoire, Mediterranean islands, the warm coastal hinterland of resorts such as Le Lavandou and St-Tropez, cooler, sub-alpine retreats north of Draguignan, and even a pocket of vines around Villars well north of Nice.

The generally cooler, limestone enclave of **Coteaux Varois**, a much more recent recruit to AC status, is sheltered from softening maritime influence by the Massif de la Ste-Baume so that some vineyards in the wooded hills north of Brignoles may not be picked until early November, while vintage time on the coast is early September. (The Burgundy négociant Louis Latour has had notable success with Pinot Noir grapes grown even further north near Aups, hinting at just how cool it is here.)

In the west, the landscape of **Coteaux d'Aix-en-Provence** (of which the university town itself is in fact on the southeastern border) is less dramatic, as the wines tend to be – although Counoise grapes add interest to some rosés. The hillside vineyards of the **Côtes du Luberon** on the other side of the River Durance enjoy cooler nights and a more Rhône-like environment and so are mapped in full on p.137. **Coteaux de Pierrevert** (see map of France, p.53) makes noticeably lighter wines.

Between Coteaux d'Aix-en-Provence and the River Rhône itself is the splinter appellation created in 1995 and named after the extraordinary hilltop tourist trap **Les Baux-de-Provence**. Warmed by the sea and buffeted by Provence's famous mistral, this area is even better suited to organic viticulture than most of the rest of Provence. It also provides a notable illustration of the current tensions between the Provençal wine fraternity and the INAO, the headquarters of the French AC system in Paris. The point at issue concerns grape varieties: whether to encourage "tradition" or sheer quality. Having been ruled by successive waves of invaders from the east, north, west, and south (Sardinians for much of the 19th century), Provence boasts a

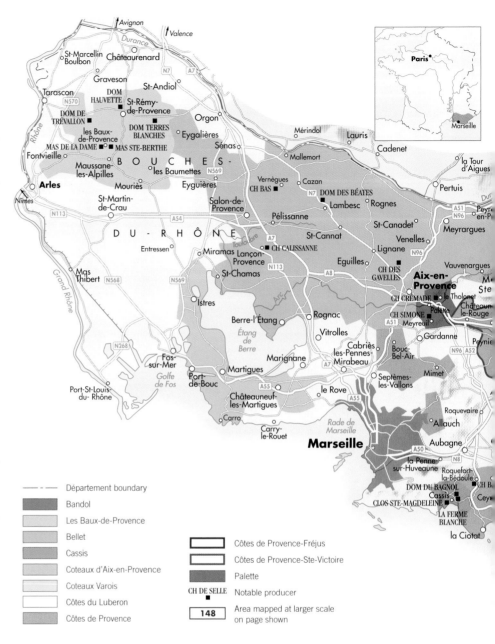

fine and varied legacy of grape varieties, some of them such as Tibouren and Calitor (Pécoui Touar) apparently unknown elsewhere. The INAO's current preoccupation seems to be to reduce and eventually eliminate the Carignan that was planted here, as in the Languedoc, to supply cheap, light reds for northern France in the early 20th century, while encouraging the Grenache and Cinsault (so useful for rosés), and the sturdier Mourvèdre and Syrah which preceded it. Cabernet Sauvignon is officially viewed as a somewhat sinister intruder, whose influence should be strictly controlled.

Many fine Provençal reds (and some whites) are therefore sold today as Vin de Pays, including all of those from Les Baux's Domaine de Trévallon, arguably the region's finest producer of all. Trailblazer of the Cabernet/Syrah blend for Provence was Georges Brunet, who arrived at a dilapidated Château Vignelaure northeast of Aix-en-Provence from Château La Lagune in Bordeaux. (Vignelaure is now in the hands of an Irish racehorse trainer.)

As might be expected of a region with a history of wine-growing that dates back to Roman times, Provence harbours some well-established individual wine zones. Perhaps the most historic is **Palette** on the north-facing, limestone-influenced bank of the River Arc just east of Aix, where the Rougier family of Château Simone has been making extraordinarily dense wine of all three colours for more than 200 years from a palette (hence the name?) of local grape varieties, more numerous even than are allowed in Châteauneuf-du-Pape.

Cassis, centred on the small port to the east of Marseille, also makes a serious effort with its white, particularly herby in this case and de rigueur with bouillabaisse. In the far east of Provence, a handful of vignerons continue to resist the encroachment of Nice on the vineyards of **Bellet**, cooled by winds from the sea and the Alps and enriched by such Italianate grapes as Braquet (Brachetto), Folle Noire (Fuella), and Rolle (Vermentino). Wines made close to tourist centres are rarely underpriced.

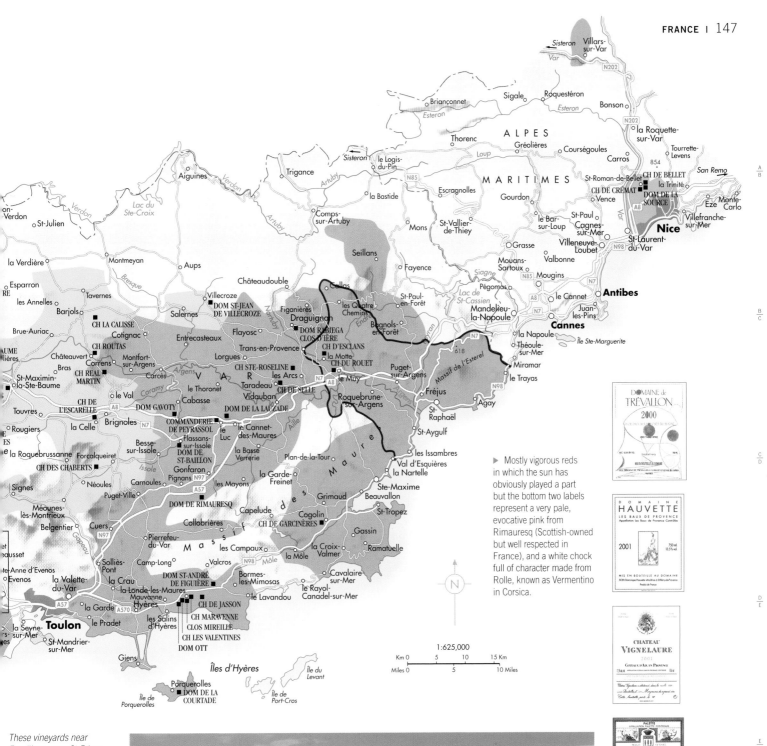

Sisteron
Villars-sur-Var
Var
N202

Briançonnet
Sigale
Roquestéron
Bonson

Esteron
Esteron

la Roquette-sur-Var
Tourrette-Levens

A L P E S

Thorenc
Gréolières
Courségoules
Carros

le Logis-du-Pin
Loup

M A R I T I M E S

San Remo

Trigance
Escragnolles
854
CH DE BELLET
la Trinité
Eze
Monte-Carlo

Aiguines
Verdon
la Bastide
Gourdon
St-Roman-de-Bellet
CH DE CRÉMAT
DOM DE LA SOURCE

Mons
St-Vallier-de-Thiey
le Bar-sur-Loup
Vence
Nice
Villefranche-sur-Mer

on-Verdon

Lac du Ste-Croix

St-Julien

Montmeyan
Aups
Seillans
Grasse
St-Paul
Villeneuve-Loubet
St-Laurent-du-Var

la Verdière

Châteaudouble
Callas
Fayence
Mouans-Sartoux
Valbonne
Mougins

Esparron

Tavernes
Villecroze
DOM ST-JEAN DE VILLECROZE
Figanières
les Quatre Chemins
St-Paul-en-Forêt
Lac de St-Cassien
Pégomas
le Cannet
Antibes

Barjols
Salernes
Draguignan
Bagnols-en-Forêt
Mandelieu-la-Napoule
Cannes

Brue-Auriac
Cotignac
Flayosc
DOM RABIEGA CLOS D'IÈRE
Massif de l'Esterel
la Napoule
Théoule-sur-Mer
Île Ste-Marguerite

Châteauvert
CH LA CALISSE
Entrecasteaux
Lorgues
Trans-en-Provence
CH D'ESCLANS
618
Miramar

Correns
CH ROUTAS
Montfort-sur-Argens
CH STE-ROSELINE
la Motte
CH-DU-ROUET
Puget-sur-Argens
le Trayas

St-Maximin-la-Ste-Baume
CH REAL MARTIN
Carcès
V A R
les Arcs
Fréjus
Agay

Touvres
le Val
Taradeau
Vidauban
le Muy
St-Aygulf

Rougiers
CH DE L'ESCARELLE
DOM GAVOTY
Cabasse
CH DE NELLE
Roquebrune-sur-Argens
St-Raphaël

la Celle
Brignoles
DOM DE LA LAUZADE
les Issambres

la Roquebrussanne
COMMANDERIE DE PEYRASSOL
le Luc
le Cannet-des-Maures
Val d'Esquières

Forcalqueiret
Flassans-sur-Issole
la Basse Verrerie
la Nartelle

CH DES CHABERTS
DOM DE ST-BAILLON
Gonfaron
Pignans
Plan-de-la-Tour
Ste-Maxime

Signes
Néoules
Carnoules
les Mayons
la Garde-Freinet
Beauvallon

Méounes-lès-Montrieux
Puget-Ville
DOM DE RIMAURESQ
Capelude
Grimaud
St-Tropez

Belgentier
Cuers
Collobrières
CH DE GARCINIÈRES
Cogolin
Gassin

Pierrefeu-du-Var
les Campaux
la Croix-Valmer
Ramatuelle

Solliès-Pont
Camp-Long
Valcros
la Môle

DOM ST-ANDRÉ DE FIGUIÈRE
Bormes-les-Mimosas
Cavalaire-sur-Mer

la Crau
Mauvanne
le Rayol-Canadel-sur-Mer

Toulon
la Garde
Hyères
CH DE JASSON
le Lavandou

la Seyne-sur-Mer
le Pradet
les Salins d'Hyères
CH MARAVENNE
CLOS MIREILLE
CH LES VALENTINES

St-Mandrier-sur-Mer
DOM OTT
Giens

Îles d'Hyères

1:625,000
Km 0   5   10   15 Km
Miles 0   5   10 Miles

Porquerolles
DOM DE LA COURTADE
Île de Porquerolles
Île du Levant
Île de Port-Cros

These vineyards near Eygalières, near St-Rémy-de-Provence in the Bouches-du-Rhône département, make it easy to see how those who never intended to invest in wine production might be persuaded to part with their money.

▶ Mostly vigorous reds in which the sun has obviously played a part but the bottom two labels represent a very pale, evocative pink from Rimauresq (Scottish-owned but well respected in France), and a white chock full of character made from Rolle, known as Vermentino in Corsica.

Bandol

On south-tilted terraces among the pines, well inland of the touristy port but open to Mediterranean breezes, the appellation Bandol feels both its isolation and its unique status keenly. In size it is dwarfed by the oceans of Côtes de Provence that make up the bulk of wine produced in this exceptionally sunny corner of southeast France. But in stature it is Provence's most important wine and one, moreover, that fulfils many modern wine drinkers' criteria for pleasure.

The wine is mainly red, made substantially from the fashionable Mourvèdre grape (the only such French appellation), and with its full-blooded almost feral herbiness extremely easy to appreciate. Thanks to a climate benign enough to ripen a vine variety with one of the longest growing cycles of all, most red Bandol is voluptuously ripe and can easily be enjoyed at

only six or seven years. A substantial, often Cinsault-dominated dry rosé is much drunk in the region and small quantities of full white Bandol are also made, mainly from Clairette, Bourboulenc, and Ugni Blanc.

Terroirs in this relatively small appellation vary enormously. On the red clay soils that predominate, the tannins of Mourvèdre can be quite marked so the wine is usually blended with some of the Grenache and Cinsault that are also grown. Grenache can easily reach such high alcohol levels here that it is a common choice for any north-facing vineyard. Soils in the northwest corner are particularly pebbly; the young soils that stretch from St-Cyr to Le Brûlat tend to produce finer, more supple wines, while the oldest soils of the appellation lie south of Le Beausset. Those at higher altitudes such as those at 1,000ft (300m) or so

around Château de Pibarnon tend to be noticeably less fertile than most and here the vintage may extend to mid-October.

If Bandol is struggling to adapt to changes in the outside world (the new oak barrique and associated special cuvées represent a highly contentious issue; larger, old oak casks are still the norm in this region), it can boast a heartening overall standard of quality. Yields are some of the lowest in France, and the Mourvèdre vines must be fully mature before they are allowed to produce red wine. Fortunately, any rain tends to be followed by a sharp mistral that blows away the risk of rot. The low-acid Mourvèdre may not be the easiest grape to vinify, with a tendency to develop an unappetizing smell if not exposed to enough air in the cellar, but the winemaking techniques in Bandol are becoming increasingly sophisticated.

▶ The most obvious omission from this range of top Bandol producers is the Peyraud family's Domaine de Tempier, which welcomed a new winemaker, Daniel Ravier, with the new century. Comte Henri de St-Victor and his family run Château de Pibarnon, with its views over the vineyards to the sea.

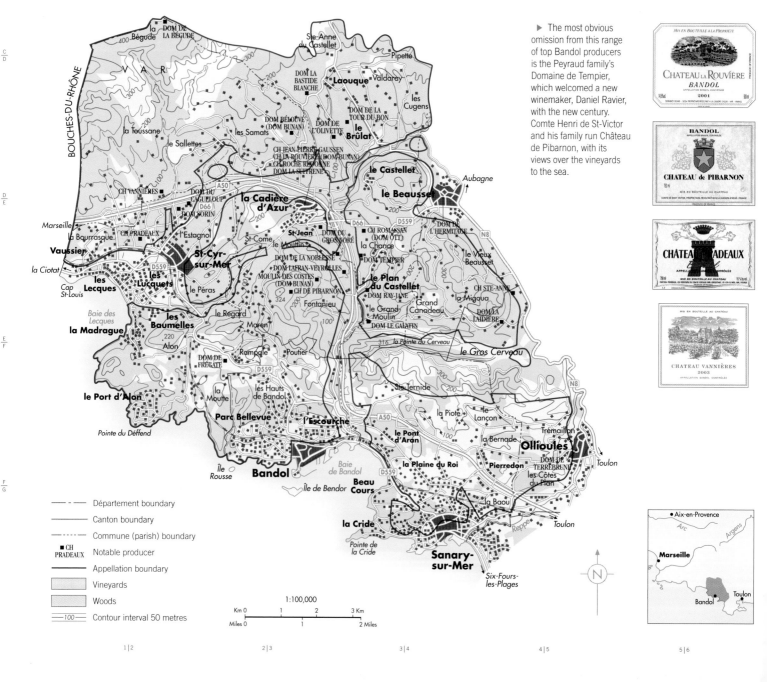

1:100,000

Département boundary
Canton boundary
Commune (parish) boundary
CH PRADEAUX Notable producer
Appellation boundary
Vineyards
Woods
—100— Contour interval 50 metres

Km 0   1   2   3 Km
Miles 0   1   2 Miles

Corsica

Corsica is sunnier and drier than anywhere in mainland France, but its mountainous terrain means its patchwork of terroirs have only an unusually dry July and August in common. The island is closer to Italy than France in many respects, including the simple one of distance, but France has been the major influence on its modern wine history. When France lost Algeria in the 1960s, an army of skilled growers migrated to the then-malarial east coast. By 1976 Corsica's vineyard area had quadrupled, covered almost entirely with bulk-producing vines.

Corsica's contribution to the European wine lake has since been stemmed and, thanks to vast subsidies from Brussels and Paris, the island's cellars are now relatively well-equipped, its winemakers trained at one of the mainland's oenological institutes, and its vineyards much reduced and planted only with vine varieties that at least have the potential to produce wines that modern consumers might actually want to drink. Even so, the great majority of all wine produced on the island is also consumed there with no more reverence than it deserves. The wine most commonly exported is basic Vin de Pays blessed only by Corsica's seductive *nom de verre*, L'Île de Beauté, under which almost half of all wine made on the island now travels.

An increasing proportion of Corsican wine, however, is serious stuff that has rediscovered its birthright in the hardy traditional grape varieties and the rocky hills where they grow best. Particularly striking is the widespread absence of oak barrels in the cellars.

Research continues into Corsica's own heritage of grapevines. Nielluccio, Tuscany's Sangiovese, which may have been imported by the Genoese who ruled the island until the late 18th century, accounts for more than one-third of the island's vines and dominates the northern appellation of **Patrimonio**, inland from the port of Bastia. The only area on the majestically craggy island to have limestone soil, Patrimonio produces some of the island's best and longest-lived wines, firm Rhônish reds, well-balanced whites, and rich Muscat Vins Doux Naturels (see p.144) of high quality. Once rather tough and unapproachable in youth, the reds are beginning to show riper tannins thanks to greater care in the vineyard and winery.

The much softer Sciaccarello grape, grown in about 15% of the island's vineyards, is associated principally with Corsica's oldest wine region on the granitic west coast around the capital Ajaccio, at Calvi, and in the Sartène region around Propriano. It makes highly drinkable, soft yet spicy red and a rosé that remains lively despite its high alcohol content.

Sweet wines, of Muscat or the local Vermentino (known as "Malvoisie de Corse" in the north of the island), are also the speciality of Cap Corse, the long northward point of the island. Rappu, a strong, sweet red made here, around Rogliano, from Aleatico grapes, also has a strong following, and not just on the island. Wines made on this northern tip of Corsica are labelled **Coteaux du Cap Corse**. Vermentino, the principal white grape in all of Corsica's ACs, also produces distinctive dry wines, varying in style from intensely aromatic to steely citrus.

The appellation of **Calvi** in the northwest uses Sciaccarello, Nielluccio, and Vermentino, as well as some of the more international grapes, to produce full-bodied table wines; **Figari** and **Porto-Vecchio** do the same in the south. It is thirsty country with wines that could scarcely be called thirst-quenching, although Figari and Sartène seem to have come furthest in making wines, particularly whites, with a degree of modern, fruity crispness.

In comparison with these concentrated wines of traditional character, the regular Vins de Corse with no further geographical suffix but typically those made around Aléria and Ghisonaccia on the eastern coastal plain are of no special interest. Blending local with international varieties has proved to be commercially successful for some of the island's better co-ops.

A new generation of growers is eager to make the most of their terroir, and a local, some would say captive, market eager to find in their wines the elusive scents of the island.

The island is quite heart-stoppingly beautiful and the climate so much drier than what the locals call "the continent" that all flavours, including those of wines good and bad, are intensified.

CORSICA: BASTIA ▼

Latitude / Altitude of WS **42.33° / 33ft (10m)**

Mean July temp at WS **74°F (23.3°C)**

Annual rainfall at WS **29in (730mm)**

Harvest month rainfall at WS **September: 2.6in (65mm)**

Chief viticultural hazard **Drought**

Principal grapes **Nielluccio, Merlot, Vermentino, Grenache Noir, Sciaccarello**

Map legend:
- Vin de Corse
- Vin de Corse-Coteaux du Cap Corse/Muscat du Cap Corse
- Vin de Corse-Calvi
- Vin de Corse-Sartène
- Vin de Corse-Figari
- Vin de Corse-Porto-Vecchio
- Ajaccio
- Patrimonio/Muscat du Cap Corse
- ▼ Weather station (WS)

◄ Muscats grown on the northern tip of Corsica are arguably some of the island's most distinctive wines. Cheerleader Antonio Arena is based in the village pictured left.

Jura

The Jura *vignoble*, a little enclave of vines scattered among woodland and meadow in what seem like France's remotest hills, may have shrivelled since the phylloxera louse invaded at the end of the 19th century, yet its wines are varied and wholly original. Its appellations Arbois, Château-Chalon, l'Etoile, and Côtes du Jura are all highly individual and hold particular fascination for students of the art of food and wine pairing.

This is a verdant land of trenchermen, heavily influenced by the gastronomic traditions and indeed soils and weather of Burgundy to the immediate west, except that in the hills here winters can be even more severe. As in the Côte d'Or, the best vineyards slope, sometimes steeply, south and southeast to catch the sun. Jurassic limestone is, not surprisingly, characteristic of Jura as well as of Burgundy (the AC l'Etoile takes its name from tiny, star-shaped fossils in the soil).

Jura grows the Burgundy grapes – some Pinot Noir and a great deal of Chardonnay, made increasingly in the imported Burgundian, non-oxidative style the locals call *floral*. The most intriguing Jura wines, however, are made from local vine varieties, particularly the late-ripening Savagnin, and are often deliberately exposed to oxygen during ageing and called *typé* or *tradition*. Savagnin, often fleshed out

with Chardonnay, brings rigour and a hazelnut note to white table wines which can be both delightful and distinctive.

This noble grape is also wholly responsible for Jura's famous strong yellow wine, *vin jaune*. To make France's answer to sherry, Savagnin grapes are picked as ripe as possible, fermented and then left in old Burgundian barrels for just over six years during which the wine evaporates and oxidizes, but on its surface grows a film of yeast, similar but by no means identical to the famous flor of the Jerez region (see p.206). The firm, intensely nutty wine is put into its signature *clavelin* 62cl bottle, supposedly the volume left of an original litre put into cask. Not for neophytes, this is a wine that can last for decades and is often best opened well in advance of sipping, preferably with a local *poulet de Bresse*. The AC **Château-Chalon** is limited to this odd but potentially excellent wine, but *vin jaune*, of distinctly varying quality, is made throughout the region.

The most common dark-skinned Jura grape is the perfumed Poulsard, often called Ploussard, especially around Pupillin (a sub-appellation of **Arbois**), where it is most popular. The reds produced are rarely very deep-coloured but can be interesting: soft, smooth, and satisfying with the local game. A considerable proportion of

These Savagnin vines growing in the Terraces des Puits-Saint-Pierre vineyard of Jean-Pierre Salvadori, just below the village of Château-Chalon, look almost feral, or at the very least a happy accident.

silky rosé, effectively a light red, is also made. Trousseau is a deeper-coloured but rarer Jura grape. It can be found in the north in Arbois, and is increasingly sold in varietal form. Pinot Noir tends to do best around Arlay due west of Château-Chalon and south of this map in the southwest corner of the region's second most important appellation after Arbois, the **Côtes du Jura**, which is used mainly for white wines, including *vin jaune*.

Jura has always produced fine sparkling wine and the relatively new appellation for traditional method fizz is **Crémant du Jura**. But this is much less distinctive than Jura's unctuous *vin de paille*, also made throughout the region from Chardonnay, Savagnin, and/or Poulsard grapes, generally picked early and dried in carefully ventilated conditions until January when these raisins are fermented (to more than 15% alcohol) and then aged in old barrels for two or three years. Like *vin jaune*, these wines are for very long keeping.

One final speciality is Macvin du Jura, a fragrant mixture of grape juice and grape spirit drunk as an apéritif in the region.

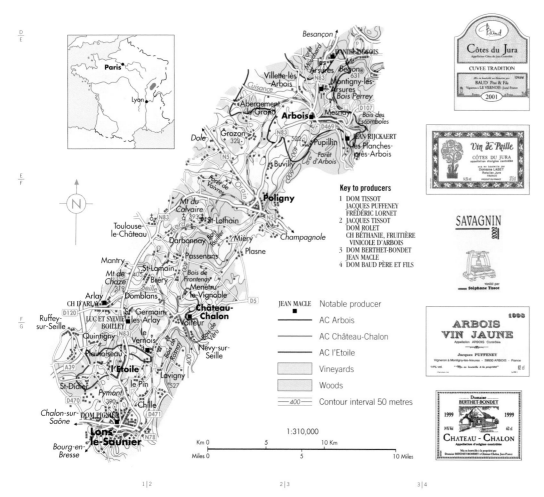

Key to producers

1 DOM TISSOT
  JACQUES PUFFENEY
  FRÉDÉRIC LORNET
2 JACQUES TISSOT
  DOM ROLET
  CH BÉTHANIE, FRUITIÈRE
  VINICOLE D'ARBOIS
3 DOM BERTHET-BONDET
  JEAN MACLE
4 DOM BAUD PÈRE ET FILS

JEAN MACLE   Notable producer

▬▬▬ AC Arbois

▬▬▬ AC Château-Chalon

▬▬▬ AC l'Etoile

    Vineyards

    Woods

—400— Contour interval 50 metres

1:310,000

Km 0   5   10 Km

Miles 0   5   10 Miles

◀ Such a small region and such a variety of wine styles, from the sherry-like *vin jaune* and Château-Chalon, to the super-sweet *vin de paille*, with particularly distinctive light reds and nutty dry whites in between.

Savoie

The area of France mapped here is almost as large as the whole of the Bordeaux wine region on p.83, and yet Savoie produces less than a fiftieth as much wine as Bordeaux – because its wine areas, and even individual vineyards, are so widely dispersed. Mountains so often get in the way. Cultivable land is at a premium. This is alpine France, complete with all the demands of tourism: winters cold enough to attract hordes of skiers and lakes that warm the nearby vineyards in summer.

A small but growing area of Savoie is now devoted to the vine but it yields wines that are so varied, from such a rich mix of local vine specialities, that it seems extraordinary to the outsider that almost all of them go under the same basic appellation, **Vin de Savoie**.

A Vin de Savoie is more than twice as likely to be white as red or rosé. It is also about ten times more likely to be light, clean, and fresh – at one with Savoyard mountain air, lakes, and streams – than it is to be deep and heady, although some producers have been experimenting with extracting more from the region's most valuable dark-skinned grape, the peppery Mondeuse. Some make their Mondeuse like Beaujolais, others give it a barrique to stiffen it; the best keep a juicy note of plums and a streak of tannin which are highly appetizing. The great majority of wine sold as straight Vin de Savoie is made from the Jacquère grape and the result is light, white, dry, and mild, like alpine Muscadet.

But within the greater Savoie region, 14 individual *crus* are allowed to add their name to the label, provided certain conditions, different for each *cru* but stricter than for basic Vins de Savoie, are met. On the southern shores of Lac Léman (Lake Geneva), for example, only the Chasselas grape, so beloved by neighbouring Switzerland, is allowed for wines labelled with the *crus* Ripaille (which can be quite a rich, golden wine), Marin, and Marignan. (**Crépy**, a similar wine made in this area, has its own small appellation.)

South of here in the Arve Valley is the *cru* of Ayze, which produces still and sparkling whites from Gringet, its own local relative of the Jura's Savagnin.

Savoie's third individual appellation is **Seyssel**. It is best-known for its sparkling wines made from Altesse (see below) with some local Molette grapes. The appellation's still wines are made mainly from Altesse. Both have a certain historic reputation.

Just north of Seyssel is Frangy, an isolated *cru* specializing in this case in the local, characterful Altesse. The superiority of the Altesse, or Roussette, grape is recognized by a special appellation for any Savoie wine made from it, within certain conditions: Roussette de Savoie. (Those *crus* authorized only for the production of Roussette de Savoie are marked in magenta on the map above.)

Key to producers
1 CH DE RIPAILLE
2 D & P BELLUARD
3 CAVE DE CHAUTAGNE
4 DOM DUPASQUIER
5 ANDRÉ ET MICHEL QUENARD
  JEAN-PIERRE ET
  JEAN-FRANÇOIS QUENARD
6 LES FILS DE CHARLES TROSSET
  LOUIS MAGNIN
7 DOM DE L'IDYLLE
8 DOM PRIEURÉ ST-CHRISTOPHE

- - - International boundary
- - - Département boundary
——— AC Vin de Savoie
AC Crépy
AC Seyssel
VDQS Bugey
● Arbin   Cru of Savoie
● Frangy   Cru of Roussette de Savoie
●   Cru of Bugey
LOUIS MAGNIN ■   Notable producer
Wine-producing areas
▼   Weather station (WS)

1:1,000,000
Km 0 10 20 30 40 Km
Miles 0   10   20 Miles

South of Seyssel are the extensive vineyards of Chautagne, a *cru* best known for its reds, particularly its grainy Gamay. To the west of the Lac du Bourget is Jongieux. A wine labelled simply Jongieux is made exclusively from Jacquère but some Altesse is grown here too.

Lying to the south of the town of Chambéry, whose herby vermouth is now all too difficult to find, is Savoie's most extensive vineyard area facing south and southeast on the lower slopes of Mont Granier. This area includes the popular *crus* of Apremont and Abymes, where, arguably, most flavour is extracted from the reticent Jacquère grape.

Following the Isère river up the Combe de Savoie is a cluster of *crus* where all of Savoie's varieties are grown, but especially Jacquère and some Altesse. Of these, Chignin is responsible for one of the best-known ambassadors of fine Savoie wine. Its speciality Chignin-Bergeron, made exclusively from the Roussanne grape of the Rhône, is one of Savoie's more powerful and powerfully scented whites. Chignin and Arbin can also ripen Mondeuse well.

Delicate sparkling wines made outside Seyssel and Ayze but also by the traditional method are sold simply as Vin de Savoie.

SAVOIE: CHAMBERY ▼
Latitude / Altitude of WS **45.39° / 754ft (230m)**
Mean July temp at WS **68°F (20°C)**
Annual rainfall at WS **48in (1,220mm)**
Harvest month rainfall at WS **September: 4in (105mm)**
Chief viticultural hazards **Underripeness, humidity in September**
Principal grapes **Jacquère, Gamay, Altesse, Chasselas, Mondeuse**

Due west of the Lac du Bourget the vineyards of **Bugey**, growing much the same grapes as Savoie together with some particularly successful Chardonnay (though not Chasselas), are delineated with equal precision and complexity. Bugey specializes in light, sparkling wines, white and pink, and smooth-scented Roussette, particularly valued in Montagnieu and Virieu-le-Grand.

▼ Just looking at these labels acts almost as a decongestant, so closely are they associated with clean mountain air and fresh, uncomplicated flavours. Bergeron is Chignin's synonym for the fashionable Roussanne grape planted in the Rhône Valley and all over southern France.

Vins de Pays

Modernism suits Skalli of Sète. Their Fortant de France operation has produced prime representatives of the contemporary face of Vin de Pays, harnessing the massive production of the Languedoc-Roussillon to produce easy-to-understand varietal wines in the modern idiom, with names and labels to match. Below is something very different, Domaine de Baron'Arques near Limoux in the Aude. Here the team from Château Mouton-Rothschild produce, among other things, Vin de Pays de la Haute Vallée de l'Aude, leaning heavily on their smart Bordeaux connections.

The category of Vins de Pays is a relatively recent creation of French wine officialdom, but a hugely successful one. If the VDQS category (see p.52) was created to distinguish ACs-in-waiting, the Vin de Pays category was created in 1973 (and formalized only in 1979) as a spur to the vast table wine, or Vin de Table, category. A Vin de Pays, or country wine, is seen by the French as a superior table wine, providing the humblest sort of French wine with the chance to earn the greatest French compliment: geographical context. By qualifying as a Vin de Pays, a table wine becomes a Vin de Pays de Somewhere Specific. The names of each Vin de Pays zone have been deliberately chosen to exclude any possibility of confusion with proper ACs, with delightfully creative results. The Vin de Pays names, more than 150 of them, read like poetry to anyone with a feeling for the French countryside: Vals, Coteaux and Monts, Gorges and Pays, Marches and Vicomtés, Balmes and Fiefs. Who could resist Vallée du Paradis (an area northeast of Corbières) or L'Ile de Beauté (Corsica's Vin de Pays name)?

Vins de Pays operate at three levels: almost 100 small local districts or zones, 54 départements (but specifically not the "fine wine" départements of Alsace, Bordeaux and Côte d'Or), and six big regions – the whole of the Loire Valley (Vin de Pays du Jardin de la France – another pretty name); the whole of Bordeaux, Cognac country and the Dordogne (Vin de Pays de l'Atlantique); most of the rest of Southwest France (Vin de Pays du Comté Tolosan); a big slice of eastern France (Vin de Pays des Comtés Rhodaniens); all of southeastern France and Corsica (Vin de Pays Portes de Méditerranée); and all of the Languedoc and Roussillon (Vin de Pays d'Oc). The last is by far the most important single Vin de Pays, subdivided into almost 60 local ones too small to be shown individually on the map – and used very much less than the portmanteau name Vin de Pays d'Oc.

There have also been plans, much discussed and hugely controversial, for a sort of super Vin de Pays – Vin de Pays des Vignobles de France – into which could be blended wines from virtually anywhere in France that meet the Vin de Pays criteria . Although the concept apparently flies in the face of French devotion to local geography, such wines would be quite different from lowly Vin de Table, which can also be a blend of wines from anywhere in France.

Vin de Pays criteria are considerably stricter than those for Vin de Table, which may not, unlike Vins de Pays, carry a vintage year. The Vin de Pays regulations stipulate the precise production area, a relatively generous maximum yield of 90hl/ha (85 for reds and rosés), minimum natural alcohol levels, and which grape varieties are officially permitted for that particular Vin de Pays – generally a wide

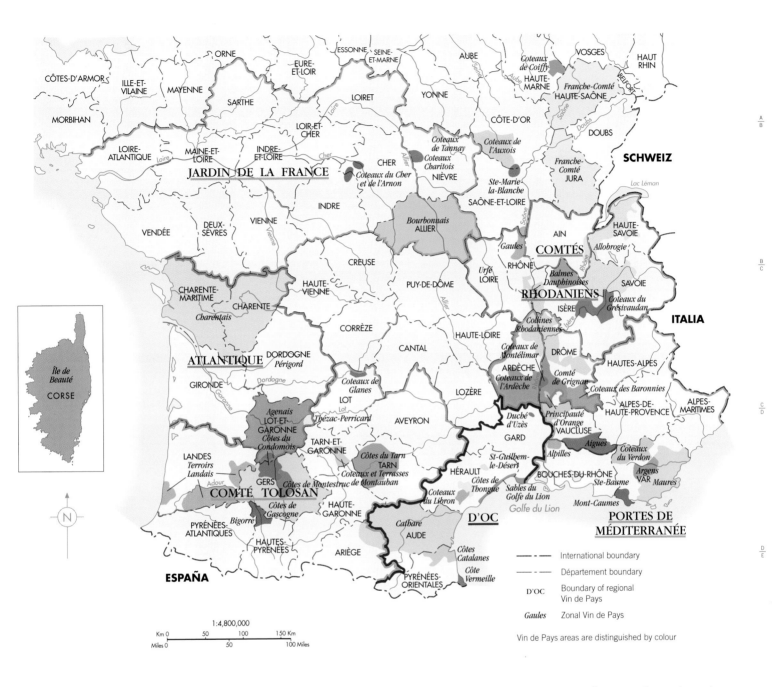

Île de
Beauté
CORSE

JARDIN DE LA FRANCE

ATLANTIQUE

COMTÉ TOLOSAN

D'OC

COMTÉS
RHODANIENS

PORTES DE
MÉDITERRANÉE

SCHWEIZ

ITALIA

ESPAÑA

1:4,800,000

Km 0   50   100   150 Km
Miles 0   50   100 Miles

— · — · — International boundary

— — — · — Département boundary

D'OC Boundary of regional
Vin de Pays

Gaules Zonal Vin de Pays

Vin de Pays areas are distinguished by colour

range of local grapes plus an appropriate selection of the major international varieties.

It is frankly admitted that some Vins de Pays have more validity than others. Some names have scarcely been used, while the annual production of Vin de Pays d'Oc approaches 350 million litres, or well over 5% of France's total annual harvest. (This explains why about 70% of all Vin de Pays is red; the south of France is essentially red wine country.)

Vins de Pays give growers an escape route from the straitjacket of AC regulations. The range of permitted grape varieties is wider, yields are higher, there is no minimum age for vines, and the geographical area is much less restricted. So a grower in the northern Rhône, for example, can sell the produce of a vine too young to produce Condrieu, or a Syrah planted on land without AC status, as a Vin de Pays des Collines Rhodaniennes. Merchants such as Louis Latour of Burgundy and Georges

Duboeuf of Beaujolais have been able to expand southwards into pastures new by, for instance, selling respectively Pinot Noir and Viognier as Vins de Pays des Coteaux de l'Ardèche. And Muscadet producers who wish to profit from Chardonnay's liking for their region can sell the wine as Chardonnay, Vin de Pays du Jardin de la France.

The Vin de Pays category could also be said to have come to the rescue of hundreds if not thousands of growers in Southwest France. Much of the embarrassing surplus of grapes originally intended for armagnac and cognac stills (see map, p.53) has already been diverted into crisp white Vin de Pays des Côtes de Gascogne and Charentais respectively. It is hoped that the recent Vin de Pays de l'Atlantique and Vin de Pays des Gaules will provide the same commercial escape route for the numerous vignerons who have been growing grapes respectively for the basic Bordeaux

and Beaujolais appellations and conspicuously failing to find a market for the resulting wines.

Vin de Pays now accounts for more than a third of all wine made in France, mopping up much of the wine that would previously have been classified as lowly Vin de Table. And its success on export markets doubtless owes much to a very un-French aspect of these wines' appeal: more than 40% of them are now sold not on the basis of their geography but as varietal wines, wines with such internationally recognizable words as Chardonnay and Merlot on their labels. The Vins de Pays provide French wine producers with a means of fighting the New World on its own ground. Most French drinkers might still regard Vins de Pays as inferior, but in many export markets, particularly Germany and the UK, the varietal versions at least are seen as hearteningly familiar, and so much easier to understand than the complexities of the AC system.

Castiglione Falletto whose majestic wines are the epitome of Barolo, Italy's king of wines and wine of kings, even if there is now a host of pretenders to the throne.

Italy

Italy

The genius of France is not just for taste: order is important too. Italy has no less taste, but order comes far down the priority list. Far below creativity. Italy has the richest variety of individual wine styles, local climates, and, most importantly, indigenous grape varieties of all the world's wine producers. She is using them to the full. France remains the mother-country of fine wine, but Italy has an equally valid, if often exasperating, wine personality. At the top end her wines have a vivacity and style all of their own. At the bottom end, like any major European wine producer, she may still have too high a proportion of dull, over-productive vines, but these are rapidly becoming a minority and it is the quality of what is produced in between that has improved so impressively, not least the white wines.

Some would say there is no excuse. Colonizing Greeks called Italy Oenotria – the land of wine (or, strictly, staked vines – a sure sign of viticultural ambition). The map reminds us that there is little of Italy that is not, at least marginally, wine country. Only France – and not in every year – makes more wine than Italy.

In terms of geography, Italy cannot fail to produce good wine in great variety, if slopes, sunshine, and a temperate climate are the essentials. Her peculiar physique, that of a long spine of mountains reaching south from the sheltering Alps almost to North Africa, means that there can hardly be a desirable combination of altitude with latitude and exposure that is absent. Many of her soils are volcanic; much is limestone or tuffeau; there is plenty of gravelly clay. But so varied is the terrain that it is virtually impossible to generalize about her wines.

Because Italy is so well suited to the vine and today produces such wonderful and wonderfully distinctive wines, it is easy to forget just how recent this phenomenon is. Hardly more than a generation ago, only a tiny proportion of Italian wine was even bottled by the producer. The great majority was shipped to the cities for domestic consumption, and such wine as was exported was mostly blended by the big shippers.

It is hardly surprising therefore that wine labels strike the outsider as distinctly unevolved, their chief inconvenience being an almost impenetrable confusion of names. Because wine is omnipresent, so much a part of everyday life, made by so many proud and independent people, every conceivable sort of name is pressed into use to mark originality. Thus one bottle may carry on it not only the name of the official denomination and producer, but also the name of the property, a part of the property, or of anything else that takes the producer's fancy. Helpful back labels are eschewed and regions rarely named on labels

where the name of an obscure town is often the only geographical reference. Italy still needs a labelling system (which is not necessarily the same thing as a new wine law) which would set out clearly who made the wine, where it was made, and which was its most significant name.

From the 1960s on, the Italian government undertook the monumental task of devising an answer to France's Appellation Contrôlée system, DOC (Denominazione di Origine Controllata), complete with boundaries (often too generous), maximum yields (ditto), and specified grape varieties and production methods. A superior form of DOC, DOCG (for which the origin was not just controlled, but guaranteed – a nice distinction) was also created, and eventually in the 1980s awarded to such obviously superior wines as Barolo, Barbaresco, Vino Nobile di Montepulciano, Brunello di Montalcino, and, as a spur to improvement, a much-revised Chianti. (See panel for the much expanded DOCG roster today.)

Over the years, though, a serious drawback in the basic DOC system became clear. What it effectively did was fossilize the current practice of most winemakers in each region, particularly over-generous

Map labels

ÖSTERREICH
SCHWEIZ
SLOVENIJA
FRANCE

Bolzano
TRENTINO-ALTO ADIGE
FRIULI-VENEZIA GIULIA
Trento
Udine
Gorizia
Lago Maggiore
Lago di Como
Sóndrio
VALLE D'AOSTA
Gattinara
Como
Bergamo
LOMBARDIA
VENETO
Trieste
Novara
Milano
Bréscia
Vicenza
Treviso
Vercelli
Pavia
Cremona
Verona
Pádova
Venézia
Torino
Alessándria
Po
Mantova
Adige
PIEMONTE
Alba
Piacenza
Parma
Ferrara
EMILIA-ROMAGNA
Cúneo
Réggio nell'Emília
Módena
LIGURIA
Génova
Bologna
Ravenna
Savona
La Spézia
159
Forlì
167
175
SAN MARINO
Pistóia
Firenze
Pésaro
Pisa
Lucca
Arno
Ancona
Livorno
Siena
Arezzo
MARCHE
Macerata
Elba
TOSCANA
Montepulciano
Perúgia
Áscoli Piceno
UMBRIA
Grosseto
Téramo
Corse
Terni
ABRUZZO
Pescara
Viterbo
L'Aquila
LAZIO
Roma
MOLISE
Latina
175
Fóggia
184
CAMPANIA
Benevento
PUGLIA
Bari
Napoli
Sassari
Isola d'Ischia
Salerno
BASILICATA
SARDEGNA
188
Isola di Capri
Cagliari
Is. Eólie o Lípari
CALABRIA
Messina
Trapani
Palermo
Réggio di Calábria
SICILIA
187
Catánia
Siracusa

Legend

— · — International boundary
— – — Regione boundary
▨ Wine-producing area
▨ Land above 600 metres
159 Regional map page number

1:6,000,000

Km 0   100   200 Km
Miles 0   50   100 Miles

A statue in the grounds of Vignamaggio, Chianti Classico. Art continues to play a more obvious role in wine in Italy than elsewhere – as witness its stylish bottles and wineries.

yields, regardless of whether it led to the best results or not. Indeed, it penalized progressive winemakers who knew that certain changes in, for example, grape varieties or maturation techniques could greatly improve their wines. The result was the proliferation in the 1970s and 1980s of Vini da Tavola that commanded more respect and higher prices than most DOC wines.

In 1992 a new law was passed to restructure the whole system of classification with restrictions, including maximum permitted yields, decreasing steadily from the pinnacle of DOCG to DOC and then to a new category, IGT (Indicazione Geografica Tipica), created for the innovative Vini da Tavola. Like France's Vins de Pays, IGTs can use the geographical and varietal name.

In theory an IGT does not have the status of a DOC, but the market says otherwise about many of them – particularly those made from the non-traditional grape varieties that are now planted all over Italy. Cabernet Sauvignon (which was first introduced in the early 19th century) and Chardonnay spearheaded this new invasion but Merlot, Syrah, and others are now almost commonplace. Of the 60-plus IGTs by far the most common are those carrying the name of one of Italy's 19 regions. IGTs are appearing on an increasing proportion of labels – not least because many of the names (Umbria, Sicilia, for example) have more market resonance than those of individual DOCs.

The map is intended as a reminder of the whereabouts of the regions and as a key to the subsequent more detailed maps. All the important current DOCs and DOCGs appear on the four pages that carve up the country into northwest, northeast, centre, and south, except those in the complex centres of quality wine-growing which are given large-scale maps of their own.

And the wine? Are all Italy's best wines still red? Most, but by no means all. Italy learned to make "modern" (that is, fresh and crisp) white wine in the 1960s. In the 1980s she began to add back the character that was lost in the process, and by the late 1990s had succeeded. Soave, Verdicchio, and Pinot Grigio are by no means the only whites that can now be found in deliciously fruity, even complex form.

Italy's red wines continue to get better and better. They range from the silky and fragile to the purple and potent, in every style and aroma from redoubtable natives to the international Cabernet standard. This extraordinarily rapid revolution in wine quality has been achieved partly with Euro-money, and largely by advice from a band, some would say too small a band, of well-travelled consultants, initially specialists in winemaking but now taking an increasingly active role in the much-needed revitalization of Italy's vineyards. Much more of outdoor Oenotria, as well as its cellars, is being converted to concentrate on quality rather than quantity, with the heavily milked overhead *tendone* vine-training system, more suitable for table grapes, gradually disappearing from the landscape.

Yet to be true to the spirit of Italy the qualities of all her wine must be seen in the context of the incredibly varied, sensuous Italian table. The true genius of Italy lies in spreading a feast. In the great Italian feast, wine plays the chief supporting role.

THE LANGUAGE OF THE LABEL

One of Italy's more straightforward labels, from a relatively new producer, although there is no clue as to which region it comes from.

QUALITY DESIGNATIONS

Denominazione di Origine Controllata e Garantita (DOCG) wines either recognized as Italy's best, or supported by the most skilful politicians

Denominazione di Origine Controllata (DOC) Italy's original answer to France's AC (see p.52)

Indicazione Geografica Tipica (IGT) Italy's relatively recent answer to France's Vin de Pays (see p.150)

Vino da Tavola table wine, Italy's most basic category

OTHER COMMON EXPRESSIONS

Abboccato lightly sweet

Amabile semi-sweet

Annata vintage year

Azienda agricola wine estate which does not buy in grapes or wine, unlike an azienda vinicola

Bianco white

Cantina cellar or winery

Cantina sociale, cantina cooperativa co-operative winery

Casa vinicola wine firm

Chiaretto very pale red

Classico original, rather than expanded, zone

Consorzio growers' association

Dolce sweet

Fattoria literally, farm

Frizzante semi-sparkling

Gradi (alcool) alcoholic strength as a percentage by volume

Imbottigliato (all'origine) bottled (at source)

Liquoroso strong, usually fortified

Metodo classico, metodo tradizionale bottle-fermented sparkling wine

Passito strong, usually sweet wine made from dried grapes

Podere very small agricultural property, smaller than a fattoria

Recioto wine made from half-dried grapes, a Veneto speciality

Riserva special, long-aged selection

Rosato rosé (relatively rare in Italy)

Rosso red

Secco dry

Spumante sparkling

Superiore wine that has undergone more ageing than normal DOC and contains 0.5–1% more alcohol

Tenuta small holding or estate

Vendemmia vintage

Vendemmia tardiva late harvest

Vigna, vigneto vineyard

Vignaiolo, viticoltore vine-grower

Vino wine

DOCG WINES

PIEMONTE
Asti and Moscato d'Asti; Barbaresco; Barolo; Brachetto d'Acqui or Acqui; Dolcetto di Dogliani Superiore or Dogliani; Gattinara; Gavi or Cortese di Gavi; Ghemme; Roero

LOMBARDY
Franciacorta; Sforzato della Valtellina or Sfursat della Valtellina; Valtellina Superiore

VENETO
Recioto di Soave; Soave Superiore; Bardolino Superiore

FRIULI
Picolit; Ramandolo

EMILIA-ROMAGNA
Albana di Romagna

MARCHES
Conero; Vernaccia di Serrapetrona

TUSCANY
Brunello di Montalcino; Carmignano; Chianti; Chianti Classico; Morellino di Scansano; Vernaccia di San Gimignano; Vino Nobile di Montepulciano

ABRUZZO
Montepulciano d'Abruzzo Colline Teramane

UMBRIA
Montefalco Sagrantino; Torgiano Rosso Riserva

CAMPANIA
Fiano di Avellino; Greco di Tufo; Taurasi

SICILIA
Cerasuolo di Vittoria

SARDINIA
Vermentino di Gallura

Northwest Italy

Northwest Italy means Piemonte (Piedmont in English) to any wine-lover but the Langhe and Monferrato hills around Alba and Asti (mapped in detail overleaf) are not the only great vineyards of the northwest. Their noblest grape, Nebbiolo, gives excellent, if different, results in several corners of the region – most notably in the hills above Novara and Vercelli (famous for rice), where under the name of Spanna it rejoices in no fewer than six different DOCs, each for a different sort of soil.

The DOCG **Gattinara** (above all from Le Colline Monsecco) is considered the noblest form of Spanna, with **Ghemme** (also DOCG) and **Lessona** as consorts and **Bramaterra** not far behind. All benefit from a subalpine climate, a southern exposure and fast-draining glacial soil that is notably more acid than the soils of the Langhe. In practice all depends on the grower and the amount of the permitted Bonarda or Vespolina grapes added. The weight and intensity of Barolo is not quite there, but perfume is not lacking. Spanna, which in the old days could become distinctly gamey in bottle, has benefited as much as any other wine from the new brooms that have been sweeping through Italy's cellars. Producers such as Proprietà Sperino in Lessona and Le Piane in Boca are doing their best to restore the region's wines to the fame they enjoyed 150 years ago when they were much more highly regarded than the wines of Langhe.

Nebbiolo also grows in the far northeast corner of the map opposite, where Lombardy meets Switzerland. In Valtellina, on south-facing suntraps on the north bank of the River Adda, the grape, known here as Chiavennasca, makes sinewy, mountain-climbing reds. The heartland, **Valtellina Superiore** DOCG, which includes the Grumello, Inferno, Sassella, and Valgella subzones, makes infinitely better wine than that sold simply as **Valtellina**. Some dry Sfursat (Sforzato) is made from semi-dried grapes.

North of Turin on the road up to the Valle d'Aosta and the Mont Blanc tunnel to France there are two more Nebbiolos, of high reputation but low output, Carema and Donnaz. **Carema** is still in Piemonte (but has its own name for Nebbiolo: Picutener); **Donnaz** is made in Donnas over the provincial boundary in the Valle d'Aosta, Italy's smallest wine region. Alpine conditions may make these Nebbiolos less potent and deep-coloured than those from lower latitudes but they have their own finesse – and their own following.

Aosta's own red grape is Petit Rouge, which tastes not unlike the Mondeuse of Savoie: dark, fresh, berryish, and bracing. It forms the basis of Enfer d'Arvier and Torrette among other wines subsumed into the **Valle d'Aosta** DOC. The Fumin grape makes longer-lived reds. The busy valley also makes some recherché whites from imported grapes: the very light Blancs de la Salle and de Morgex, some winter-weight

Just outside Sóndrio, the church of St Pietro towers above the steep slopes of the Inferno vineyard, which looks anything but hellish. This subzone of Valtellina is the Nebbiolo vines northern outpost, almost in Switzerland.

Malvoisie and Petite Arvine from Switzerland, and some Chardonnay that wins local acclaim.

Where the hilly turbulence of Piemonte merges with the Lombard plain to the east, conditions become less alpine and extreme. The fulcrum of Lombardic viticulture is Oltrepò Pavese, the part of the province of Pavia that lies beyond the River Po. Many of Italy's best Pinot Nero and some Pinot Bianco for the making of sparkling wines come from here without necessarily mentioning the fact.

The DOC **Oltrepò Pavese** Rosso calls for two-thirds Barbera mollified with a variety of local grapes, of which Bonarda (which in Oltrepò Pavese is the local alias for the Croatina grape) is the most prevalent and characterful, although Uva Rara can add spice to a blend. The zone's leading estate is Frecciarossa, "red arrow", from Castéggio. Buttafuoco and Sangue di Giuda are reds with bubbles more memorable for their names than for their flavours. Oltrepò white wines include "Pinot", which can be either Bianco or Nero (made white) or Grigio or all of these. Italian (in other words Welsch) Riesling is not unbearably dull in the Oltrepò Pavese (although Riesling Renano, "real" Riesling, is better); Moscatos are excellent and even Müller-Thurgau makes respectable wines. And see p.166 for details of Lombardy's flourishing sparkling wine industry around Brescia.

The **Colli Piacentini** south of Piacenza is bidding for recognition with international varietal bottlings and an often frizzante red made from Barbera and Bonarda.

South from Piemonte over the final curling tail of the Alps, known as the Ligurian Apennines, we are on the Mediterranean, with scarcely enough room between the mountains and the sea to grow grapes. Liguria's production is tiny, but highly individual and worth investigating. Of its grapes only Vermentino (also known as Pigato here) and Malvasia are widely grown elsewhere: the white Albarola, Bosco, and Buzzetto are as esoteric as they sound. **Cinque Terre** is the white wine served with fish on the steep coast near La Spezia. Its liquorous version is called Sciacchetrà. Other less known coastal whites should be tasted on a visit to Genoa; you will not find them elsewhere.

Potentially the most memorable Ligurian wine, however, is the red **Rossese**, whether **di Dolceacqua** near the French border or **di Albenga**, nearer Genoa. Unlike anything made west along the coast in the Alpes Maritimes, Rossese can be truly fresh, fruity in the soft-fruit or berry sense of Bordeaux, inviting to smell, and refreshing to drink. And, unlike the most famous wines of northwest Italy, it does not need any ageing.

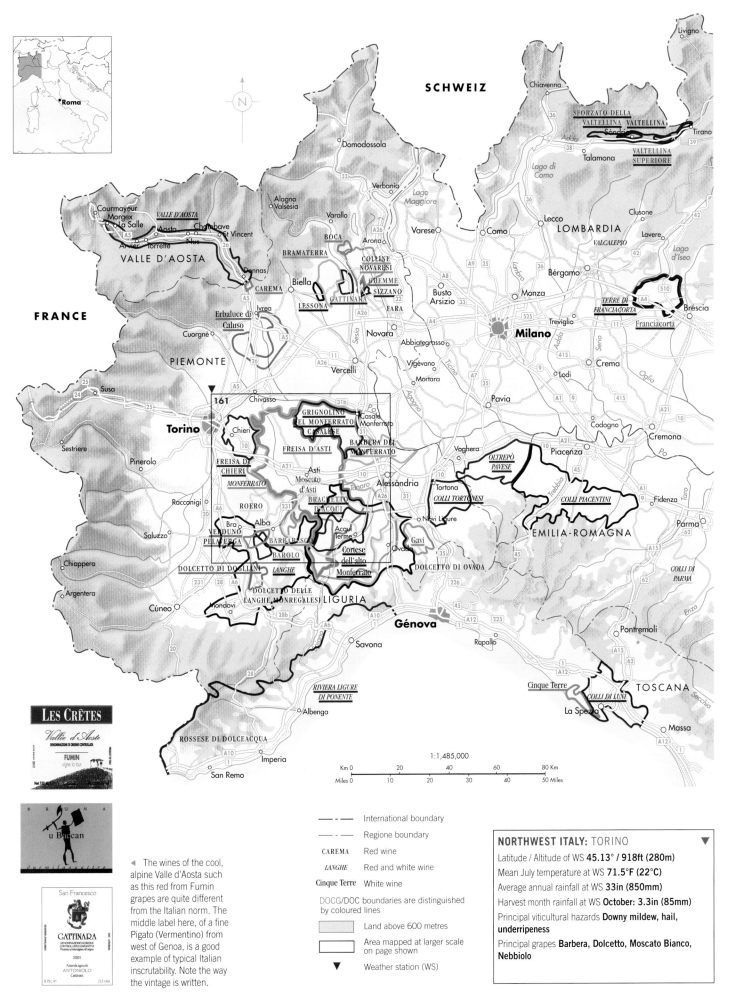

SCHWEIZ

Livigno

SFORZATO DELLA
VALTELLINA VALTELLINA
VALTELLINA
SUPERIORE

Chiavenna

Talamona Sóndrio Tirano

Lago di
Como

Domodossola

Verbania

Lago
Maggiore

Lecco

LOMBARDIA

Clusone

Como

VALCALEPIO

Lovere

Lago
d'Iseo

Alagna
Valsesia

Varallo

Arona

Varese

Monza

Bérgamo

Courmayeur
Morgex
La Salle

Aosta Chambave

St Vincent

Nus

VALLE D'AOSTA

BOCA

Colline
NOVARESI

Busto
Arsizio

Crema

TERRE DI
FRANCIACORTA

Bréscia

Franciacorta

Arnad Torrette

Donnas

VALLE D'AOSTA

BRAMATERRA

Biella

Carema

LESSONA GATTINARA

GHEMME
SIZZANO

FARA

Milano

Treviglio

Codogno

Cremona

FRANCE

Erbaluce di
Caluso

Cuorgnè

Ivrea

Novara

Vercelli

PIEMONTE

Vigévano

Mortara

Pavia

Lodi

Po

Susa

Sestriere

Pinerolo

Torino

161 Chivasso

Chieri

GRIGNOLINO
DEL MONFERRATO
CASALESE Casale
Monferrato

BARBERA DEL
MONFERRATO

Voghera

Piacenza

OLTREPÒ
PAVESE

COLLI PIACENTINI

Fidenza

FREISA D'ASTI

FREISA DI
CHIERI

MONFERRATO

Asti

Moscato
d'Asti

Alessándria

Tortona

COLLI TORTONESI

Parma

Rácconigi

ROERO

BRACHETTO
D'ACQUI

Navi Ligure

EMILIA-ROMAGNA

Saluzzo

Bra

Alba

VERDUNO
PELAVERGA

BARBARESCO

Acqui
Terme

Cortese
dell'alto
Monferrato

Gavi

Ovada

DOLCETTO DI OVADA

Chiappera

BAROLO

DOLCETTO DI DOGLIANI

LANGHE

DOLCETTO DELLE
LANGHE MONREGALESI LIGURIA

COLLI DI
PARMA

Argentera

Cúneo

Móndovi

Génova

Rapallo

Pontremoli

Savona

TOSCANA

RIVIERA LIGURE
DI PONENTE

Cinque Terre

COLLI DI LUNI

La Spezia

Massa

Albenga

ROSSESE DI DOLCEACQUA

Imperia

San Remo

1:1,485,000

Km 0 .... 20 .... 40 .... 60 .... 80 Km
Miles 0 .... 10 .... 20 .... 30 .... 40 .... 50 Miles

— · — · — International boundary

— · — · — Regione boundary

CAREMA Red wine

LANGHE Red and white wine

Cinque Terre White wine

DOCG/DOC boundaries are distinguished
by coloured lines

Land above 600 metres

Area mapped at larger scale
on page shown

▼ Weather station (WS)

◄ The wines of the cool,
alpine Valle d'Aosta such
as this red from Fumin
grapes are quite different
from the Italian norm. The
middle label here, of a fine
Pigato (Vermentino) from
west of Genoa, is a good
example of typical Italian
inscrutability. Note the way
the vintage is written.

NORTHWEST ITALY: TORINO ▼

Latitude / Altitude of WS **45.13° / 918ft (280m)**

Mean July temperature at WS **71.5°F (22°C)**

Average annual rainfall at WS **33in (850mm)**

Harvest month rainfall at WS **October: 3.3in (85mm)**

Principal viticultural hazards **Downy mildew, hail,
underripeness**

Principal grapes **Barbera, Dolcetto, Moscato Bianco,
Nebbiolo**

Piemonte

Piemontese food and wine are as inseparable as those of Burgundy. They are strong, rich, individual, mature, somehow autumnal. Truffles play an important part. One feels it must be more than coincidence that this is the Italian province nearest to France. Piemonte means at the foot of the mountains – in this case the Alps. The Alps almost encircle this hilly region, so that from its heart, the rolling Monferrato hills around Asti, they form a continuous dark – or in winter and spring, sparkling white – horizon. Less than 5% of Piemontese vineyards are officially classed as flat. Every slope of vines, it can seem, faces in a slightly different direction and is governed by a slightly different aspect and altitude. If each vineyard is characterized by its very own mesoclimate, the Piemonte region has a macroclimate of its own, with a very hot growing season followed by a misty autumn and a cold, often foggy, winter.

At vintage time in Barolo the hills are half hidden. Ramps of copper and gold vines, dotted with peach trees and the hazel that inspired the local chocolate industry, lead down to the valley of the Tanaro, lost in the fog. It is a magical experience to visit Serralunga or La Morra and see the dark grapes coming in through the mist.

The two best red wines of Piemonte, Barolo and Barbaresco, take their names from villages mapped in detail on the next pages. Most of the rest of Piemonte's most famous wines are named after the grapes from which they are made – Barbera, Brachetto, Dolcetto, Grignolino, Freisa, Moscato, Nebbiolo. If to the grape they add a district name (for example Barbera d'Asti), it means they come from a limited and theoretically superior area. The notable exceptions to this format are the relatively recent Langhe, Roero, Monferrato, and catch-all Piemonte denominations devised to avoid what the Piemontese see as the ignominy of IGT wines. The map shows the spaghetti junction of the most important *denominazione* of central Piemonte – although there are many, many more, and the perennial inclination to continue to add to them.

The haunting Nebbiolo has no rival as the finest red grape of northern Italy. It does not have to meet Barolo or Barbaresco specifications to make mellow, fragrant wine – indeed some seriously worthwhile Nebbiolo d'Alba, Langhe Nebbiolo, and red **Roero** is made nowadays. This last, made DOCG in 2004, is 95% Nebbiolo grown in the Roero hills northwest of Alba on the sandy soils of the Tanaro's left bank, together with 5% of the fragrant, pear-scented old local white grape Arneis which thrives here – a Piemontese answer to the Syrah/Viognier blends of Côte-Rôtie. **Roero Arneis** is the DOCG for the 100% varietal white.

The DOC **Langhe** on the other hand extends south of Alba on the opposite bank of the river. It has been designed for varietal Nebbiolo, Dolcetto, Freisa, Arneis, Favorita, and Chardonnay grown on the heavier clay marl soils of the Tanaro's right bank. The many geographically specific wines produced in these Langhe hills, including Barolo and Barbaresco, may be declassified to DOC Langhe, either a varietal version or merely Rosso or Bianco.

Monferrato has its own DOC, its boundaries very similar to that of Barbera d'Asti, while the Piemonte DOC is designed specifically for Barbera, Brachetto, Chardonnay, Cortese, Grignolino, Moscato, Uva Rara, and the three Pinots; not precisely an exclusive club.

Once despised as too common to inspire respect, Barbera is now Piemonte's second most glamorous red grape, and arguably its most fashionable. Nebbiolo demands time and attention; Barbera, treated to ageing in new French oak barriques (as much of it is today), conforms more closely to the modern red wine stereotype: big, bold, deep purple, and easy to appreciate in youth. Barbera grapes have traditionally been picked earlier than Nebbiolo but they need relatively warm sites and later picking to bring the acidity down to palatable levels, as growers in Asti and Alba have shown. **Barbera d'Asti**, in general the most quintessential Barbera, has three official sub-zones, Nizza, Tinella, and Colli Astini or Astiano. **Barbera d'Alba** is typically solid and ageworthy whereas most **Barbera del Monferrato**, produced in virtually the same area as Barbera d'Asti, is the opposite.

Piemonte's third red grape is Dolcetto, which will still ripen in the coolest, highest sites: soft, where Barbera often bites, but capable of a marvellous balance between fleshy, dusty-dense, and dry with a touch of bitter that goes perfectly with rich local dishes. The best Dolcetto comes from Alba, Diano d'Alba, Dogliani, and Ovada (for its most potent style).

Grignolino is consistently a lightweight cherry red but can be a fine and piquant one; at its best (from Asti or Monferrato Casalese) extremely clean and stimulating. All these are wines to drink relatively young.

Moscato is Piemonte's signature white grape, responsible for sparkling Asti and, distinctly superior, fizzy **Moscato d'Asti**, the epitome of sweet Muscat grapes in its most celebratory form. It also has the considerable merit of containing less alcohol – only about 5% – than virtually any other wine. It can amaze and delight guests after a heavy dinner.

Light-skinned Cortese grapes are grown south of Alessandria (see p.159) to produce **Gavi**, one of Italy's more fashionable dry white wines in the 1980s. Demand for whites then also led to the promotion of Arneis from a mere Nebbiolo-stretcher to make soft, light but aromatic wines not unlike Pinot Blanc. Arneis may have colonized Roero but these sandy soils are also particularly suitable for zesty Favorita, the local variant of Vermentino.

Other specialities of this prolific region include another frothy sweet red wine, Brachetto d'Acqui; light red Verduno from Pelaverga grapes; sweet pink or red Malvasia di Casorzo d'Asti; the interesting yellow wine with the DOC Erbaluce di Caluso (the sweet form, Caluso Passito, is made from semi-dried grapes); and Freisa, often from Asti, a fizzy and frequently sweet red wine not unlike a tarter, less fruity form of Lambrusco. You either love it or loathe it. No-one has ever accused Piemonte of a paucity of grapes, flavours, or names.

White dogs are used to hunt the famous white truffles of Alba so that they can easily be seen at night. (No hunter likes to give away his favourite hunting grounds in broad daylight.) Truffles are by local tradition served with plain dishes, and great Barolo or Barbaresco.

▶ Labels here are a rich cocktail of Italian and the local Piemontese dialect that owes much to French. The region was ruled by the Francophone kingdom of Savoy until well into the 19th century, which gave the Piemontese a sophistication unknown in much of the rest of rural Italy.

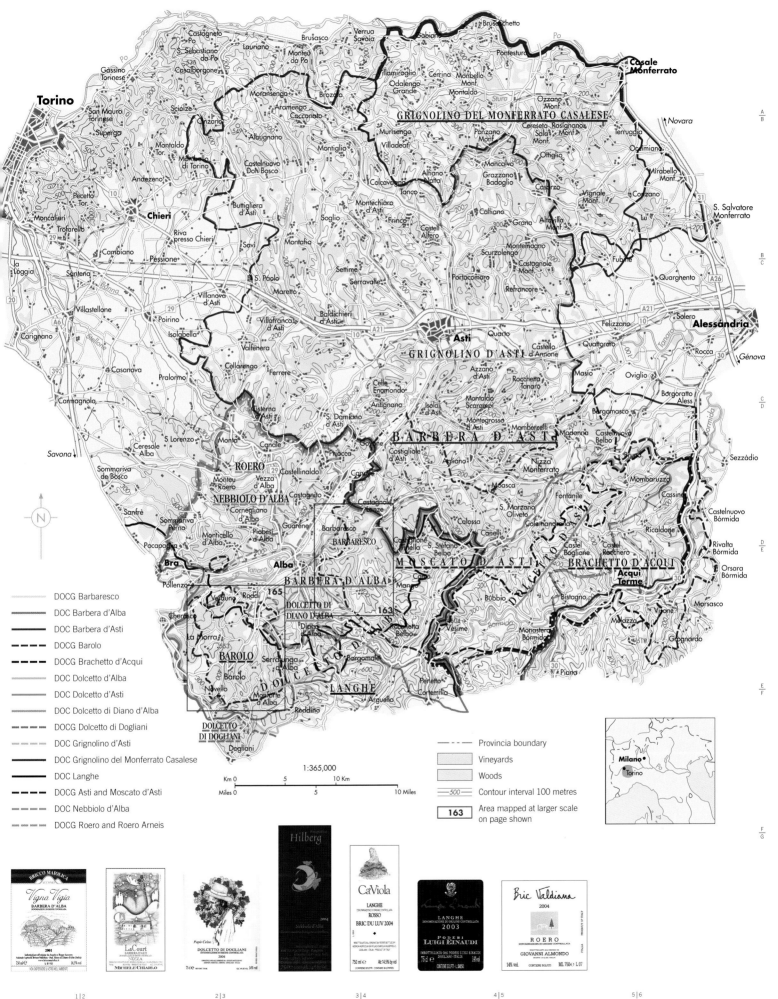

Barbaresco

Nebbiolo finds its most dazzling expression in the Langhe hills, on the calcareous clay soils of the right bank of the River Tanaro, to the northeast of Alba in the Barbaresco zone, and to the southwest of the city around the village of Barolo (mapped and discussed overleaf). The Nebbiolo grape is a particularly late ripener so the finest wine tends to come from slopes with a southern tilt that are not too high, between about 490 and 1,150ft (150 and 350m) altitude.

Today the grower and his or her vineyard (the terms *sorì* and *bricco* recur continually for distinguished sites) hold the key to Barolo and Barbaresco. Tastings reveal consistent differences of quality, of aroma, of potency, and of finesse that in the Côte d'Or would justify the term *cru*. And yet the emergence of these great wines from the limbo of legend into the critical limelight has been accomplished only since the 1980s.

It was the second time in 150 years that the region had been revolutionized. Up to the 1850s its Nebbiolos were vinified as sweet wines, their fermentation never satisfactorily concluded. A French oenologist, Louis Oudart, recruited by a reforming landowner in Barolo, demonstrated how the fermentation should be finished to make potent dry reds. His 19th-century techniques of late picking, long extraction, and endless ageing in huge old casks remained almost unaltered until the 1970s and 1980s. Around this time a newly critical public, putting "fruit" firmly on the agenda, began to turn away from wines that were vastly tannic, and of overpowering strength, but often simply dried out by having waited too long for a maturity that never came.

Modern vinification had no problem finding the solutions: choosing the right moment to pick (nowadays pushing phenolic ripeness to the limit); fermentation in stainless steel at controlled temperatures; shorter macerations; shorter ageing periods in large old oak or, more controversially, ageing in small, new or newish barrels; and, for those who invested in new-fangled rotary fermenters in the mid-1990s, maceration for days rather than the weeks or even months that were traditional.

The results are still tannic wines that need to age, but ones in which the tannin merely frames a stunning array of haunting flavours. Great Barolos and Barbarescos can overlay smoky woodland notes on deep sweetness, the flavour of raspberries on leather and spice, leafy lightness on jam-like concentration. Older wines advance to animal or tarry flavours, sometimes suggesting wax or incense, sometimes mushrooms or truffles. What unites them is the racy cut of their tannins, freshening rather than overwhelming the palate.

Although there has been considerable new planting, Barbaresco with 1,680 acres (680 ha) has less than half as much vineyard as Barolo. It is a big village of just 600 people on a ridge that wobbles west towards Alba, flanked all the way by vineyards of renown. Asili, Martinenga, and Sorì Tildin are bywords for the finest reds. A little lower and to the east lies Neive, in whose castle Oudart experimented with Nebbiolo, and in whose vineyards Barbera, Dolcetto, and, especially, Moscato, are still more important than Nebbiolo. Its finest sites in Neive include Bricco di Neive and Santo Stefano. So thrilling were the powerful wines produced from some of Neive's best sites in the 1990s that attention has been increasingly focused on the area and an increasing number of small growers are now bottling the wine produced there under their own labels.

South on higher slopes, some of which are too cool to ripen Nebbiolo and are therefore more suitable for Dolcetto, lies the commune of Treiso, whose Nebbiolo tends to be particularly elegant and perfumed. Pajorè was the most important *cru* historically. Roncagliette produces wines with the sort of balance so characteristic of those made around the village of Barbaresco to the north. The authorities have divided the entire Barbaresco zone into contiguous subzones, some of very much better quality than others. Only the best Barbaresco vineyards are marked on the map opposite, considerably more than in the last edition of this Atlas, and named as they are most likely to be found on a label (although again as in Burgundy, spellings vary – especially since Piemonte has its own dialect).

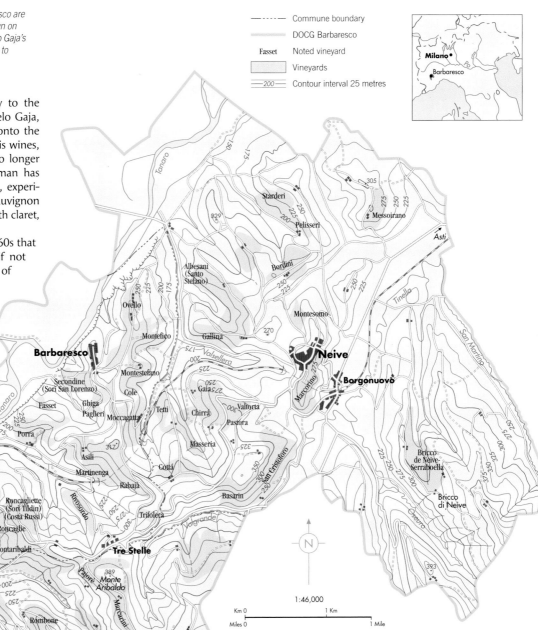

The gradients of subalpine, monocultural Barbaresco are in general less dramatic than those of Barolo shown on pages 154–55 and 164. The sheer force of Angelo Gaja's personality alone has propelled this second village to almost equal billing with Barolo.

Barbaresco once played understudy to the much more famous Barolo, until Angelo Gaja, in a dazzling Missoni sweater, strode onto the world stage. Gaja has no inhibitions: his wines, whether classic Barbaresco (though no longer labelled as such now that this showman has opted out of the DOCG's strictures), experimental Cabernet, Chardonnay, or Sauvignon Blanc, or Barbera treated like first-growth claret, state their case, and cost a fortune.

Bruno Giacosa had shown in the 1960s that Barbaresco could have the intensity if not always the sheer physical weight of Barolo, but it was Gaja who modernized the message, importing new barriques and new ideas without apparently a second thought in this most traditional of regions. In 2000 Gaja announced that he was renouncing the name he had made so famous and selling all the wine previously sold as Barbaresco DOCG, including

▼ Three of the most prominent Barbarescos, all from single well-favoured vineyards, plus a wine grown on Barolo's Cerequio vineyard but vinified in Gaja's cellars in Barbaresco. Its produce no longer carries either B word.

his fabulously expensive single-vineyard Sorì San Lorenzo, Sorì Tildin, and Costa Russi, as DOC Langhe Nebbiolo, the catch-all appellation for declassified Barolo and Barbaresco and for wines containing up to 15% of "foreign" varieties such as Cabernet, Merlot, and Syrah.

With this notable exception, and that of outstanding producers such as Giacosa and Marchesi di Gresy, overall standards of wine-making are still less evolved in Barbaresco than in Barolo, and historically a much higher proportion of the grapes were sold to the region's large merchant bottlers and co-operatives.

The vineyards of Barbaresco are generally slightly lower and warmer than those of Barolo, so the harvest is often earlier. Barbaresco is also generally released after two rather than Barolo's three years of ageing so the wines in general lack quite the staying power of Barolo at its best – which can be an advantage for today's frenetic wine consumers. It is hard to argue that they are less fine.

Commune boundary
DOCG Barbaresco
Fasset — Noted vineyard
Vineyards
200 — Contour interval 25 metres

1:46,000

Km 0 ⸻ 1 Km
Miles 0 ⸻ 1 Mile

Barolo

Barbaresco is a great example of Nebbiolo, but Barolo is the greatest. The Barolo zone starts just two miles southwest of Barbaresco, with the Dolcetto vineyards of Diano d'Alba lying between, and is subject to many of the same influences and characteristics already described on p.162. Two little tributaries of the Tanaro, the Tallòria dell'Annunziata and Tallòria di Castiglione, split Barolo into the three main though highly convoluted hill ranges mapped opposite, rising nearly 165ft (50m) higher than the Barbaresco zone.

Thanks to an increase in vineyard area of more than 40% since the late 1990s, there are now more than 4,200 acres (1,700ha) of Barolo vineyards, although some of the new ones are possibly on sites too cool to ripen Nebbiolo fully. All Barolo vineyards are concentrated in this zone, just big enough for 11 communes in the relatively populous Langhe hills. Compare the map opposite with that of the much flatter Pessac-Léognan region on p.101, which is on more or less the same scale. So many different expositions, altitudes, and mesoclimates, and two main soil types, have provided endless fodder for the discussion of possible subzones.

To the west of the Alba road around La Morra, soils are very similar to those in Barbaresco, calcareous marls from the epoch geologists know as Tortonian. These western hills of the zone in the communes of Barolo and La Morra tend to offer slightly less tense, more openly fragrant wines. The great vineyards here include Brunate, Cerequio, Le Rocche in La Morra, and La Serra in La Morra, and Barolo's most famous site, Cannubi, on slightly lower ground.

To the east, however, in the vineyards of Castiglione Falletto, Serralunga d'Alba, and those to the north of Monforte d'Alba, soils are Helvetian, much less fertile, with more sandstone. They tend to produce even more concentrated wines, Barolo's beefiest, which demand extremely long ageing, and with the years acquire a distinctive orange rim to their inky black depths. Some vineyards in Castiglione Falletto produce wines that are notably softer than those of Serralunga, while the spur of land that divides the valleys of Serralunga and Barolo again produces distinctive wines, combining the power of Serralunga and the perfume of the Barolo made in Castiglione Faletto and northern Monforte. Prime examples include Bussia and Ginestra in Monforte and, in Castiglione Falletto, Vietti's Villero and the wine that Scavino calls in Piemontese dialect Bric dël Fiasc (Bricco Fiasco in Italian). Such examples of linguistic variation/flexibility abound. The only exception to the sternness of Castiglione Falletto's Barolos might be Bricco Rocche, which, with its relatively sandy soils, can produce particularly perfumed wines.

Serralunga d'Alba is home to the former royal estate of Fontanafredda, an association that helped develop Barolo's status as "the wine of kings, the king of wines". The commune has some of Barolo's highest vineyards, but enough warmth builds up in the narrow valley that separates Serralunga from Monforte d'Alba to the west to compensate for the altitude, so that Nebbiolo can be ripened on suitable sites most years. It was in Serralunga that Angelo Gaja expanded from Barbaresco into the Barolo zone in the late 1980s, both wines having been awarded DOCG status as early as 1980.

Even before this, however, Barolo could boast dozens of dedicated grower-bottlers (domaines seems a better word than estates for this most Burgundian of Italy's wine regions). Traditions here are, as in Burgundy, that the same family who tends the vines makes the wine – even if there has been considerable evolution in the way that vivacious, expressive, almost burgundian wine is made over the last two or three decades. Barolo is arguably the world's most uncompromising wine, depending on decades of bottle age to show its true allure, its ethereal bouquet. A few traditionalists have such a faithful and knowledgeable following that they can afford to continue to make such a wine. Others have adapted Barolo to modern times to a greater or lesser degree, by reducing fermentation and barrel ageing times so that the wines can be broached earlier. No-one is right, and only those who decided to ignore the unique qualities of this grape and this place would be wrong.

Serralunga d'Alba, one of the principal villages of the Barolo zone, with the autumn mist (nebbia) that gives its name to the Nebbiolo grape that does so supremely well here. So far, it is less than convincing outside Piemonte.

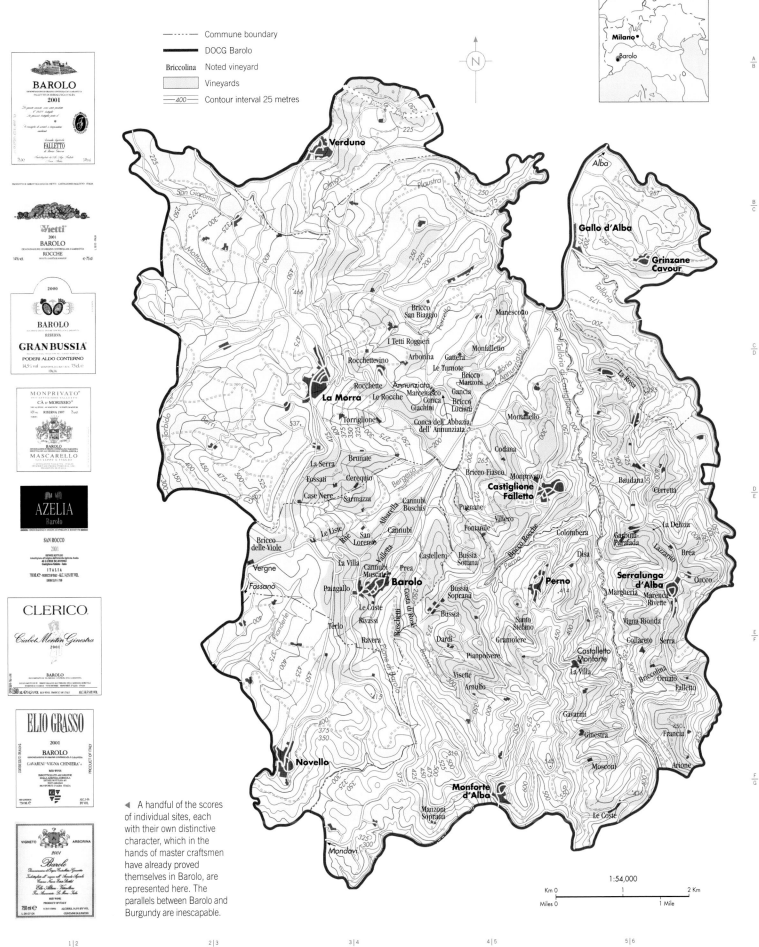

Commune boundary
DOCG Barolo
Briccolina   Noted vineyard
Vineyards
—400—   Contour interval 25 metres

Verduno

Alba

Gallo d'Alba

Grinzane
Cavour

Bricco
San Biaggio

Manescotto

I Tetti Roggieri

Arborina   Gattera   Monfalletto

Rocchettevino   Le Turnote

Bricco
Manzoni

Rocchette   Annunziata   Gancia

La Morra   Marcenasco   Bricco
Le Rocche   Conca   Luciani
Giachini

Montanello

Torriglione   Conca dell' Abbazia,
dell' Annunziata

Codana

La Serra   Brunate   Bricco Fiasco   Monprivato

Fossati   Cerequio   Baudana

Case Nere   Sarmazza   Castiglione
Falletto   Cerretta

Albarella   Cannubi
Boschis   Puenane   Villero

Fontanile   La Delizia

Le Lisse   Rue   Cannubi   Garbutti-
San   Parafada
Lorenzo   Castellero   Bussia
Sottana   Colombera   Brea

Bricco
delle Viole   La Villa   Disa
Cannubi   Prea   Bussia   Perno   Serralunga
Vergne   Muscatel   Barolo   Soprana   d'Alba   Margheria   Cucea

Fossano   Bussia   Santo   Marenca
Paiagallo   Stefano   Rivette

Le Coste   Dardi   Gramolere   Vigna Rionda
Terlo   Rivassi   Collaretto   Serra
Ravera   Pianpolvere   Castelletto
Monforte
La Villa   Briccolina

Visette   Ornato
Arnulfo   Falletto

Gavarini

Novello   Ginestra   Francia

Mosconi   Arione

Monforte
d'Alba

Manzoni
Soprana   Le Coste

Mondovi

1:54,000

Km 0   1   2 Km
Miles 0   1 Mile

◀ A handful of the scores
of individual sites, each
with their own distinctive
character, which in the
hands of master craftsmen
have already proved
themselves in Barolo, are
represented here. The
parallels between Barolo and
Burgundy are inescapable.

Milano
Po
Barolo

BAROLO
DENOMINAZIONE DI ORIGINE CONTROLLATA E GARANTITA
FALLETTO DI SERRALUNGA D'ALBA
2001

FALLETTO

Vietti
2001
BAROLO
DENOMINAZIONE DI ORIGINE CONTROLLATA E GARANTITA
ROCCHE
14% vol.   e 75 cl

2000
BAROLO
RISERVA
GRAN BUSSIA
PODERI ALDO CONTERNO
14,5% vol.   75 cl.
ITALIA

MONPRIVATO
CA' D' MORISSIO
RISERVA 1997
BAROLO
MASCARELLO
GIUSEPPE E FIGLIO

AZELIA
Barolo
SAN ROCCO
2001
ITALIA

CLERICO
Ciabot Mentin Ginestra
2001
BAROLO
1500 ML   ALC.14,5 % VOL.

ELIO GRASSO
2001
BAROLO
GAVARINI 'VIGNA CHINIERA'
RED WINE
750 ML   ALC. 14%

VIGNETO   ARBORINA
2001
Barolo
750 ml   PRODUCT OF ITALY

Northeast Italy

Once Sicily and Puglia was Italy's well of wine. In the 1980s and 1990s vast tracts of vineyard were dramatically and deliberately pulled up. Since then Northeast Italy in general, and the Veneto in particular, has become Italy's most prolific zone. The northeast has always bowed less to tradition and more to modern ideas than the rest of the country, whether because of the realism of the Venetians, the pressure of Austrian influence, or the moderate climate.

In the far west of the area mapped here, **Franciacorta** has built itself the reputation for making Italy's best *metodo classico* wine. Italy's great sparkling success story began in the 1970s on the Berlucchi family estate in direct imitation of champagne, and was taken up by farm after farm in the region south of Lake Iseo. Chardonnay and Pinot Nero are perfectly suited to a climate without extremes. The finest wines, both sparkling and still (and including wines successfully modelled on both bordeaux and burgundy) are from charismatic Maurizio Zanella of Ca' del Bosco, whose Cuvée Annamaria Clementi exhibits a finesse seen only in Champagne's greatest wines. But others such as Bellavista, Ferghettina, Gatti, Majolini, Monte Rossa, and Uberti are all pressing hard on Zanella's heels. Their varietal reds and whites are sold as **Terre di Franciacorta**.

The Veneto wine belt is described in detail on pp.170–71. Its western extreme produces an appealing dry white from the south end of Lake Garda based on its own local relative of the Verdicchio grape, known simply as Lugana. Ca' dei Frati has shown that it can even be aged and that this territory might also have potential for fully ripened reds, as well as the light **Bardolino** and pink Chiaretto traditional on this resort-lined lake. Both of these, made from the same grapes as Valpolicella, are made to be drunk young, preferably on a vine-shaded terrace, though the **Bardolino Superiore** DOCG is designed for more substantial blends. The **Garda** name has been given to the catch-all DOC that allows blending between the standard-issue Veneto zones of Soave, Valpolicella, and Bianco di Custoza. **Bianco di Custoza** made to the south can, like **Gambellara** just east of Soave, be very similar to but a surer bet than everyday Soave.

The most popular wine of the far eastern Veneto is the Venetian tourist's lubricant, sparkling **Prosecco**. Cartizze from Valdobbiane is its finest, driest incarnation, and growing finer all the time in a competitive climate. Verduzzo is the white grape of the Venetian hinterland while light Cabernet (Franc mainly) and Merlot, supplemented by the austere local Raboso, dominate the plains of Piave and Lison-Pramaggiore.

As can be seen clearly from the map, the valley of the River Po as it descends from the plain south of Milan to the Adriatic is wide and flat – not the most prepossessing wine country.

Only one Po Valley wine name is famous, for some infamous: the sparkling red **Lambrusco** from around Módena, above all from Sorbara. There is something decidedly appetizing about this vivid, grapey wine with its bizarre red foaming head. It cuts the richness of Bolognese food admirably. How its faint but unmistakable resemblance to Coca-Cola founded a great American fortune (in one year Riunite, the co-operative of Reggio nell' Emilia, shipped 11 million cases to the States, underwriting for instance Castello Banfi in Montalcino) is one of the most extraordinary success stories in the history of wine.

Wines become much more varied in the Veneto and eastwards. On green volcanic islands in the plain are the increasingly successful **Colli Berici** and **Euganei** near Vicenza and Pádova. The red grapes are the Cabernets of Bordeaux and, above all, the early ripening Merlot. White grapes are a mixture of the traditional: Garganega of Soave, Prosecco, light and sharp Verdiso, and the more solid Friulano (see p.172) and Sylvaner, Riesling, Sauvignon Blanc, and Pinot Bianco. The DOCs of the region are a series of defined areas that give their names to whole groups of red and white wines, generally varietally labelled.

Breganze, north of Vicenza, is a case of a DOC brought to prominence (like Franciacorta) by one fanatical winemaker. Fausto Maculan outstripped the traditional whites of Tocai and Vespaiolo (although he makes them) by resurrecting the old Venetian taste for sweet wines from dried grapes with his golden Torcolato, and by showing that the red Bordeaux grapes, and now even Pinot Noir, can also thrive here. For details of wines made east of here in the eastern Veneto, see p.172.

Emilia Romagna's reputation as a wine producer is steadily rising. The hills around Bologna, the **Colli Bolognesi**, now produce

This shop in the gastronomic capital of Bologna shows what Italian wines, especially the tart, bone dry, lightly sparkling true Lambrusco made nearby, are designed for. Sweetened versions exported to northern Europe and North America are quite different propositions.

some very respectable Cabernet, Merlot, and Sauvignon Blanc. The country south of Bologna and Ravenna still produces oceans of varietal Romagna wine with Trebbiano di Romagna the least remarkable. **Albana di Romagna** was the first white wine to be elevated to DOCG status, to the amazement of everyone but local politicians, in 1986. Like so many Italian whites, Albana comes in all levels of sweetness, although virtually the only interesting wines come from the hills to the east of Forlì where the grape's apple skin character can bring a certain charm to both sweet and dry wines.

More reliable than Albana by far, if highly variable, is this extensive zone's red: **Sangiovese di Romagna**. It can be thin and overcropped, but it can also be gutsy and sophisticated enough to show why some of the Sangiovese clones most popular with discerning Tuscan producers come from Romagna. Producers such as Stefano Berti, Leone Conti, Tre Monti, and Zerbina are showing the way.

▼ All but the Bellavista fizz below and the two distinctive sweet whites on the extreme right opposite are wines made in Trentino or Alto Adige, described in detail overleaf but in as restricted a space as their vineyards in these narrow subalpine valleys.

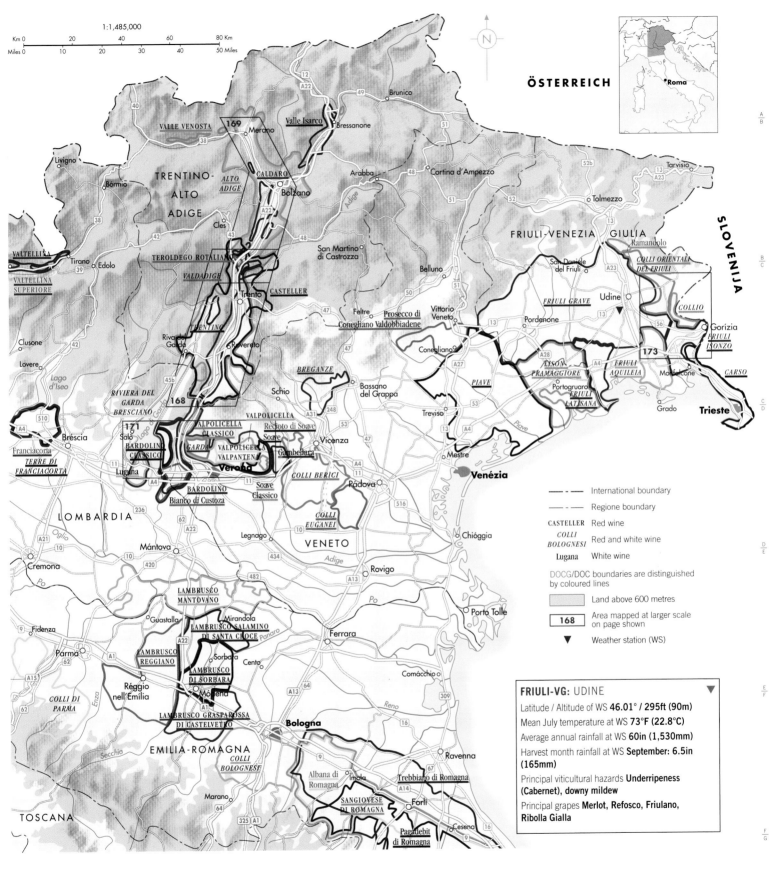

1:1,485,000

Km 0 — 20 — 40 — 60 — 80 Km
Miles 0 — 10 — 20 — 30 — 40 — 50 Miles

ÖSTERREICH

Roma

SLOVENIJA

International boundary

Regione boundary

CASTELLER Red wine

COLLI
BOLOGNESI Red and white wine

Lugana White wine

DOCG/DOC boundaries are distinguished
by coloured lines

Land above 600 metres

168 Area mapped at larger scale
on page shown

▼ Weather station (WS)

FRIULI-VG: UDINE ▼

Latitude / Altitude of WS **46.01° / 295ft (90m)**

Mean July temperature at WS **73°F (22.8°C)**

Average annual rainfall at WS **60in (1,530mm)**

Harvest month rainfall at WS **September: 6.5in
(165mm)**

Principal viticultural hazards **Underripeness
(Cabernet), downy mildew**

Principal grapes **Merlot, Refosco, Friulano,
Ribolla Gialla**

1|2 2|3 3|4 4|5 5|6

Trentino

The Adige Valley forms the dramatic corridor into the Alps that links Italy with Austria over the Brenner Pass. It is a rock-walled trench, widening in places to give views of distant peaks but, like the Rhône Valley, an inevitably crowded north–south link with all the excesses of traffic and industry that go with it.

Its vineyards form a lovely contrast to the thundering traffic below. They pile up every available slope from river to rock-walls in a pattern of pergolas which look from above like deeply leafy steps.

The catch-all DOC for the whole valley is **Trentino**. But each part of the valley has its own specialities, indeed its own indigenous grapes. Growing conditions are fine for almost any white grape, whose share of all Trentino vineyards has risen from 20% to nearly 60% since 1980. Chardonnay is by far the most planted variety, not least because of the importance of Trento DOC *metodo classico* to Italy's sparkling wine drinkers. Ferrari and Cavit make some of the best. Pinot Grigio plantings have also increased enormously along with the world's thirst for it, while Merlot is the most planted red grape.

But the native red grapes are too well-loved (as well as being too productive) to be deposed by a tide of imported varieties. On the way north to Trento the snaking gorge is known as the Vallagarina, the home of Marzemino, a dark-hued, light-bodied red that has established a following. The northern end of Trentino is the unique home of the full-blooded red Teroldego, from the grape of the same name grown on the cliff-hemmed, pergola-carpeted, gravelly plain known as the Campo Rotaliano, which lies between Mezzolombardo and Mezzocorona. **Teroldego Rotaliano** is one of Italy's great characters, a dense purple wine of high extract and good ageing qualities, smooth and even softly berry-flavoured in the mouth but too often marked, at least when young, with the unpalatably high acidity that is the telltale sign of overcropped Teroldego vines. Elisabetta Foradori is the queen of fine, fully ripe Teroldego Rotaliano thanks to pioneering work on improving the clones available.

Schiava or Vernatsch, from the Tyrol (also known in Germany as Trollinger), was once widely grown but is, fortunately, losing ground fast. Schiava is perhaps best appreciated as a *rosato* produced in the village of Faedo at the northern end of this map.

The eastern Adige slopes round San Michele are particularly successful for white grapes and, in recent years, for the international red varieties too. Some of the world's very few interesting Müller-Thurgaus are produced here.

The western arm of the valley near Trento, linking it with three small lakes, grows the same wide range of grapes (all these zones grow good

base wine for *spumante*) but specializes in sweet Vino Santo of high quality from yet another indigenous variety, Nosiola.

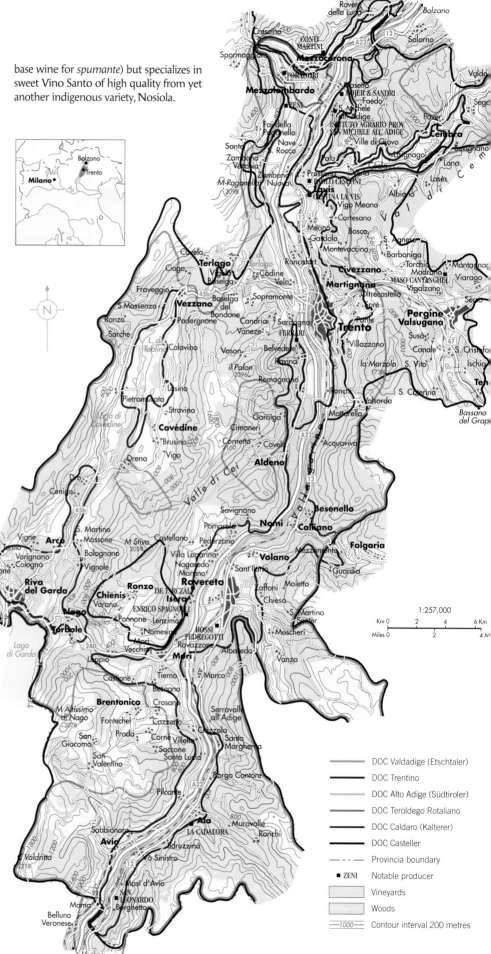

Alto Adige

The Alto Adige, the southern tip of Austria's Tyrol, is Italy's most northerly wine region and one of its most vigorous. Its Alpine peaks proclaim both a cultural and a viticultural melting pot. German is a more common language than Italian, yet French grape varieties are more widespread than Teutonic ones. Its vineyards produce both the racy varietal whites on which Alto Adige's modern reputation is currently based and varieties that will produce serious red wines in warmer areas. Most wines are sold under the blanket DOC **Alto Adige** (Südtiroler) plus the name of the grape.

Production is centred on the benchland and lower slopes of the Adige Valley. Vineyard altitudes vary from 650 to almost 3,300ft (200–1,000m) but 1,148–1,804ft (350–550m) is best for avoiding frost and optimizing ripeness.

Higher vineyards, often steep and terraced as in the **Valle Venosta** to the northwest and **Valle Isarco** (Eisack), which stretches for 15 or 20 miles (24 or 32km) northeast of Bolzano (see p.167 for both), are especially good for Riesling, the aromas benefiting from the wide fluctuations between day and night temperatures.

On slightly lower slopes Chardonnay, Pinot Bianco, and Pinot Grigio are fruity and lively, while the village of Terlano, on the way north to Merano, is highly rated for Sauvignon Blanc. Here instead of the usual white outcrops of calcareous soils moved by ancient glaciers, is hard granitic porphyry, specifically trumpeted on labels such as that shown on p.167. The Gewürztraminer grape owes its name to its presumed origin, the village of Tramin (Termeno in Italian) 12 miles (19km) south of Bolzano. The renowned producer Hofstätter shows why.

The workhorse red grape is the Schiava (alias Vernatsch), whose wines are pale, soft, and simple. The local Lagrein, originally grown round Bolzano, produces much more serious stuff, including the deeply fruity rosé Lagrein-Kretzer and darker Lagrein-Dunkel, both of which have ageing potential and a growing number of followers around the world.

Red varieties imported in the 19th century – Pinot Noir, Merlot, and Cabernet – can also be

very good, especially from growers who have abandoned the traditional pergolas for vines trained lower on wires. All of these, together with Lagrein, are replacing Schiava in the region's warmest sites east of Lake Caldaro and on the slopes above Bolzano, although benefiting from afternoon breezes off Lake Garda and the cool nights. Irrigation is generally essential.

Local co-operatives, or *cantine*, are a valuable and important force in Alto Adige and those of Bolzano, Caldaro, Colterenzio, Cortaccia, San Michele Appiano, Terlano, and Termeno can make wines just as good as the better private producers such as Franz Haas, Hofstätter, Kuenhof (in Bressanone), Lageder, and Elena Walch.

Mezzacorona's co-operative, on the border of Trentino and Alto Adige, is not quite so big as that of Colterenzio or San Michele Appiano but it is certainly one of the smartest in this border region between Italian and Teutonic cultures.

———	DOC Meranese di Collina (Meraner Hügel)
———	DOC Santa Maddalena (Sankt Magdalener)
———	DOC Caldaro (Kalterer)
———	DOC Teroldego Rotaliano
———	DOC Trentino
———	DOC Terlano (Terlaner)
———	DOC Colli di Bolzano (Bozner Leiten)
– – – –	Provincia boundary
■ FRANZ HAAS	Notable producer
▨	Vineyards
▨	Woods
—1000—	Contour interval 200 metres
▼	Weather station (WS)

ALTO ADIGE: BOLZANO ▼

Latitude / Altitude of WS **46.28° / 754ft (230m)**

Mean July temperature at WS **71°F (21.7°C)**

Average annual rainfall at WS **26in (650mm)**

Harvest month rainfall at WS **October: 2in (50mm)**

Principal viticultural hazard **Spring frosts**

Principal grapes **Schiava, Pinot Grigio, Pinot Bianco, Chardonnay, Lagrein, Gewürztraminer, Pinot Noir**

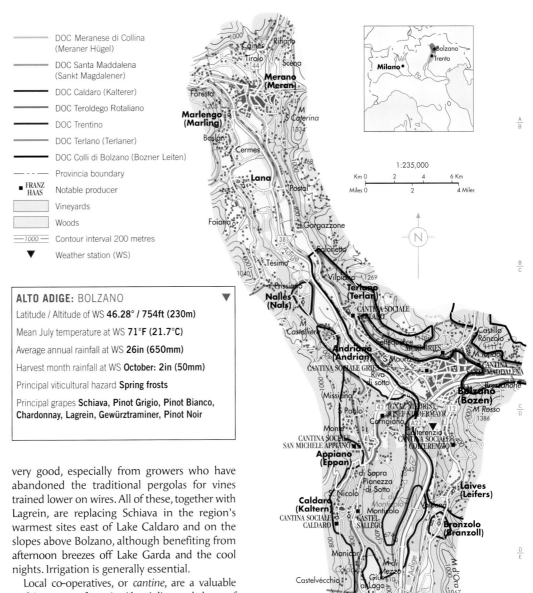

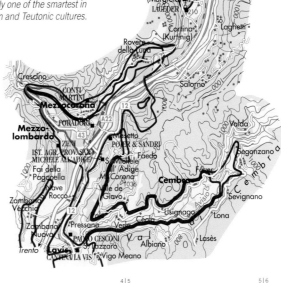

Verona

The hills of Verona, stretching from Soave westwards to Lake Garda, have such fertile volcanic soil that vegetation grows uncontrollably; the vine runs riot on every terrace and pergola, among villas and cypresses that are the image of Italian grace. But not every bottle of wine produced here is full of grace, for the Veneto is Italy's most productive wine region. High yields, with an official limit of 105 hl/ha, are the bane of quality in **Soave** DOC, the Veneto's most important wine zone. Almost 80% of the vineyards are cultivated by growers who deliver their grapes straight to the local co-op with no personal reputation for quality to uphold.

In an effort to distinguish common or garden Soave from real Soave, with its insistent combination of almonds and lemons, the authorities have devised two superior denominations. **Soave Classico** DOC, from the original historic production zone, and **Soave Superiore** DOCG, grown on wires rather than sprawling pergolas on the less fertile hillsides, have maximum yields of 98 hl/ha and 70 hl/ha respectively. Such generous yields are far higher than those actually practised by the top producers of Soave. Pieropan and Anselmi have been joined by a new band of such conscientious producers as

─ · ─ · ─	Provincia boundary
▩	Vineyards
▩	Woods
─500─	Contour interval 100 metres
▼	Weather station (WS)
────	DOC Bardolino / DOCG Bardolino Superiore
─ ─ ─	DOC Bardolino Classico
────	DOC Valpolicella
─ ─ ─	DOC Valpolicella Classico
────	DOC Valpolicella Valpantena
────	DOC Soave
─ ─ ─	DOC Soave Classico / DOCG Soave Superiore Classico / DOCG Recioto di Soave Classico
······	DOCG Soave Superiore / DOCG Recioto di Soave / DOC Soave Colli Scaligeri
────	DOC Garda
─ ─ ─	DOC Garda Classico
······	DOC Riviera del Garda Bresciano
────	DOC Bianco di Custoza
────	DOC Gambellara
────	DOC Lugana
────	DOC Valdadige

Garganega grapes are spread out to dry on rush mats to concentrate the sugars and make the deliciously revitalizing sweet white Recioto di Soave at Pieropan. Verona is arguably the world's capital of drying grapes, both for whites and reds.

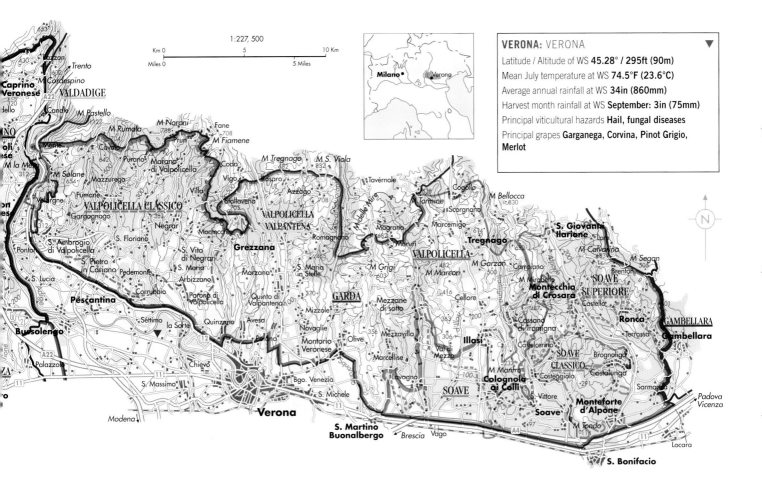

VERONA: VERONA ▼
Latitude / Altitude of WS **45.28° / 295ft (90m)**
Mean July temperature at WS **74.5°F (23.6°C)**
Average annual rainfall at WS **34in (860mm)**
Harvest month rainfall at WS September: **3in (75mm)**
Principal viticultural hazards **Hail, fungal diseases**
Principal grapes **Garganega, Corvina, Pinot Grigio, Merlot**

Cantina di Castello, La Cappuccina, Fattori & Graney, Gini, Inama, Pra, and Tamellini. They all operate in the original, classical area of Soave Classico centred on the eastern end of the Lessini Hills northeast of the village of Soave.

The important grapes are Garganega and a local form of Trebbiano which make wines of an intensity and mouth-filling texture that bring the meaning of Soave (suave) into focus. Pinot Blanc and Chardonnay are also allowed, so long as Garganega makes up at least 70% of the wine.

The best producers typically make a range of single-vineyard or *cru* bottlings, expressing such characterful local sites as Vigneto La Rocca and Capitel Foscarino, as well as experimenting with oak ageing and a wonderfully lively, and historic, sweet DOCG version made from dried grapes, **Recioto di Soave**.

Soave cohabits with **Valpolicella**, whose DOC zone has been extended far beyond the original Classico zone until it reaches the boundaries of Soave. The improving Valpantena is a permitted subzone dominated so far by Bertani and the local co-op. Plain Valpolicella should have a lovely cherry colour and flavour, a gentle sweet smell, and just a trace of almond

bitterness. The mass-produced article can often disappoint but there are now as many producers here as in Soave who recognize the need to make truly distinctive as opposed to commercially viable wine – just as the last decade of the 20th century saw a return to some of the more difficult-to-work but higher-quality hillside sites.

Valpolicella Classico, from four fingers of higher-altitude vineyard sheltering Fumane, San Ambrogio, and Negrar, has the same qualities as wine made outside this heartland but in an intensified form (although there are exceptional operators such as Dal Forno and Trabucchi outside the Classico zone). The leading estates are extremely ambitious for Valpolicella Classico, seeing it, with justice, as one of Italy's most promotable products in every sense.

Vines are being planted on white-pebbled terraces at much higher densities and vertically trained to extract more flavour from every grape, above all late-ripening Corvina, the best of the region. Indeed some producers such as Anselmi have even preferred to operate outside the DOC law, which imposed a maximum of 70% on the Corvina component and until recently demanded the inclusion of tart and

obviously inferior Molinara grapes as well as the traditional but neutral Rondinella. There is also some experimentation with rarer indigenous grapes such as Oseleta.

The most potent form of Valpolicella is as Recioto or Amarone, respectively the sweet (occasionally fizzy) and dry (also bitter) results of drying selected grapes off the vine to make highly concentrated and potent wines, the climax of every Veronese feast. Such wines are the direct descendants of the Greek wines shipped by the Venetians in the Middle Ages, adapted to the Venetian hinterland. The old practice of *ripasso* strengthens Valpolicella by refermenting it on the pressed grape skins, preferably of Corvina, after an Amarone has finished fermentation, in which case it may qualify as Valpolicella Superiore. Care is generally taken to avoid any hint of rot, and the result is a fashionable wine, often well over 15% alcohol, that deserves the title *vino de meditazione*, noble or otherwise.

▼ Three great reds, then three great whites – showing the cream of the Veneto's now exceptionally large crop, larger than any other Italian wine region's. Wines of both colours come in a wide range of levels of sweetness and alcohol.

Friuli-Venezia Giulia

Italy's northeastern corner is her powerhouse of fine white wine production. White wine-making may have progressed enormously all over the country in the last decade or so, but Friuli, or to give the region its full name Friuli-Venezia Giulia, has been famous for sleek modern whites since the early 1970s. Now it can offer some of the world's finest whites, typically varietal, perfumed, sharply etched, clean as a whistle, and by no means routinely oaked.

The country's most revered DOCs for white wines are the **Colli Orientali del Friuli**, or "COF", in the northern half of this map and **Collio Goriziano**, named after the province of Gorizia but more often than not called simply "Collio", in the southern half. The vineyards of western Primorska have also been included because although they are politically part of Slovenia (and are therefore described on p.271) they belong geographically to Friuli. Some producers even have vineyards on both sides of the border. As elsewhere in Italy, there are wine co-operatives in Friuli but, unlike Italy's other notable source of refreshing dry whites Trentino-Alto Adige, Friuli is essentially dominated by individual family-owned wine producers.

The vineyards of Colli Orientali, although protected from harsh north winds by the Julian Alps in Slovenia to the northeast, are marginally cooler and certainly more continental than those of Collio that are closer to the tempering influence of the Adriatic. These "eastern hills", or Colli Orientali, reaching altitudes of between 330 and 1,150ft (100–350m) above the sea, were once underwater and the soils still bear the traces of marl and sandstone deposits, often layered in the characteristic soil type known as "flysch of Cormons" named after the town in the centre of this map.

The principal grape grown here, now known as Friulano (the Hungarians objected to its old name Tocai Friulano), is identical to Sauvignonasse, or Sauvignon Vert. It can be rather crude elsewhere, notably in Chile, where it was for long much more common than Sauvignon Blanc, but it seems to thrive in this corner of Italy. Sauvignon Blanc, Pinot Grigio, Pinot Bianco, and the local speciality Verduzzo are also grown, but a good third of the vineyards of Colli Orientali are devoted to the production of increasingly accomplished red wine. "Cabernet" and, particularly, Merlot dominate, but the local Refosco, Schioppettino, and Pignolo can all be found in refreshing, clear-cut varietals and an increasing array of generally oaked blends. Most of the Cabernet planted in Friuli was long thought to be Cabernet Franc (sometimes spelt Frank) but some has more recently been discovered to be the old Bordeaux variety Carmenère (formerly misidentified in

The vineyards of Collio, itself a corruption of colli, *the Italian word for hills. About 85% of vines are destined to make super-clean, fragrant dry white wines with (in most cases) a good fruity core. Pinot Grigio has overtaken Friulano as the most planted variety.*

Chile as Merlot). When overcropped, as it still is routinely, Carmenère can take on a distinctly animal note. Parts of the Colli Orientali del Friuli feel more alpine than maritime, but the southwestern end between Búttrio and Manzano is warm enough to ripen even Cabernet Sauvignon. Global warming and increased winemaking competence have both contributed to the continuing increase in general wine quality here, although some of the less glorious producers can be tempted to grow a wider range of vines than suits their terrain, and at too high a yield.

In the far north of the Colli Orientali, around Nimis to the northwest of the area mapped here (see p.167), the slopes of the **Ramandolo**

DOCG are particularly steep, cool, and can be damp. Sweet amber Verduzzo is the speciality here. A great deal of local pride is also invested in **Picolit**, a strong white varietal dessert wine which could be described as the Italian Jurançon: a wine more hay-like and flowery, while less pungently honeyed, than Sauternes.

The smaller **Collio** DOC to the south of Colli Orientali makes very similar wines, including the lion's share of Friuli's finest whites, but far fewer reds, and such reds as there are can too often taste light and underripe – so early do the autumn rains arrive and prevent full ripeness. Such is worldwide demand for Pinot Grigio that this variety long ago overtook Friulano, and Sauvignon Blanc has been increasingly popular too. As in Colli Orientali, Chardonnay and Pinot Bianco are more likely to be lightly oaked than the other white wine varietals. Other local light-skinned grape specialities include Ribolla Gialla, Traminer Aromatico, Malvasia Istriana, and Riesling Italico (Welschriesling), all found over the border in Slovenia too.

On the whole the "Cabernet" of Friuli-Venezia Giulia is heartiest to the west of this region, especially in **Lison-Pramaggiore** (see p.167), where the Merlot can be a little dry and heartless for the grape that makes Pomerol. Going east, early-ripening Merlot seems better suited to the large crops and coolish climate of this part of Italy. Merlot dominates the Friuli DOCs of **Grave** and **Isonzo**. The coastal areas with their flat vineyards make less concentrated wines from these grapes than those from more limited hillside plantations in the Colli Orientali del Friuli, although some Isonzo producers on the better-drained vineyards north of the river, on the Rive Alte, are now managing to make wines as good as their counterparts in the better known hillside zones of Friuli. Indeed for many years some producers in the Colli Orientali quietly sourced their red wines from Isonzo growers. The wines made on the lower, flatter, more fertile land between the river and the sea more closely resemble those of the productive Grave del Friuli plain to the west. Competent white wines, notably Friulano and Pinot Grigio, are also made in Isonzo.

The speciality of **Carso**, along the coast around Trieste, is Refosco, known here as Terrano and widely grown just over the border in Slovenia too.

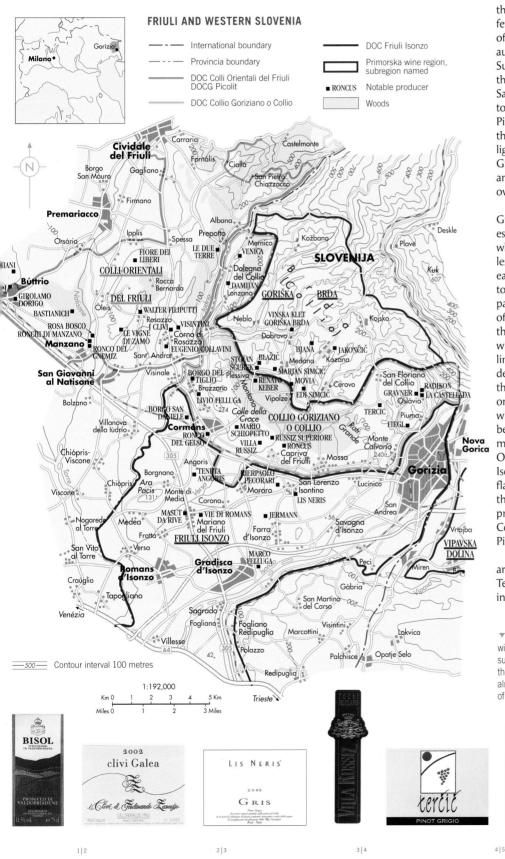

FRIULI AND WESTERN SLOVENIA

– · – · – International boundary
– · – · – Provincia boundary
――― DOC Colli Orientali del Friuli DOCG Picolit
――― DOC Collio Goriziano o Collio
――― DOC Friuli Isonzo
▭ Primorska wine region, subregion named
■ RONCUS Notable producer
▨ Woods

Contour interval 100 metres

1:192,000

▼ Most of these labels represent the aristocracy of white wines produced in the area mapped, although they are supplemented by one of the finest Proseccos made well to the west. The unusually successful red Merlot is made almost in Slovenia by Le Due Terre, who are also proponents of the local purple Schioppettino grape.

Central Italy

The heart and perhaps the soul of Italy lie in this central slightly skewed slice of the peninsula, the cities best-known to foreigners, Florence and Rome, the iconic countryside of Chianti, the tombs of the Etruscans... Does it sound predictable? It is anything but. Altitude, terrain, and above all ideas vary enormously. Ancient identities are thickly overlaid with creativity. Nothing can be taken for granted. If Italy's Apennine spine imposes strict upper limits on vine-ripening territory, the seas on either side wash maritime wine regions of wildly differing characters.

With the exception of the wine regions on the Adriatic coast, this is Sangiovese country, Italy's most planted grape variety whose wines can vary from pale, thin, tart mouthwash to the most sumptuous expressions of Italian gastronomic brio in a glass. At higher altitudes on this map it has to be coaxed to ripen fully. This was particularly true of the clones selected in the 1970s

for their huge yields, regardless of quality. The process of replacing them with better clones has revolutionized our expectations of (especially) Tuscan wine. Central Italian Sangiovese is now likely to be much deeper in both colour and flavour, but to retain the structural zest that makes such wines sit so definitively on the dinner table. The lower and more protected the vineyard, preferably south-facing, the riper are the flavours but many fine, more delicate red wines are grown at altitudes up to 1,640ft (500m) and white wines may succeed even higher than this. But Trebbiano Toscano, the workhorse white grape that has been grown in Sangiovese country for more than a century, is a poor choice at best. Its most useful purpose, it could be argued, is bulking out the sweet, dried grape speciality of Central Italy, Vin Santo.

Soils on these foothills of the Apennines vary but the two most characteristic types are *galestro*,

A storm is imminent over the green hills of Montecarotto in the Verdicchio dei Castelli di Jesi Classico zone in the Marche on the Adriatic coast. Classico is meant to denote the superior heartland but has been applied too generously within this white wine area to have much significance.

a local, particularly crumbly variant on clay-limestone, and the more solid, heavier *albarese*. Local lakes and rivers are welcome warming influences, as are, of course, the two seas.

The Adriatic coastline may be relatively flat but the pretty green hills in the hinterland can yield wines of increasing character and verve, as the wines produced at the remarkable drug rehabilitation community San Patrignano in the hills above Rimini demonstrate. South of here it is the Verdicchio grape that is responsible for the most exciting white wines. The **Verdicchio dei Castelli di Jesi** zone is extensive and the so-called Classico heart constitutes as much as

▶ These labels represent the range of wines made on the fringes of Central Italy outside the most famous zones. Except for underpinning the Poggio Valente Morellino di Scansano and the Carmignano, the ubiquitous Sangiovese is hardly represented here. Instead, various Bordeaux grapes, Vernaccia, Syrah, Montepulciano d'Abruzzo, and Verdicchio.

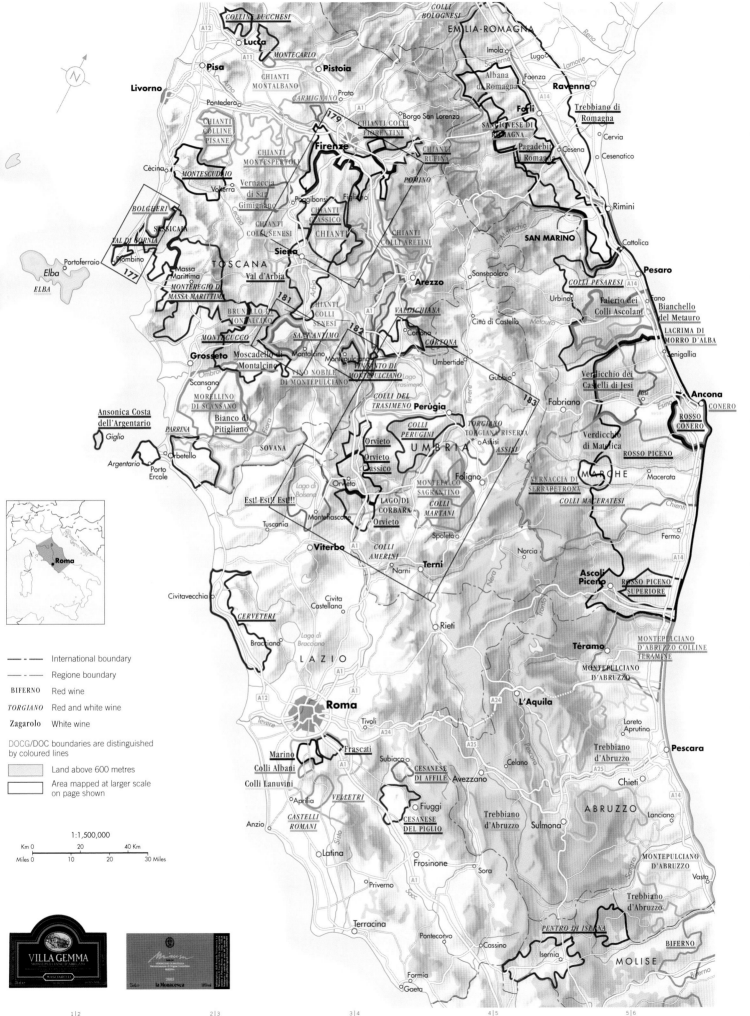

COLLI LUCCHESI

Lucca

MONTECARLO

Pisa

Pistoia

Livorno

CHIANTI
MONTALBANO

Pontedera

CARMIGNANO

Prato

Borgo San Lorenzo

Firenze

CHIANTI
COLLINE
PISANE

Cècina

MONTESCUDAIO

Volterra

Vernaccia di San
Gimignano

CHIANTI
MONTESPERTOLI

CHIANTI COLLI
FIORENTINI

CHIANTI
RUFINA

POMINO

BOLGHERI

SASSICAIA

VAL DI CORNIA

Portoferraio

Piombino

Elba

ELBA

CHIANTI
COLLI SENESI

CHIANTI
CLASSICO

CHIANTI

Siena

Poggibonsi

Fiesole

Massa
Marittima

MONTEREGIO DI
MASSA MARITTIMA

Val d'Arbia

BRUNELLO DI
MONTALCINO

MONTCUCCO

Grosseto

Moscadello di
Montalcino

Montalcino

VINO NOBILE
DI MONTEPULCIANO

Scansano

Ombr

MORELLINO
DI SCANSANO

Bianco di
Pitigliano

Ansonica Costa
dell'Argentario

Giglio

PARRINA

Orbetello

Argentario

Porto
Ercole

SOVANA

CHIANTI
COLLI
SENESI

SANT'ANTIMO

Montalcino

Montepulciano

VIN SANTO DI
MONTEPULCIANO

Lago di
Trasimeno

COLLI DEL
TRASIMENO

Perùgia

COLLI
PERUGINI

Orvieto

Orvieto
Classico

UMBRIA

Est! Est!! Est!!!

LAGO DI
CORBARA

Orvieto

Lago di
Bolsena

Tuscania

Montefiascone

Viterbo

COLLI
AMERINI

Narni

Civitavecchia

CERVETERI

Bracciano

Civita
Castellana

Lago di
Bracciano

Rieti

LAZIO

Roma

Tivoli

Marino

Colli Albani

Frascati

Subiaco

Colli Lanuvini

Aprilia

VELLETRI

CASTELLI
ROMANI

Anzio

Latina

Fiuggi

CESANESE
DI AFFILE

Avezzano

CESANESE
DEL PIGLIO

Frosinone

Sora

Terracina

Pontecorvo

Cassino

Formia

Gaeta

EMILIA-ROMAGNA

Imola

Lugo

Faenza

Ravenna

Albana
di Romagna

Forlì

SANGIOVESE DI
ROMAGNA

Cervia

Cesena

Cesenatico

Pagadebit
di Romagna

Rimini

SAN MARINO

Cattolica

Pesaro

COLLI PESARESI

Urbino

Fano

Bianchello
del Metauro

Falerio dei
Colli Ascolani

Metauro

LACRIMA DI
MORRO D'ALBA

Senigallia

Verdicchio dei
Castelli di Jesi

Jesi

Ancona

CONERO

ROSSO
CONERO

Gubbio

Umbertide

VALDICHIANA

Cortona

CORTONA

Città di Castello

Sansepolcro

Arezzo

CHIANTI
COLLI ARETINI

CHIANTI
COLLI SENESI

Torgiano

TORGIANO
RISERVA

Assisi

Assisi

ROSSO PICENO

MONTEFALCO
SAGRANTINO

Foligno

COLLI
MARTANI

Spoleto

VERNACCIA DI
SERRAPETRONA

COLLI MACERATESI

Verdicchio
di Matelica

Fabriano

MARCHE

Macerata

Fermo

Norcia

Terni

**Ascoli
Piceno**

ROSSO PICENO
SUPERIORE

Téramo

MONTEPULCIANO
D'ABRUZZO COLLINE
TERAMANE

MONTEPULCIANO
D'ABRUZZO

L'Aquila

Loreto
Aprutino

Trebbiano
d'Abruzzo

Pescara

Celano

Chieti

ABRUZZO

Trebbiano
d'Abruzzo

Sulmona

Lanciano

MONTEPULCIANO
D'ABRUZZO

Vasta

Trebbiano
d'Abruzzo

PENTRO DI ISERNA

Isernia

BIFERNO

MOLISE

Biferno

Roma

International boundary

Regione boundary

BIFERNO   Red wine

TORGIANO   Red and white wine

Zagarolo   White wine

DOCG/DOC boundaries are distinguished
by coloured lines

Land above 600 metres

Area mapped at larger scale
on page shown

1:1,500,000

Km 0   20   40 Km

Miles 0   10   20   30 Miles

VILLA GEMMA

MONTEPULCIANO D'ABRUZZO

MASCIARELLI

la Monacesca

90% of the area, but producers such as Umani Ronchi and Fazi Battaglia pull out all the stops for their top bottlings, which combine refreshment with substance. The smaller **Verdicchio di Matelica** zone tends to produce more characterful wine on its rather higher, hillier terrain.

The reds of the Marche have been slower to carve out their identity but **Rosso Conero**, based on juicy Montepulciano grapes, has shown some character. **Rosso Piceno**, made from Sangiovese with Montepulciano, generally with lower yields and judicious oaking, can be good value.

Montepulciano is the red grape of this part of the Adriatic coast and **Montepulciano d'Abruzzo** is rarely overpriced even if it is highly variable (Cerasuolo d'Abruzzo is the satisfyingly full-blooded dry pink version). The finest zone for Montepulciano grown in the wild Abruzzi hills is around the town of Téramo and in 2003 it was awarded the DOCG **Montepulciano d'Abruzzo Colline Teramane**. Superior producers include Illuminati and Villa Medoro. **Trebbiano d'Abruzzo** is also extremely variable but it can hit great heights, not least because of some confusion as to exactly which grape variety is involved. The quixotic late Eduardo Valentini of Loreto Aprutino created an international reputation for his fastidiously selected, magnificently age-worthy, full-bodied version based on the Bombino Bianco of Puglia rather than the much more common, and decidedly vapid, Trebbiano Toscano.

On the western coast, the Roman region Lazio is oddly inert in terms of wine. A handful of producers are trying hard with both imported international varieties and such local specialities as the light red Cesanese but Rome is essentially a white wine city. **Marino** and **Frascati**, from the increasingly built up Castelli Romani, are downed in vast quantities.

Moving north, Cerveteri looks much more important on the map than it is on the ground. It is north of here on, and in the hinterland of, the Tuscan coast that there has been the most dramatic change to the winescape in recent years. More details of the heartland around Bolgheri are to be found opposite but one of the fastest-growing regions has been **Morellino di Scansano**, now DOCG. Morellino is the local name for Sangiovese, raised here in balmy conditions only just above sea level. A host of outsiders has invested here in recent years, with dramatic effects on property prices. They include Florence's oldest winemaking families such as Antinori and Frescobaldi together with Barbi and Biondi-Santi (more famous for their Brunello di Montalcino), and Chianti producers Badia a Coltibuono, Cecchi, Fonterutoli, and Rocca della Macie. As at the single-estate La Parrina on the seaside, the resulting wines are much fleshier and more supple than anything made in the hills of Chianti Classico inland.

Between Scansano and the seriously fashionable stretch from Val di Cornia up to Montescudaio lies **Monteregio di Massa Marittima**. It is dominated by yet another M, the competent Moris Farms, who have spread their wings southwards to Scansano.

Tuscan Coast

It is debatable whether any wine-grower since "Chianti" Ricasoli has made such an impact on Italian wine as the founder of Sassicaia, the little vineyard near the Tuscan coast that upset the whole DOC system. Sassicaia was totally non-traditional, unmistakably superb – and at the time classed as a lowly Vino da Tavola, quite simply because there were no other other vineyards here and therefore no DOC regulations.

The Marchese Incisa della Rocchetta chose a stony hectare of the big San Guido estate in the 1940s to plant Cabernet. He hankered after the Médoc. The nearest vineyards were miles away. Bolgheri was neglected peach orchards and abandoned strawberry fields.

The estate lies six miles (10km) from the sea on the first slopes of the graphically named Colline Metallifere, a range of hills rich in minerals that forms an amphitheatre with a marvellously benign climate. Vines flower in May and grapes ripen in late September, before autumn rains end the long, dry spring and summer. When the Marchese's early wines started to lose their tannin they revealed flavours not seen in Italy before.

His nephews, Piero and Lodovico Antinori, tasted the wines. Piero talked to Professor Peynaud in Bordeaux. Antinori started to bottle and market Sassicaia with the 1968 vintage. By the mid-1970s it was world famous. Then, in the 1980s, Lodovico Antinori began planting a selection of plots with varied soils on his property, Ornellaia, with Cabernet Sauvignon, Merlot, and, less successfully, Sauvignon Blanc. The best plots have turned out to be the higher, stonier plantings, together with a patch of clay whose Merlot goes into his Masseto.

In 1990 his brother Piero produced a Cabernet/Merlot blend called Guado al Tasso from a plot on higher ground to the southwest. The soil turns sandier here; the wine lighter. This may well be the westernmost site for great reds.

New wine estates have proliferated, as the map shows; many, including the Campo di Sasso operation north of Bolgheri established by the Antinori brothers, have yet to build their reputations. Gaja of Barbaresco established Ca' Marcanda. Ruffino of Chianti is here too. Cabernet and some Merlot are the usual choices, and the prognostics all positive.

The DOC **Bolgheri** is evolving fast. (Sassicaia has its own DOC within it.) All other wines must be blends (of Cabernet, Merlot, or Sangiovese for reds) which means, for example, that the all-Sangiovese Cavaliere from Michele Satta and all-Merlot Masseto are sold as IGTs.

If Bolgheri has shown itself perfect Cabernet territory, Merlot may be the grape for the wine zone that covers large parts of the southern half of this map, the **Val di Cornia** DOC. The soils are certainly notably higher in clay than those of Bolgheri. The owner of Bellavista in Franciacorta (see p.166) has Merlot as the focus of his Petra estate. So has the San Luigi estate in Piombino right on what might today be called Tuscany's gold coast.

Angelo Gaja's Ca'Marcanda is just one, relatively discreet, brand new winery built in Bolgheri by a prospector from a quite different wine region. Great care was taken to sink it as far into the (relatively flat) landscape as possible.

Castello del Terriccio in **Montescudaio** DOC to the north of the area mapped with its minty Lupicaia Bordeaux blend was an early hit. Lodovico Antinori lost control of Ornellaia and has now bought land in Bibbona where he and his brother Piero produce Campo di Sasso.

Key:

- ----- Provincia boundary
- ——— Comune boundary
- DOC Bolgheri
- DOC Bolgheri Sassicaia
- DOC Val di Cornia
- DOC Suvereto
- ■ORNELLAIA Notable producer
- Aia Nuova Noted vineyard
- Woods
- —500— Contour interval 100 metres

1:154,000

Km 0 1 2 5 3 4 Km
Miles 0 1 2 3 Miles

▲ Bordeaux varieties dominate all the wines represented here, arranged in chronological with the longest-established producer at the top. Ornellaia's first vintage was as recent as 1985 – a baby by the standards of Italian wine history.

Chianti

The hills between Florence and Siena can come as near to the Roman poet's idea of gentlemanly country life as anywhere on earth. The blending of landscape, architecture, and agriculture is ancient and profound. The villas, cypresses, olives, vines, rocks, and woods compose pictures that could be Roman, Renaissance, Risorgimento – there is no way of telling (provided all the tourists park their cars discreetly).

In this timeless scene, once a promiscuous tangle of the crops deemed necessary to Tuscan peasant life, vineyards now march up hill and down dale, typically owned and regimented by well-heeled outsiders.

The original Chianti zone, one of the first anywhere to be delimited, in 1716, was limited to the land around the villages of Radda, Gaiole, and Castellina, with Greve added later. The red line on the map opposite shows the extended historic zone which today produces what is one of Italy's finest wines, **Chianti Classico**.

Of the six other Chianti subzones, **Chianti Rufina**, east of Florence and partly mapped here, is the most distinctive, making some particularly elegant wines for long ageing. A pass cut into the Apennines north of here that allows maritime breezes to cool the vineyards is largely responsible for the finesse of **Chianti Rufina**, and for the fact that it can need time to show its best. Some highly successful estates around San Gimignano in the **Chianti Colli Senesi** subzone, the hills above Siena, are also emerging. Chianti made in the hills above Florence, Pisa, and Arezzo (respectively the **Chianti Colli Fiorentini**, **Colline Pisane**, and **Colli Aretini** subzones) tends to be less distinguished, as are the wines of the **Chianti Montalbano** subzone northwest of Florence.

The map on p.175 shows just how large an area – almost 100 miles (160km) from north to south, more extensive than the Bordeaux wine region – is allowed to produce wine labelled simply Chianti, at best a tangy, ultra-digestible mouthful of fruit ready for drinking a year or two after it was made, but a very much less ambitious drink than Chianti Classico which is made according to much stricter conditions.

As long ago as 1872 the illustrious Baron Ricasoli (sometime Prime Minister of Italy) at his castle of Brolio distinguished between these two forms of Chianti: a simple one for drinking young and a more ambitious version aimed at the cellar. For the early-drinking Chianti he allowed some of the then prevalent white grape

The sorting table is every bit as common and crucial to widely improved wine quality in the top estates of Chianti Classico as in Bordeaux. This one is at the 10th century abbey, Badia a Coltibuono in Gaiole, run by the Stucchi family. Typically, less than 10% of the estate is suitable for viticulture.

TUSCANY: FIRENZE	▼
Latitude / Altitude of WS **43.45° / 130ft (40m)**	
Mean July temperature at WS **75.5°F (24.2°C)**	
Average annual rainfall at WS **33in (830mm)**	
Harvest month rainfall at WS **October: 4in (100mm)**	
Principal viticultural hazards **Underripeness, downy mildew, esca**	
Principal grapes **Sangiovese, Trebbiano, Canaiolo Nero**	

Firenze
Fiésole
Pistóia
Scandicci
Bagno a Ripoli
Lastra a Signa
Impruneta
Pontassieve
Pélago
Rufina
POMINO
RUFINA
COLLI FIORENTINI
MONTESPERTOLI
FIRENZE
CLASSICO
SIENA
COLLI SENESI
COLLI ARETINI
Monti del Chianti
S. Casciano in Val di Pesa
Rignano sull' Arno
Incisa in Val d'Arno
Figline Valdarno
Greve in Chianti
Panzano in Chianti
Travarnelle Val di Pesa
Certaldo
S. Giovanni Valdarno
Cavriglia
Montevarchi
Radda in Chianti
Castellina in Chianti
Gaiole in Chianti
S. Gimignano
Poggibonsi
Colle di Val d'Elsa
Monteriggioni
Castelnuovo Berardenga
Siena
Arezzo
Orvieto
Viterbo
Grosseto
Volterra
Pisa
Bologna
Forlì
Milano
Firenze
Roma
1:230,000
Km 0 4 8 Km
Miles 0 2 4 Miles
DOCG Chianti Classico
DOCG Chianti subzones:
Colli Aretini
Colli Fiorentini
Colli Senesi
Montespertoli
Rufina
DOC Pomino
Provincia boundary
FONTODI Notable producer
Vineyards
Woods
250 Contour interval 50 metres
Weather station (WS)
A/B
B/C
C/D
D/E
E/F
F/G
1|2
2|3
3|4
4|5
5|6

Malvasia into the blend with the red grapes then grown, Sangiovese and Canaiolo. Unfortunately the proportion of usefully productive white wine vines grew and the dreary Trebbiano Toscano crept in. When the DOC laws defined Chianti in 1963 they insisted on 10% and allowed up to 30% – far too much – white grapes into Chianti of any style. Pallid Chianti (too often beefed up with red imported from the south of Italy) became the rule, and it became clear that either the rules must change, or the zone's producers must make their best wine in their own way and give the wine a new name.

In 1975 the ancient Antinori family launched their rebel flag Tignanello, made, like Carmignano to the north of Florence, from Sangiovese with a small proportion of Cabernet. To underline the point they rapidly added Solaia, with the proportions of Cabernet and Sangiovese reversed. Within a few years there seemed scarcely a castello or villa in Chianti that had not followed them with a "Super Tuscan" (sold initially as a defiant Vino da Tavola, but nowadays corralled into the IGT category) of their own construction, many of them excellent and some original.

But as the character of many of these rebel wines became increasingly distant from anything obviously Tuscan, and as new, much higher quality clones of Sangiovese as well as better ways of growing them were identified, the concept of Chianti Classico – and its Riserva version, which today represents about 20% of production – as a truly fine wine emerged. Ironically, but in typical Italian fashion, this was some time after the entire Chianti production zone was awarded DOCG status in 1984 (one of the worst vintages ever). Today Chianti Classico is an extremely serious wine made substantially (80–100% of the blend) from low-cropped, top-quality Sangiovese vines, aged in wood – large and/or small oak – with a life expectancy of ten years or even more. The other varieties now allowed in Chianti Classico up to a total of 20% are the

▼ Comparison of these modern offerings from some of Chianti Classico's most admired estates and their counterparts 10 and especially 20 years ago would show that the proportion of Sangiovese in these top bottlings has increased markedly. In many cases it is 100%.

traditional Canaiolo, the deeply coloured Colorino and "international varieties", notably Cabernet and Merlot. From 2006 onwards light-skinned grapes were completely banned.

The vineyards of Chianti Classico are at altitudes of 820–1,640ft (250–500m) or even higher. At these altitudes, and in a climate with quite wet autumns, the challenge in all but the hottest, driest years is to ripen not just the sugars but the tannins of the relatively late-ripening, relatively light-coloured, high-acid Sangiovese. An increasing number of producers achieve this, with Italian brio, fashioning wines that are complex, firm, and savoury rather than voluptuous. The rest of their output often includes olive oil, a Riserva Chianti Classico to drink after extended bottle ageing (although an increasing number of producers incline to a single bottling along Bordeaux *grand vin* lines), a fairly inconsequential local dry white, perhaps a Vin Santo (Tuscany's famous dried-grape,

The towers of San Gimignano are some of the most striking landmarks in the Tuscan landscape. San Gimignano grows the Vernaccia grape to produce potent whites; an exception in a region dominated by reds.

long-aged sweet white, or rather tawny; see p.182), and perhaps a Super Tuscan IGT or two. However, this last wine style is waning as Chianti Classico, which may now be made from nothing but Sangiovese, the most Tuscan grape of all, waxes.

These wines are typically fastidiously made but nowadays larger oak vats known as *botte* are just as common as the top-quality French barriques that were the last word in fashion in the 1980s.

The map on the previous page shows, besides the chaotic hilliness of the Chianti countryside, and the scattering of vines (and olives) among woods, the cellars of most of the leading producers of Chianti Classico.

Montalcino

In the 1970s Montalcino was the poorest hilltop town in southern Tuscany. Little was heard of this part of Italy. It was purely local knowledge that the climate here was more equable than farther north – the sea is only 30 miles (50km) away – and that summers are regularly warmer and extremely dry. Monte Amiata, rising to 5,600ft (1,700m) just to the south, collects the summer storms that come from that direction. Montalcino has the double advantage of the warm, dry climate of the Tuscan coast (see p.176) with, in the best vineyards, the rockier, less fertile soils of the cooler Chianti Classico zone. This can result in the most concentrated, long-lived forms of Sangiovese on the planet.

At the same time as Ricasoli was devising an ideal formula for Chianti, Clemente Santi and his kin (now called Biondi-Santi) were establishing a model for what they labelled **Brunello di Montalcino**. Odd bottles of ancient vintages of this wine were so impressively muscular that eventually other producers emerged and from the 1980s Montalcino has been engulfed in a tidal wave of international interest in what was clearly Tuscany's answer to Barolo.

The old method was to ferment this strong, dark wine long and slowly and then age it for years in large old Slavonian oak casks and decades in bottle. The result was a wine for heroes, or rather heroic millionaires, super-charged with flavour, extract, and impact.

Even in Montalcino, however, wine laws have been adapted to modern tastes. The mandatory minimum four years in oak have been reduced to two (the wine not to be released until four years old) so that today's Brunello is much more likely to have been bottled while there was still sufficient fruit to counterbalance its power. And Montalcino was the first DOCG to be graced with a "junior DOC", **Rosso di Montalcino**, a (relatively) lighter wine that can be released at only a year old. This has swept up the less concentrated fruit and allowed Brunello to retain an average quality level that is in general admirably high.

This is all the more remarkable because the zone has been expanded so enormously, from just over 150 acres (60ha) in 1960 to more than 5,000 acres (2,000 ha) today. Altitudes vary from 490ft (150m) above sea level in the

▼ Black would seem to the colour favoured for Brunello labels, as well it might be considering the colour of the wines. Brunello is supposedly a local selection of Sangiovese although the vine selections planted in the Montalcino zone vary enormously today.

Val d'Orcia in the south, where the most potent wines tend to be made on heavy clay soils, to 1,640ft (500m) just south of Montalcino itself where wines grown on *galestro* marls are more elegant and aromatic, so some producers deliberately blend lots from different areas. Some areas are definitely better than most, but individual site classification has so far been regarded as too politically sensitive.

The only question mark over Brunello di Montalcino's future is the invasion of the new oak barrique, which has had the effect of deepening hues but smudging this zone's highly distinctive character – more obvious in its Sangiovese than in the international grapes now widely planted in Montalcino. The resulting wines may be sold under the **Sant'Antimo** DOC – same boundaries as Brunello, different name.

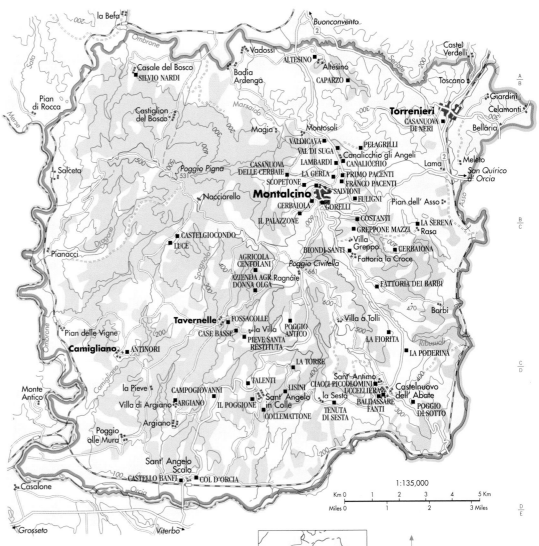

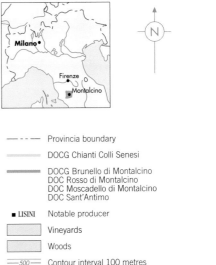

Provincia boundary

DOCG Chianti Colli Senesi

DOCG Brunello di Montalcino
DOC Rosso di Montalcino
DOC Moscadello di Montalcino
DOC Sant'Antimo

■ LISINI   Notable producer

Vineyards

Woods

500   Contour interval 100 metres

Montepulciano

Montalcino's neighbours to the east, across an intervening enclave of "mere" Chianti, have ancient pretensions of their own embodied in their *denominazione*, **Vino Nobile di Montepulciano** DOCG. Montepulciano is a hill town of great charm surrounded by vineyards planted with a mixture of its own local clones of Sangiovese, called here Prugnolo Gentile, and some local and Bordeaux varieties. Vino Nobile must contain a minimum of 70% Sangiovese – some producers prefer 100%, others a blend – so its varietal make-up is more like Chianti Classico than Brunello.

As in Montalcino, minimum oak ageing periods have been reduced (to just one year in wood for both normal and Riserva versions). If young Vino Nobile is often pretty chewy, the earlier-maturing, junior version **Rosso di Montepulciano**, can be almost surprisingly soft.

Vineyard altitudes here vary less than in Montalcino and most of the best sites are at 820–1,970ft (250–600m). The average annual rainfall, around 29in (740mm), is also slightly higher, which, with generally sandier soils, tends to make the wines more accessible, although the pervading warmth of south Tuscany leaves no shortage of ripeness.

Led by the stylish house of Avignonesi, a swelling band of accomplished wine producers here has dallied with various Super Tuscan formulae, and several of them have branched out into the **Cortona** DOC zone to the immediate east, but arguably Montepulciano's greatest triumph is its Vin Santo, the forgotten luxury of many parts of Italy, Tuscany above all. It is orange coloured, smoky scented, extraordinarily sweet, intense, and persistent, made typically from Malvasia Bianca, Grechetto Bianco, and Trebbiano Toscano – grapes that are carefully dried in well-ventilated premises at least until December before being fermented and aged for three years in tiny flattened barrels called *caratelli*. Grapes for Vin Santo di Montepulciano Riserva are dried and the wine aged even longer, while the Avignonesi Prugnolo Gentile speciality Vin Santo di Montepulciano Occio de Pernice (eye of the partridge) is often aged more than eight years before bottling.

▼ It is striking how many more notable producers have emerged from within the Brunello di Montalcino zone (see labels on p.181) than among those who make Vino Nobile di Montepulciano.

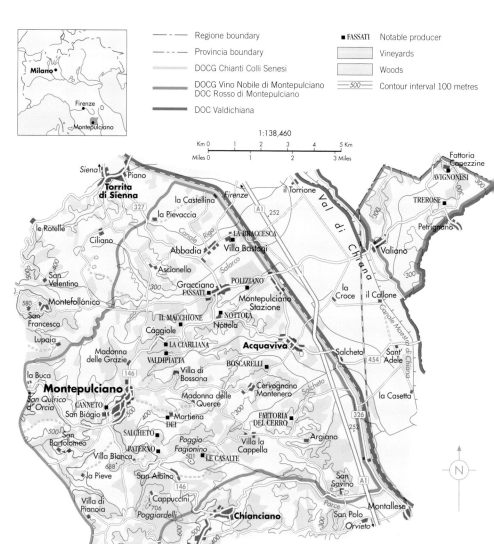

— - — - — Regione boundary	■ **FASSATI** Notable producer
— - - — - - Provincia boundary	Vineyards
DOCG Chianti Colli Senesi	Woods
DOCG Vino Nobile di Montepulciano / DOC Rosso di Montepulciano	═500═ Contour interval 100 metres
DOC Valdichiana	

1:138,460

Km 0 1 2 3 4 5 Km
Miles 0 1 2 3 Miles

Working the vineyards of Fattoria Le Casalte, which, like a substantial proportion of producers around Montepulciano, makes both red wine and a sweet white Vin Santo from dried grapes.

Umbria

Umbria's great gifts to the world of wine are its Grechetto grape for full-bodied white wines, capable of nutty intensity, and, especially, Sagrantino for reds. Sagrantino is thick-skinned, packed with flavour and potential longevity. It was for long a local secret around the town of Montefalco, where it made sweet red *passito*. But in the early 1990s Marco Caprai brought it to international attention by creating dramatic dry wines of extraordinary fruit and vivid tannins. Today **Montefalco Sagrantino** is a DOCG of more than 1,235 acres (500ha) already producing wine on well over 40 estates, with a further 740 acres (300ha) too young to yield serious wine. The flavour of Sagrantino is a new colour on Italy's palette.

Italy's only landlocked region south of the Po has wine traditions as ancient as any. Orvieto was an important Etruscan city. The magnificent cellars cut in the volcanic rock of its dramatic hilltop 3,000 years ago are unique examples of prehistoric technology, specifically designed for long, cool fermentation, the object being sweet, *amabile*, white wine. Alas for **Orvieto**, the 1960s and 1970s fashion for dry white wines turned it into yet another Central Italian blend based on Trebbiano Toscano (called Procanico here) with minimal amounts of the Grechetto that gave it character, and the fortunes of this supposed leader of Umbrian wine foundered.

Enter Dr Giorgio Lungarotti, who, on his estate at Torgiano near Perugia, was the first in modern times to prove, in the late 1970s, that Umbria could make red wine as good as Tuscany's, and even to explore what might be called Super Umbrians. His daughters, Teresa and Chiara, continue to keep **Torgiano**, whose Riserva is now DOCG, on the map.

It was in the southwest at Antinori's Castello della Sala estate that Umbrian wine history moved on again. The estate was initially designed to make Orvieto, but from the mid-1980s on winemaker Renzo Cotarella, brother of the famous consultant oenologist Riccardo, created a revolutionary range of non-traditional white wines. A barrel-fermented Chardonnay was perhaps only to be expected, but Cervaro della Sala had almost from the start a purity and singularity to establish it as one of Italy's greatest white wines. The botrytized Muffato, made from a range of international varieties plus Grechetto, showed other possibilities.

Umbria is now well on its way and today makes a truly Italian farrago of reds and whites from grapes both local and imported, including

Orvieto of some real interest once more. Patterns matching grapes and places are still emerging, but the role of consultant oenologists, the demigods of the modern Italian wine scene, will continue to be vital. The Cotarella brothers have been making particularly successful raids into Umbria from their Falesco winemaking base at Montefiascone over the border in Lazio. As innovators they are more likely to label their wines IGT **Umbria** than with a local DOC such as Colli Perugini, Colli del Trasimeno, Colli Martani (especially good for Grechetto), or Colli Amerini. Umbria, whose climate varies enormously, from cooler-than-Chianti-highland weather in the north around Lake Trasimeno, to a Mediterranean climate at Montefalco and Terni in the south, has arrived.

- – – – – Regione boundary
- ———— Provincia boundary
- <u>MONTEFALCO SAGRANTINO</u>   DOCG
- <u>ORVIETO</u>   DOC
- ■ LA FIORITA   Notable producer

DOCG/DOC boundaries are distinguished by coloured lines

- ▼ Weather station (WS)

UMBRIA: PERUGIA ▼
Latitude / Altitude of WS **43.07° / 1,673ft (510m)**
Mean July temperature at WS **73.5°F (23.1°C)**
Average annual rainfall at WS **36in (910mm)**
Harvest month rainfall at WS **September: 2.75in (70mm)**
Principal viticultural hazard **Some esca in older vineyards**
Principal grapes **Sangiovese, Ciliegiolo, Sagrantino, Trebbiano, Grechetto**

◄ The Umbrian Sagrantino grape makes particularly firm reds. The Cervaro is a dry white blend of Chardonnay and the local Grechetto. The exception here is the Montiano made by Riccardo Cotarella just over the border in Lazio, which is a luscious Merlot in a defiantly international style.

Southern Italy

Historically it was the inland parts of Campania, particularly the province of Avellino east of Naples, which set the pace for southern Italy's truly distinctive wines. Aglianico (a corruption of Ellenico, or Greek, like civilization itself down here) is arguably southern Italy's greatest dark-skinned grape, making wines with a powerful, obviously noble, brooding character. The vine ripens so late that it could not practicably be grown much further north. In the hills of the **Taurasi** DOCG zone, where it finds its finest expression, it is sometimes picked in the snow, and is naturally so high in acidity that the malolactic fermentation is no routine achievement. As everywhere in Italy, however, Aglianico is being tamed, and occasionally smothered, by the application of modern, super-soft winemaking techniques.

The name of **Greco di Tufo**, a substantial white from inland Campania of remarkably original flavour – apple peel fragrance and mineral depths – shares the credit between its long-assumed Greek origins and the tuff rock on which it grows. In the same hilly province, Avellino, the classical Fiano grape makes a more delicate, subtle white, a wine that combines emphasis with firmness and a hauntingly floral scent. Its charms are so obvious that the variety has been successfully imported into Sicily. Both Greco di Tufo and **Fiano di Avellino** are now DOCG.

These are the established names of modern Campanian wine but some encouragingly good

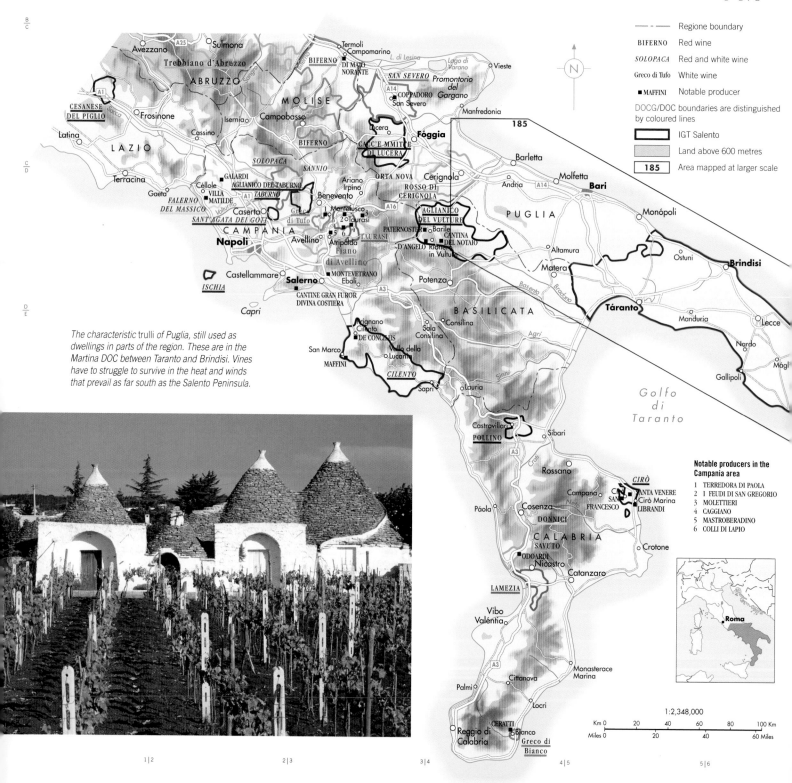

The characteristic trulli of Puglia, still used as dwellings in parts of the region. These are in the Martina DOC between Taranto and Brindisi. Vines have to struggle to survive in the heat and winds that prevail as far south as the Salento Peninsula.

------- Regione boundary

BIFERNO Red wine

SOLOPACA Red and white wine

Greco di Tufo White wine

■ MAFFINI Notable producer

DOCG/DOC boundaries are distinguished by coloured lines

IGT Salento

Land above 600 metres

185 Area mapped at larger scale

Notable producers in the Campania area

1 TERREDORA DI PAOLA
2 I FEUDI DI SAN GREGORIO
3 MOLETTIERI
4 CAGGIANO
5 MASTROBERADINO
6 COLLI DI LAPIO

1:2,348,000

wines are emerging from less obvious areas. In the hitherto unknown coastal vineyards around the temples of Paestum, producers such as Montevetrano, De Conciliis, and Maffini are making wines of world class, almost exclusively from Campania's rich heritage of indigenous grape varieties. Villa Matilde to the north in the **Falerno del Massico** zone named after Falernum, the most celebrated wine of the ancient world (see p.12), also makes the most of them, with fine reds based on Aglianico and Piedirosso and improving whites made from Falanghina grapes. Fontana Galardi's Terra di Lavoro is an impressive, highly distinctive red made in this northern corner of Campania.

Basilicata, the region to the south, has only one DOC: **Aglianico del Vulture**, grown (with unusual skill for this part of the world) on the slopes of an extinct volcano up to 2,500ft (760m) using a different selection of Aglianico from that grown in Taurasi. Less famous than Taurasi, it can often offer better value, although winemaking standards vary wildly. Leading producers are Paternoster and D'Angelo, who has had some success adding a softening dose of Merlot. Aglianico is also grown on the Adriatic coast of southern Italy in the little-known region of **Molise** where Di Majo Norante does an outstanding job – as this organic producer also does with Montepulciano and Falanghina.

The wilds of Calabria are better known for mysteriously half-built houses than for wine (although some excitement was provided by the discovery in 2004 that one of Sangiovese's parents was an obscure variety found in Campania but called Calabrese Montenuovo, and therefore presumably of Calabrian origin). There is just one strong red of reputation, Cirò on the eastern coast. The best-known producer is the family-owned firm of Librandi. It has been working hard to rescue such local grapes as the Magliocco Canino, from which it makes the velvety Magno Megonio. Calabria's most original wine, however, may be the strong, tangy, and sweetly perfumed **Greco di Bianco** made around a village itself called Bianco, near the very tip of the Italian toe.

If the wine producers of Calabria and Basilicata could do with the kick that their coastline inevitably suggests, Puglia's wine scene has been radically transformed. Thanks to generous EU grants for pulling up vines, total annual wine production has plummeted. Too often it has been at the expense of the low bush vines yielding concentrated, interesting wine rather than the region's least interesting

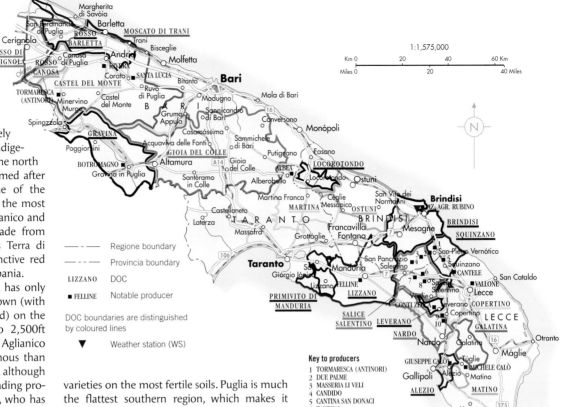

varieties on the most fertile soils. Puglia is much the flattest southern region, which makes it easy to work compared with its neighbours, but provides little in the way of altitude to afford relief from the unremitting summer heat.

Three-quarters of the region's output is still blending wine for the north (including France) or fodder for the producers of grape concentrate, vermouth, or the stills that dispose of Europe's embarrassing wine surplus. However, the proportion of Puglian wine made expressly for discerning drinkers has certainly been increasing. The flatland around Foggia in the north churns out undistinguished Trebbiano, Montelpulciano, and Sangiovese, but some more ambitious bottlings have been emerging from producers based in **San Severo**. Some promising Uva di Troia is made in the **Castel del Monte** DOC, west of Bari, and further south some producers have had success with the Abruzzi's Montepulciano.

But most of Puglia's interesting wines are made on the flat Salento peninsula where there may be no great variation in exposition and mesoclimate but the vines benefit enormously from the cooling winds that blow off both the Adriatic and Ionian seas. Today, thanks to much improved viticulture, the better grapes are rarely picked before the end of September.

At the end of the 1990s, it was the peninsula's ability to provide such anodyne shelf-fillers as IGT Chardonnay del Salento that drew international attention, but there has been a perceptible increase in interest in

Key to producers
1 TORMARESCA (ANTINORI)
2 DUE PALME
3 MASSERIA LI VELI
4 CANDIDO
5 CANTINA SAN DONACI
6 TAURINO
7 CASTELLO MONACI
8 AMATIVO
9 CANTINA SOCIALE COPERTINO
10 MASSERIA MONACI

SOUTHERN ITALY: BRINDISI ▼
Latitude / Altitude of WS **40.39° / 33ft (10m)**
Mean July temperature at WS **76.3°F (24.6°C)**
Average annual rainfall at WS **22in (550mm)**
Harvest month rainfall at WS **August: 1in (25mm)**
Principal viticultural hazards **Rapid ripening, water stress, sunburn**
Principal grapes **Negroamaro, Primitivo, Malvasia Nera, Uva di Troia**

Salento's distinctive local grapes. Negroamaro is the cautionary name of the principal red grape of eastern Salento. It makes almost port-like roasted reds in such DOCs as **Squinzano** and **Copertino**. Malvasia Nera, with different strains identified respectively with Lecce and Brindisi, is Negroamaro's usual blending partner and can add a certain velvet to the texture. But the most famous Puglian variety is Primitivo – identical to California's Zinfandel and with its historical roots now established as Croatian – traditionally a speciality of western Salento, particularly Gioia del Colle and Manduria. It can reach fiendish alcohol levels though in the right hands the wines can be positively voluptuous.

◄ More black and some creative typography in this selection of some of the more admired labels from this far southern tip of the Italian mainland. Only 25% of wine made here is bottled and labelled however; the great majority is shipped in bulk for blending, and sometimes compulsory distillation.

Sicily

After a long period of stagnation and over-production, this beautiful Mediterranean island could now claim to be Italy's most vital and improved wine region. Sicily may not have been home to more cultural influences than anywhere else but it retains the visible remnants of more civilizations more obviously than anywhere else in the world of wine – from the near-intact Greek temple of Agrigento to the Roman mosaics of Piazza Amerina, the Crusader castles and Moorish churches of Palermo to the Baroque splendour of Noto and Ragusa, and, most recently, the giant wine factories that appeared in the late 1980s and early 1990s. This is Sicily, as rich and varied culturally as it is viticulturally – with so many different terroirs and terrains that one might even suggest it should be regarded as a continent rather than a mere island.

The southeastern tip is further south than Tunis; the distant island of Pantelleria, whose Muscats are justly famous, is on the same latitude as this North African city and closer to it than it is to Palermo. Sicily can be very hot, and the sea of Catarratto vines planted in Trapani province in the west, their pale-skinned grapes originally destined for Marsala producers, is regularly warmed to boiling point by winds from Africa. Irrigation is a necessity for a good half of Sicilian vineyards – indeed so dry is the climate that the vines need little spray treatment; the island is particularly well suited to organic viticulture. But inland the landscape can be greener, and the mountains in the northeast are usually snow-capped for several winter months.

Geography is a constant but the political complexion of the island's wine industry has recently been anything but.

In the mid-1990s Sicily competed only with Puglia for the title of Italy's most productive wine region, annually churning out more than 10 million hl of usefully strong wine for blenders to the north. Ten years later the annual harvest was closer to 7 million hl (much less than the Veneto's) produced from only a slightly reduced vineyard area. The island has definitively, and sensibly in view of 21st-century economics, become more concerned with quality than quantity. The family firm of Tasca d'Almerita took the lead, sharing the fruits of their extensive researches in vineyard and cellar. More recently the regional wine institute, under the direction of Diego Planeta and through the innovative and savvy Planeta

family winery, has put modern Sicilian wine on the world map. This was achieved initially by showing that Sicily could produce world-class international varietals.

It is significant that the Planetas are now much more interested in indigenous vine varieties than in the Merlot and Chardonnay that originally won them attention. Indeed the whole island can see that this is the future, with a vine heritage as regionally varied as all of its other assets.

The Planeta winery was built on the shores of Lake Arancio, near Sambuca di Sicilia, in 1995. Apart from its excellent red and white wines, Planeta is also a producer of top-quality olive oil.

The grape that made Sicily's vinous reputation abroad is Nero d'Avola (Avola is in the southeast), making sumptuous wines with structure and ripe red fruit flavours, notably around Agrigento near the south-central coast, and in the far west too. The grape can have

◄ Three reds and three whites here, as well there might be for an island long dominated by pale-skinned varieties. The Vecchio Samperi dry Marsala *manqué* bears comparison with a Sercial Madeira for refreshment value. The Cometa is made from the Fiano grape from Campania.

difficulty ripening in the island's higher vine-yards but skilful producers (Abbazia Santa Anastasia is one) have successfully transplanted it to the north coast, where they blend it with both Syrah and Merlot.

Of potential equal interest among red wine grapes, however, is Nerello Mascalese, tradi-tionally grown on the slopes of Mount Etna, where an increasing number of ambitious vine-growers are braving the volcano's portentous rumblings and very real eruptions. Nerello can thrive here at up to 3,300ft (1,000m). Encountered most commonly in the lightly spicy **Etna Rosso**, it can produce such delicate wines that the firm of Murgo, for one, makes a traditional method fizz from it. Frappato, an important ingredient in the blend for **Cerasuolo di Vittoria** DOCG, is another grape increasingly appreciated for its lively flavour of cherries.

Catarratto has long been the workhorse white grape of the west, but the 1990s influx of flying winemakers occasionally managed to fashion interesting wines from it, and certainly from its partner Inzolia (the Ansonica of Tuscany). Grecanico can also make toothsome white and has been gaining ground in recent

years. But to judge from De Bartoli's Grappoli di Grillo and Rallo's Gruali, it may be the fra-grant, elegant Grillo, another traditional Marsala variety, which is eventually most trea-sured for fine dry whites. Some producers on Etna have managed to demonstrate that their Carricante vine, whose wines are the island's tartest, can age gracefully for up to 10 years. All this is news; exciting for Sicily's winemakers, exciting for us, but still of unknown significance to the wider world.

Moscato is not news, but it could be Sicily's most promising pale-skinned grape of all. The Planetas rescued **Moscato di Noto** from near oblivion. Nino Pupillo did the same for the dis-tinctly different **Moscato di Siracuso** – both of them made from Moscato Bianco/Muscat Blanc grapes, but in very different environ-ments. The Sicilian Moscatos perhaps best known off the island, however, are made from Muscat of Alexandria, often called Zibbibo here. Grown on the fashionable volcanic island of Pantelleria off the southwestern coast, it

makes the sumptuous **Moscato di Pantellera**. In the Aeolian Islands, however, it is Malvasia that is responsible for the sweet orange-flavoured wines. The finest example of **Malvasia delle Lipari** is produced by Barone di Villagrande.

Although not immune, Sicily is less domi-nated by the itinerant consultant oenologists who guide so many of Italy's most famous cellars. Co-operatives are still extremely impor-tant, and often benevolent. Settesoli is one which, along with Planeta, has done much to import such well-suited varieties as the Fiano of Campania to the island.

Marsala, like a very distant cousin of sherry, has been famous since Nelson's day, when he fortified the Royal Navy with it. In much of the late 20th century it seemed to be in the deepest of doldrums but Buffa shows renewed faith in this unique wine, Pellegrino persists ably, and De Bartoli is showing distinct signs of life, even if it avoids the DOC, and the rules that go with it, for its best wines, Vecchio Samperi Riserva 30 Anni and Vigna La Miccia.

--- - - - Provincia boundary

ELORO Red wine

ETNA Red and white wine

Moscato di Noto White wine

■PLANETA Notable producer

/DOC boundaries are distinguished by coloured lines

Land above 500 metres

1:1,786,000

Km 0   20   40   60 Km

Miles 0   10   20   30   40 Miles

Malvasia delle Lipari

Moscato di Pantelleria
Moscato Passito di Pantelleria

Moscato di Siracusa

Moscato di Noto

CERASUOLO DI VITTORIA

ELORO

Sardinia

Italy's northern major Mediterranean island, Sardegna in Italian, has over the centuries seen many of the same influences as Sicily but, with some increasingly exciting exceptions, has been rather slower to join the international modern winemaking party.

Wine has never played an important part in either Sardinian culture or agriculture, although there was a flurry of heavily subsidized planting in the mid-20th century to provide reds, so alcoholic they tasted almost sweet, for blending on the mainland. Sardinian reds were once fermented with the express purpose of leaving some residual sugar in the wine. Sweet reds such as Sella & Mosca's Anghelu Ruju continue this tradition and even today many of Sardinia's greatest, if least-exported, wines are sweet – rare and rich Moscatos, Malvasias, and **Vernaccia di Oristano**. During the 1980s, however, the subsidies to plant vines became bribes to pull them out and the island's total vineyard shrank by almost three-quarters to less than a third of the Sicilian total, many of them concentrated on the flat Campidano plain in the south.

For four centuries (to 1708) Sardinia was ruled by Aragón, and many of its vines came from Spain. Some were introduced by its subsequent rulers from Savoy. Bovale Sardo and Bovale Grande (Sardinian and big Bovale respectively) are thought to be cousins of the Spanish Bobal. Both make full-bodied red wines. Red Monica and Girò and white Nuragus and Nasco are typically Sardinian grapes of more obscure origin, though doubtless DNA analysis will eventually reveal all.

Cannonau, the local form of Spanish Garnacha (Grenache), a chameleon of potentially high quality, sweet or dry, accounts for 20% of production. Its DOC production zone has generously been increased to encompass the whole of the island, as has that of **Vermentino di Sardegna**, which may be produced at yields as high as 130 hl/ha and still qualify for DOC status. The light, lemony Vermentino is Sardinia's most characteristic

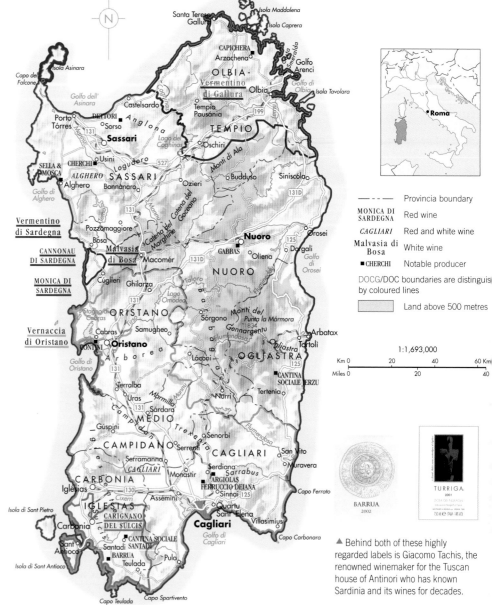

— - - - Provincia boundary

MONICA DI SARDEGNA   Red wine

CAGLIARI   Red and white wine

Malvasia di Bosa   White wine

■ CHERCHI   Notable producer

DOCG/DOC boundaries are distinguis by coloured lines

Land above 500 metres

1:1,693,000

Km 0   20   40   60 Km
Miles 0   20   40

▲ Behind both of these highly regarded labels is Giacomo Tachis, the renowned winemaker for the Tuscan house of Antinori who has known Sardinia and its wines for decades.

white grape. It can produce wines with real refreshment value, and may be found on the Ligurian coast as Pigato and all over southern France as Rollo or Rolle. In the rocky, arid northeast of Sardinia, inland from the famous Costa Smeralda, Gallura's combination of heat and marine winds concentrate Vermentino to such an extent that **Vermentino di Gallura** is the island's first DOCG.

Sardinia's most successful red wine DOC is **Carignano del Sulcis** made in the southwest of the island from the produce of seriously old Carignan (Spain's Cariñena) bushvines, although even here yields of 105 hl/ha are considered quite acceptable. This is arguably the world's most promising territory for the Carignan vine. Such is the confidence of Giacomo Tachis, the renowned oenologist behind Barrua, a joint venture between the producers of Sassicaia on the Tuscan coast and

Santadi of Sardinia, that he has based the island's most prestigious new wine on 85% Carignan. He now oversees a new planting of over 270 acres (110ha) of this old Spanish variety in the Sulcis Meridionale zone. Santadi already makes such concentrated, velvety bottlings of Carignano del Sulcis as Terre Brune and Rocca Rubia. Meanwhile, north of the capital, Cagliari, also on the flatter land in the south of the island, Argiolas was making Sardinia's modern reputation with Turriga, a combustively concentrated barrique-aged blend of old-vine Cannonau and Carignano – another Tachis project.

Sardinia undoubtedly has an unusually varied cache of raw ingredients – not least the rustic reds made in the mountains around Nuoro which one medical researcher, drawn by the unusually high concentration of centenarians there, found to contain particularly high levels of life-prolonging phenolics. Wine-lovers can only hope that the potential of this island with so many ancient bushvines of fashionable and interesting local varieties and an ideal Mediterranean grape-growing climate is increasingly realized.

Excessive vine vigour is hardly a problem in the windswept vineyards of southwest Sardinia. Bamboo windbreaks have been constructed to protect this sandy vineyard on the Isola di Sant Antioco. Bushvines predominate and yields from them are generally low.

Spain

Spain

Sum up Spain? Easier to map the movements in a beehive. At the turn of the century Spain's vineyards were humming. They still are, with unprecedented investment in the field and especially in bodegas – Spain's word for anywhere wine is made, matured, or sold. Many of the most exciting developments continue to take place outside the official *denominaciónes*: 61 DOs (as we write, though this will surely change) plus two DOCas, Rioja and Priorat (ditto).

Spanish wine is enjoying a surge in international popularity it has never known before – perhaps partly because New World wines have acclimatized the world's wine drinkers to wines made in a warm Mediterranean climate. Spanish growers rarely need to worry about

bringing their grapes to full ripeness, and costs in many regions are low so that Spain has many a bargain up her sleeve. But this prolific producer seems set on a particularly fair course because, after a period of Francophilia and an excess of technology, she is also rediscovering her indigenous strengths and traditional practices. Spain's native grape varieties may not be as numerous as Portugal's but they are once again being valued and brought into play.

Spain's great advantages for the vine are a combination of altitude and latitude. Her majestically uncivilized mountains may be too inhospitable, and parts of the north just too exposed, but the rest is perfectly suited to vines: high altitude and latitude in the low 40s. A good 90% of all Spanish vineyards lie at altitudes higher than any major French wine

region: most of Old Castile – Castilla y León and Castilla-La Mancha – for a start.

The cold winters and very hot summers, with sunshine often so relentless that the vines shut down and the grapes stop ripening, can leave the early autumn a scramble to accumulate sugar and aroma before temperatures drop. The big problem in the south, east, and some of the north of the country is summer drought. Dry soils cannot support many vines, so in most regions they are planted unusually far apart. Spain, as a result, has more land under vine than any other country – and trained (if that is the word) in bushes only just above ground level.

Since 2003 Spanish growers have officially been allowed to irrigate, albeit on a case-by-case basis: for them a major breakthrough –

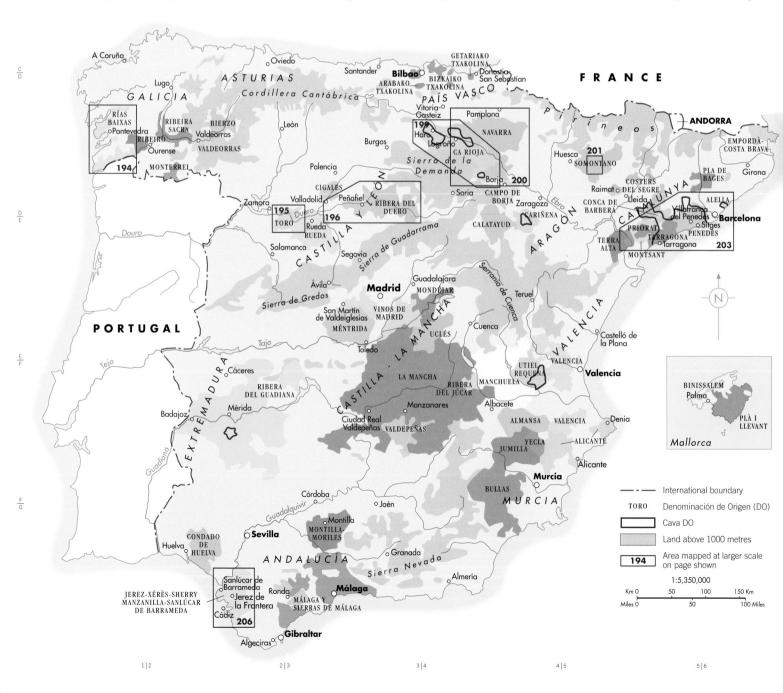

– · – · –	International boundary
TORO	Denominación de Origen (DO)
▭	Cava DO
▨	Land above 1000 metres
194	Area mapped at larger scale on page shown

1:5,350,000

Km 0   50   100   150 Km
Miles 0   50   100 Miles

although only the rich can afford to bore for water and install the systems to distribute it. Despite some dangerously dry years, irrigation has increased yields dramatically. In regions such as La Mancha that lend themselves to machine harvesting, installing wires to train the vines has made a difference too.

The DO system is very much less complicated than France's AC hierarchy – or indeed Italy's DOCs. Most DOs are so large that they include all sorts of different terrains and conditions. There is more than a streak of Latin anarchy (see Italy) in Spaniards' attitudes to these regulations too: particularly in the matter of grape varieties, where there can be some disparity between what is permitted and what is planted. In most cases this is all to the good, as so many wine producers are anxious only to improve quality. A defining characteristic, however, is that buying in grapes, and often wine, is still far more common in Spain than the practice of estate bottling. That said, Spain can already boast three DO Pagos, or single-estate denominations: Dominio de Valdepusa (see p.193), Finca Elez in Albacete, and Deheza del Carrizal near Madrid.

Spanish bodegas were traditionally places where wine was aged, often for much longer than is customary or, in some cases, advisable. Nevertheless the Spanish habit of releasing wine when it is ready to drink rather than ready to sell is appealing to say the least. But things have been changing in the bodegas. For centuries American oak was the wood of choice for barrels, thanks to the country's transatlantic seafaring. From the 1980s, however, French barrel sellers have found Spanish new wave winemakers some of their most avid customers, even if most of the barrels are actually coopered in Spain, notably at Logroño in Rioja. Not just source of oak but also time in barrel is becoming more French. The Reserva and Gran Reserva categories were devised implicitly to honour extended oak ageing, but an increasing number of producers now value intensity over antiquity and are abandoning or devaluing their Gran Reservas.

The smallest of Spain's several and very different zones in terms of wine production is Galicia in the green northwest. Traditions here are Celtic (as the Gallic name suggests) and Christian with almost no Moorish influence. The Atlantic, the hills, the wind, and a good deal of rain (see the small blue map below) are the chief physical factors. Wines are mainly light, dry, and refreshing, with the Palomino and red-fleshed Alicante Bouschet vines that were pressed into service here after phylloxera being steadily replaced by indigenous Godello, Treixadura, and Mencía. The wines which leave the region are a relatively small proportion and mainly white but locals also seem to relish Galicia's tart reds. Almost all Spanish whites need added acidity to give them zip, but not here. Rías Baixas is described in detail on

One of the most famous vineyards in Spain, the precipitous L'Ermita near Gratallops in Priorat, which Alvaro Palacios has brought to international attention. He is not the only top Spanish winemaker to have been inspired by the great wines of France, and traditional methods of viticulture.

p.194, but whites from the handful of serious producers in nearby **Ribeiro**, blended from the naturally crisp Albariño, Treixadura, Loureira, and, increasingly, the Godello of Valdeorras, deserve more attention. The almost-abandoned Ribeiro region shipped wine to England long before the Douro Valley to the south. **Ribeira Sacra** further inland still makes Galicia's potentially most interesting red wine, in archaic conditions on apparently impossibly steep terraces. Ribeira Sacra's fruitily scented Mencía grape is also grown in the small but revitalized

mm
2000
1500
1000
500

AVERAGE ANNUAL PRECIPITATION

The blue tint explains Galicia's green countryside, but note just how many regions receive less than the 20in (500mm) of rain a year deemed necessary for viticulture.

°C
28
24
20
16

AVERAGE DAILY JULY TEMPERATURE

Most of Spain, especially La Mancha and the Levante, is scorching in summer, and this map is based on statistics which predate recent climate change.

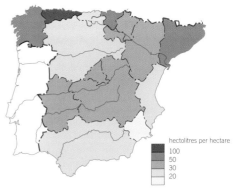

hectolitres per hectare
100
50
30
20

WINE PRODUCTION

These figures are based on average yields for producers within each region in 2006. The Catalan figure is presumably boosted by all those grapes grown for the Cava industry.

Monterrei region (which is warm enough to ripen Tempranillo) and in **Valdeorras**, whose great asset is the firm, white Godello which can yield extremely fine wines worth ageing.

Mencía is the inspiration for fashionable **Bierzo**, one Spain's fruitiest, most aromatic, distinctively refreshing reds. Alvaro Palacios, famous for his Priorat, put Bierzo on the map, intrigued by its slate terraces rather than the predominating clay. (It was originally established because it was on the pilgrims' path to Santiago de Compostela.) For Palacios, Bierzo produces Spain's answer to Burgundy, in dramatic contrast to the concentrated, heavily oaked wines that today's emergent generation of Spanish connoisseurs originally appreciated.

The majority of Castilla y León's vineyards lie in the high, landlocked Duero Valley. The serious red wine regions Toro and Ribera del Duero are mapped in detail on pages 195 and 196–97 respectively but **Cigales** just north of the Duero is already making some serious reds (as well as inexpensive traditional reds and *rosados*). Castilla y León's most famous white wines come from **Rueda**, where the local grape Verdejo, thought to have been imported from southern Spain, can yield wines every bit as refreshing as the Sauvignon Blanc that has been planted here more recently. Red Rueda is generally made from Cabernet and Tempranillo, although many winemakers keep their options open by using the Vino de la Tierra Castilla y León label.

Way up in the Bay of Biscay round the cities of Bilbao and Santander are the piercing Basque whites of, respectively, **Bizkaiko Txakolina/Chacolí de Vizcaya** and **Getariako Txakolina/Chacolí de Guetaria** (Spanish political courtesy embraces four languages: Gallego, Basque, Catalan, and mainstream Castilian). **Arabako Txakolina/Chacolí de Alava** is made in small quantities in the province of Araba/ Alava. Remarkably like Basque wines on the other side of the French border, they are served locally in delicate glass tumblers.

The River Ebro flows southeast from the Cantabrian Cordillera on the north coast to the Mediterranean in Catalunya. The Upper Ebro embraces Rioja and Navarra (see pages 198–99 and 200), where Tempranillo and Garnacha meet, but also **Campo de Borja** whose fields of old bushvine Garnacha have supplied some extremely juicy, inexpensive reds. It is now also being fashioned into much more ambitiously oaked, concentrated wines designed specifically for export to the USA. The extreme continental

The arid, baking hot vineyards of Valdepeñas in La Mancha, where for long the pale-skinned, usefully drought-resistant Airén predominated. Now, two-thirds of the wine produced here is red with Cencibel (Tempranillo) the most successful vine variety.

climate and the local *cierzo*, a cold, dry northwest wind, help. The climate is very similar in **Cariñena** to the south but Garnacha is not so dominant and incomers from places such as Rioja are making waves with Tempranillo-Cabernet blends. Neighbouring **Calatayud** is home to some of Spain's most successful co-operative exporters.

But in some ways the vineyards behind Spain's central Mediterranean coast have been making even more rapid progress in the early years of the century. For long Manchuela, Valencia, Utiel-Requena, Almansa, Yecla, Jumilla, Alicante, and Bullas were regarded as fit only to provide potent bulk wine for a dwindling export market. But many of these DOs are putting new money and ideas to good use,

▶ Just some of the rash of exciting new Spanish wines from (left–right) Valdeorras, Bierzo, Castilla-La Mancha, Campo de Borja, Manchuela, Jumilla, and two from Mallorca. Only the Finca Coronado and San Bordils depend on imported vine varieties. And only As Sortes, made from barrel-fermented Godello, is white.

resulting in fruity and even stylish reds. There is still wine made deliberately strong and sweet, but the best can compete with 'premium' super-ripe reds from California and Australia. Local grape varieties are typically blended with international imports but such growers as Julia Roch in **Jumilla** have shown how to tame varietal Monastrell (Mourvèdre). In **Alicante** Enrique Mendoza led the way, with wines varying considerably in levels of residual sugar if not in alcohol. Others have followed. The DO **Manchuela**, on a high plateau with limestone deposits, was justified by Finca Sandoval's blend of Syrah with Monastrell. The beefy Bobal (Sardinia's Bovale) is characteristic of this region and neighbouring **Utiel-Requena**, which is also more than 1,970ft (600m) above sea level.

Most central of all to Spanish life is the *meseta*, the high plateau south of Madrid whose endless flat vineyards weary the eye. The extent of **La Mancha**, its chief DO, is clear from the map. Its DO-classified vineyards alone, less than half of the total, cover more ground than all of Australia's vineyards put together. The town of **Valdepeñas** traditionally gave its name to a large part of this production: strong but pale red wine made historically from Airén (Spain's most-planted white grape on which Brandy de Jerez depends) tinted with some red. The vineyards of La Mancha have been changing just as dramatically as the rest of Spain's winescape with a marked conversion from light- to dark-skinned grape varieties from the

THE CANARY ISLANDS
These volcanic islands off the coast of Morocco have a unique viticultural heritage – vines which have never known phylloxera – and a long history of making distinctive sweet whites from low, windswept bushvines. The regional government is helping put them back on the map.

late 1990s. By 2005 more than two-thirds of all the wine made in this vast region was red, much of it inexpensive and made from Cencibel, the local strain of Tempranillo. Some Garnacha has also long been grown in the region but international varieties have also invaded with a vengeance. Cabernet, Merlot, Syrah, and even the white wine grapes Chardonnay and Sauvignon Blanc can be found here, although it can be difficult to imbue them with much character in a region where picking has to begin by mid-August. There are plenty of new ideas however: in 2005 a sparkling blend of Viura and Airén from La Mancha managed to win a medal at a significant international tasting.

Between here and Madrid are the DOs of **Méntrida**, **Vinos de Madrid**, and **Mondéjar**, presumably ripe for similar transformation. By far the most innovative vineyards here however are the Marqués de Griñon's at the first DO Pago (see panel) **Dominio de Valdepusa** near Toledo with their palette of imported grape varieties (including fashionable Syrah and Petit Verdot) and new ways of growing and watering vines.

Due west of La Mancha in Extremadura near the Portuguese frontier is the extensive and relatively recent DO **Ribera del Guadiana**. Here too there is considerable potential for robust, ripe wines, similar to those of Alentejo over the Portuguese border.

The burgeoning wine regions of Andalucía in the far south of Spain are covered in more detail on pp.205–207.

Despite being over 700 miles (1,150km) from mainland Spain, the **Canary Islands** have joined in the controlled appellation game with zest. The islands of La Palma, El Hierro, Lanzarote, and La Gomera each have one DO,

Gran Canaria has two, while the proud island of Tenerife has no fewer than five (see map below). For the moment the most exciting wines are the zesty, citrus-peel whites made from such local grape varieties as Marmajuelo (Bermejuela) and Güal (Madeira's Boal).

Nor are the Spanish Balearic islands in the Mediterranean to be left out. Mallorcan pride in its wines and its native Manto Negro and Callet vine varieties is being justifiably revived in the form of the **Binissalem** and **Plà i Llevant** DOs, valiantly resisting the developers on this holiday island.

LANGUAGE OF THE LABEL

QUALITY DESIGNATIONS

Most of the Spanish denominaciónes have their own special stamps such as this one for the DOCa Rioja just above the volume and alcoholic strength.

Denominación de Origen Calificada (DOCa) Spain's top wine distinction, so far awarded only to Rioja, and to Priorat, where it is known as DOQ

Denominación de Origen (DO) Spain's answer to France's AC (see p.52)

Denominación de Origen Pago (DO Pago) reserved for single estates producing particularly creditable wines

Vino de Calidad con Indicación Geografica (VCIG) for VdIT wines approaching DO status

Vino de la Tierra (VdIT) Spain's answer to France's Vin de Pays (see p.152); Vi de la Terra in Catalan

Vino de Mesa (VdM) table wine, the most basic Spanish wine; Vi de Taula (VdT) in Catalan

OTHER COMMON EXPRESSIONS

Año year

Blanco white

Bodega winery

Cava wine made sparkling by the traditional method

Cosecha vintage year

Crianza wine aged for a minimum of two years after the harvest, of which at least six months (12 in Rioja and Ribera del Duero) must be in oak

Dulce sweet

Embotellado (de origen) bottled (estate bottled)

Espumoso sparkling

Gran Reserva selected wine aged for at least 18 months in oak and 42 months in bottle

Joven wine sold the year after harvest having seen little or no oak

Reserva wine matured for at least three years, of which at least one is in oak and another in bottle

Rosado rosé, pink

Seco dry

Tinto red

Vendimia vintage

Vino wine

Viña, viñedo vineyard

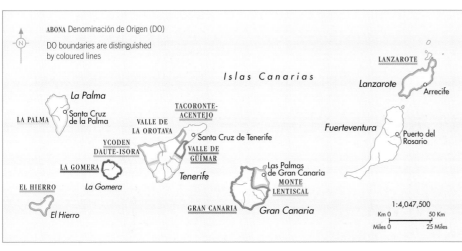

ABONA Denominación de Origen (DO)

DO boundaries are distinguished by coloured lines

Islas Canarias

LANZAROTE

Lanzarote
Arrecife

La Palma
LA PALMA
Santa Cruz de la Palma

TACORONTE-ACENTEJO

VALLE DE LA OROTAVA

Fuerteventura
Puerto del Rosario

YCODEN DAUTE-ISORA
VALLE DE GÜIMAR
Santa Cruz de Tenerife

LA GOMERA
Tenerife
Las Palmas de Gran Canaria
MONTE LENTISCAL

EL HIERRO
La Gomera

El Hierro
GRAN CANARIA
Gran Canaria

1:4,047,500
Km 0 — 50 Km
Miles 0 — 25 Miles

Alto Moncayo
2004 Garnacha

2004
Finca Sandoval
MANCHUELA

Casa Castillo
Pie Franco
2000
Jumilla
Denominación de Origen

750 ML.   ALC. 18,5% Vol.

2003
SON BORDILS

SYRAH

Galician Coast

Galicia's best-known wines are as far from the Spanish stereotype as it is possible to imagine: delicate, lively, aromatic whites that go perfectly with the shellfish that is the Galician standard diet. Their name, Rías Baixas (pronounced "ree-ass by-shuss"), is their only slight handicap.

Everything about Galician wine is small scale. Some of the best producers make only a few hundred cases of wine a year; most growers have only a few hectares of vines. This damp green corner of Spain (compare the annual rainfall of Vigo with that of any other Spanish weather station) was until recently extremely poor and virtually ignored by the rest of the country. Any Gallego with any gumption emigrated, but tended to cling fiercely to ownership of minuscule parcels of inherited land. This, and Galicia's physical isolation, meant that it was not until the 1990s that these singular wines found a ready and rapturous market outside Galicia.

Like the wines, the landscape is exceptional for Spain: irregular Atlantic inlets called *rías*, effectively shallow fjords, lined with hills densely forested with local pine and rapacious eucalyptus imported in the 1950s. Even the vines look quite different.

As in Portugal's very similar Vinho Verde country across the River Miño, vines have traditionally been trained on pergolas, horizontal trellises well above light-dappled shoulder height. The widely spaced, spindly trunks are often trained up posts of granite, so common is it in this part of the world. For the thousands of small farmers who grow vines simply to make wine for themselves, this high canopy allows them to use every square foot of precious earth, but it can also help ventilate the grapes, an important consideration here where sea mists regularly invade the vineyards even in summer. Some flatter vineyards are now trained into two curtains of hanging foliage, presumably with machine harvesting in mind.

Val do Salnés is the most important subzone, and the coolest and dampest being both northerly and right on the coast – although summers can be dry. In **O Rosal** to the south, the best vineyards are carved out of terraced clearings on the south-facing hillsides and produce wines notably lower in acidity than those of Val do Salnés. **Condado do Tea** (Tea, pronounced "tay-er," is a small tributary of the Miño) is the warmest of the subzones, being furthest from the coast, and its wines tend to be more powerful and less refined. Granite can often be found in vineyards here and in **Soutomaior**, south of Pontevedra, while the soils of **Ribeira do Ulla**, just south of Santiago de Compostela, are more alluvial.

The thick-skinned Albariño grape dominates as it can best resist the mildew that persistently threatens, and youthful varietal Albariño has a faithful following. There is increasing experimentation however with blends, oak, and deliberately aged wines.

RIAS BAIXAS: VIGO

Latitude / Altitude of WS **41.13° / 820ft (250m)**
Mean July temperature at WS **66.7°F (19.3°C)**
Average annual rainfall at WS **60in (1,520mm)**
Harvest month rainfall at WS **September: 3.5in (90mm)**
Principal viticultural hazards **Fungal diseases, high winds**
Principal grapes **Albariño, Treixadura, Loureira Blanca**

1:567,000
Km 0 — 5 — 10 — 15 Km
Miles 0 — 5 — 10 Miles

— · — International boundary
— · — Provincial boundary
Rías Baixas DO

Rías Baixas subzones:
Condado do Tea
O Rosal
Ribeira do Ulla
Soutomaior
Val do Salnés
FILLABOA Notable producer
—400— Contour interval 200 metres
▼ Weather station (WS)

◀ Ancient and modern styles of these quintessentially marine dry whites are represented here. Nora da Neve is one of the labels of the ubiquitous US importer Jorge Ordoñez.

Toro

Toro might well be called the El Dorado of the Spanish winescape. In 1998 this medieval town in the far west of Castilla y León had eight bodegas. Just two years later there were 25 and by 2006 there were 40. For years Toro the wine was regarded as a rustic, if full-throttle, provincial, but the sheer exuberance of its local strain of Tempranillo, Tinto de Toro, became just too obvious to ignore – especially in an era increasingly looking for drama rather than subtlety in the bottle.

There was a time when every bodega of note in northern Spain, whether based in Rioja or Ribera del Duero, seemed to be sniffing around the Toro region downstream of Ribera on the Duero river but perhaps the definitive seal of approval came when Vega Sicilia announced their plans to establish a bodega here to produce Pintia, one of Toro's most sophisticated and ambitious wines. Other high-profile Spanish investors include Alejandro Fernández and Mariano García, also of Ribera del Duero, and roving winemaker Telmo Rodríguez. Even higher profile outsiders to have moved in to the region include the Lurton brothers of Bordeaux with Michel and Dany Rolland (they are jointly responsible for Campo Eliseo), Bordeaux négociants Mahler Besse, whose label is Oro, and French actor Gérard Depardieu via his Bordeaux patron Bernard Magrez.

The key to Toro's quality is, as so often in Spain, its altitude. At 1,970–2,460ft (600–750m) above sea level the region's growers can depend on cool nights to "fix" colour and flavour in the grapes ripened during the torrid summers on these red clays and, particularly, sandy soils.

The average age of Toro's vines is relatively high and most of them are still grown as individual bushvines, spaced as far as 10ft (3m) apart, a record low vine density imposed by the low rainfall in Toro's near-desert conditions – at under 16in (400mm) a year, considerably less than is conventionally reckoned sufficient for successful viticulture.

Some of the Tinto de Toro that constitutes 85% of all plantings in the region is vinified quickly by carbonic maceration and sold young and juicy but the great majority of the wine is aged in oak, for at least 12 months in the case of Reservas. The deep crimson, strapping wines that result are so explosively fruity that Tinto de Toro is being planted in other parts of Spain too. Other varieties planted are Garnacha, which is sometimes blended with Tinto de Toro, and a little Malvasia and Verdejo for the region's few full-bodied white wines.

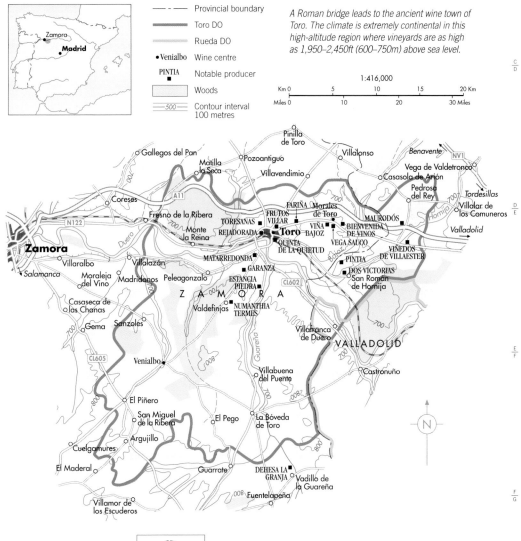

A Roman bridge leads to the ancient wine town of Toro. The climate is extremely continental in this high-altitude region where vineyards are as high as 1,950–2,450ft (600–750m) above sea level.

◄ None of the bodegas that produce these wines, now some of Spain's most admired, existed before 1998. Pintia's debut vintage was 2001, although the team had been experimenting at Vega Sicilia in Ribera del Duero for some years before then.

Ribera del Duero

Ribera del Duero is the modern red wine miracle of northern Spain. Barely known in the early 1980s, it now rivals Rioja as Spain's foremost red wine region.

The plain of Old Castile, stretching in tawny leagues north from Segovia and Avila to the old kingdom of León, is traversed by the adolescent Duero, the river that in Portugal becomes the Douro and the home of port (see pp.216–221). It is the broad valley of the Duero and its tributaries, from Valladolid upstream to Aranda de Duero, that have an ancient winemaking tradition – more, one would think, because of the thirsty population (Valladolid, as the capital of 17th-century Spain, formulated strict wine laws) than because the fierce continental climate favoured the vine. At 3,000ft (850m) the nights are remarkably cool: in late August it can be 95°F (35°C) at noon and 54°F (12°C) at night. Spring frosts are all too common. Grapes are routinely picked in late October. The light and air here have a high-altitude dryness and brightness about them, as do the wines, which have particularly lively acidity

thanks to those cool nights. These are concentrated reds of remarkably intense colour, fruit, and savour – quite different in style from the typical produce of Rioja less than 60 miles (100 km) to the northeast.

Vega Sicilia provided the initial proof that very fine red wine could be made here. The estate was initially planted in the 1860s, partly with Bordeaux varieties, at the same time as Rioja was being invaded by Bordeaux merchants and influence. Vega Sicilia's Unico, made only in good vintages, aged longer in oak than virtually any other table wine, and sold at 10 years (after some years in bottle nowadays), is a wine of astonishing, penetrating personality. But here the Bordeaux grapes were used, adding cosmopolitan glamour to the native Tempranillo (a locally adapted version known here as Tinto Fino or Tinto del País).

Rather than plant Cabernet, Merlot, and Malbec (still used at Vega Sicilia but only as a complement to Tinto Fino) the region has now won its spurs with the local grape almost single-handed, even if a little of these three Bordeaux varieties, Garnacha, and even the white Albillo are also planted. Ribera became hugely fashionable in the 1990s and while there were just 24 bodegas in the region when the DO was created in 1982, there were 215 by the end of 2005 (many of them, it should be said, unencumbered by vineyards). This wide, high plateau has seen a quite remarkable transformation of land previously given over to cereals and sugar beet to more than 49,400 acres (20,000ha) of vines. Many of the new plantings depend not on Ribera's own strain of Tempranillo but on cuttings imported from other regions, hence of more doubtful value.

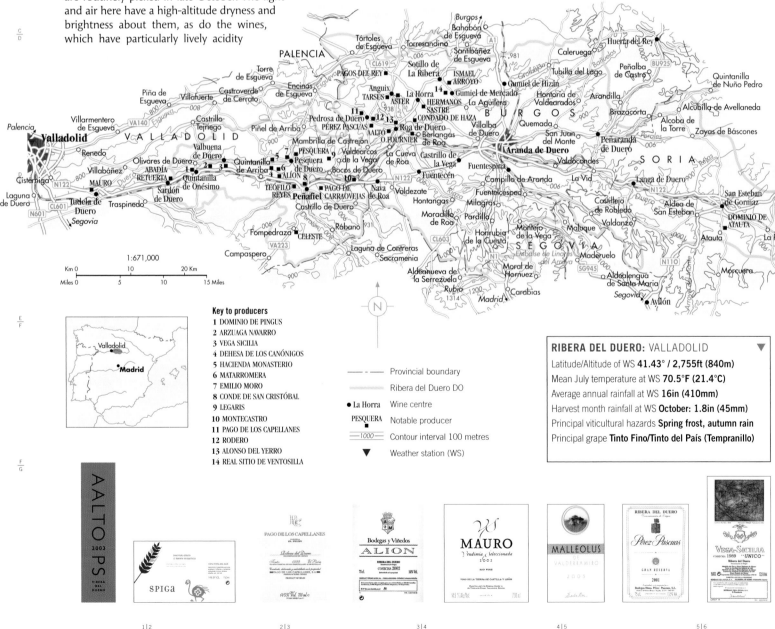

Key to producers
1 DOMINIO DE PINGUS
2 ARZUAGA NAVARRO
3 VEGA SICILIA
4 DEHESA DE LOS CANÓNIGOS
5 HACIENDA MONASTERIO
6 MATARROMERA
7 EMILIO MORO
8 CONDE DE SAN CRISTÓBAL
9 LEGARIS
10 MONTECASTRO
11 PAGO DE LOS CAPELLANES
12 RODERO
13 ALONSO DEL YERRO
14 REAL SITIO DE VENTOSILLA

------ Provincial boundary

Ribera del Duero DO

● La Horra   Wine centre

PESQUERA   Notable producer

══1000══   Contour interval 100 metres

▼   Weather station (WS)

RIBERA DEL DUERO: VALLADOLID
Latitude/Altitude of WS 41.43° / 2,755ft (840m)
Mean July temperature at WS 70.5°F (21.4°C)
Average annual rainfall at WS 16in (410mm)
Harvest month rainfall at WS October: 1.8in (45mm)
Principal viticultural hazards Spring frost, autumn rain
Principal grape Tinto Fino/Tinto del País (Tempranillo)

1|2   2|3   3|4   4|5   5|6

Viticulturists can easily be foxed by Ribera's extremely varied soils, even within a single vineyard, where grapes may ripen at infuriatingly different paces. Limestone outcrops, more common north of the Duero, help to retain rainfall that is far from generous.

The tradition of buying in grapes is just as strong here as in Rioja (even Vega Sicilia, with more than 500 acres/200ha, has contracts with other growers), and many of these new bodegas vie with each other for fruit. Some of the best comes from round La Horra, but top winemakers such as Peter Sisseck, the Dane who made Dominio de Pingus Spain's rarest

and most expensive wine, are cagey about their sources – invariably the oldest and truest of gnarled, low Tinto Fino bushes.

Two of the most successful producers in the region are not even within the DO boundaries. Abadía Retuerta, a vast property founded in 1996 by the Swiss pharmaceutical company Novartis, is at Sardón de Duero just west of the official boundary. (In 1982 when the DO regulations were being drawn up there were no vines here, but there had been vines almost continuously from the 17th century. The abbey was one of Valladolid's chief suppliers of wine until the early 1970s.) Even further west, in

Low-trained vines at Hacienda Monasterio in Pesquera de Duero make picking these Tinto Fino grapes back-breaking work. Thanks to the cool nights this elevation entails, the harvest may not take place until well into October.

Tudela, is Mauro, founded in 1980 and now established in a handsome old stone building by Mariano García, once Vega Sicilia's winemaker. García is also involved in making Aalto, just one of many relatively new names in Ribera del Duero, where, it seems, reputations can be made in a single vintage.

Recent new investors have included Felix Solis (Pagos del Rey), Alonso del Yerro, Marqués de Vargas (Conde de San Cristóbal), Torres (Celeste), Faustino – many of them already well established in other wine regions, especially neighbouring Rioja. Others, including a prominent Madrid publisher, Alfonso de Salas, the Marqués de Montecastro, could be said to be diversifying (in his case with a notably soft red radically untypical of the region).

◄ Influences on this line-up of top Ribera wines are by no means all Spanish. For example, the fabulously priced Pingus was made by the Dane, Peter Sisseck and Bordeaux-based consultant Stéphane Derenencourt makes the wines for newcomer Alonso del Yerro.

Rioja

Rioja used to have the Spanish fine wine market to itself. Those days are gone. It has always had the climate problems of a marginal region to contend with. To these it adds, today, uncertainty about the style of its wines. But its internal variety, its traditions, and its adaptability keep it in the front rank. Few great wine regions span so many difficult terrains and unite them with such recognizable character.

Without the massive wall of the rocky Sierra de Cantabria Rioja would be too buffeted by Atlantic winds for vines to survive. In the far northwest of the region some of the highest vineyards above Labastida can struggle to ripen at all. In the east, on the other hand, vines ripen fully as high as 2,600ft (800m) thanks to the warming influence of the Mediterranean, which reaches as far west as Elciego. Growers in Alfaro in the east may harvest four to six weeks before those around Haro, where the last grapes may not be picked until the end of October.

The region is divided into three zones. **Rioja Alta** is the western, higher part south of the winding, poplar-lined River Ebro, as well as the non-Basque land around San Vicente de la Sonsierra north of the river. **Rioja Alavesa**, that part of Rioja in Alava province, is Basque and, quite literally nowadays, another country, with its own language, its own police force, and like the rest of Spain recently its own substantial grants. In this case, grants have encouraged a rash of new bodegas on this northern bank of the Ebro. **Rioja Baja**, the extensive hotter, eastern section, has its own anomalous enclave carved out of it just east of the industrial capital of the region, Logroño. The historic Marqués de Murrieta Castillo Ygay bodega, like those of two more Marquéses, Vargas and Romeral, could not be allowed to belong to

Rioja has attracted some of the most ambitious recent winery architecture, as here at Bodegas Ysios, echoing the Sierra de Cantabria skyline behind. Marqués de Riscal lured architect Frank Gehry from Bilbao's Guggenheim Museum to Elciego.

Rioja Baja, which was often considered, not always accurately, to be inferior.

The soils of Rioja Baja are even more varied than those of Rioja Alta and its vines much more sparsely cultivated. In the two western subzones vines are virtually the only crop: the landscape is a spotted patchwork of small plots of low bushvines on soils variously soft clay-red and limestone white, tinted with yellow alluvial deposits. These terraces, eroded to different levels by the river (the higher the better), are more likely to be dominated by clay in Rioja Alta and limestone in Rioja Alavesa. The red soils around Fuenmayor are some of Rioja's most productive, and clay is so important there that it has spawned a huge ceramics factory.

Tempranillo is by far the most important grape of Rioja. It blends well with plumper Garnacha (Grenache), best in Rioja Alta upstream of Nájera and in Rioja Baja in the high vineyards of Tudelilla. Graciano (known as Morrastel in the Languedoc, in Portugal as Tinta Miúda) is a fine but finicky Rioja speciality that now seems safe from extinction. Mazuelo (Carignan) is allowed, and experimentation with Cabernet Sauvignon uneasily tolerated.

Oddly enough, Spain's most famous, most important wine began the 21st century with a search for its true character. The reputation of the region was made in the late 19th century when Bordeaux négociants came here to fill the embarrassing voids in their blending tanks left by phylloxera north of the Pyrenees. They had their proof of Rioja's potential in the wines of the

two Marquéses, de Riscal and Murrieta, who had established their own estates, in 1860 in Elciego and in 1872 just east of Logroño respectively.

Haro with its rail links to the Atlantic coast was the ideal centre for blending wine brought in by cart from as far away as Rioja Baja. The Bordeaux merchants showed how to age it in small barrels, and thus were born many of Haro's most important bodegas, all founded around 1890 and clustered about the railway station – some even with their own platforms.

Until the 1970s most Rioja was juicy stuff made by small-scale farmers (in villages such as San Vicente you can still see stone *lagares*, or troughs, behind half-open doors hung with the handwritten claim *Se Vende Rioja*). Blending and élevage, not even winemaking, let alone geography, were the key. Rioja was fermented fast and then aged for many years in old American oak. The result was pale wines, sweet with vanilla, that could be beguiling provided the grapes were of impeccable quality. With the bottlers' control on growers so dangerously loose however, the temptation to cut corners and increase yields has at times been overpowering.

▼ Contino is the oldest label on this page by far, and belongs to CVNE's estate in Rioja Alavesa, which was established in 1973. Fernando Remírez de Ganuza established his bodega in 1989. The other highly regarded labels are much more recent.

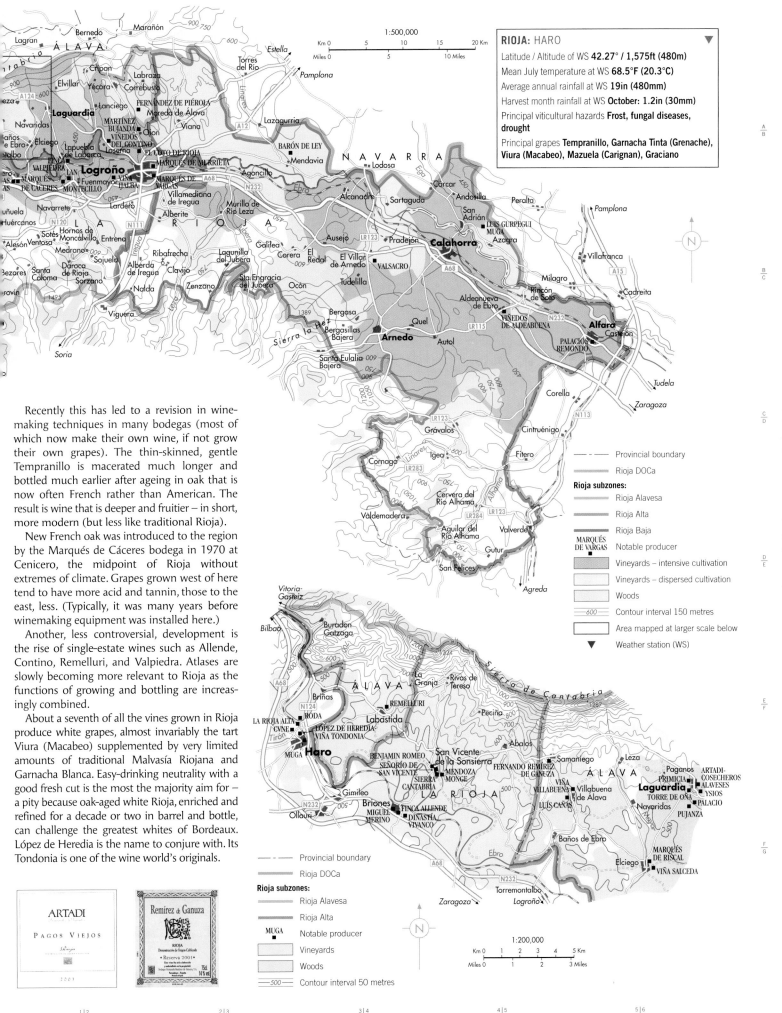

RIOJA: HARO

Latitude / Altitude of WS **42.27° / 1,575ft (480m)**

Mean July temperature at WS **68.5°F (20.3°C)**

Average annual rainfall at WS **19in (480mm)**

Harvest month rainfall at WS **October: 1.2in (30mm)**

Principal viticultural hazards **Frost, fungal diseases, drought**

Principal grapes **Tempranillo, Garnacha Tinta (Grenache), Viura (Macabeo), Mazuela (Carignan), Graciano**

Recently this has led to a revision in wine-making techniques in many bodegas (most of which now make their own wine, if not grow their own grapes). The thin-skinned, gentle Tempranillo is macerated much longer and bottled much earlier after ageing in oak that is now often French rather than American. The result is wine that is deeper and fruitier – in short, more modern (but less like traditional Rioja).

New French oak was introduced to the region by the Marqués de Cáceres bodega in 1970 at Cenicero, the midpoint of Rioja without extremes of climate. Grapes grown west of here tend to have more acid and tannin, those to the east, less. (Typically, it was many years before winemaking equipment was installed here.)

Another, less controversial, development is the rise of single-estate wines such as Allende, Contino, Remelluri, and Valpiedra. Atlases are slowly becoming more relevant to Rioja as the functions of growing and bottling are increasingly combined.

About a seventh of all the vines grown in Rioja produce white grapes, almost invariably the tart Viura (Macabeo) supplemented by very limited amounts of traditional Malvasía Riojana and Garnacha Blanca. Easy-drinking neutrality with a good fresh cut is the most the majority aim for – a pity because oak-aged white Rioja, enriched and refined for a decade or two in barrel and bottle, can challenge the greatest whites of Bordeaux. López de Heredia is the name to conjure with. Its Tondonia is one of the wine world's originals.

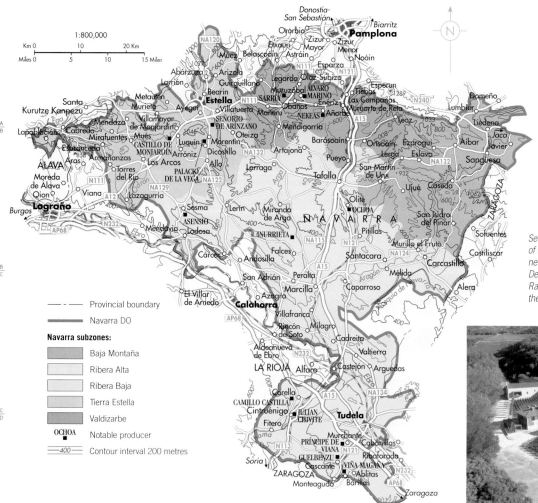

See how much space is needed to mature all the barrels of wine aged in Chivite's pride and joy, the relatively new Señorío de Arínzano estate in the north of Navarra. Designed by the head of Harvard's School of Architecture, Rafael Moneo, it encircles the three original buildings on the 750 acre (300ha) site.

Map legend:

------ Provincial boundary

—— Navarra DO

Navarra subzones:

- Baja Montaña
- Ribera Alta
- Ribera Baja
- Tierra Estella
- Valdizarbe

OCHOA — Notable producer

—400— Contour interval 200 metres

Navarra

Various parts of Spain have helped out Bordeaux over the centuries. Benicarlo from Valencia was once an important ingredient in respectable claret. Rioja and its northeastern neighbour Navarra were both in the running as principal props to Bordeaux in the dearth years of phylloxera. It was the rail link with Haro that decided the day: fertile Navarra, green land of asparagus and nurseries, lost the business to the relatively barren Rioja.

For most of the 20th century Navarra's scattered vineyards were dedicated chiefly to Garnacha and the useful *rosados* and strong, deep bulk reds that it produced. But then came a revolution in the form of Cabernet, Merlot, Tempranillo, and Chardonnay. Tempranillo has now overtaken Garnacha in total area with Cabernet Sauvignon as the region's third most planted grape. The all-important co-operatives still soak up much of the region's run-of-the-mill Garnacha, but old vines of this potent variety have their value. You see it in such wines as Chivite's Gran Feudo Viñas Viejas Reserva and Lautus from Guelbenzu, a bodega which has since withdrawn from the Navarra DO.

The most exported wines of Navarra can be seen as a bridge between Rioja and Somontano: obviously oaked but using a full palette of both Spanish and international varieties. French oak is used much more commonly than in Rioja, perhaps because oak ageing came so much later to Navarra, but also because there is so very much more acreage devoted to French vines.

Navarra is no more homogeneous than Rioja, however. There is a world of difference between the hot, dry, flat **Ribera Baja** and **Ribera Alta** subzones in the south, which lie on the banks of the River Ebro and have to be irrigated (with a system of canals initiated by the Romans) and the less-planted, cooler climes, and more varied soils, of the north. The persistence of the westerlies here has spawned virtual forests of wind-powered generators on mesas above the vineyards. Ribera Alta is a bit warmer and more exposed to the influence of the Mediterranean than Ribera Baja, which is protected by the Sierra del Moncayo to the south. The best Garnachas in Ribera Baja come from Fitero because its poor, Châteauneuf-like soils are fully exposed. Corella has earned a reputation for excellent botrytized Moscatel de Grano Menudo (Muscat Blanc) – again the work of the admirable Bodegas Chivite. Wines produced towards the north of Ribera Alta tend to be paler and less alcoholic than further south.

A day that is positively torrid in the south can be quite cool in the mountainous north, closer to the Atlantic. As in Rioja, northern Navarra's altitude means that the Bordeaux grape varieties are picked considerably later than in Bordeaux itself – sometimes as late as December in the highest vineyards. **Baja Montaña** produces mainly *rosados*. Clay with some limestone is the norm here but soils, aspects, and elevations are so varied in the northern **Tierra Estella** and **Valdizarbe** subzones that their pioneering growers have to select sites with extreme care. Spring frosts and cold autumns lie in wait for them.

◀ Guelbenzu has withdrawn from the official Navarra Consejo Regulador and sells its wines under the name of the local Vino de la Tierra, Ribera del Queiles. Like so many Navarra reds Lautus is a blend of Spanish grapes Tempranillo and Garnacha with Bordeaux varieties Cabernet and Merlot.

Somontano

Somontano means "at the foot of the mountains". On a clear day you can see the snow-covered Pyrenees in the distance. It is not the Pyrenees, however, which make viticulture possible in this well-tended, unusually cohesive wine region, but the Sierra de Guara and Sierra de Salinas. These mountains protect Somontano from cold northern influence and provide a gentle south-facing amphitheatre of suitable vineyard land between 1,150 and 2,130ft (350 and 650m) above sea level. It is centred on the villages of Barbastro, Salas Bajas, and Salas Altas, and scattered along the banks of the Vero and the Cinca.

This is an adolescent DO whose existence was initiated not by nature nor by a particularly ambitious individual but by the local government. In the late 1980s it encouraged Viñas del Vero to plant Tempranillo and international varieties to add cosmopolitan glamour to the local Moristel and Parraleta vines. The total area planted, however, has more than doubled since the late 1990s to nearly 11,000 acres (4,500ha).

Aragón has a proud history, but in terms of viticultural development it lags far behind its neighbours Catalunya and Navarra. Much of it to the west is too extreme and unprotected for vines to flourish; to the south there is desert. But the Somontano region offered the potential of a mild climate and considerably more rain than most of the central Spanish plateau, even if the historical average of about 20in (500mm) a year is only just adequate.

Today, Somontano may not have reached the heights of the best that Ribera del Duero, Rioja, and Priorat can produce, but its wines are among the most reliable and best value in Spain. Roughly three in every four bottles is filled by either Viñas del Vero, the privately owned Enate, or the model co-op Pirineos, but they have now been joined by several other quality-oriented bodegas. Blecua is the particularly ambitious estate winery in a thoroughly Napa Valley idiom built by Viñas del Vero. Laus is a stylish newcomer while Idrias from Sierra de Guara and Castillo de Monesma from Dalcamp can also impress.

Wines are attractively plump though never massive, thanks to predominantly sandy soils (although there is a bit of gravel in the lower reaches of the River Vero and some limestone south of Barbastro, the main town). Naturally crisp acidity is a distinguishing mark, not least because soils here are low in potassium, which keeps pH levels usefully low too. There are mouth-filling Bordeaux-variety reds, some savoury Tempranillo, much more convincing Chardonnay than most of Spain can manage, and some of Spain's rare but refreshingly dry Gewürztraminer. Bodega Pirineos works hardest at maintaining the region's indigenous varieties, squeezing every ounce of flavour out of the light, loganberry-scented Moristel by encouraging the malolactic fermentation in barrel.

▲ Early new wave settler Viñas del Vero produces both the all-Garnacha Secastilla and, on a separate small estate, the Blecua blend of Spanish and Bordeaux grapes. Bodegas Laus is another topnotch producer.

Pirineos also perseveres with low-yielding but more structured and mineral-scented Parraleta. Both are well worth preserving. A serious dry wine from late-picked, old-vine Macabeo is essayed too. Garnacha was the other traditional vine variety of the region; locals still make their own barrel-aged, *rancio* version of it.

Vine-growing even extends to the backstreets in the village of Graus near Barbastro. The rather rustic scene belies the very recent arrival in Somontano of such high-flying bodegas as Bestué, Estada, Meler, and Monesma, all of which are proving the Somontano doubters wrong.

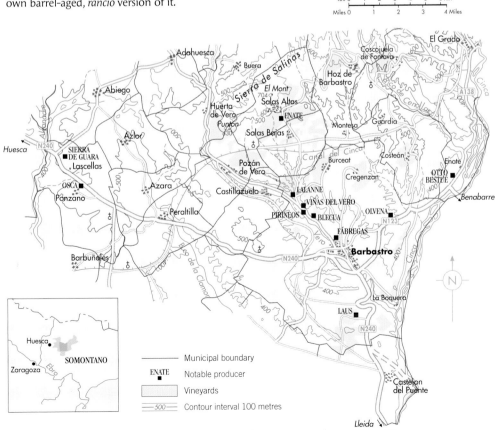

1:238,570

Km 0　1　2　3　4　5　6 Km
Miles 0　　1　　2　　3　　4 Miles

Municipal boundary

ENATE　Notable producer

　　　　Vineyards

━500━　Contour interval 100 metres

Catalunya

Are the Catalans Spanish? It is not a question for a wine book, but everything about their coastal realm feels different. Barcelona is a city with buzz; gastronomically one of the most dynamic of Europe. It is easy to forget the border that separates Catalonia (its English name) from Roussillon in Catalan France. The vineyards mapped here stretch from the hot Mediterranean coast to altitudes where cold is a useful quality factor. They produce a wider range of wine styles than any comparable tract of Spain – from the finest fizz to the richest of syrups.

For a start, most obviously on shelves and wine lists throughout Spain, there is **Cava**, Spain's answer to champagne, of which 95% is produced in Catalunya, mainly from the vineyards on the fertile plateau in and around the Penedès wine capital of Sant Sadurní d'Anoia. The industry, for that is what it is, is dominated by arch-competitors Codorníu and Freixenet. The winemaking method may be that of Champagne; the grapes are very different. Neutral Macabeo dominates most Cava blends, its late budding promising good insurance against spring frost in Penedès' relatively cool vineyards. Flavour, occasionally too much flavour, comes from the local Xarel-lo, best planted at lower altitudes. Parellada is regarded as the finest Cava ingredient, yielding appley wine of real crispness, at least in the northern Penedès, if not allowed to over-produce. Chardonnay constitutes about 5% of all plantings while Pinot Noir is permitted for the increasingly popular pink Cava. Lower yields and longer bottle ageing are steadily improving the quality of the best Cava. The great Catalan gift to the world's producers of sparkling wine – apart from its indigenous cork – was the gyropalette, the giant crate which substitutes computer-controlled riddling for painstaking and variable shaking down the sediment by hand.

For still wines, which tend to have particularly frank, direct flavours, **Penedès** is the leading DO. International vine varieties are more widespread in Penedès than anywhere else in Spain; it was here they began, in the 1960s, with such pioneers as Miguel Torres, the Catalan giant of still wine producers. Having made the point with Cabernet and Milmanda Chardonnay (Milmanda is in the quite distinct inland **Conca de Barberá** region, on limestone hills north of Tarragona known for Cava), Torres is now nurturing Catalan grapes for his finest red, Grans Muralles. The increasingly

common **Catalunya** DO, which encompasses all Catalan regions and sanctions blending between them, was introduced in 1999 largely because the expanding Torres operation found the Penedès appellation too constricting.

The hottest, lowest vineyards of the Baix-Penedès by the coast traditionally supplied super-ripe Moscatel and Malvasía grapes for dessert wines. More recently they have poured forth Monastrell, Garnacha, and Cariñena for blended dry(ish) reds which would struggle to ripen in Penedès' higher but more interesting vineyards, at altitudes up to 2,600ft (800m). At medium altitudes Cava is the main thing, but more ambitious growers, often with vineyards carved out of the Mediterranean scrub and pines on higher land, are doing their best to squeeze serious local character out of relatively low-yielding vines, both indigenous and imported varieties.

The **Tarragona** DO, immediately west of Penedès around the city of that name, also supplies raw material for Cava in its hills, but the eastern coastal plain, El Camp de Tarragona, still produces its traditional sweet, heavy red wine, sometimes long aged in barrel to take on a *rancio* character.

Since 2001 the higher, western vineyards in what was once Tarragona have had their own DO **Montsant**, encircling the exceptional Priorat DOCa described overleaf. The greatest

concentration of notable bodegas is around Falset, a high-altitude, one-horse town that is gateway to Priorat but lies just outside it. Seriously concentrated dry reds can be produced here from a wide range of grape varieties, although they lack the benefit of Priorat's distinguishing soil. The area was brought to international attention in the 1990s by the Celler de Capçanes, which continues to set the pace.

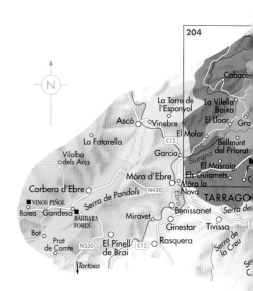

To the south and west in the high country of the hot, sunny **Terra Alta** DO imported red varieties have been replacing the region's Garnacha Blanca, which can make characterful, full-bodied whites.

The DO **Costers del Segre** is only hinted at on this map. It comprises at least four widely scattered subzones (see the map of Spain on p.190). Les Garrigues is just over the Montsant range from fashionable Priorat in similar, though slightly less wild terrain. Old Garnacha and Macabeo bushvines at altitudes of up to 2,460ft (750m) have considerable potential, but now it is Tempranillo and new international varieties that are being trellised among the almonds and olives. Breezes from the Mediterranean minimize the risk of frost. Lightish but spicy international varietals are made on lower ground to the northeast in the

Segre and Vall de Riu Corb zones, while Artesa way to the north has more in common with Somontano in Aragón (see p.201). And then there is the Raimat estate, quite literally an oasis in the semi-desert northwest of Lleida, thanks to an irrigation system developed by the Raventós family of Codorníu on this vast agricultural estate. The wines produced here are more New World than Catalan.

On the coast immediately north of Barcelona the vine-growers of **Alella** do battle with its real estate developers and have also leapt aboard the international varietal bandwagon.

Off this detailed map, but on the introductory map of Spain, is the **Pla de Bages** DO centred on the town of Manresa due north of Barcelona. Although it has some interesting old Picapoll (Languedoc's Picpoul), it too is being planted with Cabernet and Chardonnay. The northernmost of Catalunya's DOs **Empordà-Costa Brava** used to be known only for its tourist rosé made from Cariñena vines. Today it offers an increasingly exciting range of blends, both red and white. All in all, Catalunya could be said to be in full ferment.

Bushvines in spring dedicated to the production of Cava, Spain's highly successful answer to champagne that still dominates the Catalan wine scene, despite Catalunya's exciting recent rash of still wines. The region benefits from one of the most varied arrays of grape varieties in Spain.

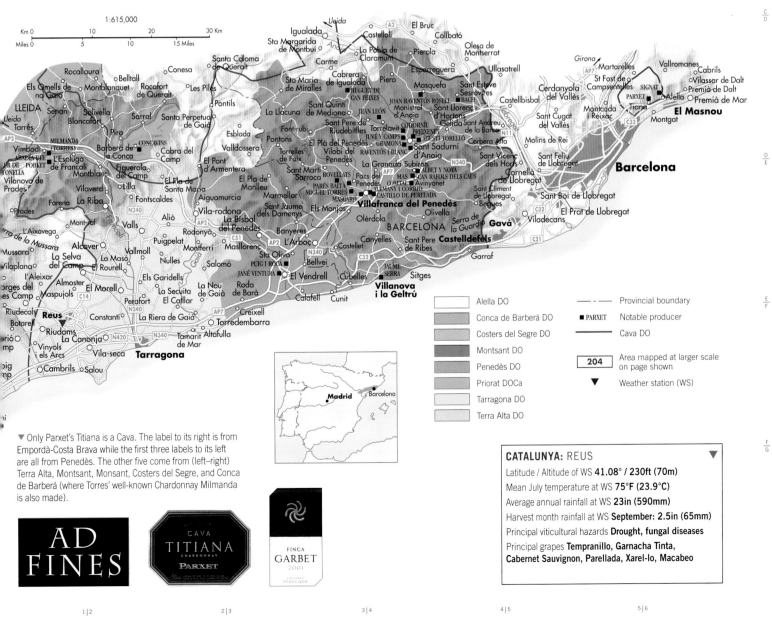

☐ Alella DO	– · – · Provincial boundary
☐ Conca de Barberá DO	■ PARXET Notable producer
☐ Costers del Segre DO	—— Cava DO
☐ Montsant DO	
☐ Penedès DO	204 Area mapped at larger scale on page shown
☐ Priorat DOCa	
☐ Tarragona DO	▼ Weather station (WS)
☐ Terra Alta DO	

▼ Only Parxet's Titiana is a Cava. The label to its right is from Empordà-Costa Brava while the first three labels to its left are all from Penedès. The other five come from (left–right) Terra Alta, Montsant, Monsant, Costers del Segre, and Conca de Barberá (where Torres' well-known Chardonnay Milmanda is also made).

CATALUNYA: REUS ▼
Latitude / Altitude of WS **41.08° / 230ft (70m)**
Mean July temperature at WS **75°F (23.9°C)**
Average annual rainfall at WS **23in (590mm)**
Harvest month rainfall at WS **September: 2.5in (65mm)**
Principal viticultural hazards **Drought, fungal diseases**
Principal grapes **Tempranillo, Garnacha Tinta, Cabernet Sauvignon, Parellada, Xarel-lo, Macabeo**

AD FINES

CAVA TITIANA *Chardonnay* PARXET

FINCA GARBET 2001

Priorat

As recently as 1990 the Catalan government published a substantial tome on 1,000 years of Catalan wine in which Priorat (Priorato in Castilian) was not even mentioned. By the late 1990s this tiny region was producing some of Spain's most exciting, and most expensive, wine. And the change was inspired by one man.

Before the arrival of phylloxera there were 12,350 acres (5,000ha) of vineyards in this dizzying landscape of crinkle-folded hills (this is not country for the nervous driver). By 1979, when René Barbier first saw the potential of this historic wine region, there were only 1,500 acres (600ha) of mainly Cariñena (Carignan) vines left. In 1989 he formed a gang of five friends who would launch five new "Clos". Initially they shared premises and grapes in the village of Gratallops. Their wines were quite distinct from the rustic, raisiny ferments that were then standard for Priorat – wines indeed very different from the oaky Spanish norm. The five were technically adept but locally inspired, and they soon set up bodegas of their own. Barbier's family firm was meanwhile sold to Freixenet and divorced from Priorat. His own Priorat bodega now is called Clos Mogador.

Such was the international acclaim for these concentrated wines (their scarcity helped too) that the region has now been invaded and quite literally reshaped by incomers – some from Penedès, some from as far away as South Africa. By the turn of this century there were 2,500 acres (1,000ha) either under vine or being bulldozed into tractor-friendly terraces ready for planting, with another 2,500 acres earmarked by planting rights. Now bodegas number 70, and all this activity has been superimposed on a region where shepherds and donkey carts were until very recently commonplace, and the best-known wine village of Gratallops has fewer than 200 permanent residents.

So why are the wines so special? Priorat is admittedly protected from the northwest by the Sierra de Montsant, a long ridge of craggy outcrops. But it is its particularly unusual soil, *llicorella*, a dark brown slate whose jagged rock-faces sparkle in the sun with their sprinkling of quartzite, which makes the best Priorat the mineral-laden essence that it is.

Annual rainfall is often less than 16in (400mm) a year, which in most wine regions would make irrigation a necessity. Priorat's soils are unusually cool and damp, however, so that the vine roots tunnel Douro-style through faults in the *llicorella* to find water. The result

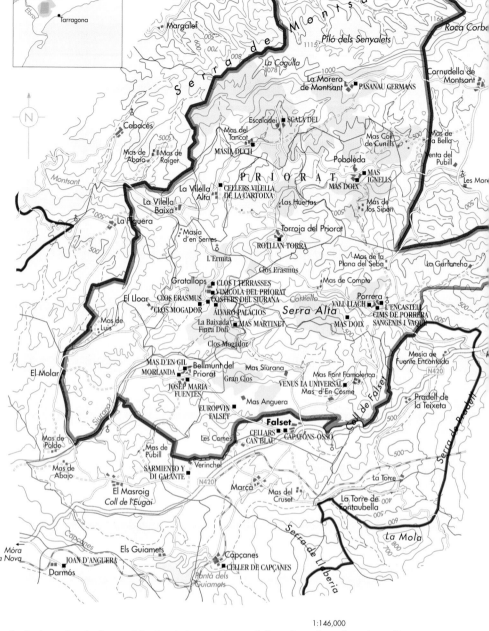

in the best sites is almost ridiculously low yields of arrestingly concentrated wine.

Cariñena is still the most widely planted vine by far, but only the oldest Cariñena vines produce wine of real quality. Ancient Garnacha planted in cooler, slower-ripening sites such as L'Ermita vineyard pictured on p.191 provides the backbone of most serious Priorat. Many of the less concentrated wines are fleshed out with some of the more recently planted Cabernet Sauvignon, Syrah, and Merlot.

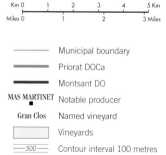

	1:146,000

——— Municipal boundary

▬▬▬ Priorat DOCa

━━━ Montsant DO

MAS MARTINET Notable producer

Gran Clos Named vineyard

Vineyards

═500═ Contour interval 100 metres

◀ All of these labels represent survivors of the original "Clos" settlers in modern Priorat except for Vall Llach, which was founded in the early 1990s rather than the mid-1980s. Today there are about 70 bodegas making Priorat whereas in the early 1980s Scala Dei, on the site of the 12th-century priory which gives its name to the zone, was virtually the only one.

Andalucía — Sherry Country

For centuries wine in Andalucía has meant *vinos generosos*, a self-translating term: sherry above all, but also the similar-but-different wines of Montilla-Moriles and Málaga. Sherry is still by far Andalucía's most famous produce – arguably, indeed, Spain's greatest wine – but modern history here has been moving in other directions. Breakneck development on the Costa del Sol has been matched by the rapid spread of vineyards destined for unfortified wines, both dry and, more surprisingly, sweet.

The key to producing wines with freshness as well as southern ripeness is, yet again, altitude. The mountains rise straight up from the villas, golf courses, and building sites along the coast. A vineyard planted just a few miles from the Mediterranean could well be more than 2,600ft (800m) above the sparkling blue sea; its nights as cool as the days are hot.

In 1998 the DO Málaga applied exclusively to seriously diminishing quantities of wine made sweet and strong either by adding grape spirit during fermentation or by drying the grapes. In 2001 the DO was transformed into Málaga and Sierras de Málaga (see the map on p.190). By 2005 the total area of vineyard had increased by 50%, partly thanks to the addition of two new subzones.

The most dynamic of these is around the hilltop tourist magnet of Ronda, where there have been considerable plantings of international varieties recently, including Petit Verdot, but also Tempranillo and the local red grape speciality Romé. For whites, the Montilla-Moriles grape Pedro Ximénez, Moscatels, and Maccabeo are allowed, as well as Sauvignon Blanc and Chardonnay, which the likes of F Schatz have made into something quite surprising considering the latitude.

The name **Sierras de Málaga** is used to denote this sort of dry wine under 15% alcohol. **Málaga** now means either a fortified wine between 15 and 22% alcohol or a natural sweet wine over 13% which depends entirely on the Andalucían sunshine for its sweetness and alcohol level.

There are other subzones: those on the coast well west of here towards Cádiz where Moscatel reigns and both Atlantic and Mediterranean influences are felt; the large plateau well north of the town of Málaga towards Montilla-Moriles where limestone under russet soils ripens Pedro Ximénez and the local Doradilla of surprising finesse; the rugged Axarquia mountains to the east, best known for Moscatel and Romé grown on slate; and the historic but almost extinct vineyards in the hills around Málaga itself.

While the Sierras de Málaga wines are remarkable for their existence, it is Málaga itself, in its two forms, light and treacly, that has a unique (if double) personality. Scholtz Hermanos, the best-known exponent of the traditional treacly version, went out of business towards the end of the last century. It looked like the end. But Lopez Hermanos (renamed Bodegas Málaga Virgen) apparently continues to flourish with a dazzling array of *vinos generosos*. At the same time Telmo Rodríguez, orginally from Rioja but a force for good in several parts of Spain, revived Málaga Moscatel as a fresh, fragrant but delicate wine with his tangy, tangerine-flavoured Molina Real. It was left to a creative US-based importer of Spanish wines, Jorge Ordoñez, himself a native of Málaga, to trump this with a nectar made from ancient Moscatel vines grown high in the hills. Almijara's Jarel is another notable example.

As fast as DOs are created they are overtaken by creative winemakers. The hinterland of the Costa del Sol, the most mountainous part of Spain, has even been described as the new La Mancha in terms of expansion. Some of the Vinos de la Tierra made around Granada, at altitudes of up to 4,270ft (1,300m), suggest that this may eventually be one of Spain's most exciting regions for unfortified wines. M Valenzuela and H Calvente are the names to look out for.

What of Jerez-Xérès-Sherry and Montilla-Moriles, the heart of Andalucía's wine industry for 2,000 years? Upwardly mobile they are not, with both a surplus of grapes and, shockingly for those of us who treasure unique qualities in wine, a deficit of customers. The sherry region, the larger of the two, is possibly feeling the pinch even more than Montilla-Moriles, whose most glorious product, dark, sweet, tooth-rotting wines based on Pedro Ximénez grapes, are currently highly fashionable within Spain. That said, and despite widespread and misplaced apathy towards sherry outside Andalucía, **Jerez** has seen the recent emergence of some exceptional new bodegas to add to its roster of great names. Fernando de Castilla, Tradición, and Valdivia are three examples.

Sherry's great distinction is finesse. It is a question of chalk, of the breed of the Palomino Fino grape, of huge investment and long-inherited skill. Not every bottle of sherry, by a very long way, has this quality – in fact the sherry aristocracy could be said to have been ruined by the high proportion of poor wine shipped from Jerez in the 1970s and 1980s. But a real fino, the finely judged produce of the bare white chalk dunes of Macharnudo or Sanlúcar de Barrameda, is an expression of wine and wood as vivid and beautiful as any in the world.

The sherry country, between the romantic-sounding cities of Cádiz and Seville, is almost a caricature of grandee Spain. Here are patios, the

Vines dedicated to Málaga, almost certainly Moscatel, creep along the ground below the Axarquia mountains. Even this sleepy, far southern Spanish zone has seen an unexpected revolution in its vineyards, cellars, and wine styles – much of it thanks to the efforts of those who do not live there.

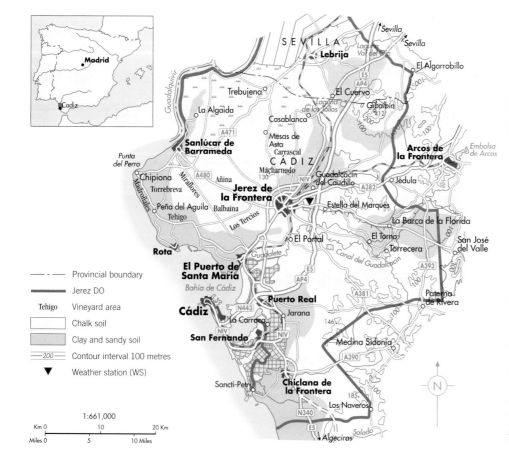

JEREZ: JEREZ DE LA FRONTERA ▼
Latitude / Altitude of WS **36.45° / 98ft (30m)**
Mean July temperature at WS **77.9°F (25.5°C)**
Average annual rainfall at WS **19in (477mm)**
Harvest month rainfall at WS **August: 0.1in (3mm)**
Principal viticultural hazard **Drought**
Principal grapes **Palomino Fino, Pedro Ximénez**

Provincial boundary

Jerez DO

Tehigo — Vineyard area

Chalk soil

Clay and sandy soil

200 — Contour interval 100 metres

▼ Weather station (WS)

1:661,000

Km 0 — 10 — 20 Km

Miles 0 — 5 — 10 Miles

guitars, the flamenco dancers, the night-turned-into-day. Jerez de la Frontera, the town that gives its name to sherry, lives and breathes sherry as Beaune does burgundy and Epernay champagne – even if consolidation, closure, and takeover have meant that there are far, far fewer sherry producers than there were even 20 years ago.

The comparison of sherry with champagne can be carried a long way. Both are white wines with a distinction given them by chalk soil, both needing long traditional treatment to achieve their special characters. Both are revivifying apéritifs, of which you can drink an astonishing amount in their home countries and only feel more alive than you have ever felt before. They are the far-northern and the far-southern European interpretation of the same equation, or the same poem: the white grape from the white ground.

Not all the ground is white. The chalk areas (*albarizas*) are best; the pagos (*districts*) of Carrascal, Macharnudo, Añina, and Balbaina the most famous. Some vineyards are on *barros* (dark lands) and sand and produce second-rank wines for blending – although sandy coastal vineyards can suit Moscatel grapes well.

The shippers' headquarters and bodegas are in the sherry towns of Sanlúcar, El Puerto de Santa María, and, especially, Jerez. There are little bars in each of these towns where the tapas, the morsels of food without which no Andalucían puts glass to mouth, constitute a banquet.

Your copita, a glass no more imposing than an opening tulip, fills and empties with a paler wine, a cooler wine, a more druggingly delicious wine than you have ever tasted.

But the most celebrated sights of Jerez are the traditional bodegas of the shipping houses. Their towering whitewashed aisles, crisscrossed with sunbeams, are irresistibly cathedral-like. In them, in ranks of butts (barrels) typically three tiers high, the new wine is put to mature. Most will not leave until it has gone through the elaborate blending process of the solera system, although wines of notable distinction may be sold unblended, either as a single vintage wine, a fairly recent revival designed to kick-start the connoisseur market for sherry, or one straight from an *almacenista*, or stockholder.

When the new wine has got over its fermentation it is sorted into categories: better or worse, lighter or more full-bodied. Then each

wine begins its journey within the solera system, which is simply a progressive topping-up of older barrels from younger of the same style, so that wine is continously being blended, thus eliminating variation.

The new wine is put into the youngest level of a specific *criadera* or nursery (the Spanish term reflecting the idea of raising children) according to its category. Each year a proportion of wine from the solera, the oldest and final stage of the *criadera*, is bottled so the younger wines move up into the next nursery class to continue their education. The more stages, the finer the wine.

All young sherry is originally classified as either a wine light and delicate enough to be a fino, or a fuller wine that is classified as an oloroso. A fino, light in alcohol, will mature under a protective, bread-like layer of a strange Jerez yeast called flor. (Flor may be vulnerable to climate change; we should be concerned.) Olorosos are matured in contact with air and deliberately fortified to more than 15.5% alcohol, normally 17.5%, to prevent the growth of flor.

The solera wines are the shippers' paint box for blending their house brands. The Spanish (and the authors) drink dry sherries straight from the solera. Sadly the export mass market has been based on blends sweetened and fortified until their character disappears – the very sherries no one (except, in folklore, aunts) wants any more.

Sherries bottled as finos are the finest and palest; distinctive, bone dry wines which need a minimum of blending. They are fast-faders; an open bottle should be drunk like any other white wine, within hours rather than days or weeks. Even lighter and drier are the manzanillas of Sanlúcar de Barrameda, made just like a fino and blessed with a faintly salty tang which is held to come from the sea. An aged manzanilla (the term is pasada) is sublime with seafood.

Amontillado, a darker more complicated wine, is the next category. The best amontillados

▼ From the left: A very respectable red table wine made just east of the sherry zone, two sweet wines from Málaga, three sherries, and two super-sweet wines from Montilla-Moriles. The driest, lightest is La Gitana Manzanilla, one of the world's most original and refreshing wine styles.

A fino in the bodega of González Byass, one of the few great sherry names to remain in the hands of the original family, who have followed the current trend by diversifying into other wine regions. The results include Beronia Riojas and a joint venture in Chile, Conde de Aconcagua.

are old finos, finos which lacked the perfect zing for drinking young and put on weight with age – although the name is more often used for export blends that are medium in every sense of the word.

True classical oloroso, dry, dark, and biting, is less common but a great favourite with Jerezanos themselves. Such wines can age superbly but are too heavy for a fino solera. Commercial brands labelled oloroso or cream are younger, coarser examples blended with sweetening wines; pale cream is similar but robbed of colour. Palo cortado, on the other hand, is a true, classical, rich-yet-dry rarity, something between amontillado and oloroso.

In a further attempt to attract fine wine drinkers to their neglected wines, sherry producers have devised a way of signalling and certifying notable age and quality: VOS and VORS sherries are more than 20 and 30 years old respectively. And 12 and 15 year-old designations of age have also been implemented.

No blend, medium-sweet or sweet as most blends are, can compare with the best natural sherries. They are as much collectors' pieces as the great domaine-bottled burgundies.

The region of **Montilla-Moriles**, just south of Córdoba, (its name incorporates two of its towns), is also shrinking. Until 50 years ago its produce was blended at Jerez as though the two

regions were one. It still had more than 20,000 acres (8,000ha) of vineyard in 2005, the best of them on chalk vineyards similar to those that give rise to the finos and olorosos of Jerez but more generally on sand.

But Montilla is different. The Montilla grape is not Palomino but Pedro Ximénez, which is still regularly shipped to Jerez for making sweet wine there. Montilla's hotter climate results in the musts' very high natural strength, which

has always allowed it to be shipped without fortification, in contrast to sherry. The wines are made very similarly to sherry. Once the two year minimum ageing period is up the wine is ready, heavier but softer than sherry, slipping down like table wine despite its high strength. People claim to find in them the scent of black olives (which are of course their perfect partners). Alvear and Pérez Barquero are the bodegas that set the standard.

THE SHERRY BODEGAS OF JEREZ DE LA FRONTERA

1 Garvey
2 Sandeman
3 Sanchez Romate
4 Rey Fernando de Castilla
5 Almocaden
6 Valdivia
7 Valdespino/Real Tesoro
8 Tradición
9 Domecq
10 González Byass
11 Williams & Humbert
12 Maestro Sierra
13 Alvaro Domecq
14 Dios Baco
15 Emilio Lustau
16 John Harvey
17 Emilio Hidalgo

Jerez can be a great place to be a tourist, provided you set your eating clock to three or four hours later than usual.

A panel of tiles at Pinhao railway station depicting the harvesting of grapes in the Douro Valley.

Portugal

Portugal

Portugal's isolation, cut off as it were behind Spain on the Atlantic fringe of Europe, has given it a Unique Selling Point a more eager marketer might never have thought of. While other countries were busy planting French grapes and joining a me-too culture Portugal stuck to its indigenous vines and its unreconstructed tastes. These vines, though, included a number with qualities capable of beguiling a much wider world.

Touriga Nacional, for example, had never been made into anything but port. A new way of thinking has already made it into great red table wines, not only up the Douro but overseas. Touriga Franca and Tinto Cão are other port grapes clearly capable of making the transition from fortified to less potent wine, while Trincadeira (the Tinta Amarela of port) has great richness and Jaen (Mencía in Spain's Galicia) can make distinguished, juicy young wine. And these are not the only ones. The grape known as Tempranillo in Spain is also extremely successful in Portugal, called Tinta Roriz in the north and Aragonês in the south. Arinto is probably Portugal's most aristocratic white grape but Bical can also age well, and Encruzado, native to the Dão region, has great potential for full-bodied whites. All this without taking into account the great white grapes of Portugal's wine island, Madeira (see p.222).

All these flavours are now more accessible to outsiders because Portugal is making much more gentle, voluptuous wines, even if acidity and tannins are still pronounced compared with the wines of Spain, for example. Portugal has retained her individuality but she has at long last joined the greater world of wine, as the following pages demonstrate.

For years Portugal was known to the world's wine drinkers only for her great sweet fortified wine, port (examined in detail on pp.220–21), and the country's other wine style conceived specifically for export – wines neither red nor white, sweet nor dry, still nor sparkling – of which Mateus and Lancers were the leading ambassadors in the mid-20th century.

The Portuguese have always been prodigious drinkers of their own wine and, knowing no other, were quite accustomed to local styles made, as they had been for centuries, often searingly high in acidity in the north and distinctly rustic in the south. The country is not

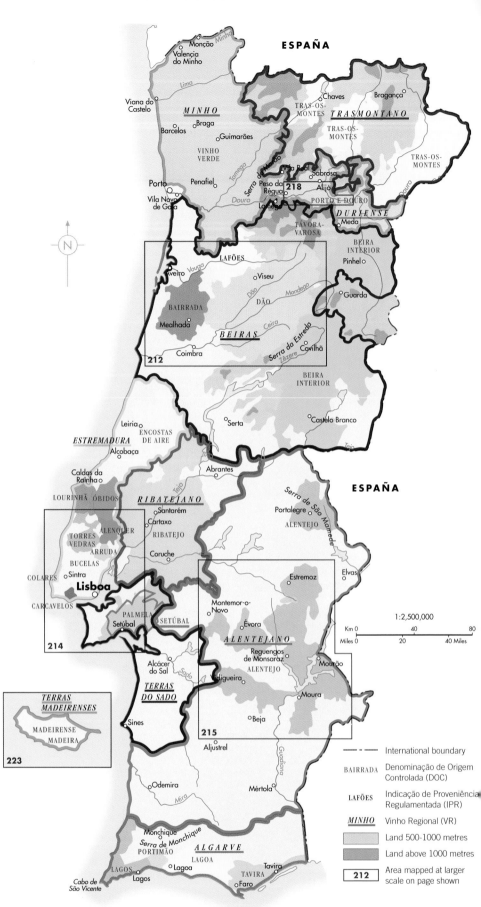

– – – – –	International boundary
BAIRRADA	Denominação de Origem Controlada (DOC)
LAFÕES	Indicação de Proveniência Regulamentada (IPR)
MINHO	Vinho Regional (VR)
	Land 500–1000 metres
	Land above 1000 metres
212	Area mapped at larger scale on page shown

◀ Labels from the far north and south of the country: three from the Minho, one from Beiras, and one from the Algarve, ignored as a wine region until British crooner Sir Cliff Richard launched his Vida Nova red, made by Alentejo-based Australian winemaker David Baverstock.

vast but different regions are subject to the very different influences of Atlantic, Mediterranean, and even continental climates. Soils, too, vary enormously, from granite, slate, and schist in the north and inland and limestone, clay, and sand by the coast and to the south.

Since the early 1990s Portugal's table wines, particularly her highly individual reds, have caught up fast with the evolution in modern winemaking. Temperature control, destemmers, new oak barrels, greater understanding of the special qualities of Portugal's shallow fermenting vats, *lagares* – all have played their part in capturing the fruit of Portugal's distinctive grape varieties in the bottle, and in producing wines that do not require ageing for a decade before they are drinkable. Although Portugal now has many talented native oenologists, Australian-trained outsiders such as David Baverstock and Peter Bright can also claim some of the credit for this in their pioneering work, respectively at Esporão and JP Vinhos (now called Bacalhôa Vinhos).

Not that Portuguese wine has been without laws and regulations. The Douro lays claim to be the world's first demarcated wine region (in

1756), and long before Portugal's entry into the EU in 1986 many other districts had been demarcated and every aspect of their wines controlled. This was not always to the benefit of their quality, or to the liking of merchants and their local clients, who routinely ignored what the law prescribed to blend the kinds of wines they preferred, typically labelled Garrafeira.

With entry into the EU Portugal's wine map, like that of Spain, has sprouted a rash of demarcated regions. The regulations of Portugal's DOCs, emulating those of France's Appellations Contrôlées, prescribe the permitted local grape varieties. Increasingly important however is the Vinho Regional category of wines from much larger regions but with more flexible regulations. In 2006 there were also four IPRs (Indicaçãoes de Proveniência Regulamentada), DOCs-in-waiting, a category which is expected to disappear eventually. The map shows the approved wine names; the key reveals their status. While some of the new regions have authentic character and important potential, others are likely to be mere straws in the wind. Time will tell.

In the far northeast, **Trasmontano** is a Vinho Regional generally used for declassified Douro wines, typically made from international grape varieties, although some basic blending wines are made by the co-ops in the remote granite uplands at the northern rim of the Douro Valley, most beautiful at their golden harvest time.

Beiras, virtually all of the northern half of the country south of the Douro Valley, is an increasingly important Vinho Regional used for wines that do not qualify as either Dão or Bairrada, usually because they contain all or some imported grape varieties. Luís Pato, for long the leader of the Bairrada DOC, now sells his wines as Beiras, as do the particularly notable Campolargo and Quinta de Foz de Arouce.

The productive **Ribatejo** region is named after the banks of the River Tagus (Tejo) which flows southwest from the Spanish border to Lisbon. The fertile river banks used to produce vast quantities of decidedly light wine, but in the late 1980s and 1990s EU subsidies persuaded hundreds of growers here to uproot

Vineyards near Amarante in the Minho, grown in very similar terrain to those of Spain's Rías Baixas, just across the river known as the Miño in Spanish. A wider range of grape varieties is grown on the Portuguese side, a phenomenon that is typical of the difference between the two neighbouring countries.

their vines. Total production has shrunk and the focus of Ribatejo wine production has now moved away from the river bank and, in some cases, towards imported grape varieties such as Cabernet Sauvignon and more recently Syrah (which seems to have a promising future in Portugal). Castelão is the most important local red wine grape although some Trincadeira is also grown. Whites are typically based on the arrestingly perfumed Fernão Pires.

In the south of Portugal the Vinho Regional category is much more important than DOC so that most Algarve wine, for instance, is sold as Vinho Regional **Algarve** rather than under the name of one of its four DOCs.

Of Portugal's many wildly differing styles of wine, the most singular remains **Vinho Verde**, the youthful "green" (as opposed to *maduro*, or aged) wine of the northernmost province, the **Minho**, which accounts for a sixth of Portugal's wine harvest. The name green describes its fresh, often underripe style, not its colour, which is red (typically astringent and mostly sold in Portugal) or almost water-white.

In this damp climate (with an average rainfall of 47in/1,200mm), vines are extremely vigorous, malic acid unusually high, and natural grape sugars relatively low, resulting in reds and whites with a low alcohol content and definite tartness, a decidedly local taste. Although most white Vinho Verde is made from a blend of grapes, typically including Azal, Loureiro, Trajadura, Avesso, and some Padernã (Arinto), some of the best is made exclusively from the white Alvarinho grape (Albariño in Spain) grown around Monção.

The grapevine is not the only plant in Portugal of interest to wine drinkers. The southern half of the country has the world's greatest concentration of cork oaks, so that Portugal is our principal supplier of wine corks.

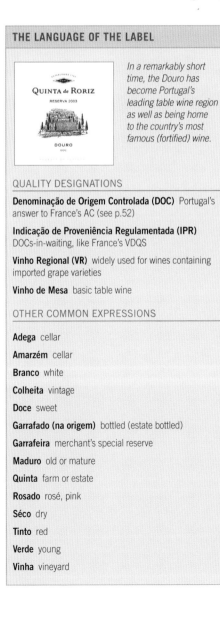

THE LANGUAGE OF THE LABEL

QUINTA de RORIZ
RESERVA 2003

DOURO
DOC

In a remarkably short time, the Douro has become Portugal's leading table wine region as well as being home to the country's most famous (fortified) wine.

QUALITY DESIGNATIONS

Denominação de Origem Controlada (DOC) Portugal's answer to France's AC (see p.52)

Indicação de Proveniência Regulamentada (IPR) DOCs-in-waiting, like France's VDQS

Vinho Regional (VR) widely used for wines containing imported grape varieties

Vinho de Mesa basic table wine

OTHER COMMON EXPRESSIONS

Adega cellar

Amarzém cellar

Branco white

Colheita vintage

Doce sweet

Garrafado (na origem) bottled (estate bottled)

Garrafeira merchant's special reserve

Maduro old or mature

Quinta farm or estate

Rosado rosé, pink

Séco dry

Tinto red

Verde young

Vinha vineyard

Bairrada and Dão

Bairrada and Dão, two of Portugal's longest-established wine regions, are currently in the throes of (entirely beneficial) transition. **Bairrada** is a thoroughly rural district lying astride the highway that links Lisbon and Oporto (convenient for those who trek to sample the region's speciality of suckling pig), filling most of the area between the granite hills of Dão and the Atlantic coast. This proximity to the Atlantic makes it one of the country's rainier wine regions and growers here have the same problems ripening grapes and keeping them free of fungal diseases as their counterparts in Bordeaux.

Bairrada's low hills encompass some extremely varied and expressive terroirs, but heavy, lime-rich clay predominates and gives body and typical Portuguese bite to its overwhelmingly (85%) red wine. The defining ingredient though is Bairrada's indigenous Baga grape. Luís Pato has been one of Bairrada's most passionate exponents, even if he is one of those who has left the DOC to sell his wines as Vinho Regional Beiras. He likens Baga to Piemonte's Nebbiolo in its uncompromisingly heavy charge

of acids and tannins. Baga produces wines of considerable character that demand patience (some of the traditional bottlings need 20 years' cellaring) and sympathy – not qualities that mark out the typical modern wine drinker. Some producers have a policy of ageing their better wines themselves and it is possible to find venerable, delicious red Bairrada from such cellars as Casa de Saima and Quinta de Baixo. All red Bairrada benefits from decanting.

Many of the region's 7,000 growers belong to the co-operatives which, along with Sogrape's vinification centre, comprise the biggest wineries. But the most ambitious smaller producers are admirably well-organized, and a serious research programme is helping to fashion Bairrada for the 21st century. Destemming has become more common and some producers are carefully thinning crops and trimming vegetation to push the grape to the limits of ripeness. Considerable investment has recently been made in upgrading vineyards here.

Increasingly complex whites are made from the local Bical grape which, like Baga, is notable for its acidity. Bical makes eminently

respectable sparkling wines as well as increasingly full-bodied still ones. Maria Gomes (Fernão Pires) is another traditional, if much less distinguished, variety. But from 2003 Bairrada may be made from such non-local varieties as Touriga Nacional, Tinta Roriz, Verdelho (for whites), and even Cabernet Sauvignon, Merlot, and Syrah.

The **Dão** DOC is at least thoroughly Portuguese in terms of permitted grape varieties. The name was until the 1990s associated with aggressively tannic, dull reds, the result of a ridiculous statute that sent all its grapes to heavy-handed co-operatives. Happily the European Union disallowed this monopoly and the result is far juicier, friendlier wines, including some of Portugal's finest. Red Dão changed more, and for the better, than any other Portuguese wine in the 1990s.

Named after the river that runs through it, Dão is effectively a granite plateau, where bare rocks show through the predominantly sandy soil – although there is some schist in the flatter south and west, which is less obvious wine country. Vineyards are only a subplot in

The very façade of the Buçaco Palace Hotel suggests that it is unlikely to bend to every whim of current fashion. The wines made, or at least blended and matured, in the cellars pictured here are one-offs – whites as much as reds. (See label, second from top right).

the landscape, cropping up here and there in clearings in the sweet-scented pine forests, ideally at altitudes of 1,300–1,640ft (400–500m) but some can be found as high as 2,620ft (800m). Its capital, Viseu, is one of Portugal's prettiest towns. The Serra do Caramulo shields the region from the Atlantic and the Serra da Estrela mountains protect it in the southeast. This means that in winter Dão is cold and wet; in summer warm and dry – much drier than Bairrada.

As is usual in Portugal, a dizzying range of grapes is grown in the Dão region to produce increasingly fruity reds – though still with a certain granitic substance – and potentially firm, fragrant whites suitable for ageing. This affinity for the cellar, in whites as well as reds, was already obvious from traditional Dãos, bottled by merchants who would buy, blend, and age wines from the co-ops before selling them as their own Reservas or Garrafeiras.

The finest individual estates such as Quinta dos Roques/Quinta das Maias and Quinta da Pellada/Quinta de Saes have been producing single varietals as well as blends as they experiment with individual grapes. Touriga Nacional has shown great promise for long ageing, Jaen (Galicia's Mencía) for fruity early drinking, and Tinto Cão for perfume. The deep-coloured Alfrocheiro is also promising with judicious blends becoming increasingly common. Full-bodied Encruzado has already proved itself one of Portugal's finest white grapes. Sogrape, pioneer of varietal wines in the region, has

invested heavily in its Quinta dos Carvalhais range. Fruit has been rediscovered in Dão.

The potential of this part of the world for truly remarkable table wines was always clear, thanks to one eccentric, mysterious, and highly idiosyncratic example. Right on Barraida's eastern boundary the Buçaco Palace Hotel has selected and matured its own red and white wines in a wholly traditional way. The reds would usually come from north of the handsome university town of Coimbra while whites were handpicked from both Bairrada and Dão, blended and aged for years in barrel in the Palace cellars. Both reds and whites on the hotel wine list still go back for decades, and the "current" vintages for both colours at the turn of the century were from the 1970s and 1960s. They look and taste like relics of another age, in the most fascinating sense.

▶ Luís Pato uses the top label exclusively for the wine he makes from a plot of ungrafted, pre-phylloxera Baga vines within the Bairrada zone but sold as a Vinho Regional Beiras, because Pato believes the Bairrada rules are no longer pure enough. The most commercial offering is represented by the bottom label, Sogrape's top Dão.

Estremadura and Setúbal Peninsula

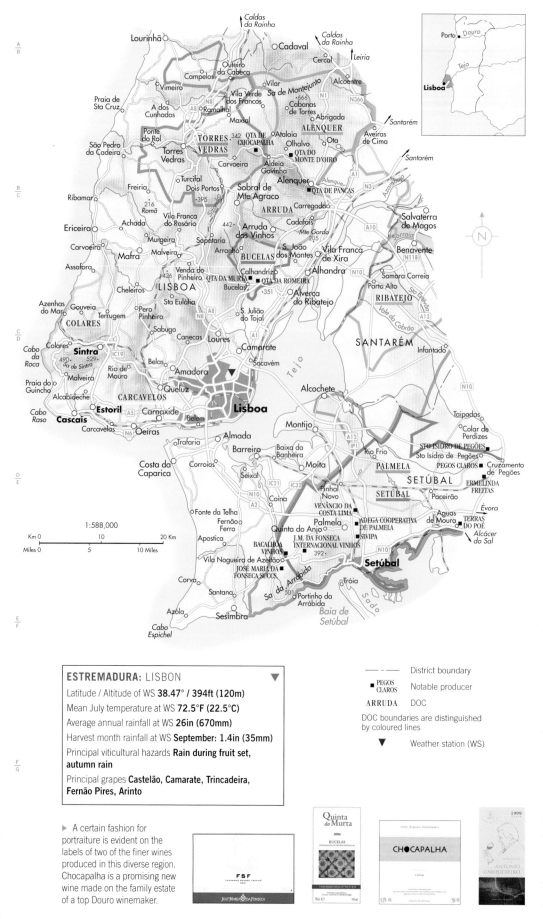

▶ A certain fashion for portraiture is evident on the labels of two of the finer wines produced in this diverse region. Chocapalha is a promising new wine made on the family estate of a top Douro winemaker.

---- District boundary

■ PEGOS CLAROS Notable producer

ARRUDA DOC

DOC boundaries are distinguished by coloured lines

▼ Weather station (WS)

Two very different wine regions are mapped here. **Estremadura**, once called simply Oeste or "the west", is Portugal's most productive wine region, even if the average holding of its more than 55,000 grape growers is not much more than a hectare. This ultra-maritime region for long made little other than very inexpensive wine, some of it good value, in its many co-ops, from sand and clay soils. Now it can boast some small estates of real interest and ambition however. Torres Vedras, Arruda, and Alenquer DOCs are mapped here but see the map on p.210 for the full northern extent of Estremadura.

For a long time this part of Portugal was famous for three historic wines, now all threatened with extinction. **Bucelas** is least threatened. Its Quinta da Romeira is successful enough to attract other investors to the region. The naturally crisp, lemony Arinto grape retains useful acidity and can provide some truly fine wine throughout Estremadura, whether varietal or blended.

Colares, right on the Atlantic coast, is one of the world's stranger wine zones. Ungrafted Ramisco vines are literally grown on the windswept cliff-tops, hugging the phylloxera-immune sand, their old limbs like driftwood, bearing small bunches of intensely blue grapes. Today the lone private investor who makes this historic wine is battling what looks like inexorable property development. To the south the similar battle to save **Carcavelos**, whose luscious amber wine became famous during the Peninsula war, is all but lost.

Much more important today than these once-famous names are the quite separate vineyards of the Setúbal Peninsula between the Tagus (Tejo) and Sado estuaries southeast of Lisbon, divided into the very different clay-limestone hills of Serra da Arrábida, whose slopes are cooled by Atlantic winds, and the much hotter, more fertile inland sandy plain of the River Sado east of **Palmela**. The local Vinho Regional Terras do Sado extends well to the south of this map towards Alentejo.

Setúbal's most important producers, Bacalhôa Vinhos and José Maria da Fonseca, were also pioneers of Portugal's new wave of modern table wines. Bacalhôa Vinhos could claim to be Portugal's most experienced producer of modern white wines, whether from Chardonnay or the local Fernão Pires, while both companies have for many years made extremely accessible, medium-weight reds from the dominant local red grape Castelão, which seems particularly at home in the sandy soils just east of Palmela. Syrah, Aragonês (Tempranillo), and Douro red grapes are gaining ground here.

The region's most traditional wine is **Moscatel de Setúbal**, a rich, pale orange Muscat that is lightly fortified and perfumed by long maceration with the headily aromatic Muscat of Alexandria skins.

Alentejo

In comparison with the tapestry of vines that seems to smother northern Portugal, in the Alentejo, the southern third of the country, vineyards are concentrated in four main enclaves: Borba, Redondo, Reguengos, and Vidigueira. Its wide, sun-browned spaces are dotted with silver olives and dark cork oaks, browsed bare by sheep, but only occasionally green with vines. Smallholdings are rare. Ranch-like estates, unknown in the densely populated north, are the norm.

Even in midwinter, this is a land of sun and open vistas. The visitor is aware that arid Spain is just over the border; winemakers do their shopping there. Rainfall is low and temperatures so routinely high that picking starts in the third week of August. Rich loamy soils are interspersed with the granite and schist to which vines are more suited.

Six of the Alentejo's eight subzones are based on an important co-op, none more important than that of **Reguengos**, which, in Monsaraz, produces a best-seller within Portugal. A significant proportion of the region's wine is sold as Vinho Regional Alentejano, often varietally labelled. **Evora** can boast a particularly long history of bottling wine, notably the Cartuxa and floridly labelled Pêra Manca of Eugénio de Almeida.

But it has been newcomers who have brought Alentejo wines to international attention. When José Roquette, owner of one of Lisbon's rival football teams, blessed his Reguengos estate Herdade do Esporão with an Australian winemaker and almost Napa-like dream winery in the late 1980s, the Portuguese took note. When the Lafite Rothschilds invested in Quinta do Carmo in **Borba** in 1992, the world took note (even if the wines were slow to shine). Oenologist João Portugal Ramos has energized the entire region, providing it with a popular and easily exportable brand, Marquês de Borba.

There are few wine traditions here and this is excellent pioneer country with the added advantage, until the recent arrival of the spotlight of fashion, of relatively low prices. By 2006 the region could boast 160 wine producers, not just on the area mapped here but also in **Portalegre** to the north where land rises to 3,280ft (1,000m) of granite and schist, and to the south on the border with the Algarve where there has also been significant investment.

Red grapes are now more popular than the floral white Roupeiro. Aragonês (Tempranillo) and the local speciality Trincadeira have risen to the fore, as has the red-fleshed Alicante Bouschet, which seems to take on a certain unaccustomed nobility in Alentejo. Touriga Nacional, Cabernet Sauvignon, and Syrah have inevitably been imported.

Cork oaks are harvested (their bark stripped to have corks punched out of it) much less frequently than vines, although some winemakers complain that the frequency has increased with worldwide demand.

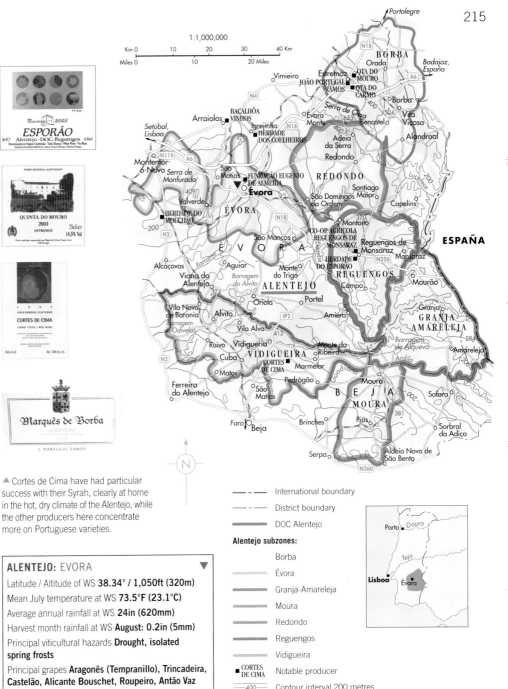

▲ Cortes de Cima have had particular success with their Syrah, clearly at home in the hot, dry climate of the Alentejo, while the other producers here concentrate more on Portuguese varieties.

ALENTEJO: EVORA ▼

Latitude / Altitude of WS **38.34° / 1,050ft (320m)**
Mean July temperature at WS **73.5°F (23.1°C)**
Average annual rainfall at WS **24in (620mm)**
Harvest month rainfall at WS **August: 0.2in (5mm)**
Principal viticultural hazards **Drought, isolated spring frosts**
Principal grapes **Aragonês (Tempranillo), Trincadeira, Castelão, Alicante Bouschet, Roupeiro, Antão Vaz**

--- International boundary
- - - District boundary
DOC Alentejo

Alentejo subzones:
Borba
Évora
Granja-Amareleja
Moura
Redondo
Reguengos
Vidigueira
■ CORTES DE CIMA Notable producer
—400— Contour interval 200 metres
▼ Weather station (WS)

Douro – Port Country

The Douro Valley, the home of port, has embraced a new vocation. After centuries of being known only for fortified wine labelled port, it is fast establishing an international reputation for its distinctive unfortified wines labelled Douro. Vineyards and wineries that were predicated on unlimited supplies of cheap labour are being redesigned to suit a region which received vast sums of World Bank capital in the 1980s. More than 6,280 acres (2,500ha) of vineyards were replanted as part of the investment programme, typically with one or two approved varieties rather than the traditional jumble. Just as significant, the quality of life and wages have improved notably in the region, dramatically increasing production costs and making the sort of cheap port sold in quantity (especially to France) almost uneconomic to produce. The economic climate of the Douro, where individual farmers, many of them smallholders, are granted the right to produce a set amount of port each year, is more fragile than ever.

The meteorological climate of the region has always been exceptional. Indeed of all the places where men have planted vineyards, the Upper Douro is the most improbable. To begin with there was hardly any soil: only 60-degree slopes of schist, flaking and unstable, baked in a 100°F (38°C) summer sun and plagued by malaria. It was a land of utter desolation and the locals were careful to settle only well above the reach of riverside mosquitoes, as can be seen by the location of most of the villages on the map overleaf.

The vine, however, is one of the few plants not quite deterred by these conditions. The harsh climate, ranging from Atlantic-influenced in the east and increasingly continental away from the coast, suits it. What was needed was simply the engineering feat of building walls along the mountainsides, thousands of them, like contour lines, to hold up the patches of ground (one could hardly call it soil) where vines could be planted. Once the ground was stabilized and rainwater no longer ran straight off, an enterprise undertaken as early as the 17th century, olives, oranges, oaks, chestnut trees, and vines flourished.

Long after phylloxera had laid waste the region's vineyards, in the efficient 1970s, some of the old stone-walled terraces were replaced by bulldozed, wider terraces (*patamares*) supported by banks of schist rather than walls. Their great advantage is that they are wide enough for tractors and mechanization (although narrow terraces also have their proponents). Their disadvantage is the reduction in vine density. Today the old stone terraces are preserved, in keeping with the region's status as a World Heritage Site, even if the old slate posts are fast being replaced by more efficient, if decidedly less picturesque, metal stakes. Along the *patamares*, and wherever the angle of elevation allows, growers are now increasingly planting vine rows up rather than across the slope, which also allows mechanization – provided the slope is less than 40% – but encourages much denser planting. Vertical planting also tends to offer more homogeneity and therefore more regular ripening within a single plot because there are fewer different aspects.

Many of the original terraces dating from the 17th century survive in the mountains above Régua, in the original port wine zone which then extended only as far as the Tua tributary. When it was given its first official limits, in 1756, they were the first such limits ever given to any wine. Today this area of the Cima Corgo remains the biggest port producer, but the search for quality has led further and further upstream.

The Douro reaches Portugal from Spain in a wilderness which has been accessible by road only since the late 1980s when funds started to flood into Portugal. The river has carved a titanic canyon through the layered rock uplands, the so-called Upper Douro, or Douro Superior, the driest, flattest, least developed part of the Douro (see regional map, p.219) which can, nevertheless, produce some very fine grapes. This easternmost part of the valley has only relatively recently been planted but vineyards in the extremely continental climate here can be much easier to work than those on the steep banks of the Cima Corgo.

To the west, the 4,600ft (1,400m) Serra do Marão stops the Atlantic rain clouds of summer from refreshing the schists of the heart of port country, Cima Corgo, mapped in detail overleaf. Average annual rainfall varies from 20in (500mm) in Douro Superior to 26in (650mm) in Cima Corgo and 35in (900mm) in the heavily planted Baixo Corgo, with the wettest, coolest climate downstream of the Corgo tributary and off the main map to the west where the basic, inexpensive ports have come from, typically grown by smallholders and produced in co-ops. See the map on p.219 for an explanation of why the rainfall noted in Vila Real, way to the north of the official Douro zone, is so much higher than even the Baixa Corgo.

It is hardly surprising that the grapes harvested from each plot, each altitude, each aspect of each slope of the Douro Valley make very different wine (very like the Mosel in Germany). It has taken time for modern viticultural techniques to be applied to this historic, fragmented wine region.

The Baixo Corgo is reckoned to be too damp for top-quality port. To make great port the vines have to be forced to insinuate their roots as far down into the schist as possible in their search for water, up to 26ft (8m) deep as at Quinta do Vesuvio in the east of the section mapped.

The vineyards that are conventionally recognized as the best of all for port are those around and above the railway town of Pinhão, including the valleys of the Tedo, Távora, Torto, Pinhão, and Tua tributaries. Because orientations and altitudes vary so dramatically, the character of wine produced even in neighbouring vineyards can be quite different. In the Tedo Valley, for instance, wine tends to be particularly tannic, while that made just across the river around Quinta do Crasto, already famous for its Douro table wine, is relatively light and fruity. The mild climate of the Torto tributary is also particularly good table wine country since maturation is slower and sugar levels tend to be lower than in the main Douro Valley. Higher vineyards wherever they are tend to ripen later and produce lighter wines, while those that face south and/or west attract the most sunlight and produce the strongest musts.

Each port vineyard is classified, from A down to F, according to its natural advantages – altitude, location, yield, soil, inclination, orientation – and the age, density, training, and varieties of vine grown on it. The higher the classification, the more money will be paid for the grapes in the highly regulated market that governs relations between the grape growers and port producers. Until pioneering work in the 1970s by José Ramos Pinto Rosas and João Nicolau de Almeida, little was known about the vines that grew in the Douro, typically a tangled jumble of different bushvines. They identified Touriga Nacional, Touriga Franca, Tinta Roriz (various clones of Spain's Tempranillo), Tinto Cão, and Tinta Barroca as those varieties which most regularly made top-quality port. These constitute the majority of the Douro's now much more disciplined vineyards, but Sousão is increasingly valued, as is Tinta Amarela in the Cima Corgo and Douro Superior, even if it is too prone to rot to be useful in the Baixa Corgo.

◀ Four particularly notable Douro table wines. They vary in style, which is only to be expected when it was hardly a generation ago that the only Douro table wine with any sort of reputation was Ferreira's Barca Velha.

To make white port – a local favourite – Viozinho, Gouveio, Malvasia, and Rabigato are some of the best light-skinned grapes that yearly do battle with the Douro's baking hot summers and freezing cold winters. An increasing proportion of them are also being used for white Douro table wine such as Dirk Niepoort's pioneering Redoma.

Vintage time anywhere is the climax of the year, but picking these grapes in the Douro, perhaps because of the hardship of life there, can be almost Dionysiac. There is an antique frenzy about the ritual, the songs, the music of drum and pipe (or, more likely nowadays, loud portable stereo), and the long nights of treading and dancing – by the light of hurricane lamps until the relatively recent advent of electricity.

The famous shipping firms have their own quintas, or wine farms, up in the hills where they go to supervise the vintage. They are rambling white houses, vine-arboured, tile-floored, and cool in a world of dust and glare. Most of the famous port quintas are shown on the map on these pages, names that have become much more familiar since the late 1980s with the rise in single quinta ports. AXA-renovated Quinta do Noval above Pinhão has been world-famous for years, but there are now scores more "single quinta ports", the products of a single estate in a single year, typically in vintages not quite fine enough to be generally declared. Taylor, for instance, sells the wine produced on their Quinta de Vargellas in lesser vintages. But many other single quinta ports are now produced, year in and year out, more like a Bordeaux château. Quinta do Vesuvio and Quinta de la Rosa are prominent examples. The main source of grapes and wine for port, however, is not the big estates but still a multitude of small farmers, even if more and more of them are being tempted to sell under the name of their own quintas.

This is particularly true for the table wines – most red, all labelled Douro – that have been emerging from the Douro since outside funds have been transformed into winemaking niceties such as temperature control, a trend encouraged by the number of oenologists trained at Vila Real. Traditionally, Douro table wines were an afterthought, made from grapes left over from making port, but light wines have become so important for producers such as Sogrape (which now owns Ferreira and Quinta da Leda), Ramos Pinto, Quinta de la Rosa, Quinta do Crasto, Quinta do Côtto, Quinta do Vale Meão, Quinta do Vale Dona Maria, Quinta de Roriz, Quinta do Vallado, and Quinta da Gaivosa (in the Baixo Corgo), that some of them have been planting vineyards specifically for table wines. Table wines, they note, call for grapes that are particularly suitable for unfortified wines rather than simply the leftovers from port production. The Bordelais have even been moving in: Chryseia is a joint venture between the Symington port-producing family and Bruno Prats (once owner of Château Cos d'Estournel); Xisto another between the Roquettes of Quinta do Crasto and the Cazes family of Château Lynch Bages. In smaller vintages there is now real competition for suitable grapes for Douro wines.

These wines vary enormously in style according to the provenance of the grapes and the intentions of the winemakers – from the almost burgundian Charme of Niepoort through the sophisticated intensity of Pintas to the schistous solidity of Quinta da Gaivosa, but there is a real air of excitement in the Douro that this extraordinary terrain can now express itself in two such different sorts of wine.

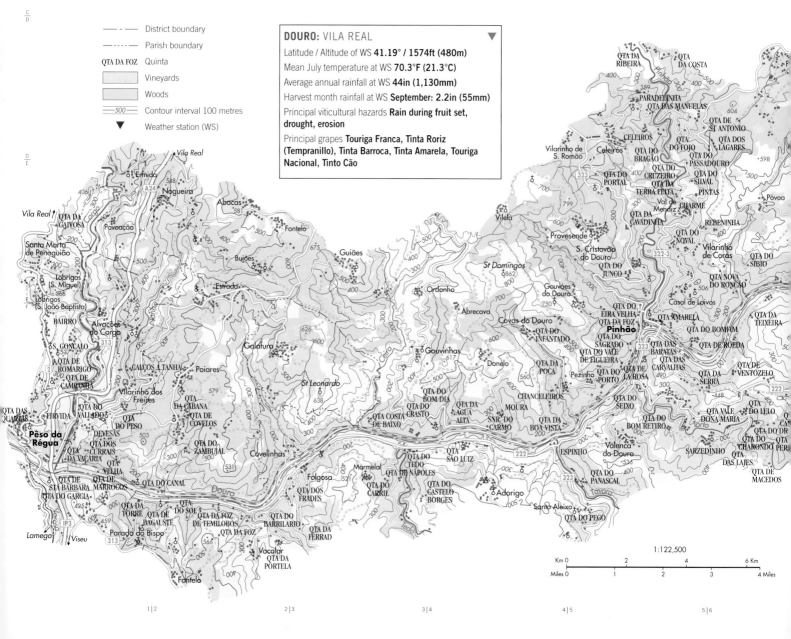

District boundary
Parish boundary
QTA DA FOZ Quinta
Vineyards
Woods
—500— Contour interval 100 metres
▼ Weather station (WS)

DOURO: VILA REAL ▼
Latitude / Altitude of WS **41.19° / 1574ft (480m)**
Mean July temperature at WS **70.3°F (21.3°C)**
Average annual rainfall at WS **44in (1,130mm)**
Harvest month rainfall at WS **September: 2.2in (55mm)**
Principal viticultural hazards **Rain during fruit set, drought, erosion**
Principal grapes **Touriga Franca, Tinta Roriz (Tempranillo), Tinta Barroca, Tinta Amarela, Touriga Nacional, Tinto Cão**

1:122,500

Km 0   2   4   6 Km
Miles 0   1   2   3   4 Miles

The Symington family, major port producers, are particularly proud of their "robotic lagares", a computer-controlled way of replicating the gentle action of the human foot on freshly picked grapes to extract maximum colour and flavour. Silicon "feet" pass up and down the tray of must at Warre's Quinta da Cavadinha.

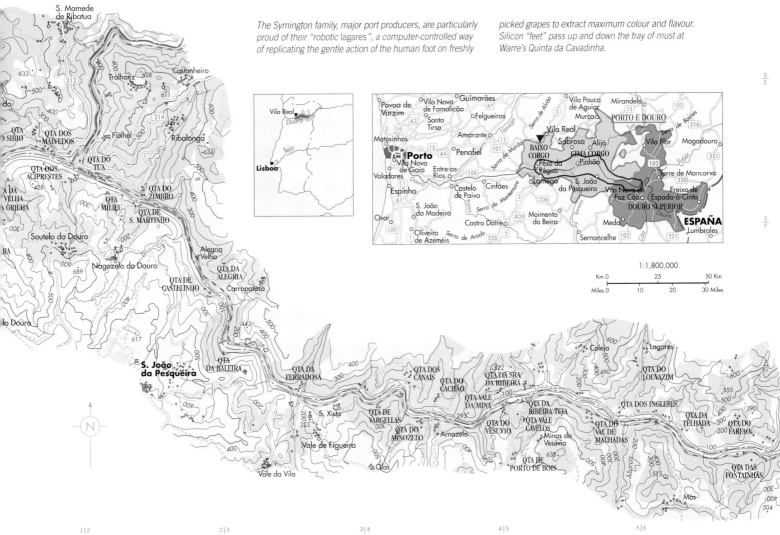

1:1,800,000

Km 0   25   50 Km

Miles 0   10   20   30 Miles

The Port Lodges

The grapes for port may be grown in the savage wilderness of the Douro Valley, but most of the wine is still aged in the huddles of shippers' lodges pictured above in Vila Nova de Gaia across the river from the recently revitalized city of Oporto, Porto in Portuguese, from which the wine takes its name. Before it can be shipped downstream however – in the old days by boat and nowadays by rumbling tanker – those grapes must be transformed into the uniquely strong sweet wine that is port (a protected name).

Port is made by running off partially fermented red wine, while it still contains at least half its grape sugar, into a vessel a quarter full of (often chilled) brandy. The brandy stops the

fermentation so that the resulting mixture is both strong and sweet. But the wine also needs the pigmentation of the grape skins to colour it, and their tannin to preserve it. In normal wines these are extracted during the course of fermentation, but since with port the fermentation is unnaturally short, pigmentation and tannin have to be procured some other way – which traditionally in the Douro means by treading.

Treading is a means of macerating the grape skins in their juice so as to extract all their valuable phenolics. The naked foot is the perfect tool for this, being warm and doing no damage to the pips, which would make the juice bitter if they were crushed. Rhythmically stamping

thigh-deep in the mixture of juice and skins in a broad stone trough (*lagar*) is the traditional treatment for giving port its colour, its grapiness, and its ability to last and improve for many years.

As living standards have risen in Portugal, even in the Douro Valley, most port producers, or shippers, have introduced some sort of mechanical substitute for treading, typically an autovinifier, a specially adapted closed fermenting vat which automatically pumps new wine over the skins – although more authentic and more recent alternatives include the various computer-controlled operations such as "robotic *lagares*" (see p.219). Some of the finest

The cramped port lodges of Vila Nova de Gaia at dawn viewed from across the river in Oporto, which is now a thoroughly modern tourist destination. The city boasts a number of attractive restaurants, bars, and cafés such as the one pictured below right, heavily branded by one of the many Portuguese port shippers whose wines are no longer also-rans, even if they may not (yet) have built up international reputations.

THE PORT LODGES OF VILA NOVA DE GAIA

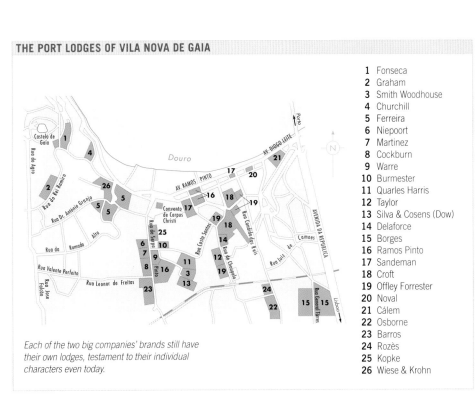

1	Fonseca
2	Graham
3	Smith Woodhouse
4	Churchill
5	Ferreira
6	Niepoort
7	Martinez
8	Cockburn
9	Warre
10	Burmester
11	Quarles Harris
12	Taylor
13	Silva & Cosens (Dow)
14	Delaforce
15	Borges
16	Ramos Pinto
17	Sandeman
18	Croft
19	Offley Forrester
20	Noval
21	Cálem
22	Osborne
23	Barros
24	Rozès
25	Kopke
26	Wiese & Krohn

Each of the two big companies' brands still have their own lodges, testament to their individual characters even today.

ports are still treated to the much more expensive, old-fashioned treading however, and this harvest ritual still takes place in some quintas, particularly in the best area, the Cima Corgo (mapped on the previous two pages).

Most port is shipped downstream in the spring to Vila Nova de Gaia, before the sweltering summer can imbue the young wine with a character known as "Douro bake". As the traffic in the narrow streets becomes worse, though, and electricity for air conditioning becomes more reliable up the Douro, more and more port is being kept and matured where it is made.

The city of Oporto and Vila Nova de Gaia across the river were once rich in English influence, with the port trade dominated by English and Anglo-Portuguese families and Oporto's handsome Georgian Factory House the weekly meeting place for British port shippers for centuries.

Across the river the port lodges with their dusty stacks of ancient, blackened barrels have much in common with the sherry bodegas. Superior tawny port is matured in barrels called pipes containing 550–600 litres (a pipe as a notional unit of commercial measurement is 534 litres), for anything from two to 50 years. Better-quality ports, in which the shipper looks for less evident signs of oxidation and woody flavour, are aged in larger vats.

Perhaps three years out of 10 conditions are near perfect for port-making. The best wine of these years needs no blending; nothing can improve it except time. It is bottled at two years like red Bordeaux, labelled simply with its shipper's name and the date. This is vintage port, and it is made in tiny but much-heralded quantities. Eventually, perhaps after 20 years, it will have a fatness and fragrance, richness and delicacy which are incomparable – although an increasing proportion of vintage port today is being drunk much younger than this, with no visible ill effects.

A great vintage port, preferably fully mature, is incontestably among the world's very best wines. Most other port, from near-vintage standard to merely moderate, goes through a blending process to emerge as a branded wine of a given character. This wine, aged in wood, matures in a different way, more rapidly, to something much mellower. A very old wood port is comparatively pale ("tawny" is the term) but particularly smooth. The best aged tawnies, usually labelled 10 or 20 years (although other permitted age claims are 30 and Over 40 years), can cost as much as vintage ports; many people prefer their gentleness to the full, fat fieriness which vintage port can retain for decades. Chilled tawny is the standard drink of port shippers.

Ports labelled Colheita (Portuguese for "harvest") are wood-aged ports from a single year, expressive tawnies which may be drunk at any point after the bottling date, which should appear on the label.

Run-of-the-mill "wood" ports labelled simply Ruby are not kept for nearly so long, nor would such age reveal any great qualities in them. Inexpensive wines labelled Tawny with no indication of age are usually a blend of particularly emaciated young ruby ports. White port is made in exactly the same way but from white grapes. France is the great market for these wines, although port at its roughest and readiest is the big seller wherever port is sold.

A noticeable notch above these basic ports are those designated Reserve, young rubies with some real guts to them and respectable tawnies bottled at under 10 years old.

As the making of vintage port does not reach its end until after bottling, the sediment forms a "crust" on the side of the bottle, generally a thicker sediment than is found in red bordeaux but one that should be separated from the wine by decanting. A port sold as a crusted or crusting port is a blend of different years bottled early enough to be sure of throwing a heavy sediment in bottle. Like vintage port, it demands a decanter.

The more common compromise between vintage and wood port is the extremely varied Late Bottled Vintage (LBV) category – port kept in barrel for four to six years, and bottled once it has rid itself of its crust. Accelerated and cleaned in this way, it is the modern man's vintage port. Most commercial LBVs have nothing like the character of vintage port, but both Warre and Smith Woodhouse produce a serious LBV, made just like vintage port but bottled after four rather than two years. They too demand decanting.

◄ The two big exporters of top-quality port are the Symington family, represented by the first four labels on the left of the previous page, and the Taylor Fladgate Partnership whose standard-bearers appear on this page. In between the two rivals are three other, very different top performers.

Madeira

The ancients knew these old off-shore volcanoes as the Enchanted Isles. They cluster 400 miles (640km) off the coast of Morocco, right in the path of sailing ships crossing the Atlantic, their modern names Madeira, Porto Santo, and the Desertas. Madeira (the only one mapped here) is the largest of the little archipelago and one of the prettiest islands in the world, as steep as an iceberg and as green as a glade.

The story goes that when the Portuguese landed on the island (in 1419, at Machico in the east) they set fire to the dense woods that gave the island its name. The fire burned for years, leaving the already fertile soil enriched with the ashes of an entire forest.

Certainly it is fertile today. From the water's edge to over halfway up the 6,000ft (1,800m) peak it is steadily terraced to make room for patches of vine, sugarcane, corn, beans, potatoes, bananas, and little flower gardens. As in northern Portugal the vines are grown in arbours, making room for yet more cultivation beneath. Hundreds of miles of *levadas*, little irrigation canals, distribute water from the peaks to the crops.

Wine has been the principal product of the Madeira Islands for 400 years. From the outset, the settlers saw them as an extension of sweet-wine vineyards to be found much further east on Crete and the Aegean Islands, the sources of Malmsey that were being enveloped by the Ottoman Empire. Porto Santo, low, sandy, and with a North African climate, looked much more promising than tall, green, rainy Madeira.

The settlers planted Porto Santo with the Malvasia grape (which is named after the southern Greek port of Monemvasia), concentrated its sugar in the sun, and found a ready market for the sweet wine that resulted – even at the court of François I of France.

The planting of Madeira itself – with both vines and sugarcane – came later. Settlement of the American colonies meant increased traffic and trade and the bigger island, with its port of Funchal, became the victualling place for westbound ships. Conditions here are very different from those on Porto Santo; rain is rarely far off, especially on the north coast unprotected from the winds off the Atlantic; Malvasia, Verdelho, and the other vines introduced often struggled to ripen. The marriage of sugar with acid and astringent wines was an obvious expedient.

The sweet-and-sour result was more than adequate as ballast on sailing ships, and an effective anti-scurvy protection into the bargain. It was travelling as ballast that made madeira. A bucket or two of brandy (or cane spirit) fortified it for its long sea voyages. One crossing of the equator would finish off any normal wine, but it was found to mellow madeira wonderfully – and a double equator crossing even more so. In the 18th century it became the favourite wine of the American colonies. Savannah, Georgia was famous for its madeira merchants and connoisseurs

Instead of long hot sea voyages, madeira today is subjected to (gentle) ordeal by fire. An effect similar to the tropical heat is produced by warming the wine to 120°F (45°C) in hot stores (*estufas*) for at least three months. (More moderate temperatures for longer periods are better; best is no artificial heat at all, but many years initially in a sun-baked loft and then in a warm wine lodge.) When it comes out it has the faintly caramel tang by which all madeiras can be recognized. Too much of a burnt sugar taste means that the *estufa* was too hot.

Today Madeira shippers blend their wine into consistent brands, most of them using the *estufagem* process. But some finer wines gain their complexity by barrel ageing alone, a process called *canteiro* after the racks on which barrels were stacked. Madeira was originally blended by a solera system like that used for sherry, a practice once again allowed by the EU. Some older bottled solera wines are very fine, if you can find them, but the very highest quality of madeira, as of port, has traditionally been the reserve wine of a single vintage – and, in the case of madeira, of a single grape variety.

Increasingly popular commercially are Colheita madeiras, made from the produce of a single year and bottled after spending five years in wood. If there is no grape variety on the label it will have been made from Tinta Negra Mole, the grape variety that invaded the island after the double disaster of oidium in the 1850s and phylloxera in the 1870s. The Russian Revolution and American Prohibition almost put an end to madeira, and for a long while interrupted the flow of good-quality wine. The vineyards were largely turned over to American hybrids (Black Spanish, the chief one, is known in Madeira as Jacquet), while the classic varieties became rarities. The most

planted vinifera vine was the Tinta Negra Mole, which today accounts for about 90% of all grapes grown on the island.

The practice until Portugal joined the EU in 1986 was to cite the classic vine varieties of Madeira on labels whether the wine was really made from them or (more likely) not. Today, unless made from one of the traditional varieties, they must be labelled simply according to age (3, 5, 10, and 15 years) and style (dry, medium, and rich, for example), nowadays generally determined, as in port production, by when the fermentation is halted by the addition of spirit.

The traditional grape varieties are associated with a particular level of sweetness. The sweetest of the four, and the earliest-maturing, is Malmsey or Malvasia: dark brown wine, very fragrant and rich, soft textured and almost fatty, but with the sharp tang that all madeiras have. Bual (the most planted white grape on the island) madeira is lighter and slightly less sweet than Malmsey – but still definitely a dessert wine. A smoky note steals in to modify its richness. Verdelho is made less sweet and softer

◄ The most exciting madeiras often have stencilled bottles rather than labels. Vintage-dated madeiras such as the Blandy's are a relatively recent modern phenomenon and those carrying the names of the traditional grape varieties represent the elite.

MADEIRA: FUNCHAL ▼

Latitude / Altitude of WS **32.41°C / 164ft (50m)**
Mean July temperature at WS **70.9°F (21.6°C)**
Average annual rainfall at WS **25in (640mm)**
Harvest month rainfall at WS **September: 1.2in (30mm)**
Principal viticultural hazard **Fungal diseases**
Principal grapes **Tinta Negra Mole, Verdelho, Sercial, Malvasia, Bual**

than Bual. The faint honey and distinct smoke of its flavour make it good before or after meals. The tiny plantings of the Sercial (Cerceal on the mainland) vine, which makes the driest, most revitalizing wine of Madeira, are in the island's highest vineyards and are harvested late. Sercial wine, the slowest-developing of them all, is light, fragrant, distinctly sharp – unpleasantly astringent young, in fact – but marvellously appetizing old. It is more substantial than a fino sherry, but still a perfect apéritif. A small but noticeable revival of the historic Terrantez vine variety is also underway.

To be labelled Vintage, a madeira must be from a single year, of a single variety, and aged in cask for at least 20 years. In practice the very finest wines may spend a century undergoing the slowest of oxidations in the barrel, or decanted into glass demijohns, before being bottled. In bottle they develop at a snail's pace.

Vintage madeira is a wine that age seems unable to exhaust or diminish. The older it is the better it is – and an opened bottle of virtually any good madeira can retain its freshness for months, even years.

Despite its steepness, the island of Madeira can offer great walks along the contour lines between the tiny plots of mixed agriculture, including viticulture, as here on the typically terraced hillside at Garachico, Câmara de Lobos, just west of the capital Funchal.

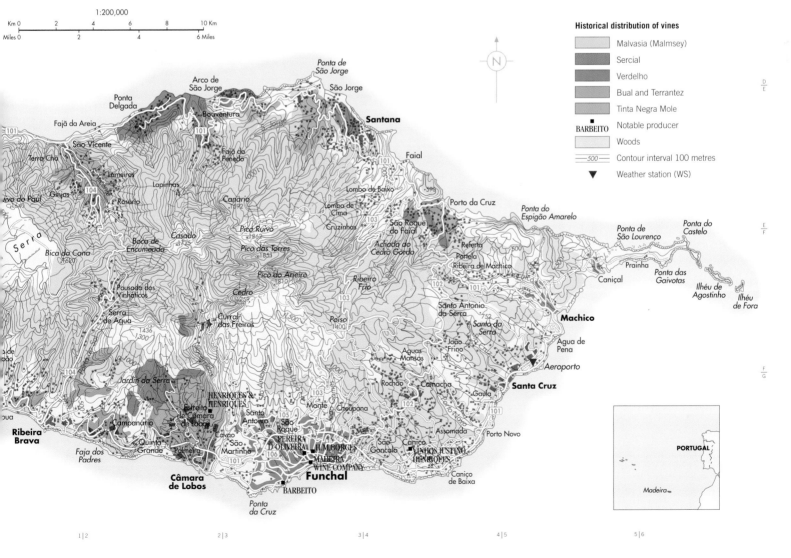

Historical distribution of vines

Malvasia (Malmsey)
Sercial
Verdelho
Bual and Terrantez
Tinta Negra Mole
BARBEITO Notable producer
Woods
500 Contour interval 100 metres
Weather station (WS)

PORTUGAL

Madeira

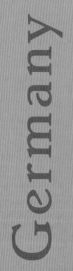
Germany

Harvested Riesling grapes being winched up the steep slopes of Weingut Dr. H Thanisch's Doctor vineyard, high above the town of Bernkastel-Kues, Mosel.

Germany

However you account for it, Germany's wine industry has been through a crisis of morale lasting a generation. Forty years ago white wines from its Riesling grapes were acknowledged the world's best. Today, for some, Australia or New Zealand is a more fashionable choice, but German wine has steadily been working its way back into international favour. A new generation of growers has taken up the reins. Its interpretation of its country's great traditions is turning the tide in Germany's favour again.

Most of Germany's best vineyards lie as far north as grapes can be persuaded to ripen. Many are on land unfit for normal agriculture: if there were no vines there would be forest and bare mountain. All in all their chances of giving the world's best white wine look slim. And yet they do, and stamp it with a racy elegance that no-one, anywhere, can imitate.

Their secret is the balance of two ingredients that sound, on the face of it, unappealing: sugar and acidity. Sugar without acid would be flat; acid without sugar would be sharp. But in good years the two are so finely counterpoised that they have the inevitability of great art. They provide the stage for a stirring fusion of essences from the grape and the ground that is more apparent in German wines than any others, perhaps because they are generally unadorned by such winemaking layers as malolactic fermentation, lees stirring, and ageing in new oak and are therefore more brilliantly transparent. Thanks to all that acidity, the best also age magnificently – far better than most other white wines.

Germany's sweeter wines are best enjoyed, unlike most wines, alone in all their glory rather than with food. They are delicate ferments, often stopping at a mere 8% alcohol, retaining much of the natural grape sugar in the wine. But this has been seen as a commercial handicap. The result? Far drier German wines; growers making many, sometimes all, of their wines completely or almost completely dry and offering them as wines for the table like any others. In 2005, a vintage that if anything favoured fruitier wines, 59% of all German wine was classified *trocken* (dry) or *halbtrocken* (medium dry).

Since the vogue for *trocken* wines began in the early 1980s the genre has advanced from thin productions (early examples of fully dry Mosel Kabinett were painfully tart) to wines of firm and convincing elegance; principally dry Spätlesen or wines labelled Grosses Gewächs (Erstes Gewächs in the Rheingau). These command enormous respect and high prices within Germany and are gradually winning friends abroad.

Germany's determined new generation of growers, inspired by the potential of historically glorious vineyard sites and often influenced by their peers in very distant countries, has also been helped by the effects of climate change. Whereas this has been a largely malign influence closer to the equator, in Germany the effects have so far been beneficial. Grapes are much easier to ripen fully and the threat of rot and other vine diseases is no longer routine. German dry wines with 12–14% alcohol are now common and the result in the right hands is wines with much more character and flavour, even if many winemakers are aware that an excess of

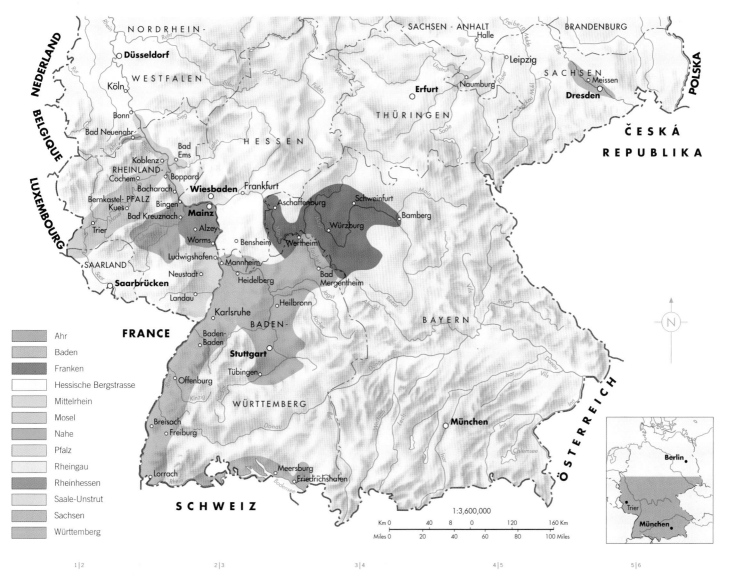

Ahr
Baden
Franken
Hessische Bergstrasse
Mittelrhein
Mosel
Nahe
Pfalz
Rheingau
Rheinhessen
Saale-Unstrut
Sachsen
Württemberg

1:3,600,000

Km 0   40   8   0   120   160 Km

Miles 0   20   40   60   80   100 Miles

alcohol can make German wines unbalanced, tasting dangerously hot or oily.

While German wine's image abroad was for long seriously damaged by the vast quantities of sugar water exported from Germany under such names as Liebfraumilch and Niersteiner Gutes Domtal, this sort of bulk wine is now in retreat. And not a minute too soon.

The German wine label (see panel), one of the most explicit yet confusing on earth, has been both cause and instrument of some of the industry's problems. The most regrettable deception was the legal creation of Grosslagen, commercially useful, large geographical units whose names are indistinguishable to most wine drinkers from those of Einzellagen, individual vineyards. But these are playing a dwindling role in the dynamic German wine scene. Progressive producers are finding more internationally acceptable (and indeed accurate) ways of labelling their wines.

Riesling (see p.20) is the great grape of Germany. A very significant proportion of Germany's best wines are made from it, and it is planted to the exclusion of almost everything else in the best sites of the Mosel-Saar-Ruwer, Rheingau, Nahe, and Pfalz. In a lesser site in a lesser year it stands no chance of ripening.

For larger and less risky production, Germany turned during the mid-20th century to Müller-Thurgau, a much earlier ripening, more productive crossing, bred in 1882. Although there has been a certain limited renaissance of the variety in Franken and around the Bodensee in the far south of Germany, Müller-Thurgau generally produces rather soft, bland wines that lack the lovely backbone of fruity acidity of the Riesling. In 1996 lovers of fine German wine had the satisfaction of seeing Riesling regain its rightful place as Germany's most planted vine and by 2005 Müller Thurgau's share of Germany's total vineyard area had fallen to just over 14%. Nevertheless standard cheap German wines with no mention of the grape on the label can be assumed to be made (at least mainly) from Müller-Thurgau.

Silvaner is now the third most planted vine for white wine, far behind these two varieties, but historically important, especially in Franken, where it makes better wine than Riesling. Silvaner brings a hint of earth and vegetation that can be coarse, but on its favourite soil type of limey clay it seems to seize the minerals to become almost like Chablis. In Franken it represents 21% of vines planted, in Rheinhessen 10%.

On many sites in Baden and some sites in the Pfalz, Grauburgunder (Pinot Gris) and Weissburgunder (Pinot Blanc) are valued above any other variety. Their fuller-bodied whites have enjoyed huge popularity in Germany in the late 20th and early 21st centuries – not least because hotter summers have given wines full enough to withstand ageing in small oak barrels, a novelty that has been welcomed.

But the most notable development in Germany's varietal make-up in the last 10 years or so has been the rise in popularity of German red wine. Plantings of Spätburgunder (Pinot Noir) have tripled in a generation so that in terms of total plantings it does not lag far behind Müller-Thurgau. And Germany's fourth most planted variety is the 1956 crossing Dornfelder, which makes particularly appetizing red wine in the Pfalz. Roughly 40% of all Germany's vineyards are now planted with red wine grapes: a revolution.

These new plantings of red wine vines have been very largely at the expense of the crossings, bred to boost ripeness levels in white wines, that enjoyed a great vogue in the early 1980s, particularly in Rheinhessen and the Pfalz. Two factors dampened early enthusiasm for them: their strident, over-obvious flavours, and the experience of very cold winters when they proved less hardy than the Riesling. This has encouraged Germany's indefatigable vine breeders to incorporate genes from cold-hardy Mongolian vines for some even newer crossings.

Kerner and Scheurebe are the most popular, and refined, of the established light-skinned crossings. But Germany is also planting newly created red wine vines, such as the rot-resistant Regent, already by 2005 planted on more than 5,000 acres (2,000ha). Cabernet Cubin is another, a cross between Cabernet Sauvignon and Lemberger bred at the Weinsberg wine school, which is already enjoying some success in the Pfalz and Württemberg.

For many years German wine law made no attempt to limit yields (which are some of the highest in the world) or to classify vineyards as the French do, but this has changed, at least within the influential VDP (Verband Deutscher Prädikatsweingüter), the association of 200 top growers. The VDP sets its members strict limits on permitted yields, and has even undertaken the politically extremely sensitive task of classifying Germany's Erste Lagen (top sites) for grape varieties specified for each region. These of course are limited to its members' holdings and, like any such classification, the VDP's list of top site and variety combinations has attracted a certain amount of criticism. In this book we continue to highlight our own selection of that small proportion of vineyards we consider consistently superior by shading them in lilac and (best of all) purple. This bold vineyard classification was made in collaboration with Germany's consortium of top-quality growers, local wine organizations, and experts, and to a certain extent the VDP, but is not identical to the classification the VDP made in 2000.

▼ Two regions left unmapped in our extensive coverage of Germany's wine regions are the Mittelrhein and the red wine region of the Ahr, represented here by two of their most able exponents. Toni Jost of the Mittelrhein has now spread his wings and owns vines in Walluf in the eastern Rheingau too.

THE LANGUAGE OF THE LABEL

The labels of this irreproachable Nahe producer split the difference between the super-traditional with its coat of arms and the more modern, easy to read examples. Gothic script is disappearing.

QUALITY DESIGNATIONS

Qualitätswein mit Prädikat (QmP) wines made from the naturally ripest grapes. Germany's best sweet wines are QmP although, depending on the character of the vintage, this category can nowdays comprise anything from 24% (1995) to 64% (2003) of the crop. No chaptalization is allowed. The additional Prädikat, or classifications, are in ascending order of ripeness:

Kabinett light, refreshing wines, ideal apéritifs

Spätlese literally "late harvest", meaning riper than Kabinett. Wines can vary from dry and fairly full to sweet and lighter. Can age well

Auslese made from riper grapes than Spätlese, sometimes botrytized, with, usually, some residual sugar. Ageing is essential

Beerenauslese (BA) rare, sweet wines, made from botrytized grapes (*beeren*)

Eiswein wines from grapes high in sugar and acidity concentrated by being frozen on the vine; less rare than TBA

Trockenbeerenauslese (TBA) very rare, very sweet, very expensive wines made from hand-picked grapes fully "dried" (*trocken*) on the vine by botrytis

Qualitätswein bestimmter Anbaugebiete (QbA) literally a "quality wine from a designated wine region", the quality level below QmP which varies enormously. Chaptalization is allowed

Grosses Gewächs (Erstes Gewächs in the Rheingau) VDP designation of top-quality dry wines of at least Spätlese ripeness from a specified top site (Erste Lage)

Classic dry-tasting wines (max 15g/l residual sugar) for everyday drinking made from a single grape variety

Selection superior dry-tasting wines (max 12g/l residual sugar) from a single variety

Landwein Germany's half-hearted answer to Vins de Pays; not a popular designation when QbA is so widely available

Deutscher Tafelwein very small category for the most basic, lightest wine

OTHER COMMON EXPRESSIONS

Amtliche Prüfungsnummer (AP Nr) every lot of wine has to be officially "tested" and gets this test number; the first digit signifies the test station, last two the year of the test

Erzeugerabfüllung or Gutsabfüllung estate bottled

Halbtrocken medium dry

Feinherb popular but unofficial term for medium dry

Trocken dry

Weingut wine estate

Weinkellerei wine company

Winzergenossenschaft/Winzerverein wine-growers' co-op

Mosel

The sinuous River Mosel is acquainted with the reflections of vines all the way from its source in the Vosges Mountains to its union with the Rhine at Koblenz. In France and then Luxembourg it is known as the Moselle. The Mosel's two great vinous side-valleys are the Saar and the Ruwer (see pages 228–29 and 234), famous for their Riesling grown on grey slate. The Mosel's other subregions are the **Obermosel**, where dry Elbling and both Grauburgunder and Weissburgunder are grown on limestone, the **Mittelmosel**, where the grey slate is planted with Riesling and other soil types with other varieties, chiefly Müller Thurgau, and, downriver, **Terrassenmosel**, which is being revitalized with sturdier Rieslings grown on harder, often quartzitic, soils.

Only on near-ideal sites will Riesling ripen this far north. With every twist and turn of the river comes a dramatic change in vineyard potential. In general all the best sites face south and slope steeply down towards the reflective river. But the gradient that makes them the source of some of the finest wine in the world also makes them near impossible to work. Many are seriously threatened by a shortage of vineyard labour as younger Germans are unwilling to spend their working days in the open, fighting gravity, hunched over truculent vines. In recent years often over-qualified vineyard workers have been imported from Eastern Europe, usually but not exclusively Poland, but this may not provide a long-term solution to this perennial problem.

All the great Mosels are made from Riesling, and this fact is increasingly acknowledged by a general uprooting of Müller-Thurgau and conversion of vineyards on less propitious, flat sites to other uses, so that the region's total area of vines has shrunk by about a third between the mid-1990s and the mid-2000s.

Most of the great wine is made between Zell and Serrig on those sections mapped in detail on the pages that follow but see p.233 for details of the increasingly exciting winescape between Zell and Cochem. Downstream of Cochem a particularly high proportion of Riesling is grown. The same is true of its virtual

continuation, the much more patchily planted **Mittelrhein** region along the banks of the Rhine centred on Koblenz.

Upstream of Trier the rolling farmland is regularly under threat from spring frosts and is almost completely devoted to the hardy, historic, if rustic, Elbling vine. Elbling makes light, acid wine, both still and (often lightly) sparkling, both in the Obermosel and in **Luxembourg** across the river. Luxembourg's growers, routine chaptalizers, are even more reliant on Rivaner (Müller-Thurgau) and are increasingly planting such inherently low-acid grapes as Auxerrois. Sparkling wine is their forte.

Vines slope down to the village of Hatzenport just upstream of Löf in the Terrassenmosel. The ripening process here benefits from some light reflected off the river's surface.

▼ Two labels from the town of Winningen, just south of Koblenz, way off the traditional areas mapped in detail. Wines from the steep slate slopes here have been firmly put back on the map by producers such as Heymann-Löwenstein, best known for mineral-laden dry Rieslings, and Knebel, who manages to make fine Trockenbeerenauslesen.

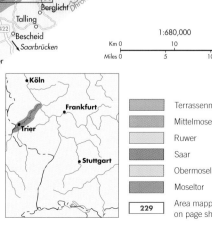

	Terrassenmosel
	Mittelmosel
	Ruwer
	Saar
	Obermosel
	Moseltor
229	Area mapped at larger scale on page shown

1:680,000

Saar

German wine, its problems and its triumphs, is epitomized nowhere better than in the valley of the Mosel tributary the Saar. The battle for sugar in the grapes rages most fiercely in this cold corner of the country. Certainly until the advent of global warming it was won only perhaps three or four years in 10, and even today the sequence of the 1995, 1997, 1998, 2001, 2003, 2004, and 2005 vintages is regarded as exceptional. Yet those years have given one of the world's superlative and inimitable white wines; every mouthful a cause for rejoicing and wonder.

A mere 1,850 acres (750ha) of vines share the valley with orchard and pasture. This is calm, open agricultural country. The map opposite shows more clearly than any other the way the south-facing slopes – here nearly all on steep hills sidling up to the river – offer wine-growers the greatest chance of enough sunshine to reach full ripeness. Unlike the Mittelmosel, the Saar valley is in many parts open to cold easterly winds. You can taste the resulting frisson in the wines.

As in the best parts of the Mosel, the soil is primarily slate and the grape is Riesling. The qualities of Mosel wine – apple-like freshness and bite, a marvellous mingling of honey in the scent and steel in the finish – can find their apogee in Saar wine. It is drier here than on the Ruwer, resulting in lower yields and more restrained aomas. If anything, the emphasis here is more on the steel than the honey.

In (increasingly rare) unsuccessful vintages even the best growers may have to sell their produce to the makers of sparkling Sekt, who need high acidity in their raw material. But when the sun shines and the Riesling ripens and goes on ripening far into October, even November, the great waft of flowers and honey which it generates would be almost too lush were it not for the rapier-like acidity. Then the Saar comes into its own. It makes sweet wine that you can never tire of: the balance and depth make you sniff and sip and sniff again.

Superlative sites are few. Most are in the hands of rich and ancient estates that can afford to wait for good years and make the most of them. The most famous estate of the Saar is that of Egon Müller, whose house appears on the map as Scharzhof at the foot of the Scharzhofberg in Wiltingen, pictured above. Müller's finest are among the world's most expensive white wines.

Geltz Zilliken singlehandedly demonstrated the greatness of the Rausch vineyard across the river from Saarburg, while rising stars include the über-traditionalist Van Volxem (Müller's neighbour in Wiltingen; he makes

Looking south from the Scharzhofberg vineyard, which nowadays produces a wide range of styles of Riesling, from classic fruity Auslesen and even sweeter wines low in alcohol to the strong, dry wines of Van Volxem that recall a past age, from what he calls "Germany's Montrachet".

only what he calls "harmonic" dry wines), Herrenberg in Schoden, and von Othegraven in Kanzem. Von Kesselstatt owns part of the Scharzhofberg vineyard while St Urbanshof in Leiwen (see p.230) also makes superior Saar Rieslings. Egon Müller also manages the Le Gallais estate, with the famous Braune Kupp vineyard, at the other end of Wiltingen.

Many of the Mosel's vineyards, particularly in the Saar, belong to a group of religious and charitable bodies in Trier. The Friedrich-Wilhelm-Gymnasium (Karl Marx's old school), the Bischöfliches Konvikt (a Catholic boarding school), the Bischöfliches Priesterseminar (a college for priests), the Vereinigte Hospitien (an almshouse), and the cathedral are all important wine-growers. The two Bischöfliches and the cathedral operate their total of 260 acres (105ha) of vineyards, here and in the Middle Mosel, together as the Vereinigte Bischöfliches Weingut. In their deep, damp Roman cellars in the city one has the feeling that wine is itself an act of charity rather than mere vulgar trade.

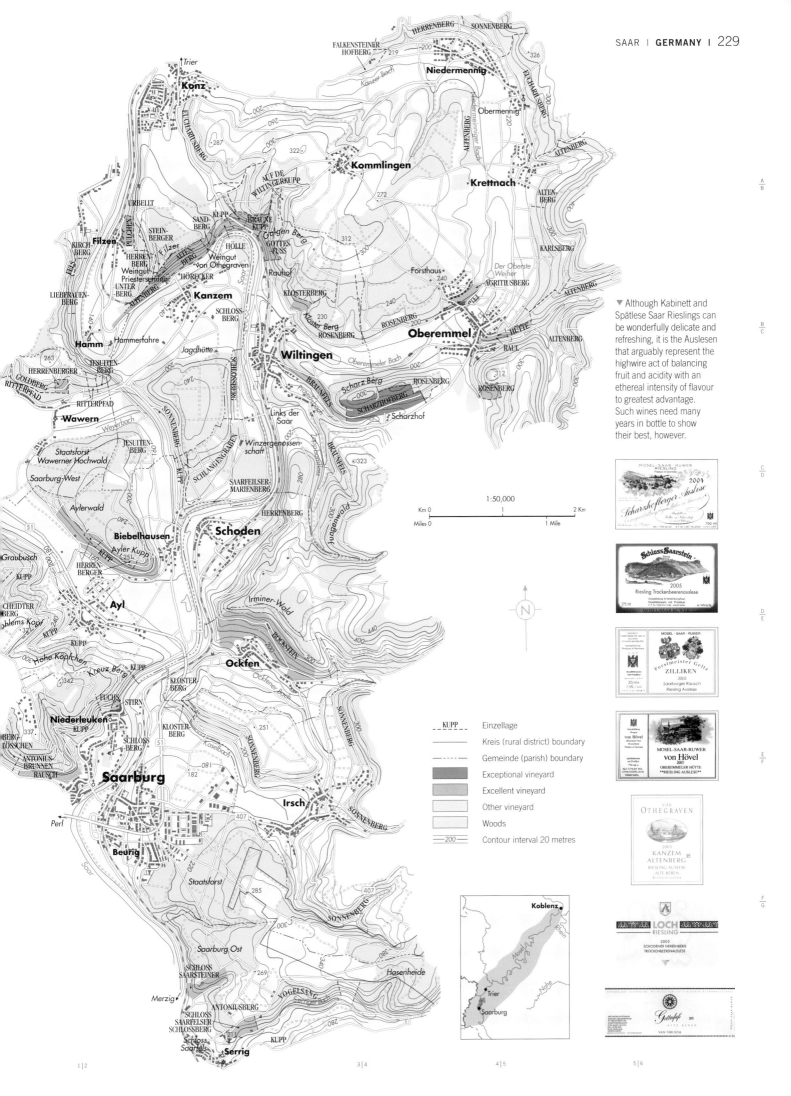

▼ Although Kabinett and Spätlese Saar Rieslings can be wonderfully delicate and refreshing, it is the Auslesen that arguably represent the highwire act of balancing fruit and acidity with an ethereal intensity of flavour to greatest advantage. Such wines need many years in bottle to show their best, however.

1:50,000

Km 0   1   2 Km
Miles 0   1 Mile

KUPP   Einzellage

          Kreis (rural district) boundary

          Gemeinde (parish) boundary

          Exceptional vineyard

          Excellent vineyard

          Other vineyard

          Woods

—200—   Contour interval 20 metres

Middle Mosel: Piesport

The spectacular river walls of slate mapped here, rising over 700ft (200m) in places, were first planted by the Romans in the 4th century. They provide perfect conditions for the Riesling vine, introduced here in the 15th century and firmly rooted in the best sites during the 18th.

The wines of the river vary along its banks even more than, say, the wines of Burgundy vary along the Côte d'Or. But all the best sites face south, held up to the sun like toast to a fire. So hot are these vineyards in midsummer that working in them after noon is unthinkable. The vineyards also benefit both from the hill north of Minheim, which effectively closes this stretch of the valley to cold eastern winds, and the wooded slopes above the vineyards, which exude cold air at night, encouraging dramatic differences between day and night temperatures and retaining acid and aroma in the wines.

There is no formal agreement on what constitutes the Mittel (Middle) Mosel. In the maps on these pages we have extended it (where space allowed) beyond the central and most famous villages to include several whose wine is often underrated.

One obvious candidate is Thörnich, whose Ritsch vineyard has been brought to glorious life by Carl Loewen. Another in this category is Klüsserath just downstream, where Weingut

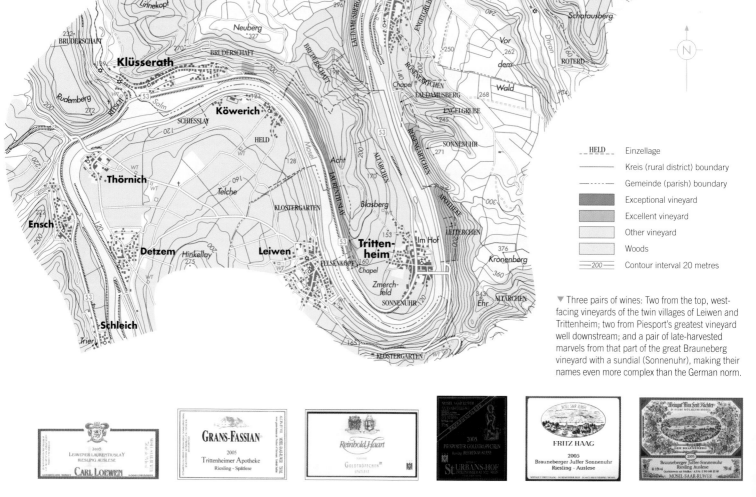

▼ Three pairs of wines: Two from the top, west-facing vineyards of the twin villages of Leiwen and Trittenheim; two from Piesport's greatest vineyard well downstream; and a pair of late-harvested marvels from that part of the great Brauneberg vineyard with a sundial (Sonnenuhr), making their names even more complex than the German norm.

HELD — Einzellage
—— Kreis (rural district) boundary
----- Gemeinde (parish) boundary
Exceptional vineyard
Excellent vineyard
Other vineyard
Woods
—200— Contour interval 20 metres

Kirsten has been making exceptional wines from the Bruderschaft vineyard, a typical Mosel steep bank curving from south to southwest. The long tongue of land which ends in Trittenheim is almost a cliff where the village of Leiwen jumps the river to claim the vineyard of Laurentiuslay – of which fine examples abound, thanks to a concentration of ambitious young vintners here.

The best-exposed site of Trittenheim is the Apotheke vineyard, which lies over the bridge next to Leiterchen, a monopoly of Weingut Milz. Like many sites here the vineyards are so steep that a monorail is necessary to work them. These are the first vineyards of the Mosel, travelling downstream, that have for long made wine of indisputable breed: always delicate but not faint.

The town of Neumagen, a Roman fort and landing place, keeps in its little leafy square a remarkable Roman carving of a Mosel wine ship, laden with barrels and weary galley slaves. The wines of Dhron, its partner, are slightly better known, particularly Dhroner Hofberger on some of the village's steepest slopes. Reinhold Haart is the outstanding producer here with fine holdings in the south-facing bowl of vines that is Piesporter Goldtröpfchen. Its dramatic amphitheatre gives Piesport a standing far above its neighbours. Its honeyed wines have magical fragrance and breed, which can, thanks to the particularly deep clay-like slate here, exude almost baroque aromas. According to our classification, half of the slopes can be regarded as exceptional, half as excellent.

Michelsberg is the Grosslage (amalgam of vineyards) name for this part of the river, from Trittenheim to Minheim. "Piesporter Michelsberg", therefore, has not normally been Piesporter at all – typical of how Grosslagen names, fortunately in retreat, have misled the consumer.

Wintrich and Kesten can all make fine wines. But there are no perfectly aligned slopes in this stretch until the beginning of the great ramp that rises to its full height opposite the village of Brauneberg. In Kesten it is called Paulinshofberg. In Brauneberg it is the Juffer and Juffer Sonnenuhr (the bit of Juffer with the sundial). One hundred years ago this was reckoned the greatest wine of the Mosel, perfectly satisfying the taste for wine that was full-bodied and golden, a taste that happily is coming back.

A typical Mosel scene: steep vineyards with a thin layer of easily eroded topsoil, in the foreground Piesport's Goldtröpfchen, facing flat, more fertile land on which only very much duller wine can be made. Vineyards on the flat, although much easier to work, are progressively being uprooted.

Middle Mosel: Bernkastel

The view from the ruined castle above Bernkastel (it was blown up by Louis XIV's troops) is of a green wall of vines 700ft (200m) high and 5 miles (8km) long. Only the Douro, in the whole gazetteer of rivers to which the vine is wedded, has anything approaching a comparable sight.

From Brauneberg to the Bernkastel suburb of Kues many of the hills are relatively gentle. One of the more notable wines produced in this stretch is the Eiswein regularly gathered by Max Ferd. Richter from the Helenenkloster vineyard above Mülheim. The top sites are exceptionally steep, however, in Lieser, a village perhaps best known for the grim mansion owned by Thomas Haag's excellent Schloss Lieser estate at the foot of the Rosenlay. In the Niederberg-Helden Schloss Lieser has a perfect south-facing slope. Just downstream, the Bastgen estate in Monzel, near Bernkastel-Kues, makes very good wine from the Weisenstein.

The Mosel's most famous vineyard starts abruptly, rising almost sheer above the gables of the tourist mecca that is Bernkastel; dark slate frowning at slate. The butt of the hill, its one straight south elevation, is the Doctor vineyard. From its flank the proudest names of the Mosel follow one another in unbroken succession. Comparison of the first-growths of Bernkastel with those of Graach and Wehlen, often with wines from the same growers in each place, is a fascinating game. The trademark of Bernkastel is a touch of flint. Wehleners, grown on shallow stony slate, are rich and filigree while those grown on the deeper, heavier slate of Graach have a more earthy, mineral distinction.

The least of these wines should be something with a very obvious personality: pale with a gleam of green and dozens of little bubbles in the bottom of the glass, smelling almost aggressively of grapes, filling and seeming to coat the mouth with sharpness, sweetness, and scent. The greatest of them, long-lived, pale gold, piquant, frivolous yet profound, are wines that beg to be compared with music and poetry.

Many world-famous producers cluster here, although a hike through the vineyards (too steep for a stroll) quickly demonstrates that not all growers here are equally conscientious. JJ Prüm has long been the leading grower of

Wehlen; Erni (Dr) Loosen of Bernkastel has won his reputation more recently. Selbach-Oster and Willi Schaefer also command worldwide respect, while von Kesselstatt continues its excellent work this far downstream too.

Zeltingen brings the Great Wall to an end. It is the Mosel's biggest wine commune, and among its best. At Urzig, across the river, red slate, in rocky pockets instead of a smooth

bank, gives the Würzgarten (spice garden) wines a different flavour, more penetrating and racy than Zeltingers. Erden's finest vineyard, the Prälat, is probably the warmest in the entire Mosel Valley, sandwiched between massive and precipitous red slate cliffs and the river. Loosen makes some of his best wines here. Wines from the Treppchen vineyard are usually more austere.

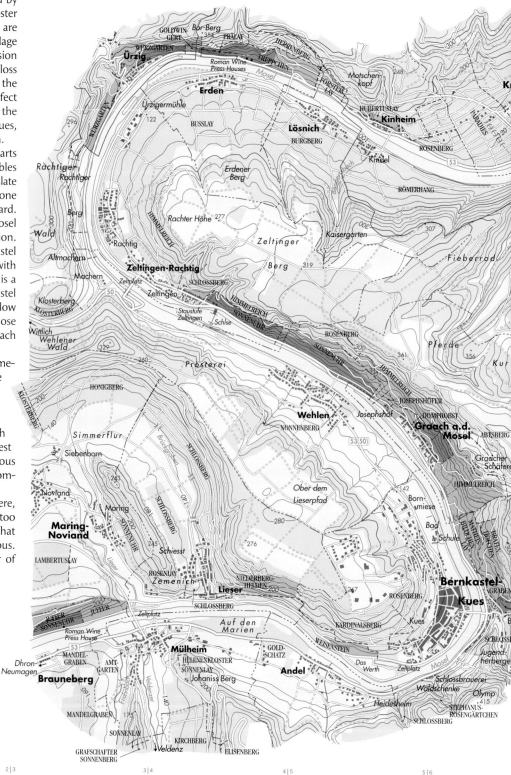

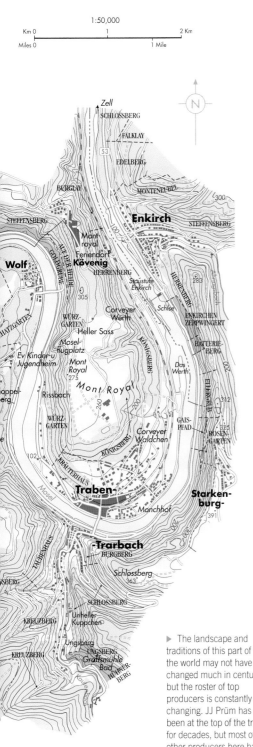

1:50,000

Km 0 — 1 — 2 Km
Miles 0 — 1 Mile

It used to be thought that the drama of Mosel wine ended at Kinheim but a new generation of producers such as Swiss-born Daniel Vollenweider of Wolf, Martin Müllen of Traben-Trarbach, Thorsten Melsheimer in Reil, and Clemens Busch in Pünderich (the latter two off the map to the north) are proving otherwise in a delicious and indeed dramatic way.

The Mittelmosel conventionally ends just downstream from here at Zell (see map on p.227). At this point the landscape changes dramatically, with most of the vineyards planted on narrow terraces, inspiring this lower section of the Mosel Valley's name Terrassenmosel.

Of the many excellent sites here the most important today are the Frauenberg in Neef, Calmont in Bremm, Gäns in Gondorf, and the Uhlen (an exceptional site) and Röttgen of Winningen. Such exciting producers as Heymann-Löwenstein and Knebel in Winningen, Franzen in Bremm, and Lubentiushof in Niederfell provide the proof in bottles of Riesling both sweet and dry.

This decorative fountain in Bernkastel alludes to medieval wine consumption but vines have been grown on the steep banks of the Mosel since at least Roman times, as described by the poet Ausonius in his 4th-century tract Mosella.

▶ The landscape and traditions of this part of the world may not have changed much in centuries, but the roster of top producers is constantly changing. JJ Prüm has been at the top of the tree for decades, but most of the other producers here have made their reputations much more recently.

UNGSBERG	Einzellage
———	Kreis (rural district) boundary
–·–·–·–	Gemeinde (parish) boundary
▓▓	Exceptional vineyard
▒▒	Excellent vineyard
░░	Other vineyard
░░	Woods
—200—	Contour interval 20 metres

Ruwer

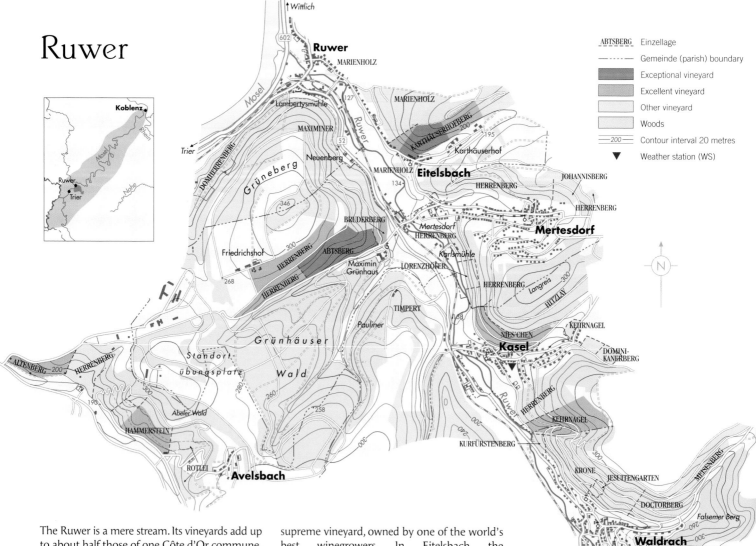

ABTSBERG Einzellage
- - - - Gemeinde (parish) boundary
Exceptional vineyard
Excellent vineyard
Other vineyard
Woods
—200— Contour interval 20 metres
▼ Weather station (WS)

The Ruwer is a mere stream. Its vineyards add up to about half those of one Côte d'Or commune. Before the advent of global warming, there were years when most of its wine was just too faint and sharp. And even today many of the lesser vineyards are being abandoned because their names are not famous enough to justify the work involved. Yet like the Saar, when conditions are right it performs a miracle: its wines are Germany's most delicate; gentle yet infinitely fine and full of subtlety.

Waldrach, the first wine village, makes good light wine but rarely more. Kasel is far more important. The extensive von Kesselstatt estate and the Bischöfliches Weingut of Trier have holdings here. There are great Kaselers in hot years. Unlike so many German wine producers, the great Ruwer estates tend to have a monopoly on the top sites. Karlsmühle of Mertesdorf, for example, are the sole owners of the Lorenzhöfer and can make wines of inspiring precision.

Mertesdorf and Eitelsbach could not be called famous names, but each has one

supreme vineyard, owned by one of the world's best winegrowers. In Eitelsbach the Karthäuserhofberg vineyard extends proudly above an old monastic manor of the same name which makes superlative wines today. Across the stream in Mertesdorf, Maximin Grünhaus echoes that situation, set obliquely to the left bank of the river with the manor house, also formerly monastic property, at its foot. The greater part of its hill of vines is called Herrenberg; the top-quality part Abtsberg (for the abbot) and the less-well-sited part Bruderberg (for the brothers). A subterranean aqueduct, still passable by foot, connects the Grünhaus property with Trier, the Roman (and actual) capital of the Mosel 5 miles (8km) upstream.

Included within the city limits off the map to the southwest is the isolated clearing of Avelsbach, belonging to the State Domain and Trier Cathedral, and the famous old Thiergarten. Avelsbach wine is similar to that of the Ruwer: supremely delicate – sometimes even more perfumed and forthcoming.

RUWER: KASEL ▼
Latitude / Altitude of WS **51.19° / 656ft (200m)**
Mean July temperature at WS **63.5°F (17.5°C)**
Average annual rainfall at WS **23in (590mm)**
Harvest month rainfall at WS **October: 2in (55mm)**
Principal viticultural hazards **Rot, underripeness**
Principal grapes **Riesling, Müller-Thurgau**

◄ Even today many top producers' names reflect the fact that it was the Church and monasteries that maintained viticultural traditions in this part of the world. Both Maximin Grünhaus, with a new winemaker for the new century, and Karthäuserhof have monastic origins and the Bischöfliche Weingüter are, of course, owned by the Church.

1|2   2|3   3|4   4|5   5|6

Rheingau

If the Rhine is one of the world's great wine rivers, it was historically the Rheingau with its castles and abbeys that once represented it most majestically. If the crown of achievement seems to have been ceded to the Pfalz and Rheinhessen today it takes nothing from the potential of this magnificent riverside vineyard. At its best the Rheingau can unite depth, subtlety, and austerity to make the river's noblest wine.

At the western end of the Rheingau the south-facing Rüdesheimer Berg Schlossberg, by far the Rheingau's steepest slope, drops almost sheer to the river. The Rüdesheimer Berg is distinguished from the rest of the parish by having the word Berg before each separate vineyard name. At their best (which is not always in the hottest years, since the drainage is too good at times) these are superlative wines, full of fruit and strength and yet delicate in nuance. In hotter years the vineyards behind the town of Rüdesheim come into their own. Georg Breuer, Johannishof, and Leitz are the outstanding names here.

The Rheingau's white wine output is even more dominated by Riesling than the Mosel's but today 13% of Rheingau vineyards are planted with Spätburgunder (Pinot Noir).

Assmannshausen, round the river bend to the northwest, is no longer the sole red wine outpost.

Ambitious, cosmopolitan growers such as August Kesseler of Assmannshausen revolutionized the colour and structure of such wines, from pale and suspiciously smoky to deep, sturdy, and barrique-aged. Dry red Assmannshäuser Spätburgunder made by the likes of Krone and Robert König is still Germany's most famous red wine, and the Staatsweingut (State Wine Domain) and von Mumm also maintain a high standard. Assmannshausen's extraordinary pink Trockenbeerenauslese is a revered rarity.

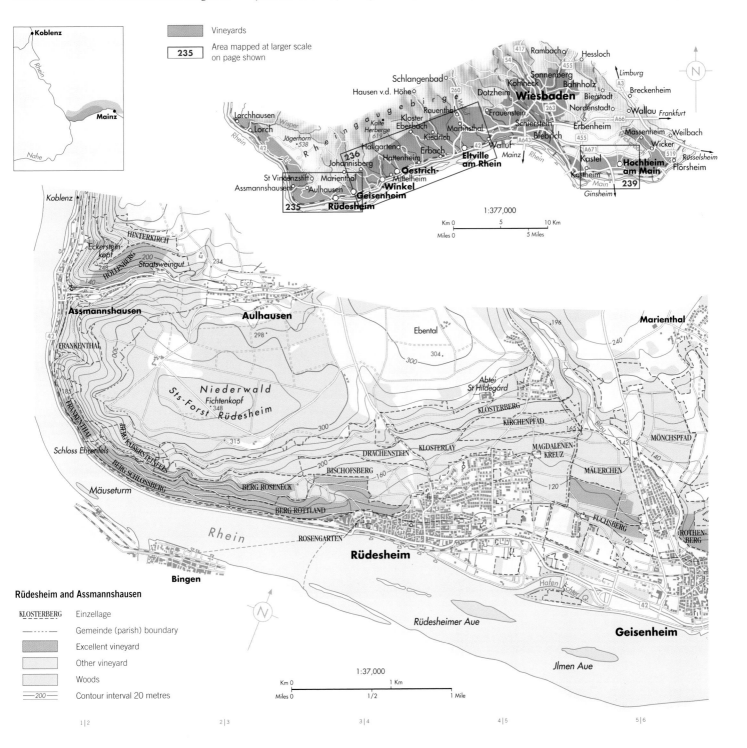

Vineyards

235 Area mapped at larger scale on page shown

1:377,000

Km 0   5   10 Km
Miles 0   5 Miles

Rüdesheim and Assmannshausen

KLOSTERBERG Einzellage

– – – – – Gemeinde (parish) boundary

Excellent vineyard

Other vineyard

Woods

—200— Contour interval 20 metres

1:37,000

Km 0   1 Km
Miles 0   1/2   1 Mile

The Heart of the Rheingau

The Rheingau wines that fetch the highest prices are the super-sweet Beerenauslesen and Trockenbeerenauslesen; wines with another purpose than accompanying food. Its less rare wines had drifted into being sweet too, before its current leaders, like so many of their peers to the south, deliberately moved away from this tradition. By 2005 84% of all Rheingau wine was dry – as it had been 100 years before. The Charta organization of top growers led the way in the 1980s, encouraging low yields and dry wines of Spätlese quality. Since 1999 this torch has been carried by the VDP growers' association, which designates the best of this style as Erstes Gewächs. This is based on their 2000 vineyard classification, which generously deemed a full 35% of all Rheingau vineyards Erste Lagen, or first growths. Rather than follow this classification we indicate on this and other German maps those vineyards that we consider to be superior to others (lilac) and those that are truly outstanding (purple).

The broad stretch of south-facing hillside mapped here, sheltered to the north by the Taunus hills and warmed to the south by reflection from the broad River Rhine, is an obvious place for vine-growing. The river, more than half a mile wide and a throbbing highway for slow strings of enormous black barges, also promotes the mists that encourage botrytis as the grapes ripen. Decidedly mixed soils include various forms of slate and quartzite as well as marls.

Geisenheim at its western end is home to the world-renowned teaching and research centre for oenology and, especially, viticulture. Just upriver and uphill from here is Schloss Johannisberg, standing above a great apron of vines, dominating the landscape between Geisenheim and Winkel. It is credited with the introduction in the 18th century of nobly rotten, sweet rarities to Germany, even if its wines no longer overshadow such neighbours as the Johannishof estate.

Schloss Vollrads, above Winkel, is another magnificent and historic property whose wines are still struggling to reach their full potential. Even Winkel's second-best site, Hasensprung (hare's leap), is capable of richly nuanced, aromatic wine.

Mittelheim lives in the shadow of its neighbours. The best wines of Oestrich, from the Doosberg and Lenchen vineyards, have

real character and lusciousness, whether sweet or dry. Peter Jakob Kühn, Spreitzer, and Querbach make both with distinction.

In Hallgarten the Rheingau vineyards reach their highest point. In the Würzgarten and Schönhell there is marly soil that gives strong, long-lived wines although many regard Jungfer as the finest site. Fürst Löwenstein and Fred Prinz are notable producers.

The boundaries of Hattenheim stretch straight back into the hills to include the high ridge of the Steinberg, the Clos de Vougeot of Germany, founded and walled in the 12th century by the Cistercians. Below in a wooded hollow stands their monastery, Kloster Eberbach, which has in its time been regarded as the headquarters of German wine. Its owners, the State Wine Domain, intent on restoring the Steinberg to full glory, are building it an entirely new winery.

Like Hallgarten, Hattenheim has marl in the soil. Mannberg on its eastern boundary is 90% owned by Langwerth von Simmern. Nussbrunnen and Wisselbrunnen are capable of producing wines just as good. Straddling the

---

RHEINGAU: GEISENHEIM ▼

Latitude / Altitude of WS **49.59° / 377ft (115m)**

Mean July temperature at WS **65.9°F (18.8°C)**

Average annual rainfall at WS **21in (537mm)**

Harvest month rainfall at WS **October: 1.8in (45mm)**

Principal viticultural hazard **Fungal diseases**

Principal grapes **Riesling, Spätburgunder**

1:37,000

Km 0   1   2 Km
Miles 0   1 Mile

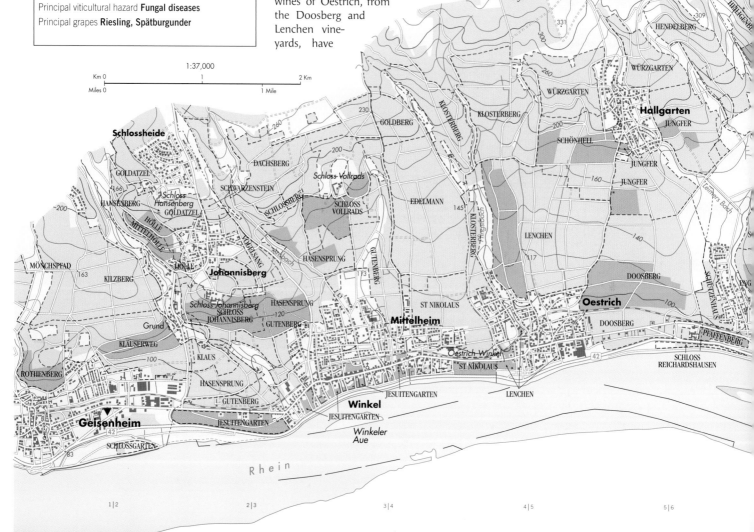

The Kläuserweg vineyard slopes but gently down to the village of Geisenheim, which is so much more famous for its academic institute than its wines. Climate change is a current focus for Geisenheim's researchers; Müller-Thurgau one of its early outcomes.

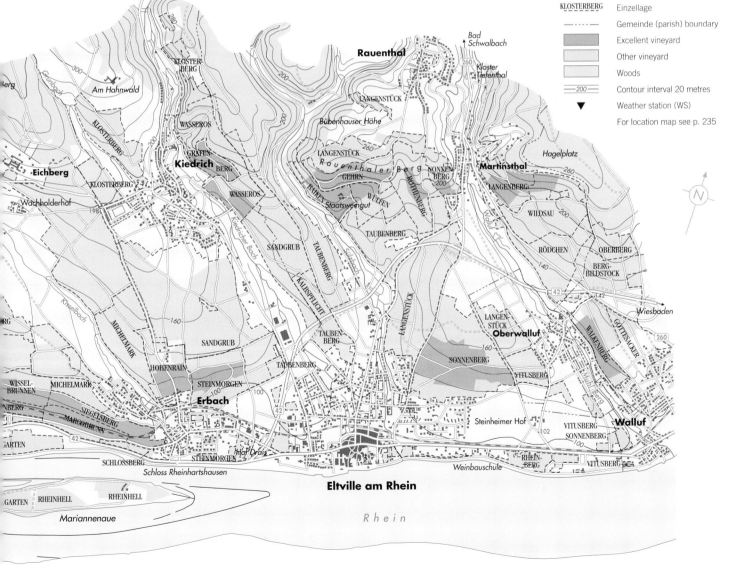

KLOSTERBERG — Einzellage

– – – – Gemeinde (parish) boundary

Excellent vineyard

Other vineyard

Woods

——200—— Contour interval 20 metres

▼ Weather station (WS)

For location map see p. 235

border with Erbach is Marcobrunn, unusually close to the river in a situation that looks as though the drainage would be far from perfect. Wine from either side of the parish boundary is very full flavoured, and often rich, fruity, and spicy. Marcobrunn, heavily influenced by marl, is owned by Schloss Schönborn, Schloss Reinhartshausen, the Staatsweingut, and the Knyphausen estate. Erbacher Siegelsberg, which lies parallel with Marcobrunn, is next in quality.

The beautiful Gothic church of Kiedrich is the next landmark, set back from the river and

▼ The Rheingau's top tier of wine producers is no longer the preserve of ancient aristocratic estates, but now includes an array of hard-working individuals too. Note the triple arches of the Charta organization, founded by Bernhard Breuer for dry wines, along the bottom of the Spreitzer label.

400ft (120m) higher. Kiedrich makes exceptionally well-balanced and delicately spicy wine. Robert Weil (part Japanese-owned) is the biggest estate of the parish and today makes many of the Rheingau's most impressive sweet wines. Gräfenberg is reckoned the best part of the vineyard, although Wasseros is almost its equal. Weil concentrates on its substantial holdings in Gräfenberg and manages to make convincing Trockenbeerenauslesen in enviable quantity.

Rauenthal, the last of the hill villages and the furthest from the river, can make a different kind of superlative wine. The complex Rauenthalers of the estate of the late Bernhard Breuer continue to be some of the most sought-after in Germany. Auslesen from two lordly growers, Baron Langwerth von Simmern and Count Schönborn, as well as those of several smaller

Kloster Eberbach, once a Cistercian abbey and still enjoying splendid isolation in the woods above Hattenheim, has been virtually untouched in its awe-inspiring nearly nine centuries of history. One of its cellars, called the Cabinet, gave rise to the term Kabinett.

growers on the Rauenthaler Berg, are prized for the combination of power and delicacy in their flowery scent and in their spicy aftertaste.

Eltville makes larger quantities of wine but without the supreme cachet. The town has been the headquarters of the Staatsweingut, whose wines (especially Steinbergers) have in the past been among the best.

Without the fame of their neighbours, Walluf and Martinsthal share much of their quality. At Walluf the stars are JB Becker and Toni Jost, the most celebrated producer of the Mittelrhein.

Hochheim

In the far east of the Rheingau, separated from the main stretch of vineyards mapped on the previous pages by the southern suburbs of sprawling Wiesbaden, the Rheingau has an unexpected outpost: Hochheim (which gave us the word hock). Hochheim vineyards lie on gently sloping land just north of the warming River Main, isolated in country that has no other vines. Good Hochheimers, with their own thrilling full-bodied earthiness, thanks to deep soils and an unusually warm mesoclimate, match the quality of the best Rheingauers and the style of those of Nackenheim-Nierstein in Rheinhessen.

Growers such as Franz Künstler and Domdechant Werner have injected new life into a region previously most readily associated with Queen Victoria, whose visit to the source of wines notably popular with her subjects is commemorated by the Königin Victoriaberg vineyard and label.

Kirchenstück grows the most elegant wines while Hölle and Domdechaney produce wines so rich they are distinctly atypical of the Rheingau's elegant signature.

Reiner Flick not only makes excellent dry and sweet wines from the vineyards of Hochheim, he is also putting the historic vineyards of Wicker to the northeast back on the map (see Rheingau map, p.235).

This church (marked on the map below) dominates the Kirchenstück vineyard. Its white walls and red sandstone corners are typical of the Rheingau's solid Gothic style.

▼ Künstler also makes some of the most admired dry Rieslings of the Rheingau from vineyards such as the Kirchenstück, shown on this page, whose wines are so completely and intriguingly different from those made in the Domdechaney vineyard right next door.

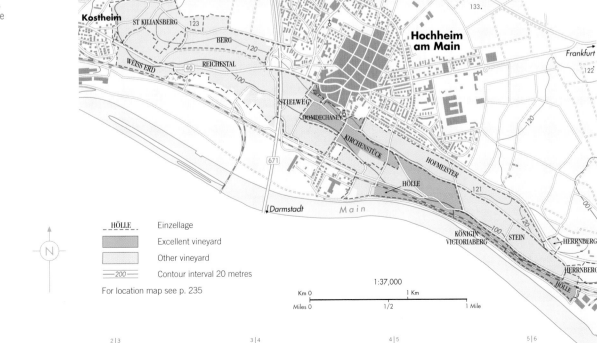

HÖLLE   Einzellage

Excellent vineyard

Other vineyard

—200—   Contour interval 20 metres

For location map see p. 235

1:37,000

Km 0   1 Km

Miles 0   1/2   1 Mile

Rheinhessen

For years Germany's most extensive wine region, in the crook of the Rhine hemmed in by the river on the east and north, the Nahe to the west, and the Pfalz to the south, seemed to be asleep. There was a small number of good producers in and around the famous wine town of Nierstein and a large amount of bland wine made in the rest of the region that went into lacklustre blends sold as Liebfraumilch, Niersteiner Gutes Domtal, and the like.

Today Rheinhessen rivals Pfalz as the most exciting wine region in Germany. By the turn of the century it was apparent that much was set

to change in and around the 150-odd Rheinhessen villages, spaced out over an area 20 by 30 miles (30 by 50km), virtually all named Something-*heim*, where wine is just one crop among many. A group of highly trained and motivated, enviably well-travelled young winemakers, many still in their twenties, have demonstrated that not just the steep terraces right on the Rhine but the dull, undulating, fertile, mixed-farming country in the hinterland can produce wines of thrilling integrity and quality to rival the best that historically more celebrated regions can manage. Many of these younger winemakers belong to organizations such as Message in a Bottle, Rheinhessen Five, and Vinovation, inspired in particular by a remarkable pair of neighbours, Philipp Wittmann and Klaus Peter Keller, in the area around Flörsheim-Dalsheim in the south.

Where the Rheinterrasse (once called the Rheinfront) around Nierstein used to be the only part of Rheinhessen we (or anyone else) troubled to map in detail, this revolution is taking place in villages no one had heard of. Dittelsheim owes its arrival to Stefan Winter, Siefersheim (far to the west in the region known as Rheinhessen's Switzerland) to Wagner-Stempel, Hohen-Sülzen to Battenfeld-Spanier, Bechtheim to Dreissigacker, and Weinheim to Gysler. In many cases they are not so much trailblazing as recovering historic sites, for the vine has been cultivated in Rheinhessen since Roman times. Charlemagne's uncle presented vineyards in Nierstein to the diocese of Würzburg in 742. Riesling (as "Russling") was mentioned here in 1402.

Typically these new wave winemakers are returning to traditional winemaking methods, including most obviously low yields and ambient

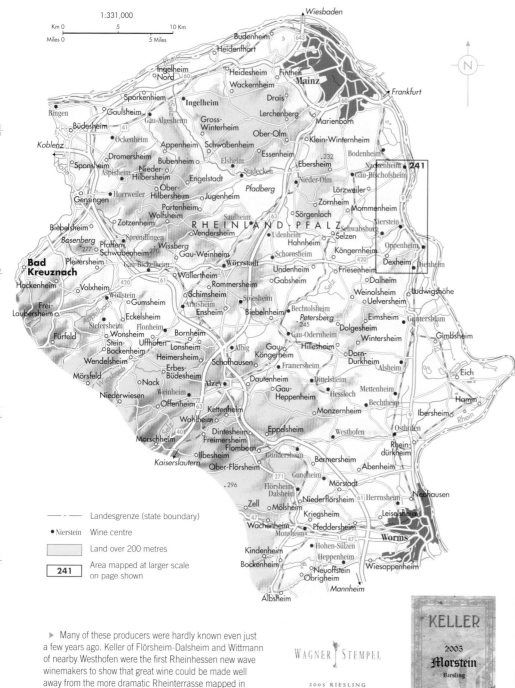

1:331,000

Km 0   5   10 Km
Miles 0   5 Miles

- – - Landesgrenze (state boundary)
- Nierstein   Wine centre
- Land over 200 metres
- 241   Area mapped at larger scale on page shown

▶ Many of these producers were hardly known even just a few years ago. Keller of Flörsheim-Dalsheim and Wittmann of nearby Westhofen were the first Rheinhessen new wave winemakers to show that great wine could be made well away from the more dramatic Rheinterrasse mapped in detail opposite.

Straw mulch between rows of Riesling vines at Freiherr Heyl zu Herrnsheim shows that this historic estate, like so many in ecology-conscious Germany, has been converted to organic viticulture.

rather than added, cultured yeasts. The result is wines that are more intense but reveal their aromas rather more slowly than the German norm. Nor do they limit themselves to Riesling.

No German wine region grows a more varied mix of vines. Even the once ubiquitous Müller-Thurgau today accounts for barely 16% of all Rheinhessen's vineyard. This region was the prime supplier of ingredients for cheap German brands and blends but now even these are likely to incorporate much more Riesling, and therefore less Müller-Thurgau, than used to be the case. Riesling is now Rheinhessen's third most planted variety, though less significant than the Dornfelder which is popular for fruity red wines. Silvaner, Portugieser, Kerner, Spätburgunder (Pinot Noir), Scheurebe, and Grauburgunder can all lay claim to between 9 and 4% of the region's vineyard.

One traditional characteristic persists. Most Rheinhessen wine is still sweeter than *halbtrocken*. Only the Mosel and Nahe produce a lower proportion of dry wine than Rheinhessen – although many of the region's finest new wave wines are bone dry.

Silvaner has a particularly long and noble history in Rheinhessen and can be found today in two distinct styles. The majority is light, fresh, reasonably fruity stuff for early drinking (notably with the early summer white asparagus the locals love). Keller and Wagner-Stempel however make a powerful, earthy, dry version strong on both extract and ageability.

For centuries Worms was one of the great Rhineland cities, seat of the famous "Diet" of 1521 which excommunicated Martin Luther, translator of the Bible into German. Its Liebfrauenstift-Kirchenstück vineyard around the Liebfrauenkirche has the doubtful distinction of having christened Liebfraumilch, the rock on which quality German wine so nearly foundered. But two growers, Schembs and Valckenberg, are now making serious wine from this vineyard.

At the other extreme of Rheinhessen, the town of Bingen, facing Rüdesheim (see p.235) across the Rhine, has excellent Riesling vineyards on the steep slopes of its first-growth Scharlachberg.

To the south, Wonnegau is now home to several good producers, not just of Silvaner, for which it was traditionally known, but also Riesling. Historically, though, the most celebrated

vineyards of Rheinhessen are concentrated in the short stretch of the Rheinterrasse mapped on this page.

The town of Nierstein is perhaps as famous as Bernkastel. This is partly through its size and the number of its growers (once 300; now declining rapidly), originally for its quality, but now principally because its name is widely and shamelessly taken in vain for Niersteiner Gutes Domtal, wine from anywhere except Nierstein. The irony is that Nierstein proper has some superb vineyards, as producers such as Heyl zu Herrnsheim, Kühling-Gillot, and Georg Gustav Huff of Schwabsburg eloquently demonstrate.

The two towns that flank it, Oppenheim and Nackenheim, have vineyards as good as most of Nierstein, but Oppenheim suffers from a dearth of winemaking ambition. The most famous stretch of vineyard here is the sand-red roll of hill, the Roter Hang, going north with the river at its foot. Hipping, Brudersberg, Pettenthal, and Rothenberg (which is in Nackenheim) can make wonderfully fragrant, luscious wine – although too many growers are content to let the vineyard name sell their wares. Gunderloch, run by the Hasselbach family, is the prime exponent of luscious, late-harvested Nackenheim Rothenberg.

Any true Niersteiner will use one of the vineyard names marked on the detailed map. The best are Rieslings, although some fine Weissburgunder and Grauburgunder have also been made here for many years.

Nahe

What would you expect of a region neatly inserted between the Mosel, Rheinhessen, and the Rheingau? Precisely. At their best, Nahe wines capture the grapey intensity of those from the Mosel, and live as long, but also reveal the body and minerality of Rhine wines. Then there is that extra ingredient: a hint of alchemical gold.

The River Nahe flows north parallel to the Mosel, out of the Hunsrück hills, to join the Rhine at Bingen. Whereas the Mosel is the very spine of its vineyards, the Nahe is sur-rounded by scattered outbreaks of wine-growing where either its own banks or its tributaries' face south. The heart of the region, mapped opposite, is the hills upstream of its only considerable town, Bad Kreuznach, once but no longer its leading name. Many of its best wines today come from newly minted areas to the west on the upper Nahe, some

— · —	Landesgrenze (state boundary)
● Norheim	Wine centre
	Land over 300 metres
243	Area mapped at larger scale on page shown

1:256,000

Km 0 — 5 — 10 Km
Miles 0 — 5 — Miles

Every August since 1987 Johannes Helle returns to the Schlossgut Diel in Burg Layen to paint new faces on the tanks in the cellars. This is the artwork for 2006, one of an unusually long series of successful vintages for so much of Germany.

from side-valleys downstream, and nearly all from talented winemakers who have enjoyed international fame only relatively recently. The best vineyards are no easier to work than the Mosel's, however, and the number of growers has been declining.

Those who are left grow the noble Riesling on about a quarter of the total vineyard area, with Müller-Thurgau's grip having been reduced to just 13% of the total vineyard. Dornfelder is the third most planted variety; a good quarter of the region's output is of red wine, sold almost exclusively within Germany. If the majority of white Nahe wine is still made in the fruity sweeter style, the likes of Helmut Dönnhoff of Oberhausen have shown that brilliant dry wines can be made from vineyards such as the Hermannshöhle of Niederhausen.

The most famous sites upstream of the detailed map are 6 miles (10km) west around Monzingen, with two first-class vineyards in the stoney, slatey Halenberg and Frühlingsplätzchen with more red loam and a certain spiciness. Emrich Schönleber is the outstanding producer of dry and sweet wines here, perhaps the Nahe's most brilliant wine-maker after Dönnhoff. Schäfer-Fröhlich is another impressive grower.

The Nahe's most concentrated stretch of great vineyards, mapped in detail here, lies on the left, south-facing bank of the river as it winds around Schloss Böckelheim,

Oberhausen, Niederhausen, and Norheim. They were classified by the Royal Prussian Surveyor in 1901 (on a map revived in the 1990s by the VDP as a blueprint for vineyard quality). Niederhäuser Hermannshöhle was rated first, encouraging the Prussian government to establish a new Staatsweingut (State Wine Domain) here the following year. Scrub-covered arid hillsides and old copper mines were cleared, using convict labour, to create several new vineyard sites, including the towering walls and terraced vineyards of the Schlossböckelheimer Kupfergrube (copper

mine). Since then its wines have challenged those of the long-established Felsenberg for Schlossböckelheim supremacy.

From the 1920s the Nahe Staatsweingut and several large estates based in Bad Kreuznach but with vineyards here produced wines of a brilliance and pungent minerality as spectacular as the rocky landscape. At last, in 1930, the Nahe was recognized as an independent wine-growing region, but the fame of the top growers was always greater than that of the region itself. From the late 1980s the Staatsweingut failed to play the leading role for

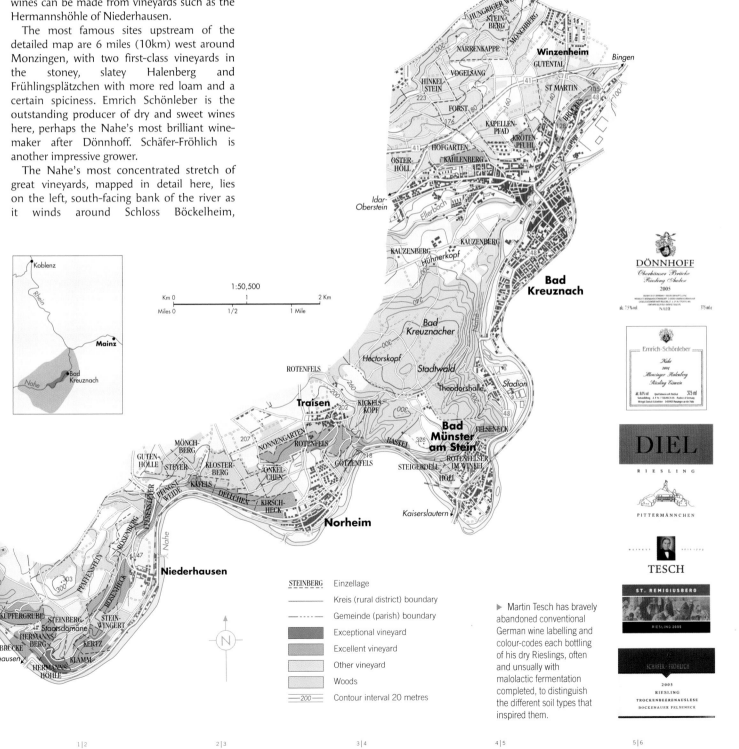

1:50,500

Km 0 — 1 — 2 Km
Miles 0 — 1/2 — 1 Mile

STEINBERG — Einzellage

——————— Kreis (rural district) boundary

----------- Gemeinde (parish) boundary

Exceptional vineyard

Excellent vineyard

Other vineyard

Woods

—200— Contour interval 20 metres

▶ Martin Tesch has bravely abandoned conventional German wine labelling and colour-codes each bottling of his dry Rieslings, often and unusually with malolactic fermentation completed, to distinguish the different soil types that inspired them.

which it was established and is now, as the longwinded Gutsverwaltung Niederhausen-Schlossböckelheim, in private hands. The once-great estates of Bad Kreuznach have also fallen by the wayside, selling many of their vineyard possessions. The major beneficiary of this turmoil has been the exceptional Hermann Dönnhoff estate of Oberhausen, run by son Helmut, which has assumed the dominant role making superlative Rieslings of all levels of sweetness.

Just upstream of the Bad Münster bend, the red precipice of the Rotenfels, said to be the highest cliff in Europe north of the Alps, blocks the river's path and can yield fine wine, notably from Dr Crusius. At the cliff-foot there is 100ft (30m) of bare fallen rubble, a short ramp of a red earth suntrap that is the once-revered Traiser Bastei.

Downstream of here, and north of the area mapped in detail, is an increasingly vibrant wine district. In Langenlonsheim Martin Tesch captures the essence of enviably mature vineyards in dramatically labelled bottles of ultra-modern, single-vineyard dry wine. Wine writer Armin Diel of Schlossgut Diel has put Dorsheim on the map with a range of sometimes dazzling wines, while Kruger-Rumpf makes exciting wine from holdings in Münster-Sarmsheim almost on the outskirts of Bingen, where the Nahe meets the Rheingau.

The Dönnhoffs have refurbished this vineyard worker's store, the Türmchen or "little tower", as a tasting room overlooking the protected, eastern end of the Felsenberg vineyard in Schlossböckelheim. A special Türmchen selection of Riesling was first made in 2006.

Pfalz

The Pfalz (once called Palatinate in English) is Germany's biggest and today arguably its most exciting wine region; a 50-mile (80-km) stretch of vineyards north of Alsace, under the lee of the German continuation of the Vosges – the Haardt Mountains.

Like Alsace, it is the sunniest and driest part of its country and has the never-failing charm of half-timbered, flower-bedecked villages among orchards, seeming part of a better, sunlit, half-fairytale world. A labyrinthine road, the Deutsche Weinstrasse, like the Route du Vin of Alsace, starts at the gates of Germany (literally: there is a massive gateway on the border at Schweigen) and winds northwards through vines and villages, culminating in the Mittelhaardt, the area mapped in detail overleaf. A great part of the wine of the area has been made by efficient co-operatives, which revolutionized casual old country methods and made the district famous as a source of good-value wine, but the Pfalz is famous for an increasing number of seriously ambitious individual wine producers. Many of the younger ones belong to organizations such as Junge Pfalz, Freunde, Pfalzhoch, and Südpfalz Connexion, which help build awareness, sales, and confidence.

Riesling is the most planted vine, but the red wine craze has swept through Pfalz too. By 2005 more than 40% of all its wine was red and the second most planted variety, Dornfelder, had decisively overtaken Müller-Thurgau. Thanks to the decline in demand for Liebfraumilch, Müller-Thurgau has fallen to almost exactly the same area as the even less distinguished red Portugieser. A rich mix of other varieties makes up 45% of the region's vines. The Pfalz is Germany's workshop for a range of whites and reds of every complexion, including the whole Pinot family, with the emphasis on dry, often barrique-aged wines for the table. Pinot in all three colours (Weissburgunder, Grauburgunder, and Spätburgunder), with and without oak influence, are firmly established and even Cabernet Sauvignon can be ripened. Two bottles in every three of Pfalz wine are dry.

Neustadt an der Weinstrasse, just south of the area mapped in detail, used to mark a sharp dividing line between country wines of little pretension to the south and the very different world of the Mittelhaardt, the home of some of Germany's biggest and most famous estates, already established in the luxury and export markets.

All this changed in the 1980s and 1990s however. Truly exciting wines throbbing with fruit started to emerge from producers such as Rebholz (particularly famous for Burgundy varieties) as far south as Siebeldingen and Müller-Catoir of Neustadt-Haardt, which under the old regime had shown that such non-classic grapes as Scheurebe, Rieslaner, and Muskateller could also be great. This trend has, fortunately, continued with a new generation, as in Rheinhessen. These young growers take reduced yields and dry styles for granted, and are determined to coax the most out of every variety and every vineyard however untried or uncelebrated. Today the quality-conscious wine drinker can find Pfalz wines of serious interest, made from the likes of Viognier and Sangiovese as well as the more traditional varieties, as far north as Laumersheim, as far south as Schweigen, and as far east as Ellerstadt on the outskirts of Ludwigshafen.

In the Mittelhaardt, however, Riesling is still king. Mittelhaardt Riesling's special quality is succulent honeyed richness and body, balanced with thrilling acidity – even when it is finished *trocken* or *halbtrocken*. It is far removed from the steely nerve of, say, Saar wine, and has more alcohol.

Historically three famous producers dominated this, the kernel of the Pfalz: Bürklin-Wolf (recently converted to biodynamic viticulture and operating outside what they see as the slacker standards of the VDP), von Bassermann-Jordan, and von Buhl. But any monopoly of quality they ever had has disappeared in a surge of ambitious and original winemaking on all sides.

The Einzellagen on the hilly west side of the villages are the ones that most often attain the summits of succulence. In the south,

◄ From top to bottom these fine wines get fuller and richer. First the five Rieslings – a Kabinett, three dry versions, and an Auslese – then one of Müller-Catoir's luscious Rieslaners, one of many hugely popular Pinot Blancs, and a top Pinot Noir.

As one might expect for such a dry region, red wine is becoming increasingly important in the Pfalz. Dornfelder, a thoroughly German 1956 crossing, has been planted so enthusiastically that it is now the region's second most planted grape variety.

Ruppertsberg is one of the first villages of the Mittelhaardt; its best sites (Linsenbusch, Hoheburg, Reiterpfad, Nussbien, Spiess) are all on moderate slopes, well exposed, and largely planted to Riesling.

Forst has a reputation as the source of the Pfalz's most elegant wine. Locals like to draw parallels with the tall, graceful spire of the village church. The top vineyards of Forst lie on usefully water-retentive clay while a black basalt outcrop above the village provides dark warm

soil, rich in potassium, sometimes quarried and spread on other vineyards, notably in Deidesheim. The Jesuitengarten, Forst's most famous vineyard, and the equally fine Kirchenstück lie just behind the church. Freundstück (largely von Buhl's) and, above it, part of Ungeheuer are in the same class. Georg Mosbacher is an outstanding Forst grower.

Historically Forst was respected as the finest wine village of the Pfalz, with its top sites – Kirchenstück, then Jesuitengarten – most

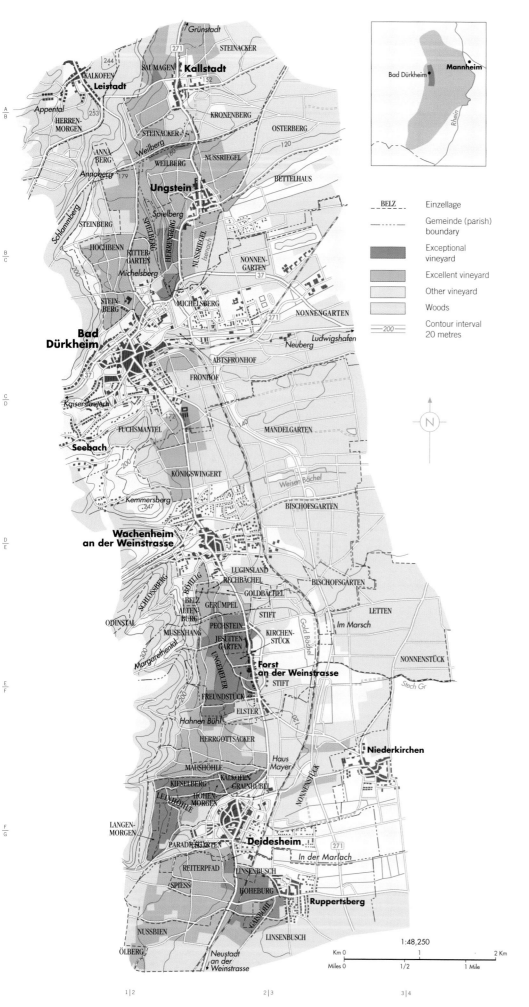

BELZ — — — — Einzellage

— · — · — Gemeinde (parish) boundary

Exceptional vineyard

Excellent vineyard

Other vineyard

Woods

—200— Contour interval 20 metres

1:48,250

Km 0   1   2 Km

Miles 0   1/2   1 Mile

highly rated in the classification of 1828. More recently the larger village of Deidesheim to the south has been rated by many the best village of the whole area, besides being one of the prettiest in Germany (this is unrivalled geranium and window box country). The best wines here have a very special sort of succulence. Von Bassermann-Jordan and von Buhl have their cellars here while Josef Biffar has a well deserved and more recently won reputation. Hohenmorgen, Langenmorgen, Leinhöhle, Kalkofen, Kieselberg, and Grainhübel are the top vineyards.

The village of Wachenheim, where Bürklin-Wolf is based and Erni Loosen of the Mosel has bought the old JL Wolf estate, marks the end of the historic kernel of the Mittelhaardt with a cluster of famous small vineyards. Belz, Rechbächel, Goldbächel, and Gerümpel are the first growths. Richness is not a marked characteristic of Wachenheim; its great qualities are finely poised sweetness and purity of flavour.

Bad Dürkheim is the biggest wine commune in Germany, with 2,000 vineyard acres (800ha). A Wurstmarkt (sausage fair) is held here before the vintage. There is red Dürkheimer (often made from the popular Dornfelder grape) to drink with the sausages as well as white. Riesling is in the minority except in the best sites of Herrenberg and Spielberg. For long Bad Dürkheim was the under-performer of the Mittelhaardt but recently producers such as Thomas Hensel and Karl Schaefer have shown what exciting wines can be produced from the terraced Spielberg and Michelsberg. Even wine producers far from Bad Dürkheim itself such as Markus Schneider of Ellerstadt and Schäfer-Frölich of Bockenau in the Nahe have been making fine wine from grapes grown here.

From here north we are in the Unterhaardt, whose most renowned parishes are Kallstadt, where the star performer is Koehler-Ruprecht, and Ungstein. Their most celebrated sites are Saumagen, planted in what was a Roman chalkpit, and Annaberg, famous for rich Scheurebe. Knipser of Laumersheim has made a wide range of thrilling wines, from barrique-aged whites and reds to substantial Grosses Gewächs dry Rieslings.

Truly outstanding wines are now found well north of what was once considered this firm line just as they are well to the south of Ruppertsberg. In short, fine, often fiery and very often dry wine is now made all over this dynamic region.

As Germany's sunniest, driest region, however, the Pfalz is feeling the effects of global warming mostly keenly. Average annual rainfall is only about 16in (400mm), less than half the total rainfall in the Mosel, and vines here have always suffered some drought stress. In really hot vintages such as 2003 and 2005, the arguments for allowing irrigation seem overpowering.

Not the Pfalz but the distinctively re-landscaped wine country of the Kaiserstuhl in Baden, another region that is suffering some adverse effects of climate change. Flurbereinigung, Germany's mid- to late-20th-century programme of vineyard rationalization, has left land such as this much easier to work.

Baden Württemberg

The far south of Germany, with its increasingly warm climate, could be expected to be more of a wine region than the northern limits of the German wine map. Certainly the style of wine produced could hardly be more different from, say, the ethereal Rieslings of the Mosel. Baden, just over the Rhine from Alsace, produces wines that are invariably dry, very full-bodied (in 2003 alcohol levels of 15% were not uncommon), and often oaked. These are incontrovertibly wines to be drunk with food and the best are keenly sought at Germany's well-kept tables, even if they are too rarely exported.

France may have provided the original models for the Spätburgunder, Grauburgunder, and Weissburgunder which are, respectively, the first, third, and fifth most planted vine varieties in Baden but a new generation of winemakers is confident enough to carve out its own local styles of wine.

Among German wine regions only the Ahr has a higher proportion of red wine than Baden and Württemberg, where 44 and 71% respectively of total vineyard area is planted with dark-skinned varieties. More than one vine in every three in Baden is Spätburgunder.

The second half of the last century saw massive restructuring of the **Baden** winescape, both physical in the form of re-landscaping of difficult-to-work steep slopes (see p.247), and social in the form of the domination of Baden's super-efficient co-operatives, which at one stage handled 90% of each crop. Today that proportion has fallen to 70%, although the mammoth Badischer Winzerkeller at Breisach, the frontier town on the Rhine between Freiburg and Alsace, is still Baden's principal marketer.

The quality of the co-ops' output has been steadily increasing but it is what is happening at the other end of the scale that has made Baden one of the most highly regarded wine regions within Germany. Talented smaller producers such as Dr Heger in Kaiserstuhl, Bernhard Huber in Breisgau, Andreas Laible in Durbach, and Salwey of Oberrotweil all pioneered Burgundian techniques and clones. They are complemented by producers such as Dutch ex-sommelier Jakob Duijn of Bühl and, in Kaiserstuhl, Karl Heinz Johner (more influenced by California than Germany) and Fritz (son of Franz) Keller, whose wine importing and gastronomic background is heavily French-influenced.

Baden is a trifle damper and cloudier than the Alsace vineyards right in the lee of the Vosges. Its vineyards skirt the evocative Black Forest with the bulk of them in a narrow 80-mile (130-km) strip between the forest and the Rhine Valley; the best of them either on privileged southern slopes in the forest massif or on the Kaiserstuhl, the remains of an extinct volcano which forms a distinct island of high ground in the Rhine Valley.

The Kaiserstuhl and Tuniberg furnish one-third of all Baden's wine. While the dominant soil type is loess, most of the finest red Spätburgunders (Pinot Noir) and full-bodied white Grauburgunders (Pinot Gris) grow on volcanic soils. This gives them such a strong character – positively stiff with flavour – that Grauburgunder has become the area's speciality. A Grauburgunder Symposium is held in Endingen every May.

Immediately east of here is Breisgau, where Bernhard Huber of Malterdingen is making some of Germany's finest Spätburgunder, notably from the precarious Bienenberg slope.

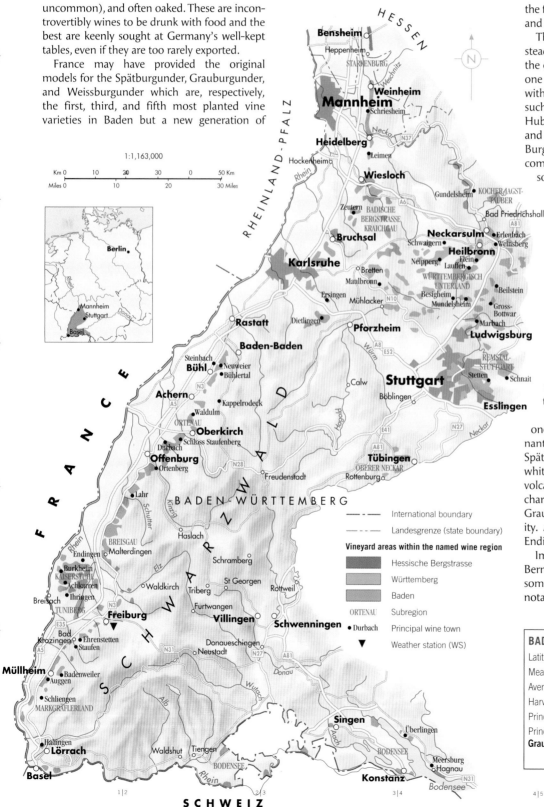

1:1,163,000

International boundary

Landesgrenze (state boundary)

Vineyard areas within the named wine region

Hessische Bergstrasse

Württemberg

Baden

ORTENAU Subregion

• Durbach Principal wine town

▼ Weather station (WS)

BADEN: FREIBURG ▼

Latitude / Altitude of WS **48° / 918ft (280m)**

Mean July temperature at WS **66.5°F (19.2°C)**

Average annual rainfall at WS **35in (880mm)**

Harvest month rainfall at WS **September: 3.3in (85mm)**

Principal viticultural hazard **Spring frost**

Principal grapes **Spätburgunder, Müller-Thurgau, Grauburgunder**

To the north, in Lahr, the Wöhrle family has breathed new life into the Weingut Stadt Lahr, which is now making particularly pure, pristine whites – Chardonnays as well as Pinots.

North again, just south of the luxurious Black Forest spa of Baden-Baden, the Ortenau is Baden's second most important pocket of vineyards with a long-established emphasis on red wine. The Durbach estates of the Margrave of Baden (Schloss Staufenberg) and of Count Wolff Metternich make worthy Klingelberger (the local name for Riesling) although they have been overtaken in local reputation by Andreas Laible and Schloss Neuweier.

Much further north, the Kraichgau and Badische Bergstrasse, disparate as they are, form an area officially regarded as one region, with their finest wines made from the minority grapes, Riesling and Grauburgunder, grown in the best sites.

Far to the south, in the Markgräflerland, the corner of Germany between Freiburg and Basel, the favourite grape has been Gutedel, the local name for the Chasselas planted across the border in Switzerland. It makes refreshing, if rather reticent, wine. Chardonnay is also very much at home here and producers such as Fritz Wassmer of Bad Krozingen-Schlatt have put the local Spätburgunder on the map.

The Seewein (lake wine) of the southernmost area of all, around Meersburg on the Bodensee, is traditionally the off-dry pink-tinted Weissherbst of Spätburgunder. Kress of Hagnau, Stiftskeller Konstanz, and Staatsweingut Meeersburg are making some remarkable Müller-Thurgau (the principal grape) here as well as fine Weissherbst and some markedly elegant white Pinots.

Württemberg, extensive though its vineyards are (it is Germany's fourth largest wine region), is very much better known in Germany than abroad, although producers such as Rainer Schnaitmann in Fellbach on the outskirts of Stuttgart suggest that Württemberg is poised for the sort of revolution just witnessed in Rheinhessen. The region, which, like Baden, extends far beyond the limits of this map (see p.225), produces mainly lightish red or pink Weissherbst. Trollinger is the most important variety here but Lemberger, the fourth most planted variety after Riesling and Schwarzriesling (Pinot Meunier), produces some thoroughly convincing and distinctive Württemberg red. The climate is more continental and not always kind to the wine-growers in Württemberg, so sites are chosen with care, lining the River Neckar and its tributaries, with three-quarters of the region's vineyards to the north of the state capital Stuttgart. Riesling, as almost everywhere in Germany, makes by far the most exciting whites although Württemberg is really red wine country and there have been some convincing experiments with Frühburgunder and even some red Bordeaux varieties.

In the far north, north of Mannheim, is the tiny wine region **Hessische Bergstrasse** (see p.225 for its full extent), which produces mainly dry Riesling and that mainly for locals.

▶ These labels tell the story of how both label design and the varietal profile of Germany have changed. All of the top eight labels, from Baden, are for various Pinots (Burgunder) red and white while the Württemberg Simonroth is a blend of Merlot and Cabernet Franc.

Harvesting in the morning mist on the restructured slopes of the Kaiserstuhl, pictured on p.247. Comparison with the gradient in the photo on p.224, for example, shows how vineyard workers must bless the re-landscaping.

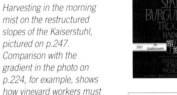

Franken

Franken (Franconia in English) is out of the mainstream of German wine both geographically and by dint of its quite separate traditions. Politically it lies in the otherwise beer-centric former kingdom of Bavaria, which gives its State cellars a grandeur found nowhere else in Germany, and its consumers high expectations. Franken is unusual in that it makes greater wines of Silvaner than of Riesling. And in savour and strength it has never been a stronghold of the light, fruity style favoured elsewhere in Germany, making its wines some of the best to drink with food.

Since its identity crisis in the 1990s, when the wines seemed to lose favour in Germany (they have never been a major export item), Franken has bounced back, with markedly enhanced quality from co-operative level up to the grandest estates, via a rash of brand new or revived enterprises.

The name Steinwein was once loosely used for all Franken wine. Stein is, in fact, the name of one of the two famous vineyards of the city of Würzburg, Franken's wine capital on the Main. The other is Innere Leiste. Both distinguished themselves in the past by making wines that were incredibly long-lived. A Stein wine of the great vintage of 1540 was still (just) drinkable in the 1960s. Such wines were Beerenauslesen at least: immensely sweet. Franken makes few such rarities today; indeed only 6% of production is anything other than *trocken* or *halbtrocken*.

Franken takes the grapevine into countryside whose climate is decidedly continental, but climate change has largely solved Franken's problem of too short a growing season. Indeed 1996 was the last vintage which saw any under-ripe Riesling – and Silvaner, the single most successful grape of Franken, is frequently as massively concentrated and alcoholic these days as some of the more substantial wines from the Austrian Wachau.

Franken's traditional bottle shape is the squat green Bocksbeutel flask. This stack of Vinum Benedictum Riesling was made specially at Schloss Saaleck of Hammelburg to celebrate the Pope's visit in July 2005.

But even in Franken, unfortunately, Müller-Thurgau seems to offer a better return, at least on less-than-ideal sites. It is the most planted variety, on about a third of all vineyard land, but Silvaner (grown on more than a fifth) is king, magically producing wines of crackling intensity here, even if it demands the most propitious vineyard sites. Franken wines may also be made of the

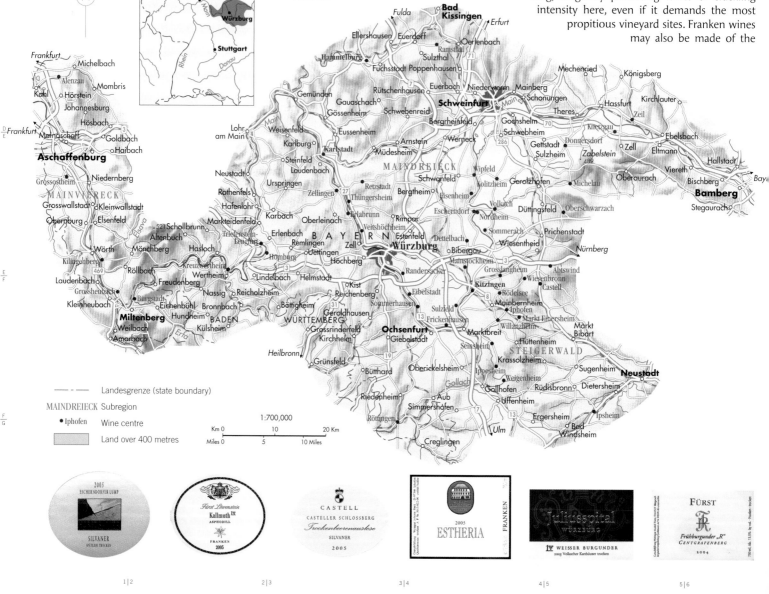

— · — Landesgrenze (state boundary)

MAINDREIECK Subregion

• Iphofen Wine centre

Land over 400 metres

1:700,000

Km 0 · · · 10 · · · 20 Km
Miles 0 · · · 5 · · · 10 Miles

super-aromatic grape varieties Kerner, and, especially, Bacchus. Scheurebe and Rieslaner, an even later ripening Silvaner x Riesling crossing, can make particularly good dessert wines and substantial dry wines here, provided they reach full ripeness.

The heart of wine-growing Franken is in **Maindreieck**, following the fuddled three-cornered meandering of the Main from Escherndorf (with its celebrated Lump vineyard, and such talented producers as Horst Sauer and neighbour Rainer Sauer) and Nordheim upstream of Würzburg, south to Frickenhausen, then north again through the capital to include all the next leg of the river and the outlying district around Hammelburg. What distinguishes all these scattered south-facing hillsides is the peculiar limestone known as Muschelkalk (whose origins are not so different from the Kimmeridgian clay of Chablis, or indeed of Sancerre). This gives the wines an elegant raciness, particularly so in the case of the famous Würzburger Stein and noticeably so even in the more honeyed wines of Eschendorfer Lump.

Würzburg is the essential visit: one of the great cities of the vine, with three magnificent estate cellars in its heart belonging respectively to the Bavarian State (Staatliche Hofkellerei), a church charity (the recently revived Juliusspital), and a civic charity (the Bürgerspital). The city is also home to the Knolls' exceptional 54-acre (22-ha) Weingut am Stein estate.

The Staatliche Hofkellerei lies under the gorgeous Residenz of the former prince-bishops, whose ceiling paintings by Tiepolo are reason enough to visit the city. There is also the noble Marienburg Castle on its hill of vines, the great baroque river bridge, and the bustling *Weinstuben* (wine bars) belonging to these ancient foundations, where all their wines can be enjoyed with suitably savoury food.

Mainviereck, further downstream to the west, has lighter loam based on sandstone. It has much less land under vine but ancient vineyards such as Homburger Kallmuth (off the map to the south) can produce extraordinary, age-worthy wines. This is also Franken's red wine area where steep, exceptionally arid terraces of red sandstone can produce Spätburgunders and Frühburgunders (an early-ripening strain of Pinot Noir) of real interest. Stars such as Rudolf Fürst and Fürst Löwenstein are based here.

In the **Steigerwald** in the east, the vine looks almost a stranger in the setting of arable fields with forests of magnificent oaks crowning its sudden hills. The seriously steep slopes are of gypsum and marl, which makes its mark in particularly strongly flavoured wines. Some of the finest wines come from the parishes of Iphofen (home of Hans Wirsching and Johann Ruck) and Rödelsee, as well as the doll's-house princedom, and wine estate, of Castell.

◀ Oval labels suit the *Bocksbeutel* particularly well. Here they are on three fine examples of Franken's signature grape Silvaner, with varying sweetness levels. Other grapes represented are Scheurebe, which can perform well here, Pinot Blanc, and the fashionable red Frühburgunder.

Sachsen and Saale-Unstrut

With the reunification of Germany, two small wine regions were added to the tight embrace of German wine bureaucracy. **Sachsen** (Saxony in English) is on the banks of the Elbe, in fine-china country between Dresden and Meissen, and **Saale-Unstrut** lies around the confluence of those two rivers southwest of Leipzig, together with an enclave of vineyards close to the Süsser See near Halle (see the map of Germany on p.225).

Both of these regions are roughly on the same latitude as London, but their much more continental climate frequently blesses them with magnificent summers, even if the risk of devastating spring frosts is high. Substantial replanting in the 1990s increased the total vineyard area to over 1,500 acres (600ha) in Saale-Unstrut and nearly 1,000 acres (400ha) in Sachsen by the mid-2000s.

By the late 1990s re-established estates such as Lützkendorf in Bad Kösen (Saale-Unstrut) and Schloss Proschwitz in Meissen (Sachsen), as well as new ones such as Günter Born in Höhnstedt, west of Halle (Saale-Unstrut), and Zimmerling in Pillnitz (Sachsen) had proved that both regions can produce dry wines with remarkable substance and character for their northerly location. Saale-Unstrut, of which a good 250,000 acres (100,000ha) were under vine in the Middle Ages, produces nothing but dry wines while Sachsen makes a tiny proportion of sweet ones.

The Herzoglicher vineyard in Freyburg is home to the sparkling wine producer Rotkäppchen, which was for long East Germany's most important wine company. These grand vineyard adornments are typical of the region.

Although the workhorse grape of both regions is the ubiquitous Müller-Thurgau, Weissburgunder, Grauburgunder, Riesling, and Traminer grapes dominate the many steep, south-facing sites with which each region is blessed. Schloss Proschwitz has even distinguished itself with prize-winning Spätburgunder (Pinot Noir). The Goldriesling crossing is a local speciality of Sachsen. These wines are often compared with those of Franken, although they are lighter, more aromatic, and less earthy.

▼ In this super-continental climate, where wines struggle to reach full ripeness, it is the most unctuous wines that have traditionally garnered most praise, although this is changing with increased regard for and proficiency in dry wines.

The Rest of Europe

Switzerland's meticulously kept vineyards near Chamoson in the Valais, the most important wine-growing canton.

England and Wales

Nyetimber in Sussex, with architecture very unfamiliar to most wine students, was established in the early 1990s by an American couple who specifically sought out conditions similar to those of Champagne.

Winemakers in more southern countries like to make little jokes about English wine. Frost, wayward summers, and poor weather during flowering can make it difficult to harvest ripe grapes this far from the equator, as vignerons in Ireland, Belgium, Holland, and Denmark know too. The fact remains, however, that in the early Middle Ages the monastic vineyards of England were extensive and by all accounts successful. Had it not been for England's acquisition of Bordeaux (by the marriage of Henry II to Eleanor of Aquitaine in 1152), they might have continued without a break. But they faded away until the modern renaissance began in the 1950s at Hambledon in Hampshire.

Now England (and Wales) have such confidence that nearly 2,470 acres (1,000ha) of vineyard are scattered widely over the southern half of the country, with the greatest concentration in the southeast – the counties of Kent, East and West Sussex, and Surrey – but also a large number of smaller vineyards (there are more than 360 in total) across the south to the West Country, along the Thames and Severn valleys, and in East Anglia, the driest part of England. The largest vineyard is Denbies, in Surrey, with 265 acres (107ha) – very much an exception in an industry where the average is

5.6 acres (2.3ha), although many of even the smaller ones depend heavily on tourism for sales. Well over 100 wineries now process the crop, which fluctuates dramatically but averages over 2.5 million bottles per year.

The great majority of wine is white and, like its original German model, is becoming progressively drier. Seyval Blanc, Reichensteiner, Müller-Thurgau, and Bacchus are the most widely grown vines, but the Champagne grapes Chardonnay, Pinot Noir, and, to a lesser extent, Pinot Meunier are now popular too. Madeleine x Angevine 7672 – a variety unique to the UK, bred by Georg Scheu in Germany in the 1930s – is also successful in blends. Early-ripening red varieties such as Dornfelder and the more recently bred Rondo are increasingly planted, with very fair results. Bottle-fermented sparkling wines – an increasing proportion of them now based on Chardonnay and Pinot – are England's strongest suit; the best match

champagne selling at the same price. There is no difference in the chalk soil between Champagne and England's Downs, and climate change has been very much in England's favour of late. Until recently, wines have routinely needed quite heavy chaptalization. But both the weather and skills have improved from a tentative start so that experienced winemakers can make good white and red wines almost every year. Imports can (easily) be cheaper, but the wines being made in England and Wales today have their own uniquely crisp, aromatic, lively style – and can age better than many a fuller white.

English and Welsh wine, officially classified as either quality wine, regional wine, or UK table wine, are quite distinct from British wine, the name confusingly given to fermented, reconstituted grape concentrate imported into Britain, generally from wherever can supply the concentrate at the lowest price.

ENGLAND: ODIHAM ▼

Latitude / Altitude of WS **51.14° / 394ft (120m)**

Mean July temp at WS **62.5°F (16.9°C)**

Annual rainfall at WS **27in (700mm)**

Harvest month rainfall at WS **October: 2.4in (60mm)**

Chief viticultural hazards **Underripeness, autumn rain, uneven fruit set**

Principal grapes **Seyval Blanc, Reichensteiner, Müller-Thurgau, Bacchus**

▼ Two of the first producers to establish first-class reputations for their fizz, made in the image of Champagne. Ridgeview name their bottling Merret after the 17th-century Englishman who supposedly taught the Champenois how to keep bubbles in a bottle.

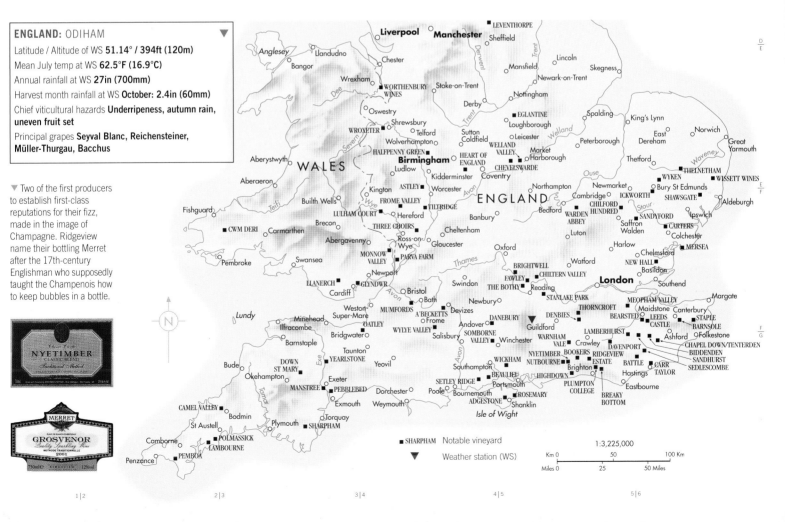

■ SHARPHAM Notable vineyard

▼ Weather station (WS)

1:3,225,000

Switzerland

Swiss wine used to be in every sense a law unto itself; a privilege not available, even to Switzerland, in the modern world. After decades of vinous isolation, Switzerland has stripped away her protective layers and, as a result, now makes more red wine than white. The wine market was fully opened in 2001, and from 2006 the once-routine stretching of Swiss with imported wine was banned.

The Swiss are enthusiastic wine drinkers. Only about 2% of their wine leaves the country. Making any sort of wine in a country with Switzerland's cost structure is inevitably expensive. The land of milk and money will never be able to produce bargains for the mass market, and Swiss wine producers are increasingly concentrating on making wine with real individuality. This should not be too difficult since every vineyard, almost every grape, is tended as and by an individual. The country's total of 37,200 acres (14,900 ha) of vineyards are divided between thousands of full- and part-time growers who ensure that their impeccable and often spectacular plots of vines are attentively gardened rather than commercially farmed.

By scrupulous care of their vines, making use of irrigation especially in the drier parts of the Valais, the Swiss have regularly achieved yields as high as Germany's. By managing to produce such big quantities, adding sugar when necessary, they make growing grapes pay in spite of the difficult terrain and the costs of a high standard of living. And in the winery, routine malolactic fermentation (unlike in Germany or Austria) compensates for any natural excess tartness.

Switzerland has the highest vines in Europe and is home to the first vineyards on two of the world's great wine rivers, the Rhine and the Rhône, which rise, remarkably close to each other, in the Gotthard Massif.

Every Swiss canton grows some grapes for winemaking. In recent years more than four-fifths of the country's wine has come from the western cantons of French-speaking Switzerland: la Suisse romande. Valais is the most productive canton, followed by Vaud and then, some way behind, Geneva. The Italian-speaking Ticino is fourth and produces virtually all red wine.

Typically Swiss scene above the Thunersee in which wine plays a part, but not a hugely important part compared with, say, the Alps and tourism. Fendant and Dôle in screwcapped bottles were standard tourist fare for many years but Switzerland has not been immune to the rise in global wine quality.

The Swiss drink twice as much red wine as white so the early 21st century saw extensive conversion of the white wine vineyards that once predominated to dark-skinned varieties, notably Pinot Noir.

The most planted white wine grape by far is the pale Chasselas, which manages to achieve real personality in Switzerland's most favoured sites (see overleaf). The grape dominates wine production in Vaud and still plays an important role in the Valais, Geneva, and Neuchâtel. Pockets of Pinot Gris, Pinot Blanc, Sylvaner, Marsanne, Chardonnay, Sauvignon Blanc, and Viognier are found in the Valais and elsewhere in Suisse romande. In German-speaking Eastern Switzerland, Müller-Thurgau, originally bred by the Swiss Dr Müller of Thurgau and often called Riesling-Sylvaner, is the most important white wine grape, though it is losing ground today to red varieties.

For Switzerland's fashionable and increasingly impressive red wines, the vine known here variously as Pinot Noir, Blauburgunder, or Clevener is grown all over Switzerland, with the exception of Ticino, which concentrates on Merlot, introduced in 1906 from Bordeaux after phylloxera all but destroyed the region's wine industry.

But the country's most distinctive wines come from her long list of historic vine specialities: for example, in the Valais, Petite Arvine, Amigne, Humagne Blanc, Païen (Heida), and Rèze for whites, and Cornalin and Humagne Rouge for reds; in German-speaking Switzerland, Completer and the old German vines Räuschling and Elbling; and in Ticino, red Bondola. Of these, Petite Arvine, Completer, and the red Cornalin and Humagne Rouge can

make some very fine wine indeed. Also being planted is a series of new Swiss crossings of pairs of popular vinifera varieties, particularly Gamaret, Garanoir, Diolinoir, and Carminoir for red wine. Some growers, particularly in the east of the country, have been planting disease-resistant hybrids.

Eastern Switzerland grows about 17% of Switzerland's wine grapes, typically in isolated, well-exposed sites able to ripen the Pinot Noir, called Blauburgunder here, which was introduced here from France during the wars of the 17th century. Quality continues to improve, with particularly fine examples available from Schaffhausen, Thurgau, and Bündner Herrschaft, where ripening benefits from the warm autumn wind, the föhn. This favoured region's white speciality is the austere but ancient Completer.

The quality spectrum in Switzerland's other red wine region, **Ticino**, is even wider, with Merlot varying from the frankly cynical to some, nurtured on the sunniest slopes, that stand comparison with Italy's Super Tuscans.

In western Switzerland, vineyards on the south-facing slopes above Lake Neuchâtel are devoted to Pinot Noir and Chasselas, for delicate wines of all three colours, often enlivened by the light bubble left by prolonged lees contact. All **Neuchâtel** producers release their unfiltered Chasselas, a welcome variation on the usual recipe, on the third Wednesday in January. Wines very similar to Neuchâtel's are grown north of Bielersee to the immediate northeast, with particularly fine Pinot Noir coming from small plots above the villages of Schafis, Ligerz, and Twann.

▶ One of the two labels from Neuchâtel is an example of the local pink speciality Oeil de Perdrix, or "eye of the partridge". The other three labels all come from German-speaking Eastern Switzerland, a dry white Räuschling flanked by some particularly impressive Pinot Noir.

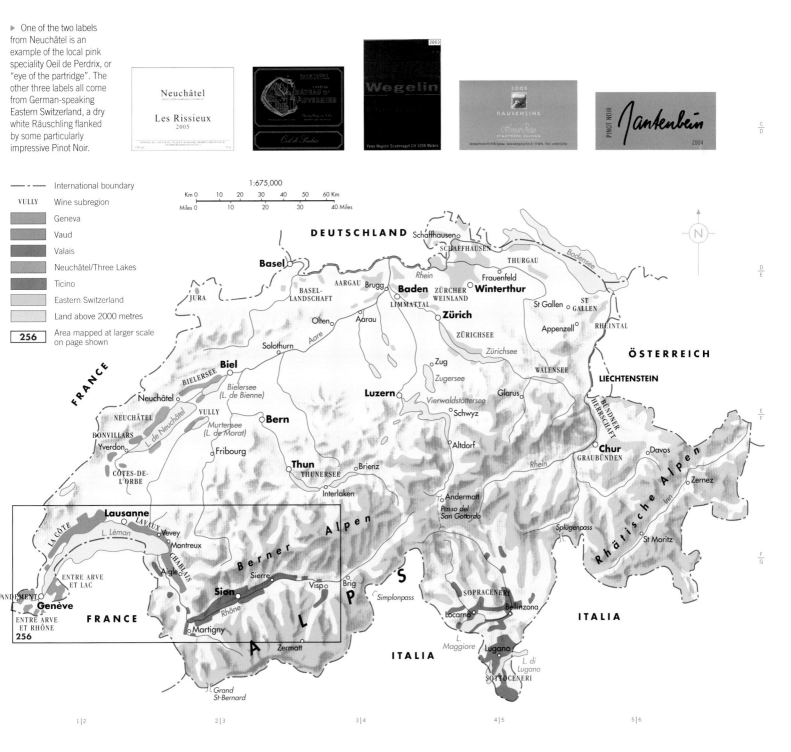

Valais, Vaud, and Geneva

The steep sides of the Valais, the valley which the young River Rhône carved through the Alps, are followed by gentler slopes in Vaud, where the waters broaden into Lac Léman (Lake Geneva). An almost continuous, south-facing band of vines hugs the north bank of the river, then the lake, all the way. The Valais is a hotbed (literally) of vinous experimentation. Vaud is the traditional heart of Swiss wine, where Cistercian monks introduced viticulture from Burgundy more than 850 years ago. Geneva has been hard at work upgrading its wines.

In the high **Valais**, peculiarly alpine conditions – brilliant sun and summer drought – can make concentrated, super-ripe wines. The average rainfall in Sion, a major wine centre, is less than two-thirds that of Bordeaux; many Valais growers build *bisses*, special channels of mountain water, to irrigate their vines.

The Rhône's first vines grow near Brig: historic varieties such as Lafnetscha, Himbertscha, Gwäss (Gouais Blanc), and Heida, throwbacks

to the age before the Simplon Tunnel and its railway transformed the Valaisian economy. Just southwest of here are Europe's highest vines at Visperterminen, at 3,600ft (1,100m) lying almost in the shadow of the Matterhorn.

Large-scale wine production begins just before Sierre (the driest place in Switzerland) and continues as far downstream as Martigny, home to many of the firms that turn out the Valais staples of white Fendant (as Chasselas is known here) and red Dôle. This mid-weight wine is usually a blend of Pinot Noir with Gamay, although some Dôles are 100% Pinot. Many of the best, containing only enough Gamay to add a certain fruitiness, come from the calcareous slopes round Sierre.

About a quarter of Valais grapes are grown by smallholders and processed by the dominant co-operative, Provins. It has taken notable steps to encourage quality but it is innovative small-scale producers who have shown the way, particularly with red wines, which now

account for more than 60% of total Valais production. Traditional varieties such as the fruity Cornalin and rustic Humagne Rouge are now increasingly supplemented not just by Pinot Noir and Gamay but by the tannic Syrah, which has travelled remarkably well upstream from its home in the French Rhône Valley.

Of the 30 light-skinned varieties grown in the Valais, Petite Arvine is the most widely successful indigenous vine. Its combination of nervy acidity and considerable extract is particularly winning in the arid climate around Sion and Martigny. Valais whites are in general extremely potent, whether Johannisberg (Sylvaner), Ermitage (Marsanne), Malvoisie (Pinot Gris; sometimes *flétri*, strong and sweet, traditionally from raisined grapes), Chardonnay, Amigne (a speciality of the village of Vétroz), Humagne Blanc (not related to Humagne Rouge) or Païen (Heida). Rèze is grown in Sierre, and aged high in the Alps in the Val d'Anniviers, to produce the rare sherry-like Vin de Glacier.

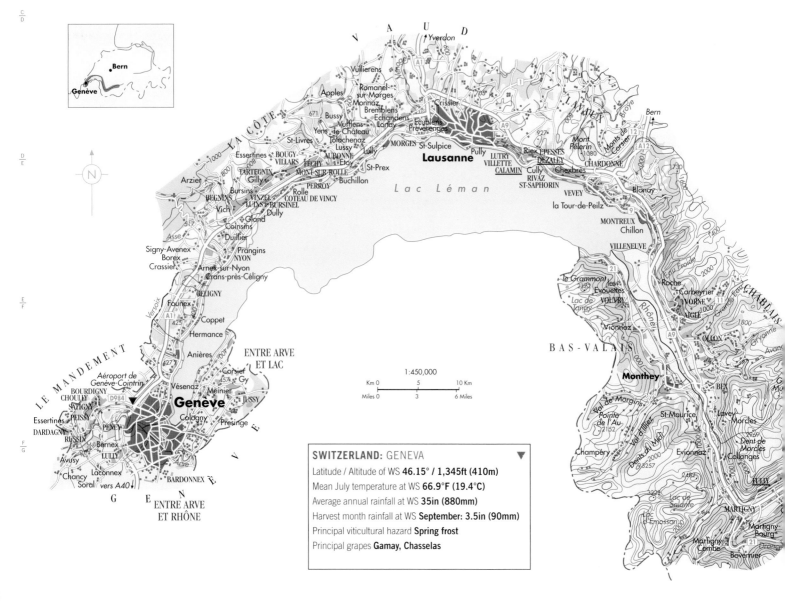

SWITZERLAND: GENEVA ▼
Latitude / Altitude of WS **46.15° / 1,345ft (410m)**
Mean July temperature at WS **66.9°F (19.4°C)**
Average annual rainfall at WS **35in (880mm)**
Harvest month rainfall at WS **September: 3.5in (90mm)**
Principal viticultural hazard **Spring frost**
Principal grapes **Gamay, Chasselas**

Vaud's vineyards are quite different, favoured by the mildness encouraged by Lac Léman's great body of water. Sixty-three per cent of them are devoted to a single grape, Chasselas – although even here red varieties are encroaching fast. Yields are still too high (averaging up to 100hl/ha) to produce much thrilling wine, but there are pockets of vineyards from which the world's most characterful expressions of this lightweight grape are regularly coaxed – which is pretty impressive considering that in many areas it belongs in the fruit basket rather than the winery.

Chablais is the easternmost of Vaud's wine regions and Chasselas can reach record ripeness levels around Aigle, Ollon, and Yvorne. The pretty vine-terraced north shore of the lake is divided into Lavaux (encompassing the area between Montreux in the east and Lausanne, where some of Switzerland's most famous and expensive white wines are grown), and La Côte, which stretches in an arc that is less glorious and spectacular from west of Lausanne to the city of Geneva.

Within Lavaux, wine villages such as, in ascending order of quality, Chardonne, Rivaz, Epesses, and St-Saphorin, luxuriate in a reputation that was established in the Middle Ages, but two specially designated Grands Crus, Calamin and Dézaley, enjoy even greater esteem, and even higher prices. Calamin, all 40 acres (16ha) of it, lies within the village of Epesses, while the 136 acres (55ha) designated Dézaley includes such estates as Clos des Abbayes and Clos des Moines, both now owned by the city of Lausanne. Within these two *crus*, Chasselas can be a nervy, smoky, flinty expression of different terroirs and expositions, all the best of which benefit from light reflected from the lake and heat radiated from the stony terraces initiated by

the Cistercians. The best wines of La Côte tend to come from such villages as Féchy, Bougy-Villars, Mont-sur-Rolle, and Morges.

Geneva's vineyards have changed more than any in Switzerland in recent years. Gamay is now the principal grape, having overtaken Chasselas, and is followed by Pinot Noir, Gamaret, and Garanoir. The co-operative, once dominant, makes mainly everyday wines and draws on three areas, the largest being Mandement (Satigny is Switzerland's biggest wine commune), which has the ripest and tastiest Chasselas. The vineyards between the Arve and the Rhône make relatively mild wine

The famous high-altitude vineyards of Visperterminen in the Valais as seen from a ski lift. The Swiss are adept at overcoming any practical obstacles involved in fully working every inch of the slopes, even at the top of mountains.

while the produce of those between the Arve and the lake is pretty dry and pallid.

As in the Valais, the pace is being set by a small group of ambitious individuals who have shown that innovation (planting Merlot and Sauvignon Blanc, for example) can be more rewarding than following local custom. The picture-book village of Dardagny, for instance, has earned itself a reputation for unusually invigorating Pinot Gris.

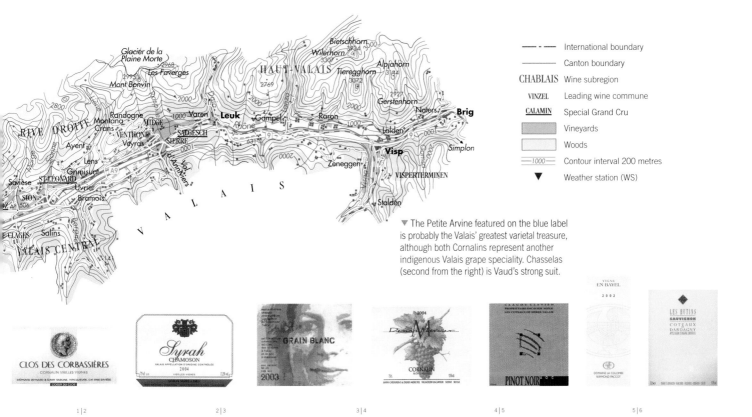

— · —	International boundary
———	Canton boundary
CHABLAIS	Wine subregion
VINZEL	Leading wine commune
CALAMIN	Special Grand Cru
▩	Vineyards
▢	Woods
—1000—	Contour interval 200 metres
▼	Weather station (WS)

▼ The Petite Arvine featured on the blue label is probably the Valais' greatest varietal treasure, although both Cornalins represent another indigenous Valais grape speciality. Chasselas (second from the right) is Vaud's strong suit.

Austria

Those fortunate wine drinkers who have been exposed to Austria's modern array of intensely pure, dry (*trocken*) wines know that in many ways they have more in common with Alsace than Germany, while having their own distinct, finely etched personality. There is something of the freshness of the Rhine in them, more perhaps of the fieriness and high flavour of the Danube, but almost nothing in common with Austria's wines of 25 years ago, before the country underwent vinous revolution – all of it benign.

So-called Weinland Osterreich in the far east of the country around Vienna, where the Alps descend to the great Pannonian Plain that reaches across Hungary, is where most Austrian wine is made, in hugely varied conditions. There is slate, sand, clay, gneiss, loam, and fertile loess, parched fields and perpetually green ones, craggy precipices above the Donau (Danube), and the tranquil shallow mere of the Neusiedler See.

Austria's fiercely continental climate and relatively modest average yields result in more potent wines than Germany's. The most commonly encountered fruit flavours are those of Austria's own white grape Grüner Veltliner, which is grown on more than a third of the country's vineyard. This is not a grape with a long history in Austria, but one that has proved over the last 50 years to be very much at home there. "Grüner" can be thirst-quenchingly fresh and fruity, with plenty of acidity and a flavour that reverberates on a wavelength somewhere between grapefruit and dill (typically in the vast Weinviertel). In the right hands and places (especially upriver of Vienna), it can also be well worth ageing in bottle.

The rolling, wooded countryside of the prolific **Weinvertel** north of Vienna, with its baroque churches and pretty villages, is the very essence of Mitteleurop. The hills of Slovakia form a barrier between it and the warming influence of the Pannonian Plain to the southeast so that wines made are Austria's freshest and lightest. Some of the best reds come from Mailberg, with a warming combination of loess, sand, and a particularly well-sheltered valley. Blauer Portugieser is the workhorse red grape, but Austria's own Zweigelt is better.

Austria introduced its counterpart to France's Appellations Contrôlées with Grüner Veltliner grown in the Weinviertel. DAC (Districtus Austriae Controllatus), like France's AC, Italy's DOC, and Spain's DO, favours geographical labelling over varietal. Traisental (for Grüner Veltliner and Riesling) and Mittelburgenland (for Blaufränkisch) have since joined the scheme, and other regions are set to follow.

Austrian wine until quite recently was almost 70% white. Grüner Veltliner was (and still is) dominant, Welschriesling and Riesling are also important, but today the market demands red. Zweigelt, Blauer Portugieser, and Blaufränkisch together make up about a fifth of all plantings. Austria's wine revolution has extended to wine geography too, with a flurry of redrawn boundaries and renaming of regions. The four most important, Wachau, Kremstal, Kamptal, and Burgenland, are considered in detail overleaf.

Although mixed farming predominates in **Traisental** and **Donauland** these regions produce seriously fine Grüner Veltliner and the unrelated, red-skinned Roter Veltliner, particularly in the Wagram subregion of Donauland. Markus Huber von Reichersdorf of Traisental, and Bernhard Ott of Feuersbrunn and Karl Fritsch of Oberstockstall in Donauland are three of the country's most admired winegrowers. On the outskirts of Vienna, but still technically in Donauland, are the monastic cellars and influential national wine school of Klosterneuburg.

Easy-drinking reds are the speciality of **Carnuntum**, the most southerly and hottest of Niederösterreich's (Lower Austria's) wine areas, with Zweigelt again the best grape. Sheltered to the north by mountains and the famous Vienna woods, it is wide open to Pannonian influence, not unlike Burgenland to the south. Göttlesbrunn and Höflein are the best-sited villages; elsewhere can be fatally cold for vines in winter or dangerously dry in summer. The best producer in the area is Gerhard Markowitsch.

No capital city is so intimate with wine as **Vienna** (or Wien), where more than 1,700 acres (700ha) of vineyards still hold their ground right up to the tramlines within the heart of the residential districts, and surge up the side of the surrounding hills into the Vienna woods. Vienna also has its own unusually elegant

▼ Following in France's AC footsteps, the DAC label on the far left deliberately suppresses the name Grüner Veltliner, as does that of Ott's own Reserve from Donauland. Three top Styrian Sauvignon Blancs below are preceded by an Austrian red wine speciality, a St Laurent from the Thermenregion.

The vineyards of Weingut Sepp Muster near Leutschach in southern Styria look for divine protection – not that they generally need it this far south, where the continental climate delivers particularly warm summers.

biennial wine fair, VieVinum, held in the grandeur of the imperial palace, with no shortage of the delicate stemware in which Austria, so close to Bohemia, specializes.

Most of Vienna's wine is drunk as *Heurige*, in *Heurigen* – for this untranslatable word means both the new wine and the leafy tavern where it is drunk, in an atmosphere that can vary from formulaic tourist-trap to idyllic. Every vintner seems to be a tavernkeeper too, and chalks up on a board the wines and their (modest) prices, to be drunk on the spot or carried away. Good *Heurige* is sensational; spirited, sprightly stuff which goes straight to your head. Most of it is Grüner Veltliner. Some is Weissburgunder (Pinot Blanc), Traminer, and Müller-Thurgau; some is Riesling, although this is the grape most likely to provide Vienna's wines for the cellar.

Vineyards continue to the south of the city in the **Thermenregion**, called after its hot springs, flanking the last crinkle of the alpine foothills facing the hot Hungarian plain. Unlike the vineyards of Vienna, those of the Thermenregion are too far from the River Danube to benefit from its refreshing influence. The Thermenregion also has the *Heurigen* tradition, however, and without nearly so many tourists. It is now concentrating on Pinot Noir and its Austrian relative St Laurent plus Chardonnay, Pinot Blanc, and, of the local white grapes, the lively Zierfandler and the heavier Rotgipfler and Neuburger.

Steiermark (Styria) in the south has little in common with Austria's northerly regions. It has produced exclusively dry wines, not unlike those over the border in Slovenia, for decades. It may have only 7% of the country's vineyards, and those widely dispersed, but its reputation for intense piercing Sauvignon Blanc (sometimes oaked), Chardonnay, and Welschriesling is unmatched within Austria. Chardonnay, some of it travelling most unusually under a local alias, Morillon, is well entrenched here. Südsteiermark has the greatest concentration of revered producers; names such as Gross, Polz, Sattlerhof, Tement, and Wohlmuth. Traminer is a speciality of the volcanic soils of Klöch in Südoststeiermark, while pink Schilcher made from the rare Blauer Wildbacher grape is that of Weststeiermark.

AUSTRIA: VIENNA ▼

Latitude / Altitude of WS **48.04° / 590ft (180m)**

Mean July temperature at WS **67.6°F (19.8°C)**

Average annual rainfall at WS **26in (665mm)**

Harvest month rainfall at WS **September: 1.5in (40mm)**

Principal viticultural hazard **Spring frost**

Principal grapes **Grüner Veltliner, Zweigelt, Blauer Portugieser, Welschriesling, Riesling, Blaufränkisch**

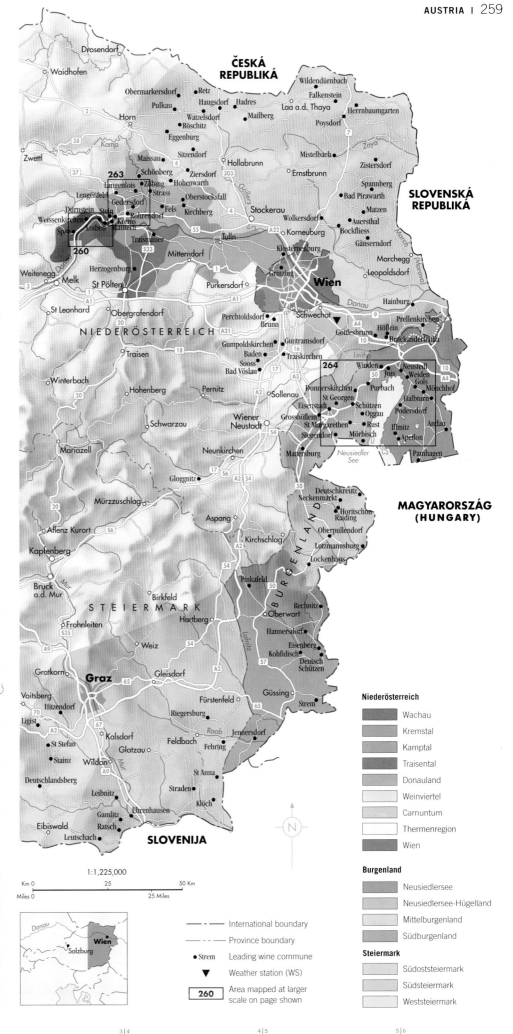

1:1,225,000

Km 0 — 25 — 50 Km
Miles 0 — 25 Miles

Niederösterreich
- Wachau
- Kremstal
- Kamptal
- Traisental
- Donauland
- Weinviertel
- Carnuntum
- Thermenregion
- Wien

Burgenland
- Neusiedlersee
- Neusiedlersee-Hügelland
- Mittelburgenland
- Südburgenland

Steiermark
- Südoststeiermark
- Südsteiermark
- Weststeiermark

——— International boundary
– – – Province boundary
● Strem   Leading wine commune
▼   Weather station (WS)
260   Area mapped at larger scale on page shown

Wachau

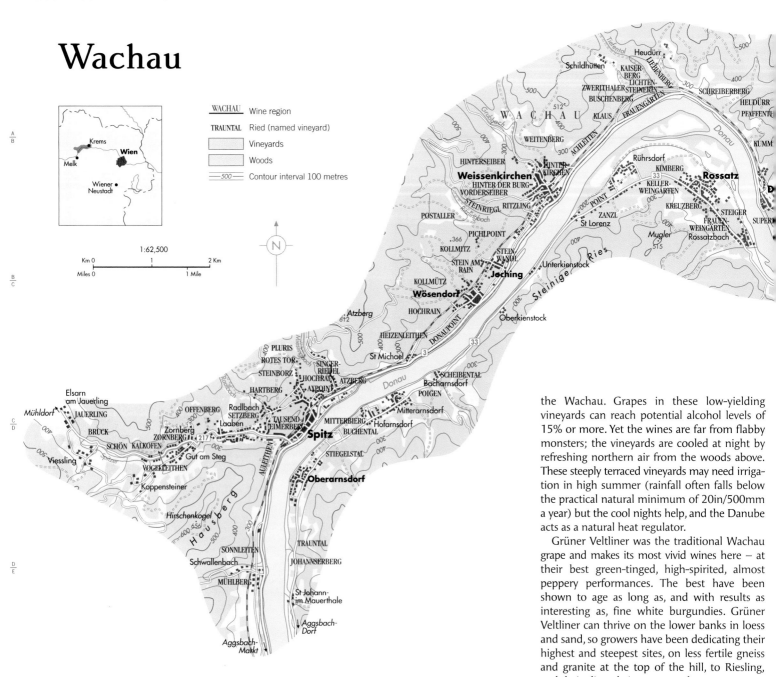

WACHAU Wine region

TRAUNTAL Ried (named vineyard)

Vineyards

Woods

─── 500 ─── Contour interval 100 metres

1:62,500

Km 0   1   2 Km

Miles 0   1 Mile

If ever a region needed an atlas to tell its story, it is the Wachau, a complex meeting point of northern and southern climates and a rich mosaic of different soils and rocks. Forty miles (65km) before it reaches Vienna, the broad grey Danube broaches a range of 1,600-ft (490-m) high hills. For a short stretch the craggy north bank of the river, as steep as the Mosel or the Côte-Rôtie, is patchworked with vines on ledges and outcrops, along narrow paths leading up from the river to the crowning woods.

There are plots of deep soil and others where a mere scratching finds rock, patches with day-long sunlight and others that always seem to be in shade. This is the Wachau, Austria's most famous wine region, even if, with 3,700 acres (1,500ha), it constitutes just 3% of the country's vineyard.

What gives the (almost invariably dry, or dryish, white) wines of the Wachau their distinction is the geography. Hot Pannonian summers reach their furthest west here, heating the Danube Valley as far as the eastern end of

the Wachau. Grapes in these low-yielding vineyards can reach potential alcohol levels of 15% or more. Yet the wines are far from flabby monsters; the vineyards are cooled at night by refreshing northern air from the woods above. These steeply terraced vineyards may need irrigation in high summer (rainfall often falls below the practical natural minimum of 20in/500mm a year) but the cool nights help, and the Danube acts as a natural heat regulator.

Grüner Veltliner was the traditional Wachau grape and makes its most vivid wines here – at their best green-tinged, high-spirited, almost peppery performances. The best have been shown to age as long as, and with results as interesting as, fine white burgundies. Grüner Veltliner can thrive on the lower banks in loess and sand, so growers have been dedicating their highest and steepest sites, on less fertile gneiss and granite at the top of the hill, to Riesling, and their clientele is enraptured.

Top Wachau Rieslings can have the steely cut of the Saar in a mouth-filling structure which is every bit as full as an Alsace Grand Cru Riesling. Growers who make such wines include Hirtzberger at Spitz, Prager at Weissenkirchen, FX Pichler at Oberloiben, Emmerich Knoll, the Tegernseerhof family, and Leo Alzinger at Unterloiben, Johann Schmelz and Josef Jamek at Joching, and Rudi Pichler at Wösendorf, as well as the famous Freie Weingärtner Wachau co-op at Dürnstein. New oak does not feature here, although there have been experiments with botrytized grapes.

◄ Just some of the top producers of the Wachau – but there are scores to choose from. Disappointing or carelessly made wines from this tight-knit district are extremely hard to find. Even the co-op is distinctly superior.

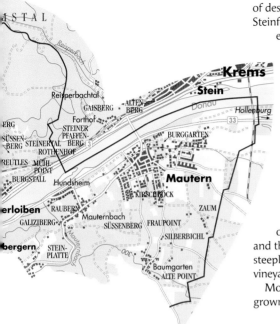

The Wachau growers have their own system of designating wines; local taste codified, in fact. Steinfeder is a light wine up to 11% alcohol for early drinking. Federspiel is made from slightly riper grapes, 11.5–12.5% (stronger than it used to be), good in its first five years. Wines labelled Smaragd (after a local green lizard), can be seriously full-bodied, with alcohol levels above – often far above – 12.5%; they repay six or more years' ageing.

Cool northern influence is at its strongest west of Spitz, while the Loibens (Unter- and Ober-) enjoy a noticeably softer climate than even Weissenkirchen. Dürnstein, in whose castle Richard the Lion-Heart was imprisoned, is the natural capital of the Wachau and the scenic climax of the valley. The baroque steeple, the ruined castle, and the village's tilting vineyards are irresistibly romantic.

Most of the Wachau's finest wines are grown on the north bank of the river, but at least one grower, Nikolaihof, makes some firm biodynamic wines around Mautern on the south bank. Fungicides are rarely called for in this dry climate, good for organic viticulture.

It is no surprise to learn that this 12-mile (20-km) mosaic of vineyards has accumulated no fewer than 900 different named sites, or *Rieden*. Their boundaries are still too debatable to map precisely here, but if one must be singled out it is Achleiten, to the northeast of Weissenkirchen. Slate and gneiss combine to give its wines a mineral signature that blind taster's should spot – or hang up their tasting cups. The Wachau wine producers' association, Vinea Wachau, swear an oath, their Codex Wachau, to make all their wines the purest and most expressive possible.

The seriously steep Schreiberberg vineyard in the foreground overlooks the broad blue Danube and its tourist traffic, with super-pretty Dürnstein downstream. It is easy to see why virtually all the vines are planted on the north bank of the river.

Kremstal and Kamptal

If the Wachau made the running in Austria's initial assault on the world's lovers of fine dry white wines, it did not take long for them to notice that the neighbouring regions of Kremstal and Kamptal produced wines of a similar quality and style – and in many cases at friendlier prices.

The pretty twin towns of Stein and Krems mark the eastern end of the Wachau and the start of the very similar but slightly less dramatic **Kremstal**. The clay and limestone vineyards round here, including the famous (Steiner) Hund, can give particular density to both Riesling and Grüner Veltliner.

The Kremstal region extends both north and south of the Danube, much of it on strangely soft loess – half soil, half rock – source of some famous Grüner Veltliners but also of full-bodied reds. Kremstal is an intermediate zone between the sharp focus of the Wachau and the greater variety of Kamptal discussed below. Parts of the region are high and steep enough to need terracing, as in the Wachau.

Among the talented producers, Malat and Nigl make racy whites with every bit as much concentration as many Wachau wines. Salomon-Undhof, which has a related wine operation in South Australia, is another notable producer with some good-value bottlings. The Stadt Krems winery and vineyards (owned by the town) are in the hands of Fritz Miesbauer, who took over in 2003 after being winemaker

at the Freie Weingärtner Wachau co-op. The municipality's ancient holdings include the 12th-century Wachtberg vineyard.

The extensive winery of Austria's largest producer, Lenz Moser, which fills 18 million bottles a year (still small by global standards) is in Rohrendorf on the lower, sandier hills of eastern Kremstal.

Kamptal, the productive buffer zone between Kremstal and Weinviertel, is the source of such outstanding wine that it has been called the K2 of Austria (Wachau being Mount Everest). Its south-facing, often loess-dominated vineyards, protected by mountains from northern chill, benefit from much the same climate and aspect as Kremstal and Wachau to the west. Kamptal is about 1.8°F (1°C) warmer than the Wachau, being lower, and produces similarly dense Riesling and Grüner Veltliner, as well as a slightly greater range of other, often lesser, varieties. The main river influence is not the broad, east-flowing Danube but its south-flowing tributary, the Kamp, which can bring cooler temperatures at night. The result is rather livelier renditions of Austria's two most famous dry white grape varieties.

The most important wine centres are Langenlois, which has been a wine town for centuries; Zöbing, famous for its Heiligenstein vineyard; and Gobelsburg, where the grand Schloss Gobelsburg has been splendidly restored since 1996 by Michael Moosbrugger,

A most unexpected vision in the middle of the vines at Langenlois in Kamptal – the famous Loisium Visitors' Centre, designed by architect Steven Holl in 2003. The Loisium Hotel combines wine, especially the local wine, with a restaurant, wine-based spa treatments, and this wine museum.

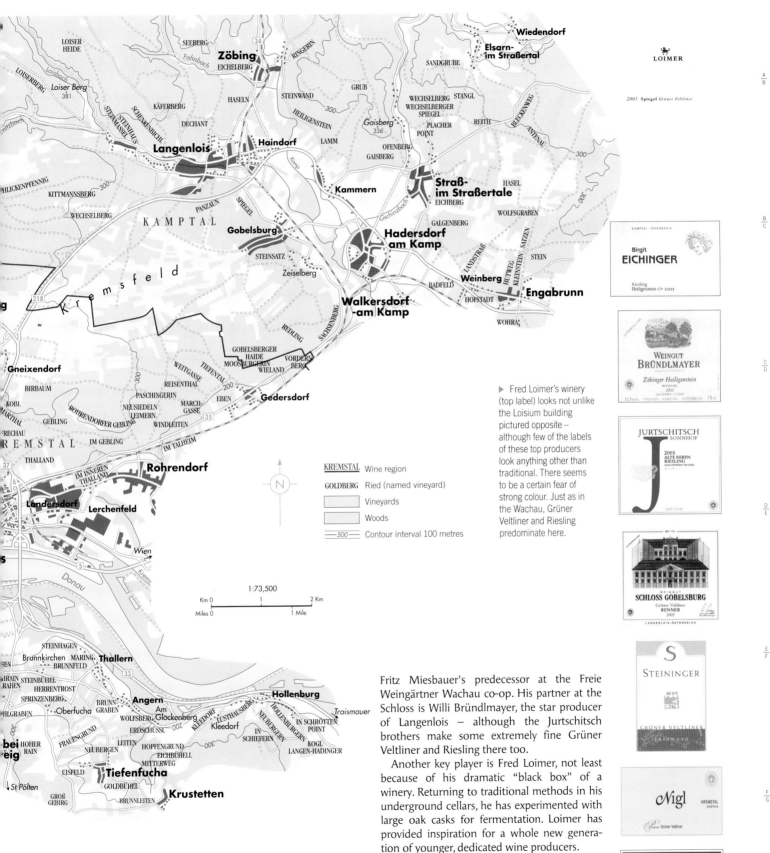

LOIMER

2005 Spiegel Grüner Veltliner

KREMSTAL Wine region

GOLDBERG Ried (named vineyard)

Vineyards

Woods

500 Contour interval 100 metres

N

1:73,500

Km 0   1   2 Km

Miles 0   1 Mile

▶ Fred Loimer's winery (top label) looks not unlike the Loisium building pictured opposite – although few of the labels of these top producers look anything other than traditional. There seems to be a certain fear of strong colour. Just as in the Wachau, Grüner Veltliner and Riesling predominate here.

Fritz Miesbauer's predecessor at the Freie Weingärtner Wachau co-op. His partner at the Schloss is Willi Bründlmayer, the star producer of Langenlois – although the Jurtschitsch brothers make some extremely fine Grüner Veltliner and Riesling there too.

Another key player is Fred Loimer, not least because of his dramatic "black box" of a winery. Returning to traditional methods in his underground cellars, he has experimented with large oak casks for fermentation. Loimer has provided inspiration for a whole new generation of younger, dedicated wine producers.

Of serious note to wine tourists in Kamptal is the exceptional Loisium Hotel in Langenlois, dedicated to wine via its wine museum, "wine spa", and restaurant with a wine list that has inspirationally well-preserved Grüner Veltliners going back to the 1930s.

Burgenland

For a long time Burgenland seemed as though it was from an earlier era of Middle Europe. It lies on the Hungarian border – indeed the Hungarian red-wine district of Sopron is carved out of it. But the flat and often sandy shores of the Neusiedl lake, an extraordinary giant marshy pool, more than 20 miles (32km) long and only a metre deep, are today the slightly improbable source of Austria's greatest sweet white and red wines: **Neusiedlersee**.

The rise of this unglamorous corner of the wine world to international fame has been extraordinarily rapid. After the Second World War, fewer than 250 acres (100ha) of vines were grown between the marshy ponds on the east shore of the lake around villages such as Illmitz and Apetlon, which then knew only dirt roads and had no electricity. Wide village streets are still flanked by simple, single-storey cottages thatched with local reeds. Horse-drawn vehicles are no surprise. The country is so flat here, and the lake so surrounded by waist-high reeds, that views of the lake are few and far between. One small 80-ft (25-m) rise is revered as a hill.

This may sound an unlikely description of great wine country. The secret is the shallow lake, enveloped by mist through its long, warm autumns, encouraging so much botrytis, or noble rot, that bunch after bunch of grapes look as though they have been dipped in ash. This is Austria's hottest wine region (too hot for early-ripening Riesling), wide open to Pannonian warmth, so red grapes (grown in a landscape not too dissimilar to the Médoc's) ripen reliably each year, yet morning mists help keep them reasonably crisp. And the final ingredient is some of the world's most thoughtful, curious, and well-travelled winemakers.

Alois Kracher, father and son, have done most to put Illmitz on the world wine map with an extraordinary range of sweet white wines (often carefully designed blends) created in the vineyard and a simple winery-cum-laboratory. Each year a series of selections are made according to the depth of botrytis – the higher the number of the Cuvée the more extraordinarily sweet the wine. Chardonnay and Welschriesling are a particularly successful combination for his world-famous Trockenbeerenauslesen. Kracher also now produces wine in California (K&K) and Málaga. Angerhof-Tschida is another notable Illmitz producer, and Willi Opitz makes waves too. These richly dramatic, intensely sweet wines are made both traditionally in large old oak casks and in the more concentrated modern style that brings a smile to French coopers' faces.

Burgenland grows a wider range of different grapes than any other Austrian region, with the red wine grapes Blaufränkisch and Zweigelt now considerably more widely grown than Grüner Veltliner. Welschriesling, Chardonnay, and Weissburgunder (Pinot Blanc) are also popular for white wines of all levels of sweetness. Neuburger, Muskateller (Muscat Ottonel), St Laurent, Sämling 88 (Scheurebe), and Cabernet Sauvignon also feature in the Burgenland wine range, but the region's historic speciality is sweet wines.

The best Neusiedlersee red wines tend to come from (slightly) higher ground further away from the lake around the villages of Frauenkirchen, Mönchhof, and Gols. Here, too, the introduction of new French oak barrels has added rigour to the local grapes Zweigelt and St Laurent, neither of which is naturally high in tannin. Producers such as Paul Achs, Gernot Heinrich, Hans and Anita Nittnaus, Juris, Umathum, Josef Pöckl, and Schloss Halbturn seem to make better quality red wines with every vintage.

Across the lake in **Neusiedlersee-Hügelland** there are real hills (which often encourage real rain) in the form of the Leithaberg Range, which gives its name to a group of particularly terroir-driven Burgenland producers, some much grander baroque architecture, and a serious history of fine winemaking. The most historically famous wine of Burgenland comes from Rust, where Feiler-Artinger is the leading producer. Ruster Ausbruch was regularly compared with Tokaji (see p.268), despite having less acidity and more alcohol, and ranks in sweetness between Beerenauslese and Trockenbeerenauslese.

Vineyards slope east down to the villages of Purbach, Donnerskirchen, Rust, and Mörbisch

International boundary
Province boundary
Parish boundary
NEUSIEDLERSEE Wine region
UNTERE LÜSS Ried (named vineyard)
Vineyards
Woods
Marsh
250 Contour interval 50 metres

◄ The most famous wines of Burgenland are Alois Kracher's remarkably rich, clean, and vibrant sweet whites, but fine sweet white is also made across the lake in Rust, while vineyards in the northeast of this map are best for plump reds. Velich have carved out a reputation for their full, dry Chardonnay from the Tiglat vineyard at Illmitz.

and, being higher than those on the east of the lake, are slightly less prone to botrytis. Serious amounts of red wine are made here and in the vineyards that stretch west almost as far as Wiener Neustadt and south past Mattersburg. Andi Kollwentz of the Römerhof estate in Grosshöflein is considered Austria's best all-round cellarmaster.

In **Mittelburgenland** to the immediate south, one vine in every two is Blaufränkisch, which really comes into its own here. The result has been increasingly sophisticated versions of this invigorating red grape, using oak in a style pioneered by the late Hans Igler. Thanks to a succession of excellent vintages in

the early years of this century, there has been considerable investment here, not least in smart winery buildings, by, for example, Albert Gesellmann, Johann Heinrich, Paul Kerschbaum, and Franz Weninger.

Blaufränkisch also reigns in **Südburgenland**, a much more dispersed wine region well south of the lake. The wines are lighter than in Mittelburgenland, with distinct minerality and spice, a reflection of the high iron content in the soil. The best producers are the Krutzler family, whose best-known bottling is Perwolff, while Uwe Schiefer's single vineyard Reihburg Blaufränkisch is also notable.

No Austrian winemaker stands still.

Such reliable and heavy infections of noble rot, or botrytis, concentrate the sugars in these grapes on the vines so carefully tended by Alois Kracher Senior. The local bird population is well aware of this and the quantities of ultra-rich Burgenland wines made by any producer depends on how effectively he or she can net them in the last few weeks of the growing season.

Hungary

Budapest is a thrilling city again; Hungary has revived – leading the longed-for awakening of Central and Eastern Europe from its communist nightmare. For centuries Hungary has had the most distinctive food and wine culture, the most developed native grape varieties, and the most refined wine laws and customs of any country east of Germany. A late 20th-century flirtation with inexpensive and rather anodyne international varietals therefore seemed a particular threat, but there are now definite signs that Hungary's extraordinary palette of indigenous white grape varieties is beginning to be recognized as an asset rather than a liability. Today, Hungarian wine producers confidently offer light, aromatic, fresh wines, especially in the north of the country; much fuller, spicier wines reminiscent of traditional styles; and oak-aged examples of both international and middle European varieties.

The characteristic traditional Hungarian wine is white – or rather warmly gold – and spicy. It tastes, if it is a good one, distinctly rich, not necessarily sweet but full of fire and even a shade fierce. It is wine for meals cooked with more spice and pepper and fat than a light wine could stand. These are dishes for Hungary's savage winters. The grapes are ripened in warmer autumns than in many parts of continental Europe, although the climate is relatively cool and the growing season shorter than in most Mediterranean regions. Average annual mean temperatures are warmest in the south, reaching 52.5°F (11.4°C) around the town of Pécs, and coolest in the north, reaching a low of around 49°F (9.5°C) at Sopron. (See over for Tokaj.) Almost all of the country's historic wine regions have evolved in the shelter of high ground; varied terrain results in a range of mesoclimates, reflected in the diversity of each region's wines. The map opposite shows the 22 wine regions defined by law in 1997, several of which now have new names.

Hungary's great grape varieties begin with the strong, acidic Furmint and the softer, more perfumed Hárslevelű – the grapes of Tokaji, but not only of Tokaji. Quite different – lighter – are the aromatic, lively Leányka (the Fetească Albă of Romania) and the even grapier Királyleányka (Fetească Regală). Other varieties grown mainly for crisp, lighter, unoaked whites are Sauvignon Blanc and the popular crossing Irsai Olivér, while Furmint, Hárslevelű, Olasz Rizling (Welschriesling), Chardonnay, Szürkebarát (Pinot Gris) and some newly planted Viognier are more likely to be fuller-bodied and oaked.

Specifically Hungarian varieties, in most cases rare today, include Kéknyelű ("blue-stalk") of Lake Balaton; the fresh, even tart, Ezerjó of Mór; Mézesfehér ("white honey"), which is rich, mouthfilling, and usually sweet; and the aromatically restrained Juhfark of Somló, which needs

time in wood to soften. Zeta, Zeus, Zenit, and Zefír are other easy-to-spot Hungarian crossings.

Hungarian red varieties are still in the minority, and grown mainly in Eger, Villány, Sopron – and on the Great Plain, the Alföld. Traditional clones of the workmanlike Kadarka (called Gamza in Bulgaria) produce agreeable, early-maturing wines for the table, notably in Szekszárd in the south, and as a seasoning in Bikáver blends. Kékfrankos is Austria's Blaufränkisch and does well in Szekszárd, as well as in Sopron. Pinot Noir shows promise around Eger, while the Cabernets are best suited to the soils and climate of sunny Villány. Merlot and the much lighter Portugieser (formerly called Kékoportó) are also grown.

Half of Hungary's vineyard area lies on the easily mechanized Great Plain, between the Duna (Danube) and the Tisza in the southern centre of the country, the regions now known as **Kunság** and **Csongrád**, on sandy soil which is little use for anything but vines. Great Plain wine, the red mainly Kadarka, the white Olasz Rizling or Ezerjó, is the day-to-day wine of Hungarian cities, although producers such as Frittmann Testvérek show that better wines are possible.

Hungary's better quality vineyards are scattered among the hills that cross the country from southwest to northeast, culminating in the Tokaj region (previously known as Tokajhegyalja, or the Tokaji foothills).

In the south the districts of Szekszárd, Villány, Pécs, Tolna, and Hajós-Baja grow both red and white wines in Hungary's warmest climate. Kadarka is the historic grape, with Kékfrankos well-entrenched. **Villány** is southernmost, warmest, and makes the running with full-bodied reds of increasing interest and complexity; with Eger in the north, it is the region that shows

Typically steep roofs rise alongside vineyards in the village of Markaz east of Gyöngyös, which is sheltered from cold northern winds by the Mátra Hills. This is definitively white wine country, on the same latitude as Chablis.

up on foreigners' radar and top wine lists in Budapest. Such growers as Attila Gere, Ede Tiffán, and Vylyan have substantial followings for Cabernet Sauvignon, Cabernet Franc (especially), and Merlot, sometimes blended with Kékfrankos or Zweigelt or even Portugieser for a Magyar twist. On the slopes of **Szekszárd**, the deep, reddish loess produces tannic Kadarka, Merlot, and the Cabernets. The names to look for are Vesztergombi, Ferenc Takler, and Péter Vida. Antinori of Tuscany has invested in Tolna nearby. Szekszárd also produces a Bikáver blend of (usually) Kékfrankos with Cabernet and Merlot. The appellation is otherwise limited to Eger.

Egri Bikáver was once Hungary's famous wine in the West, a rugged red sold as Bull's Blood. **Eger**, at the eastern end of the Mátra Hills in the northeast of the country, is one of Hungary's most important wine centres, a baroque city with huge cellars, magnificent caverns cut in the hills' soft, dark tuff. Hundreds of time-blackened oak casks, 10ft (3m) across and bound with bright red iron hoops, line 8 miles (13km) of tunnels. Their age and less-than-pristine condition played a part, along with the substitution of Kékfrankos for Kadarka, in an apparent thinning of the blood in this historic wine, but the 21st century has seen a renaissance in red wine making here. György Lőrincz, Gróf Buttler, and Tibor Gál's GIA (continued by his family after his fatal car accident), are the modern face of Eger, with Bikáver only part of much larger red and white portfolios, including some very promising Pinot Noir. Of the whites, the winner is the charming, fragrant Leányka. The sweet white Hárslevelű of Debrő, a district of Eger, was its great historic wine.

West of Eger along the south-facing slopes of the Mátra range is Hungary's second-biggest vineyard region, **Mátra**, with the town of Gyöngyös at its heart. White wines make up 80% of its output; Olasz Rizling, Tramini, and Chardonnay are successful, but standards are not notably high.

In the far west, almost on the Austrian border, is **Sopron**, a red wine outpost growing Kékfrankos, which has been revitalized by producers such as Franz Weninger from across the Austrian border in Burgenland. His redevelopment of the best sites has been followed by locals Luka, Pfneiszl, and Ráspi.

To the east of Sopron, **Aszár-Neszmély** was best-known for dry whites from traditional grapes but today produces a range of thoroughly international varietals from several new, ultra-modern wineries (of which Hilltop is the best known) designed with exports in mind. **Etyek-Buda**, just west of Budapest, is another

flourishing source of largely internationally styled whites, including sparkling wine, vast quantities of which are made in the cellars of Budafok, just south of the capital. Chateau Vincent is probably the best.

The small, isolated hill districts of **Somló** north of Lake Balaton, growing Furmint and Olasz Rizling on volcanic soil, and **Mór** to the northeast, growing Ezerjó on limestone, also have very distinct characters: Mór for tart, fresh, high-flavoured wine; Somló for more firm and mineral flavours, especially in its now-rare Juhfark. Both are among Hungary's "historical wine regions".

Lake Balaton, besides being the biggest lake in Europe, has a special significance for Hungarians. In a country with no coast, it is the sea and chief beauty spot. Balaton's shores are thick with summer villas and holiday resorts, fragrant with admirable cooking. It has good weather and a busy social life. The north shore of Lake Balaton has all the advantages of good southward exposure and shelter from cold winds, as well as the air-conditioning effect of a big body of water. It is inevitably a vineyard.

Its special qualities come from the climate, and from the combination of a sandy soil and extinct volcano stumps (Mount Badacsony is the most famous) that sprout from otherwise flat land. The steep slopes of basalt-rich sand drain well and absorb and hold the heat. Except in exceptional years when botrytized sweet wines – above all Szürkebarát – are made, most wines made here are dry, and with their strong mineral element can benefit from aeration. Olaszrizling is the common white grape. Its wine can be very good when it is only a year old; dry but fresh and clean and not too strong. Rhine Riesling can be excellent.

The Lake Balaton region has been divided into four appellations. On the north shore are the classic **Badacsony**, where Huba Szeremley's Szent Orban and József Laposa are the most renowned producers, and **Balatonfüred-Csopak**, where Mihály Figula and István Jásdi are notable. On the south shore, **Balatonboglár** is best-known on export markets for Chapel Hill. The best grower is János Konjári. Various outlying vineyards to the west, where the finest producer is Lászlo Bussay, are grouped as **Zala**.

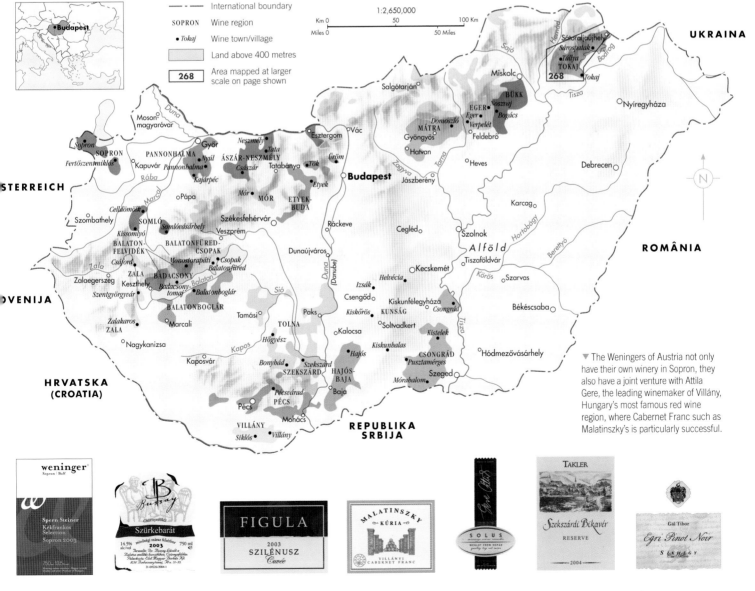

▼ The Weningers of Austria not only have their own winery in Sopron, they also have a joint venture with Attila Gere, the leading winemaker of Villány, Hungary's most famous red wine region, where Cabernet Franc such as Malatinszky's is particularly successful.

Tokaj

The word legend is more often used about Tokaji than any other wine. (Tokay is the old English spelling; the town that inspired the name, at the bottom of the map below, Tokaj.) And with good reason. When Hungary became communist in 1949 the quality of what all agreed was the greatest wine of Eastern Europe was compromised. The famous vineyards and great estates of the Tokaji hill range, Tokajhegyalja, southernmost bastion of the Tatra, the western extension of the Carpathians, lost their identity. Most were confiscated and their wines homogenized in the vast collective cellar operations that took control. Vineyards moved from steep slopes to flat land, reduced from 10,000 to a lazy 2,500 plants per hectare, and forced to spew out absurd quantities. The wine was allowed to oxidize. It was as if all the châteaux of the Médoc sent their wines to be finished and bottled in one cellar – which then pasteurized them. After 50 years, memories of even Lafite and Latour would become dim.

Tokaji, though, has been legendary for 400 years. Only champagne has spawned as many anecdotes. History relates how the sumptuous Tokaji Aszú, made from botrytized grapes, was first produced – methodically, rather than by chance – by the chaplain of the Rákóczi family in their vineyard called Oremus (his name was Szepsy; the year 1650). How in 1703 the patriot Prince Rákóczi of Transylvania used Tokaji to woo Louis XIV and drum up support against his Habsburg overlords. How Peter and Catherine (both Great) kept Cossacks in Tokaj to escort their supplies – and how its restorative properties led potentates to keep Tokaji at their bedsides.

Tokaji was the first wine knowingly to be made from botrytized or "nobly rotten" grapes; over a century before Rhine wine, and perhaps two before Sauternes. The conditions that cause the rot, the shrivelling of the grapes, and the intense concentration of their sugar, acid, and flavour are endemic to Tokaj.

The Zemplén Mountain range is volcanic, rising in typically sudden cones from the north edge of the Great Plain. Two rivers, the Bodrog and the Tisza, converge at the southern tip of the range, where Mount Kopashegy rises above the villages of Tokaj and Tarcal. From the plain come warm summer winds, from the mountains shelter, and from the rivers the rising autumn mists that promote botrytis. October is usually sunny.

Of the three grape varieties in Tokaj today, some 70% of the vines are the late-ripening, sharp-tasting, thin-skinned Furmint, highly susceptible to botrytis infection. Another 20–25% is Hárslevelű ("lime-leaf"), less susceptible but rich in sugar and aromas. Furmint and Hárslevelű are often harvested, pressed, and fermented together. Between 5 and 10% is Muscat Blanc à Petits Grains, known locally as Sárgamuskotály – either used as a seasoning grape, as Muscadelle is in Sauternes, or as a sumptuous speciality on its own.

The vineyards of Tokaj (formerly known as Tokajhegyalja) were first classified in 1700 by Prince Rákóczi. By 1737 they were divided into first, second, third, and unclassed growths. The map shows the principal villages of the region (there are 27 in all) whose slopes form a

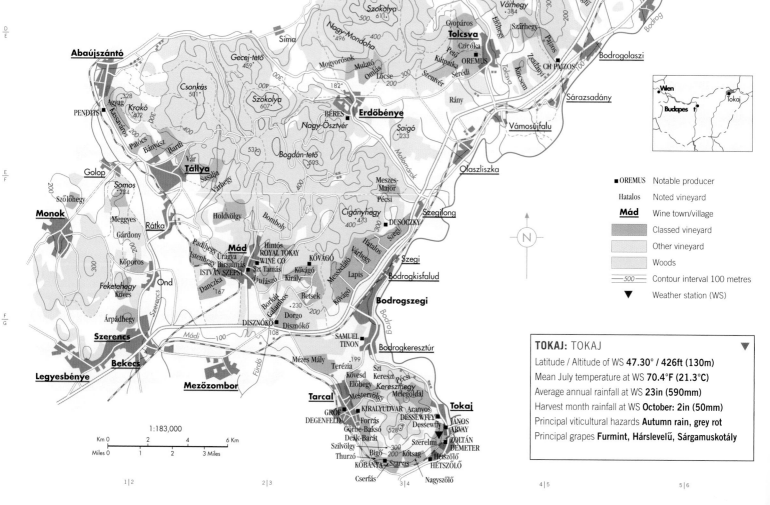

Legend:
- ■ OREMUS — Notable producer
- Hatalos — Noted vineyard
- **Mád** — Wine town/village
- Classed vineyard
- Other vineyard
- Woods
- —500— Contour interval 100 metres
- ▼ Weather station (WS)

TOKAJ: TOKAJ ▼
Latitude / Altitude of WS **47.30° / 426ft (130m)**
Mean July temperature at WS **70.4°F (21.3°C)**
Average annual rainfall at WS **23in (590mm)**
Harvest month rainfall at WS **October: 2in (50mm)**
Principal viticultural hazards **Autumn rain, grey rot**
Principal grapes **Furmint, Hárslevelű, Sárgamuskotály**

1:183,000
Km 0   2   4   6 Km
Miles 0   1   2   3 Miles

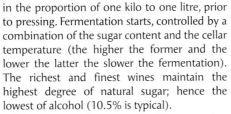

wide V, thus facing southeast, south, or southwest. The northernmost make delicate and fine *aszús* from sandy soil. It was here that the original Oremus vineyard of the Rákóczis made the first of all Aszú wines. The new Oremus cellar, owned by Vega Sicilia of Spain, has moved south to Tolcsva.

In Sárospatak, with a splendid Rákóczi castle on the river, Megyer and Pajzos were two of the first vineyards to be privatized. Kincsem is the great vineyard of Tolcsva, named after Hungary's greatest racehorse. The old Imperial Cellars in Tolcsva were still owned by the state co-op at the beginning of this century but were partly privatized in 2006 under the old name Tokaj Kereskedőház. It is still the largest producer in the region.

Olaszliszka ("Olasz" means Italian) is a 13th-century Italian settlement; more legend says the Italians introduced winemaking. Here the soil is clay with stones, producing more potent wines. Erdőbénye lies up by the oak forests, the source of barrels. Szegilong has a number of classed growths, and is seeing a revival. Bodrogkeresztúr and Tokaj itself, by the river, have the most regular botrytis.

From Tokaj, round the south side of Mount Kopashegy into Tarcal, the steep and sheltered vineyards are the Côte d'Or of the region; a succession of once-famous site names (the greatest is Szarvas) which continues through Tarcal onto the road to Mád with Terézia and the great growth Mézes Mály. In Mezőzombor, Disznókő was one of the first vineyards to be privatized and spectacularly restored by AXA of France. Mád, the former centre of the wine trade, has the famous first growths Nyulászó, Szt Tamás, Király, and Betsek, as well as the steep, abandoned Kővágó.

If the current renaissance of Tokaji has a figurehead, it is István Szepsy, an excitingly innovative grower. If it has a market leader, it is Royal Tokaji, also in Mád, founded in 1989 by Hugh Johnson and others, and the first independent company of the new regime.

Tokaji is made by a unique two-stage process. Vintage starts in late October. Shrivelled *aszú* grapes and unaffected grapes full of juice are picked at the same time but kept apart. The latter are then pressed and fermented to make various styles of dry or semi-dry wine, including a powerful base wine. The *aszú* grapes meanwhile are stored in an almost-dry heap, gently leaking the fabulous Eszencia – juice with up to 850g/l of sugar – to be reverently kept as the region's greatest treasure.

As the harvest ends, the vintner soaks the crushed *aszú* berries for 16–36 hours in fresh must or in partly or fully fermented base wine,

in the proportion of one kilo to one litre, prior to pressing. Fermentation starts, controlled by a combination of the sugar content and the cellar temperature (the higher the former and the lower the latter the slower the fermentation). The richest and finest wines maintain the highest degree of natural sugar; hence the lowest of alcohol (10.5% is typical).

The measure of sweetness is still expressed as the number of 20-kilo *puttonyos*, or vineyard hods, of *aszú* added to 137 litres (one *gönci* barrel) of base wine, although today sweetness is, more conventionally, measured in grams of residual sugar per litre and wines are fermented in barrels of various sizes, sometimes even in stainless steel. Wine sold as a 6-*puttonyos* Aszú must have more than 150g/l sugar; Aszú Eszencia is effectively 7-*puttonyos* wine, in which second fermentation is minimal, intensity phenomenal. Three *puttonyos* make it the rough equivalent of a German Auslese (at least 60g/l), four or five put it into the Beerenauslese class of sweetness and concentration. The minimum age for these Aszú wines is three years, two in barrel and one in bottle. Traditionally they were aged much longer but earlier bottling for faster turnover is now the fashion, producing wines with fresher fruit flavours but less complexity. If no *aszú* has been added, the wine is Szamorodni (literally "as it comes") – developing rather like a light sherry and either *száraz* (dry) or *èdes* (fairly sweet). The unregulated use of the term Late Harvest (*Késői szüretelésű*) on labels has added to an already complicated picture. Such wines are sweet, unaffected by noble rot, and matured only briefly.

Two more peculiarities of circumstance give Tokaji Aszú its unique character. The tradition is (or was) to leave the casks with a little headspace,

Is this the prettiest tractor shed in the world? When French insurance group AXA took over Disznókő winery in the 1990s they brought in the Hungarian architect Dezső Ekler and transformed the estate beyond all recognition.

and the pitch-black, small-bore tunnels are thickly veiled in a particular cellar mould, *Cladosporium cellare*. A rich store of yeasts and bacteria can therefore feed on the oxygen in the wine, rather as flor does on fino sherry but much more slowly, weaving a complex web of flavours.

Eszencia, the most luxurious Tokaji, is so sweet it will hardly ferment at all. And of all the essences of the grape it is the most velvety, oily, peach-like, and penetrating. Its fragrance lingers in the mouth like incense. In the old days Eszencia was stabilized with brandy. Today it has the lowest degree of any wine – if you can call it wine at all. No age is too great for it (or indeed for any great Aszú wine).

What does the future hold? Privatization of land and cellars is almost complete; some have been restored to their historic owners, some sold to newcomers. Six new ventures were begun by 1993, three of them by French insurance companies. Huge amounts of capital have been poured into upgrading vineyards, renewing equipment, and researching the finest qualities of the land. Estate-bottled Tokajis are again on the market and the names of the first growths are again becoming familiar.

As a second string to its bow, Tokaji is discovering the qualities of Furmint treated as Chardonnay. The result is dry, intense, perfumed and mineral-laden.

▼ These labels represent the full gamut of wines that have been emerging from the Tokaj region since about 2003, from full bodied and dry on the extreme left, to almost unbelievably sweet and hardly wine on the right. So high in acidity are the Furmint grapes that those intended for dry wines are sometimes picked after those for the most luscious.

Czech Republic and Slovakia

The Czech and Slovak republics, just north of such incorrigibly vinous countries as Austria and Hungary, seem destined to make good wine. But for a long time the potential was much more inspiring than the reality, all too often in the form of an undistinguished litre of lean Müller-Thurgau. The Czech wine market is dominated by two German-owned blenders and packagers with little interest in the quality-orientated family concerns whose cult offerings can be found only in the very best Czech wine shops. But wine quality and consumption continue to rise, thanks to the mastery of malolactic fermentation, oak ageing, lees contact, and making both Icewine and sweet straw wine (from dried grapes).

Across Germany's eastern border from Sachsen, **Bohemia** has about 1,800 acres (720ha) of vines, mainly along the right bank of the Elbe north of Prague, making light, Germanic-style wines, most notably at Mělník, Roudnice (famous for Sylvaner), Most, and Velké Zernoseky, which is notable for its Ryzlink Rýnský (Riesling).

Moravia, with 44,000 acres (18,000 ha) of vineyard, makes by far the majority of Czech wine from vineyards that are just over the border from Austria's Weinviertel, concentrated south of the capital Brno. They spread east from Znojmo across the peaceful Pálava Hills for some 70 miles (110km). Warm limestone slopes here are locally famous for their flora. The most successful wines of the Znojmo subregion are Sauvignon Blancs (which have real zest without exaggerated aromas) from well-equipped cellars at Nový Saldorf and Nové Bránice, and also Veltínské Zelené (Grüner Veltiner) and Riesling from Satov. Ryzlink Vlašský (Welschriesling), Chardonnay, and the two pale Pinots are the flagship wines of the Mikulov subregion. The northern part of Slovácko grows Riesling, while the southern part is better at reds such as Frankovka (Austria's Blaufränkisch). The aromatic white Pálava (from Rakvice, Lechovice, and Satov) and Muškát Moravský (Moravian Muscat) also have a certain following.

Moravian reds are not usually so interesting, although Svätovavřinecké (St Laurent) and Zweigeltrebe (Zweigelt) from the Velké Pavlovice subregion and Frankovka from Kobylí, Bořetice, and Dolní Kounice are the most satisfactory grapes at present. Pinot Noir has in general performed better than Cabernet Sauvignon, while Dornfelder shows promise in Velké Bílovice and Pavlovice.

Slovakia has much the biggest wine region of the formerly united country, with about two-thirds of its acreage and production. Slovakia's vineyards cluster round Bratislava and scatter east along the Hungarian border, enjoying a marginally warmer climate and adding the Hungarian varieties Ezerjó, Leányka, and Cserszegi Füszeres to their repertoire.

Skalica on the border with the Czech Republic is known for hearty red Frankovka, St Laurent, and André. Pezinok makes good Veltliners and Rieslings of all sorts including a popular Silvaner blend (Limbach), while Modra has the best name for Riesling, Alibernet, and Cabernet Sauvignon. Nitra grows an assortment of white grapes plus Cabernet Sauvignon. Further south, Sered' has produced Hubert sparkling wine since the early 19th century, while there is even a little enclave of Tokaji production on the far eastern border with Hungary.

The most exciting wine to have been exported from Slovakia, however, is Kastiel Belá Riesling made near Stúrovo by Egon Müller of the Saar.

▼ Egon Müller's Riesling below right reached Auslese quality in its debut (2001) vintage although in most years it is as crisp as the crunchiest green apple. The Modrý Portugal (Portugieser) is a relative rarity – a sufficiently fruity red.

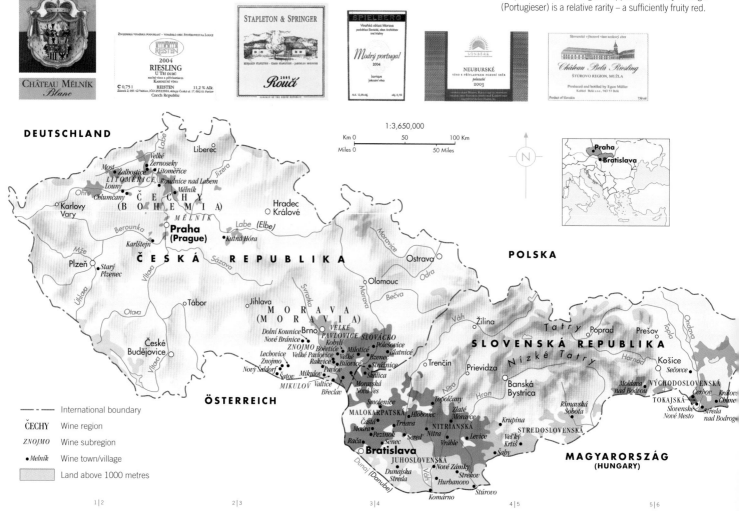

Slovenia

Even under the communists it was hard to tell where Italy stopped and Slovenia began. It was the first Yugoslav country to declare independence (in 1992) and the only one whose wine has always been acknowledged and drunk in western Europe. This relatively prosperous nation (mapped in its entirety on p.273) stretches eastwards from the Adriatic to the Pannonian Plain. The rolling foothills here provide some excellent grape-ripening sites that are grouped into three distinct wine regions: Primorska (on the coast), Posavje (along the Sava river) and, the one mapped here, Podravje (along the Drava river).

Wines made in **Podravje**, Slovenia's most important and continental wine region, are still almost exclusively white, with the dominant varieties being Laški Rizling (Welschriesling) and Šipon (Furmint) with some Renski Rizling (Rhine Riesling). Other international varieties such as Chardonnay, Sauvignon Blanc, and Pinots of all three hues are grown around Ljutomer, Ormož, Maribor, and Radgona, where Ranina (Austria's Bouvier) and Dišeči Traminec (Gewürztraminer) are particularly treasured. The wines tend to have relatively low alcohol and crisp acidity, often masked by unfermented sugar, with some seriously sweet botrytized wines and even Icewines made in favourable years. Radgona has been Slovenia's sparkling wine capital since 1852.

Wines from **Posavje**, the country's smallest though very varied wine region with a strong French influence in winemaking, can be even lighter and tarter, notably the white Rumeni Plavec, which is a speciality of the Bizeljsko Sremič subregion. The standard issue in Posavje is pink Cviček, a popular local answer to the Austrian Schilcher. In the Bela Krajina subregion the climate is partly influenced by the Gulf of Kvarner so that wines grown here tend to be stronger and even red grapes, notably Modra Frankinja (Blaufränkisch), will ripen.

The westernmost and currently most exciting Slovenian wine region is **Primorska**, part of which is mapped with Friuli on p.173. Predictably it favours the Friulian style of aromatic dry varietal whites and firm reds, which, unusually for Slovenia, represent as much as half of production. Indeed in some cases, Slovene regions are simply a continuation of their neighbours across the border in Friuli. Ribolla Gialla is the dominant white wine grape here, though red Bordeaux blends are increasingly impressive. Kras, the harsh karst limestone plateau above Trieste with its red, iron-rich soils, is the eastern extension of Carso, famous for its dark, tart Teran

Older wine drinkers in Britain may associate the village of Ljutomer with the vast quantities of over-sulphured Laski Riesling shipped there in bulk in the 1960s and 1970s, but its Jeruzalem vineyard is one of Slovenia's most venerable.

made from Refošk (Refosco) grapes, which are also grown around Koper on the Istrian coast.

Summers here are hot but autumn rains arrive early. Most of the Primorska vineyards are influenced both by the sea and the Alps and tend to produce particularly aromatic, powerful wines. As in Friuli, a wide variety of local and international varieties are grown, including Sauvignonasse (previously known here as Tokaj and as Tocai Friulano in Friuli).

1:540,000

Km 0 — 10 — 20 Km
Miles 0 — 10 Miles

- - · - · International boundary
——— Boundary of Okoliš (Appellation)
■ VINAG Notable winery
Vineyard
—600— Contour interval 150 metres

◄ Aleš Kristančič is Slovenia's best-known ambassador and a fervent convert to biodynamics. His Veliko is, like so many wines made on the borders of Friuli and Slovenia, a white blended from a host of varieties, but his varietal (Modri) Pinot Noir is also a revelation.

The Western Balkans

The winemaking traditions of the countries mapped in this strife-torn corner of Europe are as varied as one would expect of such a complex mosaic of different cultures – although there are similarities between the wine history of Croatia and that of Slovenia (which is discussed separately on the previous page).

Croatia (Hrvatska) is an important wine producer and a country full of original, if elusive, rewards, with marked distinctions between the majority of wines made along the Adriatic and Dalmatian coasts and those from the continental interior. White wines predominate except in the southern Dalmatian coastal area.

Istria (Istra) is closer in many ways to coastal Slovenia and northeast Italy. It makes mainly Merlot, Cabernet, and Teran (Refosco) reds, and whites from the particularly characterful local Malvasia, Malvazija Istarska. These full-bodied whites often have the tang of apple skins and are made, generally very competently, in a wide variety of sweetness levels. They may be unoaked or even aged, with some success, in acacia barrels. Some Muskat Momjanski is also made.

The beautiful islands along the Adriatic coast and Dalmatia to the south are a treasure trove of indigenous vines. Crljenak Kaštelanski, unearthed at Kaštela near Split, achieved international fame in the early years of this century when DNA profiling showed it was none other than the Zinfandel of California. Its close relative Plavac Mali is more commonly grown and among its most potent manifestations are dense and sweetish Dingač and pungent Postup from the steep, seaside terraces of the Pelješac Peninsula north of Dubrovnik.

Notable white wine grapes found here include Pošip and Grk on the island of Korčula, Vugava on the island of Vis, Bogdanuša on the island of Hvar, and Maraština grown all along the coast. Pošip and Bogdanuša can produce zesty white wines – such as those made by Mike Grgich, who returned to his native-Croatia from the Napa Valley in 1996. The island of Krk's speciality is Zlahtina. With Dalmatian food – tiny oysters, raw ham, grilled fish, smoky and oniony grilled meats, and mounds of sweet grapes and figs – the fire and flavour of such local wines can seem ambrosial.

Inland, continental Croatia produces rather less distinctive, mainly white, wines, typically from the local workhorse grape Graševina (Welschreisling), which tend to follow the traditions of central Europe. Wines similar to those of inland Slovenia across the border are made north of the capital in Varaždin and Sveti Ivan Zelina. Most of Croatia's best Chardonnays come from here.

Slavonia (Slavonija), more famous in the greater world of wine for the oak it provides for Italy's beloved *botte*, or larger casks, is slowly trying to re-establish its vinous traditions. Traminac (Traminer) and Riesling seem the best bets, although some Silvaner and Austria's red Zweigelt are also grown. The Kutjevo region is an important grower of Graševina.

Mountainous **Bosnia and Herzegovina** was once an important wine producer. The Austro-Hungarians developed vineyards in the late 19th century near Trebinje, particularly the characterful Vranac vine (see below) for red wines and Zilavka, which still produces some memorable, full-flavoured, dry, apricot-scented whites around Mostar. But the dominant grape today is the much more ordinary dark-skinned Blatina, whose wines tend to lack structure. Bosnia and Herzegovina continued to export considerable amounts of wine until the Second World War. The civil war of the early 1990s left a much-reduced domestic wine industry but this is now being actively rebuilt with official help from the USA, Switzerland, and the EU. Vineyards and the republic's 30-odd wineries are concentrated in Herzegovina and there are ambitious plans to increase the total vineyard area from 10,000 acres (4,000ha) in 2006 to 25,000 acres (10,000ha) by 2010.

Wine production in **Serbia** (Srbija) has a chequered history determined by its various conquerors, the Muslim Turks having done their best to rout the vine while the Hapsburgs positively encouraged it. Today, Serbia has even more vineyards than Croatia, according to OIV figures; they are concentrated on the valleys of the Danube and its tributary the Morava.

The northern autonomous province of Vojvodina shares the torrid characteristics of the Pannonian Plain with Hungary to the north and Romania to the east. Its grapes and wine styles show heavy Magyar influence in mainly full, sweetish whites plus some promising Pinot Noir. The vineyards with the best potential are on the Fruška Gora, the hills that relieve the flatness of Vojvodina along the River Danube north of Belgrade.

The countryside along the Danube here is very similar to that of inland Croatia across the border to the west, while the sandy Subotica-Horgoš and Čoka wine regions in the far north are both geographically and culturally much more Hungarian than Serbian, and the wines distinctly Magyar in character. The town of Smederevo south of Belgrade gives its name to the white Smederevka, producing scarcely memorable off-dry whites, but south of here, throughout much of southern Serbia, more invigorating red wines are made from the local Prokupac grape. This may be blended with Pinot Noir or Gamay grown in the Morava Valley, while Cabernet and Merlot with intriguing potential can also be ripened, notably around Vranje, Niš, and Leskovac in the south. To the east, towards the Bulgarian border, Timok also has potential as a red wine region although so far it is much less developed.

Until the disintegration of Yugoslavia, **Kosovo**'s wine industry was maintained largely by exports of Amselfelder, a sweet red blend designed expressly for the German market. **Albania**'s ancient wine industry is in equal turmoil but certainly has potential, which some Italian advisors are hoping to realize. The country's historic Kallmet grape produces deep-coloured, distinctively perfumed wines in the Shkodra (Shkodër) region, and is probably the

The most basic cultivation techniques at Albania's Fidal vine nursery in Lezhe, where no fewer than 140 indigenous vine varieties are said to be available. Fidal's manager advises vineyard owners what to plant where.

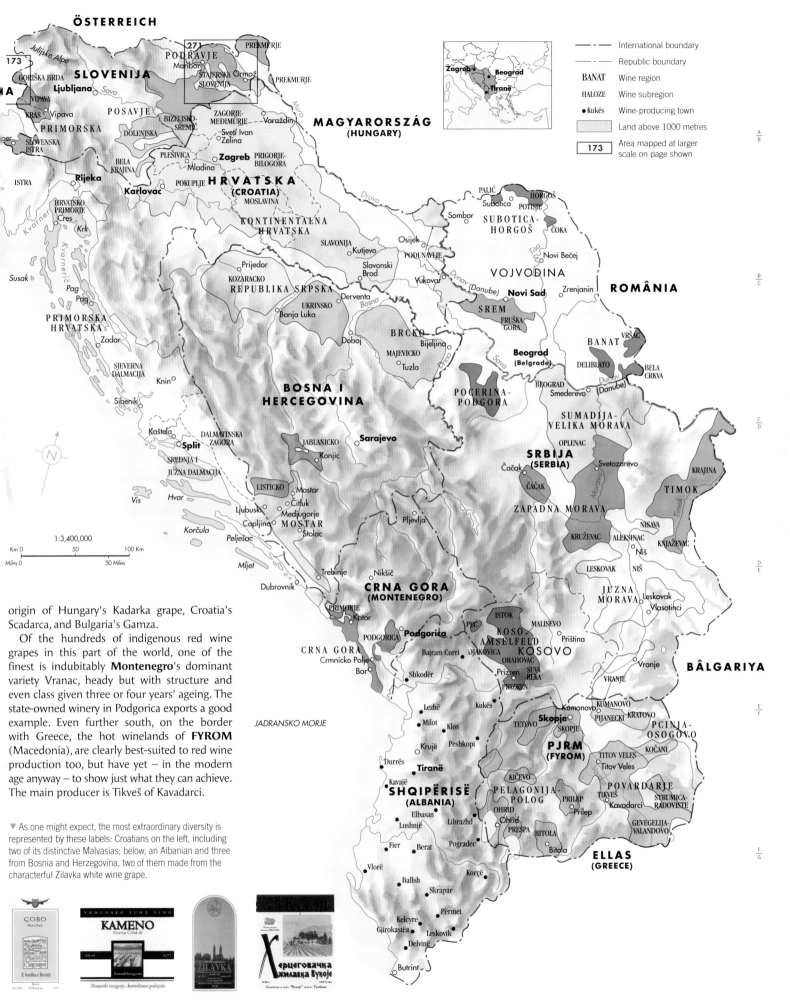

origin of Hungary's Kadarka grape, Croatia's Scadarca, and Bulgaria's Gamza.

Of the hundreds of indigenous red wine grapes in this part of the world, one of the finest is indubitably **Montenegro**'s dominant variety Vranac, heady but with structure and even class given three or four years' ageing. The state-owned winery in Podgorica exports a good example. Even further south, on the border with Greece, the hot winelands of **FYROM** (Macedonia), are clearly best-suited to red wine production too, but have yet – in the modern age anyway – to show just what they can achieve. The main producer is Tikveš of Kavadarci.

▼ As one might expect, the most extraordinary diversity is represented by these labels: Croatians on the left, including two of its distinctive Malvasias; below, an Albanian and three from Bosnia and Herzegovina, two of them made from the characterful Zilavka white wine grape.

Bulgaria

Of all the wine countries of the Soviet Bloc, Bulgaria was the most single-minded in directing its wine industry towards exports and designing it to earn hard currency. Its Cabernet became a byword for value. In the 1980s it lost the plot. At last there are signs Bulgaria is coming back, to offer good value wines from both international and indigenous varieties.

Massive plantings of international varieties on fertile land in the 1950s were intended to pump out a river of everyday wine for the Soviet Union (and later for the West). For a time the plan succeeded beyond anyone's dreams. By the late 1970s Bulgaria had begun to make a serious impression on British claret-lovers in search of a bargain. Wine exports reached a peak in 1996, and even now constitute almost half of all wine produced.

By the end of the 1990s Bulgarian wineries had started to benefit from an EU investment programme in vinification technology – resulting in such modernisms as these stainless steel tanks at Sliven, the giant East Thracian winery.

But Gorbachev's 1980s anti-alcohol purge had a profound effect on Bulgaria. As the economy foundered and the market for its produce shrank, the country's vineyards were simply neglected or abandoned. It is difficult to know exactly how much wine is today consumed or privately sold by those who grow it, but according to official figures, total plantings in 2005 were just 222,400 acres (90,000ha) and average yields had fallen to under 30hl/ha; barely half the French average. Today there are increasing signs that new vineyards are being planted and maintained to international standards and many old vineyards are now better tended.

During the 1990s the wineries and bottling plants that were once state-owned were privatized, some of the better wineries attracting investors from Western Europe and EU investment funds. Millions of dollars poured in. There is still no shortage of investors seeking to use cheap Bulgarian wine to financial advantage, but the country is in the process of drawing winemaking and grape-growing activities closer together to regain its old reputation for robust, fruity wines. The majority of wine producers realize that control over grapes is paramount and are acting accordingly. The first of the larger enterprises to invest in vineyards to any great extent were Suhindol, Stork Nest Estates, and Haskovo.

The big old wineries that persist from the communist regime continue to be bought and sold, split up and combined. A roster of hopeful investors from Bulgaria and, mainly, abroad includes Italian textile magnate Edoardo Miroglio, whose new plantings of Pinot Noir on a boutique estate at Elenovo in the mountains show promise, and the French distribution company Belvedere has been a major force. Bessa Valley has benefited from investment by the owner of Château Canon-la-Gaffelière in St-Emilion, and Château de Val is owned by a US robotics manufacturer.

In anticipation of EU entry in 2007, Bulgarian officials drew up a complex quality wine scheme around 47 listed wine regions (the associated term Controliran is sometimes used on the label). Only the most significant of these are shown on the map opposite. The term Reserve is limited to wines made from a single variety aged for a least a year before being sold.

Bulgaria, if the figures are to be believed, still has 32,000 acres (13,000ha) of Cabernet vineyard. It was unadulterated, frank, unusually vigorous Cabernet Sauvignon that built Bulgaria's reputation for value in the late 1970s and early 1980s. Merlot has since joined the party and by the beginning of this century, thanks to long overdue investment in temperature control and an influx of foreign winemaking expertise, some Bulgarian producers had finally, and rather late in the day, begun to master fresh, fruity reds and Chardonnay. Other minor imported grapes are Riesling and Sauvignon Blanc.

But Bulgarian winemakers' attention is increasingly turning to their own extremely respectable grape varieties. Mavrud is a fine, late-ripening, characterful red grape that can produce strapping spicy reds suitable for a long life. It is increasingly appreciated, and planted, mainly in the south around Plovdiv and Assenovgrad as it needs a long growing season. Melnik is another southern speciality grown exclusively in the hot Struma Valley right on the

▼ As an example of the extent to which the Bulgarian wine industry has attracted foreign investment, the owners of these labels live variously in the USA, Germany, Italy, and France – and Bulgaria. Enira is produced by Bessa Valley, while Maxxima is a relatively new Bulgarian-owned négociant.

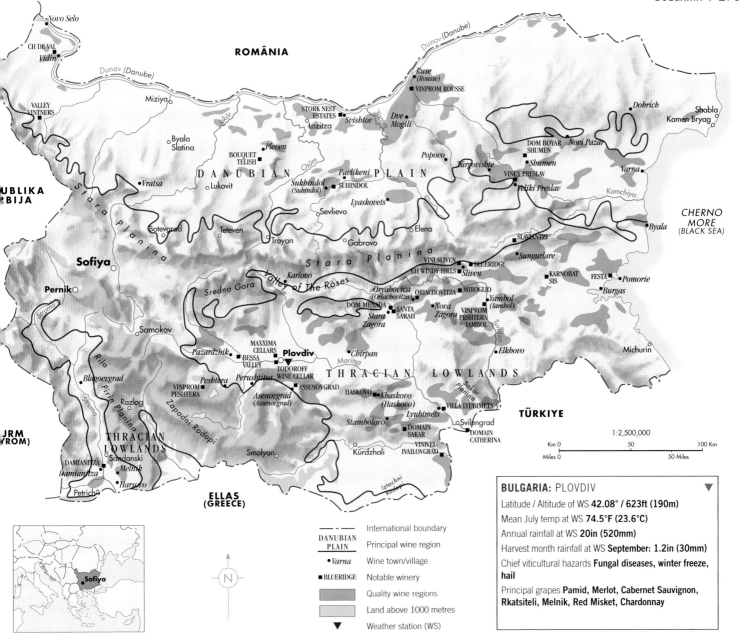

Novo Selo
CH DE VAL
Vidin
VALLEY VINTNERS
UBLIKA RBIJA

ROMÂNIA

Dunav (Danube)

Miziya
Byala Slatina
Vratsa
Botevgrad
Sofiya
Pernik
Samokov

Stara Planina

Dunav (Danube)

Lukovit
BOUQUET TELISH
Pleven
Sukhindol (Suhindol)
SUHINDOL
Sevlievo
Teteven
Troyan
Gabrovo
Valley of the Roses
Karlovo
Sredna Gora

Ruse (Rousse)
VINPROM ROUSSE
STORK NEST ESTATES
Lozitza
Svishtov
Dve Mogili
Pavlikeni
Lyaskovets
Elena

D A N U B I A N   P L A I N

Popovo
Turgovishte
SUHINDOL

Osům

Iskŭr

Dobrich
Shabla
Kamen Bryag

DOM BOYAR SHUMEN
Novi Pazar
Shumen
VINEX PRESLAV
Veliki Preslav
Varna

Kamchiya

CHERNO MORE (BLACK SEA)

Stara Planina

SLAVIANTZI
Sungurlare
VINI SLIVEN   BLUERIDGE
CH WINDY HILLS   Sliven
KARNOBAT SIS
FESTA
Pomorie
Burgas
Byala

Oryahovica (Oriachovitza)
ORIACHOVITZA
MIROGLIO
DOM MENADA
SANTA SARAH
Stara Zagora
Nova Zagora
VINPROM PESHTERA IAMBOL
Yambol (Iambol)
Elkhovo
Michurin

Pazardzhik
MAXXIMA CELLARS
BESSA VALLEY
Plovdiv
TODOROFF WINE CELLAR
Peshtera
VINPROM PESHTERA
Perushtitsa
ASSENOVGRAD
Asenovgrad (Assenovgrad)
Chirpan
Maritsa

T H R A C I A N   L O W L A N D S

Elkhovo
Michurin

Blagoevgrad
Razlog
Struma
Rila
Pirin Planina
Zapadni Rodopi

THRACIAN LOWLANDS
DAMIANITZA
Damianitza
Sandanski
Melnik
Harsovo
Petrich

Smolyan
Kŭrdzhali
Stambolovo
HASKOVO
Khaskovo (Haskovo)
Lyubimets
DOMAIN SAKAR
Svilengrad
DOMAIN CATHERINA
VINNEL-IVAILOVGRAD

VILLA LYUBIMETS

TÜRKIYE

Iztochni Rodopi

ELLAS (GREECE)

JRM (ROM)

1:2,500,000

Km 0 ...... 50 ...... 100 Km
Miles 0 ...... 50 Miles

International boundary

DANUBIAN PLAIN — Principal wine region

• *Varna* — Wine town/village

■ BLUERIDGE — Notable winery

Quality wine regions

Land above 1000 metres

▼ Weather station (WS)

BULGARIA: PLOVDIV ▼
Latitude / Altitude of WS **42.08° / 623ft (190m)**
Mean July temp at WS **74.5°F (23.6°C)**
Annual rainfall at WS **20in (520mm)**
Harvest month rainfall at WS **September: 1.2in (30mm)**
Chief viticultural hazards **Fungal diseases, winter freeze, hail**
Principal grapes **Pamid, Merlot, Cabernet Sauvignon, Rkatsiteli, Melnik, Red Misket, Chardonnay**

Greek border (see below). It makes scented, powerful wines, some of them strangely sweet but impressive survivors of long ageing in old oak. Much more common than either of these though is Pamid, which gives pale gulping wine. Rubin is a promising Bulgarian crossing of Nebbiolo and Syrah whose best examples can display more than a whiff of Nebbiolo's perfume and velvety texture.

The great majority of Bulgaria's Cabernet, Merlot, and Pamid grapes are grown in the south of the country where wines typically are riper and more structured, while the reds produced on the best sites in the north have more finesse.

Red wines predominate in all regions apart from those on the Black Sea. Most of Bulgaria's best white wines come from around Shumen and Veliki Preslav in the coolest, northeast part of the country, although Belvedere has shown that their new plantings in the Sakar Mountains can yield truly aromatic Sauvignon Blanc (see label, far right). Among whites, the dominant local varieties are Dimiat and Georgia's crisp Rkatsiteli. Red Misket (a local crossing of Dimiat and Riesling) and Muscat Ottonel are popular, as is Aligoté.

The Valley of the Roses between the Balkan and Sredna Gora mountains, famous for its damask roses, which are grown for their essential oils, or attar, produces perfumed wines too: both Misket and Muscat as well as some Cabernet Sauvignon.

Over the Rhodope and Pirin mountains (Zapadni Rodopi and Pirin Planina) in the warm southwest of the country, close to the borders of Greece and Macedonia, the Struma Valley produces only a small amount of wine. The Damianitza winery in Melnik is famous for the Shiroka Melnishka Losa ("broadleafed vine of Melnik"), and the earlier maturing variety known simply as Melnik, which makes what are surely Bulgaria's most original, tangy red wines.

Romania

Romania will surely export some great wine again one day. It is not only a matter of situation – although Romania lies on the same latitudes as France – but of temperament. Romania is a Latin country in a Slav sandwich. It has long enjoyed a natural affinity with the culture of France – and France a weakness for Romania. Its wine literature shares the sort of hard-headed lyricism of much of French gastronomic writing.

There is admittedly a great difference between the Atlantic influence, which makes France moist and mild, and the continental influence, which dominates Romania and its hot, dry summers. But there are local moderating influences: the Black Sea and the height of the Carpathian Mountains.

The Carpathians curl like a conch in the middle of Romania. They occupy almost half the country, rising from the surrounding plain to about 8,000ft (2,400m) at their peaks, and enclosing the high Transylvanian plateau. Across Wallachia, the south of the country, the Danube (Dunărea) flows through a sandy plain, turning north towards its delta and isolating the Black Sea province of Dobrogea.

In Romania, as in the old Soviet Union, a great planting programme in the 1960s turned huge tracts of arable land into vineyard, but by the mid-2000s Romania's total vineyard area was shrinking again, even if the country's 445,000 acres (180,000ha) of vines still made it the sixth largest grower and producer of wine in Europe, and by far the most important in the old Soviet Bloc. Unlike Bulgaria and Hungary, which have in their time been serious exporters of wine, Romania still drinks most of her wine herself, although capital for upgrading wineries has been flowing into the country.

Seventy per cent of the wine consumed in Romania is white, made mainly from local vine varieties. Fetească Albă (famous in Hungary as Leányka) and Fetească Regală (a 1930s crossing of the Grasă of Cotnari and Fetească Albă) are the most widely planted and, with Tămâioasă Românească, most favoured for the future, but Welschriesling and Aligoté are also common, as is Merlot. Cabernet Sauvignon, Sauvignon Blanc, Pinot Gris, and Muscat Ottonel are other international grape varieties with a track record in Romania. There is also a little Chardonnay and Pinot Noir. Of Romania's own red varieties, Babească Neagră makes light, fruity wines, and Fetească Neagră more serious stuff.

Like Hungary, Romania has one wine whose name was once famous all over Europe. But while Tokaji struggled on through socialism to re-emerge in splendour, Cotnari, which was described as "green" and known in Paris as "Perle de la Moldavie", faded from sight. It is now being resurrected. Cotnari was traditionally a natural white dessert wine made in the northeast of the country. It is like Tokaji but only medium sweet and without oak influence: pale, delicate, and aromatic; the result of botrytis attacking the indigenous "fat" Grasă and tart Frâncusa, scented with what is considered the indigenous and highly perfumed Tămâioasă (the frankincense grape) and Fetească Albă. Barrel ageing is brief: complexity develops in the bottle. Cotnari comes from the part of Moldavia that was left to the Romanians after first the Tsars then the Soviets had annexed its northern half – annexation that led to intense planting further south.

The country today is divided into seven wine regions, of which Romanian **Moldova**, to the east of the Carpathians, is by far the biggest, with over a third of all Romania's vineyards. Hilly Muntenia and Oltenia, the southern ramparts of Transylvania, come next with about a quarter.

Northern Moldova is white wine country, with Cotnari as its pearl. The great concentration of production, though, is further south in the central Moldavian Hills: Vrancea, with Focşani as its capital and 50,000 acres (20,000ha) under vine. Coteşti, Nicoreşti, Panciu (known for sparkling wine), and Odobeşti (a brandy centre) are the lilting names of its wine towns. The terrain varies but much of it is sand, as in the Great Plain of Hungary. The vines have to be planted in pockets dug deep enough for their roots to reach the subsoil, sometimes as much as 10ft (3m) below the surface. It seems a desperate expedient, especially as it takes the vine some time to grow up to ground level and come to bear fruit. But good light wines are being made where nothing would grow before.

Following the curve of the Carpathians, Moldova gives way to **Muntenia** and **Oltenia**, the former better known by the name of its most famous vineyards at Dealu Mare. These hills, well-watered, south-sloping, and with the highest average temperatures in Romania, are largely dedicated to Cabernet, Merlot, and Pinot Noir, as well as full-bodied Fetească Neagră,

This plaster relief on a typically Transylvanian house at Hogilag in the Târnave area reminds us just how important wine production, and consumption, has been (and still is) to Romania. Until now, however, it has been something of a domestic secret.

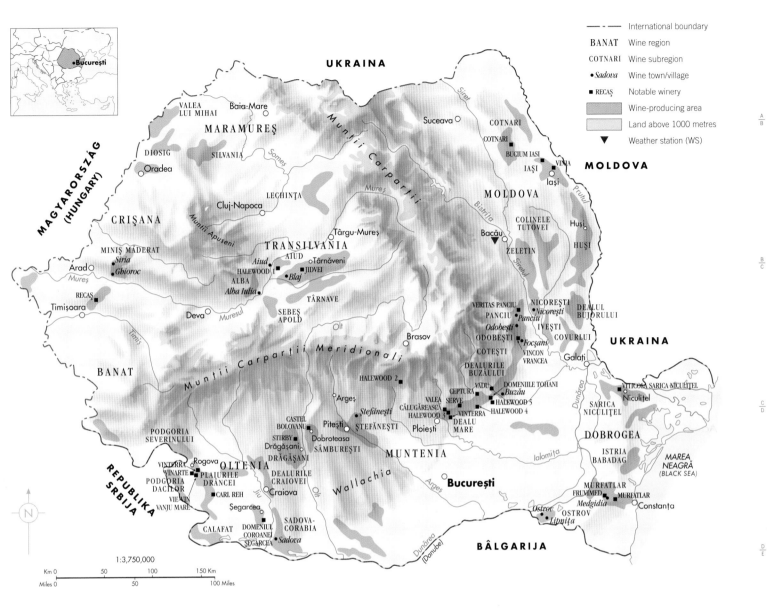

Burgund Mare (Austria's Blaufränkisch), and, more recently, some appetizing Sangiovese. In Soviet days, red wines from here were generally made sweet to suit the Russian market. Exports to the West, particularly of well-priced Pinot Noir and Cabernet, have helped to correct this. One white speciality stands out: unctuous and aromatic dessert Tămâioasă from Pietroasa (northeast of Dealu Mare).

Romania's short Black Sea coast gives **Dobrogea**, across the Danube to the east, the country's sunniest climate and lowest rainfall. Murfatlar has a reputation for soft red wines and luscious white ones, even sweet Chardonnays, from exceptionally ripe grapes grown on limestone soils, tempered by on-shore breezes.

The outcrops of Carpathian foothills scattered through Muntenia and Oltenia each have their own specialities. Piteşti is known for aromatic white wines (particularly from Stefăneşti); Drăgăşani for Cabernet Sauvignon, Merlot, and Pinot Gris, especially from Sâmbureşti. Vânju Mare to the west has an established name for Cabernet, and a growing one for Pinot Noir.

In the western corner of Romania, the Hungarian influence is plainly felt; many of the red wines of **Banat** are made from Pinot Noir, Merlot, and Cabernet Sauvignon. The best come from Recaş. The principal white grapes are Fetească Regală, Welschriesling, and Sauvignon Blanc.

Transilvania, meanwhile, remains like an island in the centre of the country: a plateau 1,500ft-plus (460m) above sea level, cool and relatively rainy, favouring much fresher and crisper whites than are produced in the rest of Romania. Târnave makes the best dry Fetească; Alba Iulia the most aromatic Muscat Ottonel and Gewürztraminer.

It remains to be seen what effect Romania's entry to the EU will have on its wine industry.

ROMANIA: BACAU ▼

Latitude / Altitude of WS **46.35° / 623ft (190m)**

Mean July temp at WS **67.8°F (19.9°C)**

Annual rainfall at WS **21in (540mm)**

Harvest month rainfall at WS **September: 1.8in (45mm)**

Chief viticultural hazards **Spring frost, drought, September rain, winter freeze**

Principal grapes **Fetească Regală, Merlot, Welschriesling, Fetească Albă, Băbească Neagră, Aligoté, Cabernet Sauvignon**

▼ Romania has traditionally exported much less than 10% of her substantial wine production. All these labels are, unusually, designed for export markets, with La Cetate, for example, owned by Carl Reh of Germany.

The Former Soviet Republics

In the 1970s the Soviet Union was the world's third biggest wine producer. By the end of the 20th century it was reduced to producing a mere 3% of the global total. President Gorbachev's campaign to cut alcohol consumption included domestic wine producers (and neighbouring suppliers), with devastating effect.

When the Soviet Union broke up in the early 1990s, many vineyards had already been pulled up and others abandoned for lack of a market. There are still many chronic and apparently contradictory difficulties: an anarchic commercial environment allied with an excess of bureaucracy; outdated and obstructive analytical standards but a dangerous lack of controls over exactly what goes into which wines – some of them on sale in Russia containing no grapes whatsoever. In 2006 Russian president Vladimir Putin used this last as an excuse to ban wine imports from Moldova and Georgia altogether, a crushing blow for both wine industries.

Serious wine producers are pressing for some sort of wine regulation to combat the fraud that is so widespread, and in some quarters at least there is real interest and investment in the regions that gave Russia her best wines in the past. Without exception, these lie in the broad sweep mapped below around the north coast of the Black Sea as far east as the Caspian Sea.

Moldova in the extreme west is the ex-Soviet republic with the most vines and the most obvious potential. This is largely thanks to the efforts of French colonists, who, at the end of the 19th century, ensured that the great majority of vines planted here, as in neighbouring Romania, are the most saleable varieties in the world: Cabernet Sauvignon and Merlot.

The Kremlin cellars of the Tsars looked to what was then Moldavia (and anciently Bessarabia) for their finest table wines. Moldova's history has been a tug-of-war between Russia and Romania. Happily for its (largely Romanian) people, neither side prevailed and Moldova won the prize of independence in 1991. (See p.276 for details of wine production in Romanian Moldova.)

During the Soviet years, Moldova's natural affinity for the vine had been paid the back-handed compliment of a colossal, indiscriminate planting programme, reaching almost 600,000 acres (240,000ha), and in the early 1980s furnishing one-fifth of the Soviet Union's wine-drinking requirements. A combination of particularly severe winters with Gorbachev's anti-alcohol campaign still left Moldova with 370,000 acres (150,000ha) in the mid-2000s, an extraordinary one-twelfth of the area of the country.

The elements that combine to grow first-class grapes in Moldova are the latitude of Burgundy, relatively poor soils, the slopes of the many valleys, and a climate tempered by the Black Sea. Winters are occasionally cold enough to kill unprotected vines, but long-established vineyards in the best sites have an almost model climate.

The great majority of vines are planted in southern and central Moldova around the capital Chisinău. Moldova's most famous vineyard today is at Purcari in the southeast, where Cabernet and Saperavi, the splendid red Georgian grape producing dark, plummy, acidic wines for long ageing, make a formidable claret-like blend. Only the country's lack of stable commercial environment has frustrated most foreign attempts so far to capitalize on Moldova's most obvious asset. Cricova Acorex is a notable exception, however, exporting very competent international varietals, notably Pinot Gris.

The second most important vine-grower among the ex-Soviet republics is Moldova's eastern neighbour **Ukraine**, although its wine industry is yet to attract much outside investment. While there are significant vineyards around the Black Sea ports of Odessa and Kherson, by far the most interesting wine region is the Crimea (Krym).

The Crimea became part of the Russian Empire under Catherine the Great at the end of the 18th century. The Mediterranean climate of its south coast soon made it the natural resort

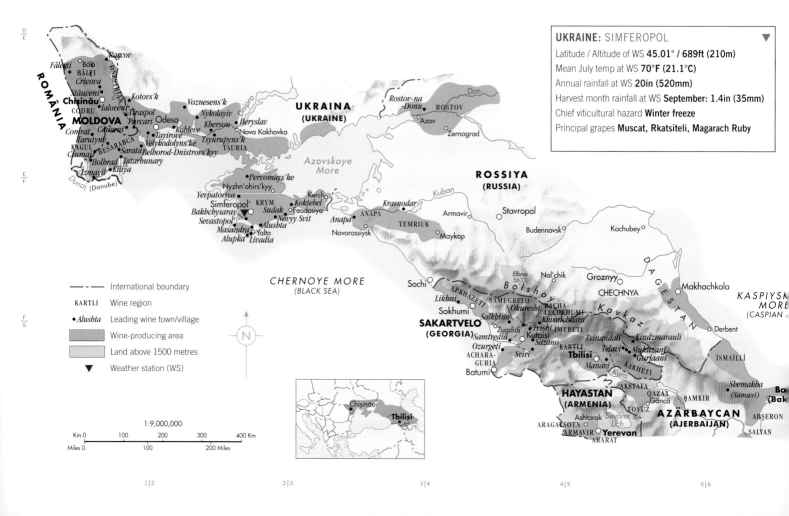

UKRAINE: SIMFEROPOL

Latitude / Altitude of WS **45.01° / 689ft (210m)**

Mean July temp at WS **70°F (21.1°C)**

Annual rainfall at WS **20in (520mm)**

Harvest month rainfall at WS **September: 1.4in (35mm)**

Chief viticultural hazard **Winter freeze**

Principal grapes **Muscat, Rkatsiteli, Magarach Ruby**

- International boundary
- KARTLI Wine region
- •Alushta Leading wine town/village
- Wine-producing area
- Land above 1500 metres
- ▼ Weather station (WS)

1:9,000,000

Km 0   100   200   300   400 Km

Miles 0   100   200 Miles

area for the more adventurous aristocracy. It was developed by the famously rich and cultured anglophile Count Mikhail Vorontzov in the 1820s. Vorontzov built a winery, and later his palace, at Alupka, southwest of Yalta, and founded a wine institute (wine being his passion) at Magarach nearby, which continues to be the most important in the ex-Soviet republics.

In a precise parallel with what was going on in Australia at the same time (and California a generation later), Vorontzov began by imitating as closely as possible the great wines of France. His success was as limited as someone trying to make burgundy in Barossa. The south coast was too hot. Only 6 miles (10km) inland, on the other hand, it was too cold. Winter temperatures go down to -4°F (-20°C) and vinifera vines have to be completely buried to survive at all. Notwithstanding, there were vast inland plantings by the Soviets, not just of the white Georgian grape Rkatsiteli, but also of winter-hardy crossings bred specially for the rigours of the local climate at Magarach.

A generation after Vorontzov, Prince Lev Golitzin was more scientific. After the Crimean war of 1853–56, the Tsar built a summer palace, Livadia, between Alupka and Yalta. Golitzin had remarkable success making Russia's second favourite drink, sparkling "shampanskoye", 30 miles (50km) east along the south coast at his Novy Svet ("New World") estate – a tradition that continues.

But the destiny of the Crimea clearly lay in dessert wines. In 1894 the Tsar built "the world's finest winery" at Massandra, near Livadia, with Golitzin in charge, to develop the potential of the south coast, a narrow 80-mile (130-km) belt between mountains and sea, for strong sweet wines of all sorts.

These wines established a fabulous reputation in pre-revolutionary Russia. They were called "Port", "Madeira", "Sherry", "Tokay", "Cahors" (a wine with historic status within the Russian Orthodox church), or even "Yquem", as well as Muscats, White, Pink, and Black. The Massandra winery still houses nearly a million bottles of these wines, in what must be the world's largest, and certainly most distinctive, collection of old wines.

Russia itself has rather less land devoted to the vine than Ukraine, according to official OIV figures. Most of Russia's vines are planted somewhere on this map, not too far from the tempering influence of the Black and Caspian seas on the country's harshly continental climate, which generally means vines have to be painstakingly buried each winter for protection.

Krasnodar, with a thriving wine culture, is Russia's most important wine-producing region, with Rostov-on-Don second. The vines in Stavropol, Chechnya, and Dagestan are mainly devoted to brandy.

While the old industrial wineries of the Soviet regime were rapidly becoming too obsolete even for reliable bottling, let alone winemaking, by the mid-2000s there were already signs of increasing interest in modern wine production with revamped old enterprises such as Myskhako and Fanagoria, and new, French-influenced ones such as Château Le Grand Vostock and Château Tamagne. Myskhako is already exporting Chardonnay to the West and developing wine tourism possibilities on the Black Sea coast.

The majority of new vines planted are imported from France but some growers are exploring the potential of such indigenous varieties as Pinot Franc, Golubok, and Krasnostop (meaning the same as Piedirosso – red foot – in Italian). Georgia's Saperavi also grows well in the Russian south. The principal white wine varieties are Chardonnay, Sauvignon Blanc, Aligoté, and Rkatsiteli.

As was long the Soviet tradition, semi-industrial plants near the major cities process wines and grape concentrate imported in bulk from all over the world, catering particularly to Russians' historic love of sparkling wines. Nevertheless, traditional method all-Russian examples can still be found at the Abrau Durso winery (also founded by Golitzin) in Krasnodar, while the Tsimlianskiy plant in Rostov-on-Don is working on its rather less sophisticated sparkling wines.

In the past, a heavy dose of sweetening, in reds just as much as whites, covered a multitude of winemaking sins but as more and more Russians are exposed to western influences and tastes, not least via the vibrant restaurant scene in Moscow and St Petersburg, it is to be expected that Russian taste in wine will increasingly favour drier styles.

The Armenian diaspora has ensured that wine labelled Armenian has long enjoyed cachet in Russia, even if **Armenia** has only about 32,000 acres (13,000ha) of vines, the

Modern bottling lines may not be the distinguishing marks of wineries in most of the world but in Russia equipment as relatively new and efficient as this at the Fanagoria winery, which lies on the Taman Peninsula between the Black and Azov seas, northwest of Anapa, is still comparatively rare.

The Chandrebi vineyard at 1,700ft (520m) above sea level near the village of Ikalto in Kakheti, Georgia, was completely redesigned in 2001, and is now divided into blocks that are monitored, picked, and vinified separately. The mainly Saperavi grapes are bought by Orovela (see label below).

Muscovites rate Georgian Saperavi their old empire's most reliable red. This blow fell at the same time the Kremlin banned Moldova's potentially excellent wines.

Georgia has three historic wine regions. Kakheti, where more than two-thirds of all Georgian grapes are grown, is the driest, spanning the easternmost foothills of the Caucasus. Kartli, where *kwevri* are rare, lies on flatter land round the capital, Tblisi, and Imereti, to the west, has more humid conditions.

North of here in Racha-Lechkumi the climate is much wetter and local Alexandreuili and Mujuretuli grapes mainly produce naturally sweet wines. Local varieties and naturally sweet wines also predominate in the humid, subtropical zone around the Black Sea coast.

Modern winemaking came to Georgia with Russian settlers early in the 19th century. Pushkin preferred the results to burgundy, and such estates as Tsinandali became famous. Under the Soviets, decline was inevitable, but since independence progress has been slow. A joint venture between the Georgian Wine & Spirit Company and Pernod Ricard, based on a combination of traditional winemaking techniques and modern quality control methods applied in a modern winery in the Kakhetian city of Telavi, is Georgian wine's most energetic exporter.

The red Saperavi is an extremely promising variety, in a global context, and gives the best available wines – many but by no means all of them sweet, but with lively tannins and acidity that keeps them fresh in the mouth. Rkatsiteli has proved itself a useful and adaptable grape throughout the Black Sea zone and even in the New World. Georgian winemakers are very self-aware, and despite shortages of equipment (and even of bottles) compete to exhibit better and better wines, both the old style and the new. For the moment politics stand in the way of real progress, but no one doubts that Georgia's grapes, its climate, and its temperament have extraordinary potential.

great majority of them supplying raw materials for the even more popular Armenian brandy. Vineyards here are at altitudes of up to 5,250ft (1,600m) and are attracting interest from expatriate investors, even if in the mid-2000s there was still a shortage of modern winemaking equipment and most grapes were still processed in old Soviet-style wine factories. The indigenous Areni grape is particularly promising and can yield some impressively fresh, delicate, almost burgundian reds in the Yeghegnadzor region, which lies to the southeast of the Armenian capital, Yerevan.

Azerbaijan also produces wine, much of it sweet red, notably from its Matrassa grape.

Georgia is a very different case from the other former Soviet republics. The Georgians may not be the only people to think that they invented wine, but they have a better archaeological case than most. There are grape-pip findings suggesting winemaking at least 5,000 years old, and artefacts of that age proving an extraordinary respect for vine cuttings. They have had time and motivation to develop at least 500 different vine varieties, and uniquely still employ pre-classical methods of winemaking. A

visit to a Georgian *marani*, the outdoor "cellar", where wine is fermented in *kwevri*, earthenware vessels buried to their brims in the soil, has a Homeric feel.

Everything goes into the *kwevri*: trodden grapes, skins, stalks and all. It stays there until a celebration calls for supplies. The result, whether fermented dry or not, is seriously tannic, a taste to acquire, but at best is remarkably good wine. This is not the way industrial wine is made, and is unlikely to survive without a miracle, but the flavours of Georgia's best grapes need no such intervention: pale-skinned Mtsvane, the sterling, red-fleshed Saperavi, and characterful, reliably crisp Rkatsiteli. These and the sweet, fizzy shampanskoye lubricate a lively social life.

Georgians are notorious for their relish and capacity for wine, seeing a natural connection between their famously long lives and the potency and nutritional value of Saperavi. Georgian wine has commanded a premium within Russia since the time of Pushkin. Sadly the temptation to fake it seems to have been too strong. That at least is the reason the Kremlin (no friend to Georgia) gave in 2006 for banning its import, despite the fact that

▼ From the left: Two Moldovan labels, one (a 1929) from the Crimea, a Russian Merlot from Fanagoria (presumably applied by the equipment pictured overleaf), a Russian Cabernet, and three Georgian specialities. Teliani Valley in Tsinandali, Kakheti, is the modern successor to a winery built for the Russian Romanovs in the 1880s.

Greece

The modern winescape of Greece is even more exciting than most because it holds such potential for going backwards as well as forwards in time. In the past decade, Greece has built a newly respected name not on imported international grapes – although these are certainly grown – but on indigenous grapes. Some of them (they are predominantly white) may well be able to trace their lineage back to Ancient Greece, the cradle of modern wine culture as we know it.

This new era for Greek wine began in 1985 with the return of a handful of agronomists and oenologists from formal training in France. An influx of funds from both the EU and ambitious individuals allowed them to upgrade technology in some of the larger négociants (notably Boutari and Kourtakis) and to establish new, much smaller wineries in cooler areas where land was relatively cheap. Their successors are just as likely to have learnt their skills at Adelaide in Australia or Davis in California as in Athens. An increasingly affluent middle class has provided willing buyers for these robustly priced new wines – aeons away from the oxidized ferments once typical of Greek wine.

Many outsiders may intuitively feel that Greece must be too hot and dry to make good-quality wine, but growing grape varieties that can cope with local conditions has been key to successful wine production, and altitude and exposure usually play their part. In fact some wines made in cooler vintages on the Mantinia plateau in the Peloponnese interior have to be deacidified, and in Naoussa in Macedonia in the north of Greece, some vintages have been critically plagued by rain and rot, while some north-facing vineyards can have trouble ripening the fruit at all.

Greece now has a quality designation system modelled on the French one, with eight OPEs, equivalent to ACs, and a generous 25 OPAPs, supposedly equivalent to VDQSs. When devising the system, the authorities designated as OPE those products they considered in most need of protection, which is why all eight are sweet Muscats or Mavrodaphnes. Most sweet Greek wines today, incidentally, are made as Vins Doux Naturels (see p.144) rather than from dried grapes as they were traditionally.

Northern Greece is the area with the most unrealized potential – and where the Greek wine revolution was heralded most conspicuously in the 1960s at Château Carras.

Physically **Macedonia** relates more to the Balkan landmass than to the Aegean limbs of Greece. This is red wine country, dominated by one variety, Xinomavro, whose name ("acid black") denotes sourness but whose slow-maturing wines are some of the most impressive in the country. **Naoussa** is the most important appellation and the country's first (1971). With age the best-made wines can acquire a bouquet as haunting as all but the finest Barolo – although many wineries here in the north are still poorly equipped. There is snow on the slopes of Mount Vermio in winter but summers are so dry that irrigation is essential. The land is sufficiently varied and extensive for individual *crus* to deserve identification.

Gouménissa, at slightly lower altitudes on the slopes of Mount Piako, produces a rather plumper version of Naoussa. **Amindaio** on the northwest-facing side of Mount Vermio is so cool that it can produce aromatic whites, a denominated Xinomavro rosé, and good sparkling wine. Fine, dense, cool-climate Xinomavro does exist, as Boutari has shown.

An increasing number of international Vins de Pays are made around Kavála. Biblia Chora makes super-zesty blends, and in Drama in the far northeast of the country Lazaridi is an example of modern Greeks' confidence in their wine, seen in isolated developments all over

A terraced vineyard on the island of Sámos, where nearly all the vines were replaced by Muscat after phylloxera devastated the vineyards at the end of the 19th century. All winemaking is in the hands of the co-operative, which produces a competent range of styles and sweetnesses.

northern Greece. Gerovassiliou of Epanomí, just south of Thessaloníki, is experimenting with Petite Sirah and Viognier as well as the indigenous white Malagousia.

Zítsa is the only appellation in **Epirus** in the northwest, with Debina the most planted white grape for still and fizzy dry wines. Epirus has Greece's highest vines at Métsovo, at nearly 4,000ft (1,200m), and the oldest Cabernet Sauvignon, planted at Katogi Averoff in 1963. Rapsáni is the area's flagship red.

Négociants and co-ops dominate **Central Greece**. The traditional Athenian wine, from the capital's backyard, **Attica** (Attiki), is retsina, the curious resinated ferment that for so long dogged Greece's vinous reputation. Attica is the country's biggest single wine region, with

▼ Of this varied selection made all over Greece and its islands, only the Hatzimichalis Merlot is based on an imported international grape variety – although the other notable wine of Alpha Estate, near the Albanian border, is based on particularly fine Sauvignon Blanc.

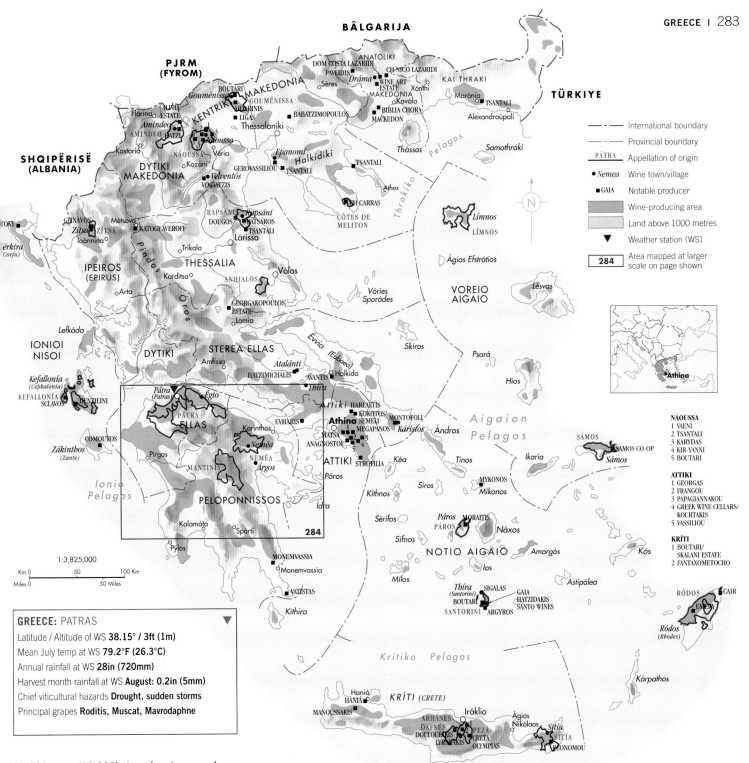

BÂLGARIJA

PJRM (FYROM)

TÜRKIYE

SHQIPËRISË (ALBANIA)

ANATOLIKI
DOM COSTA LAZARIDI   CH NICO LAZARIDI
PAVLIDIS   *Dráma*
WINE ART   Xánthi   KAI THRAKI
ESTATE   Kavála
MAKEDONIA   Marónia   TSANTALI
BIBLIA CHORA   Alexandroúpoli
MAKEDON

BOUTARI   GOUMÉNISSA
ALPHA   Gouménissa
ESTATE
Flórina   VIDARINIS
AMINDEO HATZI   LIGAS
Amindeo   BABATZIMOPOULOS
Kastoriá   Náoussa   Thessaloníki
NÁOUSSA   Véria   Epanomi
KENTRIKI MAKEDONIA   Halkidiki   *Thássos*   *Thrakiko Pelagos*   *Samothráki*
DYTIKI   Kozáni   EPANOMI
MAKEDONIA   Siátista   Velventós   GEROVASSILIOU   TSANTALI   TSANTALI
VOGIATZIS   HALKIDIKI   *Athos*
GRINAVOS   Métsovo   CÔTES DE
Zítsa   ZÍTSA   KATOGI AVEROFF   MELITON
Ioánnina   RAPSÁNI   *Rapsáni*   KARI CARRAS
DOUGOS   MATSAROS
IPEIROS   Trikala   TSANTALI
(EPIRUS)   Lárissa   *Límnos*
érkira   Pindos   Oros   LÍMNOS
Corfu   THESSALIA   *Ágios Efstrátios*

Lésvos

ANHIALOS
Vólos
Vóries
Sporádes   VOREIO
IONIOI   Karditsa   AIGAIO
NISOI   GEORGAKOPOULOS   *Skíros*
DYTIKI   ESTATE   *Psará*   *Híos*
Lefkáda   STEREA ELLAS   Lamía   *Ewia (Euboea)*
Arta   Amfissa
Atalánti
HATZIMICHALIS   AVANTIS   *Thiva*
Kefallonía   Pátra   Ávantis   Halkída   *Tínos*
(Cephalonia)   (Patras)   Égio   HARLAFTIS   *Kárystos*   *Aigaion Pelagos*   SÁMOS
KEFALLONÍA   PÁTRA   KOKOTOS   MONTOFOLI   SÁMOS CO-OP
SCLAVOS   GENTILINI   ELLAS   Korinthos   SEMELI   *Ándros*   *Sámos*
EVHARIS   Athina   MEGAPANOS   *Kéa*
COMOUTOS   MANTINIA   MATSA   ANAGNOSTOU   ATTIKI   STROFILIA   *Mykonos*   *Ikaría*
Zákinthos   Neméa   *Mikonos*
(Zante)   Pírgos   NEMÉA   *Póros*   *Kíthnos*   *Síros*
Ionio   Argos   *Sérifos*   *Páros*   MORAITIS   NOTIO AIGAIO   *Náxos*
Pelagos   PELOPONNISSOS   *Sífnos*   PÁROS   *Kós*
Kalamáta   284   *Idra*   *Milos*   *Ios*   *Amorgós*
Pylos   *Astipálea*   RÓDOS   CAIR
Spárti   *Kritiko Pelagos*   EMERY
MONEMVASSIA   *Thíra*   SIGALAS   *Ródos*
Monemvassía   *(Santorini)*   GAIA   (Rhodes)
BOUTARI   HATZIDAKIS
VATISTAS   SANTO WINES
Kíthira   SANTORINI   ARGYROS   *Kárpathos*

Kámathos

Haniá   *KRÍTI (CRETE)*
HÁNIA   Iráklio
MANOUSSAKIS   ARHÁNES   Ágios
DÁFNES   PEZÁ   Nikólaos   Sitía
DOULOUFAKIS   CRETA   SITÍA
LYRARAKIS   OLYMPIAS   ECONOMOU

1:3,825,000

Km 0   50   100 Km
Miles 0   50 Miles

GREECE: PATRAS ▼

Latitude / Altitude of WS **38.15° / 3ft (1m)**

Mean July temp at WS **79.2°F (26.3°C)**

Annual rainfall at WS **28in (720mm)**

Harvest month rainfall at WS **August: 0.2in (5mm)**

Chief viticultural hazards **Drought, sudden storms**

Principal grapes **Roditis, Muscat, Mavrodaphne**

Legend:

— · — International boundary

— — Provincial boundary

PÁTRA Appellation of origin

• *Nemea* Wine town/village

■ GAIA Notable producer

▬ Wine-producing area

▬ Land above 1000 metres

▼ Weather station (WS)

284 Area mapped at larger scale on page shown

NÁOUSSA
1 VAENI
2 TSANTALI
3 KARYDAS
4 KIR-YANNI
5 BOUTARI

ATTIKI
1 GEORGAS
2 FRANGOU
3 PAPAGIANNAKOU
4 GREEK WINE CELLARS/ KOURTAKIS
5 VASSILIOU

KRÍTI
1 BOUTARI/ SKALANI ESTATE
2 FANTAXOMETOCHO

27,000 acres (11,000ha) under vine, mostly on the arid, infertile plain of Mesogia. An increasing number of fine unresinated wines are now made in Attica, although Savatiano, the base for retsina and the country's most widespread vine variety, accounts for 95% of plantings.

Of the Greek islands, **Crete** (Kríti) is much the biggest wine producer, famous in Venetian times for its sweet Malmseys. These seem, alas, to be extinct, but the island's moribund wine industry has recently attracted much-needed funds and enthusiasm. Boutari's Fantaxometocho estate, outside Heraklion (Iráklio), is a hopeful sign. The best vineyards are relatively high. A recent trend on Crete has been the cultivation of Rhône grape varieties, often for blends with local varieties such as Kotsifali.

Cephalonia (Kefallonía) and its Ionian neighbour **Zante** (Zákinthos), with its own lively red Avgoustiatis grape, come next in importance, especially for fresh white Robola and Tsaoussi, as well as for imported grapes. Corfu is not an island for wine tourists.

In the Aegean, several islands make sweet wines of Muscat. **Sámos** is the best and most famous, and the prime exporter, with utterly clean young wines and some tempting oak-aged ones, virtually all made from the small-berried Muscat Blanc. **Lemnos** (Límnos) makes both dry and sweet Muscats. **Páros** grows its own grape, Monemvasia, thought to be related to at least one Malvasia. Mandilaria is another tough island red grape found on Páros, Crete, and Rhodes.

On **Rhodes** (Ródos) white wine is more important than red: the full-bodied white Athiri has recently made some remarkably elegant whites when grown at high altitudes.

Santorini, though, of all the islands, is the most original and compelling. Its potent and intense wines, white, scented with lemon and minerals and (very) dry, are made mainly from ancient Assyrtiko vines, trained in little nests crouching on the windswept heights of this dormant volcano. Sigalas, Hatzidakis, and Gaia's Thalassitis are all fine examples. The island also produces a particularly rich white Vinsanto. The problem on Santorini is not shortage of winemaking enthusiasm and ingenuity but that the thriving tourist business has pushed up land prices, calling into question the very survival of these unique vineyards (see photo on p.281).

Peleponnese

This new map highlights the northern half of the Peleponnese, the area that has seen even more energy and activity than any other part of Greece in recent years. It is also Greece's best-known wine region thanks to its beautiful coastline, accessibility from Athens, and the lure of its ancient sites.

Neméa, near Mycenae, is the most important appellation, making luscious red wines exclusively from Agiorgitiko (St George) grapes grown in such varied terrains that areas such as Koútsi, Asprókambos, Gimnó, Ancient Neméa, and Psari are already starting to earn their own reputations. Neméa has milder winters and cooler summers than one might expect thanks to the influence of the sea (and rains that can threaten the harvest in some parts). It can be roughly divided into three zones. The fertile red clays of the Neméa valley floor produce perhaps the least interesting wines. The mid-altitude zone seems best suited for the most modern, richest, most dramatic styles, although even here there is wide variation in character. And some vineyards in the highest zone, even as high as 2,950ft (900m), which were once thought fit only for rosé production, are now producing some fine elegant reds. It will take more than one symposium to sort out a just system of subregions.

Pátra in the northern Peloponnese is predominantly a white wine region and source of

the finest Roditis, its principal variety. The rediscovered mineral-scented white Lagorthi grape has also been making waves, thanks to Antonopoulos's Adoli Ghis (meaning "guileless earth") bottling. Oenoforos is another producer buying in grapes from the cool, north-facing Aighialia plateau. They are keeping up the pace of change in a region that was long associated only with sticky Muscat and Mavrodaphne – which have the potential to be just as good as the Muscat of Sámos, given more care.

The **Mantinía** plateau in the south of the area mapped is the home of the Moschofilero vine, whose grapey wine is today also grown on the Ionian islands of Cephalonia and Zante to the west. Producers such as Tselepos make both oaked and sparkling versions of this delicate grape variety. Like so many ambitious Greeks, they grow a range of international grape varieties too.

Papaioannou Vineyards in what is so obviously Ancient Neméa are organic, Thanassis Papaioannou being a viticulturist at heart. When he started out in 1984 he was one of the first of Greece's new generation of urbane, quality-conscious wine producers. His son Giorgos continues the tradition.

▶ Black seems to be the colour of choice for Neméa neighbours Gaia and Driopi, while white surely suits Burgundy-trained Yiannis Tselepos's delicate white varietal Moschofilero, *the grape of Mantinia's high-altitude vineyards. Mercouri's Italian history brought the zesty red Refosco grape to the northwest of the Peloponnese.

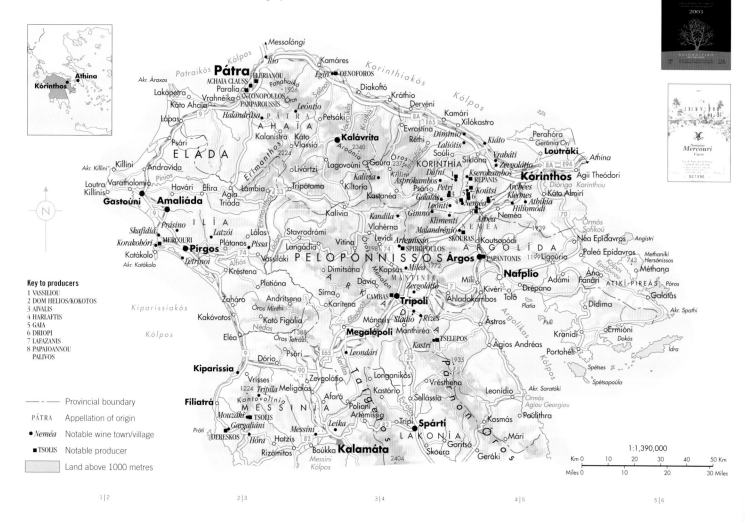

Key to producers
1 VASSILIOU
2 DOM HELIOS/KOKOTOS
3 AIVALIS
4 HARLAFTIS
5 GAIA
6 DRIOPI
7 LAFAZANIS
8 PAPAIOANNOU
PALIVOS

— - — Provincial boundary

PÁTRA   Appellation of origin

● *Neméa*   Notable wine town/village

■ TSOLIS   Notable producer

        Land above 1000 metres

1:1,390,000

Km 0   10   20   30   40   50 Km

Miles 0   10   20   30 Miles

The Eastern Mediterranean

Whether it was in Turkey, Georgia, or Armenia that the first wine was made, there is no doubt that the Middle East is wine's birthplace. The Eastern Mediterranean was the France and Italy of wine in the ancient world – until the 8th century and the advent of Islam. Today, **Turkey** has the fourth largest vineyard acreage in the world, but hardly 3% of the grapes are made into wine. The rest are eaten, fresh or dried. The wine industry has been held back by lack of a domestic market in this Muslim country but tourism, the abolition of a ban on foreign imports, and the early 21st-century privatization of the state monopoly Tekel, now called Mey, is changing that. Kemal Atatürk, founder of the secular republic, built state wineries in the 1920s in the hope of per-suading his people of the virtues of wine and ensured the survival of indigenous Anatolian grape varieties, which may yet yield clues to the origins of viticulture itself. Younger Turks are beginning to take an interest in wine rather than raki, the country's aniseed-flavoured spirit.

Turkey's climate varies enormously. Thrace's Marmara in the hinterland of Istanbul is the most significant region in terms of amount of wine produced. This is the most European part of the country in every way, including its wine-friendly soils and warm coastal climate, which are similar to those of Bulgaria's Black Sea coast to the north and the northeastern corner of Greece. More than two-fifths of all Turkish wine is grown here, and the proportion of imported grape varieties grown is higher than elsewhere, with Syrah an interesting newcomer. The first Turkish producer to concentrate exclu-sively on international grapes is Sarafin, inspired by the Napa Valley, with its own vineyards in Marmara (while most producers buy in the majority of their grapes). Gülor, with Pascal Delbeck of St-Emilion as consultant, is also here.

About one-fifth of all Turkish wine is made from productive vines grown around Izmir in the Aegean, rich in classical relics and remains. White wines tend to be better than red, espe-cially those made from Misket (Muscat) and Sultaniye. Pamukkale near Denizli in the south-west is the best producer.

Some vines are grown in the northeast around Tokat, but most of the rest of Turkey's wine is grown in the higher-altitude vineyards of Central Anatolia, where winters are very cold, summers extremely dry, and yields notably low. The most promising varieties here are Kalecik Karasi for reds and Emir for whites.

Doluca and Kavaklidere are the biggest and best-known Turkish producers. Doluca operates in Marmara (its Villa Doluca brand is reliable). Kavaklidere operates near Ankara and concen-trates on Anatolia's own vines: Narince, Emir, and Sultaniye whites (including a very fresh Primeur) and Boğazkere, Oküzgözü, and, especially, Kalecik

Karasi reds. Southeast Anatolia, however promising its red grapes, has practically no wineries; its grapes have to be trucked west. Turkey's wine map will become more precisely defined as membership of the EU beckons.

Cyprus joined the EU in 2004 and its wine industry is in the throes of revolution as a result. Where subsidies were paid for exporting vast quantities of nondescript wine in bulk to manu-facturers of cheap drinks (the Soviets were big customers), grants are now available for grubbing up the worst vineyards and planting in the

mountainous interior. The whole south-facing side of the Troodos Mountains is potential wine-producing country; the mountains, attracting rain, make viticulture possible on what would otherwise be too dry an island. The vineyards lie where the rains fall, in valleys at 1,980ft (600m) up to nearly 4,950ft (1,500m) in the hills.

The four big wineries are moving winemaking facilities away from Limassol and Paphos on the coast and closer to the most promising wine regions, still for the moment dominated by small-scale producers with a lack of modern expertise. Nevertheless by 2006 there were already about 50 boutique wineries on Cyprus and an appella-tion of origin scheme is being developed.

Change has come suddenly to one of the world's oldest wine-growing cultures, which dates from at least 3500BC, according to arche-ological evidence recently unearthed.

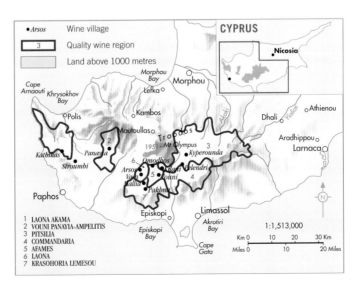

▲ Modern Cyprus (top) is represented by Vasa's reworking of an indigenous vine and modern Turkey by one of Sarafin's Cabernets.

Cyprus has never been invaded by phylloxera, so its ungrafted vines have been protected by strict quarantine – slowing the introduction of international varieties. Over 70% of the island's wine-grape vineyards (for Cyprus is also a considerable grower of grapes for the table) is planted with the indigenous and rather unexciting grape Mavro, so common that its name simply means "black". The local Xynisteri and Muscat of Alexandria and now Palomino are used for both fortified and light white wines, Xynisteri in particular making delicate dry whites if grown at high altitudes. Cabernet Sauvignon, Syrah, and Grenache are the most significant incomers for red wine but the indigenous Maratheftiko and Lefkada are making increasingly interesting, nervier reds. Earlier picking is gradually making fruitier wines.

The most individual of Cyprus wines is the liquorous Commandaria, made of raisined Mavro and Xynisteri grapes, grown in 14 designated villages on the lower slopes of the Troodos. Commandaria, which must be aged in oak for at least two years, can be simply sticky, or almost alarmingly concentrated, with four times as much sugar as port. The best have a haunting fresh grapiness, however.

Technical advance and modern demand have been good for both the Lebanese and Israeli wine industries. If pressed to name an Eastern Mediterranean wine, many drinkers would cite Chateau Musar of **Lebanon**, which one remarkable man, Serge Hochar, somehow continued to produce through the country's 20 years of civil war in the last century. From dry-farmed Cabernet Sauvignon, Cinsault, and Carignan he produced extraordinarily aromatic wines, like rich and exotic Bordeaux, long-aged before sale and capable of ageing for decades after.

Several other Lebanese wineries are also based on vines in the war-ravaged western Bekaa Valley and in the hills above Zahlé, where vineyard altitudes of around 3,280ft (1,000m) help to produce fresh wines not spoiled by sun-baked flavours. Château Kefraya makes refreshing rosé, as well as a serious Bordeaux/Rhône combination red. The senior and biggest operation is Chateau Ksara, while Massaya (set up by an impressive triumvirate from Bordeaux and the Rhône), Domaine Wardy, and Clos St Thomas are all serious, albeit much newer, enterprises.

Across the much-disputed border, **Israel** is the other seat of wine revolution in this part of the world. It has only about a quarter as much land planted with vines as Lebanon, but exports far more, largely to satisfy world demand for kosher wine. Sweet red kiddush wines were for years the standard output of the original co-operative wineries of Carmel at Rishon le Zion and Zichron Yaacov in the coastal regions of Samaria (Shomron) and Samson (Shimshon), a gift to Israel from Baron Edmond de Rothschild. They still control just under half of all grapes in the most traditional wine-growing areas, increasingly supplemented nowadays by more modern vineyards in the northern Negev Desert near Ramat Arat and in Upper Galilee.

Until the 1980s, Israeli wines were of sacramental interest only. But late-1970s planting on the volcanic soils of the Golan Heights, from 1,300ft (400m) above the Sea of Galilee up to 4,000ft (1,200m) towards Mount Hermon, signalled a new direction. California technology and expertise was shipped in by the pioneering Golan Heights Winery, and their top Galilee wines, under the Yarden and Gamla labels, set a new international quality standard.

A wine culture is now well and truly established in Israel – a culture that celebrates Israeli wine rather than solely kosher wine – complete with wine magazines, international wine lists in restaurants, recognized wine regions, and scores of small but ambitious new wineries. Castel and Flam are two in the cool Mediterranean climate of the Judean Hills near Jerusalem, Margalit is in the Sharon Plain, and Yatir in the northern Negev. Improvements in quality and consistency since the mid-1990s have been remarkable.

The range of climatic conditions is extreme for a small country, but the region with the most obvious potential is Galilee (Galil). The three leading wineries are supporting the wine-quality revolution by diligent vineyard site selection and by investment in technology. In a joint venture with Kibbutz Yiron, Golan Heights has built the new Galil Mountain winery on the Lebanese border; Carmel has built three hi-tech wineries near key vineyards; while Barkan, the second biggest producer after Carmel, has developed a modern winery near Rehovot in the heavily planted Samson coastal region, as well as planting in the semi-arid soils of the Negev. Israeli farming prowess and determination is good at coaxing wine that will stand international comparison from challenging environments. Cabernet, Merlot, Chardonnay, and Sauvignon Blanc are clearly at home, Shiraz is gaining ground, and Cabernet Franc shows promise. Attempts are now being made to bring an Israeli identity to the country's wines without the benefit of indigenous grape varieties.

▲ Flam wines are made by the Italian- and Australian-trained son of Israel Flam, chief oenologist at Israel's dominant Carmel winery, while the Hochars of Chateau Musar in the Lebanon were originally inspired by a visit to Bordeaux.

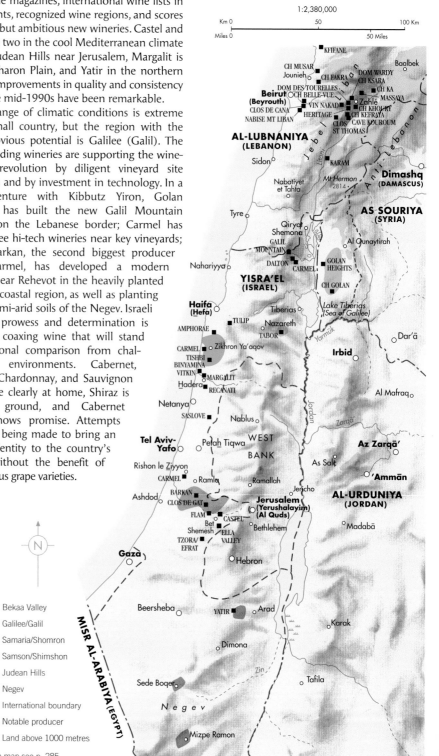

For location map see p. 285

1:2,380,000

Bekaa Valley
Galilee/Galil
Samaria/Shomron
Samson/Shimshon
Judean Hills
Negev
——— International boundary
■ CH MUSAR Notable producer
Land above 1000 metres

North Africa

The rather unlikely possible saviour of the beleaguered Algerian wine industry is French actor Gérard Depardieu, seen here in the St Augustin vineyard from which he and Magrez of Bordeaux coax a heady red.

North Africa, or more specifically Morocco, is at long last recovering from a sleep that has lasted for 50 years, ever since the French left. In the mid-20th century, Algeria, Morocco, and Tunisia between them accounted for no less than two-thirds of the entire international wine trade. Almost all of this vast quantity of wine went to Europe (mainly to France) as usefully strong, dark red for blending. The lack of domestic demand in these substantially Muslim countries meant that after independence the decline was immediate. In each country (and also in **Egypt**, where Gianiclis has a virtual, and not particularly virtuous, monopoly), the state took over the shrivelling wine industry with the result that there was almost no investment.

Morocco is already en route for revival via a number of joint ventures – although the big money, from Castel of Bordeaux, is being spent on planting new, mechanizable vineyards – and much-needed modern equipment. Common sense would in any case suggest that of North Africa's three most important wine producers, Morocco should have the best vineyards, benefiting from altitude and the influence of the Atlantic. The dominant Moroccan-owned producer Celliers de Meknès opened a high-tech winery, Château Roslane, in 2003.

Morocco has 14 Appellations d'Origine Garantie (AOG) and now one Appellation d'Origine Contrôlée (AC), Les Coteaux d'Atlas, each with its own specified grape varieties. Only four – Guerrouane, Beni M'Tir, Berkane, and Coteaux d'Atlas – are much used, however. The vineyards around Meknès, which accounts for 60% of Morocco's production, and Fès have the best reputation, with altitudes of around 2,000ft (600m) bringing a welcome night-time drop in temperature.

Most of the wine is red, but much more popular than the increasingly crisp whites is Morocco's pale pink *vin gris*, its prototype "blush wine" made of short-macerated red grapes, often Cinsault. South of Casablanca, the fortified village of Boulaouane within the Doukkala AOG gives its name to one of the best-known *vins gris* brands in France, now being modernized by Castel.

Tunisia is also trying to improve quality to generate exports. The state has been active in encouraging joint ventures, whereby expertise and capital are imported from Europe. By the turn of the century, at least seven were under way; Château St Augustin, Domaine Neferis, and a project by Calatrasi of Sicily were the most notable. The results include the introduction of much-needed temperature control in wineries and upgraded vineyards, most now having irrigation. Tunisia has good supplies of water. Carignan, Grenache, Mourvèdre, and Syrah are typical red varieties.

The coolest regions are those on the coast. The ocean breezes and unusually cool clay soils of northern Bizerte can result in reasonable white wines, well-balanced reds, and some fine sweet Muscat, Tunisia's speciality – probably since Carthaginian times. Dry Muscat, often oxidized, is the speciality of the sandy soils of Cap Bon, otherwise known as Kelibia, on the east coast.

The westernmost vineyards of Jendouba south of Béja are Tunisia's hottest. Wineries there are most prone to the faults associated with primitive equipment and non-existent cooling systems. There is real potential for powerful, deep-flavoured reds, however, from the better-equipped wineries of Grombalia, the terra rossa hills between here and Tunis, maritime Mornag just southwest of Tunis, and Tébourba, west of the city, whose speciality is the very pale pink Gris de Tunis.

Algeria, once by far the world's biggest wine exporter, lags far behind its neighbours in terms of modernization. So many of its vineyards have been either neglected or pulled up that between 1966 and 1997, when 80% of her vines were more than 40 years old, the crop shrank from 16 million hectolitres of wine to less than half a million. This is not to say that Algerian wine has to be of poor quality; the problem is infrastructure. The State Monopoly, which still controls production tightly, claims to have planted 24,700 acres (10,000ha) of international grape varieties in the mid-1990s, mainly in the traditional areas of Tlemcen, Médéa, and Zaccar, and in very difficult social conditions is attempting to develop the wineries necessary to turn them into exportable wine.

▶ Both the Moroccan labels are French-owned, by Bernard Magrez and Castel, while Selian (far right) uses some old-vine Carignan in northern Tunisia, finishing the wine at their winery in Sicily. France has a long tradition of drinking North African wine thanks to creative blending in the early to mid-20th century.

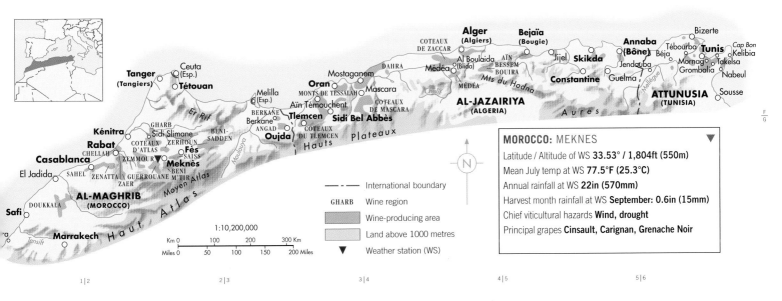

International boundary

GHARB — Wine region

Wine-producing area

Land above 1000 metres

▼ Weather station (WS)

1:10,200,000

MOROCCO: MEKNES ▼

Latitude / Altitude of WS **33.53° / 1,804ft (550m)**

Mean July temp at WS **77.5°F (25.3°C)**

Annual rainfall at WS **22in (570mm)**

Harvest month rainfall at WS **September: 0.6in (15mm)**

Chief viticultural hazards **Wind, drought**

Principal grapes **Cinsault, Carignan, Grenache Noir**

North America

North America

The vine must be a tenacious plant to persist in its hold on a continent where it has been so prone to pests, disease, climatic extreme, and disaster as it has in North America. Today the USA is the world's most important wine producer, and consumer, outside Europe. Only France, Spain, and Italy make more wine. Canada's wine industry is in dynamic transformation, and one of these days Mexico may also catch up.

When the early colonists first landed, they were impressed by the rampant grapevines whose fruit festooned the forests. The grapes were sweet, if strange to taste. It was natural to assume that wine would be one of the good things of the New World.

Yet more than 300 years of American history are a saga of the shattered hopes of would-be wine-growers. Wine made from American vines tasted distinctly odd, while European vinifera vines planted in the new colonies withered and died. The colonists did not give up. Having no notion what was killing their vines, they assumed it was their fault and tried different varieties and methods.

As late as the Revolution, Washington tried, and Jefferson, a great amateur of wine and one of France's early wine tourists, made a determined attempt. Nothing came of it. The American soil was riddled with the European

vine's deadliest enemy, phylloxera. The hot, humid summers of the south and east encouraged diseases unknown in Europe. In the north, European vines were prey to the harsh winters. Native American vines had developed resistance to all of these hazards.

We now know of well over a dozen vine species indigenous to North America, many of them (and particularly *Vitis labrusca*) producing wine so feral that it has long been described as "foxy" – a flavour familiar today in grape juice and jelly but offputting to wine drinkers weaned on Europe's only vine species, *Vitis vinifera*.

Now that American and European vines coexisted on this continent new to wine, their genes commingled in random and spontaneous combinations from which various grape varieties with less obvious foxiness emerged. The Alexander grape, discovered in Pennsylvania and grown in Indiana, was the earliest of these accidental American–European hybrids; Catawba, Delaware, and Isabella followed. Norton is an all-American grape still producing powerfully distinctive reds.

Settlers tried vine-growing and winemaking wherever they were, especially in New York (where winters were bitterly cold), Virginia (where summers were sultry), and New Jersey (somewhere in between). But it was at Cincinnati, Ohio, that the first commercially successful American wine was born: Nicholas Longworth's famous Sparkling Catawba. By the mid-1850s the wine was celebrated on both sides of the Atlantic and, with 1,200 acres (485ha) of vineyard, he was making a fortune.

Success was short-lived. Black rot, the Civil War, and finally Longworth's death in 1863 ended Cincinnati's challenge to Reims. But the point was made. Longworth's "champagne" makers soon found new employers: the new Pleasant Valley Wine Co of Hammondsport on New York's Finger Lakes. This time American wine had found a permanent home – still important today (and described on p.320).

By the time of the Civil War, vine-breeding had become a deliberate activity, resulting in scores of new varieties especially adapted for American conditions, including the almost rudely hardy but extremely foxy Concord, introduced in 1854 and today the mainstay of the great grape belt along the southern shore of Lake Erie through northern Ohio, Pennsylvania, and New York, which supplies America's grape juice and jelly.

In the South, the Carolinas and Georgia had their own indigenous Muscadine vines, particularly Scuppernong, whose viscous juice made wine even further from the European model than these American hybrids, although they are

A vineyard reaches almost to the base of the Grand Mesa at Palisade, near the Colorado River. Colorado is not the most obvious habitat for the vine but wine is now made in every single American state.

at least resistant to Pierce's Disease, which is currently a serious threat to some of America's vinifera vines (see p.19).

Winemaking reached the West Coast by a quite different route. The earliest Spanish settlers in Mexico had imported vinifera there in the 16th century with tolerable success. Their primitive vine, known as the Mission and identical to Argentina's Criolla Chica, flourished in Baja California. But not for 200 years did the Franciscan fathers move north up the coast of California. In 1769 the Franciscan Junípero Serra, founding the San Diego Mission, is said to have planted California's first vineyard.

With the notable exception of Pierce's Disease, originally called Anaheim Disease (it appeared in the mid-19th century near Los Angeles), there were none of the problems of the East Coast here. *Vitis vinifera* had found its Promised Land. The well-named Jean-Louis Vignes brought better vines than the Mission from Europe to Los Angeles. The Gold Rush brought massive immigration. By the 1850s northern California had been well and truly conquered by the vine.

Thus by the mid-19th century America had two wine industries, poles apart. California, where vinifera had displaced Concord by the late 19th century, enjoyed an early golden age in the 1880s and 1890s, only to see its burgeoning wine industry besieged by the scourges of mildew and phylloxera – just like Europe.

But then came a blow greater than any of these: Prohibition of alcohol throughout North America between 1918 and 1933. Both western and eastern vine-growers limped through, making supposedly sacramental wine and shipping huge quantities of grapes, juice, and concentrate to a nation which suddenly discovered home winemaking, with the warning "Caution – do not add yeast or the contents will ferment".

The lasting legacy of the culture that spawned this outright ban on all things alcoholic, long after Repeal in 1933, has been a wine industry for long thwarted by unnecessarily complex organization, obstructive legislation, and extreme suspicion on the part of the substantial proportion of 21st-century Americans who are teetotal and those who drink only spirits or beer.

Despite this, and despite phylloxera and Pierce's Disease, wine is currently basking in the glow of fashion and enthusiasm bordering on obsession among the growing proportion of Americans who do own a corkscrew. This has been translated into a flurry of activity and experiment on the part of would-be wine producers all over the continent. Ever since the development of the railroads, grapes and wine have been shipped from viticulturally well-endowed states, particularly California, for blending and bottling in less fortunately situated wineries, some of which grow relatively few vines. All 50 states, including Alaska, now produce some wine, even if 15 of them have

fewer than 10 wineries, and about 20 of them have over 1,000 acres (400ha) of vines – a sign of considerable vinous activity.

The mushrooming wine industries of Canada, Mexico, Texas, New York, and all of the USA west of the Rockies are considered in detail on the following pages, but there are hundreds of wineries (some of them producing wines from fruits other than grapes too) and thousands of acres of vines elsewhere. They may produce juice or jelly or heavily flavoured drinks based on the produce of American vines or, increasingly, more subtle and sophisticated ferments from either vinifera or the so-called French hybrids. This new generation of varieties such as white Vidal, Seyval Blanc, and Vignoles, and red Baco Noir and Chambourcin, was bred in post-phylloxera Europe from American and vinifera vines and introduced to North America (where they have enjoyed far more success than in Europe) by Philip Wagner of Boordy Vineyards, Maryland, in the mid-20th century.

French hybrids dominate vine-growing in the Midwest, although the American variety Norton also thrives here. **Missouri** is the only state with a long history of vine-growing on any scale and was Ohio's only serious 19th-century rival east of the Rockies. Augusta made this point when in 1980 it became America's first AVA, or American Viticultural Area, and continues to improve in vineyard and cellar. These 180-plus vine-growing areas (often delineated with more regard for political than natural boundaries, and producer rather than consumer sensitivities) represent the first steps towards a controlled appellation system for US wine.

Michigan, surrounded by the Great Lakes, is today the fourth most important vine-grower of all the states (after California, Washington, and New York). Most vines are Concord, but vinifera, especially Chardonnay, and a shrinking minority of French hybrids on the lake-girt Old Mission and Leelanau peninsulas are promising.

Pennsylvania has almost as much vineyard (more than Oregon, in fact), and **Ohio** is also important. But the eastern state that, after New York, offers the most excitement today is unquestionably **Virginia**, home to more than 100 small, intensely ambitious wineries, with Merlot and the Cabernets being particularly successful. **New Jersey**'s wine industry has almost as long a history but is much smaller; that of **Maryland** smaller still. Both hedge bets between vinifera and French hybrids.

The rest of the South, those states bordering on the Gulf of Mexico as far as Texas, has a small but growing wine industry of its own, expanding from the usefully loose-berried Muscadine vines native to its hot, damp woods to French hybrids, vinifera, and newer Muscadine hybrids which can produce quite mainstream flavours. Cooler, higher parts of the South can have conditions very similar to Virginia's.

All over this great and thrilling continent, an exciting trend is discernible: to produce wines that will be appreciated outside their region while truly expressing their origins.

▶ Wollersheim's Dry Riesling is made in Wisconsin from fruit shipped across the country from Washington state – not atypical of the American wine scene, also represented by, from left to right, Michigan fizz, Virginia's "terroiriste" Linden, and a fine Norton from Missouri.

California

"If California is not at present the favourite grape-growing country of the world, it is certainly destined to attain that rank, and also to become one of the most extensive." So wrote Ben Truman in *The New York Times* in 1868. In 2007 California is as important to the world of wine as wine is important to California. Ninety per cent of all American wine is grown in the state, more wine than in any country outside Europe – and the planting goes on.

Here at the vine's western limit there is a distinct shortage of geographical generalities and physical truisms. Few of the dozens of California cult wines that command three- and four-figure dollar sums per bottle existed in the 1980s, for example. Wine now basks in the glow of social approbation and a wine-friendly economy. Problems have not gone away, though: California's vine-growers have had more than their fair share.

In the 1990s phylloxera returned after a century to haunt vineyards in fashionable Napa and Sonoma. And now the even more deadly Pierce's Disease threatens vineyards throughout the state (see p.19). Meanwhile, wine production is inextricably bound up with disputes over land development, labour, and water use.

California's wine geography presents a series of surprises, and much more variety than outsiders give it credit for. The potential of a vineyard site is linked hardly at all to latitude but is crucially determined by what lies between it and the Pacific. The more mountains there are between the site and the sea, the less chance there is of the sea air, often fog, reaching it to moderate the climate.

So cold is the inshore water of the Pacific here that it causes a perpetual fog bank all summer just off the coast. Each day that the temperatures approach 90°F (32°C) inland, the rising hot air draws the fog inland to fill its space. The Golden Gate Bridge straddles its most famous pathway, but everywhere up and down the coast that the Coast Ranges dip below about 1,500ft (460m), the fog, or at any rate cold Pacific air, spills over and cools the land. Certain valleys that are end-on to the ocean act as funnels to allow sea air to invade as far as 75 miles (120km) inland. So effectively are cool winds sucked off the Pacific over San Francisco Bay that they even have an effect on the climate in the Sierra Foothills, nearly 150 miles (240km) east of the coast.

Since foggy San Francisco Bay is northern California's chief air conditioning unit, vineyards close to the waters of the Bay, such as those of Carneros skirting the south of Napa and Sonoma counties, can be rather cool too. Within the inland Napa Valley, sheltered from Pacific influence by its almost unbroken ridge of western hills, it is those most southerly vineyards just north of the town of Napa that are the coolest due to the breezes off the Bay, and those around Calistoga at the northern limit of the valley that are hottest.

For similar reasons, if the result of different topography, the vineyards of the Santa Maria Valley way down the coast in Santa Barbara County, 140 miles (225km) northwest of Los Angeles, are some of the coolest in the state.

The Central (or San Joaquin) Valley on the other hand, the flat farmland that still makes agriculture California's most important economic activity (and grows three-quarters of the state's wine grapes), is too far inland to be directly influenced by Pacific fog. It is one of the world's sunniest wine regions with a hotter, drier climate than anywhere logged in this book. Irrigation, increasingly expensive, is essential. Dry farming is the dream of terroir-driven growers everywhere; it is a distant one in California.

The key facts panels show that summers are very much drier than those of most European wine regions. Total annual rainfall is not exceptionally low but it does tend to be concentrated in the first few months of the year, topping up dams used throughout the summer for irrigation. This being California, however, a roughly decade-long cycle of damaging flood and drought results respectively in erosion of the most fashionable hillside vineyards, then both a water shortage and – thanks to thick skins and a lack of juice – tough wines. And in the warmth that is typical of a California September, atypical rain can wreak havoc. Autumn rains are very unusual, however, allowing growers to prolong the grapes' "hang time" almost as long as they like, or are asked to by the wine producers to whom they sell. This is just one, important, reason why California's wines tend to be especially potent.

The most important of California's roughly 100 AVAs are mapped opposite and on the following pages but even those marked should not be given too much significance. Some of the viticultural areas are so small that they affect only one winery while North Coast, for example, encompasses much of

The four main protagonists in the influential 2004 film of the book Sideways, *a lyrical celebration of the virtues of (California) Pinot Noir set not in Napa or Sonoma but in the Central Coast. Closer to Hollywood after all.*

THE CLIMATE REGIONS OF CALIFORNIA WINE-GROWING

Viticultural academic Winkler classified California's wine regions on a scale of "degree days" which measures the length of time the thermometer remains over 50°F (10°C) between 1 April and 31 October. Thus if the mean temperature over a five-day period was 70°F (21°C), the "summation" of heat would be (70 - 50 = 20) x 5 = 100 degree days.

	Region I 2,500 degree days or fewer
	Region II 2,501 to 3,000 degree days
	Region III 3,001 to 3,500 degree days
	Region IV 3,501 to 4,000 degree days
	Region V More than 4,000 degree days

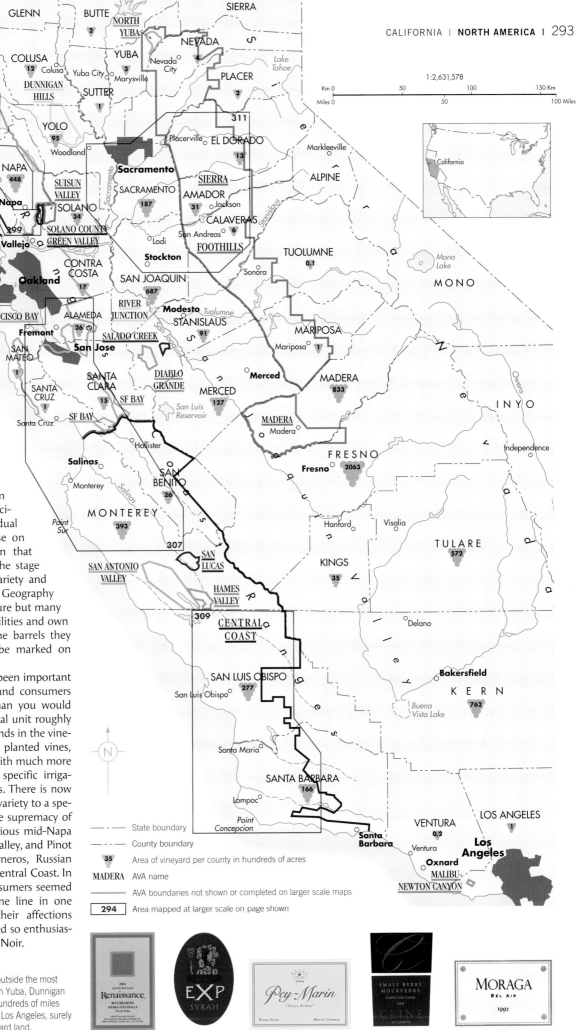

Lake, Mendocino, Napa, and Sonoma counties.

There are excellent winemakers who still ignore AVAs, preferring to use good grapes from wherever they can get them while others relish vineyard specificity. Hundreds of individual vineyard names are now in use on labels – powerful confirmation that California is moving on from the stage where it was only the grape variety and the brand name that counted. Geography has definitively entered the picture but many producers use custom crush facilities and own little other than a label and the barrels they store there, so they will not be marked on these maps.

Fashion, however, has always been important in California. Wine producers and consumers tend to act more uniformly than you would normally expect in a geographical unit roughly half as big as France. Current trends in the vineyard are towards more densely planted vines, from a wider variety of clones, with much more open, controlled foliage, more specific irrigation, and later and later harvests. There is now much better matching of grape variety to a specific site. This has confirmed the supremacy of Cabernet Sauvignon in the glorious mid-Napa Valley, Zinfandel in Dry Creek Valley, and Pinot Noir and Chardonnay in Carneros, Russian River Valley, and much of the Central Coast. In the mid-2000s, meanwhile, consumers seemed to have been persuaded by one line in one movie, *Sideways*, to transfer their affections from the Merlot that was planted so enthusiastically in the late 1990s to Pinot Noir.

▶ These very varied wines are all made outside the most famous wine regions in (left to right) North Yuba, Dunnigan Hills, Marin County, Contra Costa, and, hundreds of miles further south, Malibu in a canyon west of Los Angeles, surely some of the world's most expensive vineyard land.

Legend:

— · — · State boundary

— — — County boundary

35 Area of vineyard per county in hundreds of acres

MADERA AVA name

—— AVA boundaries not shown or completed on larger scale maps

294 Area mapped at larger scale on page shown

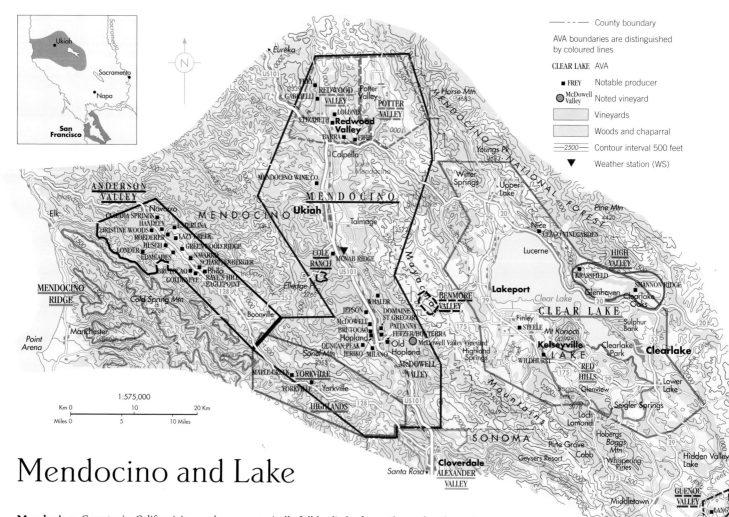

Mendocino and Lake

Mendocino County is California's northern-most outpost of the vine. Its most distinctive wine region is the **Anderson Valley**, where ocean fogs can drift in easily through the coastal hills to hang thick and low. The little Navarro River tumbles down the valley through resin-scented redwoods. A few reclusive Italian families discovered long ago that Zinfandel ripens splendidly on hillsides well above the fog line, but most of Anderson Valley has a super-cool, sometimes too cool, ripening season – particularly in its lower reaches below Philo. As Navarro Vineyards continues to prove, Riesling and Gewurztraminer are perfectly in tune with the climate (if not the market), but it took a French company to put Anderson Valley on the map, in the shape of Roederer of Champagne. In 1982 Roederer chose to set up shop here and not, like so many of its peers, in Carneros. The quality of Roederer Estate's sparkling wines justifies the choice; so does still Pinot Noir, especially Duckhorn's from their Goldeneye winery at Philo.

There is good natural acidity too in wines from **Yorkville Highlands** to the southeast, but the bulk of Mendocino's plantings are to be found well tucked in behind the coastal hills that rear up to 3,000ft (900m) north of Cloverdale and the Sonoma county line, protected from Pacific influence and therefore in much warmer, drier conditions. The fogs do not reach Ukiah, nor very often the Redwood Valley, and their wines (from some deep alluvial soils) are

typically full-bodied, often rather soft reds made from Cabernet, Petite Sirah or, from particularly ancient vines above Ukiah, spicy Zinfandel. The distinctly cooler, not-yet-famous Potter Valley can also make very fine botrytized wines.

The oldest winery in Mendocino is Parducci. It was founded in 1932, a date that proclaims a visionary, for Prohibition was still in force (these days it is owned by the Mendocino Wine Co.). Fetzer set down roots in 1968 to become justly celebrated as a source of dependable value and as one clear, confident voice in favour of organic wine production in a state so well suited to it. The winery is now owned by distillers Brown-Forman, while the Fetzer family grow increasing quantities of organic grapes for labels such as Patianna and Ceàgo.

McDowell Valley is a tiny appellation, a charming alcove of inland Mendocino, established by eponymous early specialists in Rhône grape varieties. Petite Sirah was first planted here in 1919.

Lake County to the east is another warm region, comparable to the head of the Napa Valley and valued for its fruity Cabernet Sauvignon, Zinfandel, and Sauvignon Blanc at attractive prices. Steele and Langtry are leading winery names.

▼ The two labels on the left, for Pinot Noir and Riesling, bear testimony to the coolness of the Anderson Valley, while the relatively new Ceàgo label is sold on its organic credentials – which have been more common in this part of California than any other.

MENDOCINO: UKIAH ▼
Latitude / Altitude of WS **39.09° / 590ft (180m)**
Mean July temp at WS **73.7°F (23.2°C)**
Annual rainfall at WS **38in (964mm)**
Harvest month rainfall at WS **September: 0.8in (20mm)**
Chief viticultural hazards **Over-winter drought, rain at harvest**
Principal grapes **Chardonnay, Zinfandel, Cabernet Sauvignon, Merlot**

Northern Sonoma

The California Climate Rule – coast equals cool – tells you Sonoma should be cooler than its inland neighbour, Napa. Overall it works. **Sonoma County** grows far more grapes than Napa County in more varied conditions, with much more potential for planting in newer, cooler areas. Sonoma is also where fine wine started in California, early in the 19th century, even if in the late 20th century it was eclipsed by Napa's seminal role in the state's wine renaissance.

As elsewhere in California, climate is a function of the penetration of Pacific fogs and the resultant cloud cover. Just south of the area mapped overleaf, there is a wide dip in the Coastal Ranges known as the Petaluma Gap. Thanks to this opening, the vineyards in the south are the coolest, often being shrouded in mist until 11 in the morning and from 4 in the afternoon. The boundary of the **Russian River Valley** AVA, one of Sonoma's coolest, was extended southwards in 2005 to incorporate all those vineyards south of Sebastopol within the fog zone, with some of those in the southwest corner being most affected by marine incursions. It can even be a struggle to ripen a commercial crop here, as Marimar Torres and Joseph Phelps of Napa Valley have found with their new vineyards near Freestone.

Away from the Petaluma Gap, the Russian River Valley gradually warms up, so that Williams Selyem, Rochioli, and Gary Farrell, some of the first to draw attention to this characterful region and all clustered on West Side Road on the heavier soils of the banks of the Russian River itself, enjoy warmer conditions than many of the newcomers. That said, the majority of Russian River producers are still at the planning stage with their own premises. Their early efforts are made in one of the custom crush facilities that have been fashioned out of apple processing stores. Apples, not grapes, were until recently the crop along the winding valley with its old oaks and banks of flowers. As elsewhere, and not just in California, it is quite feasible to set up a wine business with neither winery nor vines – especially since professional

Above the morning fog, high in the hills at the head of Sonoma Valley east of Santa Rosa, it is easy to see that the precise topography between individual vineyards and the Pacific is critical for the rate at which grapes ripen.

growers, notably the Dutton family here, are in business specifically to sell well-grown grapes to third parties.

Chardonnay, still by far Sonoma County's most planted grape, was initially the most celebrated variety here, planted in the white wine boom of the 1970s and 1980s, but it was the richness of Russian River Pinot Noir with its red berry fruit flavours that drew critical attention to the region. This is one of California's serious Pinot Noir sources, where the best producers have etched a Burgundian tradition of vineyard-designated bottlings, albeit in a distinctly unburgundian style: open, jewel-like fruit not without some promise of longevity. Thanks to the regular fog shroud, the levels of acidity usually remain notably and refreshingly high here – unless heat spikes in August rush ripening – so that Russian River can offer structured wines from both the Burgundy varieties. The lowest vineyards tend to be the coolest, because this is where the fog hangs longest. Vineyards above the fog line such as Jack Ass Hill and Morelli Lane have long provided notable Zinfandel from vines originally planted by Italians who settled here to log the redwoods into railway sleepers. Higher elevation vineyards are now showing promise with Syrah.

If West Side Road, sometimes called the Northern Reach, is the warmest, oldest subregion of Russian River Valley, **Green Valley** is the coolest, an optionally used AVA within Russian River Valley itself, which was originated

by Iron Horse in the 1970s when they specialized in sparkling wine production. The Sebastopol Hills, sometimes called southern Sebastopol, next door and now included in the Russian River AVA, is almost as cool – slap bang in the

path of the fog that swirls in through the Petaluma Gap. Both of these subregions are on sandy Goldridge soils, while Laguna Ridge just east of Green Valley has the sandiest, fastest-draining soils of all.

------- County boundary

AVA boundaries are distinguished by coloured lines

CHALK HILL AVA

■ KORBEL Notable producer

● Hirsh Vineyard Noted vineyard

▨ Vineyards

▨ Woods and chaparral

═800═ Contour interval 400 feet

▼ Weather station (WS)

NORTHERN SONOMA: HEALDSBURG ▼

Latitude / Altitude of WS **38.37° / 98ft (30m)**

Mean July temp at WS **71.5°F (21.9°C)**

Annual rainfall at WS **42in (1,073mm)**

Harvest month rainfall at WS **September: 0.6in (15mm)**

Chief viticultural hazard **Autumn rain**

Principal grapes **Chardonnay, Zinfandel, Pinot Noir**

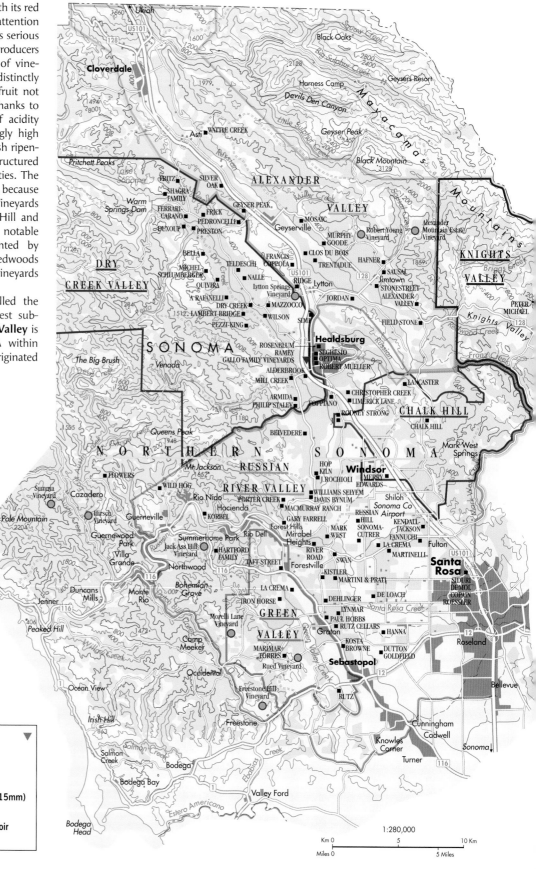

1:280,000

Km 0   5   10 Km

Miles 0   5 Miles

Chalk Hill to the northeast has its own AVA and is somewhat anomalously included in Russian River Valley, being much warmer and having volcanic soils. It is the fiefdom of one winery, called Chalk Hill, whose greatest strength is its particularly direct medium-weight Chardonnay, although it has made some good Sauvignon Blanc too, even if it is less zesty than Merry Edwards' version in the cooler reaches of the Russian River Valley. The inclusion in the Russian River AVA of the northern loop of the Russian River around Healdsburg, far from the cooling influence of fog, is equally difficult to justify climatologically.

On this map, between Russian River Valley and the ocean, are some of the most exciting producers in the coolest reaches of the absurdly extensive Sonoma Coast AVA (see p.293), which incorporates a total of half a million acres from Mendocino down to San Pablo Bay. The AVA was initially created to enable producers such as Sonoma-Cutrer, now owned by distillers Brown-Forman, to sell wines blended from their very varied holdings in this region as estate bottled but there is now pressure to develop more geographically specific AVAs within it. The Fort Ross-Seaview AVA is likely to be the first.

Site selection is critical here with exposure to marine influence, altitude, and orientation the crucial factors. If some of the finest fruit in the Russian River Valley comes from east-facing vineyards where the risk of raisining is minimal, south-facing sites help to maximize ripening in the even cooler conditions here. High-profile pioneers include Marcassin, Littorai, Flowers, and Fort Ross Estate. The Hirsch vineyard has long provided exceptional fruit for Russian River Valley producers and others.

Perceptibly warmer are the densely planted AVAs to the north of Russian River Valley, even if, as in Chalk Hill, Dry Creek Valley's valley floor is cooler than the hillsides. It can be positively damp at times, particularly at the southern end. (Compare Healdsburg's annual rainfall with that of somewhere as close as the town of Sonoma.) As in Russian River Valley, this encouraged 19th-century Italian settlers to plant the rot-prone Zinfandel above the fog-line and farm it without irrigation, thus earning Dry Creek Valley a (continuing) reputation for some of the finest examples of this finicky variety. Throughout these northern California valleys the east side, kept hotter for longer by the caress of the setting sun, tends to make fuller wines than the west. The best sites in the canyon enclosing Dry Creek Valley with substantial benchland are distinguished by a particularly well-drained mixture of gravel and red clays known as Dry Creek Valley conglomerate. Zins and Cabernet thrive here, while the valley floor is left to white

varieties, particularly Sauvignon Blanc. Dry Creek Vineyards was an early exponent while more recently Quivira, like Phelps an early convert to biodynamic viticulture, makes both good Sauvignon Blanc from valley floor vineyards and fine hillside Zinfandel. Rhône varieties have also been added to the mix, with maverick winemaker Lou Preston of Dry Creek leading the way. Some interesting Cabernet Sauvignon is made on the hillsides too.

The broader, more open Alexander Valley is very much warmer still, thanks to some low hills just northeast of Healdsburg that shelter it. On its alluvial soils Cabernet is consistently ripened to distinctive, almost chocolatey richness while lower ground near the river can yield some appetizing Sauvignon Blanc and Chardonnay. There are even some old Zinfandel and, much more unusual, Sangiovese vines in the northern Alexander Valley. Stonestreet's Alexander Mountain Estate, once known as Gauer Ranch, supplies some of California's most celebrated Chardonnay and has quite different, cooler conditions from the valley floor 450ft (140m) below.

A typical Sonoma scene: one of northern California's native oaks drenched in the morning sunshine on the Knights Valley property of British entrepreneur Sir Peter Michael. His Chardonnays, Cabernets, and now Pinot Noir and Sauvignon Blanc have won considerable acclaim.

Knights Valley, its Napa-wards offshoot and almost an extension of the head of the Napa Valley, is warmer than Dry Creek Valley but cooler (because higher) than Alexander Valley. Peter Michael is the only winery in the AVA, with estate vineyards of Chardonnay and Cabernet on volcanic soils up to 2,000ft (600m) and 1,500ft (450m) above sea level respectively. Beringer pioneered Knights Valley Cabernet and now also make a white Bordeaux blend from their Knights Valley vineyard called Alluvium, after the alluvial soils in this relatively warm site.

▼ All of these producers are well-established, even if the Dutton of Dutton Goldfield is better known as a large-scale grape grower than a wine producer. The "Dutton Ranch" cited on a number of producers' labels is not one vineyard but many, all in Northern Sonoma.

Southern Sonoma and Carneros

This is where fine wine, or the first attempt at it, began in California, round the former mission, garrison town, and one-brief-time state capital of Sonoma. It was at Mission San Francisco de Solano, founded in 1832, that the Franciscan monks, moving up the Pacific coast, planted their last and most northerly vineyard, introducing the vine to one of its friendliest environments on earth.

The town of Sonoma has all the atmosphere of a little wine capital – in fact of the capital of a very little republic: the original if short-lived Bear Flag Republic of California. Sonoma's tree-shaded square, with its old mission buildings and barracks, its stone-built City Hall and ornate Sebastiani Theatre, is faintly Ruritanian in style, and thickly layered with history.

The hills overlooking the town were the site of Agoston Haraszthy's famous pioneer estate of the 1850s and 1860s. Part of his Buena Vista cellars still stands in the side-valley to the east, although the winery has migrated to Carneros. Another famous 19th-century winery, Gundlach-Bundschu, was revived in the 1970s on the same southern slopes. Winemaking in northern California started here, even if in modern times much more attention is focused on Russian River Valley and Sonoma Coast to the north.

Like the Napa Valley, but in a smaller compass, the **Sonoma Valley** is cooled in the south by fogs and wind off San Pablo Bay and is progressively warmer towards the north, in this case into the lee of Sonoma Mountain, which shelters the valley from western storms and cooling maritime breezes. The Mayacamas Mountains, Napa Valley's western edge, constitute the eastern boundary. Landmark Vineyard's local

output, Kistler's Durell bottling, and Sonoma-Cutrer's Les Pierres vineyard (just west of Sonoma town) are all evidence that this AVA can grow excellent Chardonnay. Hanzell made history here with oak-aged Pinot Noir and Chardonnay that Joseph Heitz bottled to spectacular acclaim.

Evidence of excellent Cabernet first came from Louis Martini's famous Monte Rosso vineyard about 1,100ft (335m) up in the eastern hills, and more recently from the outstanding Laurel Glen Cabernets from **Sonoma Mountain**, a significant upland appellation in the west whose best wines seem to benefit from unusually thin, rocky soil, altitude, and long sunshine hours. The key to Cabernet and Zinfandel quality here again is to be above the fog line. Benziger are creating waves in Sonoma Mountain with their enthusiasm for biodynamic viticulture.

Just north of Sonoma Mountain the new AVA **Bennett Valley**, whose best known winery is Matanzas Creek, has similar soils to Sonoma Valley but much more cooling marine influence thanks to the proximity of the Crane Canyon wind gap (west of this map). The area is too cool to ripen Cabernet reliably and Merlot is the dominant variety. In general in Sonoma, unlike Napa, mountain vineyards are routinely picked long before those on the valley floor.

At Sonoma Valley's southern end, and included in the AVA, is the part of the cool **Carneros** district that lies in Sonoma County. Politically, Carneros straddles the Napa–Sonoma county line. Both Sonoma Carneros and Napa Carneros are mapped here as they have so much more in common with each other than with the rest of each county to the north.

On the low, rolling hills north of San Pablo Bay, Los Carneros (commonly known as Carneros), literally "the rams", is dairy country that was suddenly colonized by the vine in the late 1980s and 1990s. Winemakers Louis Martini and André Tchelistcheff had bought Carneros fruit as early as the 1930s and Martini first planted Pinot Noir and Chardonnay there in the late 1940s. Shallow clay-loam soils, much less fertile than, for example, the Napa Valley floor, help to regulate vine vigour and productivity. Strong winds off the Bay rattle the vine-leaves when hotter weather to the north sucks in cool air, particularly in the afternoons. They slow the ripening process to such an extent that Carneros produces some of California's most delicate wines, making them some of the state's better base wines for sparkling wine blends. Much hope and capital were invested here, particularly by sparkling wine producers, many of them from Champagne (notably Taittinger's Domaine Carneros) and from Spain's Cava country (Artesa and Gloria Ferrer are owned by Codorníu and Freixenet respectively). Following champagne traditions, Pinot Noir and, especially, Chardonnay are the dominant grape varieties, in vineyards regularly plundered by wineries in warmer country to the north.

The best still wines from Carneros can be delicious too, the Chardonnays having more ageing potential than most in California with

Taittinger's California outpost Domaine Carneros is almost spookily like their Château de la Marquetterie back home in Champagne. The focus of Carneros production has switched from sparkling wine to Pinot Noir to follow the market.

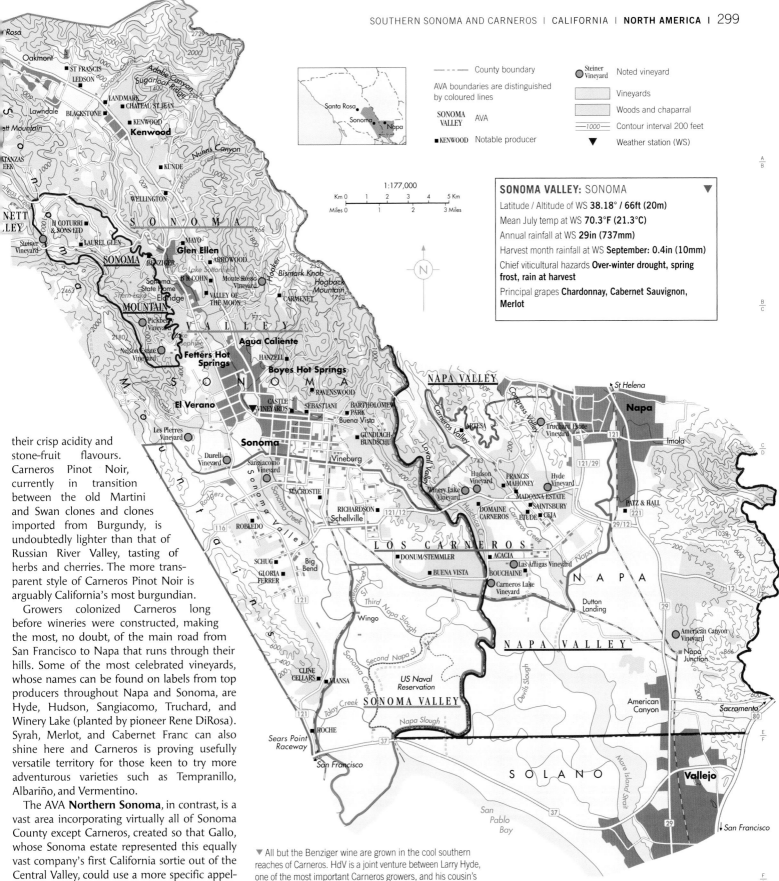

County boundary

Steiner Vineyard — Noted vineyard

AVA boundaries are distinguished by coloured lines

Vineyards

SONOMA VALLEY — AVA

Woods and chaparral

1000 — Contour interval 200 feet

■ KENWOOD — Notable producer

▼ Weather station (WS)

1:177,000

Km 0 1 2 3 4 5 Km

Miles 0 1 2 3 Miles

SONOMA VALLEY: SONOMA ▼

Latitude / Altitude of WS **38.18° / 66ft (20m)**

Mean July temp at WS **70.3°F (21.3°C)**

Annual rainfall at WS **29in (737mm)**

Harvest month rainfall at WS **September: 0.4in (10mm)**

Chief viticultural hazards **Over-winter drought, spring frost, rain at harvest**

Principal grapes **Chardonnay, Cabernet Sauvignon, Merlot**

---

their crisp acidity and stone-fruit flavours. Carneros Pinot Noir, currently in transition between the old Martini and Swan clones and clones imported from Burgundy, is undoubtedly lighter than that of Russian River Valley, tasting of herbs and cherries. The more transparent style of Carneros Pinot Noir is arguably California's most burgundian.

Growers colonized Carneros long before wineries were constructed, making the most, no doubt, of the main road from San Francisco to Napa that runs through their hills. Some of the most celebrated vineyards, whose names can be found on labels from top producers throughout Napa and Sonoma, are Hyde, Hudson, Sangiacomo, Truchard, and Winery Lake (planted by pioneer Rene DiRosa). Syrah, Merlot, and Cabernet Franc can also shine here and Carneros is proving usefully versatile territory for those keen to try more adventurous varieties such as Tempranillo, Albariño, and Vermentino.

The AVA **Northern Sonoma**, in contrast, is a vast area incorporating virtually all of Sonoma County except Carneros, created so that Gallo, whose Sonoma estate represented this equally vast company's first California sortie out of the Central Valley, could use a more specific appellation than Sonoma for its estate brands.

▼ All but the Benziger wine are grown in the cool southern reaches of Carneros. HdV is a joint venture between Larry Hyde, one of the most important Carneros growers, and his cousin's husband Aubert de Villaine of Domaine de la Romanée-Conti.

Napa Valley

Twenty per cent of the value of all California's wine comes from the Napa Valley – from only 4% of its volume. Such is the reputation of the world's most glamorous, most cosseted, and most heavily capitalized wine region. Its modern history starts in 1966, with the construction of the Robert Mondavi winery. The Mission-style adobe arch and global ambitions of this iconic cellar signalled the start of the transformation of a sleepy farming community of walnut and prune orchards. But its 44,000 acres (18,000ha) of vines would fit seven times into Bordeaux. For all the noise made about it, it is really quite small, and yet far more varied than most outsiders realize.

Detailed surveys undertaken in recent years have established that half of the soil orders on earth are to be found in the Napa Valley. In broad terms the valley is the result of the Napa River, now a lazy trickle, eroding its way between the Mayacamas Mountains on the west and the Vaca Range on the east. Their respective peaks are the igneous outflows of Mount Veeder and Atlas Peak, responsible at various times for a wide range of mineral deposits. (That volcanic activity continues is obvious at the head of the valley in Calistoga, where visitors frolic in mud baths and hot springs.) Soils as a consequence are thinnest, oldest, and least fertile on the sides of the valley while the valley floor is dominated by deep, fertile alluvial clays. There are some deep but well-drained soils on the piedmonts on both sides of the valley.

As for climate, as elsewhere in northern California, the open (in this case southern) end of this narrow valley is much cooler than the

northern end, by an average of at least 10°F (6.3°C) during the summer. In fact Carneros (see previous page) is virtually at the coolest limit of fine wine production while Calistoga is as hot as any fine wine producer would care for. Much of the land in between is just right, especially for the late-ripening Cabernet Sauvignon. As the air heated by the long summer season rises, it draws in cooling draughts of ocean air, whether from Sonoma's Russian River Valley via the Chalk Hill gap (see p.297) around Diamond Mountain and Spring Mountain or, more persistently, from Carneros as far north as Stags Leap. Eastern slopes benefit from sunshine during the warmer afternoons, resulting in softer wines than those made on the west side from grapes ripened by morning sun. The latter generally have more definition.

Wines tend to taste progressively richer with riper tannins as you move north. As you move up into the hills, they have more structure and concentration than the valley floor counterparts they look directly down on. The less fertile, dry-farmed hillsides have been colonized by the vine to a certain extent despite problems with erosion and land use disputes. High-altitude vineyards both east and west of the valley often benefit from strong morning sunshine above a valley floor shrouded in fog. Then cool breezes bathe the mountaintops in the late afternoon while the valley floor radiates heat trapped below an inversion layer.

This is the theory. What gets in the way of matching geography to bottle is less natural caprice – although vintages vary here far more than many wine drinkers realize – than how the Napa Valley is organized. To the millions of

The social highlight of the Napa Valley calendar is the charity wine auction held each June. It has funnelled millions of dollars from dot-com fortunes to healthcare programmes and low-income housing for vineyard workers and their families. Auction lots are viewed here at the St Supéry winery.

tourists attracted to "The Valley" each year, there seems an infinity of wineries flanking the traffic-jammed Highway 29 and its eastern counterpart, the quieter Silverado Trail. In fact there are fewer than 400 wineries, but more than 700 grape-growers. The symbiotic functions of selling wine and growing vines are more distinct here than in most fine wine districts. Some wineries have but a line of ornamental vines of their own. They will buy in fruit, sometimes wine, and very possibly blend different lots so that these expressive nuances are lost. Even if the wine is, unusually, labelled with a more specific AVA than Napa Valley, unless the vineyard is named, it can be difficult to locate the precise grape source.

Cabernet Sauvignon is the Napa Valley's grape. In fact Napa's best Cabernets are incontrovertibly some of the world's most successful. They have unparalleled opulence and exuberance, yet the finest examples have rigour too. Some of the more austere hillside examples apart, these are Cabernets that can be drunk with pleasure when only three or four years old, although the great mid-20th century vintages from pioneers such as Beaulieu and Inglenook aged beautifully for 50 years. Time will tell how the super-ripe, super-alcoholic Cabernets that now result from fashionably prolonged "hang time" will last in bottle.

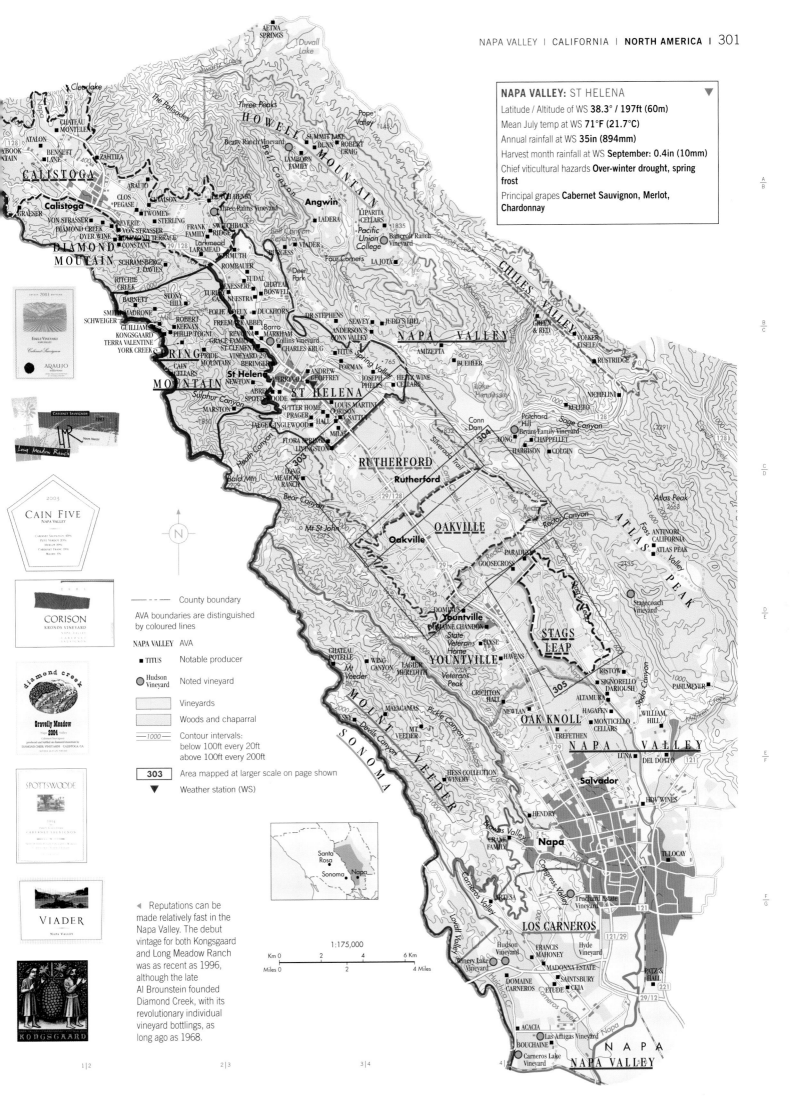

NAPA VALLEY: ST HELENA

Latitude / Altitude of WS **38.3° / 197ft (60m)**

Mean July temp at WS **71°F (21.7°C)**

Annual rainfall at WS **35in (894mm)**

Harvest month rainfall at WS **September: 0.4in (10mm)**

Chief viticultural hazards **Over-winter drought, spring frost**

Principal grapes **Cabernet Sauvignon, Merlot, Chardonnay**

— · — · — County boundary

AVA boundaries are distinguished by coloured lines

NAPA VALLEY AVA

▪ TITUS Notable producer

⬤ Hudson Vineyard Noted vineyard

Vineyards

Woods and chaparral

—1000— Contour intervals:
below 100ft every 20ft
above 100ft every 200ft

303 Area mapped at larger scale on page shown

▼ Weather station (WS)

◀ Reputations can be made relatively fast in the Napa Valley. The debut vintage for both Kongsgaard and Long Meadow Ranch was as recent as 1996, although the late Al Brounstein founded Diamond Creek, with its revolutionary individual vineyard bottlings, as long ago as 1968.

1:175,000

Km 0   2   4   6 Km

Miles 0   2   4 Miles

Most Napa-labelled Chardonnay now comes from the cooler climes of Carneros, but some good Sauvignon Blanc is produced just north of Yountville. Syrah is being planted on some hillside sites, notably Mount Veeder, and some fine Zinfandel is produced in various Napa vineyards, particularly around Calistoga and on Mount Veeder, but Napa does not have a cohesive answer to Sonoma's Dry Creek Valley.

That said, Napa County has one of the more highly developed and cogent sets of AVAs – certainly more logical than Sonoma's. Napa Valley is the general AVA and includes not just the world-famous main valley with its extraordinary concentration of modish restaurants, art galleries, and gift shops as well as wineries, but also a considerable area of quite separate land. The very warm Pope Valley to the northeast and the **Chiles Valley** AVA will surely be colonized by would-be vignerons, as American Canyon, southeast of Napa town (mapped with Carneros on p.299) already has been. This southern territory towards the town of Vallejo has proved warm enough for extensive viticulture on land that is much more exposed and therefore cooler than most of the Napa Valley but is entitled to the name.

Rutherford, Oakville, and Stags Leap in the middle stretch of the valley are considered in detail overleaf. **Oak Knoll District**, a relatively new AVA, is the coolest, southernmost, and has the distinction of being able to produce fine examples of both Riesling and long-lived

TEMPERATURE VARIATION IN THE NAPA VALLEY

The two diagrams below left and centre, supplied by California viticultural consultants Terra Spase, show actual morning and afternoon temperatures on one particular day, illustrating the typical variance between the two sides of the Napa Valley. Note how the south of the valley is consistently cooler than the north, and the land above the fog line is much warmer than the valley floor in the early morning.

Cabernet – as Trefethen can attest. **Yountville** immediately north of here is slightly warmer and has a good affinity with Merlot, which thrives on some of the clay-rich alluvial fans found in this AVA, characterized by massive blocks of intact rock that make up the area's distinctive knolls.

A little warmer than Rutherford, **St Helena** is not just the largest and busiest of the Napa Valley's wine towns, it is also the address of many of the valley's biggest wineries. Many ship in wine or grapes from well outside the area. The fortune of Sutter Home was built on palest pink "White" Zinfandel bought in from the Central Valley. Beringer, for long a source of fine, geographically designated reds and whites, is now owned by Australian brewers Foster's; V Sattui thrives on tourists, and so does the once-great Louis Martini. St Helena can also boast the vineyards of some of the smallest, most cultish labels such as Grace Family, Vineyard 29, and Colgin Herb Lamb, although Spottswoode and Corison among others show that this area can also produce wines with real restraint and subtlety.

At the northern end of the valley, **Calistoga**, now with its own AVA, is all but surrounded by mountains, notably Mount St Helena to the north, which capture cold winter air at night and bring spring frosts, a perennial threat to all valley floor vineyards. Sprinkler systems and, particularly, wind machines and propellers are an eye-catching local feature of the vineyards on the volcanic soils around Calistoga. Most tourists give up long before they reach this end of the valley.

This means that such a distinctive region as **Diamond Mountain District**, just southwest of the town, is not too overrun. Diamond Creek Vineyard was an early exponent of occasionally impenetrable vineyard-designated bottlings from its extremely mixed soil, which includes volcanic elements. Sparkling wine pioneer Schramsberg

(now sourcing virtually all its base wines from much cooler areas) is an unlikely neighbour.

Mountain vineyards have become increasingly important in Napa Valley. All along the western ridge are single-minded individuals perceived, not least by themselves, as very different creatures from those on the valley floor below. **Spring Mountain District** benefits not just from altitude but from cool Pacific air too. Stony Hill became the prototype for Napa Valley cult wines with its long-lived Chardonnays back in the 1960s and is still going strong. Today, many of Spring Mountain's most supple wines carry the Pride Mountain label. Still within the Spring Mountain District AVA, York Creek makes fine Zinfandel as well as Cabernet.

Mount Veeder to the south produces altogether tougher but highly distinctive wine from very thin, very acid soils with a strong volcanic element not dissimilar to those found over the ridge in the western Sonoma Valley (Monte Rosso, for example).

On the gentler east side of the valley, vines are being planted and wineries constructed as fast as local planners will allow. Dunn, La Jota, and Liparita are some of the highest achievers on the cool, quiet, generally fog-free uplands of **Howell Mountain**. Just a few metres outside the Howell Mountain AVA, Delia Viader makes superb examples of Napa mountain Cabernet, Franc as well as Sauvignon.

The sheltered Conn Valley benefits from benchland soils and is clearly well suited to Cabernet. Chappellet on Pritchard Hill was the pioneer here. **Atlas Peak** to the south is even higher, and cooler, with breezes straight from the Bay. Its thin soils were planted with a slew of Italian grape varieties by Antinori at Atlas Peak Vineyards. Cabernet, however, with particularly bright fruit and good natural acidity, is now the Atlas Peak speciality. From edge to edge Cabernet is Napa's own grape.

EARLY MORNING TEMPERATURES

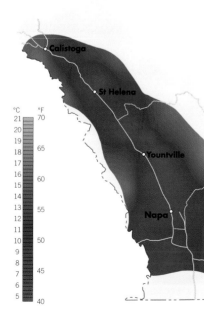

LATE AFTERNOON TEMPERATURES

CUMULATIVE GROWING DEGREE DAYS
(See p.292)

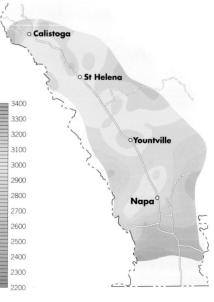

Rutherford

To explain Rutherford to a visitor schooled in French wine, you might describe it as the Pauillac of Calilfornia. This is Cabernet country par excellence. Nearly two-thirds of the 4,000 acres (1,600ha) of vines here are Cabernet Sauvignon and most of the rest are other Bordeaux dark-skinned grapes grown to complement it.

Not that the Cabernet ripened in Rutherford's warm summers is left with any of the holes on the palate that may require Merlot and Cabernet Franc to fill them in the Médoc. Rutherford's is full-throttle Cabernet in terms of ripeness, even if it typically tends to have more structure, backbone, and longevity than almost any other California Cabernet.

Rutherford has produced great, ageworthy Cabernet since the first half of the 20th century when names such as Inglenook and Beaulieu carved California's reputation. The proof is still there, behind labels printed in the 1940s. Other famous specific vineyards include Bosché, Bella Oaks, and, with a rather more youthful but deserved reputation, Livingston's Moffett vineyard. In Rubicon Estate film director Francis Ford Coppola has revived Inglenook, once the district's most famous winery and vineyards.

All of these are on the so-called Rutherford Bench on the west side of the valley, a slightly elevated stretch of sedimentary gravelly sand and alluvial fans carved out by the influential Napa River. They are deep and particularly well-drained, so conducive to lower crop loads, earlier ripening, and greater intensity of flavour than the valley norm. Many tasters detect a mineral element in wines produced here, known in shorthand as "Rutherford dust" – although the trend towards prolonged hang time has in some cases tended to blur Rutherford's distinction.

The Rutherford AVA is more homogeneous than most because elevation, up to 600ft (180m), is pretty uniform, although another notably successful district within Rutherford is on the east side between the Napa River and Conn Creek, where afternoon rays linger longest. Gravelly deposits washed down from the Vaca Range have resulted in a particularly well-drained cluster of vineyards such as that used by Caymus to source their Special Selection Cabernet. Some cooling marine influence from the Bay reaches as far north as this, but not as much as in districts further south.

The famous "Rutherford dust", seen here with typically widely spaced vine rows in the Rutherford Bench district. It is true that many of Rutherford's majestic Cabernets – and this is very much Cabernet country – have a certain earthiness about them.

▶ The Staglin family and Agustin Huneeus's Quintessa are relatively new kids on the Rutherford Bench, but film director Francis Ford Coppola grows Rubicon on much the same vineyards as produced the most legendary Inglenook bottlings when Gustave Niebaum owned the estate.

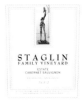

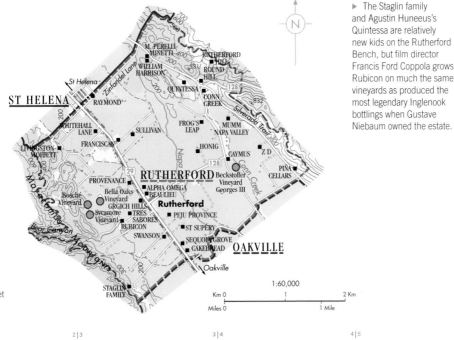

AVA boundaries are distinguished by coloured lines

RUTHERFORD AVA

■ CAYMUS   Notable producer

◉ Bosché Vineyard   Noted vineyard

▢ Vineyards

▢ Woods and chaparral

═ 500 ═ Contour interval 100 feet

1:60,000

Oakville

There may not be much more to Oakville than the admirable Oakville Grocery store (one of the Napa Valley's best places to buy wine and food for your picnics) and the Napa Wine Company (a particularly popular custom crush facility). But it was in Oakville, in 1966, that the California wine revolution began when Robert Mondavi built his striking winery. Sadly it is no longer a family enterprise, just one of hundreds of subdivisions of Constellation, the world's largest wine company.

Going north up the valley, Oakville is where serious, meaty Cabernet begins. The wines may not have quite the weight and backbone of the best that Rutherford can offer but they certainly offer the Napa Valley's quintessential opulence. Oakville can also produce some vote-catching Chardonnay and Sauvignon Blanc, even some convincing Sangiovese, but Cabernet is its essence.

The AVA is far enough south to benefit from some marine influence from San Pablo Bay, although the knoll southeast of Cardinale has a bearing on exactly where those cooling fogs and breezes go.

As in Rutherford there is a marked difference between the west and east sides of Oakville. Alluvial fans predominate in the west with, closest to the hillsides, large particles washed out of the Mayacamas Mountains providing relatively good drainage and not too high a level of fertility. Closer to the valley floor the richer Bale loams predominate. Ripening grapes is easy here.

It is even easier on the eastern side – in fact the warmth of afternoon sunshine on the lower slopes of the Vaca Range in the east can be a threat to freshness of fruit. (The AVA boundary goes up to the 600ft/180m contour line whereas much of the valley floor is at an altitude below 200ft/60m.) Soils here in the east are heavier and have more volcanic influence.

The To Kalon vineyard, which lies in the west, was first planted as long ago as 1870. Such is the sheer, exuberant quality of its Cabernet that its precise boundaries, ownership, and name continue to be fought over. It is currently partly owned by growers Beckstoffer and partly by the Robert Mondavi winery.

The first Napa Valley vineyard to achieve international fame in the modern era was Martha's Vineyard, bottled and label-designated by Joe Heitz, who consistently denied that its minty overlay had anything to do with the eucalyptus trees planted on its edge.

Today the name of Oakville is so potent that several of its producers allocate their wines rather than sell them, then donate a small proportion to America's charity auctions and marvel at the zeroes. Screaming Eagle in the east and the increasing range of wines from the Harlan stable on the opposite side of the valley are the most obvious but by no means the only examples.

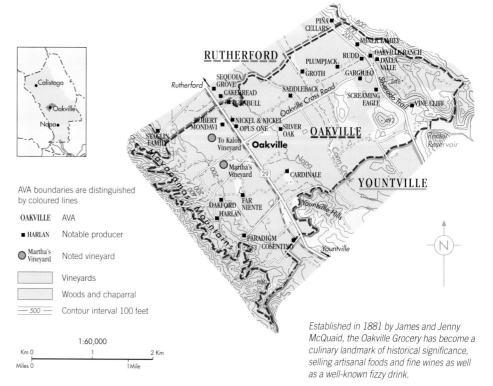

AVA boundaries are distinguished by coloured lines

OAKVILLE   AVA

■ HARLAN   Notable producer

◉ Martha's Vineyard   Noted vineyard

Vineyards

Woods and chaparral

500   Contour interval 100 feet

1:60,000

Km 0 ___ 1 ___ 2 Km
Miles 0 ___ 1 Mile

Established in 1881 by James and Jenny McQuaid, the Oakville Grocery has become a culinary landmark of historical significance, selling artisanal foods and fine wines as well as a well-known fizzy drink.

▶ The Mondavi/Mouton joint venture Opus One and this Paul Hobbs wine (which set a new record for grape prices) are based on the famed To Kalon vineyard, while Dalla Valle's Maya Cabernet comes from west-facing vines.

Stags Leap

and Clos du Val. The knoll above Stag's Leap Wine Cellars protects some vineyards from this cooling influence. Indeed the AVA's rumpled series of hills and ridges makes generalizations more difficult than elsewhere in the Napa Valley. But the area is warm enough to see the vines start leafing a good two weeks ahead of more northerly areas, even though the ripening process is gentler, with the result that harvest tends to be at about the same time as, say, Rutherford's.

Soils are moderately fertile, volcanic, gravel-loams on the valley floor with rockier, particularly well drained terrain on the heavily protected hillsides. Shafer, another one of the district's top performers, benefits from its highly regarded hillside vineyard that was carved out of the eastern slopes before restrictions started to bite.

Stags Leap Merlot is also notable but the area seems too hot for Chardonnay.

Cabernet Sauvignon grapes being harvested in the Stag's Leap Wine Cellars vineyard, which is named after a local legend. According to the Wappo tribe, a noble stag, which was being pursued by hunters on the cliffs above the valley, was able to leap to safety across a chasm in the rocks.

Stags Leap is the eastern opposite number to Yountville; the AVA for an enclave contained behind a high knoll on the valley floor and climbing the eastern hills. Its reputation might make you expect something more imposing or extensive. Fame came overnight in 1976, when a Cabernet from Stag's Leap Wine Cellars came first in a Paris tasting that still makes the news 30 years later. It pitted some of what were then California's better-known wines against some of the best of Bordeaux. Much to everyone's surprise, including the authors of this book, who were on the panel of judges, the California wines repeated the performance in a re-run exactly 30 years later. Perhaps if the winery had been named after its thoughtful owner, Warren Winiarski, Stags Leap District might not trip off tongues as it does.

It deserves its fame, though. Of all Napa Cabernets, those of Stags Leap (the district as well as Winiarski's winery) have arguably the most recognizable character: a silky texture, a certain aroma of violets or cherries, tannins that have always been supple, power with more delicacy than is usual in Napa Cabernet. Some make comparisons with Margaux.

The district, barely three miles by one, takes its name from a run of bare rocks, a basalt palisade, on the eastern edge of the valley, an afternoon suntrap, from which warm air radiates. This is moderated by marine breezes, another afternoon phenomenon, that are funnelled through the Golden Gate Bridge, over San Pablo Bay and turned by the hills behind Berkeley straight up towards Chimney Rock

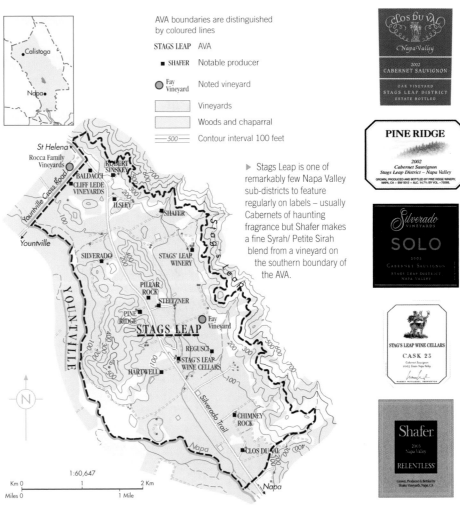

AVA boundaries are distinguished by coloured lines

STAGS LEAP AVA
■ SHAFER Notable producer
⬤ Fay Vineyard Noted vineyard
  Vineyards
  Woods and chaparral
—500— Contour interval 100 feet

▶ Stags Leap is one of remarkably few Napa Valley sub-districts to feature regularly on labels – usually Cabernets of haunting fragrance but Shafer makes a fine Syrah/ Petite Sirah blend from a vineyard on the southern boundary of the AVA.

South of the Bay

The other sides of San Francisco Bay, east and south, are nothing like the Napa and Sonoma valleys, either in terms of the wines they produce or their social history. Nor are they similar to each other. To the east the windswept, dry gravels of the **Livermore Valley** have been famous for white wine, especially Sauvignon Blanc with perhaps the most individual style in the state, ever since they were planted with cuttings from Château d'Yquem, no less, in 1869. The creative Wente family dominates the 1,600 acres (650ha) of vines under constant threat from urban development, and have carried an unappreciated torch for Livermore Sauvignon Blanc for well over a century. It remains a fresh but foursquare white, worth maturing two or three years, and as close as California gets to white Graves.

The grey sprawl of urban development on the map has spread rapidly south of San Francisco Bay as Silicon Valley wallowed in a period of extraordinary growth. High above it in the **Santa Cruz Mountains** is quite incongruous wine country, older than the Napa Valley. Its isolated wineries are far fewer, and vineyards fewer still, but several of them are among California's most famous names.

In the 1950s Martin Ray of Mount Eden was the first winemaker of the modern era to bring renown to these beautiful forested mountains. His eccentric, expensive wines, like those of his ex-cellarhand David Bruce, caused arguments and amusement in exactly the opposite proportion to those caused by their spiritual successor, Randall Grahm of Bonny Doon, whose ocean-cooled vineyards just northwest of the "alternative" town of Santa Cruz succumbed in 1994 to Pierce's Disease. No matter. Grahm is an agent provocateur and an inspired improviser, scouring not just the state but the world now for the raw ingredients for his highly original blends with names such as Le Cigare Volant and Il Fiasco.

The established leader in the region is Ridge Vineyards, high above the fog-line on a ridge overlooking the ocean one way and the Bay the other. Cabernet from the highest patch, Monte Bello, is often as fine and long-lived a red wine as any in California, thanks to old vine stock and the infertile soils on these steep slopes. Aged almost exclusively in seasoned American oak, it can taste disconcertingly like Bordeaux with the bottle age it demands. Ridge also painstakingly trucks fruit, especially from ancient Zinfandel vines, from all over the state

up to the winery at 2,600ft (790m), to treat it in the same uncompromising way. Santa Cruz has hundreds rather than thousands of acres, but it has determined growers. A small band of them has led a revival of brooding, mountain-grown Pinot Noir.

Just east of the Santa Cruz Mountains AVA is **Santa Clara Valley**, a wine region almost squeezed out of existence by the electronic revolution, yet just a little further south, near "the garlic capital of the world", Gilroy, in the unofficial Hecker Pass district, ancient Rhône vines persist. The local wineries can sell everything they make at the cellar door. As a result, few realize how good its wine can be, which makes the grey sprawl all the more of a threat.

The reason **Monterey** County produces almost as much wine as the whole of Napa County lies on the valley floor, from Gonzales south beyond King City, a monument to 1970s corporate madness. The then large companies (several are now defunct) and private investors pursuing tax breaks were encouraged by the University of California at Davis and its preoccupation with degree days to plant in what promised to be a wonderfully cool-climate zone. The Salinas Valley, with its mouth open to the ocean on Monterey Bay, forms a highly efficient funnel for a regular afternoon visitation of cold sea air. The valley, with its short history of salad and vegetable growing and long history of exploitation (remember Steinbeck?), was enthusiastically turned over to vines in a planting spree that took in nearly 40,000 acres (16,200ha) – far more than Napa Valley.

Flying in the face of fashion, Ridge has consistently favoured tight-grained American oak over French and yet makes some of the state's most French-tasting reds. The choice is based on research in century-old archives and obsessive attention to how the oak is seasoned before being made into barrels.

Unfortunately, in the short term at least, the funnel proved all too efficient. On a hot day inland, clammy coastal air comes rushing up the valley with such force that it actually tears off vine shoots. The valley is extremely dry (with irrigation water aplenty from the underground Salinas River) but fiendishly cold. Vines regularly bud two weeks earlier than the California norm and are picked at least two weeks later, giving Salinas Valley one of the longest growing seasons in the world of wine.

These huge vine farms stretch for miles between the bottom of the map opposite and the top of the one overleaf. The most notable is the record 12,640-acre (5,100-ha) San Bernabe vineyard of which 5,500 acres (2,200ha) are planted; Scheid and Lockwood are two other monster vineyards. The excessively herbaceous wines that initially resulted seriously sullied the name and reputation of Monterey. Even today, with viticultural practices much improved, a substantial amount of the production of Salinas Valley is sold in bulk to the Central Valley giants, to be blended with wine from warmer regions and sold under the basic California appellation. At best, with fine tuning in the vineyard, it can produce medium-quality varietals that are certainly not overpriced. As so often in California, Chardonnay predominates, by a wide margin.

◄ While most of the grapes represented in this varied line-up were grown somewhere on the map opposite, the provenance of Randall Grahm's Cigare Volant has varied over the years. The name is a reference to a flying saucer supposedly spotted in Châteauneuf-du-Pape, the inspiration for this wine.

Arroyo Seco has an even longer growing season thanks to its notably low average daytime temperatures. The western section is more sheltered from the winds, and Riesling and Gewurztraminer vines on its pebbly vineyards have been persuaded to rot nobly every year, giving botrytized wines with particularly refreshing acidity.

Nowadays there are vines as far south as hot **Hames Valley** (see p.293) near the San Luis Obispo county line and up on the valley's western slopes in the **Santa Lucia Highlands**. Thanks to their glacial alluvial soils, southeast-facing terraces, and exposure to Pacific fogs and breezes, they yield some Pinot Noir and Chardonnay of real quality. Caymus of Napa Valley ended up here for their Mer Soleil vineyard, for example. In general this is vine-farming, not winemaking, country.

Chalone Vineyard, with its own AVA, lies on a sun-scorched 2,000-ft (600-m) limestone hilltop on the road from Soledad to nowhere – except the Pinnacles National Monument. Chalone has, with varying degrees of success, made Chardonnay and Pinot Noir with the conviction that Burgundy's Corton has somehow migrated west. Burgundy, or more precisely limestone, was the inspiration for Josh Jensen's Calera, founded in equally splendid, equally arid isolation to grow Pinot Noir just 20 miles (32km) north in the same range (**Mount Harlan** AVA). The soil is right; the rainfall almost ruinously low. Calera estate wines have long been subsidized by imports from the rapidly expanding Central Coast region to the south. Since Chalone was acquired by Diageo in 2005 it has leaned heavily on cheaper fruit from Monterey.

1:710,000

Km 0 — 10 — 20 — 30 Km
Miles 0 — 10 — 20 Miles

County boundary

AVA boundaries are distinguished by coloured lines

CHALONE   AVA

■ RIDGE   Notable producer

◉ Pisoni Vineyard   Noted vineyard

Vineyards

Woods and chaparral

—4000—   Contour interval 1000 feet

Central Coast

There are traces of ancient Mission vineyards in the fashionable Central Coast, but its modern life started only in the early 1990s as a cheaper alternative to vineyard expansion in Napa and Sonoma. The name applies all the way from the vineyards south of San Francisco in the north (see previous page for a map of these and of Monterey County) to the subtropical climate of greater Los Angeles (whose wine country is discussed on p.312).

The two counties in between, San Luis Obispo and Santa Barbara, mapped opposite, are in full viticultural spate. The view from Highway 101, which winds through them, was transformed by the end of the 20th century from scrub oaks and cattle grazing to an undulating strip of vineyards that continues for miles on end.

This part of California is distinctive geologically: the San Andreas Fault runs down the eastern side of the region; its vineyards are based on quite different, more marine-influenced, carbonate-infused soils, which, according to some authorities, is one of the reasons their wines have a certain voluptuousness. There is a parallel in textural differences and acidity levels between North and Central Coast wines and between those of Chianti Classico and the Tuscan Coast.

The climate here is also primarily maritime, with very mild winters (vines may not always get the chance of a restorative sleep) and summers that are much cooler than the California norm (see the key facts panel, which shows a mean July temperature roughly the same as that of the Mosel Valley).

San Luis Obispo County has at least three distinct zones, two of them in the crudely drawn **Paso Robles** appellation, which includes such a wide stretch of country. The rolling grassland east of Highway 101 is decidedly hot with no direct access for cooling ocean breezes. Its deep fertile soils are now home to a sizeable area of vineyard that supplies supple, fruity, though hardly demanding varietals, largely for North Coast wineries and contract bottlers. The big companies Constellation (Mondavi et al) and Foster's (Beringer et al), as well as the locally

Vines in Edna Valley, where cattle used to graze until America became a wine-producing and wine-consuming nation and so much of its west coast was converted to viticulture from other forms of agriculture. Thanks to the proximity of the Pacific, this is one of California's most humid wine regions.

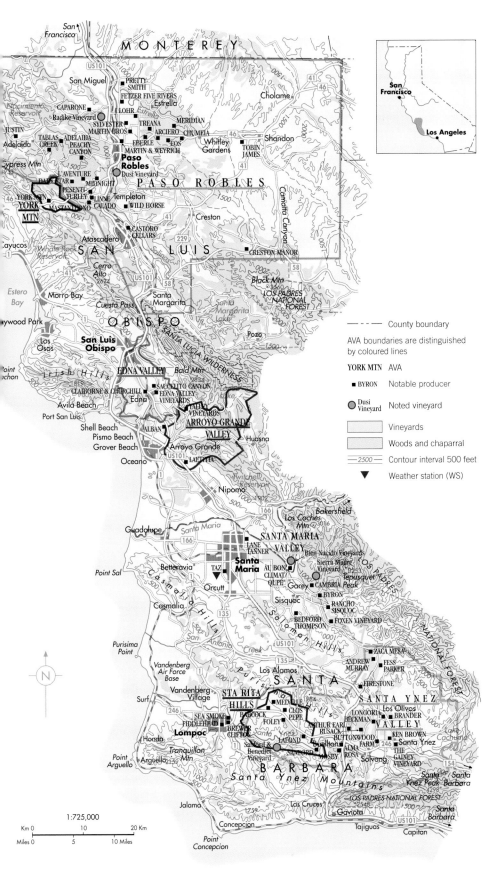

CENTRAL COAST: SANTA MARIA ▼
Latitude / Altitude of WS **34.54° / 230ft (70m)**
Mean July temperature at WS **63.1°F (17.3°C)**
Average annual rainfall at WS **12in (314mm)**
Harvest month rainfall at WS **September: 0.4in (10mm)**
Principal viticultural hazard **Late ripening**
Principal grapes **Chardonnay, Pinot Noir**

based J Lohr, are all big players in the district. Beringer's Meridian winery (formerly called Estrella River) stands out for its hilltop site, a vantage point dominating the increasingly viticultural landscape to the southeast.

The wooded hill terrain of the western section of Paso Robles on the other side of the highway has much more interesting soil and, being cooled by marine air (if rarely fog), has rather more in common with the Santa Clara Valley west of the San Andreas Fault. The historic fame of Paso Robles, such as it is, comes largely from potent Zinfandels, which are dry-farmed following Italian immigrant tradition and taste not unlike Amador Foothill Zinfandel (see p.311). This was the area chosen by the Perrin family of Château de Beaucastel in Châteauneuf-du-Pape to plant with a wide range of French clones of Rhône grapes at their Tablas Creek nursery and winemaking operation. Larry Turley of Turley Wine Cellars and Chateau Potelle are notable investors from the Napa Valley.

Edna Valley, over the Cuesta Pass to the south, is different again. Sea air swirls in from Morro Bay, providing perfect conditions for the development of fungal diseases, and renders the valley as cool as any California wine region. It somehow manages to produce some quite luscious Chardonnays, albeit with a fine streak of lime to keep them lively. Edna Valley Vineyards (related to Chalone) was once its prime local winemaking operation, but it has been joined by other wineries, most notably Alban, one of the Central Coast's most proficient exponents of red and white Rhône varieties, who manage to coax Syrah to ripeness levels unimaginable in the Rhône Valley.

To the immediate southeast, the more varied but generally even cooler **Arroyo Grande** is increasingly recognized as a source of particularly fine Pinot Noir and Chardonnay from the likes of Talley and Laetitia, once the champagne house Deutz's California venture.

▼ All manner of grapes here but not a trace of that northern California staple Cabernet Sauvignon. It would have great difficulty ripening in these fog-cooled vineyards. The Fess Parker comes from the new Sta (sic) Rita Hills appellation.

Moving south again across the county line into Santa Barbara, the **Santa Maria Valley**, southern California's riposte to the Côte d'Or, provides conditions that are, if anything, cooler still. Its river runs out to sea in flat land that offers no opposition at all to the Pacific air. Some of its vineyard land is so low-lying that sea fog moves in at midday and overcropped fruit can easily be underripe and over-acid. This countryside is far from the stereotype of southern California, and indeed from balmy, palmy Santa Barbara itself. Santa Barbara lies in the lee of the crucial mountains that run off the southeast corner of the map on p.309, shielding it from the cold ocean fogs that influence the Santa Maria and Santa Ynez Valleys. What is common to all of Santa Barbara County, however, in contrast to Sonoma's Pinot country, is remarkably low rainfall (as the key facts panel shows). This means that there is no hurry to harvest before autumn rains. Santa Barbara's grapes, like those grown further north in Monterey and San Luis Obispo, benefit from an extremely long growing season, building flavour over months and months.

Almost all the thousands of acres of grapes in Santa Maria Valley are owned by farmers rather than wineries, making vineyard names unusually prominent. Bien Nacido, for one, crops up on a range of different winery labels, while many of the region's wineries also buy grapes up and down the Central Coast. Cambria (part of the Kendall-Jackson empire) is notably warmer than Bien Nacido because it is further

from coastal influence. Rancho Sisquoc is the most sheltered, except for the positively secluded Foxen in its own canyon. The best grapes, Pinot Noir and Chardonnay in the main but Syrah too, are grown on slopes high enough – 600ft plus (180m) – above the valley floor to be on the fringe of the fog belt. Their naturally high acidity is offset by a fruity intensity which has something in common with the best of New Zealand. Much the most exciting winery in Santa Maria, with an air of frenetic experimentation matched only by Bonny Doon in Santa Cruz, is Au Bon Climat and its partner in the same modest premises, Qupé. Heavily influenced by Burgundy, Jim Clendenen of Au Bon Climat makes a wide range of different styles of Chardonnay and Pinot Noir (sourcing some grapes from Oregon), but also Pinot Gris, Viognier, and many an Italian varietal.

Just south of Santa Maria, in similarly cool, intensely rural conditions, is the (unofficial) Los Alamos region where several thousand acres of vineyard produce particularly lively Chardonnay. Conditions are a bit warmer and more stable over the Solomon Hills, particularly (as in Paso Robles) east of Highway 101. The **Santa Ynez Valley**, within easy reach of wine tourists and property developers from Los Angeles, is no obvious physical feature, but a sprawl of vineyards in rolling, oak-dotted hills around and to the north of Solvang, a town as peculiarly Danish as its name. East of the highway are some particularly well-favoured sites with warm days and cold

Au Bon Climat's premises, originally a dairy shed, have always been defiantly unglamorous – very un-Napa. And for many years the company owned no vines but simply operated on contracts with the handful of extensive vineyards in Santa Barbara County.

nights that can yield impressive red wines, both Syrah and the Bordeaux varieties, as well as the Roussanne of Andrew Murray.

Things get even better in the much cooler and relatively recent AVA Santa Rita Hills (officially **Sta Rita Hills** in deference to the powerful Chilean producer Santa Rita), a series of rolling hills in the far west of Santa Ynez Valley between Lompoc and Buellton, where a bend in the Santa Ynez River marks the end of intense ocean influence. Soils are a patchwork of sand, silt, and clay. Pinot Noir, with Chardonnay as support, is the principal grape variety here. The AVA boundaries were established with Pinot Noir in mind, but Bryan Babcock showed that the high acidities that are common here suit Sauvignon Blanc, Riesling, and Gewurztraminer well. Kathy Joseph is another to do well with Sauvignon Blanc under the name Fiddlehead.

It was the Sanford & Benedict vineyard that first drew attention to the Santa Rita Hills. It lies in a sheltered north-facing niche that perfectly suits Pinot Noir. The Richard Sanford who lent it his name, a screwcap pioneer, now grows the Burgundian varieties organically at Alma Rosa nearby.

Sierra Foothills, Lodi, and the Delta

The Central Valley is a vast, flat, extremely fertile, heavily irrigated tract of industrial farmland, one of the planet's most important growers of citrus, stone fruit, tomatoes, cotton, cattle, rice, nuts, and grapes. At its northern end the grapes become more interesting.

The Sacramento Delta has a very different character and style from the rest of the valley. The influence of the nearby San Francisco Bay is felt in much cooler nights than are found either south or north. **Clarksburg** in the northwest portion of the Delta manages to produce good honeyed Chenin Blanc.

Lodi lies on higher land, on soils washed down from the Sierras, both factors for better wine. Growers, many with a century-old history, have worked so hard on researching which district is best suited to which variety that no fewer than seven AVAs within Lodi were approved in 2006. Cabernet is good, but old-vine Zinfandel is Lodi's traditional strength.

Being coolish, fragmented, and distinctive, the **Sierra Foothills** is precisely the opposite of the Central Valley. In the foothills of the Sierra, where the Gold Rush gave California its first notoriety, the wine industry that slaked the miners' thirst is quietly and determinedly being revived. In the late 19th century there were more than 100 wineries in these hills that promised so much. During Prohibition there was just one, and the vines, many of them Zinfandel, were all but abandoned. But the land was (and is still) of such relatively low value that it was not worth pulling many of the vines out. This is California's treasure chest of Zinfandel plants with a long, long history – culminating, today, in some characterful wines at reasonable prices.

The wines of **El Dorado** County, its name a hopeful reference to the hills' most desirable natural resource, share a streak of natural acidity – not least because of the altitude of its rapidly expanding vineyards, which, at above 2,400ft (730m), are the highest in California. Rain, or even snow, is commonplace, temperatures are low, and the wines from the thin soils tend to be relatively (mercifully, some think) light.

The vineyards of Amador County are at distinctly warmer, lower elevations of 1,000 to 1,600ft (300–490m) on a plateau where the altitude has little chance to temper the heat. This is especially true of **Shenandoah Valley**, west of Amador's other AVA, **Fiddletown**.

About three-quarters of the county's vines are Zinfandel, some of them pre-Prohibition. Old or young, dry or rich, almost chewable, Amador Zinfandel tends to taste as though it has come from a miner's bucket, and is none the worse for that. Syrah also works well here, as does Sangiovese and the occasional Sauvignon Blanc. Calaveras County vineyards to the south have an elevation, and therefore climate, somewhere in between those of El Dorado and Amador, although in some places soils are more fertile than in either.

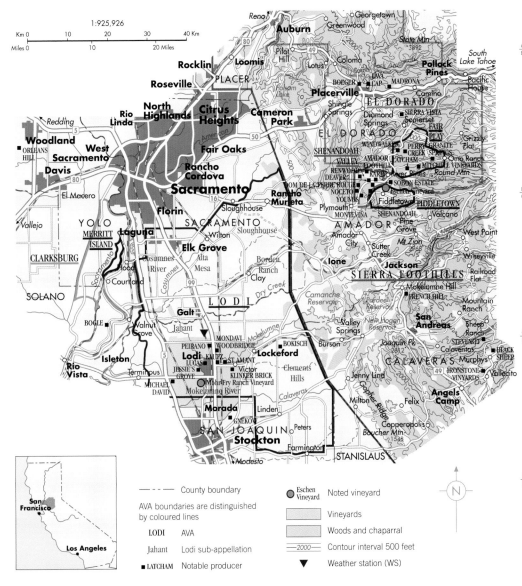

LODI: JAHANT WOODS
Latitude / Altitude of WS **38.12° / 52ft (16m)**
Mean July temp at WS **74°F (23.3°C)**
Annual rainfall at WS **17in (432mm)**
Harvest month rainfall at WS **September: 0.4in (10mm)**
Chief viticultural hazards **Botrytis, powdery mildew**
Principal grapes **Zinfandel, Chardonnay, Cabernet Sauvignon**

▼ From left to right these wines come from increasingly inland locations. The Clarksburg Chenin has a real raciness about it, then come two of Lodi's best. The Amador Zin is a California original which has in its time been made in the style of port.

Southwest States and Mexico

California's first Mission vines were planted between what is now downtown Los Angeles and the city of Pasadena to its north. The Mission San Gabriel still stands, but subdivision and smog have long since driven vineyards out of their original California home. Los Angeles' vines migrated east into what was then the desert area of Cucamonga. Early in the 20th century, Cucamonga was a vast and prosperous vineyard, producing "common table wines and fine dessert wines". The road maps still credit it as the "Oldest winery in California".

Since 1650, long before even the Mission grape reached California, however, it was being fermented for the needs of Spanish missionaries in Arizona, New Mexico, and near El Paso in Texas. **Texas** has a special place in the history of the vine, if not of wine. It is the botanical heart of America – and can boast more indigenous grapevine species than any other region on earth. Of 36 species of the genus Vitis scattered around the world, no fewer than 15 are

Texas natives – a fact that was turned to important use during the phylloxera epidemic. Thomas V Munson of Denison, Texas, made hundreds of hybrids between *Vitis vinifera* and indigenous grapes in the search for immune rootstock. Working with Professor Viala of the University of Montpellier he introduced many of the resistant rootstocks that saved not only France's, but also the world's wine industry.

That of Texas itself was killed by Prohibition. In 1920 the state had a score of wineries. Revival after Repeal was slow and painful; a quarter of the state's 254 counties are still "dry" today. In the early 1970s a new start was made with experimental plantings of vinifera and hybrid vines in the High Plains region at nearly 4,000ft (1,200m) near Lubbock at what would become Llano Estacado and Pheasant Ridge wineries. They chose well. Despite the infinite exposure and dismal flatness of the region, its soil is deep, calcareous, and fertile, its sunshine brilliant, its nights cool (and its

winters very cold). Abundant water from the Ogalala aquifer feeds drip irrigation and helps offset extreme weather such as freeze, hail, and high temperatures. Constant wind keeps disease at bay and helps cool the vineyards at night. Llano Estacado is now Texas's second-largest winery, making competent, bright-flavoured reds that have something in common with Washington State's best.

Texas's biggest wine enterprise by far is 200 miles (320km) south near Fort Stockton, where the land-rich University of Texas planted an experimental vineyard in the late 1970s. The 1,000-acre (400-ha) vineyard was once run by Domaines Cordier of Bordeaux, but is now leased by a Texas company, Mesa Vineyards. Their inexpensive varietals, which constitute more than half of all wine produced in the state, are labelled Ste Genevieve. Peregrine Hill is their more ambitious label.

▶ From the top, particularly respectable representatives from Arizona, New Mexico, Texas, and then two from Baja California in Mexico, where there seems to be all to play for.

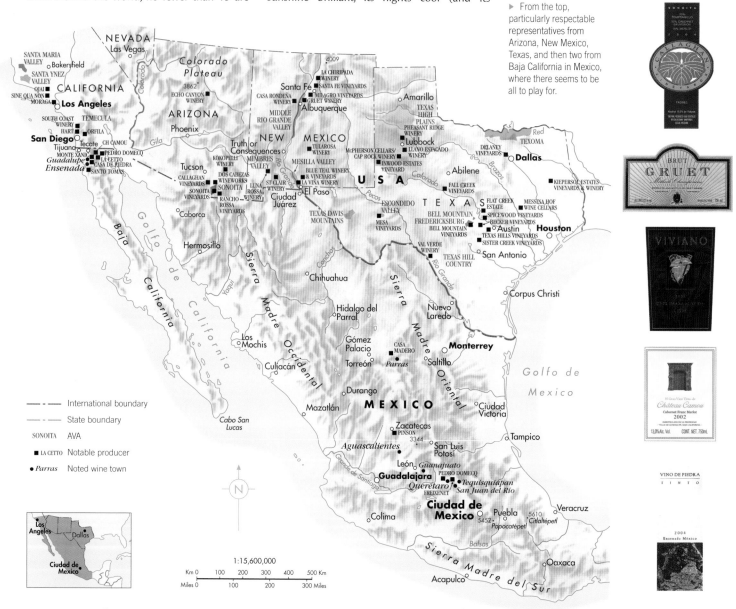

International boundary — State boundary

SONOITA AVA

■ LA CETTO Notable producer

● *Parras* Noted wine town

1:15,600,000

Km 0   100   200   300   400   500 Km

Miles 0   100   200   300 Miles

More promising for quality is the Hill Country west of Austin in the heart of Texas, which has staked out three AVAs: Texas Hill Country, Fredericksburg, and Bell Mountain (the last for a single estate winery of the same name specializing in Cabernet). These three AVAs include a possible million acres (405,000ha), of which only about 500 (200ha) are planted, and a fluctuating roster of about 20 wineries operate. Although Pierce's Disease and humidity plague various parts of the state, Texas shows every symptom of wine-mania and now boasts over 100 wineries. Many of them are clustered round the cities, processing grapes trucked from distant vineyards, and often wine produced even further away. An energetic pro-wine state initiative in the early 21st century now allows wineries to make and sell wine even in dry areas, provided the wine contains at least 75% Texas-grown fruit.

It is the Rockies that allow **New Mexico** to even think of growing wine: elevation cools the climate down to the point where, in the north of the state, only French hybrid vines will survive. The Rio Grande Valley provides almost the only agricultural land, falling from over 7,000ft (2,000m) at Santa Fe to 4,500ft (1,300m) at Truth or Consequences. Its three AVAs are Middle Rio Grande Valley below Albuquerque, and Mimbres Valley and Mesilla Valley almost on the Mexican border. Insofar as New Mexico has any national reputation for wine it is, surprisingly but quite justifiably, for the fine sparkling wine made by the Gruet winery.

Southeast **Arizona**, with its one AVA, Sonoita, shares much of the character of southern New Mexico, although the unofficial Sulphur Springs Valley wine region about 50 miles (80km) east of Tucson is even warmer. The Callaghan winery has had some success with Cabernet and Merlot.

To the north, wineries have been sprouting in **Colorado**, most of them in the shelter of the Grand Valley AVA of the Colorado River near Grand Junction at an elevation of 4,000ft (1,200m). Winter freeze and phylloxera threaten the mainly vinifera vines here, of which Chardonnay, Merlot, and Riesling are most common, although Viognier and Sangiovese are hardly surprising in a state as modish as this.

Meanwhile in **southern California** the vine is under greater threat than ever before from Pierce's Disease, although most remaining growers have upgraded clones and vineyard design to combat it. The principal AVA Temecula rises in bumps and hillocks to elevations of up to 1,500ft (450m), a mere 20-odd miles (32km) from the ocean and linked to it by the vital corridor known as Rainbow Gap. Every afternoon ocean breezes cool this essentially subtropical area to temperatures no hotter than the upper Napa Valley. The cool nights help too.

Thanks to the Spanish colonists, **Mexico**'s is the oldest wine industry of the New World, founded in the 1530s when Governor Hernando Cortés decreed that all farmers plant

10 grapevines a year for every Indian slave on their estate. However, in 1699 the King of Spain banned new vineyards in Mexico, fearing competition to Spain's wine industry, thus halting the development of a wine culture in Mexico for three centuries. Veracruz, where the first vines were planted, proved too tropical for long-term viticulture, just as many of the higher-altitude sites essayed later were too wet to produce healthy grapes. In Parras Valley to the south, however, there were indigenous vines in abundance, and here Casa Madero, built in 1597, can claim to be the oldest winery of the Americas, while making thoroughly modern Rhône-like reds and fresh white wines today. But it is an exception. Barely 10% of Mexico's 100,000 acres (40,000ha) of vines are dedicated to table wine; the great majority produces table grapes, raisins, and, especially, brandy.

In the 18th century, Basque immigrants brought the likes of Grenache, Carignan, and Pedro Ximénez to Parras and these, and other vinifera varieties, subsequently found their way to the northern end of the long finger of land, cooled by the Pacific, known as Baja California. Although the first modern winery in Baja California was Santo Tomas, established in 1888, the pioneer of modern Mexican table wine was LA Cetto, begun by Italian immigrants in 1926. LA Cetto now owns 2,500 acres (1,000ha) of vineyards in the Guadalupe Valley, planted with equal parts red and white wine grapes. Cetto makes remarkably successful wines from the Nebbiolo of the family's native Piemonte, as well as Cabernet and very palatable Petite Sirah. The white wines are fair, but not as fresh and fruity as those of Casa Madero.

World music enthusiast John R Calvin was inspired to set up Casa Rondeña near Albuquerque in New Mexico as an arts centre initially, turning grapes grown elsewhere in the state into wine. Today, he grows his own vinifera vines on his increasingly Italian-influenced estate.

LA Cetto was for many years a supplier to Pedro Domecq, Mexico's dominant brandy producer and second-biggest wine producer after Cetto. The Spanish firm Pedro Domecq invested heavily in the mid-20th century, like Martell, in brandy production in response to import controls, buying grapes and wine rather than vineyards. Today the company is controlled by Pernod Ricard.

The Guadalupe Valley is the home of Mexico's first "boutique winery" Monte Xanic, founded in 1988, although today the intense reds of Casa de Piedra and Château Camou provide the most significant inspiration for the new small but ambitious wineries sprouting in Baja California.

Vinifera varieties were also planted in Mexico's highland vineyards, specifically in Querétaro province north of Mexico City, at altitudes of up to 6,500ft (2,000m). Here and in Zacatecas province to the immediate north, days are hot while nights are cool but wines can suffer as a result of heavy rains at vintage time. Oaked reds are best so far but Freixenet and others hope to make decent sparkling wine in these provinces.

Mexican taste and drinking habits have for long lagged behind the increasingly exciting achievements of Mexico's modern vineyards and wineries, although this is slowly changing in the major cities and tourist areas.

Pacific Northwest

This striking sculpture marks the entrance to Nk'Mip (pronounced "Ink-a-meep") Cellars, overlooking Osoyoos Lake in the Okanagan Valley. The vineyard was first planted by the Osoyoos Indian Band in 1968, Nk'Mip being North America's first aboriginal owned and operated winery.

Oregon, Washington, Idaho, and British Columbia over the border in Canada are planting vinifera vines at an extraordinary pace, and producing some startlingly good wines from them. Northern Oregon's are perhaps the most distinctive. The Coast Range lines up as a sheltering sea wall, as it does in the wine regions of northern California, but here the ocean's warm North Pacific current brings rain instead of fog, modifying what might otherwise be more severe temperatures. The Willamette Valley, the heartland of Oregon wine production, suffers the same sort of perplexing weather as Burgundy, whereas southern Oregon is warmer, drier, and altogether more Bordeaux-like.

Both Oregon and Washington's wine industries have grown prodigiously since the late 20th century, although at the beginning of 2006 Oregon had just 14,000 acres (5,700ha) of vinifera vines compared with Washington's total of more than 50,000 acres (20,000ha). But Oregon has always been the home of the craftsman winemaker, vinifying grapes grown in small, personally managed, mainly estate vineyards, many of which are organic. Eastern Washington on the other hand originally operated on a quasi-industrial scale, with heavily irrigated grapes grown by farmers who might just as well have been growing cereals or apples, picked mechanically and shipped back to Seattle.

The roots of this difference lay in the terrain. The great concentration of Oregon's wine-growing is in the settled valleys west and south of Portland that have raised cattle, fruit, nuts, and a wide range of crops for more than a century. Vineyards have been slipped piecemeal into this busy, well-worked landscape. But when the grapevine came to Washington, it moved straight out east onto the steppe-like wastes beyond the Cascade mountain range where monoculture under irrigation was the primary form of agriculture. Washington (described in detail on pp.318-19) has been changing fast, however, and artisan operations are now much more common, with as much emphasis on growing, or at least finding, great grapes as on making wine.

Oregon meanwhile is becoming less homespun in its organization, with the injection of capital and marketing skills from the big wide world outside. One of the biggest operations, King Estate, was built in a distinctly un-Oregonian French château style but with an associated nursery, Lorane Grapevines, that has

played its part, with others, in introducing much more suitable clones to the state's wine industry.

The Willamette Valley AVA, around and south of Portland, is by far the most developed (see overleaf for more details). To the south the **Umpqua Valley** benefits from more shelter, warmer summers, and drier autumns. Pinot Noir, Pinot Gris, Cabernet Sauvignon, and Syrah are the main varieties. The past is represented by HillCrest vineyard, which was established in 1961; the future may be closer to the dynamic Abacela winery, which has made toothsome Tempranillo, Albariño, Cabernet Franc, and Syrah. The cumbersomely named **Red Hill Douglas County** AVA is a relatively wet sub-appellation.

South again, near the California border, the slightly more densely planted **Rogue Valley** is even warmer, and the annual rainfall (about 12in, or 300mm) in the east of the region is almost as low as that of far eastern Oregon. Cabernet Sauvignon and Merlot will usually ripen here (in contrast to the Willamette Valley) and are the favoured red grapes. Chardonnay and Syrah are also popular, notably in the **Applegate Valley**, the middle of the three valleys that roughly define the Rogue Valley and which has its own AVA. Some Gewurztraminer and Riesling are grown in the west of the Rogue Valley where the climate is closer to that of the Willamette Valley.

Southern Oregon is a large AVA designed to give an identity to the state's warmer, drier wine country and to demonstrate that there is more to Oregon than Pinots Noir and Gris.

One of the more surprising wine regions in the US is in the **Snake River Valley**, which is mainly in Idaho but also encompasses a bit of eastern Oregon. As in eastern Washington, the climate is continental, all the more extreme for being further south, and also considerably higher, at nearly 3,000ft (900m). Summer days

can be very hot, the nights usefully cool, but winter arrives early. Nearly 30 wineries now flourish in Idaho, and there is considerable cross-border traffic in grapes and wine with eastern Washington, although Idaho's own vineyard area is over 1,500 acres (600ha).

British Columbia now has almost 7,000 acres (2,800ha) of vinifera vines and 130 wineries. The centre of Canada's flourishing western wine industry is the **Okanagan Valley**, 200 miles (320km) east of Vancouver, where the long, narrow, deep Lake Okanagan wards off winter freeze. This is holiday country so land prices are higher but natural conditions are very similar to those of eastern Washington – in fact the south of the Okanagan Valley is so dry that some of it qualifies as desert. Irrigation is essential, diurnal summer temperature variation is exceptional, early-ripening grapes are favoured (for the same reasons as in Idaho), and acidities are naturally high. The pungency and acidity of Okanagan wines recall New Zealand in refreshment value and immediacy of appeal. Chardonnay and Merlot are the most popular varieties and while it can be difficult to ripen Cabernet Sauvignon in northern Okanagan, some very successful Bordeaux blends are made, not all of them red. Icewine is made here but in much smaller quantities than in Ontario (discussed on p.321).

Similkaneen Valley to the southwest of Okanagan is British Columbia's second most important wine region and favours red wine varieties. In the far west on **Vancouver Island** and the **Gulf Islands**, the climate may be much cooler and wetter than Okanagan's but winemaking enthusiasm is by no means dampened.

▼ Some of British Columbia's exciting panoply of emerging fine wines with a lone southern Oregonian on the far left. See overleaf for the story of the rest of Oregon and p.321 for that of eastern Canada's much more established wine regions.

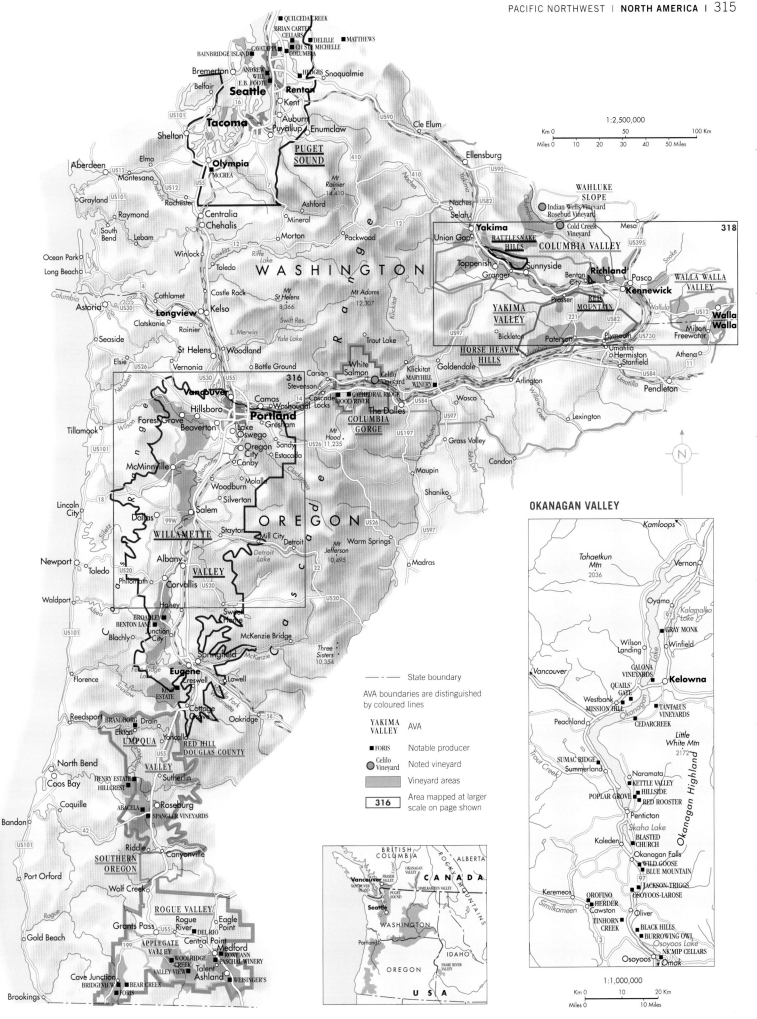

QUILCEDA CREEK
BRIAN CARTER CELLARS
DELILLE
MATTHEWS
CAVATAPPI
CH STE MICHELLE
COLUMBIA
BAINBRIDGE ISLAND
HEDGES
ANDREW WILL
E.B. FOOTE
Bremerton
Belfair
Seattle
Renton
Kent
Tacoma
Shelton
Auburn
Puyallup
Enumclaw
Olympia
McCREA
PUGET SOUND

Aberdeen
Elma
Montesano
Grayland
Raymond
South Bend
Lebam
Ocean Park
Long Beach

Centralia
Chehalis
Rochester
Mineral
Ashford
Mt Rainier 14,410

Ellensburg

Naches
Selah
Yakima
Union Gap
Toppenish
Granger
Sunnyside

WAHLUKE SLOPE
Indian Wells Vineyard
Rosebud Vineyard
Cold Creek Vineyard

Mesa

COLUMBIA VALLEY
RATTLESNAKE HILLS
Richland
Pasco
Benton City
Kennewick
Prosser
RED MOUNTAIN

318

WALLA WALLA VALLEY

YAKIMA VALLEY

Bickleton
Paterson
Plymouth
Milton
Freewater
Walla Walla

WASHINGTON

Winlock
Toledo
Castle Rock
Kelso
Longview
Cathlamet
Astoria
Clatskanie
Rainier

Mt St Helens 8,366
Mt Adams 12,307

Riffe Lake
Morton
Packwood

Trout Lake

White Salmon
Celilo Vineyard
MARYHILL WINERY
Klickitat
Goldendale

Carson
Stevenson
Cascade Locks
CATHEDRAL RIDGE
HOOD RIVER
COLUMBIA GORGE

Goldendale
Arlington
Wasco
Grass Valley
Condon
Lexington
Shaniko
Madras

HORSE HEAVEN HILLS

Umatilla
Hermiston
Stanfield
Pendleton
Athena

Seaside
St Helens
Vernonia
Battle Ground
Vancouver
Hillsboro
Forest Grove
Beaverton
Portland
Gresham
Camas
Washougal
316
Lake Oswego
Sandy
Oregon City
Canby
Estacada
Tillamook
McMinnville
Woodburn
Molalla
Silverton
Dallas
Salem
Stayton
Mill City
Detroit
WILLAMETTE VALLEY
Albany
Corvallis
Philomath
Halsey

OREGON

Mt Hood 11,235

Mt Jefferson 10,495
Detroit Lake
Warm Springs

Lincoln City
Newport
Toledo
Waldport

Sweet Home
McKenzie Bridge

Three Sisters 10,354

BROADLEY
BENTON LANE
Junction City
Blachly

Springfield
McKenzie

Florence
Eugene
Creswell
Lowell

KING ESTATE
Cottage Grove
Oakridge

BRANDBORG
Drain
Reedsport
Elkton
Yoncalla
UMPQUA VALLEY
North Bend
Coos Bay
Sutherlin

RED HILL DOUGLAS COUNTY

Coquille
HENRY ESTATE
HILLCREST
ABACELA
Roseburg
SPANGLER VINEYARDS

Bandon
Riddle
Canyonville

Port Orford
SOUTHERN OREGON
Wolf Creek

Gold Beach
Grants Pass
Rogue River
Eagle Point
DEL RIO
Central Point
Medford
ROXY ANN
PASCHAL WINERY
WOOLRIDGE CREEK
VALLEY VIEW
Talent
WEISINGER'S
APPLEGATE VALLEY
Ashland
ROGUE VALLEY

Cave Junction
BRIDGEVIEW
BEAR CREEK
FORIS

Brookings

1:2,500,000
Km 0   50   100 Km
Miles 0 10 20 30 40 50 Miles

OKANAGAN VALLEY

Kamloops
Tahaetkun Mtn 2036
Vernon
Oyama
Kalamalka Lake
GRAY MONK
Wilson Landing
Winfield
CALONA VINEYARDS
QUAILS' GATE
Westbank
MISSION HILL
Kelowna
TANTALUS VINEYARDS
CEDARCREEK
Peachland
Little White Mtn 2172
SUMAC RIDGE
Summerland
Naramata
KETTLE VALLEY
HILLSIDE
POPLAR GROVE
RED ROOSTER
Penticton
Skaha Lake
Kaleden
BLASTED CHURCH
Okanagan Falls
WILD GOOSE
BLUE MOUNTAIN
Keremeos
JACKSON-TRIGGS
OSOYOOS-LAROSE
OROFINO
HERDER
Cawston
Oliver
TINHORN CREEK
BLACK HILLS
BURROWING OWL
Osoyoos Lake
NK'MIP CELLARS
Osoyoos
Omak

Okanagan Highland

Vancouver
Trout Creek
Similkameen

_____ State boundary

AVA boundaries are distinguished by coloured lines

YAKIMA VALLEY AVA

■ FORIS Notable producer

⬤ Celilo Vineyard Noted vineyard

Vineyard areas

316 Area mapped at larger scale on page shown

BRITISH COLUMBIA
ALBERTA
OKANAGAN VALLEY
Vancouver
VANCOUVER ISLAND
PUGET SOUND
FRASER VALLEY
SIMILKAMEEN VALLEY
Seattle
CANADA
ROCKY MOUNTAINS
WASHINGTON
Portland
OREGON
SNAKE RIVER VALLEY
IDAHO
USA

1:1,000,000
Km 0   10   20 Km
Miles 0   10 Miles

1|2   2|3   3|4   4|5   5|6

Willamette Valley

Oregon prides itself on how unlike California it is. But most of the state, and certainly the **Willamette Valley**, is very unlike Washington to the north too. While summers are much cooler and cloudier than those of the sunny state to the south (see key facts boxes), its winters are considerably milder than those of Washington's heavily continental wine country deep inland. Pacific influence washes in to Oregon's wineland, especially the north of the Willamette Valley, through breaks in the Coast Range, so that cool summers and damp autumns rather than winter freeze are the perennial threats.

The discovery (or invention) of the Willamette Valley as a modern wine region was made in the late 1960s at Dundee in Yamhill County by David Lett with his Eyrie Vineyards. Had Lett planted Chardonnay and Cabernet, fame would have been slow to follow (especially since the latter would hardly ever have ripened properly). But he hit on Pinot Noir. Since 1970 Oregon and Pinot Noir have been inextricably linked. The grey skies of this lush pastoral country can do what California had found next to impossible: conjure up the illusion of drinking fine red burgundy, even if Oregon Pinots are in general softer, more obviously fruity, and earlier maturing than their European counterparts.

Almost as though this was the way Pinot Noir liked to be grown, the Willamette Valley has largely remained small-scale. The area attracted a different type of would-be wine-maker from the high-rollers who head for Napa or Sonoma. Small means and big ideas produced a range of unpredictable wines, from the fascinating to the seriously flawed. Most of the early wines were fragrant but ethereal.

But by the mid-1980s it was obvious that some of the Pinots had exciting staying power.

Whether or not this was what convinced them, high-profile foreigners moved in: from California, a succession of wine producers looking for a moodiness in Pinot that sunny skies could not give them; from Australia, Brian Croser of Petaluma, who set about making Argyle sparkling and still wines in an old hazelnut drying plant next to Dundee's fire station; and, most importantly for Oregonian pride, from Burgundy itself, Robert Drouhin and his daughter Véronique at Domaine Drouhin. Pinots made today vary from the suave, gently understated Drouhin style (which has well withstood comparison with Drouhin's wines back home) to the richly oaky style initially adopted at Beaux Frères, the winery part-owned by Oregon's other internationally famous outside investor, wine guru Robert Parker.

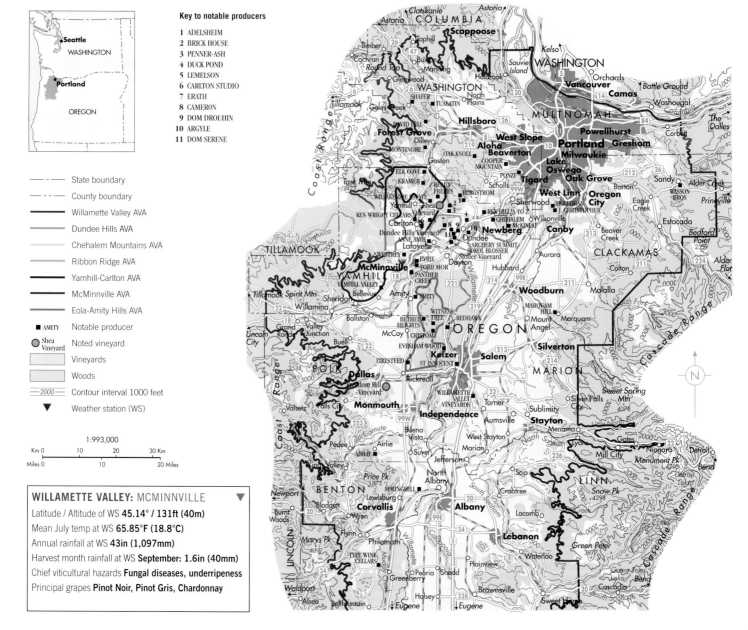

Key to notable producers

1 ADELSHEIM
2 BRICK HOUSE
3 PENNER-ASH
4 DUCK POND
5 LEMELSON
6 CARLTON STUDIO
7 ERATH
8 CAMERON
9 DOM DROUHIN
10 ARGYLE
11 DOM SERENE

State boundary
County boundary
Willamette Valley AVA
Dundee Hills AVA
Chehalem Mountains AVA
Ribbon Ridge AVA
Yamhill-Carlton AVA
McMinnville AVA
Eola-Amity Hills AVA
■ AMITY Notable producer
● Shea Vineyard Noted vineyard
Vineyards
Woods
2000 Contour interval 1000 feet
▼ Weather station (WS)

1:993,000
Km 0 10 20 30 Km
Miles 0 10 20 Miles

WILLAMETTE VALLEY: MCMINNVILLE ▼
Latitude / Altitude of WS **45.14° / 131ft (40m)**
Mean July temp at WS **65.85°F (18.8°C)**
Annual rainfall at WS **43in (1,097mm)**
Harvest month rainfall at WS **September: 1.6in (40mm)**
Chief viticultural hazards **Fungal diseases, underripeness**
Principal grapes **Pinot Noir, Pinot Gris, Chardonnay**

Broadly, the Willamette summer is coolest and dampest in Washington County's vineyards that are most open to Pacific incursion, making them particularly favourable for aromatic varieties. Pinot Noir tends to be fine rather than fat here. The Ponzi family has shown that such wines can last, however.

After considerable debate and degustation, several sub-appellations are now officially recognized within the 150-mile (240-km) long Willamette Valley. **Dundee Hills**, based on the famous, heavy, red-tinged Jory loam Red Hills of Dundee, constitutes the most established combination of good drainage and propitious exposure to rainfall and light that is so crucial in cloudy Oregon. **Yamhill-Carlton** District has very slightly more warmth but more frost problems, so vines are planted well above the frost-prone valley floor, ideally on east-facing slopes on the west side of the valley at between 200 and 700ft (60 and 210m). **McMinnville** is named after the university town that is a focus for the Oregon wine industry, while **Ribbon Ridge** lies to the northeast, just above the Dundee Hills. Both **Eola-Amity Hills** to the northwest of Salem and **Chehalem Mountains** in the north of the Willamette Valley gained AVA status in 2006.

Successful grape growing in the Willamette Valley is about ripening grapes fully and early enough to pick them before the autumn rains arrive. Just when that happens, and how damaging the rains are, varies enormously each year. Many grape varieties such as Cabernet Sauvignon and Sauvignon Blanc are too late-ripening to be viable here. But even for early-ripening varieties, Willamette Valley's vintage pattern is as wilful as any in France and arguably more wildly varied than in any other American wine region. Wine drinkers outside Oregon tend to fall in and out of love with the state's Pinot Noirs according to the success, or at least the obvious fruitiness, of the vintage on offer.

But there is another, superficially surprising, problem: summer drought. The rains can arrive in September or October, but generally only after a cool, grey but often very dry summer. This means that many older vineyards can be starting to turn a nastily inconvenient yellow long before the photosynthesis needed for ripening is completed. Newer vineyards therefore tend to be designed with irrigation systems in place so that the vines are stressed only if and when the grower deems it useful.

The early pioneers, often operating on extremely limited budgets, tended to establish vineyards as cheaply as possible, but higher-density planting is now reckoned to be a worthwhile luxury. Another relatively recent change to Oregon vineyard design is the use of rootstocks. Ever since phylloxera was first spotted here in 1990, sensible growers have planted vines grafted on to rootstocks that will both resist the fatal root-muncher and limit the amount of vegetation that distracts from the grape-ripening process.

Yields in these vineyards therefore tend to be more consistent and vines tend to ripen earlier, but the most important influence on the continually improving quality of Oregon Pinot Noir and Chardonnay has been the introduction of Burgundian clones of each variety.

For at least the first two decades most Oregon Pinot Noir was made from the Wädenswil clone originally from Switzerland and/or the clone, so popular in California, known as Pommard. They tended to yield wines that had fruit and charm (in a good year) but not necessarily structure and subtlety. The introduction of smaller-clustered clones such as (for fans of detail) 113, 114, 115, 667, 777, and 882, called Dijon clones in Oregon, has added new dimensions to Oregon Pinot, even if in most instances they are used as elements in a blend.

One of the reasons Oregon Chardonnays have been relatively disappointing is probably the principal clone planted, Davis 108, whose main attribute in California was the length of its growing season before ripening. Most years in Oregon this is a distinct disadvantage and many Chardonnays have seemed rather thin and tart. More suitable, and subtle, Dijon clones 76, 95, and 96 are now planted but most white wine hopes are firmly pinned on Pinot Gris. Oregon Pinot Gris is generally more like an aromatic Chardonnay than a rich Alsace Pinot Gris, although this is slowly changing.

To its credit, and despite a notably humid climate, Oregon viticulture is today distinguished by widespread commitment to sustainable, often organic and sometimes biodynamic, practices.

One quirky institution that has done much to put the Willamette Valley on the international wine map and emphasize Oregon's distinction, however, is the International Pinot Noir Celebration held every July. This three-day Pinotfest sees fans (see photo above) and producers from all over the world congregate in the town of McMinnville to worship at the altar of Pinot and mutter about the iniquities of Cabernet- and Merlot-mania.

In an "Everybody's a Critic" session in 2005, such luminaries as Michel Bettane of France and Michael Broadbent of the UK took participants at the International Pinot Noir Celebration through their own personal process of tasting Oregon's signature grape.

◀ Some gold standards in Oregon wine production. Ex-newsman Doug Tunnell at Brick House was an early adopter of the more wholemeal viticultural practices that distinguish Oregon, despite its relatively high humidity and the risk from fungal diseases of the vine.

Washington

Eastern Washington, where all but 80 acres (30ha) of the state's vines are grown, does not look like wine country. Most visitors reach it from the city of Seattle, round which so many of the state's wineries still cluster. They drive through damp Douglas fir and ponderosa pine forests, over the mighty Cascades and descend suddenly into semi-desert, where in summer the sun shines reliably for up to 17 hours each day and where in winter an arctic chill settles for months on end.

During eastern Washington's relatively short growing season, the arid wheatfields which look as though they roll all the way to Kansas are punctuated by oases of green; growing apples, cherries, hops, and, increasingly, vines. This is low-cost farmland (far cheaper than California,

for example) irrigated by water from the Columbia Basin. Many of the vines may be Concords for juice and jelly, but the total area of vinifera vines has been expanding fast, surpassing 50,000 acres (20,000ha) in 2005. Washington is definitively the USA's second-biggest vine-grower and producer of vinifera wine, albeit making only a few per cent of California's output.

The continental climate here has proved excellent for ripening fine wine grapes, on a latitude between those of Bordeaux and Burgundy, with the very important proviso that there is access to irrigation water – from rivers, reservoirs, or from much more expensive wells. Rainless summers and autumns minimize disease problems while the hot days and cold nights of the desert induce good colour and singularly well-defined flavours in some (not all) varieties. Winters are icy and can kill vines but at least they help keep phylloxera at bay (virtually all

vines are planted on their own roots), as do the fast-draining, relatively uniform sandy soils.

Vine-growing here was initially even more distinct from winemaking than in most American states but this has been changing. For example, the dominant wine company, which owns Chateau Ste Michelle, Columbia Crest, Snoqualmie and many other labels, now grows almost two-thirds of the grapes it needs. The great majority of wineries buy in some grapes, however, often trucking them west over the Cascades, although the number of wineries – and estate vineyards – in eastern Washington has been increasing recently. They also tend to buy from a wide range of growers and blend heavily so that winery location is rarely much clue to wine provenance. Partly so as to keep all blending options open, the giant **Columbia Valley** AVA (encompassing eastern Washington's more specific AVAs mapped here) and the ultra-flexible term Washington State are widely used in preference to more specific appellations such as **Yakima Valley**.

This valley of scrub overlooked by snowy Mount Adams, carved by the Yakima River

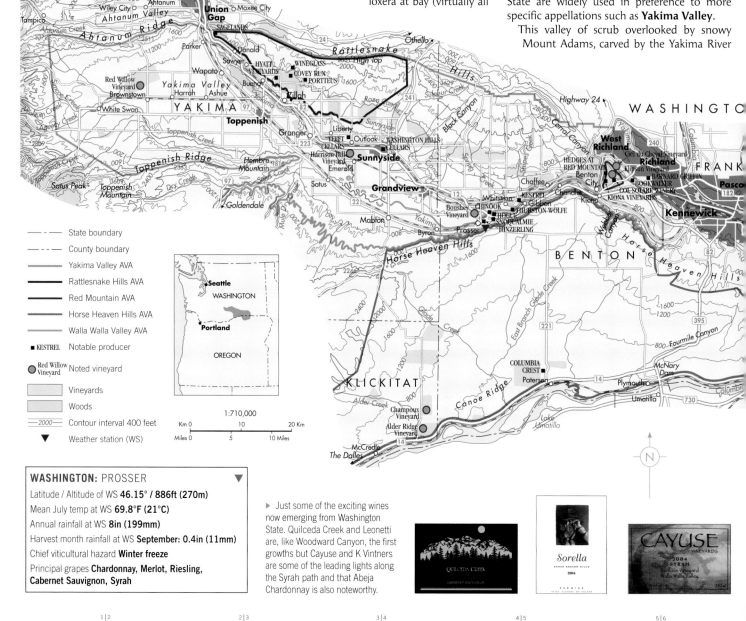

Legend

State boundary
County boundary
Yakima Valley AVA
Rattlesnake Hills AVA
Red Mountain AVA
Horse Heaven Hills AVA
Walla Walla Valley AVA
■ KESTREL Notable producer
● Red Willow Vineyard Noted vineyard
Vineyards
Woods
—2000— Contour interval 400 feet
▼ Weather station (WS)

1:710,000
Km 0   10   20 Km
Miles 0   5   10 Miles

WASHINGTON: PROSSER ▼
Latitude / Altitude of WS **46.15° / 886ft (270m)**
Mean July temp at WS **69.8°F (21°C)**
Annual rainfall at WS **8in (199mm)**
Harvest month rainfall at WS **September: 0.4in (11mm)**
Chief viticultural hazard **Winter freeze**
Principal grapes **Chardonnay, Merlot, Riesling, Cabernet Sauvignon, Syrah**

▶ Just some of the exciting wines now emerging from Washington State. Quilceda Creek and Leonetti are, like Woodward Canyon, the first growths but Cayuse and K Vintners are some of the leading lights along the Syrah path and that Abeja Chardonnay is also noteworthy.

on its way east to join the Columbia, is Washington's coolest and oldest wine region. Chardonnay is the grape variety most popular with Yakima Valley farmers, but the results can easily be insipid. Red Willow vineyard was one of the first to show that Syrah, now being planted furiously throughout the state, as elsewhere in the Pacific Northwest, has considerable potential as a savoury but fruity addition to the state's more traditional roster of grapes. **Rattlesnake Hills** is a new AVA along the western part of the eponymous ridge within Yakima Valley. In the far southeast of Yakima Valley, the town of Prosser, site of the new Walter Clore Wine and Culinary Center, is rapidly establishing itself as the focus of the state's wine industry.

Between Yakima Valley and the Columbia River, the **Horse Heaven Hills** are particularly promising. The upper reaches such as those of Champoux ranch are predominantly clay. The lower, south-facing slope of Canoe Ridge is the source of fruit for the Chalone group's Canoe Ridge Vineyard winery in Walla Walla (a typical example of Washington's disregard for geographical precision) and many of Chateau Ste Michelle's better reds. It is also close enough to the broad Columbia River, in effect a series of lakes dammed for irrigation water and hydro-electricity, to be saved the worst extremes of weather, particularly winter freeze.

To the north and east of Yakima Valley are some of the state's warmest vineyards of all, including the famous **Wahluke Slope** (see map, p.315), which runs down from the Saddle Mountains to the Columbia River, tilting vines southwards for maximum radiation in summer and encouraging cold winter air to drain away from them in winter. And it was from just north of the Tri-Cities of Richland, Pasco, and Kennewick that the original Sagemoor vineyard supplied grapes for some of the state's very first wines. Merlot is the most widely planted variety here but the small, water-limited **Red Mountain** AVA has a reputation for supple Cabernet Sauvignon. The AVA is the home of Col Solare ("shining hill"), the smartly housed joint venture between Chateau Ste Michelle and Antinori of Italy.

Summers as far inland as **Walla Walla Valley** are also decidedly warm; winters are dangerously cold, and rainfall high for eastern Washington. The genteel college town of Walla Walla is where a marked concentration of the state's most sought-after reds are made, and the fact that many of them have been based on grapes grown outside the AVA seems to have done nothing to harm its reputation. Wines grown here tend to be powerfully fruity but with sturdy tannins too. The AVA, pioneered in the early 1980s by Leonetti and Woodward Canyon, spills south into Oregon to include the Seven Hills vineyard.

The new **Columbia Gorge** AVA in the southwest of Columbia Valley (see map, p.315) also includes a good portion of Oregon and is particularly suitable for Chardonnay, aromatic white wine varieties, Lemberger (also known as Blue Franc, a nod to its Austrian name Blaufränkisch), Merlot, and Zinfandel. Lying in the north of the Columbia Valley, Chelan Valley is a promising and distinctive area pioneered by CR Sandidge that is expected to be granted its own AVA.

A new Washington winery is bonded every 15 days so that the total number almost quadrupled, to nearly 400, in the first six years of this century – rather more than the number of grape growers. This rapid growth means that many vines are young. They are planted on young, light soils, often from single clones. Most vines are grown, and yields decided, by fruit farmers rather than winemakers so that some wines can lack nuance, but the best wines, while sharing the deep colour, crisp acidity, and bright, frank flavours that typify Washington wine, have admirable intensity of rich, soft fruit that can last in bottle for up to eight years, even if it tends to fade fast after that.

Chardonnay then Merlot are Washington's most planted grapes, but Riesling plantings have increased so rapidly in the last few years to supply bottlings such as the popular Eroica (a joint venture between Chateau Ste Michelle and Erni Loosen of Bernkastel) that Riesling has overtaken Cabernet Sauvignon to become the third most planted variety in the state. In the mid-2000s, Syrah was a definitive fifth but rising fast.

Only certain sites in this continental climate will ripen Cabernet Sauvignon fully, while Merlot, which has a much clearer identity here than in California, is more flexible, although it is inconveniently susceptible to winter freeze. Cabernet Franc has its followers, and not just because it is hardier. Lemberger has long been a local speciality because of its naturally low acidity and can produce delicious purple wines redolent of dusty blackberries. Sauvignon Blanc can be truly bracing, and Semillons such as L'Ecole 41's show that the grape could really shine – if given the chance.

Grapes grown back west in the **Puget Sound** AVA around Seattle are completely different – early ripeners such as Müller-Thurgau, Madeleine Angevine, and Siegerrebe (increasingly supplemented by Pinot Noir and Pinot Gris) – a crew familiar to those who also live in a cool, rainy climate.

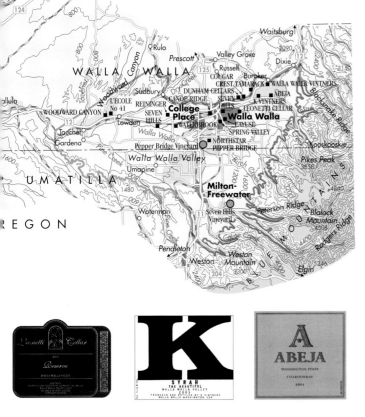

No mistaking what country this Walla Walla vineyard is in although one might have expected to see more mechanization here.

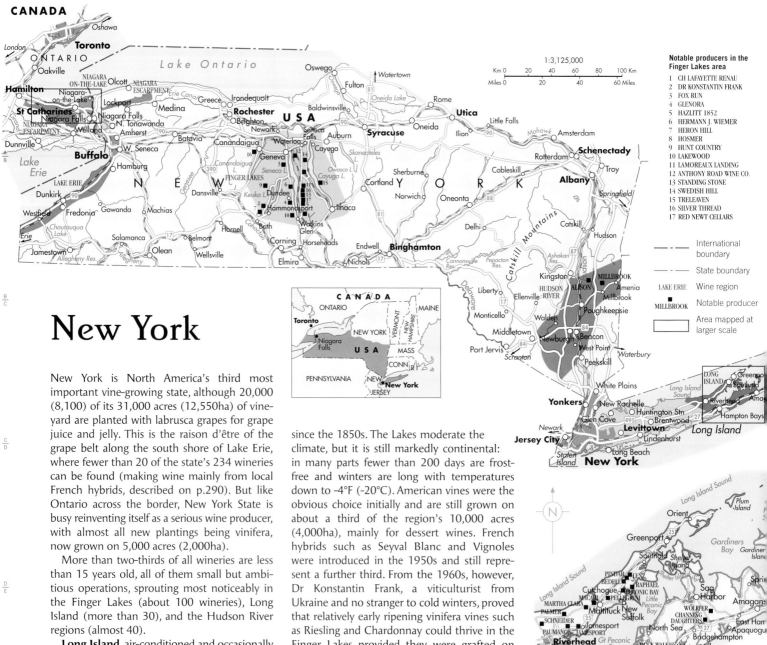

CANADA

Notable producers in the Finger Lakes area

1 CH LAFAYETTE RENAU
2 DR KONSTANTIN FRANK
3 FOX RUN
4 GLENORA
5 HAZLITT 1852
6 HERMANN J. WIEMER
7 HERON HILL
8 HOSMER
9 HUNT COUNTRY
10 LAKEWOOD
11 LAMOREAUX LANDING
12 ANTHONY ROAD WINE CO.
13 STANDING STONE
14 SWEDISH HILL
15 TRELEAVEN
16 SILVER THREAD
17 RED NEWT CELLARS

1:3,125,000

- - - International boundary
— State boundary
LAKE ERIE — Wine region
■ MILLBROOK — Notable producer
▭ Area mapped at larger scale

North Fork AVA
The Hamptons AVA
■ LENZ Notable producer

1:769,230

New York

New York is North America's third most important vine-growing state, although 20,000 (8,100) of its 31,000 acres (12,550ha) of vine-yard are planted with labrusca grapes for grape juice and jelly. This is the raison d'être of the grape belt along the south shore of Lake Erie, where fewer than 20 of the state's 234 wineries can be found (making wine mainly from local French hybrids, described on p.290). But like Ontario across the border, New York State is busy reinventing itself as a serious wine producer, with almost all new plantings being vinifera, now grown on 5,000 acres (2,000ha).

More than two-thirds of all wineries are less than 15 years old, all of them small but ambitious operations, sprouting most noticeably in the Finger Lakes (about 100 wineries), Long Island (more than 30), and the Hudson River regions (almost 40).

Long Island, air-conditioned and occasionally battered by the Atlantic, is New York's answer to Bordeaux, both in terms of its maritime climate and the amiable and refreshing build of its wines. The ocean influence blurs the seasons and maintains the mild weather for so long that the growing season here is much longer than inland. Long Island now has 2,500 acres (1,000ha) of vines, all vinifera (mainly Chardonnay, Merlot, and the Cabernets). The island has three AVAs: the original North Fork, the cooler (and smaller) Hamptons, or South Fork, and the over-arching Long Island. All the mapped wineries have good track records, however many changes of owner-ship and names there have been recently.

Vines have been grown commercially in upper New York State, around the deep glacial trenches known collectively as the **Finger Lakes**, just south of the great inland sea of Lake Ontario,

since the 1850s. The Lakes moderate the climate, but it is still markedly continental: in many parts fewer than 200 days are frost-free and winters are long with temperatures down to -4°F (-20°C). American vines were the obvious choice initially and are still grown on about a third of the region's 10,000 acres (4,000ha), mainly for dessert wines. French hybrids such as Seyval Blanc and Vignoles were introduced in the 1950s and still repre-sent a further third. From the 1960s, however, Dr Konstantin Frank, a viticulturist from Ukraine and no stranger to cold winters, proved that relatively early ripening vinifera vines such as Riesling and Chardonnay could thrive in the Finger Lakes provided they were grafted on the right rootstocks. Today, some particularly fine, almost Saar-like dry, age-worthy Rieslings are made by producers such as Red Newt Cellars, Standing Stone, Hermann J Wiemer, and Dr Frank's Vinifera Wine Cellars. The research station at Geneva is known internationally for its work on vine-training and winter-hardy varieties, and the Finger Lakes wine region remains the commercial hub of the New York industry, not least thanks to the presence, since 1945, of the original headquarters of what is now the world's largest wine company, Constellation. Once called Canandaigua, it is now the Centerra Wine Company.

The **Hudson River**, where New York's first recorded commercial vintage took place in 1829 at what is now Brotherhood winery, is also a region of small wineries. Vinifera vines

can be vulnerable here in a climate unmoder-ated by either ocean or lake and until recently most of the nearly 1,000 acres (400ha) have been French hybrids. Operations such as Millbrook, however, have demonstrated a vinifera future for this pretty upstate region too, while Clinton Cellars has shown that diver-sification into other fruit wines can also pay.

A new AVA, **Niagara Escarpment**, just over the border from Ontario's principal wine region, already boasts about 10 wineries.

◄ Two top Rieslings from the Finger Lakes, a region which has shown itself exceptionally well suited to the variety, and a selection of Long Island's best: a Channing Daughters Chardonnay flanked by Merlot, which ripens nicely in this moderate, Atlantic-tempered climate.

Ontario

Canada, much of it frozen for much of the year, may on the face of it seem a decidedly chilly place to grow vines, but wine is made, with increasing élan, in four different provinces. (See p.314 for details of the vibrant British Columbia wine industry in the Pacific Northwest.)

In the southeast corner of the country, Nova Scotia has a few hundred acres of vines, mainly winter-hardy hybrids (some of them Soviet-bred from Mongolian stock) planted in particularly sheltered corners on the Atlantic seaboard. Québec also has a small wine industry, also dependent on winter-hardy hybrids, with the best wineries around the town of Dunham on the US border.

Much more important is Ontario, however, which, although it can barely produce enough wine for the local market, is emerging on to the world stage, not least thanks to the prodigious quantities of Icewine produced each year. Canada's most important wine region, with 15,000 acres (6,000ha) of vineyard dedicated to wine, is the **Niagara Peninsula**, mapped in detail below. A combination of geographical quirks makes viticulture possible in the semi-continental climate here. This narrow mosaic of glacial deposits is protected by vast lakes both north and south and the deep Niagara River to the east. These large bodies of water delay bud-burst in spring thanks to the accumulated cold of winter, and prolong ripening in autumn by storing summer sunshine in relatively warm

Picking frozen grapes for Icewine (liquid gold in more than one sense) in Henry of Pelham's vineyards in St Catharines. Global warming may start to affect just how much of this Canadian speciality is produced each year but quantities will surely continue to dwarf Germany's Eiswein output.

water. Lake Ontario in particular moderates the effect of Arctic air masses in winter, while the temperature difference between this cooler lake and the warmer Lake Erie to the south encourages cooling breezes in summer. The lake's offshore breezes are kept circulating by the Niagara Escarpment (responsible for the famous Niagara Falls), which helps minimize frost damage and fungal disease. The land here tilts slightly north so that vineyards benefit even more from Lake Ontario's influence.

Summers in Niagara are increasingly warm and long but Ontario still manages to make an average of half a million litres of tinglingly sweet Icewine every year, either from Riesling or, more commonly, from the luscious curranty French hybrid Vidal, whose wines tend to mature early. Riesling is increasingly recognized as Niagara's strength for bone dry wines too, although individual producers have shown brilliance with Chardonnay and even Syrah. Most Niagara vines are grown on the Lake Iroquois Plain but the well-protected Benches with their calcareous soils are particularly suitable for

delicate Riesling and Pinot Noir. An ambitious series of 12 Niagara Peninsula sub-appellations is already in place.

Ontario's other small appellations lie too far from the Niagara Peninsula to be mapped here. **Lake Erie North Shore** depends solely on Lake Erie to temper its climate, as does **Pelee Island**, Canada's southernmost point, and completely surrounded by the lake. Hopes are pinned on the emerging **Prince Edward County** wine region on Lake Ontario's north shore, not least because of its shallow limestone soils so suitable for members of the Pinot family, although vines are buried to protect them in winter.

Wines made exclusively from Canadian-grown, good-quality grapes are designated VQA (Vintners Quality Alliance), although larger Canadian vintners have a long tradition of bottling imported wine too.

▼ Inniskillin and the family-owned Cave Spring are some of Ontario's longest-serving trailblazers, while Le Clos Jordanne is a relatively new joint venture between Vincor and Boisset of Burgundy. Lailey's Cabernet Franc is matured in Canadian oak.

NIAGARA PENINSULA: ST CATHARINES ▼

Latitude / Altitude of WS **43.1° / 295ft (90m)**

Mean July temp at WS **71°F (21.7°C)**

Annual rainfall at WS **34in (860mm)**

Harvest month rainfall at WS **October: 2.6in (65mm)**

Chief viticultural hazards **Winter freeze, underripeness, Asian ladybirds**

Principal grapes **Chardonnay, Cabernet Franc, Riesling, Cabernet Sauvignon, Merlot, Pinot Noir**

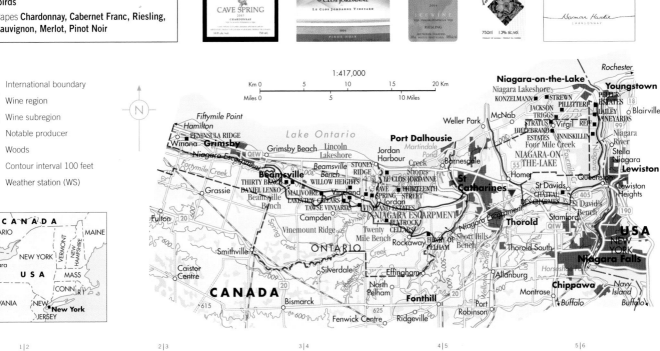

Legend:

- – · – · International boundary
- NIAGARA-ON-THE-LAKE Wine region
- Niagara River Wine subregion
- ■ CAVE SPRING Notable producer
- Woods
- —500— Contour interval 100 feet
- ▼ Weather station (WS)

1:417,000

Km 0   5   10   15   20 Km
Miles 0   5   10 Miles

An alpaca peers through the vines at Viña Carmen in the Rapel Valley, Chile. The winery is organic and alpaca manure is used as fertilizer.

South America

South America

After Europe, South America is the world's most important wine-producing continent. European vines were grown here, in Peru in 1531, long before they reached any other part of the New World apart from Mexico. The continent's wine industries, just like its culture, continue to be heavily influenced by immigrants and their descendants – initially Spanish and Portuguese, more recently Italians, French, and Germans.

The most important South American wine producer in terms of quantity is, by quite a mile, Argentina (see p.330), even if Chile (see overleaf) preceded it onto the international stage and is still a more significant exporter.

Unknown to the rest of the world, **Brazil** is the continent's third most important producer in terms of quantity. The local industry has until recently concentrated on supplying light, sweetish, Italianate fizz to the domestic market. The greatest spur to produce better quality wine came in the early 1990s when Brazil opened its market. It was immediately obvious, even to the less discerning consumers that many, though not all, imported wines were of higher quality and reasonably priced once the import tariffs had been reduced. Producers began to invest in vineyards and wineries and brought in respected foreign oenologists.

Brazil has yet to try its hand at wine exporting in any serious fashion, although there are signs that this may change, just as interest in imported fine wines has never been greater. A population of over 180 million constitutes a huge potential market, even if average wine consumption is only 2 litres a year and the cane spirit cachaça and beer are currently much more popular.

The size of the domestic market attracted Chandon (as in Moët) to Brazil as long ago as 1973. Traditionally, however, vine-growing has long been divided between thousands of small-scale farmers, mainly in the humid and mountainous Serra Gaúcha region in the state of Rio Grande do Sul, where rainfall is exceptionally high, almost 69in (1,750mm) a year, and soils tend to drain poorly. For this reason, hybrids, particularly Isabella, are a common choice for their resistance to rot and mildew. Indeed, in 2005, more than 80% of wine was made from American hybrids. Yields here are generally too high to result in wine of exportable quality, and the grapes struggle to ripen fully. (The Vale dos Vinhedos – "vineyard valley" – subregion does best.) Merlot, however, can usually be harvested before the rains arrive at the end of March, and its affinity with the clay soils of Serra Gaúcha means that it is the region's rising star.

The most exciting new region is Fronteira (formerly called Campanha) in the far south, where almost 2,500 acres (1,000ha) of vinifera vines are planted on less fertile sandy soils which offer good drainage – just like those over the border in Uruguay. Rainfall is lower here and longer sunshine hours make ripening easier.

There are also significant developments along the border of the states of Bahia and Pernambuco in the hot, dry Vale do São Francisco in the northeast of the country. The valley is less than 10 degrees south of the equator and historically was considered beyond the pale for viticulture. However, with very little temperature fluctuation, essential irrigation, and increased understanding of the demands of tropical viticulture, vines produce two harvests a year. Moscatel is the most common grape here, for very sweet and fresh sparkling wines, but both Syrah and Cabernet Sauvignon look promising.

The newest wine region is the mountainous Vale do Rio do Peixe in Santa Catarina state, where most vines are planted at 1,300–2,000ft (400–600m) above sea level. Bold, modern wineries are attracting tourists, and early results include surprisingly good Cabernet and Syrah and aromatic Sauvignon and Chardonnay.

Brazil's equivalent of France's Appellation Contrôlée system, Indicação de Procedência

— · — · —	International boundary
MENDOZA	Wine region
▨	Wine-producing areas
▨	Land above 2000 metres

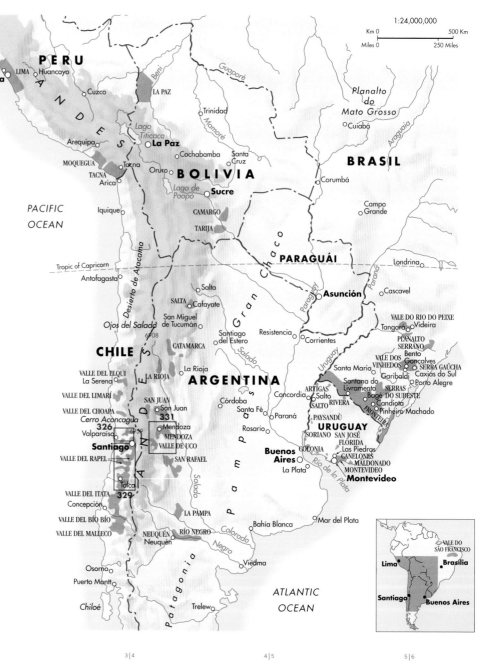

(Indication of Origin), had been awarded only to Vale dos Vinhedos at the time of writing, but both Vale do São Francisco and Pinto Bandeira have applied for official status.

Unlike Brazilians, the people of **Uruguay** are some of South America's most dedicated wine drinkers (second only to the Argentines), making the country's unusual wine industry the continent's fourth largest. The modern era began in 1870 with Basque immigration and the import of superior European grape varieties such as Tannat, called Harriague after its original promulgator. In a direct parallel to Malbec's softening transformation under the sunny skies of Argentina, the Tannat produced in Uruguay is much plumper and more velvety than in its homeland in southwest France, and can often be drunk when only a year or two old – most unlike the prototype Madiran.

Not that Uruguay's climate and topography have much in common with those of Argentina's wine regions. It is sunny but much wetter, and nights in the southern, most important wine districts of Uruguay are cooled by the influence not of altitude – most of the country undulates only very gently – but by Antarctic currents in the south Atlantic. Evenings are often breezy and cool, ripening slow and gradual. Except in years when the autumn rains arrive early, acidity levels are attractively refreshing. This freshness of aromas and flavours is one of the welcome distinctions of well-balanced Uruguayan wines of all hues. The conditions and the will to produce both elegant and characterful wines are evident.

About 90% of Uruguay's wine is grown in the maritime climate of the southern coastal departments of Canelones, San José (in both of which there has been recent French investment), Florida, and Montevideo, whose low hills offer a wide variety of different terroirs on generally loamy soils. In the Colonia department in the far southwest of the country, across the Río de la Plata estuary from Buenos Aires, the alluvial soils can be so fertile that vines are too vigorous to ripen grapes fully. A significant proportion of Uruguayan vineyards use the lyre trellis to balance this tendency by increasing the sun's access to more bunches, but maintaining the health and openness of such canopies is very time- and labour-consuming. Cover crops are also used to good effect to compete with the vine for water and other nutrients. The temperate, generally sunny but also humid, climate makes organic viticulture virtually impossible, but passionate, highly educated growers such as Reinaldo De Lucca manage without herbicides and fungicides (generally very widely needed and used to counteract rot and mildew).

The original importations of Harriague succumbed to virus disease and have been virtually replaced by vines more recently imported from France, called Tannat to distinguish them. However, Gabriel Pisano, a member of the youngest generation of this winemaking family, has developed a liqueur Tannat of rare intensity from surviving old-vine Harriague. There is also

Viognier, Trebbiano, and Torrontés – as well as the usual "international" suspects, including Chardonnay, Sauvignon Blanc, Cabernet, Syrah, and Merlot, which makes a juicy blending partner with the dominant Tannat. And isolated plantings of Pinot Noir are producing one or two excellent wines in a uniquely Uruguayan style.

In the Rivera department in the far northeast is a relatively new area that is viticulturally indistinguishable from Brazil's promising Fronteira region. Bodegas Carrau, which is involved in a joint venture with Freixenet of Spain, has one of its two wineries up here. The vine has also invaded sugar plantation country in the northwest and the centre of the country where poor soils and good diurnal temperature variation may yield interesting results. In this hotter, drier and less maritime climate, where Harriague was first planted, H Stagniari produces a rich, rounded style of Tannat in the Salto department.

The Uruguayans are making a concerted effort to join the international wine party so obviously being enjoyed by Chile and Argentina. However, volumes produced by these family-owned companies tend to be quite small and only about 10% of the 270 or so producers are exporting their wines. Small-scale newcomers such as the Bouza family are focusing on exports and high quality, as are the longer-established small and medium-sized family producers such as Marichal, Pizzorno, De Lucca, Castillo Viejo, Pisano, and Juanico (which has a joint venture with Bernard Magrez of Bordeaux). Larger family companies such as Traversa are

Harvesting grapes, grown in the traditional overhead pergola style, at Fazenda Santa Maria in Brazil's new Vale do São Francisco wine region, just nine degrees south of the equator. Vines here have to be prevented from producing crops too frequently.

▶ From top to bottom: One of Peru's rare wines of interest, three Brazilians, of which Miolo's Quinta do Seival bears a remarkable resemblance to a Portuguese label, then three from Uruguay, with Pisano's innovative liqueur Tannat first.

also taking steps to expand their range away from high-volume domestic production.

Venezuela has one winery growing its own grapes, but perhaps the greatest surprise in this roll call of regions is wine of remarkable quality from **Peru**, birthplace of pisco, the Chilean national spirit. The Tacama vineyards in Ica province benefit from the cold Pacific alongside in much the same way as those of California's Central Coast. They provide yet another revelation of what the least expected quarters of the globe can be persuaded to do.

Chile

To the visiting European, Chile seems comfortingly familiar culturally, but geographically it is the very essence of isolation. It is this isolation, thanks to the inhospitable Andes to the east, the Pacific to the west, the sands of the Atacama Desert to the north, and the wastes of Antarctica to the south, that has given Chilean vineyards what was once their most frequently touted distinction: freedom from the phylloxera louse. The vines can safely grow on their own roots, which means that a new vineyard can be planted simply by sticking cuttings straight into the ground, without the time and expense of grafting on to resistant rootstock.

Chile has a reliable Mediterranean climate, with day after day of uninterrupted sunlight in a dry, largely unpolluted atmosphere, and it is the special qualities of this grape-growing environment, together with some propitious vine importing in the 19th century, that make Chile today such a valuable source of inexpensive, fruity, reliably ripe wine. Moreover, wine that is made from some of the world's most popular grape varieties, both red and more recently white. A whirl of plantings of superior clones and new varieties has dramatically widened the range of flavours available from these particularly healthy vineyards. The Cabernet, Merlot, and Carmenère that dominated exports in the late 20th century have now been joined by very respectable, mid-priced Chilean Syrah, Pinot Noir, Malbec, Sauvignon Blanc, Chardonnay, and even Viognier, Gewurztraminer, and Riesling. Rot and mildew are not unknown, but are much rarer than they are in most of Europe and even Argentina just across the Andes.

Chile's latitudes may seem rather low for good quality wine production (about the same as North Africa's, for example), but as a comparison of the factfiles of Meknès (see p.287) and Santiago (see overleaf) shows, the central slice of the country in which vines are grown is not excessively hot, and both the Pacific and the Andes exert a significant influence on the climate (see panel opposite). Chile's day–night temperature variation is unusually wide, and this is almost certainly a factor in the clarity of the fruit flavours.

For decades vineyards were concentrated on a corridor of fertile flatland between the Andes and the much lower Coastal Range, which reaches only 3,300ft (1,000m) at most, but today Chile's restless wine entrepreneurs are much more experimental. Although the official Chilean wine map is divided into appellations split politically north to south, it is increasingly evident that local soil and climatic conditions in fact vary much more from west to east, according to a site's geology and proximity to the cooling influences of the Pacific and the Andes.

The cool, near-coastal Casablanca Valley, developed at a rapid rate in the 1990s, is just one of Chile's coastal-influenced wine regions now, and today's wine map extends as far

north as Limarí and Elqui at latitudes that were originally considered far too low for high-quality wine production (see p.324). In the far south of this, the world's longest, thinnest country, the cool southerly subregion of Bío Bío is being colonized by the vine, with the southernmost plantings to date being a full 200 miles (320km) south of the Malleco Valley at Osorno in Chile's Lake District. And in the long Central Valley in between, vines are creeping uphill, both towards the Coastal Range in the west but particularly on the sunnier, drier eastern slopes of the foothills of the Andes.

If Chile's wine country has any natural agricultural disadvantage it is that the summers are virtually rainless. Earlier farmers spotted this possible problem and dug an astonishing network of canals and gullies to flood the land with water from the snow that each year melts in the Andes (even if less plentifully nowadays). This admirable, if imprecise, sort of irrigation is being replaced in newer vineyards by drip irrigation, which can both apply fertilizer (often necessary in Chilean soils) and respond more sensitively to each vine row's needs. With light but fertile soil and complete control of the water supply, grape growing is absurdly easy, even if the most quality-conscious producers are now actively seeking poorer soils, such as those of Apalta in Colchagua for their best wines.

Irrigation is absolutely essential in most of the vineyards north of those mapped on these pages, in the Atacama and Coquimbo regions, whose

main products have been table grapes and pisco, Chile's curiously addictive Moscatel-based spirit, but they are now producing some exciting wines. Along the Limarí River, for example, where vineyards 9–15 miles (15–25km) inland are systematically cooled by marine incursions, some particularly fine Chardonnay and Syrah produced. Chile's leading wine company, Concha y Toro, invested heavily in **Limarí** in 2005, and Tamaya has ambitious plans there. Choapa Valley just south of Limarí is being planted and Viña Falernia has shown that **Elqui** even further north can also produce fine wine, at altitudes over 6,600ft (2,000m).

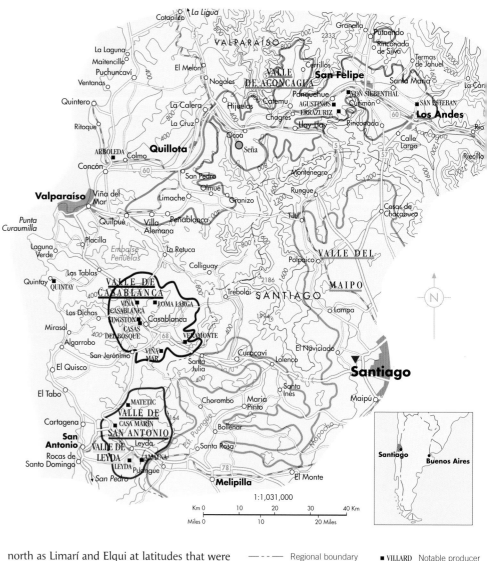

– – – – – Regional boundary	■ VILLARD Notable producer
──────── Valle de Aconcagua	◎ Seña Noted vineyard
──────── Valle de Casablanca	══1200══ Contour interval 400 metres
──────── Valle del Maipo	
──────── Valle de San Antonio	▼ Weather station (W
──────── Valle de Leyda	

CHILE: SANTIAGO ▼

Latitude / Altitude of WS **33.23° / 1,542ft (470m)**

Mean January temp at WS **69.5°F (20.8°C)**

Annual rainfall at WS **13in (330mm)**

Harvest month rainfall at WS **March: 0.2in (5mm)**

Chief viticultural hazard **Nematodes**

Principal grapes **Cabernet Sauvignon, Chardonnay, Merlot, Carmenère**

Between here and Santiago is the region of Aconcagua (named after the highest peak of the Andes, at 23,000ft/7,000m). It is mapped separately opposite, showing clearly the east–west contrasts in local conditions. The region is made up of three contrasting subregions, the warm Aconcagua Valley itself and the particularly cool Casablanca and San Antonio Valleys.

The warmth of the broad, open **Aconcagua Valley** is tempered by winds that regularly sweep cool mountain air coastward in the early afternoons and funnel ocean air up from the river mouth most evenings to cool the west-facing foothills of the Andes. In the late 19th century the Errázuriz family's property at Panquehue was reputed to be the biggest single wine estate in the world. Today about 2,500 acres (1,000ha) of wine grapes are grown in the Aconcagua Valley, and the hillsides are being converted to vineyards under Errázuriz's auspices. There are also notable new plantings west of Colmo, just 10 miles (16km) from the ocean (and about as cool as Marlborough in New Zealand). Panquehue was the site of Chile's first planting of Syrah, in 1993, closely followed by Montes' much further south in Apalta.

The **Casablanca Valley**, between Santiago and the port of Valparaiso, has become almost synonymous with Chilean white wine. It was long thought to be too cold for viticulture, but in 1982 Pablo Morandé, then winemaker at Concha y Toro, converted his table grape vineyard with its traditional pergola to vertically trellised wine grapes and proved that Casablanca could produce white wines with a finesse quite unprecedented in Chile.

Today dozens of bodegas, and almost all of the big ones, buy or grow fruit here. The valley is too far from the Andes for cool mountain air in the evening, or even for access to meltwater for irrigation (so expensive bore-holes have to be sunk deep below the thin topsoils, and access to water is the limiting factor in developing the valley for wine). It is so close to the sea, though, that cool breezes can be relied upon to lower afternoon temperatures by as much as 18°F (10°C), which, with the valley's mild winters, makes Casablanca's growing season up to a month longer than most vineyards in the Central Valley. Aromatic crisp whites are the usual result, from plantings that totalled about 10,000 acres (4,000ha) by the mid-2000s. The valley is a natural home to increasingly fine Sauvignon Blanc, but Chardonnay is in such demand that it still dominates Casablanca's vineyards – without necessarily having a particularly distinctive style.

Spring frost is a perennial and inconvenient threat, and it is not unknown for vineyards on the frost-prone open valley floor to suffer frost a week before harvest. The water shortage makes anti-frost sprinklers a luxury, however. The naturally low-vigour vines are also prey to worm-like nematodes so that vines have to be grafted on to resistant rootstocks. Growing costs are higher here than elsewhere, but Casablanca, Chile's answer to Carneros, has irrefutably widened the range of wines available from this ambitious wine exporter.

CENTRAL VALLEY'S CLIMATE

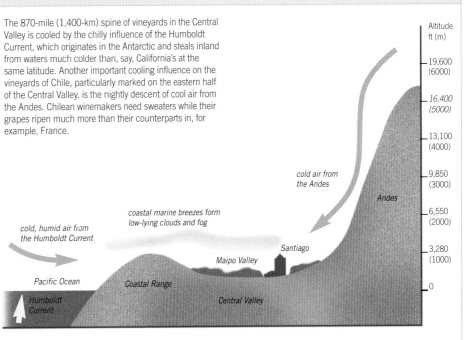

The 870-mile (1,400-km) spine of vineyards in the Central Valley is cooled by the chilly influence of the Humboldt Current, which originates in the Antarctic and steals inland from waters much colder than, say, California's at the same latitude. Another important cooling influence on the vineyards of Chile, particularly marked on the eastern half of the Central Valley, is the nightly descent of cool air from the Andes. Chilean winemakers need sweaters while their grapes ripen much more than their counterparts in, for example, France.

Altitude ft (m)
19,600 (6000)
16,400 (5000)
13,100 (4000)
9,850 (3000)
6,550 (2000)
3,280 (1000)
0

cold air from the Andes

Andes

coastal marine breezes form low-lying clouds and fog

cold, humid air from the Humboldt Current

Santiago

Maipo Valley

Pacific Ocean

Coastal Range

Central Valley

Humboldt Current

The success of Casablanca encouraged the development of the rolling coastal hills of the **San Antonio Valley**, first planted in 1997 by Viña Leyda and officially recognized in 2002. The varied topography makes San Antonio even more subject to the cool, damp ocean influence than western Casablanca. Along with Viña Leyda, the most important pioneers were Casa Marin, Matetic, and Amayna, but many other companies source grapes here, particularly Sauvignon Blanc, Chardonnay, and Pinot Noir. Syrah, too, can be ripened in the Rosario Valley, where Matetic is based. The infertile soils consist mainly of thin layers of clay on granite, as in the westernmost part of Casablanca, and irrigation water is just as scarce. **Valle de Leyda** is an officially recognized zone in the south of the San Antonio Valley.

The map on p.329 shows the most important of Chile's five wine-growing areas by far: the Central Valley, with its four regions named after the Maipo, Rapel, Curicó, and Maule valleys that cross the central plain, like gradations on a thermometer, to pierce the low Coastal Range and find the sea.

Maipo has the hottest climate, an atmosphere occasionally polluted by the smogs of Santiago, and the smallest vineyard area of the Central Valley's regions, but a high concentration of bodegas. Its proximity to the capital spawned a tradition of grand plantations and extensive homesteads belonging to Chile's 19th-century gentlemen-farmers, some of whom established such longstanding and important wine com-

panies as Concha y Toro, Santa Rita (which belongs to the same group as Chile's only bottle producer), and Santa Carolina.

It was here, just a convenient ride south of Santiago, that Chile's first generation of serious wine was made. Not from the common País grape (Criolla Chica in Argentina, Mission in California), which is still widely grown for the tetrapak wine so popular within Chile, but from cuttings imported directly from Bordeaux in the mid-19th century before phylloxera ravaged the vineyards of Europe.

This is why Chile is such a rich repository of long-adapted Bordeaux grape varieties: Cabernet Sauvignon (which overtook País in total vineyard area in the late 1990s), "Sauvignon Blanc" (much of which was actually Sauvignon Vert or Sauvignonasse), Merlot, and the notably vigorous old Bordeaux variety Carmenère, which is generally best suited to poor soils and as an ingredient in blends rather

A Carmenère vine in flower in early summer, when the vineyards are heady with the smell of vine blossom. Until the mid-1990s, when a visiting French vine specialist identified it, Carmenère was thought to be a strain of Merlot and was labelled as such.

The distinctive amphitheatre of Apalta in Colchagua with the Tinguiririca River in the foreground. Grapes for both Montes Folly and Casa Lapostolle's Clos Apalta (see labels below) are grown on these south/southwest-facing slopes.

than as a varietal. Maipo is essentially red wine country where Bordeaux varieties flourish, and when yields are restricted can produce wines reminiscent of some of the Napa Valley's output. Maipo Alto is where vineyards are creeping up the Andean foothills and the mountain influence is most keenly felt. Its relatively chilly mornings, and poor soils, have already resulted in some of Chile's most admired reds such as Almaviva, Aurea Domus, Casa Real (Santa Rita), Haras de Pirque (Quebreda de Macul), and Viñedo Chadwick (Errazuriz).

The burgeoning and varied region of Rapel to the immediate south encompasses the valleys of **Cachapoal** in the north (including the Rancagua, Requínoa, and Rengo areas – all names occasionally found on labels), and fashionable **Colchagua** to the south, including San Fernando, Nancagua, Chimbarongo, Marchigüe (Marchihue), and Apalta. Cachapoal and, especially, Colchagua are names more often found on labels than Rapel, which tends to be reserved for blends from both subregions. Colchagua, where Luis Felipe Edwards has planted as high as 3,300ft (1,000m), has earned itself a reputation for Chile's most succulent and concentrated

Merlot. Soils vary enormously in Chile even within small zones such as Colchagua, but there is some clay here, Merlot's classic partner, as well as the usual Chilean cocktail of loam, limestone, and sand with some volcanic areas. Red and white blends such as Anakena Ona's are an increasingly respected product of Cachapoal.

Quite a way down the Pan-American Highway, with its ancient trucks and unpredictable fauna, are the vineyards of **Curicó**, including the subregion of Lontué, which is also often specified on wine labels. Here the climate becomes slightly more temperate and irrigation is less likely to be a necessity. Average rainfall is 10 times higher here than in Elquí Valley, the frost risk is very much higher, and the Coastal Range extends far enough east to effectively block any Pacific influence. Miguel Torres of Catalonia famously invested in a winery here in 1979 (the same year that Baron Philippe de Rothschild struck another seminal transatlantic deal with Robert Mondavi of California), and this act of faith in wine country once thought of as being impossibly far south has been followed by many others. The San Pedro winery at Molina was dramatically upgraded and

expanded in the 1990s, with the funds of Chile's dominant brewer and the expertise of Jacques Lurton of Bordeaux. It is surrounded by South America's largest block of vines (3,000 acres/1,200ha) and run, like much in the Chilean wine industry, with a technical precision far from any Latin American stereotype.

The southernmost region of the Central Valley and Chile's oldest wine region, **Maule**, has three times the rainfall of Santiago (although the same dry summers) and Chile's greatest area of vines on substantially volcanic soils. Many of them are basic País, but Cabernet Sauvignon is now the most planted variety, with Merlot and then Carmenère some way behind. Many of these grapes are included in wines labelled simply Central Valley. After much scouting, Torres discovered a Priorat-like slate-dominated terroir in Empredado in western Maule.

South of the area mapped opposite, with less protection from the Coastal Range and in even cooler, wetter conditions which favour such grapes as Riesling, Gewurztraminer, Sauvignon Blanc, Chardonnay, and Pinot Noir, are the three subregions of the Sur (Spanish for South), **Itata**, **Bío Bío**, and **Malleco** (see map on p.324). They are still dominated by País and (especially in Itata) Moscatel, but there has been serious pioneering work on the part of producers such as Viña Gracia, Viña Porta, and Concha y Toro at Mulchén. The quality of Viña Aquitania's Sol de Sol Chardonnay from Malleco has encouraged those who would extend the Chilean wine map even further south.

Since the early, well-publicized incursions of Torres and the Lafite-Rothschilds' investment in the Peralillo estate of Los Vascos, dozens of foreigners have invested in Chile's wine, and scores of flying winemakers have flown in and out. The most heartening aspect of all, however, is that Chile's own, often peripatetic, viticulturists and oenologists are so well-qualified, well-travelled, and competent, often backed by well-funded operators with experience in general fruit farming.

New vineyards have proliferated, but with much more careful site selection and matching of variety to environment. In the vineyards,

▼ A selection of some of Chile's best, arranged left to right from north to south according to where the grapes are grown rather than where the wine is made. (Sol de Sol Chardonnay, for instance, is grown in the country's southernmost wine region but is made on the outskirts of Santiago.)

the temptation was to over-use fertilizers and irrigation, although this has become rarer for vines weighed down by Chile's naturally dense canopy. Too many grapes have a nasty habit of failing to ripen properly. Moreover the strength of the peso has meant that Chilean wines have if anything to over-deliver.

Rootstocks are much more prevalent, both for resistance to problems such as nematodes, and just in case the recent influx of visitors from other wine regions – particularly during harvest, when northern hemisphere wine producers have little to do at home – should unwittingly import the phylloxera louse. Facilitated by the unusually benign climate, an increasing proportion of Chilean vines are cultivated organically, even if relatively few growers take the trouble to gain certification. Concha y Toro can afford the necessary time and money, however, and their subsidiary Viñedos Organicos Emiliana (VOE) operates the world's largest single biodynamic vineyard, Los Robles estate in Colchagua, run by Chile's organic pioneer Alvaro Espinoza.

In the cellars, since the emergence of an export-orientated economy – Chile exports as big a percentage of its production as Australia (about 60%) – there has been extraordinary investment in winery hardware, and oak is now more likely to be harnessed than flaunted. Average yields have declined, and grape prices risen, in recent years. The fruit is usually, although not always, robust enough to take considerable oak influence, whether from expensive new barrels or much cheaper oak chips or inner staves. Much recent effort has been expended on mastering technology in Chile. Nature needs so little taming here.

– – – – –	Regional boundary
————	Valle del Maipo
————	Valle de Casablanca
————	Valle de San Antonio
————	Valle de Leyda
————	Valle del Cachapoal (within the Valle del Rapel)
————	Valle de Colchagua (within the Valle del Rapel)
————	Valle de Curicó
————	Valle del Maule
Lolol	Wine subregion
■ CANEPA	Notable producer
▨	Vineyards
–1200–	Contour interval 400 metres

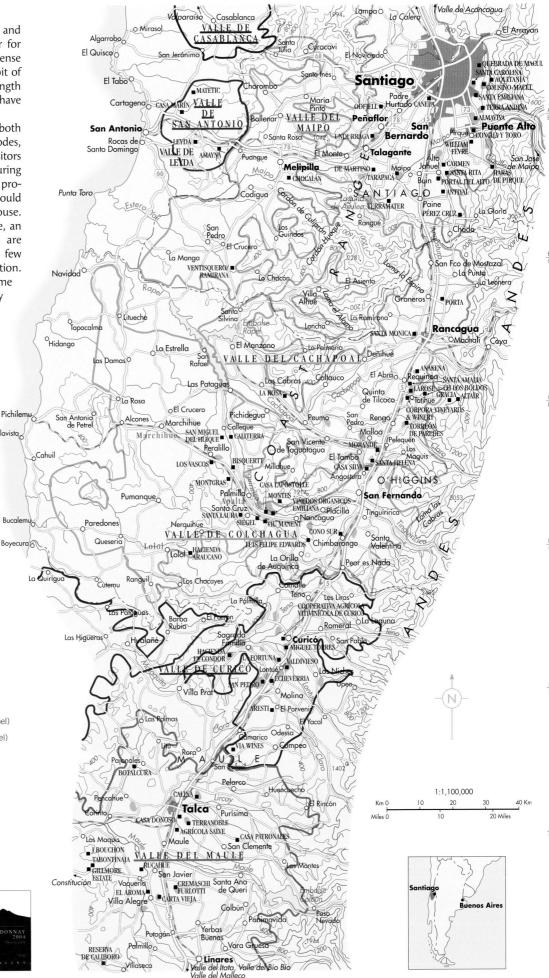

Argentina

Argentina, a promising blend of extreme landscapes with a uniquely wide range of cultural influences, has put itself on the international wine map remarkably recently. Blessed with an enviable diversity of grape varieties thanks to mid-19th century immigration from Spain and Italy, Argentina had little or no export aspirations before the mid-1990s, no sense of belonging to a wider world, and in wine terms at least, contented itself with producing vast quantities of mediocre wine, often oxidized and aged for years in vast old vats.

The 1990s saw a remarkably rapid change of pace for what is now the world's fifth biggest wine producer. After a long period of economic instability, old cellars were rejuvenated, glamorous new ones created by investors from all over the world, and new vineyards were planted at a fiendish rate at ever higher altitudes. Argentines themselves began to drink less but fruitier wine, and abroad Argentina's intensely flavoured, full-bodied reds, and some whites, became first more familiar and then admired.

The economic crisis of 2001–02 provoked a dramatic devaluation, slowed inward investment, made imported barrels and other winemaking equipment much more expensive, and did not seem to be reflected in lower prices for exported Argentine wines. But these external factors have apparently done little to curb the continuing rise in wine quality, and Argentine wine continues to put pressure on Chilean wine, its longstanding rival.

The tree-lined city of Mendoza (officially acknowledged one of the world's eight Great Wine Capitals) is only 50 minutes by air from the Chilean capital Santiago – so close that shopping bags are a common sight on the crowded flights. Yet the plane has to clear the highest ridge of the Andes, a 20,000-ft (6,000-m) serrated blade of rock and ice. The centres of Argentine and Chilean wine may be cheek by jowl, yet they are poles apart in terms of natural conditions. Both lie in the low latitudes for wine-growing, but while Chile's wine regions owe their ideal growing conditions to their isolation (they are sandwiched between the cold Andes and the cold Pacific), Argentine vineyards, typically oases of green set in uncompromisingly arid semi-desert, exist because of altitude.

The altitudes at which Argentine vineyards flourish would be unthinkably high in Europe: from 2,300 up to 4,600ft (700 to 1,400m), and even up to 9,080ft (3,015m) in the northern province of Salta. Indeed the average elevation of Argentine vineyards is over 2,950ft (900m) above sea level. At this height, overnight temperatures are regularly low enough to give well-flavoured, deeply coloured grapes for red wine and in the cooler areas, especially in the north, aromatic whites. With little or no disease in the dry mountain air, usually on ungrafted roots, provided there is abundant water, crops

can reach yields virtually unknown elsewhere. The current challenge in Argentine viticulture, which is slowly moving to more widespread adoption of wires and shoot positioning, is to harness irrigation so as to deliver quality before quantity. Traditional vineyards and irrigation channels were sited so that the vines were routinely flooded with meltwater off the Andes. Today, as less and less snow seems to fall on the mountains and vineyards are increasingly sited in completely new districts, supplies of water are much more restricted. Local authorities may limit irrigation to certain periods. Expensive bore holes may have to be factored into wine-making economics. Traditional flood irrigation is being replaced by both furrow and drip irrigation systems whose relative merits are the subject of much debate.

Most new plantings are on rootstocks, for phylloxera is not absent from Argentine vineyards – a source of worry for Chilean growers now that Chilean wine companies have invested in Argentina's vineyard land, which is cheaper than Chile's – but it has so far posed no great threat. That flood irrigation was so common and soils are relatively sandy may be pertinent. Such plants as are affected seem to recover, growing new roots, in contrast to the experience of vine-growers elsewhere. An OIV study in 1990 confirmed Argentina's remarkably low incidence of vine disease; Argentine vines had developed hardly any tolerance to common vineyard chemicals.

But conditions in Argentine vineyards are not perfect and the weather is far from predictable. At these altitudes winters are cold (importantly, cold enough for vine dormancy) but spring frosts can present real danger. But summers in some of the lower-altitude, lower-latitude regions such as parts of San Juan and La Rioja provinces, and eastern San Rafael in the south of Mendoza (see map on p.324) can be just too hot for fine wine production. And as the key facts box shows, Argentina's annual precipitation may be very low (even in El Niño years) but is concentrated in the growing season. In some areas, particularly in the province of Mendoza, where almost 70% of Argentina's vines are planted, it has a nasty tendency to fall as hail, which can devastate an entire year's crop. One area particularly prone to hail is the east of San Rafael between the Diamante and Atuel rivers. Some growers have invested in special hail nets which can also usefully reduce the risk of sunburn in Argentina's intense sunlight. The zonda, a fearsome hot, dry wind from the northeast, is another liability, particularly at high altitudes, and particularly at flowering.

Soils tend to be relatively young and alluvial with quite a high proportion of sand in many areas. The intensity of flavour that the best wines demonstrate comes not from below but

Catena's Pirámide vineyard in Agrelo, where the first small lot of Catena Alta, based on Cabernet Sauvignon, was grown in the mid-1990s. It was also used as a testing ground for choosing the superior clones of Malbec which are now responsible for Catena's top wine.

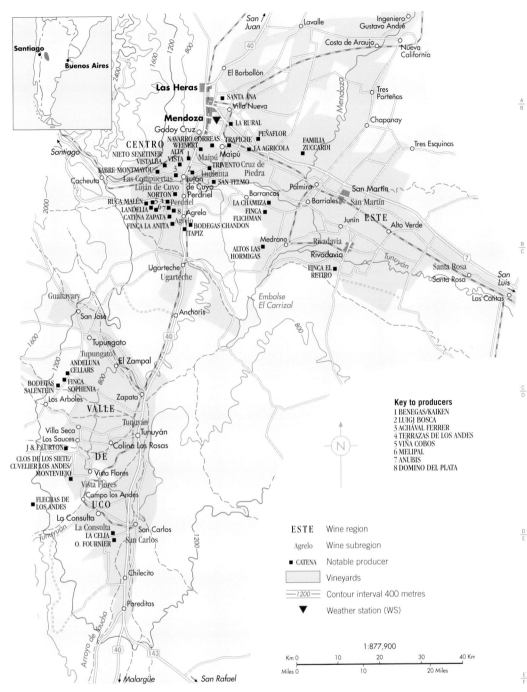

Key to producers
1 BENEGAS/KAIKEN
2 LUIGI BOSCA
3 ACHÁVAL FERRER
4 TERRAZAS DE LOS ANDES
5 VIÑA COBOS
6 MELIPAL
7 ANUBIS
8 DOMINO DEL PLATA

ESTE   Wine region
Agrelo   Wine subregion
■ CATENA   Notable producer
▢   Vineyards
═1200═   Contour interval 400 metres
▼   Weather station (WS)

1:877,900
Km 0   10   20   30   40 Km
Miles 0   10   20 Miles

from above, from the intense sunlight, the dry air, and the diurnal temperature differences at these altitudes. At up to 36°F (20°C) temperature variation is higher in Argentine vineyards than practically anywhere else in the world. This is often because of altitude, but in Patagonia in the south it is because of the high latitude. Apart from in the most southerly vineyards of Patagonia, in Neuquén and Río Negro, full ripeness is easy to achieve. In fact, dedicated viticulturists may deliberately slow ripening by controlled drip irrigation in order to coax more flavour out of each vine. Argentina's high temperatures can be tasted in particularly soft tannins in the red wines, and sometimes rather aggressive alcohol in the whites.

The country's wine reputation rests largely on its most planted red wine grape Malbec,

ARGENTINA: MENDOZA   ▼
Latitude / Altitude of WS **32.5° / 2,493ft (760m)**
Mean January temp at WS **75°F (23.9°C)**
Annual rainfall at WS **8in (200mm)**
Harvest month rainfall at WS **March: 1.2in (30mm)**
Chief viticultural hazards **Summer hail, zonda**
Principal grapes **Bonarda, Malbec, Criolla Grande, Cereza, Cabernet Sauvignon, Barbera, Sangiovese**

introduced to Mendoza in the mid-19th century, possibly via Chile's pre-phylloxera importations of vines from Bordeaux. (In the 18th century Malbec dominated in Bordeaux.) The opulent Malbec grown today in Argentina not only tastes very different from that which now dominates the vineyards of Cahors in

Southwest France, it also looks different, with much smaller, tighter bunches and smaller berries. Early South American growers must have selected particular plants that seemed to perform well and these have since adapted perfectly to local conditions, although to keep its acidity and intensity of flavour Malbec is best grown at slightly higher altitudes than, say, Cabernet Sauvignon.

In enviable contrast to that of Chile, Argentina's palette of grape varieties is varied and colourful. Deep-coloured Bonarda, probably identical to Charbono, is Argentina's second most planted red wine grape, and arguably the country's most underdeveloped wine resource (although Catena and La Agrícola pioneered serious versions). Other significant reds, in declining order of land claimed, are Cabernet Sauvignon, Syrah (which seems particularly promising), Merlot, Tempranillo, Sangiovese, Pinot Negro (sic), and Barbera, all of them producing rich, savoury wines with powerful ripe flavours often far from those of the European archetypes but sometimes none the worse for that. Pinot Negro/Noir is so far limited to Patagonia or Mendoza's higher altitudes but some promising examples are beginning to emerge.

This rather obvious case apart, for a long time there was relatively little discipline in matching grapes to local conditions. An increasing number of producers, however, led by the likes of Alta Vista, Achával Ferrer, and particularly the high-profile Catena, have pioneered single-vineyard wines designed to display the characteristics of, typically, Malbec in different wine areas.

The country's most distinctive light-skinned grape (other than the coarse, pink-skinned Criolla Grande, Cereza, and Criolla Chica or Mission, and the light-skinned Pedro Giménez, which are grown strictly for local consumption) is Torrontés. The name is applied to three distinct varieties. Torrontés Riojana, named after La Rioja province, is the finest and reaches its apogee, albeit in a style of wine that is not especially fashionable at present, in the high vineyards of Salta province, notably around Cafayete. The origins of this florally perfumed but naturally crisp wine are still obscure but probably Spanish.

Other widely grown grapes for "fine white wine", as Argentine authorities call anything pale and conceivably exportable, are Chardonnay (planted with particular enthusiasm recently), Chenin Blanc, Ugni Blanc, and an increasing acreage of Sauvignon Blanc – a sign perhaps of just how high and therefore cool some of the new plantings are. The odd Viognier has also emerged.

The northernmost of Argentina's wine-growing provinces is **Salta**, home to what are claimed to be the highest vineyards in the world. They produce Donald Hess's Colomé mountain wine in the Valle de Calchaquies, although Raúl Dávalos, his predecessor on this primitive estate and now neighbour in this wild land close to the Bolivian border, continues to challenge him for this particular crown. At rather lower altitudes, the holiday country of Cafayete has a fine reputation for aromatic white Torrontés, and San Pedro de Yacohuya has shown that vine age and low yields provide the key to red wine quality here. Just to the south, **Catamarca** is better known for table grapes than wine.

La Rioja province is best known for, logically, Torrontés Riojana, which is typically trained on pergolas and vinified by the local co-op. The dry, windy Famatina Valley is its best-known wine region.

The only province that makes wine in any quantity to rival that of Mendoza is **San Juan**, which is even hotter and drier (just 3.5in/90mm of rain in an average year) than Mendoza to the immediate south. Almost a quarter of all Argentine wine is made here, much of it based on Moscatel de Alejandria or Muscat of Alexandria, the predominant Muscat in Argentina. Syrah is increasingly popular here, although much of the land is too hot to yield wines with much varietal definition. Just as in Mendoza, however, quality-conscious producers have begun to plant vines at ever higher altitudes in the Ullum, Zonda, Calingasta, and Pedernal valleys, with promising results.

Mendoza, centred on the vibrant city of the same name, is by far the dominant Argentine wine province, with many very different regions within it.

Central Mendoza has the longest tradition for fine wine, and a high proportion of Argentina's most famous producers are based here. Vineyards on either side of the avenues that radiate from the city, in the Luján de Cuyo department (which has its own appellation), have developed a reputation for especially fine Malbec. Vineyard districts within this area which have carved out their own reputations for Malbec include Vistalba, Perdriel, Agrelo, and Las Compuertas, where soils are particularly poor. The average age of vines here, many of which escaped Argentina's enthusiastic vine-pull schemes in the late 20th century, has contributed to wine quality. The department of Maipú may be better for Cabernet Sauvignon.

In Central Mendoza the climate is temperate (almost cool in Agrelo) and the soils unusually gravelly for Argentina (especially in Maipú) when elsewhere in Mendoza soils are typically

alluvial and sandy. And there are none of the salinity problems that can cause difficulties in the lower districts, which churn out oceans of table wine from Cereza, the Criollas, Pedro Giménez, Moscatel Alejandría, and the high-yielding Bonarda.

East Mendoza is better known for quantity than quality. Vineyards here are at lower altitudes and the cooling influence of the Andes is at its weakest. The Mendoza and Tunuyán rivers traditionally provided ample, grape-swelling irrigation for the pergola vines that spewed forth wine for the local market.

About 60 miles (100km) southeast of Mendoza, San Rafael has a similar reputation and its lower altitude, down to below 1,650ft (500m), means that acid additions, routine for the fruit of all but Argentina's highest vineyards, are particularly necessary.

The most exciting part of Mendoza from the fine wine lover's point of view is the Uco Valley, named not after a river but after a pre-Columbian Indian chief reputed to have introduced irrigation here. Although the first vines were planted as recently as the 1980s, the Uco Valley now has well over 25,000 acres (10,000ha) of vineyard, much of it notably youthful, at altitudes of 3,300–5,600ft (1,000–1,700m). Producers such as Catena and the LVMH-owned Terrazas de los Andes specify precise altitudes on their front labels.

The highest vineyards are in the Tupungato subregion, where much of Argentina's surprisingly fine Chardonnay is grown. Tupungato has been the focus of sophisticated modern vineyard development, and some of the older wineries are at a distance from the vineyards. Nights are sufficiently cool to produce delicate fruit flavours and acidity levels are sufficiently high to make malolactic fermentation desirable. The frost-free period lasts no longer than in New York's Finger Lakes region, however, and late frosts are a particular threat in the east of the Uco Valley on the slightly lower slopes of the San Carlos subregion.

Other notable plantings include Clos de los Siete near Vista Flores, a vast red wine estate designed by Michel Rolland of Pomerol with fellow investors, and various vineyard sites around La Consulta, San Carlos, and Tunuyán.

The upper limits of vine cultivation in Mendoza are still being tested, but a shortage of irrigation water is another potential hazard. To compensate, however, much is made of the intensity of sunlight in this unpolluted area high in the Andes, which seems to act as a spur to photosynthesis and naturally ripens phenolics such as colour, flavour, and tannins. It is a rare Argentine wine, however young,

that is uncomfortably astringent. The prevailing texture of Mendoza red is velvet.

The wines of **Patagonia** in the south of the country, in the provinces of Neuquén and especially Rio Negro, tend to have their own distinctive character – chewier if no less intense. Antarctic influences keep temperatures down but strong winds keep vine disease at bay. These are bright, distinctively sculpted wines strong on structure and character. Several of the relatively few wineries in Patagonia have some non-Argentine connection: Bordeaux-inspired Fabre Montmayou have Infinitus; Noemia is Cinzano funded and operated by a Dane; Bodega Familia Schroeder has its origins in Europe; and Bodega Chacra, which is developing an old, once-abandoned Pinot Noir vineyard in Rio Negro, is owned by the Tuscan Piero Incisa della Rocchetta.

Peñaflor, with its associated Trapiche bodega, is the country's biggest producer, while Dr Nicolas Catena, whose interests include Catena

Zapata, Alamos, Gascon, and La Rural, is arguably Argentina's best-known producer abroad, with a joint venture with the Rothschilds of Lafite and an increasing respect for Malbec over Cabernet Sauvignon. There has been no shortage of outside investment to join that of champagne house Moët, which has operated Bodegas Chandon for decades, and now has Cheval de los Andes made by Pierre Lurton of Cheval Blanc as its flagship wine at Terrazas de los Andes. The Swarovski family of Austria acquired Norton in 1989. There is also Donald Hess (Colomé) and Paul Hobbs (Viña Cobos) from California; the Lurtons (near Tunuyán in high country), Jean-Michel Arcaute (Alta Vista), Hervé Joyaux (Fabre Montmayou), Michel Rolland (Clos de los Siete), the Cuvelier family (Cuvelier de los Andes), Catherine Péré-Vergé (Monteviejo), and Rothschild-Dassault (Flechas de los Andes) from Bordeaux; Codorníu (Septima) and O Fournier from Spain; Sogrape from Portugal (Finca Flichman); Alberto

Carlos Pulenta has extended his original family property into a state-of-the art winery with ample attractions for visitors, including the thoroughly modern restaurant La Bourgogne. All symptomatic of Mendoza's transformation into a top tourist destination – the Napa Valley of South America?

Antonini (Altos las Hormigas) from Italy; and Pernod Ricard (Etchart, Balbi, Graffigna) and Seagram (San Telmo) from their corporate stratosphere. From over the Andes have come a growing number of Chilean investors including Montes (Kaiken), Viña San Pedro (Finca La Celia), and Concha y Toro (Trivento).

Not that the Argentines themselves have been inactive. Some of the recent significant developments have been by Susanna Balbo and Pedro Marchevsky (Dominio del Plata), Patricia Ortiz (Tapiz), Santiago Achával Becu and partners (Achával Ferrer), and Roberto de la Mota (Mendel). Argentina will continue to challenge Chile for pole position as South America's leading wine innovator.

◄ The six labels on the near left represent some of Mendoza's finest Malbecs and Malbec blends (which have become increasingly sophisticated and elegant in recent vintages), while the three on the far left come from (left to right) Patagonia, San Juan, and Salta. The Bramare Chardonnay demonstrates Californian Paul Hobbs' admiration of Perdriel in Mendoza as Chardonnay territory, whereas Lindaflor's Chardonnay comes from Tunuyán.

Australia

Salvation Jane blooms between the vines in Penfolds' organic vineyard in the Clare Valley, South Australia, heralding spring.

Australia

In 1996 Australia set itself a target: to achieve annual wine sales (both export and domestic) worth A$4.5 billion by 2025. The target was met in 2003. Soon afterwards Australia overtook France to become the biggest exporter of wine to the UK – and seemed set to do the same in the USA. In not much more than a decade it became one of the most potent forces in the wine world.

Stability was harder to achieve. While sales soared, the confidence and tax incentives that had encouraged Australians to double the country's vineyard area to 410,000 acres (167,000ha) in the 10 years to 2006 took their toll. Australian growers were hit by a glut of grapes. Vast vineyards went unpicked. Within Australia, sales of "cleanskins", parcels of surplus wine of indeterminate provenance at knock-down prices, soared. With its relatively small domestic population, Australia depends on exports for 60% of its wine sales, a proportion that is unlikely to fall as more and more Australian wine companies, big and small, fall into non-Australian hands.

Meanwhile, Australia's wine colleges continue to spew out a new crop of technically adept winemakers each year, by no means all of them Australian, unleashing them every September on cellars throughout the northern hemisphere.

There (during the quiet season in southern hemisphere wineries) they have spread the gospel of super-hygienic, ultra-efficient Australian vinification, forging useful links across the equator. Their science is highly saleable; the Commonwealth Scientific & Industrial Research Organization (CSIRO) and the Australian Wine Research Institute (AWRI) have earned international respect.

One of the most notable aspects of Brand Australia, as the ever market-conscious Australians call it, is its consistency. Every single bottle of Australian wine reaches a certain minimum, perfectly acceptable level of quality, of exuberant if sometimes eventually tiring fruit, even if, as is statistically most likely, it comes from the heavily irrigated vineyards in the interior of the country. Almost two-thirds of every year's grape harvest is grown in one of the three big irrigated areas where canalized river-water turns bush into orchard and vineyard. They are, in decreasing order of volume produced: **Murray Darling**, which, with Swan Hill, straddles the Victoria–New South Wales border; **Riverland** in South Australia; and **Riverina** in New South Wales (see map, below right).

The Australian wine industry is crucially dependent on irrigation water in general and the Murray River in particular. Availability of good-quality irrigation water is the principal constraint on those who

would convert this, the driest country on earth, into one big vineyard. Current preoccupations include pollution of the river, drought, and the dangerously high level of salt in Australia's underground water, the legacy of wholesale clearance of the land by two centuries of settlers.

The large, inland irrigated areas, with their effortless mass-production of increasingly fresh, varietally distinct, everyday wines (and even some especially distinctive specialities such as botrytized Riverina Semillons from Griffith), have become a centre of industrial power. Australia's most successful 21st-century brand [yellow tail] (sic), for example, is owned by Casella Wines of Riverina. It seduced the American market from a standing start when it was taken up by the US distributors of the previous leading Australian Chardonnay, Lindemans Bin 65 made at Karadoc in Murray Darling. Riverland meanwhile is home to such famous brands as Banrock Station and Oxford Landing – and even more own-label bottlings.

Australians believe in economies of scale. Between 1996 and 2006 the number of wineries

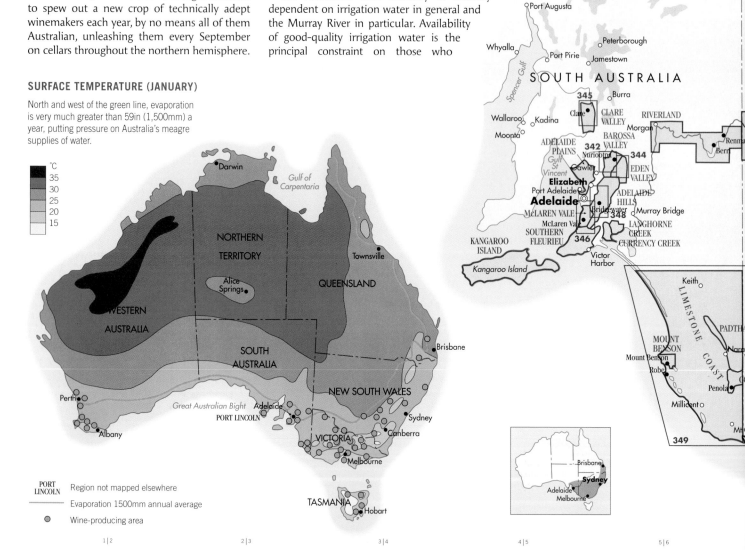

SURFACE TEMPERATURE (JANUARY)

North and west of the green line, evaporation is very much greater than 59in (1,500mm) a year, putting pressure on Australia's meagre supplies of water.

°C
35
30
25
20
15

PORT LINCOLN — Region not mapped elsewhere

—— Evaporation 1500mm annual average

● Wine-producing area

swelled from 900 to 2,000, but even this was not enough to keep pace with the almost feverish planting of vines at the end of the 20th and beginning of 21st centuries. Many new labels have no bricks and mortar winery behind them. No worries: shipping grapes or grape must long distances from vineyard to corporate cellar is Australian tradition.

The produce of geographically quite distinct vineyards is often blended into a single wine, one of the many carefully segmented brands that have been so dear to the Australian international marketing plan. Although almost all the wineries in Tasmania and Queensland are relative minnows, crushing fewer than 100 tonnes of fruit each autumn, the commercial landscape is essentially dominated by five big wine companies – Hardys, Foster's, McGuigan Simeon, Pernod Ricard Pacific, and Casella – which between them account for 64% of the annual crush and 75% of exports. As the number of big retail outlets has shrunk worldwide, these companies have been trapped in an orgy of price cutting at home and abroad.

That said, there is a creeping sense of geography throughout the Australian wine business, and certainly among Australia's avid wine consumers – so much so that it has acquired its own term: regionality. This is well-timed, for the Australian wine map has been changing fast (as a comparison of this one with its predecessor reveals) and Australia has been devising its own answer to the controlled appellation system. Geographic Indications, inevitably called GIs, do not of course attempt to dictate anything other than a, sometimes hotly contested, boundary. There would be no point, though, if no one were interested.

The wine regions (like the wine drinkers) hug the southern coast of Australia, which can offer a combination of lowish temperatures and rainfall. **Queensland** is the exception; quietly developing its own increasingly dynamic wine industry, now even further north than the cooler, higher western slopes of the Great Dividing Range.

Much of **South Eastern Australia** (a GI used liberally for wine made from the blended produce of virtually anywhere other than Western Australia) has the Mediterranean-type climate in which the vine luxuriates. Melbourne is on the same latitude as

1:5,300,000

Km 0   50   100   150 Km

Miles 0   50   100 Miles

— · — · — State boundary

• Penola Notable wine town

HUNTER Geographical Indication (GI)

  Land 500-1000 metres

  Land above 1000 metres

342 Area mapped at larger scale on page shown

Western Australia map p. 339

Tasmania map p. 355

Córdoba in Spain. The Hunter Valley is on much the same latitude as Rabat, the capital of Morocco. Strong wines full of sugar but lacking acidity are what you would expect – and what Australia, for more than a century, was happy to produce, until strapping tonic wines fell out of favour and the country's wineries rapidly equipped themselves with refrigeration and switched to table wines. Nowadays the vine is increasingly colonizing new, cooler areas, including many that have never known viticulture before. Roughly half of all Australia's GIs qualify as cool-climate regions. Sauvignon Blanc, Pinot Noir, and Pinot Gris, varieties that suffer in the heat, are becoming commonplace.

With the noble exception of some ancient vines in Barossa and McLaren Vale, the average vine age in Australia is notably young. Plantings have tended to swing from whim to whim of fashion. For example, not a Chardonnay vine was known in South Australia in 1970, but in the 1980s and early 1990s it sometimes seemed as though little else was planted. In the mid-1990s the pendulum swung again, the red wine craze was officially recognized, and so much Shiraz and Cabernet Sauvignon was planted that in the early 21st century there was a Chardonnay shortage. This immediately spurred such a flurry of planting of white wine grapes that a glut of them is already forecast. Among white wine grapes, Semillon, Riesling, and Verdelho were all established Australian favourites long before Chardonnay was first planted, in New South Wales.

Australia's most planted variety, Shiraz, benefited from a complete rehabilitation in the 1990s. Previously scorned for its ubiquity, even at times denatured for use as base wine for cheap white, sparkling, and fortified wine, it was finally recognized as what Australia does best, in red wine at least. Margaret River and Coonawarra (see pages 340–41 and 350) may have a special way with Cabernet Sauvignon, but the nation had collectively abandoned its belief in the necessary superiority of things imported and French by the 1990s. Nowadays, even wineries with considerable history are dropping such Frenchified terms as Chateau.

The Australian wine industry has always been notable for its flexibility and in the early 21st century has embraced grape varieties from all over the world. Pinot Gris, Viognier, and Sangiovese are already commonplace, while growers scramble for (necessarily quarantined) cuttings of such exotica as Aglianico, Albariño, Fiano, Graciano, and Lagrein. Blends, usually of two often unusual varieties, are common.

Australia is now understandably proud of its own cultural identity, vibrant Asian-influenced cuisine, and wine ethos, complete with BYOs (bring your own), cardboard "casks" at the bottom end of the market, and the much-hyped show system with its medals and trophies for best of breed.

Australia was also the first major wine country to embrace screwcaps, for red wines as well as whites, spurred on initially by the much smaller New Zealand wine industry. Exporters may offer the choice of traditional cork or screwcap but the great majority of Australian producers, and the all-important show judges, are completely converted to the virtues of Stelvin, referring to it by the name of the dominant brand.

There could hardly be another image that encapsulates so much of what Sydney has to offer today: the Harbour Bridge in the background and the Opera House with its typically innovative Bennelong restaurant offering superlative food and wine. Bennelong was the first native Australian to fraternize with the European settlers and lived on this very site.

◀ Two of Queensland's most impressive wines, along with an example from the quite staggeringly successful [yellow tail] range for which no specific wine region is cited. In 2004, one of its stablemates even won the coveted Jimmy Watson Trophy for Australia's best young red.

Western Australia

West to east is the way this atlas travels. "WA" is our landfall; not the first in importance of Australia's wine regions, with less than 5% of the country's wine output, but in quality terms very near the top, with a distinctive lightness of touch combined with ripeness of fruit – an unusual combination in Australia. Margaret River, its single most important region, is mapped overleaf.

The first colonists of Western Australia were almost as quick to start winemaking as those of New South Wales. The Swan Valley, just upstream from the state capital, Perth, saw its first vintage in 1834. From the searing heat of the summer, with dry winds from the interior keeping temperatures close to 100°F (38°C) for weeks, the early vintners realized that their forte for many decades would be dessert wines.

It was however an experimental lot of dry white wine, made from Chenin Blanc in 1937, that put Western Australia on the nation's wine map. Houghton's White Burgundy (renamed Houghton's White Classic for export markets sensitive about the appropriation of European place names) became an Australian staple even in the east of the continent, recognized by all as a consistent bargain. Originally it was a huge golden wine of intense flavour. It has since been tamed to be soft yet lively, dry yet faintly honeyed in character; a blend of Chenin Blanc with all manner of other grapes including Muscadelle, Semillon, Verdelho, and (recently) Chardonnay that has remained year after year Australia's best-selling dry white. The extraordinary bonus for such a keenly priced wine is that for many years it has been even more delicious after six to eight years in bottle.

It is hard to imagine primitive techniques producing a better white wine from so hot a region. Perhaps this is why it took Western Australia another 30 years to realize what potential lay in the cooler parts of this vast, almost empty, state. When the move to cool-climate areas began in the late 1960s, Western Australia had plenty to offer. It still has. Perth, around which is still clustered a small warm-climate wine industry, has blistering summers, but southwards down the coast the influence of Antarctic currents and onshore westerlies is felt in much more temperate conditions.

The **Great Southern** region, first staked out at Mount Barker in the 1960s and progressively extended, offers some of the coolest, wettest terrain in Australia with some grapes still on the vine well into May. Plantagenet was the pre-eminent pioneer but the region has since been invaded by an army of small growers, many of whom rely on one of several sizeable contract winemaking operations here. Unusually for Australia, Great Southern has been divided into subregions: Albany, Denmark, Frankland River, Mount Barker, and Porongurup.

The most obvious strengths of Mount Barker (not to be confused with the Mount Barker of

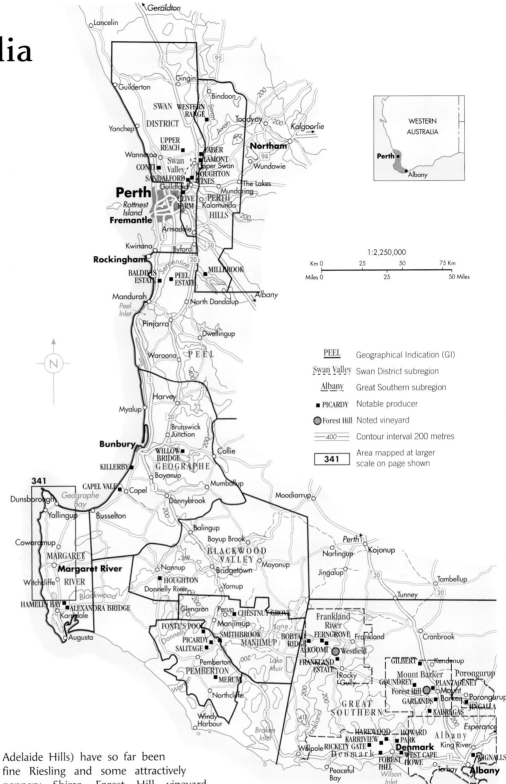

Adelaide Hills) have so far been fine Riesling and some attractively peppery Shiraz. Forest Hill vineyard, planted in 1966, recently revived, and supplying the winery of the same name in Denmark, qualifies as one of the Western Australian wine industry's historic landmarks. Goundrey, via a rapid series of acquisitions, is now part of Constellation.

Denmark on the coast is even wetter but often warmer. The cluster of small vineyards in this subregion grows early-maturing varieties in the main; most promising are Pinot Noir and Chardonnay although Merlot may work too. The celebrated winemaker John Wade and the substantial Howard Park operation are both based here.

Albany is the region's principal population centre, and Western Australia's first European settlement. Shiraz and Pinot Noir both seem at home here. Porongurup boasts a string of vineyards producing fine Riesling and Pinot Noir. But these are early days.

Boom-time arrived at the Frankland River in the late 1990s, largely driven by tax incentives. This subregion, inland and west of Mount Barker, now has Great Southern's greatest concentration of vineyards (and a 1,000-acre/400-ha olive estate), though few wineries. The

Margaret River

Australia has few landscapes as green or forests as splendid as the soaring karri and jarrah woods of Western Australia's most famous wine region, dotted with brilliantly coloured birds and lolloping kangaroos. Surf reliably laps the rocky coastline and the introduction of vineyards surely tilted the whole package slap-bang into paradise. Tourists seem to agree.

The first wines emerged in the early 1970s, from Vasse Felix followed by Moss Wood and then Cullen – all of them, true to Australian wine history form, created by doctors. Critics immediately recognized a quite remarkable quality in the wines, particularly in the Cabernets. Sandalford, Houghton's neighbour and rival in the Swan Valley, rapidly moved in with a large plantation. Robert Mondavi of California became enthused and encouraged Denis Horgan to develop the ambitious Leeuwin Estate, which rapidly became as famous for its creamily authoritative Chardonnay as for its annual, world-class outdoor concerts.

Today there are more than 100 producers and another 60 grape growers, on wildly varying soils, of which the infertile red loams are most prized. If Margaret River has a clima-tological problem it is that, thanks to the influence of that beautiful Indian Ocean, winters are so mild that vines may struggle to achieve useful, fortifying dormancy. Spring can be so windy as to affect flowering and reduce the crop, one of the reasons for the concentra-tion of flavour in wines from the heartland of Margaret River. Summers are dry and warm, tempered by the onshore wind known as the Fremantle Doctor. Grapes may be picked as early as February.

The Cabernet heartland of the Willyabrup Valley is particularly heavily planted and the vine now extends south past the Margaret River itself all the way to the south coast, where the dominant influence is Antarctica rather than the Indian Ocean. This is classic white wine country although Suckfizzle, McHenry Hohnen, and others have demonstrated that fine reds can also be produced in the southern half of this map.

Plantings are also increasing north of Willyabrup, where it is milder, and, more con-troversially, inland in an area known as Jindong, where Evans & Tate have built an extensive and ambitious winery. Margaret River has seen more than its fair share of speculative invest-ment in recent years and the era of enthusiastic hobbyists seems very distant.

Margaret River's reputation has been built on Cabernet Sauvignon. It joins such other west coast wine regions as Bordeaux, Bolgheri, Napa Valley, and the Limestone Coast (see p.349) in its propensity to turn the rays of the setting sun into some of the most satisfying, and age-worthy, red wine in the world. There is both finesse and ripeness in Margaret River's

relatively youthful Ferngrove is by far the biggest operation; Alkoomi has an established reputation for Sauvignon Blanc (and olive oil). Frankland Estate's strength is Riesling and a Bordeaux blend known as Olmo's Reward in recognition of the California professor who first suggested back in the 1950s that the area would be suitable for viticulture. The Westfield vineyard has long provided fruit for Houghton's superlative red blend named after Jack Mann, even if, as so often, Great Southern is not acknowledged on the label.

Vines are going into all manner of areas between here and Margaret River on the Indian Ocean coast. Most significant are the plantings at Manjimup and Pemberton. **Manjimup** is certainly warmer, further from the cooling influence of Antarctic currents on the coast, and can make some fine Verdelho at Chestnut Grove. Land even further inland around Perup is also being planted. In **Pemberton** producers such as Picardy and Salitage are concentrating on Burgundy varieties with some fine results, whereas Smithbrook has replaced its Pinot Noir with Merlot.

The most important sector of the expanded **Geographe** region is the coastal strip between

The Southern Ocean, seen here pounding Isthmus Bay south of Albany, brings currents straight from Antarctica and cooling influences on the southern stretches of Great Southern, responsible for the raciness of the Plantaganet Riesling whose label appears below.

Bunbury and Busselton, which is dominated by Capel Vale. As in Margaret River, the climate is thoroughly influenced by the Indian Ocean, but the soils here are rather more fertile, notably the dusty grey soil known as Tuart Sands. The inland area around Donnybrook with its cool nights has consider-able potential while Willow Bridge to the north has shown that a wide range of grape varieties can thrive here. **Blackwood Valley** is essentially the land between Geographe and Manjimup but it suffers from a shortage of non-saline irrigation water; availability of water is a brake on expansion in this corner of Australia. Western Australia's underground water is naturally high in salt (the land has been vigorously cleared) and a dam is a pre-requisite for irrigation.

◀ The range of grape varieties represented in these three very fine wines shows just how varied the mesoclimates in the southwestern corner of Western Australia are. The ripening demands of the varieties in the Jack Mann Bordeaux blend are high, while the Pinot Noir has almost Burgundian delicacy.

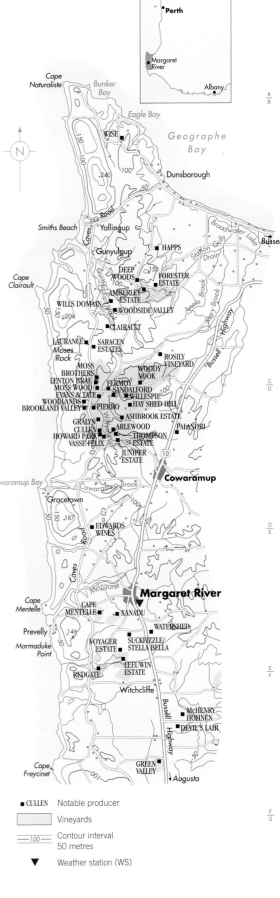

most admired Cabernets, although most producers also make a Bordeaux blend, usually Cabernet/Merlot (of which Cullen is the prime exponent).

The Margaret River region's obvious affinity with Cabernet has not hindered plantings of Shiraz, which is almost as important and typically reaches an appetizing halfway house of ripeness between Barossa heft and white pepper. Chardonnay shines here too, not just at Leeuwin Estate but notably at Pierro, Moss Wood, and others. The region has also established a national if not international reputation for its very own vibrant, tropical fruit-flavoured blend of Semillon and Sauvignon Blanc. The range of grape varieties planted and taken seriously has been expanding as rapidly in Margaret River as elsewhere.

The inhabitants of Perth used to say that their nearest good out-of-town restaurants were in Singapore. Not any more, thanks to the likes of Leeuwin Estate, which has played a vital role in making Margaret River the tourist draw it is today.

1:350,000

Km 0   5   10 Km

Miles 0   5 Miles

MARGARET RIVER: MARGARET RIVER ▼

Latitude / Altitude of WS **33.57° / 295ft (90m)**

Mean January temp at WS **68.6°F (20.4°C)**

Annual rainfall at WS **45in (1,150mm)**

Harvest month rainfall at WS **March: 1in (25.4mm)**

Chief viticultural hazards **Wind, birds**

Principal grapes **Cabernet Sauvignon, Shiraz, Chardonnay, Semillon, Sauvignon Blanc**

■ CULLEN   Notable producer

⬚   Vineyards

━100━   Contour interval 50 metres

▼   Weather station (WS)

◀ Margaret River is such an established, if small, fine wine region that it even has its own aristocracy, whose labels appear here. The three on the far left were founded by doctors with a hunch and a strong thirst.

South Australia: Barossa Valley

South Australia is to Australia what California is to the USA: the wine state. It crushes an increasing proportion, already almost half, of every vintage and houses all the most important wine and vine research organizations. Adelaide, the state capital, is fittingly surrounded by vineyards. The landscape on the 35-mile (55-km) drive northeast to South Australia's answer to the Napa Valley, Barossa Valley, is filled with vines. Founded by German-speaking immigrants from Silesia in what is now Poland, much in the Barossa Valley, including a sense of community and an appetite for hard work and Wurst, is still Germanic to this day.

Barossa is Australia's biggest quality wine district. It follows the North Para River for almost 20 closely planted miles (nearly 30km), and spreads eastwards into the next valley, Eden Valley (see overleaf), from the 750ft (230m) altitude of Lyndoch to 1,800ft (550m) in the east Barossa Ranges. The Barossa Zone encompasses these two contiguous wine regions, so a wine labelled just "Barossa" may be made from a blend of Eden Valley and Barossa Valley grapes.

Barossa summers are hot and dry, and irrigated vines need to be supplied with enough water to compensate for a fierce evaporation rate – an increasingly difficult feat. Unirrigated bushvines were traditionally the norm and, partly thanks to a malaise in the 1970s and early 1980s when the Australian wine industry neglected Barossa's old Shiraz vines for fashionable Cabernet, some of them date back to the 19th century. Because there is a stringently imposed quarantine, South Australia is yet to be invaded by phylloxera, so ungrafted vines are planted directly into the soil, many of them cuttings from older vines.

Such vines can produce the most concentrated form of what has become one of the world's most distinctive wine styles, Barossa Shiraz. Rich and chocolaty, spicy and never shy, these wines can range from intriguing essences to unctuously alcoholic elixirs. Grapes ripen fast under the blistering sun, so fast that acidity often plummets before the grapes are picked, although there is an increasing

sensibility about this; some producers are now deliberately picking grapes earlier for fresher aromas and more natural acidity. Some Barossa winemakers add tannins as well as acid, however, so the typical Barossa Shiraz is a demanding mouthful, especially in youth. Instead of the long post-fermentation maceration

that Bordeaux producers give their wines while extracting colour and tannins, Barossa reds are typically encouraged to finish their fermentation in American oak barrels, imbuing them with a heady sweetness and smoothness. Although here again, the Australian winemaker's constant quest for evolution can be

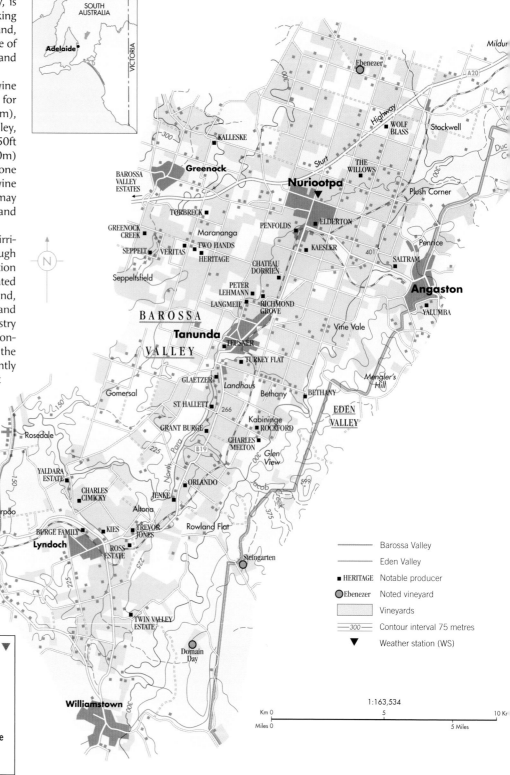

BAROSSA VALLEY: NURIOOTPA ▼

Latitude / Altitude of WS **34.29° / 899ft (274m)**

Mean January temp at WS **70°F (21.1°C)**

Annual rainfall at WS **20in (501mm)**

Harvest month rainfall at WS **March: 1in (25.4mm)**

Chief viticultural hazard **Drought**

Principal grapes **Shiraz, Cabernet Sauvignon, Grenache Noir, Semillon, Chardonnay**

Barossa Valley
Eden Valley
■ HERITAGE Notable producer
⊙ Ebenezer Noted vineyard
Vineyards
═══300═══ Contour interval 75 metres
▼ Weather station (WS)

1:163,534

Km 0 ... 5 ... 10 Kr
Miles 0 ... 5 Miles

seen in the increasing use of French oak for Barossa Valley's super-ripe fruit. Another current winemaking fashion, apparent throughout Australia but especially prevalent here, is to co-ferment Shiraz with Viognier grapes, for added perfume and stability of colour.

In sheer volume Barossa is dominated by the large subsidiaries of even larger global corporations. Beer company Foster's for example owns Penfolds (which blends its flagship Grange here from wines produced all over South Australia), Wolf Blass, and a host of other brands. French pastis makers Pernod Ricard own the old Orlando, whose most famous brand by far is Jacob's Creek, named after a trickle near Rowland Flat. The biggest family-owned company, Yalumba, is based in Angaston on the border between Barossa and Eden Valleys, but there is a host of others, of varying sizes. These range from Peter Lehmann, who virtually rescued the reputation of old-vine Barossa Shiraz single-handedly in the late 1980s (but whose company was eventually taken over by Donald Hess of Switzerland in 2003), down to a host of ambitious young winemakers who may produce only a few hundred cases a year from bought-in grapes, and then only on their days off from working for the big companies.

There are old Grenache vines too (capable of even higher alcohols) and old Mourvèdre, for long called Mataro. "GSM" blends of both grapes with the ubiquitous Shiraz are popular. Semillon, some of it Barossa's very own pink-skinned clone, is more common than Chardonnay and can produce stunningly rich white wines. Cabernet Sauvignon can shine when planted on the most favoured dark grey-brown soils but Shiraz is more dependable, summer in and summer out, on the clay and limestone soils of the valley.

Some of the most admired Shirazes come from around Ebenezer in the northeast of the valley, where ancient stocks of dry-farmed Shiraz can yield wines of real complexity. However, such a high proportion of vines are owned by growers rather than winemakers, that there is a particularly delicate tension between grape prices and quality. And here it is the ability of producers to get their hands on the produce of the oldest, least greedily tended vine stocks that can be more important than the small geographical distinctions between different parts of the valley. Most of these ancient vines have been farmed all their lives by the same family, and many are hidden from view of the thousands of tourists who flood the valley every week.

▼ Some of the finest wines made in the Barossa are represented below, even if the production of Grange returned from Nuriootpa to Magill on the outskirts of Adelaide in 2001, the only vintage to be composed entirely of Barossa Valley fruit.

Seriously ancient Shiraz vines such as these at St Hallett are a Barossa speciality – in fact there are probably more centenarians here than anywhere else in the world. Their concentrated produce is sought by a swelling roster of ambitious young and not-so-young winemakers.

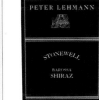

Eden Valley

The Eden Valley is in pretty, higher country than the Barossa Valley floor. Its vineyards are scattered among rocky hills, dusty lanes, and eucalyptus groves. Historically, though, it is an eastern extension of the Barossa Valley. Captain Joseph Gilbert established the Pewsey Vale vineyard as early as 1847; the site now belongs to Yalumba of Angaston, the family company that has played such a large part in developing Eden Valley's potential for Riesling.

When modern times called for table wines rather than the fortified dessert wines (of which Yalumba still has impressive museum stocks, despite having sold off its fortified wine business in 1993), it was the Rhine Riesling, strangely enough, that Barossa did best. With the Silesian settlers came a fondness for the grape, and growers found that the higher they went into the hills to the east the finer and more crisply fruity the wine became. In the early 1960s Yalumba moved the focus of its Riesling production from the warmer Barossa Valley to the Eden Valley, and Colin Gramp (whose family owned Orlando until 1971) planted a patch of schistous hilltop that a sheep would scarcely pause on, called it Steingarten, and gave Australian Riesling a new dimension. Today, the produce of this vineyard adds lustre to the Jacob's Creek range and has certainly shown ageing ability.

One notable relatively new Eden Valley Riesling is Mesh, a joint venture between Yalumba and Jeffrey Grosset, Australia's king of Riesling from South Australia's other Riesling redoubt, Clare Valley. The aim with this bottling, screwcapped from the start, is to present Eden Valley Riesling characteristics in powerful but early-maturing form. Eden Valley Riesling

at its best has a floral, sometimes mineral, top note to it when young. Like the Clare Valley Riesling with which it is inevitably compared, it becomes increasingly toasty after time in the bottle. According to Grosset, Eden Valley Riesling tends towards grapefruit whereas Clare Valley Riesling is characterized more by lime.

Eden Valley offers more than Riesling, however, particularly at lower altitudes. Indeed Shiraz is the region's leading grape and Henschke grows some of Australia's very best examples: Mount Edelstone, well up in the hills, and above all from century-old vines in the (actually rather flat) Hill of Grace vineyard south of Moculta. Chardonnay grown here can also be very fine, as Mountadam was one of the first to demonstrate in the **High Eden** subregion in the south of the valley. Eden Valley is one of Australia's very rare regions to have established any sort of reputation for Merlot, chiefly thanks to Irvine Wines.

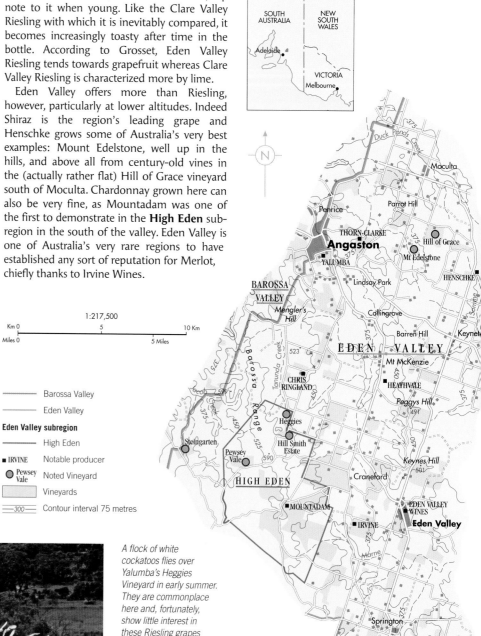

1:217,500

| Km 0 | | 5 | | 10 Km |
| Miles 0 | | | 5 Miles | |

—————— Barossa Valley
—————— Eden Valley
Eden Valley subregion
—————— High Eden
■ IRVINE Notable producer
⬤ Pewsey Vale Noted Vineyard
▢ Vineyards
═300═ Contour interval 75 metres

A flock of white cockatoos flies over Yalumba's Heggies Vineyard in early summer. They are commonplace here and, fortunately, show little interest in these Riesling grapes even when fully ripe.

▼ Although Rieslings such as those on the left are some of Eden Valley's most characteristic wines, the valley also produces one of Australia's most haunting Shirazes from Henschke's Hill of Grace vineyard planted in the 1860s. Irvine's is one of Australia's very few Merlots with a reputation.

Clare Valley

Riesling is even better entrenched in the prettily pastoral Clare Valley, well north of the Barossa's northernmost limit, than in the Eden Valley but Clare has the unique distinction of making world-class Shiraz and Cabernet as well as one of Riesling's great archetypes.

Clare Valley is in fact a series of narrow, mainly north–south valleys on an elevated plateau with very different soil types in each. In the southern heartland of the region between Watervale and Auburn, considered classic Riesling country, is some of the famous limestone-based terra rossa (see p.350), while a few miles north around Polish Hill the rocks are much softer and red loam overlays clay soils. The northern, more open part of the Clare Valley is influenced by westerlies blowing in from the Spencer Gulf, whereas the southern part, from Watervale south, is subject to cooler breezes from Gulf St Vincent. Clare is only about a third of the size of Barossa Valley but with its notably higher altitude has a more extreme climate. The particularly cool nights help to preserve acidity; in many vintages routine acid adjustments are unnecessary.

There is keen rivalry between the winemakers of Clare Valley and those in the much more visited and visible Barossa Valley. Its history is as long as that of Barossa – vines were first planted by John Horrocks from England in 1840 and he was soon followed by Lutheran Silesians escaping persecution (hence Polish Hill).

Clare is isolated, and feels like it. Local wine producers are proud to be distant from the influence of fashion and big company politics. Only Leasingham, part of Hardys and therefore owned by Constellation, and Annie's Lane, now controlled by Foster's, have any connection with large corporations. This is farming country in the hands of small farmers in the main who form an unusually cohesive group of wine producers. They were the first in Australia to agree to move to screwcaps in an effort to preserve the particular steely purity of their Rieslings.

In the hands of literally dozens of Riesling producers as capable as Grosset, Kilikanoon, Tim Knappstein (TK Wines), Leasingham, and Petaluma (owner of Knappstein Wines), Clare Riesling has established itself as Australia's most distinctive: firm and dry, sometimes almost austere in youth, but usually with a rich undertow of lime that can mature to toastiness after years in bottle. These are the wines for which Australia's famous fusion food has surely been designed.

Great, plummy reds with particularly good acidity and structure are also made, provoking discussion as to whether Shiraz or Cabernet is Clare's most eloquent dark expression. Particularly smooth-talking Cabernets and Shirazes come from Jim Barry, Grosset, Kilikanoon, Leasingham, and Skillogalee, while the reds of pioneer Wendouree continue to be positively and distinctively chewable.

The slate in Grosset's Polish Hill vineyard recalls the Mosel Valley in Germany, and may help to explain why the Rieslings grown here, as in the Mosel, need so much time to develop in bottle.

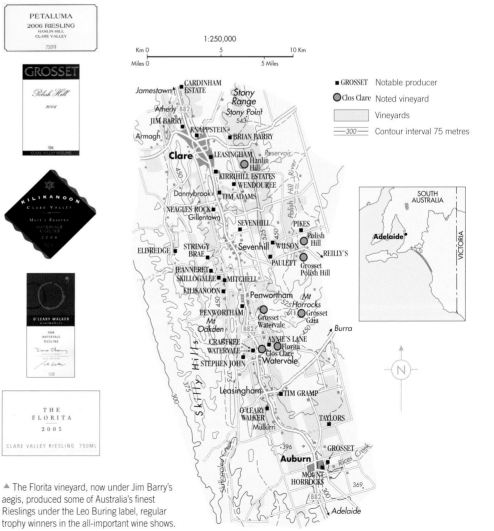

▲ The Florita vineyard, now under Jim Barry's aegis, produced some of Australia's finest Rieslings under the Leo Buring label, regular trophy winners in the all-important wine shows.

McLaren Vale and Beyond

The Fleurieu Zone, named after the Fleurieu Peninsula, points southwest from Australia's wine city, Adelaide, through McLaren Vale and Southern Fleurieu to Kangaroo Island, which has a growing reputation for tourism and gastronomy. It also extends southeast to include Langhorne Creek and Currency Creek (see map on p.336). As the world heats up we can expect to see more wine operations sprouting in both **Kangaroo Island**, where French flying winemaker Jacques Lurton is the most renowned producer, and **Southern Fleurieu**, which has attracted ex-Petaluma luminary Brian Croser.

But for the moment by far the most prominent and historic wine region in the Fleurieu Zone is **McLaren Vale**, so popular with commuters to Adelaide that the motorway here is one-way and reverses direction in the middle of the day. John Reynell, who gave his name to Chateau Reynella, planted South Australia's first vines in 1838, and Mclaren Vale can still boast many old vines, some more than 100 years old. For most of the intervening decades, Reynella claret and fortified wines were respected names, and the original underground cellar that Reynell built is one of the historic landmarks of Australian wine. Today, it is the headquarters of the almost equally ancient firm of Thomas Hardy & Sons (now part of the world's largest wine company Constellation) along with the Tintara winery bought by the original Thomas Hardy in 1876. Ryecroft (established in 1888) and the Amery vineyards (acquired by the Kay brothers in 1890) are also located on the loam-covered limestone and ironstone ridges that dominate the north of the region. Soil types vary enormously throughout McLaren Vale, as does wine quality and style.

Around Blewitt Springs, deep sandy soils over clay can yield particularly good Grenache. Kangarilla to the east produces more elegant, tarter Shiraz than the McLaren Vale norm. The area north of the township of McLaren Vale has some of the thinnest topsoil, resulting in low yields and intense flavours. Willunga, lying to the south of the town, yields relatively late ripening fruit thanks to a strong marine influence.

Natural meteorological conditions could hardly be better for the vine than in this coastal zone, a narrow band between the heights of Mount Lofty Ranges and the temperate sea. There is a long warm growing season, good air drainage to prevent frosts, and about 20% of vineyards survive without the irrigation water that is in increasingly short supply. The ocean supplies some cooling influence, particularly in the form of afternoon breezes, which help to retain acidity. Some vineyards even have a history of growing fine Sauvignon Blanc, thanks to a particularly low-yielding clone.

There is a confidence in McLaren Vale's glossily seductive reds, with old-vine Grenache, Shiraz, Cabernet Sauvignon, and more recently Merlot performing with brio. Chapel Hill, d'Arenberg, Pirramimma, Tatachilla, Wirra Wirra, and Woodstock all make good examples. And Coriole and Kangarilla Road demonstrated quite some time ago that the palette of varieties could be widened to include Sangiovese and Zinfandel respectively. At least 80 wineries are based in McLaren Vale although more than half the fruit grown here is plundered by others – some located as far afield as the Hunter Valley – to add plump ballast to blends. McLaren Vale's Shiraz is said to contribute a mocha and warm-earth character.

If the rolling countryside of McLaren Vale has a blight it is in the unlovely form of the double, and occasionally even triple, cordon system of vine training adopted by the greedier growers and all too visible on the fertile flat land. Recent plantings, many of which are in the flat southeastern sector of the region (although some nudge up into the Sellicks foothills that overlook the coast), have avoided this blot on the landscape. Grapes here tend to ripen faster than the norm and often have a herbal note. Harvesting begins in February and may continue well into May for some of the classic Grenache and Mourvèdre vines.

Langhorne Creek, it could be argued, is South Australian wine's big secret. Less than a fifth of the wine made here is sold with the region's name on the label even though it is as productive as McLaren Vale. Most wine disappears into the blends put together by the big companies, all of which have built large wineries here to take advantage of the region's

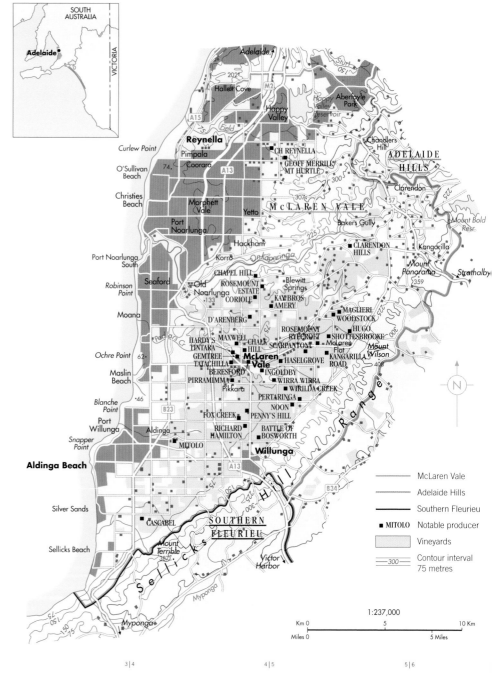

soft, gentle, mouth-filling Shiraz and, especially, Cabernet fruit. Originally this fertile bed of deep alluvium was irrigated by deliberate late-winter flooding from the diverted Bremer and Angas rivers, an unreliable water supply that limited expansion. It has only been since the early 1990s, when licences were granted to transport irrigation water from Lake Alexandrina at the mouth of the mighty Murray River, that Langhorne Creek has seen rapid development.

The older vines tend to be close to the river-banks. They include the famous Metala vineyard owned by the Adams family, of Brothers in Arms, since 1891 and those planted by Frank Potts at Bleasdale once he had felled

the titanic red gums growing by the Bremer River. But ambitious new plantings such as those of Step Road and Angas Vineyards pipe water to their hi-tech irrigation systems via a complex network of ditches on the pancake flat land here.

The so-called Lake Doctor, a reliable after-noon breeze off the lake, slows ripening here so that grapes are typically picked two weeks later than those of McLaren Vale.

Currency Creek to the immediate west also depends crucially on irrigation but is so far the domain of small, relatively low-profile wineries. It is slightly warmer than Langhorne Creek but even more maritime.

Frank Potts, pictured below, sailed on HMS Victory and eventually built the original Bleasdale winery which, inside as well as out, has hardly changed since – except that the fortified wines that once constituted the entire production now account for about 1%. Only Yalumba has been in the same family for longer, and Potts' great-great-grandson and team offer some of Australia's best wines.

▼ Although the minuscule Noon winery is in McLaren Vale, the fruit for the Cabernet Reserve has long come from some particularly treasured blocks in the Borrett Family vineyard in Langhorne Creek. Mitolo is a relatively new operation whose wines are made by Ben Glaetzer of Barossa Valley, while the two all-Langhorne Creek labels are on the right.

Adelaide Hills

When Adelaide warms up in the summer there is always somewhere nearby to cool off: the Mount Lofty Ranges just east of the city. Clouds from the west collect here to give a climate cool enough for very different wines. The southern tip of the **Adelaide Hills** region may skirt the northeastern boundary of McLaren Vale but they are worlds apart. Adelaide Hills was the first Australian region to establish a reputation for reliably citrus-fresh Sauvignon Blanc. The 1,300ft (400m) contour line provides the appellation's boundary except to the north. At altitudes above this, grey mist is common, as is spring frost, and chilly nights, even in summer. Rainfall is relatively high (see the key facts panel below) but concentrated in winter. Generalizations are difficult, however, about a wine region that stretches 50 miles (80km) from northeast to southwest.

The **Piccadilly Valley** on Mount Lofty was originally staked out in the 1970s by Brian Croser, founder of Petaluma, as a defiantly cool area for Chardonnay vines, then a novelty in Australia. Today the wooded hills east of Adelaide are being planted at a lick to supply the needs of corporations calling for cool-climate blending ingredients. But only a handful of individuals have been permitted to build wineries in what is effectively an eastern suburb of the city.

Only the southwestern corner of the Adelaide Hills is mapped in detail here. To the north, vineyards around Gumeracha are warm enough to ripen Cabernet Sauvignon, and some particularly Rhône-like Shiraz comes from Mount Barker, southeast of Stirling. Indeed, even though the dominant characteristic of Adelaide Hills wine is sleek acidity, almost half of all the grapes planted in the region are dark-skinned. Cabernet and, particularly, Merlot are important varieties here, although not widely grown, while Pinot Noir is even more important, as producers such as Jeffrey Grosset, Tim Knappstein (TK Wines), Henschke, Nepenthe, and Leabrook Estate have shown.

The region is cool enough to provide sparkling wine producers with their raw material, and even the Chardonnays, common ingredients in some of Australia's more admired blends, can be Sauvignon-like with their brisk nectarine flavours and lissom build. Producers such as Nepenthe and The Lane have been experimenting with a wide range of such aromatic varieties as Viognier and Pinot Gris and have met with considerable success. Riesling clearly thrives here too, although South Australia is not short of Riesling.

Piccadilly Valley and **Lenswood** are the only two official Adelaide Hills subregions to date but many locals consider that Birdwood, Charleston, Echunga, Hahndorf, Kuitpo, Macclesfield, Mount Barker, and Paracombe all have discernible and distinctive characteristics.

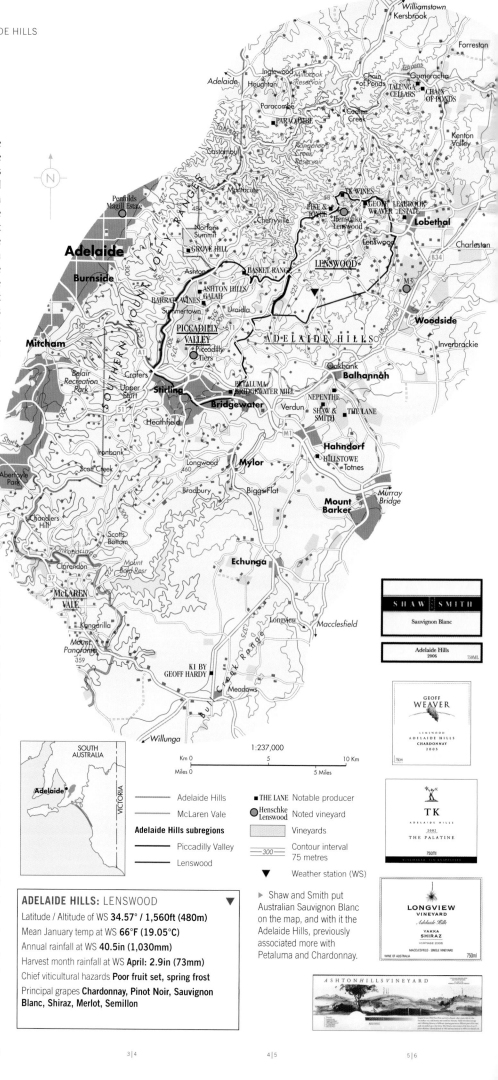

ADELAIDE HILLS: LENSWOOD ▼

Latitude / Altitude of WS **34.57° / 1,560ft (480m)**

Mean January temp at WS **66°F (19.05°C)**

Annual rainfall at WS **40.5in (1,030mm)**

Harvest month rainfall at WS **April: 2.9in (73mm)**

Chief viticultural hazards **Poor fruit set, spring frost**

Principal grapes **Chardonnay, Pinot Noir, Sauvignon Blanc, Shiraz, Merlot, Semillon**

Adelaide Hills
McLaren Vale
Adelaide Hills subregions
Piccadilly Valley
Lenswood

■ THE LANE Notable producer
● Henschke Lenswood Noted vineyard
Vineyards
300 Contour interval 75 metres
▼ Weather station (WS)

▶ Shaw and Smith put Australian Sauvignon Blanc on the map, and with it the Adelaide Hills, previously associated more with Petaluma and Chardonnay.

Limestone Coast

There can be little doubt about what growers in this southeastern corner of South Australia are most proud of: limestone. The remains of ancient seabeds underpinning the famous terra rossa soils is the most distinctive feature of the wine regions that together make up this wine zone. The official regions within the geometrically drawn **Limestone Coast** are Coonawarra (mapped overleaf), Padthaway, Mount Benson, Wrattonbully, and Robe, but Bordertown and Mount Gambier are distinct vine-growing areas which have yet to seek individual recognition.

Of all the two dozen wine zones delineated by Australian wine officialdom, Limestone Coast is the one most likely to be seen on wine labels – perhaps because of its evocative name, perhaps because with the exception of Coonawarra its constituents' names lack magic, and perhaps mainly because it usefully allows blending between them.

Padthaway was the first limestone-rich alternative to Coonawarra to be scouted out in this remote corner of Australia's wine state. While the soils were not dissimilar to Coonawarra's, the climate was usefully warmer, although it took the big companies that have dominated vineyard ownership here some time to work out what the region was best at, and indeed what to call it. Most of the fruit grown here is vinified far from the vineyards but in 1998 Hardys built the Stonehaven winery just off the highway – quite a signal of faith in the region. Initially irrigated, it produced serviceable Chardonnay, Cabernet, Shiraz, and Riesling for blends in even more serviceable quantity, usually blended with fruit from other regions.

Wrattonbully just north of Coonawarra is cooler and more homogeneous than Padthaway and may yet prove even more interesting – provided the temptation to over-irrigate is resisted – although it has less than half the vineyard area of Coonawarra and very much less than the more established Padthaway. Some Shiraz from deliberately devigorated vines has shown particular promise.

A few plantings around Mount Gambier have proved that this southern outpost is too cool to ripen Bordeaux grapes but shows potential for Pinot Noir.

There are several extensive vineyards, the warmest of Limestone Coast, just west of Bordertown, to the northeast of Padthaway, and at Elgin near the coast, due west of Coonawarra, as well as scattered plantings at Mundulla and Lucindale. But perhaps the most promising new

wine country is on younger limestone on the west coast south of Cape Jaffa. **Mount Benson** has almost a score of individual growers, while **Robe**, the remarkably similar region to the south, has been virtually colonized by Foster's. Wine made from fruit grown right on the coast here is much juicier, if less concentrated, than the sinewy ferments of Coonawarra, although admittedly the average vine age is much lower. Soils are just the sort of gentle, infertile slopes beloved by the vine. Sea breezes cool the vineyards almost constantly although they can be dangerously salty this close to the sea. At least the underground water table is free of salinity, and the prospects, give or take a frost or two, are good for both red and white wines.

Biodynamic preparations 502–507 (pre-prepared yarrow, chamomile, nettle, oak bark, dandelion, and valerian) are added to the compost at Cape Jaffa in Mount Benson.

▼ Limestone Coast is so new that it has been developed by outsiders such as (left to right) Chapoutier of the Rhône Valley, Kreglinger of Belgium, the Fowlers of the Hunter Valley, and a triumvirate including the Bollinger and Lynch-Bages families.

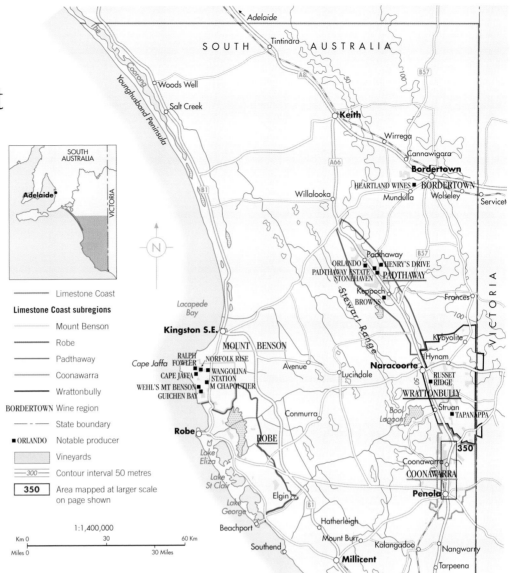

Limestone Coast
Limestone Coast subregions
Mount Benson
Robe
Padthaway
Coonawarra
Wrattonbully
BORDERTOWN — Wine region
State boundary
■ORLANDO — Notable producer
Vineyards
300 — Contour interval 50 metres
350 — Area mapped at larger scale on page shown

1:1,400,000
Km 0 — 30 — 60 Km
Miles 0 — 30 Miles

1|2   2|3   3|4

Coonawarra

The story of Coonawarra is to a large extent the story of terra rossa. As far back as the 1860s early settlers became aware of a very odd patch of ground 250 miles (400km) south of Adelaide and its essentially Mediterranean climate. Just north of the village of Penola, a long, narrow rectangle, only 9 miles by less than one (15 by 1.5km), of completely level soil is distinctively red in colour and crumbly to touch. A mere 18in (45cm) down, the red soil changes to pure free-draining limestone and, only 6ft (2m) below, there is a constant table of relatively pure water.

No land could be better designed for fruit growing. The entrepreneur John Riddoch started the Penola Fruit Colony and by 1900 the area, under the name of Coonawarra, was producing large quantities of an unfamiliar kind of wine, largely Shiraz, but brisk and fruity with moderate alcohol: in fact, not at all unlike Bordeaux.

This great resource, an Australian vineyard producing wines with a structure quite different from most, was for a long time appreciated by very few. Only with the table wine boom in the 1960s was its potential fully realized and the big names of the wine industry began to move in. Wynns is by far the biggest single winemaking landowner, although its owner

Machines are inevitable in Coonawarra with its acute labour shortage but they have done little for the quality or reputation of its wines. At one stage "minimal pruning", leaving the vines like a thicket, was encouraged to counter this problem.

Foster's controls a good half of all the vineyard through Penfolds, Lindemans, and Jamiesons Run as well. Partly because of this, considerable amounts of Coonawarra fruit end up in wines blended and bottled many miles away. Producers such as Balnaves, Bowen, Hollick, Katnook, Leconfield, Majella, Parker, Penley, Petaluma, Rymill, and Zema on the other hand offer something much closer to the estate model.

Shiraz was the original Coonawarra speciality but since Mildara demonstrated in the early 1960s that conditions were just as close to ideal for Cabernet Sauvignon, Coonawarra Cabernet has been one of Australia's remarkably few touchstone combinations of variety and place. And since almost six vines in every 10 in Coonawarra are Cabernet Sauvignon, the fortunes of Coonawarra have tended to rise and fall with the popularity of Australian Cabernet.

Coonawarra's soil was not the only reason for this marriage apparently made in heaven. The area is considerably further south, hence cooler, than any other South Australian wine region, and only 50 miles (80km) from an exposed coast, washed by the Antarctic currents and fanned by westerlies all summer. Frost is a problem in spring and rain at vintage time – enough to make a French grower quite nostalgic. Indeed Coonawarra is cooler than Bordeaux and sprinkler irrigation is more likely to be used to counter the threat of frost than to swell yields, which have declined since a spurt in the 1980s caused by the high proportion of productive new vines. If the will is there, vigour can be fine-tuned on terra rossa, unlike the darker and naturally damper rendzinas to the west.

Coonawarra, limited by the extent of its eccentric soil (itself a matter of controversy), has another problem: its isolation. The population is sparse to say the least. Penola is not much more than a hamlet. Labour is a scarce resource. This means that many vines are pruned, or at least pre-pruned, and picked mechanically, and the region can all too easily seem cold and inhuman, although there are more than 20 cellar door sales outlets valiantly aimed at such tourists as make it this far south – quite a feat considering that there are only 16 working wineries and a 17th under construction in the region at the time of writing.

COONAWARRA: COONAWARRA ▼

Latitude / Altitude of WS **37.17° / 164ft (50m)**

Mean January temp at WS **65.9°F (18.9°C)**

Annual rainfall at WS **22in (570mm)**

Harvest month rainfall at WS **April: 1.4in (35mm)**

Chief viticultural hazards **Underripeness, spring frost, harvest rainfall**

Principal grapes **Cabernet Sauvignon, Shiraz, Merlot, Chardonnay**

◀ The winery bought and renamed by David Wynn in the early 1950s was materially responsible for establishing the reputation of Coonawarra's distinctively long-lived style of Cabernet Sauvignon, although the company's top Shiraz, Michael, is also very fine.

Victoria

In many ways Victoria is the most interesting, the most dynamic, and certainly the most varied of Australia's wine states, even if today it is nowhere near as quantitatively important as it was at the end of the 19th century, when it had as much vineyard as New South Wales and South Australia put together. The gold rush of the mid-19th century helped to establish a wine industry (just as it had done in California), but then phylloxera arrived in the 1870s and was fatally destructive. Panicked, the government encouraged widespread destruction of vineyards so that today Victoria produces less than half as much wine as South Australia, which has never known phylloxera, even if Victoria has almost twice as many wineries. Three hundred – almost half – of all Victorian wine producers crush fewer than 25 tonnes of grapes.

The state is the smallest and coolest on the Australian mainland, but it can boast the most diverse conditions for vine-growing. These range from the arid, heavily irrigated inland Murray Darling region around Mildura, which straddles the Victoria–New South Wales border and grows 80% of all Victorian grapes by volume, to wine regions as cool as the Macedon Ranges, and Henty on the remote southwest coast. The most exciting recent developments in Victoria have almost entirely

resulted from the search for good vineyard land in cooler regions. The move has been either south towards the sea, or up into hilly areas.

The most important survivor of phylloxera, however, was the incontrovertibly hot North East Victoria Zone, which continues to specialize in fortified dessert wines unlike anything produced anywhere else. Most of these sticky elixirs are based on raisined dark-skinned Muscat and the more caramelised "Tokay" (the Muscadelle of Sauternes and Bergerac). After years of ageing in old wooden casks, often under tin roofs in baking hot conditions, they can achieve astonishingly silky richness, none more so than Rutherglen's Rare Muscats. Some truly boot-strapping reds are also made around **Rutherglen** and **Glenrowan**, the Jerez and Oporto of Australia, with the ancient Rhône variety Durif a speciality of Rutherglen.

The zone now includes three more, much higher, cooler wine regions: King Valley, Alpine Valleys, and Beechworth – all of potential interest to skiers as they head hopefully towards the snowfields of the Great Dividing Range. The family-owned Brown Brothers of Milawa is by far the dominant company of **King Valley** and has played an important part in experimenting with a wide range of grape varieties until recently regarded as exotic in Australia, but which are now increasingly mainstream. Italian

varieties have become a particular speciality here, not least thanks to the pioneering work of the Pizzini family, who came from the Italian alps in the 1950s to grow tobacco. Dal Zotto has a similar Italian heritage.

Many of these producers source grapes in the even higher vineyards of the **Alpine Valleys** region. Vines are planted at altitudes of over 1,000ft (300m) and the resulting wines can have particularly sharp, bright, indeed alpine, flavours. Gapsted is the label of the Victorian Alps Wine Company, a contract winery much used by companies outside the region – not least because this region is still plagued by phylloxera.

At rather lower altitudes around the historic gold-mining town of **Beechworth** some superlative California-influenced Chardonnay is made by Giaconda, which is fast building a reputation for Roussanne and its reds, while some ambitious Shiraz is made by Castagna. Some gloriously intense grapes, including some unusual Gamay, are grown at Sorrenberg, one of the first of the modern wave of vineyards, which still cover just a tiny fraction of the area planted in the early 19th century.

Like the North East wine country, Great Western, the district made famous by Seppelt's "champagne", never gave up either. Now called **Grampians**, the region lies 1,100ft (335m) up

Who ate all the grapes? A grey kangaroo and her joey at the top of one of Coldstream Hills' steep vineyards in the Yarra Valley, as caught on camera by the viticulturist. Kangaroos are a perennial threat for Australian vignerons.

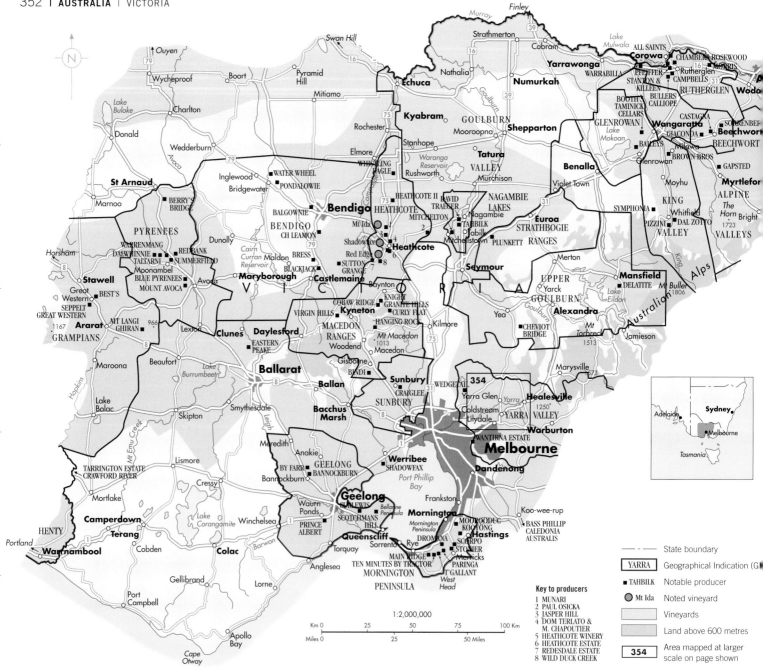

at the westernmost end of the Great Dividing Range, on lime-rich soil. Seppelt and Best's, a miniature by comparison, have a long record of producing good still and sparkling wines in deep, cool caves here. Grapes for the oceans of fizz made at Seppelt Great Western come partly from Padthaway over the heavily patrolled (for phylloxera) border in South Australia and partly from irrigated vineyards along the Murray, but those for its extraordinary and deservedly celebrated sparkling Shiraz are grown locally. Mount Langi Ghiran's authoritatively peppery Shiraz eloquently explains why.

Pyrenees is the (ironic?) name of the rolling landscape to the east of the Grampians. This region is not notably cool (except sometimes at night) and its showpiece wines are big reds from Redbank and Dalwhinnie, which has also made a fine Chardonnay.

Henty, the third region of the Western Victoria Zone, is the coolest and perhaps the most exciting. Seppelt pioneered the region, calling it Drumborg, and were at times tempted to give up but climate change has worked in Henty's favour. Crawford River, planted in 1975 by an ex-grazier, has shown that exceptionally fine, ageworthy Riesling can be produced here while Tarrington has demonstrated extraordinary devotion to duty with Burgundian varieties.

Heading back inland, **Bendigo** in the Central Victorian Zone is much warmer. Its wines are epitomized (and were launched) by Balgownie's sumptuous reds. Then Jasper Hill and others showed what could be done in slightly cooler country to the east with its own special red Cambrian soils. They added such lustre to **Heathcote** as a wine address that it is now recognized as a separate region making hauntingly rich Shiraz from dry-farmed vines.

Also in this zone is **Goulbourn Valley**, where David Traeger, Mitchelton, and Tahbilk, once the sole survivor of the region and called Château Tahbilk, cluster in the far south. The special qualities here have earned it the status of a subregion called **Nagambie Lakes** where, belying its name, a shortage of water is perennial. As in so much of Australia, irrigation is essential. Tahbilk is old enough to be classed a national monument – it still has some vines that were planted in 1860.

Upper Goulburn is another wine region overlooked by ski country. Its higher altitudes (at Delatite, for example) can make wines with unusually fine definition. The memorably named **Strathbogie Ranges** lies between the two Goulburn regions. It includes some extensive vineyards at up to 1,970ft (600m), where acidities are so high that Domaine Chandon grows Pinot Noir and Chardonnay as base wines for fizz.

The Port Phillip Zone is now the name for the regions clustered round the epicurean city of Melbourne. For all the excitement elsewhere in Victoria, this is the epicentre. The historic Yarra Valley is considered separately overleaf, but the long-established **Sunbury**, on the plains just north of Melbourne airport, is even closer to the city centre. Its standard-bearer has long been Craiglee, whose particular style of defiantly dry Shiraz has for decades remained admirably constant, savoury, and long-lived.

North of Sunbury, towards Bendigo, lies the **Macedon Ranges**, which encompasses some of Australia's coolest vine-growing conditions and can be almost too cold. Bindi's efforts near Gisborne and Curly Flat's near Lancefield (whatever makes you think Australians have a tin ear for names?) show that this is good country for both Chardonnay and Pinot Noir.

Pinot Noir is also the grape of choice for many growers in Victoria's new coastal wine regions, particularly in the barren, warmer, windy wine country of **Geelong**, where maritime influence is paramount, and By Farr, Bannockburn, and Scotchmans Hill ripen bumptious Pinot. Shadowfax is another ambitious winery on the western edge of Melbourne which buys fruit in this district.

South of Melbourne the definitively maritime **Mornington Peninsula** is home to many admirably ambitious growers and makers of Pinots Noir and Gris and Chardonnay – too

Notably wide spacing and lowering skies high up in the Grampians in one of the vineyards that belongs to Mount Langi Ghiran, now part of the Rathbone group, which includes Yering Station in the Yarra Valley and Xanadu in Margaret River – geographical diversification indeed.

many to fit on the map. Wines made here have crystalline, well-defined structure, no excess of body, and fine, pure acidity. Many vineyards are subject to almost constant wind, whether off Port Phillip Bay or from the east, but exact location can determine more variation than the map suggests. For much of the late 20th century, Mornington Peninsula was a sort of playground for Melbournites who liked to get their fingers sticky with grape juice, but as vines have matured and the people growing them have been sucked into the absorbing minutiae of wine culture, quality has perceptibly risen so that this is one of Australia's most rewarding sources of handcrafted wine.

Finally **Gippsland**, so big it's both a zone and a region that stretches far off this map to the east (see p.337), contains another vast array of different environments – so many that the region is ripe for subdivision. The most convincing, if highly variable, wine so far has been Bass Phillip Pinot Noir grown just south of Leongatha.

◀ The wines behind these labels become increasingly assertive from left to right. But the progression from the steeliest of Rieslings to the stickiest of stickies shows just how wide a range of flavours and styles the coolest mainland state can offer. The Chambers Muscat is arguably Australia's most distinctive wine style of all.

Yarra Valley

By far the best-known wine region within striking distance of the restaurants and concert halls of Melbourne is the Yarra Valley, which firmly sets its cap at visitors from the city, only 28 miles (45km) away, and houses many of those who work there. The map with its measles-like rash of little squares shows just how many habitations there are here compared with Australia's other wine regions. The valley's topography is complex, with steep, shallow slopes at altitudes of 160–1,540ft (50–470m) and facing all points of the compass. The upper slopes are cool and cool nights follow hot days here. Rainfall is also relatively high (see the key facts panel), although recent years have been drier than these figures indicate. Soils range from grey sandy or clay loam to vivid red volcanic earth so fertile that enormous "mountain ashes" (*Eucalyptus regnans*) along the creeks tower above the blue-leaved wattle.

The rebirth of the valley dates from the 1960s, when the once-powerful St Huberts reopened its doors, rapidly followed by the customary clutch of doctors fanatical about wine (see also Margaret River, p.340). Three of them, Drs Carrodus at Yarra Yering, Middleton at Mount Mary, and McMahon at Seville Estate, all set impeccable standards on a tiny scale. Those who followed included Dr Lance at Diamond Valley and the wine writer James Halliday at Coldstream Hills (now owned by Foster's), both fired with the desire to grow Australia's first great Pinot Noir.

Pinot Noir is clearly one of the Yarra Valley's strongest suits (Beaune in style rather than Nuits) even if the Yarra no longer has the distinction of being one of Australia's very rare examples of Pinot territory. Indeed the Yarra has been able to ride the recent rosé wave largely thanks to its substantial area of Pinot Noir. Chardonnay is just as widely planted, however, and there is no shortage of fine, harmonious examples. Fewer now undergo malolactic fermentation in a widespread move to greater finesse for this variety, which particularly thrives in the elevated southern end of the valley. Cabernet Sauvignon is the second most planted red wine grape. The Yarra style is especially

▼ The contrasts between the styles of these wines, from the delicacy of the fizz and the Giant Steps and Diamond Valley Chardonnays to the density of Yarra Yering's Bordeaux blend Dry Red No 1, illustrates just how much conditions vary throughout the Yarra Valley.

clean-cut although the variety is best grown on warmer sites. Yarra Shiraz has benefited from the Australians' newfound enthusiasm for cooler climate Shiraz, and here too there has been a fashion for fermenting it (best from the valley floor) with a small proportion of Viognier.

It was in the Yarra Valley that the foundations for Australia's best-yet sparkling wine were laid when, in 1987, Moët & Chandon established Domaine Chandon there. Today Chandon also produces Green Point still wine, but 50% of the fruit for its sparkling wines is still grown in the valley's cool upper reaches. Virtually all of the big companies have bought their slice of Yarra subsequently, with family-owned De Bortoli having established a particularly enviable reputation. The standard of winemaking has never been higher.

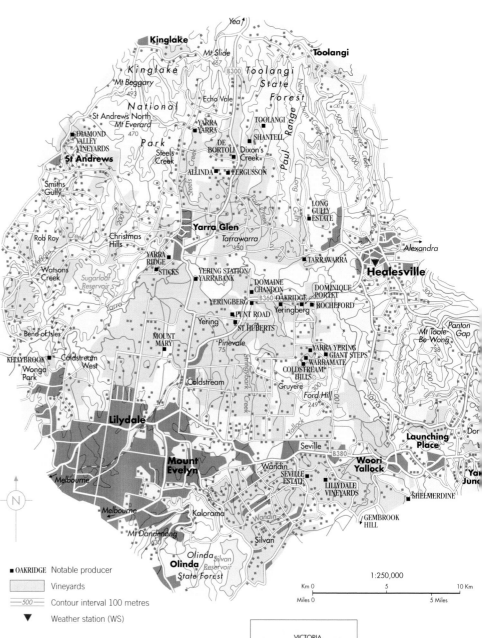

■ OAKRIDGE Notable producer

Vineyards

—500— Contour interval 100 metres

▼ Weather station (WS)

1:250,000

Km 0 — 5 — 10 Km
Miles 0 — 5 Miles

VICTORIA

Melbourne ● Healesville

YARRA VALLEY: HEALESVILLE ▼

Latitude / Altitude of WS **37.41° / 426ft (130m)**

Mean January temp at WS **65.5°F (18.6°C)**

Annual rainfall at WS **40in (1,010mm)**

Harvest month rainfall at WS **March: 2.5in (65mm)**

Chief viticultural hazards **Underripeness, fungal disease, frost**

Principal grapes **Pinot Noir, Chardonnay, Cabernet Sauvignon, Shiraz**

Tasmania

The continuing search for cooler climates in Australia logically leads to its southernmost, and sea-girt, state: Tasmania. In stark contrast to the mainland, this quaint island can boast grass that stays green all summer and a ready market for woolly knitwear, which makes it the envy of many mainland winemakers. Its cities of Launceston and Hobart are on the same latitudes as Marlborough and Christchurch in New Zealand respectively.

For the moment Tasmanian wine producers are officially limited to just one geographical appellation, Tasmania, but the unofficial sub-regions shown here have very distinct characters. The sheltered Tamar Valley and the wooded, later-ripening Pipers River subregions in the northeast of the island are reckoned to be some of Australia's most propitious areas for cool-climate wine production. Most of the island's biggest and most ambitious producers are based here. But there are sites on the southeast coast so sheltered by the principal mountains that the fact that there is no land between them and the Antarctic seems hardly relevant. Even Huon Valley, Australia's southernmost wine region, has produced some fully ripe medal winners, while Derwent Valley and Coal River to the north and northeast of Hobart respectively are quite warm enough to ripen Cabernet Sauvignon, as the fanatical owners of Domaine A have proved. Around Freycinet on the East Coast is a natural amphitheatre that seems pre-ordained for viticulture and has yielded some exceptionally pretty Pinot Noir.

For most of the late 1980s and 1990s when Tasmania emerged as a wine producer, it was reckoned that the grapes' high natural acidity made it primarily a useful source of base material for sparkling wine producers. The island, particularly northern Tasmania, still plays an important part in Australia's growing reputation for fine fizz such as the Jansz label owned by Yalumba of South Australia and that of Hardys' Bay of Fires winery in Pipers River. Juice and base wine is regularly transported to the mainland by some of the larger companies for further transformation into a wide range of sparkling wines. But of all the Australian wine regions, Tasmania has most to gain from global warming, even if by the early 21st century there was a danger that some of the earlier-ripening varieties such as Chardonnay could actually become overripe.

No one now doubts that the island can also make still wines that are extremely distinctive in an Australian context. The Alsace grapes Riesling, Pinot Gris, Gewurztraminer – and Pinot Noir in particular, which accounts for 40% of production – can be exceptionally lively with a natural raciness and delicacy often lacking on the mainland. Tasmania has a light touch with Pinot Gris, and Tasmanian Riesling, the island's third most important variety, has almost the delicacy of the Mosel – or New Zealand's South Island.

The number of Tasmanian wine producers is now approaching 250, most of them on a miniature scale and only 28 with more than 25 acres (10ha) of vines, which contributes to the relatively high production costs. The most important producers include Kreglinger (the Flemish-owned company that now owns Pipers Brook and its Ninth Island label) and Tamar Ridge, now run by Andrew Pirie, who used to run Pipers Brook and now also has his own label.

Pipers Brook vineyard has never been short of viticultural expertise. Here vines are trained on a U-shaped "lyre" system to curb their natural enthusiasm to sprout leaves instead of ripening fruit. This trick is widely used in other high-vigour wine regions.

The coastal winds provide a natural limit to yields in the vineyards carved out of Tasmania's rich and floriferous bush. Screens are necessary in some places to preserve the vine leaves on the seaward slope. But ripening is as slow and sure as any vintner could hope for, and flavour correspondingly intense.

TASMANIA: LAUNCESTON ▼
Latitude / Altitude of WS **41.32° / 558ft (170m)**
Mean January temp at WS **63.9°F (17.7°C)**
Annual rainfall at WS **27in (680mm)**
Harvest month rainfall at WS **April: 2.2in (55mm)**
Chief viticultural hazards **Botrytis, coulure**
Principal grapes **Pinot Noir, Chardonnay, Riesling**

▼ An exceptional oaked Sauvignon Blanc with real complexity and longevity, plus three great sparkling wines with a finesse that only Domaine Chandon of Yarra Valley seems to be able to achieve on the mainland.

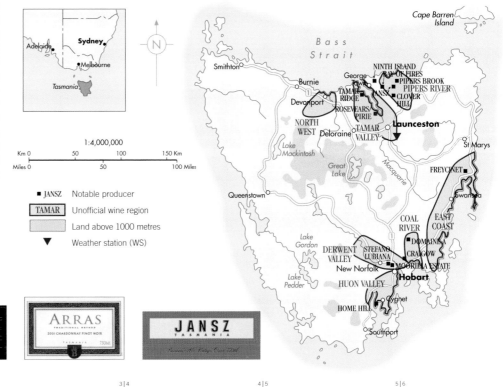

■ JANSZ   Notable producer
TAMAR   Unofficial wine region
   Land above 1000 metres
▼   Weather station (WS)

1:4,000,000
Km 0   50   100   150 Km
Miles 0   50   100 Miles

New South Wales including the Hunter Valley

New South Wales, Australian wine's birthplace, has long since been overtaken by South Australia as the nucleus of the industry. But there remains one district 100 miles (160km) north of Sydney as famous as any in the country, even if it grows only a tenth as many grapes as the inland wine factory that is Riverina (see p.337) and is progressively being overtaken by the state's swelling roster of new wine regions.

The Lower Hunter Valley around Branxton and the mining town of Cessnock represents a triumph of proximity over suitability. The **Hunter**, as it is known, is a far from ideal place to grow grapes. It is subtropical; the most northerly of Australia's traditional wine regions: summers are invariably very hot and autumns can be vexingly wet. The prevailing northeast winds from the Pacific counter the extreme heat to some extent and summer skies are often cloud-covered so the direct sun is diffused. More than two-thirds of the region's relatively high annual rainfall of 29in (750mm) falls in the crucial first four months of the year, harvest time. There is plenty for the farmer to curse: vintages are as uneven as they are in France.

The reason for the rash of wineries on the map, an unparalleled proportion of which have changed their names since our last edition, is not so much a natural affinity with the vine as the fact that they are just two hours' drive from Sydney and a mecca for wine tourists and investors. No other Australian wine region sets its cap so obviously at the casual visitor. Restaurants, guesthouses, golf courses, and, of course, cellar doors proliferate.

Surprisingly, being so far north, the Hunter was one of the first regions in Australia to concentrate entirely on table wines – perhaps because it for so long housed the movers and shakers in the nation's wine industry.

Vines were planted here (at Dalwood, near the river just east of Branxton) as early as 1828, but the soil that gave the Hunter Valley its reputation is found to the south in the foothills of the Brokenback Range. Around the east side of the hills there is a strip of weathered basalt, the sign of ancient volcanic activity, that restricts vine vigour and concentrates often distinctly mineral flavour into the grapes. The red volcanic soils on higher ground, such as those of Pokolbin, are particularly suitable for Shiraz, the classic red grape of the Hunter, based on some particularly old clones. Semillon grown on the white sands and loams on lower ground is the traditional white, even if it has been overtaken quantitatively by Chardonnay. No more than medium-bodied, Hunter Shiraz is often beefed up with stronger stuff imported from South Australia, up to the permitted maximum of 15%. Soft and earthy but long and spicy, Hunter Shiraz from a successful vintage may ripen relatively early but lasts well and grows complex and leathery with time. Cabernet, no

friend of wet autumns, is far less important here than in other areas.

Hunter Semillon is one of Australia's classic, if under-appreciated, wine styles. The grapes are picked at conveniently low ripeness levels, fermented in vat, and bottled fairly early at around 11% alcohol without any softening (and accelerating) malolactic fermentation. These grassy or citrus, relatively austere young wines age in bottle quite magnificently into green-gold, toasty, mineral-laden bombs packed with explosive layers of flavour, although the style is not for neophytes. Verdelho also has a long history in the Hunter although there is some dispute as to whether it should be made as bone dry as Semillon.

The Hunter was in the forefront of Australia's love affair with imported French grapes. In the early 1970s, Murray Tyrrell, inspired by Len Evans (see photo, p.49), the impresario not only of the Hunter but of modern Australian wine at large, did with Chardonnay what Max Lake had done in the 1960s with Cabernet: put down a marker no winemaker could ignore, his Vat 47. It launched a thousand – make that a million? – Australian Chardonnays.

Chardonnay is also by far the principal, some might say only, grape variety in the Upper Hunter, put resoundingly on the map in the 1970s by Rosemount. It lies 40 miles (60km) to the northwest on higher ground around Denman and Muswellbrook. Rainfall is lower and irrigation freely practised. The Broke

Not what the Australian tourist posters show but a winter reality in a high-altitude wine region such as Orange. This is the entrance to Brangayne winery, an enterprise begun by fruit farmers who have become increasingly seduced by the grape.

▼ Some of New South Wales' more interesting wines produced outside the Hunter Valley: two refined wines from Orange, a Hilltops answer to Amarone, Canberra's finest, and a stickie from Riverina.

Fordwich subregion half an hour's drive west of the area mapped here is currently much more dynamic, producing distinctive Semillons on sandy, alluvial soils.

To the west, about 1,500ft (450m) up on the western slopes of the Great Dividing Range, **Mudgee** has also made its mark since the 1970s (see p.337 for the location of all New South Wales wine regions, considered here from north to south). Its origins are almost as old as those of the Hunter Valley, but Mudgee dwelt in obscurity until the hunt began for cooler districts to make wines of more pronounced grape flavours. Intense, long-established Chardonnay and Cabernet are its real successes. Craigmoor (now Poet's Corner) is the oldest cellar in the region, Huntington the best (though unknown outside Australia), and Botobolar admirably organic.

New South Wales has seen a sustained and vigorous quest for new wine regions, all of them in promising cooler, often higher, corners of the state. **Orange**, at high altitude and with volcanic soils on the slopes of Mount Canobolas (now extinct), was first planted in 1983 by wine-crazy librarian Stephen Doyle at Bloodwood. Notably pure natural acidity is the hallmark of whatever grows here, and the range is wide. Altitude is what defines the appellation. Uniquely for Australia, it is ring-fenced at about 2,000ft (600m). Promising red wine vineyards planted with the usual suspects straddle the appellation's lower boundary and are sold under the name Central Ranges.

Cowra has a much longer history for lush, fulsome, exuberant Chardonnays grown at fairly high yields and much lower altitudes: on average only about 1,150ft (350m). **Hilltops**, a little to the south, around the town of Young, and higher than Cowra, is much more recent and, like most of these more obscure New South Wales wine regions, tends to grow fruit – notably red grapes, Chardonnay, and Semillon – for wineries outside the region. There are half a dozen small enterprises, by far the most important being Barwang, now owned by McWilliam's, along with Tyrrell's, De Bortoli, and Casella of Riverina, one of the bigger family-owned wine companies based in New South Wales.

The great surprise about **Canberra District**, the cluster of vineyards round the nation's capital, is firstly that there are so many of them, secondly that almost all are actually in New South Wales, and thirdly that they have been in existence for so long. John Kirk planted the first vines at Clonakilla as long ago as 1971 and his son Tim virtually pioneered Australia's popular Shiraz/Viognier blend modelled on Côte Rôtie. The government seems keen for this dark horse of a region to emerge into the limelight: Hardy

were lured to establish a wine tourism centre within the Australian Capital Territory itself under the aboriginal name Kamberra. The highest vineyards such as Lark Hill's are not just cool but cold (frost can strike), and the result can be some of Australia's most delicate Pinot Noir. Helm is one of the country's most passionate exponents of Riesling.

Shoalhaven Coast is also developing fast although, like **Hastings River** around Port Macquarie to the north, it suffers from high humidity. Hybrids such as Chambourcin offer potential of a sort. **Tumbarumba** is another extremely cool high-altitude region, of particular interest to blenders of such renowned Chardonnays as Penfolds Yattarna and Eileen Hardy as well as bottlers of sparkling wine and Sauvignon Blanc.

Key to producers

1 CONSTABLE & HERSHON
2 HONEYTREE
3 TYRRELL'S
4 GLENGUIN
5 McGUIGAN
6 TEMPUS TWO
7 THOMAS WINES
8 TAMBURLAINE
9 PEPPER TREE
10 TOWER
11 HUNGERFORD HILL

POKOLBIN — Unofficial wine subregion
■ ADINA — Notable producer
● Mount View — Noted vineyard
▢ — Vineyards
—300— — Contour interval 75 metres
▼ — Weather station (WS)

LOWER HUNTER: CESSNOOK ▼
Latitude / Altitude of WS **32.49° / 197ft (60m)**
Mean January temp at WS **74.7°F (23.7°C)**
Annual rainfall at WS **29in (750mm)**
Harvest month rainfall at WS **February: 3.8in (95mm)**
Chief viticultural hazards **Harvest rainfall, fungal disease**
Principal grapes **Chardonnay, Shiraz, Semillon**

▼ The Hunter Valley high achievers are represented by these labels, the two on the right evidence of a particularly active nucleus of young Turks in the long-established wine region, which bodes well for the future. McWilliam's and Tyrrell's are the old hands, and very sure ones.

New Zealand

Few wine countries have quite so sharp an image as New Zealand. The word sharp is apt, for the wines are characterized by piercingly crystalline flavours and bracing acidity. But then many of the world's wine drinkers will never have experienced proof of this, for New Zealand is not just one of the most isolated countries on earth (more than three hours' flight from its nearest neighbour Australia), but it is a newcomer to wine. And it is small, producing less than 0.3% of the world's crop. New Zealand has colonized as much space in this book as it has because it is now exporting seriously – most of its wine is now sold abroad – and because so many of those who try the wines fall madly in love with their unusually powerful, direct flavours.

In historical terms this is Stop Press news. In 1960 the country had fewer than 1,000 acres (400ha) of vines, mainly in Auckland and Hawke's Bay, and too many of them hybrids. By 1980 there were 14,000 acres (5,600ha), 2,000 of which were in the brand-new Marlborough region on the South Island (see p.362). In the 1990s it seemed as though anyone with a few acres wanted to try their hand at vine-growing so that by 2006 the total area in production was more than 54,000 acres (22,000ha), and there were 530 wine producers. This is a relatively small average holding and a high proportion of producers have a label but no winery of their own; contract winemaking is big business.

It was New Zealanders who coined the term and bought the concept of a "lifestyle winery": a bucolic way of life whereby, typically, a fine education is focused on producing, in the most pleasing environment, one of life's more delicious commodities from the earth.

New Zealand had some natural problems to contend with before this enthusiasm could be positively harnessed. Only 150 years ago much of this long, thin country was covered with rainforest. Soils here tend to be so rich in nutrients that vines, like everything else, grow too vigorously for their own good, a phenomenon exacerbated by the country's generous rainfall. Canopy management techniques were sorely needed, and were introduced in the 1980s most notably by the then state viticulturist Dr Richard Smart, allowing light to shine both literally and figuratively on New Zealand's unique style of wine.

Wine-growing New Zealand lies, in terms of the northern hemisphere, on latitudes between those of Morocco and Bordeaux (see the key facts panels on pages 360 and 362). The effects of latitude are countered, though, by the Pacific, by strong prevailing westerlies, and by the effects of the mountains on their rain-clouds: factors that give the two islands a wide range of growing conditions – almost all cooler than the statistics suggest.

Wine regions

- Auckland/Northland
- Waikato/Bay of Plenty
- Gisborne
- Hawke's Bay
- Wairarapa
- Nelson
- Marlborough
- Canterbury
- Otago

– · – Region boundary
Kumeu Wine subregion
360 Area mapped at larger scale on page shown

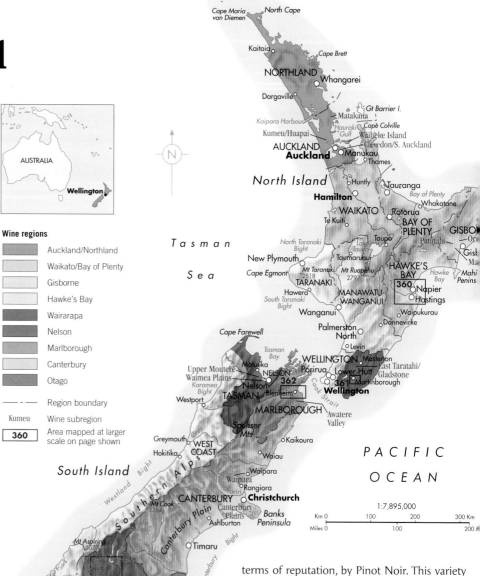

It was Sauvignon Blanc that made the world take notice of New Zealand. After all, a cool climate is needed if it is to be lively, and the cool, bright, sunny, and windy northern tip of the South Island seems to have been designed to intensify the scarcely subtle twang of Sauvignon. Early examples of Marlborough Sauvignon in the 1980s opened a Pandora's box of flavour that no one could ignore and, most importantly, no other part of the world seems able to replicate. Today Sauvignon Blanc is the country's most important grape, and for the moment it seems that no matter how much is planted, demand will always be greater.

Chardonnay, enlivened by the country's trademark zestiness, was for long New Zealand's other calling card but it has recently been overtaken in terms of vineyard area, and certainly in terms of reputation, by Pinot Noir. This variety has enjoyed success for much the same reason as Sauvignon Blanc: New Zealand's cool climate. In a surprisingly wide range of wine regions, this finicky grape has provided Kiwi growers with another chance of succeeding where so many other regions (most importantly, most of Australia) have failed.

Merlot overtook the inconveniently late-ripening Cabernet Sauvignon in 2000. Bordeaux blends are in general more popular with Kiwis themselves than outside in the big, wide, Cabernet-saturated world. Other significant grapes include Riesling, which can be very fine here, both dry and sweet; and a significant number of producers and growers are now investing their hopes in Gewurztraminer, Viognier, and, especially Pinot Gris and Syrah (see Hawke's Bay). Isolation has proved no defence against vine pests and diseases; most of these new plantings are grafted onto phylloxera-resistant rootstocks.

New Zealand wine has come a long way since it was known locally as "Dally plonk", a reference to settlers from Dalmatia, lured from the kauri gum forests of the far north to plant vineyards near **Auckland** in the early 20th century. They persisted despite a rainy subtropical climate; several of the families in what is now a surprisingly good red wine area have Dalmatian names. As in Australia's Hunter Valley, cloud

cover moderates what could be too much sunshine and gives steady ripening conditions. Vintage-time rain and rot are problems, although Waiheke Island to the east misses some of the mainland rain. Stonyridge has shown the island's potential with Bordeaux grapes, but prospects for Syrah look if anything even brighter. Te Whau is another winery to watch.

In the early years of this century, New Zealand wine was paid the compliment of more interest from multinational corporations than ever before. In 2005 Pernod Ricard New Zealand became the owner of the country's giant Montana and several other labels (including Brancott Estate, which substitutes for Montana for obvious reasons in the USA), thus producing more than a third of all New Zealand wine. The company's wines are fermented and generally aged at regional wineries and bottled in Auckland – common practice for the larger companies. Its Gisborne winery processes 60% of the region's production and is home to the country's largest cooperage.

Gisborne on the east coast of the North Island (like so many of New Zealand's wine regions it has another name, Poverty Bay) is a good example of a region plundered by the bottlers. In terms of vineyard area, it is the country's third most important wine region, admittedly a long way behind Marlborough

and also behind Hawke's Bay, New Zealand's answer to Bordeaux, but it has relatively few wineries, fewer even than Nelson and far fewer than Central Otago. Warmer but wetter than Hawke's Bay, especially in autumn, Gisborne grows almost exclusively white grapes on relatively fertile loamy soils. It has a particular reputation for lush Chardonnay, generally picked two to three weeks before Hawke's Bay and Marlborough for example, but also produces some of the world's finest Gewurztraminer as well as intense Semillon and relatively rich Chenin Blanc. Merlot and Syrah are notably approachable too.

If Poverty Bay is Gisborne, the Bay of Plenty is otherwise known as **Waikato** and produces bumptious Chardonnay in relatively small quantity. The North Island's other wine regions are considered in detail overleaf.

Just across the windy Cook Strait on the South Island, the little **Nelson** region to the west of Marlborough has higher rainfall and richer soil than Wairarapa but does well with similar (Burgundian) grape varieties.

Meanwhile, well south of Marlborough, on the relatively cool plains surrounding Christchurch and an hour's drive north in undulating terrain at Waipara, **Canterbury**'s winemakers are producing crisp, flinty Rieslings and some unusually well-structured

The sun also rises in New Zealand, and shines brilliantly through unpolluted air. The hole in the ozone layer above Marlborough is said to play a part in creating those pungent wine flavours.

Chardonnays (from Mountford, for example), as well as Pinot Noir that ranges from disappointingly herbal to tantalizingly promising in extremely varied environments. The east of the region is dominated by alluvial gravels, often covered with thin loess, but some isolated outcrops of limestone, so revered in Burgundy, have been assiduously sought out further west by some of Waipara's most ambitious growers such as Bell Hill and Pyramid Valley. And the fact that Montana has planted several hundred hectares of vineyard in the region is surely significant. The isolation of most vineyards, the reasonably dry climate, and persistent winds make organic viticulture relatively easy here.

Another embryonic, limestone-dominated wine region has been scouted even further south. Waitaki Valley in northeastern Otago is discussed with Central Otago, on p.363.

▼ Some particularly fine offerings from regions not mapped in detail on subsequent pages. Left to right they run north to south, with only one red wine among them: the Waiheke Bordeaux blend. Neudorf is a standard-bearer for the northwest of the South Island.

Hawke's Bay

In New Zealand terms, Hawke's Bay is an historic wine region, having been planted by Marist missionaries in the mid-19th century. But it was Cabernets made here in the 1960s by the celebrated Tom McDonald for the Australian wine company McWilliam's (at a winery revived in 1990 by Montana for their Church Road label) that hinted at the long-term promise of the area. When serious planting began in the 1970s, Hawke's Bay was a logical place to expand, especially with the Cabernet Sauvignon that was then de rigueur.

Hawke's Bay has been the Kiwi standard-bearer for claret-style reds ever since, but it was only in the late 1990s that the region began to make wines that demanded attention. The 1998 vintage, so hot and dry that Hawke's Bay's sheep had to be trucked west over the mountains to greener pastures, produced wines that not only had New Zealand's usual crisp definition, but they were obviously made from fully ripe grapes, and had the gentle but insistent tannins to suggest a serious future.

It was also in the late 1990s that growers began fully to understand and take advantage of the complexities of Hawke's Bay soils. It had long been obvious that the maritime climate of this wide bay on the east coast of the North Island, sheltered from the westerlies by the Ruahine and Kaweka ranges, could offer one of the country's most favourable combinations of relatively low rainfall and high temperatures (albeit lower than Bordeaux's – see key facts panel). What happened underground took longer to understand.

An aerial view of Hawke's Bay vividly shows the remarkable variety of rich alluvial and less fertile, gravelly soils and their distribution in a pattern flowing from mountain to sea. Silt, loams, and gravel have very different water-holding capacities; one vineyard can be at saturation point, shooting forth vegetation at an embarrassing rate, while another needs to be irrigated. It became clear that the ripest grapes were grown on the poorest soils, which limited vine growth and on which irrigation could carefully control just how much water each vine received (even if summers seem now to be getting hotter and red grape ripening more reliable).

There are none poorer than the 2,000 acres (800ha) of deep, warm shingle that remain where the Gimblett Road now runs, northwest of Hastings, along what was the course of the

Ngaruroro River until a dramatic flood in 1870. The late 1990s saw a viticultural land grab on these so-called Gimblett, or Twyford, gravels, a frenzy during which the last three-quarters of available land was bought and planted in readiness for virtually hydroponic cultivation.

Other fine areas for ripening red grapes include Bridge Pa just south of and slightly cooler than here, selected sites on the limestone hills of Havelock North, such as that colonized by Te Mata early on, and a cool, late-ripening strip of shingle along the coast between Haumoana and Te Awanga.

New Zealand suffered excessive Cabernet Sauvignon worship like everywhere else in the 1980s, but even in Hawke's Bay this variety does not always ripen fully, and plantings of the much more reliable, earlier-ripening Merlot are now more than double those of Cabernet Sauvignon. Malbec also thrives here and ripens

even earlier, although it is prone to poor fruit set. Future hopes, however, are pinned on that midseason ripener Syrah. Two in every three of the country's Syrah vines are planted in Hawke's Bay's poor soils, ripening satisfactorily most years. Brookfields' Hillside bottling is an example of how juicy Syrah can be here. Like Bordeaux, this is a region of exaggerated annual variation; and for much the same reasons as in Bordeaux, most of Hawke's Bay's best-balanced reds are sensitively oaked blends.

Chardonnay rivals Merlot as Hawke's Bay's most planted variety, however, and the region grows some of the country's finest, often more opulent than elsewhere.

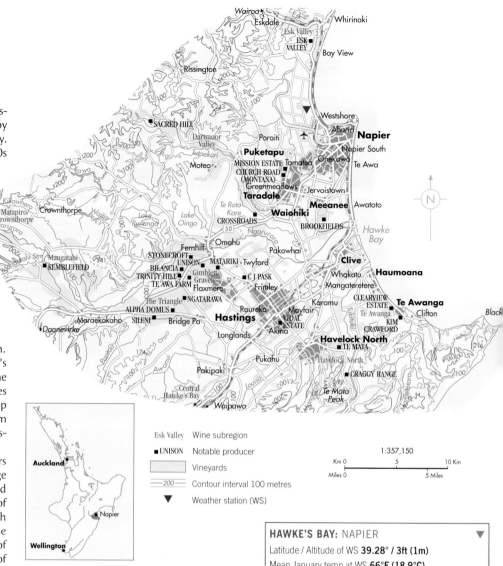

Esk Valley — Wine subregion
■ UNISON — Notable producer
Vineyards
200 — Contour interval 100 metres
▼ Weather station (WS)

1:357,150
Km 0 — 5 — 10 Km
Miles 0 — 5 Miles

HAWKE'S BAY: NAPIER ▼
Latitude / Altitude of WS **39.28° / 3ft (1m)**
Mean January temp at WS **66°F (18.9°C)**
Annual rainfall at WS **35in (890mm)**
Harvest month rainfall at WS **March: 3in (75mm)**
Chief viticultural hazards **Autumn rain, fungal diseases**
Principal grapes **Chardonnay, Merlot, Sauvignon Blanc**

◀ This is New Zealand's answer to Bordeaux and the Rhône rolled into one with all these most celebrated labels dedicated to red wines. Stonecroft was the Syrah pioneer. Craggy Range (Le Sol) is a relative parvenu but is enviably well-funded – New Zealand's version of a Napa Valley winery?

1|2   2|3   3|4   4|5   5|6

Martinborough

The North Island's most exciting area for Pinot Noir, and the first in New Zealand to establish a reputation for it, is variously called Wairarapa, Martinborough (a subregion named after Wairarapa's wine capital), and Wellington. It is just an hour's drive east of the nation's capital, over the mountains and into the island's eastern rain shadow. Temperatures may be so much lower here than other North Island regions that ex-research scientist Dr Neil McCallum of Dry River is able to observe drily: "We're very like Edinburgh in terms of our heat summation." Thanks to the mountains to the west, however, Martinborough's autumns are the country's most reliably dry, giving its 55 wineries the chance to make some of the most vivid and Burgundian Pinot Noir, the region's dominant vine. It has ranged from potently plummy to lean, dry, and earthy; but then so does burgundy.

The Burgundian parallel extends to the structure of the wine business here, with wines typically being made by the same people as grew the grapes. Grape farmers would be more likely to be attracted to the steady and generous yields of Marlborough than the Martinborough average of barely 2 tonnes/acre. The region has thin, poor soils on free-draining deep gravels, silts, and clay, and the prevailing westerlies in this windy area are particularly persistent at flowering time, generally after a cool spring during which frosts are a perennial threat. Grapes are routinely treated to a particularly long growing season, however, thanks to the long autumns and because Martinborough enjoys New Zealand's greatest difference between average day and night temperatures. As elsewhere, the current challenge is to produce subtle wines of real interest but without an excess of ripeness.

Many of the leading wineries, Ata Rangi, Martinborough Vineyard, and Dry River, were established in the early 1980s. The individuals behind them have built consistent and very personal reputations, *à la bourguignonne*, although Larry McKenna, once of Martinborough Vineyard, has now established a second-generation operation in Escarpment.

The region has also shown real proficiency in New Zealand's latest varietal darling, Pinot Gris, particularly those wines based on the original clone imported into New Zealand for the Mission winery in the 1880s, even though Sauvignon Blanc is Wairarapa's second most planted variety after Pinot Noir. In the hugely self-conscious world of New Zealand Pinot Noir, there is considerable rivalry between Martinborough and Central Otago, each organizing major international events to celebrate the variety, according to carefully alternating cycles.

▶ Martinborough was long considered Pinot Noir country – in fact, it was New Zealand's first region to establish a reputation for that wildly popular variety – but, as elsewhere, Pinot Gris such as Palliser's is increasingly fashionable.

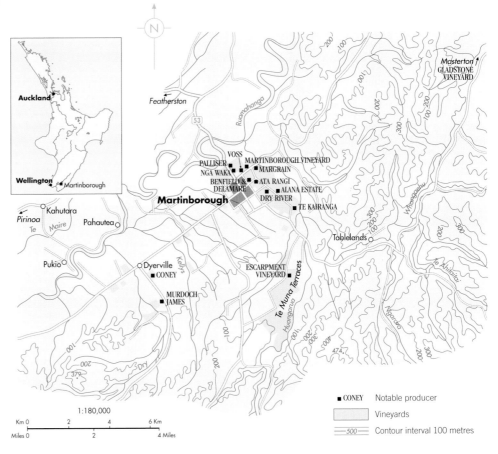

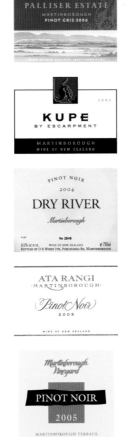

For New Zealanders wine is inextricably intertwined with leisure activities. Leisure is energetically pursued at the Toast Martinborough wine, food, and music festival held every November – so popular that tickets sell out within hours of release. Shuttle buses between tastings are essential.

1:180,000

■ CONEY Notable producer
          Vineyards
  500   Contour interval 100 metres

Marlborough

At the northern tip of the South Island, Marlborough has seen such feverish vine planting in recent years that it has pulled ahead of all other regions to come to epitomize New Zealand wine. Roughly half of all the country's vineyards lie in this very particular corner of the wine world – quite an achievement given that, apart from one settler who planted vines at Meadowbank Farm around 1873, the vine was unknown here until 1973, when Montana, the country's dominant wine producer, cautiously established a small commercial vineyard.

Lack of irrigation caused teething problems but by 1980 the first release had been bottled and the special intensity of Marlborough Sauvignon Blanc was too obvious to ignore. Such an exhilarating, easy-to-understand wine clearly had extraordinary potential, rapidly realized by, among others, David Hohnen of Cape Mentelle in Western Australia. In 1985 he launched Cloudy Bay, whose name, evocative label, and smoky, almost chokingly pungent flavour have since become legendary.

By 2007 Marlborough had more than 27,000 acres (11,000ha) under vine, nearly three times the area planted at the turn of the century. The number of wine producers passed 100 in 2005 and the proportion of fruit leaving the region in bulk to be shipped across Cook Strait for processing in the North Island has plummeted – much to the benefit of the resultant wine. Today an increasing proportion of the growers who once sold their grapes to one of the big companies have their own label, which may well be applied at one of the region's busy contract wineries.

The wide, flat **Wairau Valley** has become a magnet for investors and those who simply like the idea of making wine their life – even if some of them have been planting so far inland that grapes may not necessarily ripen every year, and on land where the valley's precious water supply is scarce. The need for frost protection on the wide, flat valley floor has been another stumbling block for the multitude who want to join in.

What makes Marlborough special as a wine region is its unusual combination of long days, cool nights, bright sunshine, and, in good years, dryish autumns. In such relatively low temperatures (see key facts panel) grapes might have difficulty ripening wherever autumn rains threatened, but here they can usually be left on the vine to benefit from a particularly long ripening period, building high sugars without, thanks to the cool nights, sacrificing the acidity that delineates New Zealand's wines.

This diurnal temperature variation is most marked in the drier, cooler, and windier **Awatere Valley**, which is too far south to be included on our map. It was pioneered by Vavasour and has expanded enormously in recent years, thanks to a new privately funded irrigation scheme. Both budbreak and harvest tend to be later in the Awatere Valley than on the Wairau Valley floor but summers can be long and hot enough to ripen Bordeaux varieties – in contrast to the main swathe of vineyards in the Wairau Valley. (Montana's much-photographed Brancott vineyards also tend to lag behind those on the valley floor because of their elevation.)

But perhaps the most significant variation in Marlborough is that of soils. North of Highway 6/63, with a few exceptions round Woodbourne, soils are very much younger than those to the south. In places the water table can be dangerously high and the best vineyards on these young, stony soils are the best drained, on light loams over the shingle that was once the river bed. Mature vines develop deep root systems although young vines need irrigation to survive the dry summers.

South of the highway, the lowest-lying older soils are too poorly drained for fine wine production, but higher-altitude vineyards on the exposed, barren southern edge of the valley can produce interesting fruit from much drier soils.

Big producers of Sauvignon Blanc typically blend fruit grown on different soils in slightly different climatic conditions in an attempt to differentiate their produce in what can sometimes seem a rather monotone category. Careful and limited use of oak and malolactic fermentation can help, and a growing number of single-vineyard Sauvignons provide a counterpoint.

Marlborough has produced some fine Pinot Gris, a variety that is becoming increasingly popular, and Riesling, including some inspiring late-harvest examples, but Chardonnay and Pinot Noir are quantitatively much more important. They are both grown for sparkling as well as still wine, and the fruity Marlborough Pinots are gaining in stature as the vines age.

MARLBOROUGH: BLENHEIM ▼

Latitude / Altitude of WS **40.31° / 66ft (20m)**

Mean January temp at WS **63.9°F (17.7°C)**

Annual rainfall at WS **29in (730mm)**

Harvest month rainfall at WS **April: 2.3in (60mm)**

Chief viticultural hazard **Autumn rain**

Principal grapes **Sauvignon Blanc, Pinot Noir, Chardonnay**

▶ Marlborough now boasts hundreds of different labels so making a Sauvignon or Pinot that stands out from the crowd here can be a challenge. Dog Point is owned by two of the people originally behind Cloudy Bay. The Fromms are Swiss. Gravitas is New Zealand-owned but its soils were analyzed in the USA.

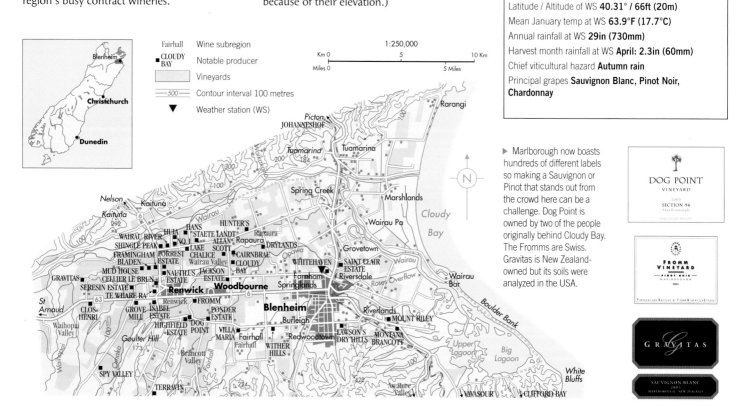

Fairhall Wine subregion
■ **CLOUDY BAY** Notable producer
Vineyards
500 Contour interval 100 metres
▼ Weather station (WS)

1:250,000

Central Otago

Central Otago (or "Central" as the locals call it) is the world's southernmost wine region and is rivalled only by the Cape wine country of South Africa as the world's most scenic. Brilliant turquoise rivers tumble through wild thyme-scented gorges, overlooked by snowcapped mountains even in summer. In winter, Queenstown, a magnet for tourists all year, is New Zealand's ski capital and Central Otago's remarkably cohesive band of winemakers take an hour or two's skiing before work as their right.

In 1997 there were just 14 wine producers and fewer than 500 acres (200ha) of vines. By 2006 official figures saw the number of producers rise to 82 drawing on 2,800 acres (1,150ha) of vineyards, planted mainly with particularly youthful Pinot Noir vines, much of whose produce is vinified at contract wineries.

Unlike the rest of New Zealand, Central Otago has a dramatically continental rather than maritime climate, which makes summers sunny and dry but short. Frosts are a threat throughout the year and in cooler areas, such as Gibbston, even the early-ripening Pinot vine can have difficulty reaching full maturity before the advent of winter.

On the other hand the summer sunlight is blinding. The hole in the ozone layer over this isolated part of the world may account for this unusually high solar radiation, but reliably cool nights keep acidities respectable. The result is dazzlingly bright fruit flavours, and such ripeness that wines with less than 14% alcohol are relatively rare. Central Otago Pinot Noir, like Marlborough Sauvignon Blanc, may not be the subtlest wine in the world but it is easy to like almost as soon as it's bottled.

The region's summers and early autumns are so dry that even the rot-prone Pinot Noir rarely suffers fungal diseases, and there is no shortage of irrigation water in a ski area. The soils' water-holding capacity is very limited, however; they are mainly light, fast-draining loess with some gravels over schist (the same rock base, 200 million years ago, as that of Marlborough).

The southernmost subregion is Alexandra. Relatively cool, it was first planted in the 1980s at Black Ridge, the winery closest of any to the South Pole. Gibbston, slightly northwest of here, is even cooler, but the vines are planted on north-facing slopes of the stunning Kawarau Gorge. In longer growing seasons wines from here can have some of the most complex flavours of all. Bannockburn, where the Gorge meets the Cromwell Valley, is the most intensively planted subregion. Like so many fine wine regions, this was once gold mining country. Bendigo to the north is also relatively warm and is rapidly being planted with vines even if there are no wineries here yet. There is also great potential in Lowburn, the valley south of Bendigo.

The most northerly subregion of all, Wanaka, was one of the first to be developed. Rippon's vineyards are right on the lake, which usefully reduces the risk of frost, and have provided fodder for thousands of photographers since they were first planted in the early 1980s.

Northeast Otago now has its own wine region, Waitaki Valley (see map, p.358), where prospectors are banking on the limestone of Burgundy, unknown in "Central", although they too have to cope with the disadvantages of perennial frost risk and (so far) young vines. The future should be as bright as the wines.

No doubt about chilly winters here at one of Chard Farm's vineyards in Gibbston. The crucial factor each year for the cool Gibbston region is whether the grapes ripen fully before winter arrives.

▼ Felton Road, established in the early 1990s, is the winery that has done most to put Central Otago on the international map. Mt Difficulty is another very reliable producer and, founded in 1998, another old hand in this very new region.

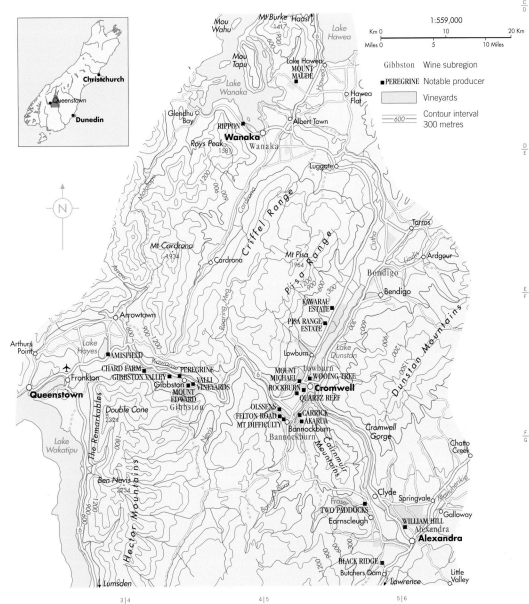

South Africa

Looking across Neetlingshof estate towards the town of Stellenbosch. The "tablecloth" cloud formation draped over the Groot Drakenstein mountains in the distance is a sign of the prevailing southeasterly blowing in cool air from False Bay.

South Africa

There are many contestants in the world's vineyard beauty contest, but South Africa is always in the finals. Blue-shadowed stacks of Table Mountain sandstone and decomposed granite rise from vivid green pastures dotted with the brilliant white façades of 300-year-old Cape Dutch homesteads. To the casual observer the Cape winelands may look just as they did in the decades leading up to 1994, but in reality the wine map, the vineyards, the cellars, the people, and the wines have changed out of all recognition.

Most South African vines thrive in an almost perfect Mediterranean climate, cooler than their latitudes suggest thanks to the cold Benguela Current from Antarctica that washes the western Atlantic coast. Climatologists predict furthermore that of all New World wine producers South Africa is least likely to be seriously affected by climate change. Rain is usually concentrated in the winter months, but exactly how much falls varies considerably according to the Cape's extremely diverse topography. Prevailing winter westerlies temper the climate; the further south and west – and nearer the sea – the cooler and better supplied with rain. Rainfall can be heavy on either side of mountain chains such as the Drakenstein, Hottentots Holland, and Langeberg ranges, yet dwindle to as little as 8in (200mm) a year within only a few miles. The mountains also play a part in funnelling the famous Cape Doctor, a powerful southeaster that can ward off rot and mildew but can also batter young vines.

The Cape boasts the oldest geology in the wine-growing world: ancient, weathered soils, typically based on either granite, Table Mountain sandstone, or shale, which naturally curtail the vigour of the wines. Much is now also made of the fact that these soils nurture the richest floral kingdom on the planet so that biodiversity has become the mantra of the South African wine industry. The Biodiversity and Wine Initiative is a scheme designed to make both biodiversity and geography key elements in what distinguishes Cape wine. Wine producers are encouraged to preserve natural vegetation and add features to their land of interest to ecotourists. Registration of single vineyards, which must be smaller than 12 acres (5ha), is encouraged and official study of their individual characteristics and favoured grape varieties is well underway. (Vineyard names first appeared on wine labels in 2005.) An ambitious plan envisaged all exported wine being sustainably grown by the end of 2008. Lacking the equivalent of, for example, Australia's vast mechanized inland wine regions, South African wine needs to deliver something more valuable than low prices to survive. But only part of the South African grape harvest is sold as wine, the rest being low-grade stuff consigned either to distillation or grape-juice concentrate of which South Africa is the world's largest producer. The proportion sold as wine continues to increase but was still only 70% in 2005.

This phenomenon is a hangover from the stifling regime that governed wine-growers in South Africa for most of the 20th century. For much of the 19th, wine exports, and the Cape in general, flourished but phylloxera, the Anglo-Boer War, and the collapse of the all-important British market for Cape wines brought intense hardship to wine farmers. This was alleviated in 1918 by the formation of the KWV, a giant co-operative organization designed to provide

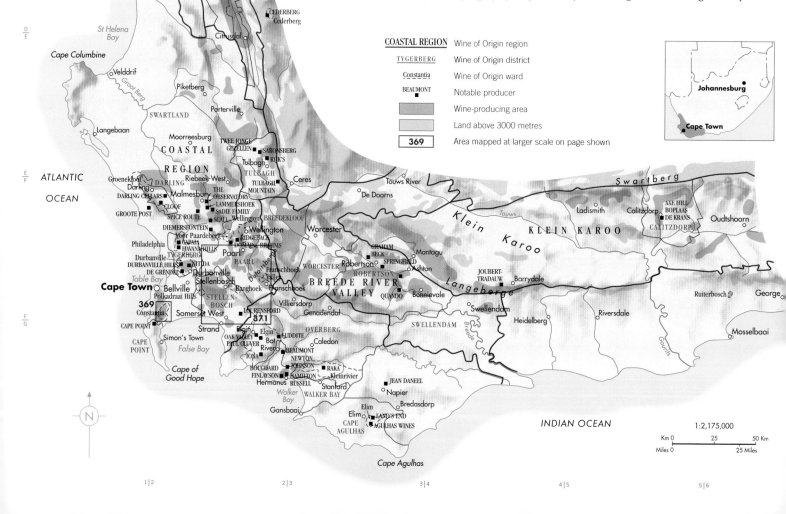

COASTAL REGION — Wine of Origin region
TYGERBERG — Wine of Origin district
Constantia — Wine of Origin ward
BEAUMONT — Notable producer
Wine-producing area
Land above 3000 metres
369 — Area mapped at larger scale on page shown

1:2,175,000
Km 0   25   50 Km
Miles 0   25 Miles

Paul Cluver, whose De Rust Estate is seen here, was a pioneer of the cool Elgin region and one of the first established wine producers to effect a black empowerment scheme in the form of the successful Thandi label, whose wines are made at the Cluver winery.

Neil Ellis. Like Constantia and Stellenbosch and Paarl, considered in detail overleaf, Darling is virtually on Cape Town's doorstep, making this beautiful part of South Africa of particular interest to wine tourists.

Durbanville is practically in the Cape Town suburbs and can easily be underestimated, but the nearby ocean brings nights cool enough to yield particularly refreshing whites and well-defined Cabernet and Merlot. Philadephia too, another ward of the **Tygerberg** district, with dramatic views over the city, should have a bright future, thanks partly to German investment in its flagship Capaia winery.

Another rediscovered wine district is **Tulbagh**, to the immediate east of Swartland in one of the most distinctive settings, hemmed in on three sides by the Winterhoek Mountains. Soils as well as exposures and elevations vary enormously, but diurnal temperature variation is reliably high, even if mornings can be particularly cool as cold overnight air sits trapped in the amphitheatre formed by the mountains.

Further north the WestCorp co-operative at Vredendal has shown that decreased latitude need not mean decreased quality. Much of the crisp Chenin and Colombard that can make South Africa seem the world's best source of bargain white wines comes from the **Olifants River** region, with its **Citrusdal** and **Lutzville** districts. Bamboes Bay, a ward on the west coast, produces much finer Sauvignon Blanc than might be expected at this latitude. Altitude is the trump card of the separate Cederberg ward just east of Olifants River.

Lower Orange, off the map to the north, is even hotter in summer and depends heavily on irrigation from the Orange River. Much work has gone into vine trellising to protect the grapes from the relentless sunlight here.

Summer temperatures in **Klein Karoo**, the great eastern sweep of arid inland scrub, are so high that fortified wines, made possible only by irrigation, are the local speciality, along with some red table wines and ostriches (for their meat and feathers). Muscats and such Douro Valley grapes as Tinta Barocca (Barroca in Portugal), Touriga Nacional, and Souzão thrive here. Portugal's port producers have been keeping a wary but respectful eye on developments, notably in the **Calitzdorp** district that routinely produces the trophy winners in South Africa's fortified wine classes.

a market and control prices for everything produced on Cape vineyards, no matter what the quality.

Today the structure of the wine industry is quite different. As soon as apartheid and isolationism were abandoned, a new generation of young wine producers travelled the world, soaking up techniques and inspiration with unparalleled curiosity. Considerable new capital has been invested in the Cape's wine industry so that today there are more than 500 private wineries – twice as many as at the turn of the century. There are still more than 60 co-ops, many of which have worked hard to raise their standards. Three hundred of the wineries, many of them the personal labels of winemakers at larger enterprises, crush fewer than 100 tons of grapes. Freedom is palpably being celebrated.

Until 1992 the KWV also operated a quota system that stifled attempts to plant new vines in new places. But the KWV as regulator no longer exists and there has been a rash of experimental planting in new, typically cooler, regions. Just as significantly, some of the older wine regions are being re-evaluated. The Wine of Origin scheme of 1974, which first gave

official recognition to regions, districts, and wards (the smallest geographical entities), continues to develop. The most significant ones are mapped here and on the following pages.

The **Swartland** district is perhaps the most obvious example of this re-evaluation. For long associated with nothing more distinguished than robust red ingredients for the co-ops' blends, this swathe of cereal-growing north of Cape Town is now home to some of South Africa's most admired vineyards, patches of green punctuating the rolling grain-fields. Charles Back of Fairview lit the torch, which is now being carried by the likes of Eben Sadie, who is also fashioning powerful dry whites such as Palladius from Swartland fruit, in addition to his well-known Columella red. Dry farming is the norm here, where sea air from the Atlantic steals in from the west. So far Syrah and old-vine Chenin Blanc have made the most waves.

An enclave within Swartland called **Darling**, with its ward Groenekloof, is particularly well exposed to cool influence from the Atlantic to the west and has built up quite a reputation for its crystalline Sauvignon Blanc, pioneered by

◀ Of these fine wine regions outside the classic Cape wine heartland, Hamilton Russell's Walker Bay is arguably the most established, although Elgin and Elim, where the Sauvignon Blancs are grown, are even cooler. TMV's White and the Sadies' Columella are proof of Swartland's newfound respectability.

A little closer to the gentle influence of the Atlantic, but still so warm and dry that irrigation is *de rigueur*, is **Worcester**, a district in the **Breede River Valley** region. More wine is made here than in any other Cape region, more than a quarter of the country's entire wine output. Much of it ends up as brandy, but this is the source of some well-made commercial red and white too.

If one region outside the immediate Cape area stands out for having established the quality of a clutch of estates, and good co-op wine too, it is **Robertson**, further down the Breede River Valley towards the Indian Ocean. Add to this sufficient limestone to support substantial stud farming and you have a district that is useful for white wine, particularly juicy Chardonnay, with a growing reputation for reds. Rainfall is low, summers are hot, but southeasterlies help to funnel cooling marine air off the Indian Ocean into the valley.

Perhaps the most exciting potential lies to the south, closer to the Antarctic. **Walker Bay** near Hermanus is a relatively recent district, but it can already boast wines with a track record of elegance. Tim Hamilton Russell was the pioneer who showed that South Africa could produce serious Pinot Noir and eerily burgundian Chardonnay. Weathered shales characterize the Hemel-en-Aarde Valley, which varies considerably in altitude and exposure so that Sauvignon Blanc, Merlot, and Shiraz can also be grown successfully here. Walker Bay includes some of the finest whale-watching country in Africa – another reason for tourists to visit Cape wine country.

To the east even cooler land has been prospected with particularly elegant Sauvignon Blanc now coming from the hinterland of **Cape Agulhas** around the breezy village of Elim and at least as far east as Ruiterbosch.

To the immediate north and west of Walker Bay is the **Overberg** district, where the apple-growing country of Elgin has been substantially converted to vineyards. They seem well suited to Sauvignon Blanc, Semillon, Pinot Noir, and cool-climate Shiraz. The Kleinrivier ward near Stanford is also promising, for much the same grape varieties.

Not that long ago most South African wineries, no matter where, used to produce a wide range of different varietals and blends, particularly the controversial "Cape blend" red, designed to show Pinotage tempered with other dark-skinned grapes, no matter where they were located. Today there is greater awareness of what each vineyard is best at and smaller producers increasingly dare to specialize in just one or two wine styles.

The most noticeable trend in Cape grapes has been the wholesale substitution of red, of which there was a virtual glut in the mid-2000s, for the white, especially Chenin Blanc, that once dominated South African vineyards. Chenin is still the most planted variety, but now represents fewer than one vine in five. To pull up more would be a mistake; old bushvine Chenin is still the Cape's most original contribution; wine of real style and substance at a relatively bargain price. Chenin does best where coastal influence helps maintain its high natural acidity. Ken Forrester, Rudera, and De Trafford make some of the finest examples in Stellenbosch, while the Sadie Family's Palladius blend, based on old bushvines in Paardeberg in Swartland, is setting a new standard.

Colombard is the Cape's third most planted variety, much used for distillation. Chardonnay and Sauvignon Blanc are grown in almost equal quantities and with equal promise. Chardonnays in all but the hottest vineyards can exhibit a finesse, and in some cases ageing potential, that is rare outside Burgundy. Sauvignon Blancs also benefit from high levels of natural acidity. Blended whites have a long history in South Africa; today Rhône varieties are increasingly being harnessed for full-bodied examples.

Cabernet Sauvignon is the most planted red wine grape. Plantings doubled between 1998 and 2005 but Shiraz (sic) is catching up fast, so popular are South African variations on this theme, from the determinedly peppery northern Rhône-style "Syrahs" of Boekenhoutskloof to the much richer, brighter, sweeter, often American-oaked style favoured by Saxenburg and Fairview.

Plantings of Merlot have increased sharply, while the area devoted to Pinotage, South Africa's own crossing of Pinot Noir and Cinsaut, is static. This often pungent grape variety can be found either as an answer to Beaujolais or as a more seriously oaked, if still fleshy, mouthful. The debate as to which is the more successful style is ongoing.

The country's red wine production was for long plagued by leafroll virus in the vineyards, which stops grapes ripening fully. By the mid-2000s almost half of all South African vineyards had been replanted with new clones of virus-free varieties perceived as more fashionable than the old Chenin and Colombard mix, on rootstocks carefully selected for local conditions. One of the greatest challenges for South African viticulture will be to ensure that this new, heavily quarantined plant material proves robust and healthy well into the 21st century.

But without doubt the potentially greatest evolutionary step in South Africa is social. It has not proved easy to share more equitably ownership and management of an industry run for so long by the white minority. There have been plenty of setbacks, but now there is a very real will to transform the wine industry – not least so that the black majority of South Africans will become a significant market for South African wine. Black empowerment schemes and joint ventures are under way, albeit sometimes developing slowly. Labels such as Fair Valley, Tukulu, Bouwland, Yammé, and, more emotively, Freedom Road, Thandi (Xhosa for "cherish"), and Winds of Change bear witness to the start of a new era for South African wine. Mentoring and training schemes are specifically designed to encourage wider participation in the wine industry, while more winery funds are being directed at better housing, conditions, wages, and general social upliftment, as they call it. Nevertheless, impatience is understandable.

Flocks of domesticated ostriches are a common sight in the Klein Karoo. These inquisitive birds benefit from a surprisingly varied diet, although it probably does not include the impressive fortified wines that are this region's speciality.

Constantia

Historically the most famous wine name of South Africa is Constantia, a legendary dessert wine which by the late 18th century was recognized as one of the greatest wines in the world. The original extensive vineyard, which at 1,850 acres (750ha) is far bigger than the total area of vines in Constantia today, was established in 1685 by the Cape's second Dutch governor, Simon van der Stel. (He also gave his name to Stellenbosch, the focus of fine wine production today; see overleaf.)

Constantia is now effectively a suburb, a particularly pretty southern suburb, of Cape Town. As such it is heavily developed and it is unlikely that the total vineyard area will grow substantially, and it may even continue to contract. Land prices are high and vines are increasingly driven uphill on to the steeper eastern, southeastern, and northeastern slopes of Constantiaberg, which is effectively the eastern tail of Table Mountain. But this corner of the Cape winelands produces some of its most distinctive wines, from what is in effect a mountain amphitheatre that opens directly on to False Bay. It is constantly cooled by the Cape Doctor, the southeaster that blows in from the ocean. This same wind helps to mitigate the fungal diseases that can be relatively common here as the annual rainfall is more than 40in (1,000mm).

Sauvignon Blanc is the grape of choice in Constantia's 1,040 acres (420ha) of vineyard. It represents a third of all the region's vines, with Chardonnay and Cabernet Sauvignon a long way behind. The Cape Doctor is thought to encourage the retention of pyrazine, which is responsible for the grassy range of aromas associated with Sauvignon. Perhaps the most dramatic example of Constantia Sauvignon is at Steenberg, a particularly windswept site. Semillon, by far the most planted grape variety in South Africa in the early 19th century, can be outstanding, with both Steenberg and Cape Point making particularly fine examples.

Soils here are deeply weathered, acid, and reddish brown with a high clay content, except around Uitsig, where sand predominates and vines in these soils, the warmest and lowest in Constantia, tend to ripen first.

Despite the pressures of encroaching urban development and the occasional marauding baboon from the nearby nature reserves on Table Mountain, two new wineries opened in Constantia in the early 21st century, bringing the total to seven. Klein Constantia continues the dessert wine tradition with its Vin de Constance, made from small-berried Muscat grapes grown on the site of those first planted by Simon de Stel, and sold in bottles moulded from an original 200-year-old flask.

Cape Point is a one-winery wine district just south of Constantia (see map p.366) which is even cooler but has made some wonderfully distinctive Sauvignon and Semillon.

A batik rendering of the four seasons of Constantia by Linda Jooste, daughter of the owner of Klein Constantia, which has been in the forefront of providing its workers with their own, superior accommodation on a nearby housing development. This in a Cape wine area with the highest land prices of all.

▲ This cool region is a natural home for vivacious, aromatic Sauvignon Blanc, but in warmer vintages Buitenverwachting (pronounced Bay-ten-ver-vak-ting) shows that Constantia can also yield Bordeaux blends with real complexity and ageing potential.

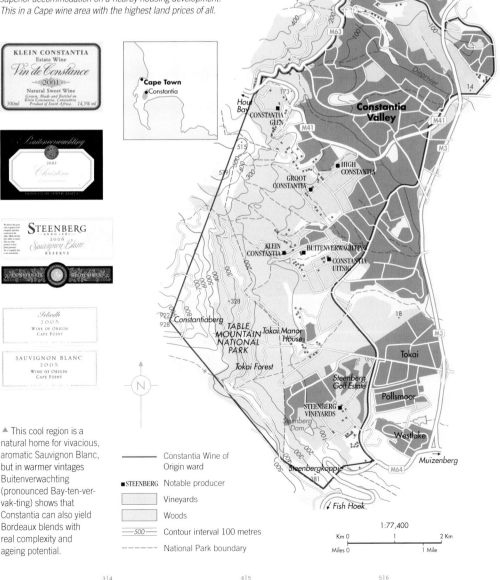

Constantia Wine of Origin ward

■ STEENBERG Notable producer

Vineyards

Woods

—500— Contour interval 100 metres

------ National Park boundary

1:77,400

Stellenbosch and Paarl

The area mapped opposite is the traditional hub of Cape wine activity, even if today fine wine is made in a much wider area all the way from Swartland to Walker Bay. However exciting the results from some of South Africa's recent plantings in cooler areas elsewhere, the great concentration of South African winemaking is likely to remain centred on **Stellenbosch**, a leafy university town surrounded by Arcadian countryside whose curling white Cape Dutch gables have been captured in thousands of tourist photographs. The town is also the centre of South African wine academe, with increasing numbers of students representing the new multiracial South Africa, as well as the Nietvoorbij research centre.

The soils of Stellenbosch vary from light and sandy on the western valley floor (traditionally Chenin Blanc country) to heavier soils on mountain slopes and decomposed granite at the foot of the Simonsberg, Stellenbosch, Drakenstein, and Franschhoek mountains in the east (the last two ranges in Paarl rather than Stellenbosch). The contour lines and distribution of blue on the map opposite are enough to hint at just how varied a range of terroirs can be found here. At this stage in South African wine evolution, however, it can be dangerous to associate a winery's location too closely with a likely terroir effect, since so many producers vinify fruit from a wide range of different locations, often blending the wine so that the appellation Coastal Region, and sometimes the even larger Western Cape, is common on labels.

North, further from the sea, temperatures tend to be higher, but the climate is in general pretty perfect for growing wine grapes. Rainfall is just about right, and concentrated in the winter months; summers are just slightly warmer than Bordeaux. So fashionable have red wines become that Cabernet Sauvignon (definitively), Shiraz, and Merlot have all overtaken Chenin Blanc in terms of total vineyard acreage in Stellenbosch, as has Sauvignon Blanc, which can produce fine white wines here, especially in cooler spots. Chardonnay is not as widely planted but can also reveal finesse. Blends have long been important too, particularly the infamous red Cape Blend, although white blends are increasingly and justifiably admired.

So established and varied are the vineyards of Stellenbosch that there has been time to subdivide what is, according to official South African wine nomenclature, a district in the Coastal Region into wards (they have changed a little since the last edition of this book). And just to keep us on our toes, there are other geographically distinct entities within Stellenbosch which are not official wards.

The first ward to gain official recognition was Simonsberg-Stellenbosch, including all the cooler, well-drained southern flanks of the imposing Simonsberg Mountain (although the heavy-hitting Thelema, not a wine farm when the boundaries were drawn up in 1980, is excluded). Jonkershoek Valley is a small but long-recognized area in the eponymous mountains east of Stellenbosch, while the equally minute Papegaaiberg sits on the opposite side of the town, buffering it from the thriving ward based on the sheltered Devon Valley. The much larger, flatter, and more recent Bottelary ward to the north borrows its name from the hills in its far southwest corner. Banghoek was the newest ward until Polkadraai Hills to the west gained recognition in 2006 (see map on p.366).

On the whole the best wines come from estates around the town of Stellenbosch, which is open to southerly ocean breezes from False Bay, or high enough in the hills for altitude and cooling winds to slow down the ripening process. The imposing Helderberg Mountains running northeast of Somerset West are an obvious factor in local wine geography, for example, and on their western flanks are many winemaking high-fliers. Anglo American's spectacular and much-garlanded Vergelegen winery (below) lies on the mountains' southern slopes.

Paarl, further from the cooling influence of False Bay, may not be the focus of the Cape wine scene that it was in the KWV and fortified wine era, but fine table wines are made here by producers such as Fairview, Glen Carlou, Rupert & Rothschild, and Villiera. Chenin Blanc and Cabernet Sauvignon are planted in almost equal quantity, with Shiraz and Merlot lying third and fourth respectively.

Wards within Paarl include the detached and higher settlement of Franschhoek Valley (only partly mapped here), originally farmed by Huguenots and still distinguished by its French place and family names. Today the valley, enclosed on three sides by mountains, is more readily associated with restaurants and pretty scenery than with wine, but it can boast a handful of top performers. Boekenhoutskloof is based in Franschhoek Valley, even if the fruit for its mould-breaking Syrah is sourced from one of the cooler corners of Wellington, a much less fashionable ward of Paarl, in the north. Wellington, with greater diurnal temperature variation than areas closer to the coast, is made up of a varied mixture of alluvial terraces, which stretch towards Swartland's rolling cereal country, and some more dramatic sites in the foothills of the Hawequa Mountains.

In addition to Simonsberg-Paarl, which lies on the foothills of the Simonsberg Mountain and is contiguous with Simonsberg-Stellenbosch discussed above, Paarl's other ward, Voor Paardeberg, is effectively an extension of Swartland to its immediate west.

Vergelegen itself looks pretty spectacular, but the views from the winery across False Bay towards Table Mountain are, if anything, even more so. Combine this with an unbeaten record on the show circuit and you have a wine estate that seems almost absurdly over-endowed.

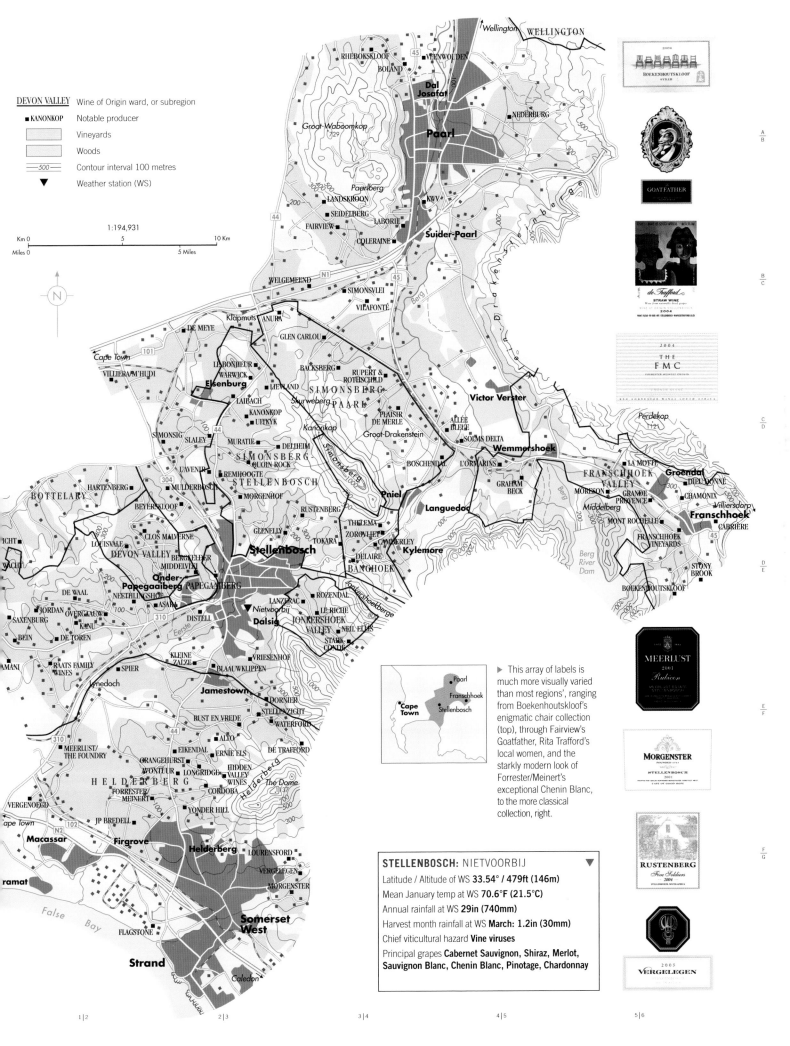

DEVON VALLEY Wine of Origin ward, or subregion

■ KANONKOP Notable producer

Vineyards

Woods

─500─ Contour interval 100 metres

▼ Weather station (WS)

1:194,931

Km 0 — 5 — 10 Km
Miles 0 — 5 Miles

N

WELLINGTON

RHEBOKSKLOOF
BOLAND
VEENWOUDEN
Dal Josafat
NEDERBURG
Groot-Waboomkop 729
Paarl
Paarlberg
KWV
LANDSKROON
SEIDELBERG
FAIRVIEW
LABORIE
COLERAINE
Suider-Paarl
WELGEMEEND
SIMONSVLEI
VILAFONTÉ
Klapmuts ANURA
DE MEYE
GLEN CARLOU
VILLIERA M'HUDI
LE BONHEUR
WARWICK
BACKSBERG
RUPERT & ROTHSCHILD
Elsenburg
LIEVLAND
SIMONSBERG-PAARL
Skurweberg
Victor Verster
LAIBACH
KANONKOP
UITKYK
PLAISIR DE MERLE
ALLÉE BLEUE
SIMONSIG SLALEY
MURATIE
Kanonkop
Groot-Drakenstein
SOLMS DELTA
Wemmershoek
DELHEIM
SIMONSBERG-STELLENBOSCH
QUOIN ROCK
REMHOOGTE
L'AVENIR
MULDERBOSCH
MORGENHOF
BOSCHENDAL
L'ORMARINS
GRAHAM BECK
Middelberg
FRANSCHHOEK VALLEY
Groendal
DIEU DONNÉ
MORESON GRANDE PROVENCE
CHAMONIX
Villiersdorp
Perdekop 1121
HARTENBERG
BOTTELARY
BEYERSKLOOF
RUSTENBERG
Pniel
Languedoc
MONT ROCHELLE
Franschhoek
CLOS MALVERNE
GLENELLY
THELEMA
ZORGVLIET
CAMBERLEY
Kylemore
FRANSCHHOEK VINEYARDS
CABRIÈRE
ICHT
LOUISVALE
DEVON VALLEY
BERGKELDER MIDDELVLEI
Stellenbosch
TOKARA
DELAIRE
BANGHOEK
STONY BROOK
WACHT
Onder-Papegaaiberg PAPEGAAIBERG
NEETHLINGSHOF
ASARA
LANZERAC
ROZENDAL
LE RICHE
BOEKENHOUTSKLOOF
DE WAAL
JORDAN OVERGAAUW
KANU
DISTELL
Dalsig
Nietvoorbij
JONKERSHOEK VALLEY
SAXENBURG
BEIN
DE TOREN
STARK-CONDÉ
NEIL ELLIS
AMANI
RAATS FAMILY WINES
KLEINE ZALZE
VRIESENHOF
SPIER
BLAAUWKLIPPEN
Lynedoch
Jamestown
DORNIER
STELLENZICHT
RUST EN VREDE
WATERFORD
MEERLUST/THE FOUNDRY
ALTO
EIKENDAL
ERNIE ELS
DE TRAFFORD
ORANGEHURST
AVONTUUR
LONGRIDGE
HIDDEN VALLEY WINES
CORDOBA
The Dome
HELDERBERG
FORRESTER MEINERT
VERGENOEGD
YONDER HILL
JP BREDELL
Cape Town
Macassar
Firgrove
Helderberg
LOURENSFORD
VERGELEGEN
MORGENSTER
False Bay
ramat
FLAGSTONE
Somerset West
Strand
Caledon

▶ This array of labels is much more visually varied than most regions', ranging from Boekenhoutskloof's enigmatic chair collection (top), through Fairview's Goatfather, Rita Trafford's local women, and the starkly modern look of Forrester/Meinert's exceptional Chenin Blanc, to the more classical collection, right.

Paarl
Franschhoek
Stellenbosch
Cape Town

STELLENBOSCH: NIETVOORBIJ ▼

Latitude / Altitude of WS **33.54° / 479ft (146m)**

Mean January temp at WS **70.6°F (21.5°C)**

Annual rainfall at WS **29in (740mm)**

Harvest month rainfall at WS **March: 1.2in (30mm)**

Chief viticultural hazard **Vine viruses**

Principal grapes **Cabernet Sauvignon, Shiraz, Merlot, Sauvignon Blanc, Chenin Blanc, Pinotage, Chardonnay**

China

One of the more potent symbols of the westernization of China has been the extent to which the staggeringly numerous Chinese have taken to wine. Consumption is rising at such a rate, estimated at 15% a year, that Shanghai and Beijing are now as common a destination for French wine exporters as New York and London. And China's love affair with grape wine (*putaojiu*), as opposed to mere *jiu*, meaning any alcoholic drink, has been so effectively encouraged by the state in recent years, partly in an effort to reduce cereal imports, that according to OIV figures, China's total vineyard area tripled in the 10 years to 2003. Those same figures suggested that China was already the world's sixth most important wine producer.

The vine was known to gardeners in western China at least as early as the 2nd century AD when wine, very possibly grape wine, was certainly made and consumed. European grape varieties were introduced to eastern China at the end of the 19th century, but it was only in the late 20th century that grape-based wine insinuated itself into Chinese (urban) society.

China's vastness can offer a staggering range of soils and latitudes. Climate is more problematical. Inland China suffers typical continental extremes, while much of the coast, especially in southern and central areas, is subject to monsoons.

In **Xinjiang** province in the far northwest, where about a fifth of all China's vines are planted, many of them recently, winters are so bitterly cold that vinifera vines have to be painstakingly banked up, one by one, every autumn. Ingenious irrigation systems harness meltwater from some of the highest mountains in the world. The biggest operator here is Vini Suntime, which now manages about 25,000 acres (10,000ha) of vineyard (from a standing start in 1998). Western China, including Xinjiang and as far east as **Gansu** and **Ningxia** provinces, is becoming increasingly important for wine, and many wineries in the east also have grape-processing plants here.

State wineries still operate all over China, but it was only from the early 1980s, when foreign expertise was invited to participate in joint ventures, that wines of a sort recognizable to western palates (dryish, fruity, and entirely based on grapes) began to be made in China – some of them using imported must.

Rémy Martin was the first Western company to collaborate with the Chinese, based in **Tianjin** but drawing heavily on grapes from nearby **Hebei** province, home to just under 15% of all Chinese vines. The success of

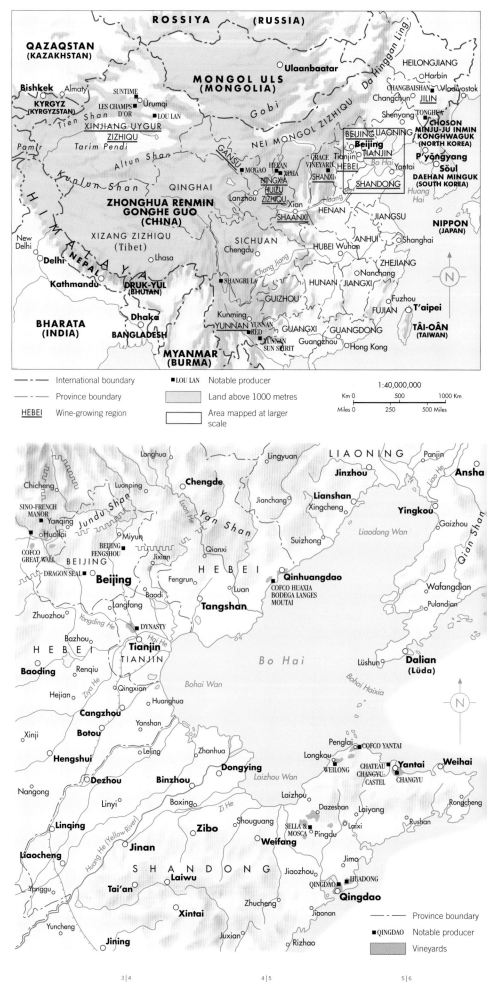

International boundary

- - - Province boundary

HEBEI   Wine-growing region

■LOU LAN   Notable producer

Land above 1000 metres

Area mapped at larger scale

1:40,000,000
Km 0   500   1000 Km
Miles 0   250   500 Miles

1:5,128,000
Km 0   50   100   150 Km
Miles 0   50   100 Miles

Province boundary

■QINGDAO   Notable producer

Vineyards

Dynasty, a white wine of local Long Yan (Dragon's Eye) grapes flavoured with Muscat (brought from Bulgaria in 1958) encouraged them to plant classic European varieties. Long Yan is widely used for western-style wines while *shan putao*, literally "mountain grape", is the staple of more traditional ferments. So far only just over 10% of all vines planted are international varieties, with Cabernet Sauvignon and to a lesser extent Merlot predominating. The typical 21st-century Chinese wine has been red, and not unlike a very pale imitation of red Bordeaux, although plantings of Shiraz have been increasing. For white wines, Welschriesling was for long the dominant vinifera wine grape but plantings of Chardonnay have accelerated in recent years.

A second venture with European input at least in the form of winemaking advice produced Great Wall, also in Hebei. A third, Dragon Seal, in the western suburbs of Beijing, involved Pernod Ricard. The French company withdrew from the venture in 2001, but its influence continues in the form of the French winemaker, Jérôme Sabaté.

On the face of it the **Shandong** Peninsula in eastern China looks one of the more likely places to grow European grapes. With a truly maritime climate that requires no winter protection of vines, it offers well-drained, south-facing slopes. Shandong province is where almost a third of China's roughly 500 wineries are now based, but fungal diseases in late summer and autumn are the main drawback. Changyu was the pioneer and is still by far the dominant producer; the Italian drinks group Saronno took a third-share in 2005. Chateau Changyu-Castel is a separate joint venture with Castel of Bordeaux.

The first modern, western-style winery was established by a Hong Kong businessman in the early 1980s and was owned at one time by Allied Domecq. Today Huadong is best known for its Chardonnay and Gamay.

The winery that could claim to make China's most impressive wine in the early 21st century was also Hong Kong-owned. Grace, nothing to do with the Japanese winery of the same name, produces convincing reds from Bordeaux varieties grown in coal-mining country southwest of Beijing.

Merlot grapes are picked for Bodega Langes in Hebei province, owned by the same Austrian family as owns Swarovski crystal and runs Norton in Argentina. The property includes a wine school, a luxury hotel, and an ultra-modern winery.

▼ Some of the labels on Chinese wine that are more intelligible to westerners. Despite western perceptions that Chinese food is best suited to white wine, most Chinese consumers feel that the first duty of a wine is to be red.

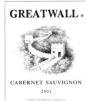

Japan

In constructing Japan, nature seems to have had almost every form of pleasure and enterprise in view except wine. Although the latitude of Honshu, the main island of the Japanese archipelago, coincides with that of the Mediterranean, its climate does not. Like the eastern USA (lying in the same latitudes), it suffers from having a vast continent to the west. Caught between Asia and the Pacific, the greatest land and sea masses in the world, its predictably extreme climate is peculiar to itself. Winds from Siberia freeze its winters; monsoons from the Pacific and the Sea of Japan drench its springs and summers. At the precise moments when the vines most need sunshine they are lashed by typhoons.

The land the typhoons lash is hard-boned and mountainous, almost two-thirds of it so steep that only the forests prevent the acid soil from being washed into the short, turbulent rivers. The plains have alluvial paddy soils, washed from the hills, poor-draining and good for rice, not vines. Such little gently sloping arable land as exists is consequently extremely valuable and demands a high return.

It is not surprising, therefore, that Japan has hesitated about wine; hesitated, that is, for about 1,200 years. History is exact. Grapes were grown in the 8th century AD at the court of Nara. Buddhist missionaries spread the grapevine around the country – although not necessarily with wine in mind. In 1186, near Mount Fuji, a seedling vinifera vine with thick-skinned grapes was selected and named Koshu. It remains the variety best suited to Japanese conditions: although basically a table grape it can make confident, delicate wine, both oaked and non-oaked, sweet and dry.

A wine industry, in the modern sense, has existed for 130 years, much longer than any other in Asia. Japan's first outward-looking government sent researchers to Europe in the 1870s to study methods and to bring back vines. It soon became clear that American vines did better than French or German. Nor were the Japanese averse to the "foxy" flavour of eastern American grapes. Delaware is still planted on almost 20% of Japan's declining total vineyard area, second only to the popular

hybrid Kyoho. Vinifera varieties account for much less than 20% of all varieties planted, of which some of the more notable are a relative of Kyoho called Pione, Campbell Early, Muscat Bailey A, and Neo Muscat, a crossing of Koshu Sanjaku and Muscat of Alexandria.

The wine industry was based from the start in the hills around the Kōfu Basin in Yamanashi prefecture – within view of Mount Fuji and convenient for the capital. Yamanashi also has the highest average temperatures and the earliest budbreak, flowering, and vintage. More than half of Japan's 175-odd genuine wineries (as opposed to blending and bottling plants or production centres for rice-based sake) are here. Japan is an enthusiastic importer of bulk wine and grape must, though imported content must now be specified on labels.

Up to the 1960s, many small firms in Yamanashi made wine as sweet as possible for an unsophisticated market. Today the Japanese wine market is dominated by Mercian, Suntory (which has wine holdings elsewhere, notably the Bordeaux classed-growth Château Lagrange), Sapporo, and Manns. All have access to the best Japanese-grown European grapes, from some of the world's most manicured vines. Cabernets and Merlots can have formidable tannin and acidity. Chardonnays are less distinctive.

Nearby Nagano is less prone to monsoons, grows some of the finest Japanese wine, and can now boast 25 wineries although it also supplies grapes to many of the bigger Yamanashi-based wineries. Hokkaidō, the northernmost island with particularly cold winters, has 10 wineries and is also an important grape grower.

The number of wineries has been increasing and wine is now made in 36 of Japan's 43 prefectures, even on the semi-tropical island of Kyūshū in the southwest, where the Tsuno winery is managing to conjure fine wine out of varieties such as Muscat Bailey A and Campbell Early.

▼ Grace's version of Kai Noir, a Japanese hybrid vine variety, has done particularly well in wine competitions. Tsuno is a new winery on Kyūshū Island in the far south while Château Mercian is an old-timer and Koshu is Japan's signature white wine grape.

1:10,700,000

Km 0 — 100 — 200 — 300 Km
Miles 0 — 100 — 200 Miles

Notable producers in Nagano	
HAYASHI NO-EN	ST COUSAIR
IZUTSU	VILLA D'EST
OBUSE	

Notable producers in Yamanashi	
ALPS	KIZAN
CH LUMIÈRE	MANNS
CH MERCIAN	RUBAIYAT
GRACE	SADOYA
IKEDA	SAPPORO
KATSUNUMA	SOLEIL
KITANORO	SUNTORY

■ TSUNO — Notable producer

▢ — Land above 1000 metres

▼ — Weather station (WS)

JAPAN: KUMAGAYA ▼

Latitude / Altitude of WS **36.09° / 98ft (30m)**

Mean July temp at WS **76.5°F (24.7°C)**

Annual rainfall at WS **50in (1,260mm)**

Harvest month rainfall at WS **September: 9in (230mm)**

Chief viticultural hazards **Rain, summer typhoons, fungal diseases**

Principal grapes **Koshu, Neo Muscat, Cabernet Sauvignon, Merlot, Chardonnay, Kyoho, Delaware**

The Rest of Asia

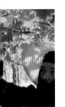

It seems only yesterday that Asia was regarded as the one continent of no relevance to the world of wine. By common consent it was for long agreed that grape wine would never be of interest to Asian producers or consumers. How wrong we were. The Asian market played a major part in driving up the price of fine wine in the 1990s. And wine is now produced not just in the Central Asian republics of Uzbekistan, Tajikistan, Kazakhstan, Turkmenistan, and Kyrgyzstan, which have a long history of growing vines and making (traditionally rather syrupy) wines, but in such unlikely countries as India, Thailand, Vietnam, Taiwan, and Indonesia – each of which has a fledgling wine industry based on tropical or near-tropical viticulture. In many cases vines are persuaded to produce more than one harvest a year, by judicious pruning, trimming, watering, withholding water and/or the application of various chemicals and hormones.

India's swelling, increasingly westernized, and increasingly prosperous middle class is encouragement enough for the local wine industry, although the imposition of heavy duties on imported wines in 2005 provided another spur to the likes of Château Indage and Sula (both in the state of Maharashtra) and Grover, the three companies that between them have been responsible for about 90% of sales of Indian wine. Since 2001 the state of Maharashtra has actively encouraged wine production via various financial incentives. As a result, 38 of Maharashtra's 41 wineries (in 2007) are new ventures. Half of them are in the Nashik district, where relatively high altitudes offset the low latitude.

Château Indage was the pioneer of modern Indian wine production, notably with an off-dry sparkling wine sold under such names as Marquis de Pompadour and Omar Khayyam, with expertise and grape varieties imported from Champagne. It has grown considerably, produces a wide range of varietal still wines, and has a new winery at Himachal Pradesh in the foothills of the Himalayas as well as contract plantings in Andra Pradesh and Orissa.

Rajeev Samant returned to India from Silicon Valley with California wine sensibilities and set about making fresh, fruity, dry white wines, most notably Sula Sauvignon Blanc. Sula's debut vintage was 2000, producing 5,000 cases, but by 2006 125,000 cases were made, supplied by a total of 1,200 acres (485ha) of vineyard.

These "floating vineyards", islands of vines alternating with a series of canals, in the Chao Phraya Delta in southern Thailand, are some of the world's most visually distinctive. Malaga Blanc grapes, grown on pergolas to keep fungal diseases at bay in the humid climate, are shipped out by boat for Siam Winery's Monsoon Valley label.

The Grover family's highly successful wine operation is one of relatively few based outside Maharashtra, in this case in the hills above Bangalore in the state of Karnataka (although they are now investing in Maharashtra for a second line of wines). As long ago as the mid-1990s they hired Michel Rolland of Pomerol as winemaking consultant and the result was La Réserve, a red that would not look remotely out of place on a Bordeaux merchant's tasting bench. The vines are never dormant but careful pruning results in just one harvest each year in April or May.

Thailand's wine industry is much smaller but the nine winery members of the Thai Wine Association form a cohesive whole, as well they might in a country with some powerful forces dedicated to banning alcohol altogether. Its roots go back to the 1960s when vines were planted, mainly for table grapes in the Chao Praya Delta just west of Bangkok. The Siam Winery initially produced coolers from the resulting grape juice, but a serious operation dedicated to wine production followed, Château de Loei, whose first vintage, from vines grown in the far north near the Laos border, was 1995.

Today there are vineyards in the Khao Yai region northeast of Bangkok at altitudes up to 1,800ft (550m), and Siam Winery also has some vineyards at 330ft (100m) in the hinterland of the resort of Hua Hin in the south of the country at only 10 degrees north of the equator.

Total vineyard area in Thailand is still well under 2,500 acres (1,000ha), however, with Shiraz/Syrah by far the most planted variety, followed by Chenin Blanc. Wines are certainly competently made and the most conscientious producers try to harvest just once every 12 months even though it is quite possible to pick five crops every two years. Hard pruning during the extremely hot months of March to May and the following three rainy months encourages the vines to treat this as their dormant period. Any early fruit produced is dropped, the vines are pruned again in late September or early October in order to encourage a "vintage" of the most concentrated, ripest fruit in February.

Vines are also grown for wine in Bhutan, Cambodia, Indonesia, Korea, Myanmar, Sri Lanka, Taiwan, and Vietnam, often on a tiny and embryonic scale, but there is no doubt that wine has colonized the continent of Asia.

◀ The owner of the Sula label cut his wine-drinking teeth in California and so was determined that the design should be thoroughly western, albeit with an oriental twist. Monsoon Valley and GranMonte are directed chiefly at Thailand's substantial tourist industry while Hatten has manged to establish a similarly tourist-oriented wine business in Bali, Indonesia.

Glossary

The aim of this list is to give you an insight into the most commonly used wine jargon. Terms used only in one region are explained in the relevant part of the Atlas. There are more French terms here than, say, Italian or Spanish, because they have been more widely adopted – and occasionally adapted. See also the Language of the Label boxes. Cross-references to other entries in the Glossary are denoted by italics.

acid vital component of wine and one that gives it zip and refreshment value. Most common wine acids are tartaric acid, malic acid, and to a lesser extent lactic acid.

acidify add *acid* to wine or *must* to improve its balance.

acidity total measure of *acids*.

Amarone style of wine made from dried grapes, originally from the Veneto, Italy.

appellation controlled, geographical wine name.

BA commonly used abbreviation for Beerenauslese, sweet German wine. See p.226.

bacterial diseases diseases (of the vine) spread by bacteria.

barrel any container for liquids made from wood although usually a *barrique* or *pièce*.

barrel ageing, barrel maturation process of maturing wine for months in *barrels* after *fermentation*.

barrel fermentation popular winemaking technique whereby the alcoholic *fermentation* takes place in *barrels*. Such wines (usually white) are said to be **barrel fermented**.

barrica, barrique standard Bordeaux *barrel* with a capacity of 225 litres.

base wines ingredients in a blend.

bâtonnage French for *lees stirring*, from *bâton*, French for stick.

blush wine see *rosé*.

bodega Spanish word for cellar or winemaking enterprise.

botrytis (Botrytis cinerea) generic term for certain *fungal diseases* of the vine known colloquially as rot. The benevolent form, noble rot, infects the grapes with a mould which concentrates the sugar and acidity in grapes, resulting in potentially magnificent, long-lived, very sweet **botrytized** wines. The malevolent form, grey rot, infects the grapes with mould which spoils flavour and, in dark-skinned grapes, destroys colour too.

bottle standard unit of wine volume containing 75cl.

bottle ageing, bottle maturation process of maturing wine in *bottle* (cf *barrel ageing*). Such a wine is said to have **bottle age**.

bottle deposit insoluble deposit that sticks to the inside of a bottle after *bottle ageing* (cf *sediment*).

bottling information generally mandatory on wine labels. See *château bottled*, *domaine bottled*, *estate bottled*.

calcareous one of the most used, and misused, descriptions of vineyard soils. Calcareous soils are based on limestone (prized in Burgundy) and occasionally include chalk (prized in Champagne).

canopy the green bits of a vine: shoots and, especially, leaves.

canopy management widely used vine-growing technique whereby the position and density of the *canopy* is deliberately managed so as to maximize wine quality and optimize wine quantity.

capsule alternative word for *foil*.

carbonic maceration winemaking technique whereby grapes are fermented whole in a sealed container under the influence of carbon dioxide. See p.33 for more details.

case standard container of 12 wine *bottles*, 24 halves, or 6 *magnums*. Smartest in wood, more often made of cardboard.

CB common abbreviation for *château bottled*.

chai French, particularly Bordeaux, word for the building in which wine is stored, usually in *barrel*.

chaptalization winemaking process named after French agriculture minister Chaptal whereby the alcohol level of the resulting wine is boosted by sugar added before or during *fermentation*. Such a wine is said to have been **chaptalized**.

château loose French (especially Bordeaux) term for a property on which wine is grown and, usually, made. Its vineyards are not necessarily a single, contiguous plot.

château bottled wine bottled at the same property where it was grown, or at least made.

classed-growth English for *cru classé*.

climat Burgundian word for an individual vineyard or *appellation*.

clone of a vine, plant specially selected for some particular attribute.

clos French (particularly Burgundian) term for a specific, walled vineyard. Also used by the pioneers in Priorat, Spain.

close spacing vine-growing technique dedicated to high *vine density*.

concentration winemaking process whereby some water is eliminated from the *must* or wine, thereby making it more **concentrated**.

contract winery see *custom crush facility*.

corked used to describe musty-smelling wines tainted by the compound trichloroanisole (TCA), usually via the cork.

coulure vine-growing phenomenon whereby a significant proportion of the potential fruit fails to set when the vine flowers in early summer, usually due to unsettled weather. The effect is reduced yield.

cru French word meaning literally growth, but in wine terms generally a specific vineyard.

cru classé a generally Bordeaux term for a vineyard included in one of the region's important classifications, most often but not necessarily the 1855 Classification of the Médoc and Graves (see p.82), which divided the top properties into five divisions. Thus first-, second-, third-, fourth-, and fifth-growths.

crush New World term for the annual grape harvest and business of winemaking.

custom crush facility contract winery making wines to order for a number of different vine-growers. Particularly common in California.

cuve French for vat or tank.

cuvée widely used, originally French term for a blend, used particularly for the final blend in sparkling winemaking.

cuvier French, particularly Bordeaux, term for the building where *fermentation* takes place – where *cuves* are to be found.

deacidify winemaking process undertaken only after very cool summers whereby the *acidity* of a wine or *must* is deliberately reduced, usually by adding calcium carbonate (chalk) or occasionally water.

diurnal temperature variation difference in average day and night temperatures. High variation is thought to result in deep colours and firm *acidity*.

domaine French (particularly Burgundian) term for a wine-producing property.

domaine bottled wine bottled by the same person or enterprise as grew it.

dosage amount of sweetening added to a sparkling wine before bottling.

Eiswein sweet wine made from grapes frozen on the vine, a German and occasionally Austrian speciality.

élevage the winemaking process of "raising" a wine from *fermentation* to release.

enology US spelling of *oenology*

en primeur offer of a wine for sale before it is even bottled, most common in Bordeaux, generally in the spring following the *vintage*.

esca debilitating *fungal disease* that weakens vines.

estate bottled wine bottled at the estate on which it was grown.

extraction important process of getting colour, *tannins*, and flavours out of the grape skins in various ways.

fermentation generally synonymous with the alcoholic fermentation during which *yeast* act on the sugars in ripe grapes to transform sweet grape juice into much drier wine. See also *malolactic fermentation*.

field grafting vine-growing operation of *grafting* another, more desirable, variety onto an existing root system in the vineyard.

filtration controversial winemaking operation designed to filter out any potentially harmful yeast or bacteria.

fining winemaking operation designed to clarify the wine by adding a **fining agent** such as albumen, casein, or a type of clay called bentonite which attracts solids in suspension in the wine and precipitates them as sediment.

first-growth see *cru classé*.

flor *yeast* that forms a thick film on the surface of a wine. Vital to the production of lighter sherries.

foil the (largely superfluous) covering of the top of a *bottle* neck and cork. Useful for identification in bottle racks.

fortified wine wine made extra strong by spirit added at some point during the production process. Some of the best known are port, sherry, and madeira.

fungal diseases diseases spread by fungal infections, to which the vine is particularly prone. See p.18.

futures wines sold *en primeur*.

garagiste see *microcuvée*.

generic wine named after a region or wine style (eg madeira, hock) rather than a *varietal* or one which qualifies for an *appellation*.

grafting vine-growing technique whereby one plant, usually a *vinifera* cutting, is **grafted** onto another, usually a *phylloxera*-resistant *rootstock*.

Grand Cru widely used term which in Burgundy is designed to denote the very finest vineyards of the Côte d'Or and Chablis, as it is in Champagne and Alsace.

gris very pale *rosé*.

Guyot vine-training system especially popular in Bordeaux, where the fruiting shoots grow from a cane or branch that is renewed each year.

hang time American expression for the (often extended) time grapes are allowed to stay on the vine in order to achieve full *physiological ripeness*.

hybrid vine variety bred by crossing one species (often *vinifera*) with another (often American). Hybrids are frowned on within Europe, sometimes unfairly.

Icewine Canadian term for *Eiswein*.

jeroboam large bottle size containing 4.5 litres or the equivalent of six standard *bottles* in Bordeaux; 3 litres or four bottles in Champagne.

Keller German term for cellar.

lay down to deliberately give a wine *bottle ageing*, usually for some years.

late harvest style of wine, generally sweet, made from very ripe grapes.

lees the deposit left in the bottom of a vat, tank, or *barrel*.

lees stirring winemaking operation of stirring up the *lees* to encourage aeration and interaction between them and the wine.

macération carbonique French for *carbonic maceration*.

magnum large bottle size containing 1.5 litres or two standard *bottles*.

malolactic fermentation softening winemaking process which follows alcoholic *fermentation* in virtually all red wines and many whites whereby harsh malic (appley) *acid* is converted into softer lactic (milky) acid under the influence of lactic bacteria and heat. Often known simply as the **malolactic**, or just **malo**.

mesoclimate the climate of a small patch of land such as a vineyard (cf **microclimate** of a single vine, or **macroclimate** of a district or region).

méthode traditionnelle, méthode classique see *traditional method*.

microcuvée very small Bordeaux *château*, often without its own winemaking facilities; a garage is popularly imagined to suffice. In this book we have defined *microcuvée* as producing no more than 1,000 cases, at least initially.

mildew downy mildew (peronospera) and powdery mildew (oidium) are two *fungal diseases* which persistently plague the vine and vine-grower. Spraying is the usual treatment.

millerandage uneven setting of fruit during flowering which can result in inconveniently uneven ripening.

mise the bottling process in French. **Mis(e) en bouteille au château/domaine** means *château/domaine bottled*.

must the interim, pulpy stage between grape juice and wine during winemaking.

négociant French term for a merchant bottler (cf *domaine*).

noble rot see *botrytis*.

non-vintage used particularly for sparkling wines and champagne to denote a wine that is not vintage-dated but is a blend of the produce of different years. A common abbreviation is **NV**.

oaked used of wines subjected in some way to the influence of oak, whether full-scale *barrel maturation* or, much cheaper, some contact with oak chips, inner staves, or the like. See p.35.

oenology the science of making wine.

old vines thought to imbue concentration and quality in a wine, mainly because *yields* are low.

owc common abbreviation in auction catalogues for original wooden *case*.

pH important winemaking measure in juice and wine of the strength of *acidity*, which can also affect colour and ageing potential. Water has a pH of 7, wine is usually about 3.5.

phenolics general term for the potentially astringent *tannins*, pigments, and flavour compounds in a grape or wine. In grapes they are concentrated in the skins.

physiological ripeness stage reached by a grape when the flavours and *phenolics* are fully ripe; the stem is brown rather than green, a grape can easily be pulled off the bunch, and the skin may start to shrivel.

phylloxera deadly vine pest of American origin, an aphid that feasts off vine roots. Its prevalence has made *grafting* onto resistant *rootstocks* essential in most wine regions. See pp.18–19.

pièce traditional Burgundy *barrel* holding 228 litres.

Pierce's Disease fatal vine disease spread by insects, especially in the southern states of the USA and increasingly in California. See p.19.

Premier Cru widely used term which in Burgundy and Champagne denotes some of the best vineyards (though not as good as *Grand Cru*). In Bordeaux, a *first-growth* may be known as a **Premier Grand Cru (Classé)**.

punt indentation in the base of most bottles, useful for stacking.

racking transferring wine off the *lees* from one container to another. See pages 29 and 35.

raisin dried grape, out of which a wide range of wines are made including *Amarone* and *Vin Santo*. Grapes may be said to be **raisined**, or to raisin on the vine.

remuage French for *riddling*.

Reserve much-used term which generally has very little meaning.

residual sugar one of wine's vital statistics, the amount of unfermented sugar remaining in the wine. A wine with an **RS** (common abbreviation) of 2g/l or less tastes dry.

reverse osmosis common technique for making wine more, or less, alcoholic.

riddling sparkling winemaking operation whereby the *sediment* deposited by the second *fermentation* in *bottle* has to be shaken into the bottle neck for removal. It is increasingly mechanized today.

rootstock vine root specially chosen for some attribute, typically resistance to *phylloxera*, although it may also be chosen for particular soil types or to devigorate particularly *vigorous* vine varieties.

rosé common name for wine made pink by brief contact with red, black, or purple grape skins.

rot see *botrytis* for details of this *fungal disease*.

saignée French term for bleeding, literally bleeding off some liquid from the fermentation vat to make the resultant wine more *concentrated*.

sediment the detritus of *bottle ageing*, particularly significant if the wine was not *filtered* or *fined* too heavily and the wine has been in bottle for years.

settling allowing juice to stand (usually over night) so that the bigger solids fall to the bottom of the *settling tank*.

sommelier wine waiter.

stirring see *lees stirring*.

sur lie French description of a wine kept deliberately in contact with the *lees* in order to add flavour.

TA *total acidity*.

tannins cheek-drying *phenolics* from grape skins, stalks, and pips which preserve wine and contribute to the ageing process.

TBA common abbreviation for Trockenbeeren-auslese, German term for very sweet wine made from individually picked *botrytized* grapes.

terroir physical environment. See pp.26–27.

tight spacing high *vine density*.

tirage process of leaving a *traditional method* sparkling wine on the yeast *lees* to mature, encouraging complex flavours.

top grafting *grafting* a new variety onto a mature vine in the vineyard.

total acidity the sum of all the many sorts of *acid* in a wine. One of wine's vital statistics.

traditional method sparkling winemaking operation whereby the bubbles are formed through the second *fermentation* taking place in *bottle*.

ullage headspace between a liquid and its container, whether a *bottle* or *barrel*. As wines age, ullage tends to increase.

varietal wine sold under the name of the grape variety from which it was made (cf *generic*). Not to be confused with the **variety** itself, which is a plant.

vendange tardive French for *late harvest*.

vieilles vignes French for *old vines*.

vigneron French for vine-grower.

vigour vine's propensity to grow leaves or *canopy*. A **vigorous** vine may be too leafy to ripen grapes properly.

vin de cépage French for *varietal* wine.

vin de garde French for a wine made to be aged.

vin de paille sweet dried grape wine traditionally made by drying grapes on straw mats.

Vin Doux Naturel sweet, strong wine made by adding spirit to grape juice before it has fully fermented. See p.144.

vine density measure of how closely vines are planted.

vinifera European species of the grapevine genus *Vitis* responsible for well over 95% of all wine, wherever it is grown (cf *hybrid*).

vinification making wine.

Vin Santo dried grape wine speciality of Italy.

vintage either the process of harvesting grapes or the year in which the grapes were harvested. All wine is therefore "vintage wine".

vintner originally someone who **vinted**, or made wine but now more usually someone who sells it.

viticulture science and practice of growing vines.

white how wines that are not red or pink are described, although in practice they vary from colourless to deep gold.

yield measure of how productive a vineyard is, usually in tonnes per acre or hectolitre per hectare. Multiply the former by about 17.5 to convert to the latter.

Index

Châteaux, domaines, etc appear under their individual names. Main treatments are indicated in **bold**, page numbers in *italics* relate to illustration captions.

wine: additives 16, 32, 34; alcoholic strength 16, 34, 261; collecting 41; colour and age 42–3, *43*; consumption of 10–11; coolers 45, *47*; "corked" (TCA) 40; development of 15–17; and food 206; global production 10–11; history of 12–17; kosher wine 286; laying down *15*, 41; serving 44–7, *44*; storage 41; tasting 14, 15, 29, *48*, **48–9**; and time 42–3
winemaking **32–9**; Alsace 126; Australia 342–3; Beaujolais 33, 72; calendar 28–9; California 16–17, 293; Chablis 76; Champagne 78–9; Georgia 280; Germany 240–1; Hungary 269; Italy 162; Madeira 222; Madiran 114; medieval 14; micro-oxygenation 35, *35*; port 220–1; Portugal 212; racking 29, 35; refrigeration 16; science and industry 16–17; sherry 206–7; Spain 198-9, 206–7; Switzerland 254, *see also* fermentation
viticulture **28–31**; biodynamic 19, 27, 31, *31*, 55, 57, 60, 115, 120, 123, 144, 245, 261, *271*, 297, 298, 317, 329, *349*; Bordeaux *31*, 82; California 293; Champagne 80; frost protection 24, *25*, 29, 76, 302, 327, 350; hail damage 24, 331; organic 27, 57, 146, 185, 186, *241*, 261, 284, 294, 310, 314, 317, *323*, 325, 329, 357; spraying 19, 27; vineyard zoning 27, *see also* organic viticulture; vine training
Vitis labrusca 22, 290, 320
Vitis vinifera 18, 22, 279, 290, 320

Gazetteer

This gazetteer includes place name references of vineyards, châteaux, quintas, general wine areas, and other information appearing on the maps in the Atlas, with the exception of minor place names and geographical features that appear as background information in sans serif type. All châteaux are listed under C (eg château Yquem, d') and quintas under Q (eg quinta Noval, do) in the gazetteer. Domaines, wineries, etc appear under their individual name. The alphanumeric before the page number refers to the grid reference system on the map pages. Vineyards, etc are indexed under their main name (eg Perrières, les). Identical names are distinguished by either the country or region being indicated in italic type. Alternative names are shown in brackets: Praha (Prague), etc. Wine producers whose names appear on the maps are also listed.

Carvalhais, dos E5 212
Carvalhas, das F5 218
Carvalheira, da F6 218
Castelinho, de F2 219
Castelo Borges, do G4 218
Cavadinha, da E5 218
Charondo, do F6 218
Chocapalha, de B2 214
Costa de Baixo F3 218
Costa, da D5 218
Covelos, de F2 218
Crasto, do F4 218
Cruzeiro, do E5 218
Currais, dos F1 218
Dr Christiano, do F6 218
Eira Velha, do F5 218
Encontro, do F2 212
Farfao, do G6 219
Ferrad, da G3 218
Ferradosa, da G3 219
Fojo, do D5 218
Fontainhas, das G6 219
Foz de Arouge, de G3 212
Foz de Temilobos, da G2 218
Foz, da F5, G2 218
Frades, dos G3 218
Gaivosa, da E1 218
Garcia, do G1 218
Gricha, da E1 219
Infantado, do F4 218
Ingleses, dos G5 219
Junco, do E5 218
Lagares, dos D6 218
Lajes, das G6 218
Lelo, do F6 218
Louvazim, do G6 219
Macedos, de G6 218
Maias, das F5 212
Malvedos, dos E1 219
Manuelas, das D5 218
Marrocos, de G1 218
Merouco, do E1 219
Milieu E2 219
Monte d'Oiro, do B3 214
Mouro, do A5 215
Murta, da C2 214
Nápoles, de G3 218
Nova do Roncão E6 218
Noval, do E5 218
Panascal, do G5 218
Pancas, de B3 214
Passadouro, do D5 218
Pedrogão, do G6 218
Pego, do G5 218
Pellada, da F5 212
Perdiz, da F6 218
Peso, do F1 218
Poca, da F4 218
Portal, do E5 218
Portela, da G2 218
Porto de Bois, de G5 219
Porto, do F5 218
Quarias, das F1 218
Quietud, de la E5 195
Ribeira Teja, da G5 219
Ribeira, da D5 218
Roeda, de F5 218
Romaneira, da E6 218
Romarigo, de F1 218
Romeira, da C2 214
Roques, dos F5 212
Roriz, de E1 219
Rosa, de la F5 218
Sagrado, do F5 218
San Martinho, de E2 219
São Luiz G4 218
Seixo, do F5 218
Serra da Ribeira, da G5 219
Serra, da F6 218
Sibio, do E6 218, E1 219
Silval, do E5 218
Sol, do G2 218
St Antonio, de D6 218
Sta Barbara, de G1 218, F1 219
Tedo, do G3 218
Teixeira, da F6 218
Telhada, da G6 219
Terra Feita, da E5 218
Torre, da G1 218
Tua, do E2 219
Vacaria, da G1 218
Val de Malhadas, do G5 219
Vale Cavelos G5 219
Vale da Mina G4 219
Vale de Figueira, do F5 218
Vale Dona Maria F6 218
Vallado, do F1 218
Vargellas, de G4 219
Velha G1 218
Ventozelo, de F6 218
Vesúvio, do G4 219
Vila Velha, da E1 219
Zambujal, do F2 218
Zimbro, do E2 219

Quintay B3 326
Quintessa F3 303
Quivira C4 296
Quoin Rock D3 371
Qupé E3 309

Raats Family Wines E1 371
Rabajà D3 163
Rabat G2 287
Rabiega, Dom C3 147
Rača G3 270
Racha-Lechkumi F4 278
Radgonske Gorice A5 271
Radike Vineyard A2 309
Radikon D4 173
Rafanelli, A D4 296
Ragot, Dom E5 68
Raguenières, les C3 122
Ragusa G5 187
Raiding D5 259
Raignots, aux E4 65
Raka G3 366
Rakvice G3 270
Ralph Fowler C4 349
Ramandolo B5 167
Ramey D5 296
Ramirana C4 329
Rampa di Fugnano, la E1 179
Ramsthal D4 250
Rancagua C6 329
Ranché, en la D3 60
Rancho Rossa Vineyards E2 312
Rancho Sisquoc E3 309
Rancy, Dom de B3 145
Randersacker E3 250
Rány E4 268
Rapaura F3 362
Rapazzini D4 307
Raphael D5 320
Rapitalà E2 187
Rapsáni B3 283
Raşcov E1 278
Raspail-Ay, Dom C4 139
Rastatt D2 248
Rasteau C3 137, A4 139
Ratausses, les D1 63
Rátka F2 268
Ratosses, les D1 63
Ratsch F3 259
Rattlesnake Hills B5 315
Raubern B1 261
Rauenthal D4 237
Raul C5 229
Rausch F1 229
Ravelles, les F4 60
Ravenna F4 167, A5 175
Ravenswood C3 299
Raventós i Blanc D4 203
Ravera E5 165
Raviolles, aux F3 65
Raye's Hill C2 294
Ray-Jane, Dom E3 148
Raymond F3 303
Raymond Usseglio & Fils E2 139
Razac-de-Saussignac B4 115
Real Sitio de Ventosilla D4 196
Réas, aux F3 65
Réas, le Clos des F3 65
Rebeninha E6 218
Rebichets, les F2 60
Recanati E4 286
Recaş C2 277
Réchaux, la D4 67
Rechbächel E2 246
Rechnitz E5 259
Recioto di Soave D3 167
Rectorie, Dom de la D6 145
Red Edge B3 352
Red Hill Douglas County F2 315
Red Hills C5 294
Red Mountain B5 315
Red Newt Cellars A3 320
Red Rooster F6 315
Red Willow Vineyard D2 318
Redbank B2 352
Redesdale Estate B3 352
Redgate E5 341
Redhawk E4 316
Redling C3 263
Redman B5 350
Redondela D4 194
Redondo B5 215
Redrescut B1 63
Redwood Valley A3 294
Refène, la F6 61, C1 62
Referts, les G4 60
Reggio di Calabria G4 184
Réggio nell'Emilia E2 167
Régnié F5 55, C3 73, E3 74
Regrippière, la F4 119
Reguengos B5 215
Reguengos de Monsaraz E5 210, B5 215
Regusci F4 305
Rehberg D6 262
Reichestal F3 239
Reif F6 321
Reilly's F5 345
Reims B4 53, A4 79, A4 81
Reininger E2 319
Reinsport C5 230
Reisenthal D2 263
Reiterpfad G2 246
Reith B4 263
Rejadorada E5 195
Reland, le Clos C6 59, G1 60
Réméjeanne, Dom la C1 137
Remelluri F4 199
Remhoogte D3 371
Remilly, en F3 60
Remstal-Stuttgart E4 248
Renardes, les C5 63
Renato Keber D3 173
René Bourgeon E5 68
René Noël Legrand F3 121
René, Clos D3 107
Renmark E6 336
Renton A3 315
Renwick G2 362
Renwood B5 311
Réole, la G5 83
Repanis E4 284
Republika Srpska C3 273
Reserva de Caliboro G3 329
Ressier, le Clos E6 71
Restigné D3 122
Retz A4 259
Retzlaff A3 307
Retzstadt E3 250
Reugne E2 61
Reuilly C3 119
Reus F1 203
Revanna C3 301
Reverie B2 301
Reversées, les D3 62
Rex Hill E4 316
Reynella D4 346
Reysses, les C5 71
Rezé C2 118, F2 119
Rhebokskloof A4 371
Rheinberg G5 237
Rheingarten G1 237
Rheingau E2 225
Rheinhell G1, G2 237
Rheinhessen E2 225
Rheintal E5 255
Rhodt F4 244
Rias Baixas D1 190
Ribagnac C5 115
Ribatejano D4 210
Ribatejo D4 210, C3 214
Ribaudy, la F1 133
Ribeauvillé D4 127, F4 129
Ribeira Brava G1 223
Ribeira Sacra D2 190
Ribeiro D1 190
Ribera del Duero D3 190
Ribera del Guadiana F2 190
Ribera del Júcar F4 190
Ribonnet, Dom de D5 113
Richard Hamilton F4 346
Richarde, en la F3 60
Richardson D4 299
Richaume, Dom C1 147
Riche, le E3 371
Richebourg, le E4 65
Richemone, la E3 65
Richland B5 315, D5 318
Richmond Grove D4 342
Richou, Dom E3 120
Rickety Gate F5 339
Ridge, *Northern Sonoma* D4 296
Ridge, *Santa Cruz* B2 307
Ridgeback F2 366
Ridgeview Estate G5 253
Riecine E5 179
Riefring E2 264
Riegersburg E4 259
Rierpaolo Pecorari E3 173
Rignano sull' Arno B5 179
Rijeka B1 273
Rijk's E2 366
Rilly-la-Montagne B4 81
Rimauresq, Dom de D2 147
Rimavská Sobota G5 270
Rimbert, Dom A3 141
Ringerin A3 263
Rio E3 284
Rio Grande D5 183
Río Negro G4 324
Rioja Alta, la F3 199
Rioja, Ca D4 190
Rioja, la F4 324
Riojanas, Bodegas B1 199
Rios-Lovell A3 307
Riotte, la E4 66
Riottes, *les, Beaune* C1 62
Riottes, *les, Meursault* E3 61
Ripaille A6 151
Rippon D4 363
Riquewihr D4 127, F3 129
Riscal, Marqués de G6 199
Ristow E5 301
Ritchie Creek B2 301
Ritsch E1 230
Rittergarten B2 246
Ritterpfad C1, C2 229
Ritzling B4 260
Riudoms F1 203
Riva del Garda E3 168
Rivadavia B5 331
Rivas de Tereso E4 199
Rivassi E4 165
Rivaux, les E3 61
Rivaz E4 256
Rive Droite F1 257
River Junction B3 293
River Road E5 296
River Run D3 307
Rivera, *Puglia* A3 185
Rivera, *Uruguay* F5 324
Riverhead C6, E5 320
Riverina E2 337
Riverland E6 336
Rivesaltes B4 145
Riviera del Garda Bresciano C2 167, B5 170
Riviera Ligure di Ponente F3 159
Rivière, au dessus de la F3 65
Rivolet E3 73
Rivoli Veronese B1 171
Rivosordo D3 163
Rixheim G4 127
Rízes F4 284
Rizzi E2 163
Roa de Duero D3 196
Roaix C3 137, A5 139
Robardelle F4 61
Robe F6 336, C4 349
Robe Ranges C4 349
Robert Craig A3 301
Robert Keenan B2 301
Robert Mondavi B4 304
Robert Mueller D5 296
Robert Plageoles et Fils B6 113
Robert Sinskey E4 305
Robert Talbott F4 307
Robert Young Vineyard C5 296
Robert-Denogent, Dom C5 71
Robertson F3 366
Robinvale E1 337
Robledo D3 299
Robyn Drayton D4 357
Roc d'Anglade A5 143
Roc des Anges B3 145
Rocalière, Dom la F5 138
Rocca di Castagnoli F5 179
Rocca di Montegrossi F4 179
Rocca Family Vineyards E3 305
Rocche, le D4 165
Rocchette D4 165
Rocchettevino D4 165
Rocfort E5 123
Rochains, les B5 133
Roche E3 299
Roche aux Moines, la D2 120
Roche Vineuse, la E1 70
Roche, Clos de la E5 66
Roche, sur la A4 71
Rochecorbon E2 123
Rocheford C5 354
Rochefort-sur-Loire B4 118, E2 120
Rochegude C2 137
Rochelle, la F3 61
Rochelles, Dom des D5 120
Rochère, la E5 123
Roches Neuves, Dom des F3 121
Roches, les E3 123
Rocheservière C2 118
Rochester A2 320
Roche-sur-Foron, la B5 151
Rochette-St-Jean F4 122
Rochioli, J E5 296
Rockburn F5 363
Rockford E4 342
Rockingham B4 339
Rockpile A1 293
Rocoule C5 135
Roda F3 199
Rödchen E5 237
Rödelsee F4 250
Rodern D4 127
Rodero D3 196
Rodney Strong D5 296
Ródos (Rhodes) E6 283
Roederer B2 294
Roero D3 159, D3 161
Roessler E6 296
Roger Lassarat, Dom A3 71
Roger Sabon, Dom E2 139
Rognet-Corton, le C5 63
Rogue River G2 315
Rogue Valley G2 315
Rohrendorf B4 259, D2 263
Rohrendorfer Gebling D2 263
Roi, Clos du C6 62
Roi, le Clos du C4 63
Roichottes A2 63
Rolet, Dom E3 150
Roma F3 175
Romagniens, les E3 61
Romanèche-Thorins C4 73, C6 74
Romanée St-Vivant E4 65
Romanée, la, *Gevrey-Chambertin* C1 67
Romanée, la, *Nuits-St-Georges* E4 65
Romanée, la, *Santenay* C5 59
Romanée-Conti, la E4 65
Romans d'Isonzo F2 173
Rombauer B3 301
Rombone E2 163
Römerhang D5 232
Römerstein-Martinhof F3 264
Romorantin-Lanthenay B3 119
Ronca C5 171
Roncaglie E2 163
Roncagliette D2 163
Roncé G6 122
Roncée, Dom du G6 122
Ronceret, le F4 61
Ronchevrat A3 71
Ronchi di Manzano D2 173
Roncière E6 64
Roncières E3 77
Ronco del Gelso E2 173
Ronco del Gnemiz D2 173
Roncus E3 173
Ronda G3 190
Rondières, les B6 60
Roque Sestière C3 141
Roquemaure F1 139
Roquemaure, la C5 59
Roquete, Dom la E2 139
Rosa Bosco D2 173
Rosa, la, *Barolo* D5 165
Rosa, la, *Chile* C4 329
Rosacker F4 129
Röschitz A4 259
Rosebud Vineyard B5 315
Roseburg F2 315
Rosella's Vineyard F4 307
Rosemary G5 253
Rosemount Estate E4 346
Rosemount Ryecroft E5 346
Rosenberg, *Bernkastel* C6, E5, F5 232
Rosenberg, *Nahe* F2 243
Rosenberg, *Piesport* C5 230
Rosenberg, *Rheinhessen* C4 241
Rosenberg, *Saar* B4, C3, C4 229
Rosenblum D5 296
Rosengärtchen E4 230
Rosengarten, *Bernkastel* D2 233
Rosengarten, *Rheingau* F3 235
Rosenheck G2 243
Rosenlay F4 232
Rose-Pauillac, la C5 91
Rosettes, les G3 122
Rosevears F5 355
Rosily Vineyard C6 341
Ross Estate F3 342
Rossano F5 184
Rossatz B6 260
Rossese di Dolceacqua F2 159
Rossiya (Russia) E4 278
Rosso Barletta A3 185
Rosso Canosa A3 185
Rosso Conero D6 175
Rosso di Cerignola D4 184, A2 185
Rosso Piceno D6 175
Rosso Piceno Superiore E6 175
Rostov E4 278
Rostov-na-Donu E3 278
Rota B2 206
Rotenfels E3, F3 243
Rotenfelser im Winkel F4 243
Roterd D4, E5 230
Rotes Tor C3 260
Rothenberg, *Rheingau* F6 235, G1 236, E4 237
Rothenberg, *Rheinhessen* B5 241
Rothenberg, *Wachau* B1 261
Rothenhof B1 261
Rotier, Dom C6 113
Rotlei D2 234
Rotllan Torra C5 204
Rotorua B5 358
Röttingen F3 250
Roudnice nad Labem E2 270
Roudon Smith C2 307
Rouffach F4 127, F3 128
Rouffignac-de-Sigoulès B5 115
Rouge Garance, Dom E1 137
Rouge Gorge, Clos du B3 145
Rougeots, les F1 61
Rougeotte, la F5 61
Rouges du Bas, les E5 65
Rouges du Dessus, les E5 65
Round Hill F3 303
Rousselle, la G4 60
Rousset-les-Vignes B3 137
Rouvrettes, les B1 63
Rovellats E3 203
Rovereto E4 168
Rovigo E4 167
Roxheim B5 242
Roxy Ann G3 315
Royal Tokaj Wine Co F2 268
Rozendal E3 371
Rozier A5 133
Rubaiyat F5 374
Rubbia al Colle E5 177
Rubicon G3 303
Rubino, Az. Agr. B5 185
Ruca Malén B4 331
Rucahue G3 329
Ruchots, les E4 66
Ruchottes du Bas E1 67
Ruchottes du Dessus D1 67
Rudd A5 304
Rüdesheim D3, F4 235
Rué E3 165
Rue au Porc G6 61
Rue aux Vaches, la G4 60
Rue de Chaux E1 65
Rue de Vergy F4 66
Rue de Vergy, en la E4 66
Rue Rousseau G3 60
Rued Vineyard F4 296
Rueda E3 190
Ruffieux B4 151
Ruffino A5 179
Rúfina A5 179
Rugiens-Bas, les F5 61
Rugiens-Hauts, les F5 61
Ruiterbosch F6 366
Rully D5 55, B6 68
Rumilly B4 151
Rupert & Rothschild C4 371
Ruppertsberg E4 244, G3 246
Rural, la B4 331
Rusack F3 309
Ruse (Rousse) A4 275
Russet Ridge C6 349
Russian Hill E5 296
Russian River Valley E4 296
Russin F1 256
Russiz Superiore E3 173
Russo E5 177
Rust C5 259, F2 264
Rust en Vrede F3 371
Rustenberg D3 371
Rustridge C5 301
Rutherford C4 301, G3 303, A4 304
Rutherford Hill F3 303
Rutherglen F3 337, A6 352
Rutz F5 296
Rutz Cellars F5 296
Ruwer F4 227, A3 234
Rymill A5 350

Saale-Unstrut D4 225
Saarbrücken F2 225
Saarburg G3 227, F2 229
Saarfeilser-Marienberg D3 229
Sables du Golfe du Lion D5 153
Sablet C3 137, B5 139
Sablonettes, Dom des G3 120
Sablons, les D2 122
Sachsen D5 225
Sachsenberg C3 263
Sackträger G5 241
Sacramento A3 293, B4 311
Sacred Hill A4 360
Sacy B3 81
Saddleback B5 304
Sadie Family F2 366
Sadova D3 277
Sadova-Corabia D3 277
Sadoya F5 374
Saering D1 128
Sag Harbor E6 320
Sagelands D2 318
Sahel G2 287
Sahy G4 270
Saillon G6 256
St-Aignan B2 119
St Amant D4 311
St-Amour F5 55, B4 73, A6 74
St-Amour-Bellevue G2 70, A6 74
St-Andelain C5 125
St-André de Figuière, Dom D2 147
St-André-de-Cubzac E3 83
St-Andrieu, Dom B1 143
St Anna F4 259
St-Anne F3 91, E3 92
St-Antonin, Dom D5 142
St-Aubin D5 55, D2 60
St-Aubin de Luigné F1 120
St-Baillon, Dom de C2 147
St-Barthélémy-d'Anjou B4 118
St-Bouize C4 125
St-Brice E5 87
St-Bris, *Bordeaux* B4 101
St-Bris, *Burgundy* B3 55
St Catharines A1 320, G5 321
St Charles Vineyard C2 307
St-Christol B4 143
St-Christoly-Médoc C5 87
St-Christophe E6 109
St-Christophe-des-Bardes C3 105
Saint Clair Estate G3 362
St Clair Winery E3 312
St Clement C3 301
St-Clément-de-la-Place B4 118
St-Corbian D4 89
St-Cyr-en-Bourg G3 121
St-Cyr-sur-Mer E2 148
St Cousair F5 374
St David's Bench G5 321
St-Denis, Clos, *Morey-St-Denis* E4 66
St-Denis, Clos, *Vosne-Romanée* E5 65
St-Désiré C2 62
St-Didier-sur-Beaujeu C2 73
St-Drézéry B4 143
Ste-Agathe C3 133
Ste-Anne, Dom C1 137
Ste-Baume D5 153
Ste-Croix-du-Mont G4 83, B5 103
Ste-Foy-la-Grande E6 83, B4 115
Ste-Gemme-en-Sancerrois A3 125
Ste-Magdeleine, Clos D6 146
Ste-Marie-la-Blanche B5 153
Ste-Maure-de-Touraine C1 119
St-Émilion E5 83, D2 105, F5 107
Ste-Radegonde-de-Touraine F1 123
Ste-Rose, Dom D6 142
St-Estèphe C2 83, D5 89, A4 91
St-Estève B4 145
St-Étienne-des-Ouillères D3 73
St-Étienne-la-Varenne D3 73
St-Fiacre-sur-Maine F2 119
St-Florent-le-Vieil B3 118
St Francis A1 299
St Gallen E5 255
St-Gayan, Dom B5 139
St-Gengoux-de-Scissé B2 70
St-Geniès-de-Comolas E6 138
St Georgen C5 259
St-Georges E5 83
St-Georges, les E5 64
St-Georges-d'Orques C3 143
St-Georges-St-Émilion B5 109
St-Georges-sur-Loire B4 118
St-Germain-d'Esteuil F4 87
St-Gervais C1 137
St Gregory, Dom C4 294
St-Guilhem, Dom de C2 113
St-Guilhem-le-Désert D4 153
St Hallett E4 342
St-Herblain B2 118
St Helena C3 301, F2 303
St-Hilaire-St-Florent B5 118
St-Hippolyte, *Alsace* D4 127, G6 129
St-Hippolyte, *Loire* C2 119
St Huberts C4 354
St-Hune, Clos F4 129
St-Imer, Clos E4 128
St Innocent F4 316
St-Jacques, aux F2 65
St-Jacques, le Clos D2 67
St-Jean de l'Arbousier, Dom B4 143
St-Jean de Villecroze, Dom B2 147
St-Jean, Clos F2 60
St-Jean, *Médoc* C2 87
St-Jean, *Santenay* A2 59
St-Jean-d'Ardières E6 74
St-Jean-de-Braye A3 119
St-Jean-de-Duras C4 115
St-Jean-de-la-Croix D2 120
St-Jean-de-la-Porte C5 151
St-Jean-des-Mauvrets D5 120
St-Jeoire-Prieuré C4 151
St-Joseph B4 131, F1 133

Acknowledgments

We would like to thank the following, and particularly apologize to those we may have overlooked.

Introduction *Terroir* Laurent Lebrun; *Anatomy of a Winery* Frédéric Engerer, Hélène Genin, Sonia Favreau

France Chris Skyrme, Pierre Morel, Amina El Abbassi (Sopexa UK); Elodie Pastie (INAO); *Burgundy* Soizic Pinczon du Sel; Tina Sellenet (BIVB); *Pouilly-Fuissé* Jean Rijckaert; *Beaujolais* Clive Coates MW; Anne Masson (UIVB); *Chablis* Rosemary George MW; *Champagne* Michael Edwards; Brigitte Batonnet (CIVC); *Bordeaux* James Lawther; Kees van Leeuwen; Tim Unwin; Aurélie Chobert (L'Alliance des Crus Bourgeois du Médoc); Anne Marbot (CIVB); *Southwest France* Paul Strang; Jérôme Pérez; *Loire Valley* Charles and Philippa Sydney; *Alsace* Oliver Humbrecht MW; Thierry Fritsch (Conseil Interprofessional des Vins d'Alsace); *Rhône* John Livingstone Learmonth; François Drounau (Inter Rhône); *Languedoc* Christine Behey-Molines (Comité Interprofessional des Vins du Languedoc); Paul Strang; *Roussillon* Eric Aracil (Comité Interprofessional des Vins du Roussillon); Tom Lubbe; *Provence* François Millo (Comité Interprofessional de Vins de Provence); *Corsica* Patrick Fioramonti; *Jura, Savoie, and Vins de Pays* Wink Lorch

Italy David Gleave MW; Michèle Shah; Federico Vincenzi; *Trentino* Sabrina Schenchl *Alto Adige* Thomas Augscholl; *Verona* Emilio Fasoletti; *Friuli* Barbara Rosso; *Chianti* Silvia Fiorentini (Consorzio Vino Chianti Classico); *Puglia* Mark Shannon; *Sicily* Kate Singleton

Spain John Radford; Maria-José Sevilla, Margarita Perez Vilanova (Wines of Spain); Alison Dillon; *Somontano* Martin Abell; *Rueda* Arancha Zamácola; *Priorat* René Barbier; *Jerez* Jesús Barquín

Portugal Richard Mayson; Filipe Neves; *Douro and Madeira* Ben Campbell-Johnson

Germany Stuart Pigott; Michael Schemmel, Steffen Schindler (DWI); Hilke Nagel (VDP); *Pfalz* Markus Heil

England and Wales Stephen Skelton MW; Julia Trustram Eve (English Wine Producers)

Switzerland Pierre Thomas

Austria Peter Moser; Susanne Staggl (OEWM)

Hungary Gabriella Meszaros; Diana Sidlovits (Hegyközségek Nemzeti Tanácsa)

Czech Republic and Slovakia Helena Baker; Pavel Heimlich; Martin Kristek; Ondrej Kuchar

Slovenia Robert Gorjak, Mojca Jakša

The Western Balkans Lisa Shara Hall; *Croatia* Irina Ban, Darrel Joseph; *Albania* Andreas Shundi

Bulgaria Caroline Gilby MW; Lilia Stoilova; Julia Kostadinova

Romania Caroline Gilby MW; Basil Zarnoveanu (Provinum)

The Former Soviet Republics Shalva Khetsurani; Bisso Atanassov; John Worontschak; *Ukraine* T Postoain; *Azerbaijan* Mail Amanov; *Georgia* Shalva Khetsuriani; Gia Sulkhanishvili

Greece Konstantinos Lazarikis

Eastern Mediterranean *Turkey* Yakip Icgoren; Oktay Onderer, Ozlem Atak; *Cyprus* Caroline Gilby MW; *Lebanon* Michael Karam; Charles Ghostine; *Israel* Adam Montefiore

North America *USA* Rebecca Murphy; Doug Frost MW,MS, Bill Nelson, Jenny Mattingley (Wine America); *California* Larry Walker; Linda Murphy; Emma Rice; Gladys Horiuchi; *Napa* Terry Hall; *Sonoma* Phil Bilodeau; *Lodi* Mark Chandler; *Arizona* Todd Bostock; *Michigan* David Creighton; *Missouri* Ann Miller; *Ohio* Donniella Winchell;

New York Jim Tresize, Susan Spence (NYWGF); *Pacific Northwest* Lisa Shara Hall; Susan O'Hara; *Texas* Dacota Julson; *Canada* Janet Dorozynski; Igor Ryjenkov; *British Columbia* John Schreiner; *Ontario* Prof Tony Shaw (Brock University), Linda Bramble, Laurie Macdonald (VQA); *Mexico* John Worontschak

South America *Brazil* Arthur Azevedo; *Uruguay* Daniel Pisano; Lauro Arias; José Osvaldo do Amarante; Luiz Horta; *Chile* Patricio Tapia; Michael Cox (Wines of Chile); *Argentina* Enrique Chrabolowsky; James Forbes, Fernando Farré, Ariel Menniti (Wines of Argentina)

Australia Kirsten Moore (Wines of Australia); Peter Bailey (AWBC); *Western Australia* Peter Forrestal; *Margaret River* Janine Carter; *South Australia* Max Allen; *McLaren Vale* Sandie Holmes; *Adelaide Hills* Katie Cameron; *Limestone Coast and Coonawarra* Brian Croser; Ian Hollick; *Victoria* Max Allen; Joanne Butterworth; *Geelong* Diana Sawyer; *Yarra Valley* Anna Aldridge; *Tasmania* Andrew Pirie; Kim Seagram; *New South Wales* Stuart McGrath-Kerr; *Hunter Valley* Iain Riggs; Christopher Barnes; Paul Stuart

New Zealand Michael Cooper; Warren Adamson (Wines of New Zealand); *Auckland* Michael Brajkovich MW; *Hawke's Bay* Gordon Russell; *Martinborough* Larry McKenna, Sarah Sherwood; *Marlborough* Sarah Booker; *Central Otago* Lucy Thomson

South Africa Tim James; Sophie Waggett (WOSA UK); Su Birch, Andre Morgenthal (WOSA South Africa); *Constantia* Di Botha; Lowell Jooste

Asia Denis Gastin